GUM

Grammar, Usage, and Mechanics

Conventions of Standard English

ZB Zaner-Bloser

Grade Level Consultants

S. Elaine Boysworth
Lincolnton, North Carolina

Linda Crawford
Calhoun, Georgia

Martha Swan Novy
Florissant, Missouri

Heather Stanton
Colorado Springs, Colorado

Jaqueline Xavier
Cleveland, Ohio

Illustration: Tom Kennedy, Tracy Greenwalt

ISBN: 978-1-4531-1219-9

ZB Code 16

Zaner-Bloser, Inc.
1-800-421-3018
www.zaner-bloser.com

Printed in the United States of America

1 2 3 4 5 19750 18 17 16 15 14

SFI® Certified Chain of Custody
Promoting Sustainable Forestry
www.sfiprogram.org
SFI-01042

Teacher Edition Table of Contents

GUM

Grades 2–8

Grammar, Usage, and Mechanics

Conventions of Standard English

Are Your Students Ready to Write?

With *G.U.M. (Grammar, Usage, and Mechanics)*, students master the **conventions of standard English** critical for success on **next-generation assessments** and **college- and career-ready** writing.

In as little as 15 minutes per day of **targeted, systematic, self-guided** instruction and practice, students will master these skills and meet the new academic standards.

The Right Choice for Grammar Instruction!

- Provides **targeted, systematic, self-guided** instruction and practice in **under 15 minutes a day**

- Meets 100% of the **conventions of standard English**

- Reinforces skills from grade to grade to ensure a **cumulative progression of skills** and **greater retention and skill development**

- Features **writing and spelling practice** in every unit

- Prepares students for high-stakes **next-generation assessments**

- Includes **English Language Learner support** in each lesson

- Fits easily into any reading or language arts curriculum

Five-Step Lessons for Self-Guided Instruction

The easy-to-follow, five-step lesson format provides explicit instruction in the conventions of standard English and includes opportunities for students to practice, apply, and reinforce skills.

Step 1

Provides an example of the skill in context for students to read and analyze

Step 2

Explains key skill information in clear, concise language

Step 3

Provides skill practice in the context of high-interest, nonfiction topics

Step 4

Provides an opportunity to apply skill knowledge

Step 5

Reinforces learning through writing, puzzles, and other fun activities

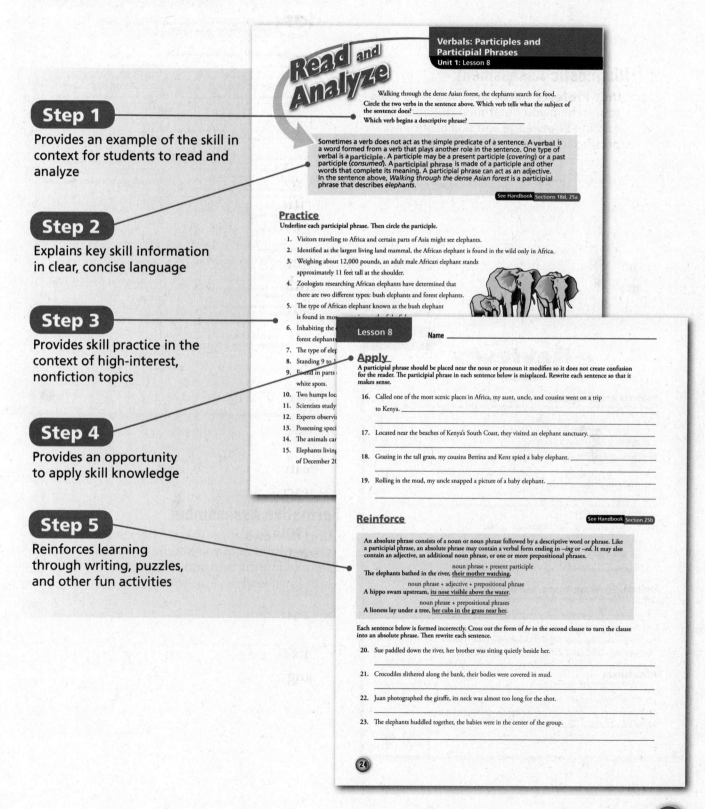

Read and Analyze

Verbals: Participles and Participial Phrases
Unit 1: Lesson 8

Walking through the dense Asian forest, the elephants search for food.
Circle the two verbs in the sentence above. Which verb tells what the subject of the sentence does? _____
Which verb begins a descriptive phrase? _____

Sometimes a verb does not act as the simple predicate of a sentence. A **verbal** is a word formed from a verb that plays another role in the sentence. One type of verbal is a **participle**. A participle may be a present participle (*covering*) or a past participle (*consumed*). A **participial phrase** is made of a participle and other words that complete its meaning. A participial phrase can act as an adjective. In the sentence above, *Walking through the dense Asian forest* is a participial phrase that describes *elephants*.

See Handbook Sections 18d, 25a

Practice

Underline each participial phrase. Then circle the participle.

1. Visitors traveling to Africa and certain parts of Asia might see elephants.
2. Identified as the largest living land mammal, the African elephant is found in the wild only in Africa.
3. Weighing about 12,000 pounds, an adult male African elephant stands approximately 11 feet tall at the shoulder.
4. Zoologists researching African elephants have determined that there are two different types: bush elephants and forest elephants.
5. The type of African elephant known as the bush elephant is found in mos...
6. Inhabiting the ... forest elephants ...
7. The type of elep...
8. Standing 9 to 1...
9. Found in parts ... white spots.
10. Two humps loc...
11. Scientists study...
12. Experts observin...
13. Possessing speci...
14. The animals car...
15. Elephants living... of December 20...

Lesson 8   Name _____

Apply

A participial phrase should be placed near the noun or pronoun it modifies so it does not create confusion for the reader. The participial phrase in each sentence below is misplaced. Rewrite each sentence so that it makes sense.

16. Called one of the most scenic places in Africa, my aunt, uncle, and cousins went on a trip to Kenya. _____

17. Located near the beaches of Kenya's South Coast, they visited an elephant sanctuary. _____

18. Grazing in the tall grass, my cousins Bettina and Kent spied a baby elephant. _____

19. Rolling in the mud, my uncle snapped a picture of a baby elephant. _____

Reinforce

See Handbook Section 25b

An absolute phrase consists of a noun or noun phrase followed by a descriptive word or phrase. Like a participial phrase, an absolute phrase may contain a verbal form ending in *–ing* or *–ed*. It may also contain an adjective, an additional noun phrase, or one or more prepositional phrases.

noun phrase + present participle
The elephants bathed in the river, their mother watching.

noun phrase + adjective + prepositional phrase
A hippo swam upstream, its nose visible above the water.

noun phrase + prepositional phrases
A lioness lay under a tree, her cubs in the grass near her.

Each sentence below is formed incorrectly. Cross out the form of *be* in the second clause to turn the clause into an absolute phrase. Then rewrite each sentence.

20. Sue paddled down the river, her brother was sitting quietly beside her.
_____

21. Crocodiles slithered along the bank, their bodies were covered in mud.
_____

22. Juan photographed the giraffe, its neck was almost too long for the shot.
_____

23. The elephants huddled together, the babies were in the center of the group.
_____

24

Assessment Options

The assessment options in *G.U.M. (Grammar, Usage, and Mechanics)* prepare students for next-generation, high-stakes tests and can be used for diagnostic, formative, and summative assessment.

Diagnostic Assessment

Unit Pretests can be used as a diagnostic tool to help you determine students' existing knowledge and skill proficiency prior to instruction.

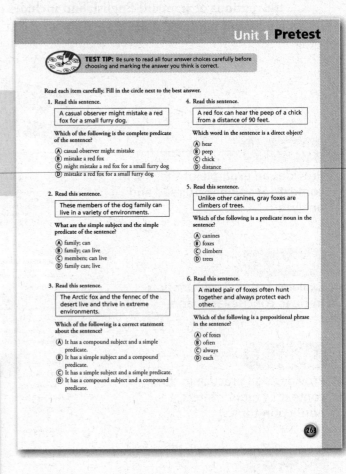

TEST TIP: Be sure to read all four answer choices carefully before choosing and marking the answer you think is correct.

Read each item carefully. Fill in the circle next to the best answer.

1. Read this sentence.

   A casual observer might mistake a red fox for a small furry dog.

   Which of the following is the complete predicate of the sentence?

   (A) casual observer might mistake
   (B) mistake a red fox
   (C) might mistake a red fox for a small furry dog
   (D) mistake a red fox for a small furry dog

2. Read this sentence.

   These members of the dog family can live in a variety of environments.

   What are the simple subject and the simple predicate of the sentence?

   (A) family; can
   (B) family; can live
   (C) members; can live
   (D) family can; live

3. Read this sentence.

   The Arctic fox and the fennec of the desert live and thrive in extreme environments.

   Which of the following is a correct statement about the sentence?

   (A) It has a compound subject and a simple predicate.
   (B) It has a simple subject and a compound predicate.
   (C) It has a simple subject and a simple predicate.
   (D) It has a compound subject and a compound predicate.

4. Read this sentence.

   A red fox can hear the peep of a chick from a distance of 90 feet.

   Which word in the sentence is a direct object?

   (A) hear
   (B) peep
   (C) chick
   (D) distance

5. Read this sentence.

   Unlike other canines, gray foxes are climbers of trees.

   Which of the following is a predicate noun in the sentence?

   (A) canines
   (B) foxes
   (C) climbers
   (D) trees

6. Read this sentence.

   A mated pair of foxes often hunt together and always protect each other.

   Which of the following is a prepositional phrase in the sentence?

   (A) of foxes
   (B) often
   (C) always
   (D) each

26

Subjects and Predicates
Underline the complete subject in each sentence. Circle the simple subject. If the understood subject is *you*, write *you* on the line.

1. Come with us to the marine animal park. _____

2. The star of the show is a bottle-nosed dolphin. _____

Underline the complete predicate in each sentence. Circle the simple predicate.

3. These acrobats of the marine world leap in formation.

4. Dolphins swim in large groups in the wild.

Draw one line under each compound subject in these sentences, and circle each simple subject in the compound subject. Draw two lines under each compound predicate, and draw a box around each simple predicate in the compound predicate.

5. A dolphin breathes and expels water through a blowhole on its head.

6. Herring, sardines, and other fish are favorite dolphin foods.

7. Agile dolphins swim very fast and leap high out of the water.

8. Happy passengers and members of the crew spot dolphins in front of their ship.

Objects, Predicate Nouns, and Predicate Adjectives
Circle the term in parentheses that correctly describes the boldfaced word in each sentence.

9. Many varieties of tuna are **valuable** to fishermen. (direct object/predicate adjective)

10. Dolphins often accompany the **schools** of tuna. (direct object/predicate noun)

11. One of the tools used to ensnare dolphins is a **net**. (direct object/predicate noun)

12. New kinds of nets give **dolphins** an escape route. (indirect object/direct object)

Appositives
Underline the appositive in each sentence.

13. The sound waves bounce off the object and return to the dolphin, a creature sensitive to such waves.

14. From the echoes, the returning sound waves, the dolphin can tell an object's size, shape, and location.

15. Bats, flying mammals, use a similar system.

33

Formative Assessment

Unit Reviews allow you to check students' progress and help you determine when targeted instruction and support for individual learners is needed.

Summative Assessment

Unit Posttests, modeled after next-generation assessments, can be used as a summative assessment to evaluate students' achievement.

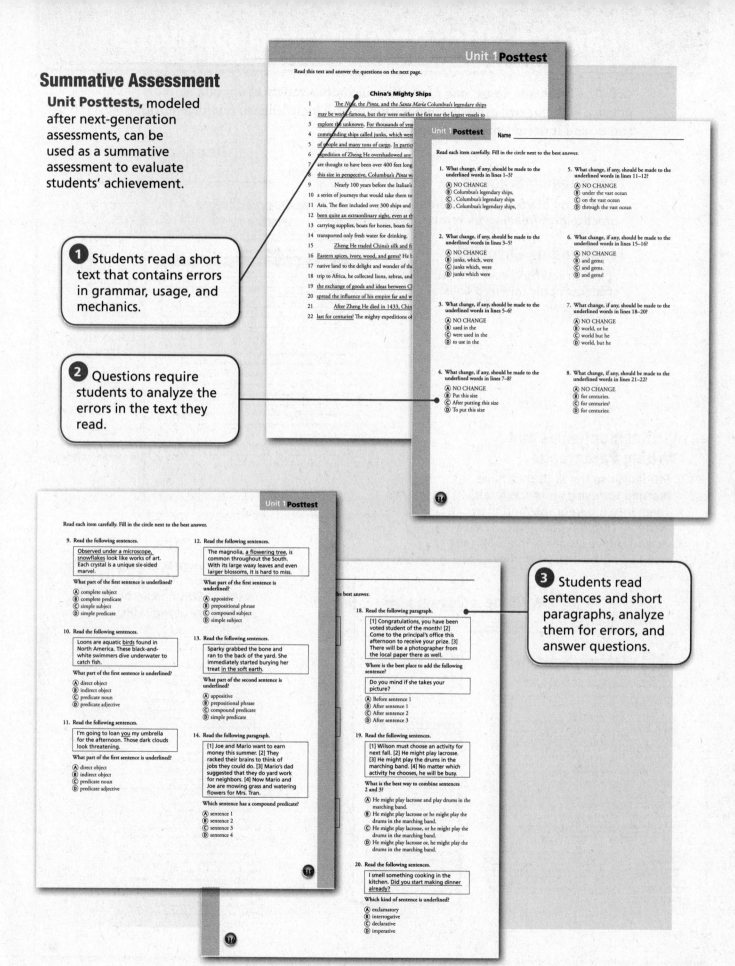

1 Students read a short text that contains errors in grammar, usage, and mechanics.

2 Questions require students to analyze the errors in the text they read.

3 Students read sentences and short paragraphs, analyze them for errors, and answer questions.

Practice and Application Options

G.U.M. (Grammar, Usage, and Mechanics) includes a variety of options for more practice with targeted skills and application of skill knowledge to reinforce learning and extend it to students' own writing.

Proofreading Practice

At the end of each unit, students practice proofreading for errors.

Proofreading Checklist

A proofreading checklist helps students apply targeted skills to their own writing.

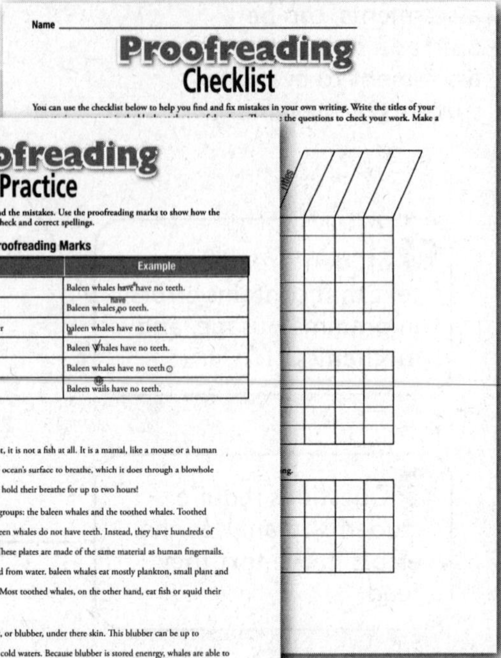

Name
Proofreading
Checklist
You can use the checklist below to help you find and fix mistakes in your own writing. Write the titles of your

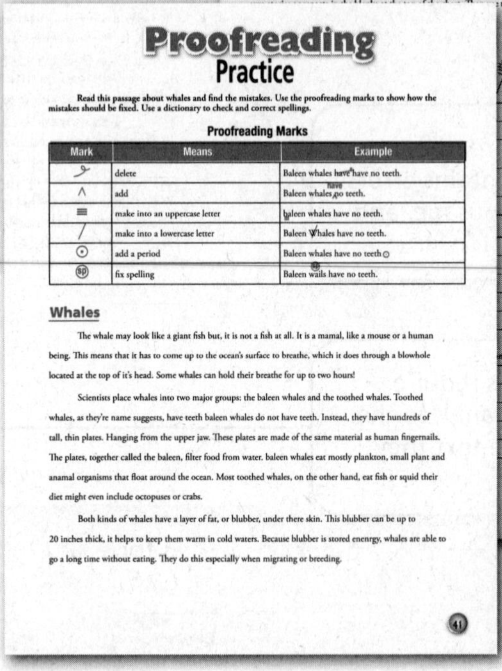

Proofreading
Practice
Read this passage about whales and find the mistakes. Use the proofreading marks to show how the mistakes should be fixed. Use a dictionary to check and correct spellings.
Proofreading Marks
Mark | Means | Example
delete | Baleen whales have have no teeth.
add | Baleen whales no teeth.
make into an uppercase letter | baleen whales have no teeth.
make into a lowercase letter | Baleen Whales have no teeth.
add a period | Baleen whales have no teeth
fix spelling | Baleen wails have no teeth.
Whales
The whale may look like a giant fish but, it is not a fish at all. It is a mamal, like a mouse or a human being. This means that it has to come up to the ocean's surface to breathe, which it does through a blowhole located at the top of it's head. Some whales can hold their breathe for up to two hours!
Scientists place whales into two major groups: the baleen whales and the toothed whales. Toothed whales, as they're name suggests, have teeth baleen whales do not have teeth. Instead, they have hundreds of tall, thin plates. Hanging from the upper jaw. These plates are made of the same material as human fingernails. The plates, together called the baleen, filter food from water. baleen whales eat mostly plankton, small plant and anamal organisms that float around the ocean. Most toothed whales, on the other hand, eat fish or squid their diet might even include octopuses or crabs.
Both kinds of whales have a layer of fat, or blubber, under there skin. This blubber can be up to 20 inches thick, it helps to keep them warm in cold waters. Because blubber is stored enenrgy, whales are able to go a long time without eating. They do this especially when migrating or breeding.
41

Writing Sentences and Writing Paragraphs

Students use the skills they have learned to revise sentences, craft them into a paragraph, and then write an original paragraph. These activities give students the tools they need to become successful writers.

Extra Practice

Additional practice exercises for each lesson in the back of the Student Edition can be used to reteach targeted skills.

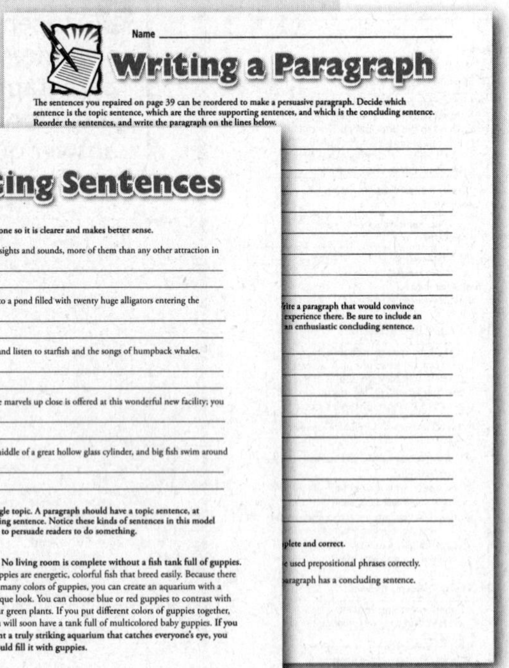

Name
Writing a Paragraph
The sentences you repaired on page 39 can be reordered to make a persuasive paragraph. Decide which sentence is the topic sentence, which are the three supporting sentences, and which is the concluding sentence. Reorder the sentences, and write the paragraph on the lines below.

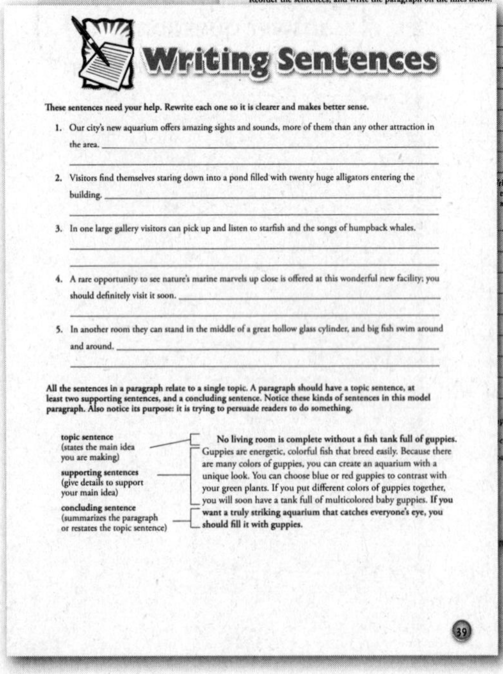

Writing Sentences
These sentences need your help. Rewrite each one so it is clearer and makes better sense.
1. Our city's new aquarium offers amazing sights and sounds, more of them than any other attraction in the area.
2. Visitors find themselves staring down into a pond filled with twenty huge alligators entering the building.
3. In one large gallery visitors can pick up and listen to starfish and the songs of humpback whales.
4. A rare opportunity to see nature's marine marvels up close is offered at this wonderful new facility; you should definitely visit it soon.
5. In another room they can stand in the middle of a great hollow glass cylinder, and big fish swim around and around.
All the sentences in a paragraph relate to a single topic. A paragraph should have a topic sentence, at least two supporting sentences, and a concluding sentence. Notice these kinds of sentences in this model paragraph. Also notice its purpose: it is trying to persuade readers to do something.
topic sentence (states the main idea you are making)
supporting sentences (give details to support your main idea)
concluding sentence (summarizes the paragraph or restates the topic sentence)
No living room is complete without a fish tank full of guppies. Guppies are energetic, colorful fish that breed easily. Because there are many colors of guppies, you can create an aquarium with a unique look. You can choose blue or red guppies to contrast with your green plants. If you put different colors of guppies together, you will soon have a tank full of multicolored baby guppies. If you want a truly striking aquarium that catches everyone's eye, you should fill it with guppies.
39

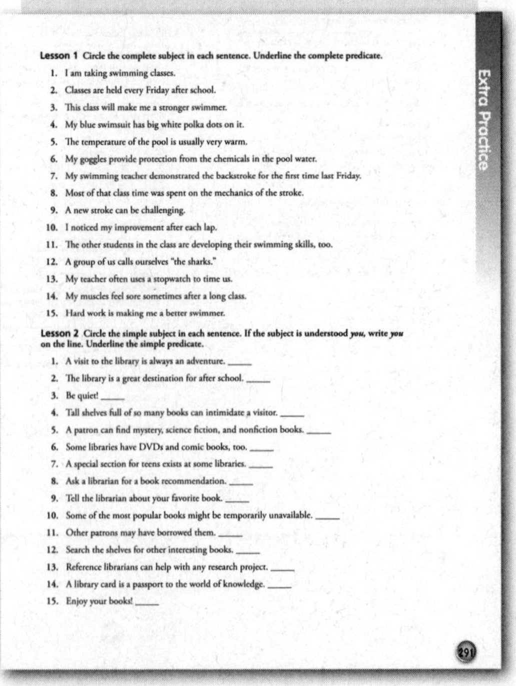

Extra Practice
Lesson 1 Circle the complete subject in each sentence. Underline the complete predicate.
1. I am taking swimming classes.
2. Classes are held every Friday after school.
3. This class will make me a stronger swimmer.
4. My blue swimsuit has big white polka dots on it.
5. The temperature of the pool is usually very warm.
6. My goggles provide protection from the chemicals in the pool water.
7. My swimming teacher demonstrated the backstroke for the first time last Friday.
8. Most of that class time was spent on the mechanics of the stroke.
9. A new stroke can be challenging.
10. I noticed my improvement after each lap.
11. The other students in the class are developing their swimming skills, too.
12. A group of us calls ourselves "the sharks."
13. My teacher often uses a stopwatch to time us.
14. My muscles feel sore sometimes after a long class.
15. Hard work is making me a better swimmer.
Lesson 2 Circle the simple subject in each sentence. If the subject is understood you, write you on the line. Underline the simple predicate.
1. A visit to the library is always an adventure.
2. The library is a great destination for after school.
3. Be quiet!
4. Tall shelves full of so many books can intimidate a visitor.
5. A patron can find mystery, science fiction, and nonfiction books.
6. Some libraries have DVDs and comic books, too.
7. A special section for teens exists at some libraries.
8. Ask a librarian for a book recommendation.
9. Tell the librarian about your favorite book.
10. Some of the most popular books might be temporarily unavailable.
11. Other patrons may have borrowed them.
12. Search the shelves for other interesting books.
13. Reference librarians can help with any research project.
14. A library card is a passport to the world of knowledge.
15. Enjoy your books!
291

Spelling Practice

Many adolescents today will undoubtedly choose to do their reading on a tablet instead of in a book.

Underline the two words in the sentence that have a silent consonant. Circle each silent consonant.

Spelling Patterns: Words With Silent Consonants
Some words have **silent consonants** that are not pronounced. For example, the g is silent in *gnarled* and *resign*, the c is silent in *fascinate* and *discipline*, and the p is silent in *raspberry* and *pneumonia*.

Word Sort
Use the words below to complete the word sort.

adjust	campaign	psychology	miscellaneous	subtle	acknowledgement
ascend	mortgage	undoubtedly	adjoin	raspberry	adjourn

Silent *c* or *k*	Silent *p* or *t*

Silent *d* in the first syllable	Silent *b* or *g*

> Students practice **word sorting** or using **spelling words in context**.

> Activities focus on **pattern practice** and **dictionary skills**.

Sentence Diagramming

Sentence diagramming activities help students understand the relationships between words and phrases within sentences.

```
(you) | Diagram | sentences
```

A **sentence diagram** is a picture of a sentence that shows how the parts of the sentence fit together. Diagramming sentences can help you understand how the words in a sentence are related.

Diagramming Subjects and Verbs
A short sentence consisting of a simple subject and a simple predicate is diagrammed this way:

Owls hoot.   Owls | hoot

Look at the structure of the diagram. Based on its structure, complete these sentences.

1. The simple subject and simple predicate go on a _____ line.
   horizontal/vertical

2. A _____ line separates the subject and predicate.
   horizontal/vertical

3. The subject goes to the _____ of the vertical line, and the predicate goes to the
   left/right
   _____
   left/right

Use what you have learned to diagram these sentences. Include only the simple subject and the simple predicate. Ignore all the other words in the sentences.

4. The sun disappeared.

5. The owls awoke.

6. Rodents scurried.

Diagramming Adjectives and Articles
An adjective (describing word) or an article (*a, an, the*) goes on a slanted line below the word it modifies. Look at the way this sentence has been diagrammed.

The **bright** sun disappeared.   sun | disappeared

Now diagram these sentences.

7. The sleepy owls awoke.

37

Spelling Practice

Each unit includes a spelling practice lesson that focuses on grade-level spelling skills and strategies as required by the new standards.

Name _____

Pattern Practice

acquisition	undoubtedly	acknowledge	adjourn	psychology
adolescent	discipline	acquaintance	subtle	miscellaneous
raspberry	fascinate	pneumonia	adjust	

Write the word above that belongs in each group. Circle the silent consonant.

1. cranberry, blueberry, strawberry _____
2. positively, certainly, definitely _____
3. biology, geology, zoology _____
4. assorted, diverse, various _____
5. addition, purchase, possession _____
6. hypnotize, captivate, interest _____
7. juvenile, youth, minor _____
8. influenza, measles, mumps _____

Write the word above that best completes each sentence.

9. Sanjay is a new _____ I met at summer camp.
10. It takes a lot of time and _____ to learn a new language.
11. The lemon flavor is so _____ I can hardly taste it.
12. The class will _____ for the day at noon.
13. You can _____ the volume with this remote control.
14. Mr. Ito didn't _____ the whispering in the back of the room.
15. Two quarters, a gum wrapper, and a receipt are among the _____ items in my pocket.
16. A _____ is a type of fruit that grows on a bush.
17. It is important to go to the doctor right away if you think you have _____.

Use the Dictionary

Circle the word in each boldfaced pair that is spelled correctly. Check your work in a print or an online dictionary.

18. Trevor's **asma/asthma** keeps him from playing soccer.
19. We'll have to **hussle/hustle** to get to the movie on time.
20. Your blouse will go perfectly with my **khaki/kahki** pants.

80

Community Connection

These activities can be sent home anytime during the unit to reinforce unit skills and to involve families and the community in student learning.

In Unit 1 of *Grammar, Usage, and Mechanics*, students learned about different types of sentences and sentence structures and used what they learned to improve their own writing. The content of these lessons focuses on the theme Astounding Animals. As students completed the exercises, they learned about numerous creatures with remarkable attributes. These pages offer a variety of activities that reinforce skills and concepts presented in the unit. They also provide opportunities for students to make connections between the information presented in the lessons and animal-related activities going on today in the community.

A Pal to a Pet
Find out which pet care facilities in your area allow students to volunteer. You may be able to volunteer at a local Humane Society to play with pets and take them for walks. Dogs and cats need regular human attention and can become stressed and unhappy if left alone for too long. You'll have fun as you perform a valuable service.

Watch the Birds
Go on a bird-watching expedition. Wherever you live, you can easily find somewhere to observe birds. In dense urban areas, birds congregate at places they might find food and water, such as parks, outdoor café tables, and public fountains. In the country, you don't need to look far to find birds. Different types of birds live in fields, scrubby brush, and wetlands. You may even have a bird feeder at your own house. Wherever you go bird watching, take a notebook and a pencil with you and write descriptive information about each bird you see.

Differentiating Instruction

The Teacher Edition features lesson plans that make it easy to differentiate and target instruction to meet the needs of individual learners.

Lesson 1 (student pages 9–10)
Complete Subjects and Complete Predicates

Objectives
- To learn that every sentence has a subject and a predicate
- To learn what words make up the complete subject and what words make up the complete predicate
- To identify the complete subject and the complete predicate
- To complete sentences by adding a subject or a predicate
- To write and evaluate original sentences with long or short subjects and predicates

English Language Learners
Invite students to share what they know about penguins and Antarctica. Introduce the words *conditions (climatic conditions), insulation, abdomen,* and *endure.*
Read the sentences in **Practice** aloud and invite volunteers to paraphrase the information. Then reread each sentence, one at a time, and ask students to identify the complete subject and complete predicate in each by asking *Whom or what is this sentence about?* to identify the subject and *What happened?* or *What did the subject do?* to identify the predicate.
Read the phrases in **Apply** aloud, and ask volunteers to suggest a subject or predicate that could complete each phrase. (Example: item 20: The icy waters off the coast *are full of fish and other sea creatures.*) Pair students with English-proficient partners to complete the activity.
For **Reinforce**, read the boxed text and the instructions aloud. Have students work with partners to plan and outline their short paragraphs. Tell them that it may help to compose their sentences orally before they write. Then have students work independently to write their paragraphs and expand them.

Speaking and Listening
Invite volunteers to read aloud the short and long paragraphs they wrote in **Reinforce**. Have students discuss which of each pair they think is more effective and why. Then have volunteers write sentences from their paragraphs on the board. Invite students to identify the complete subject and the complete predicate in each.

Extra Practice
For more practice, see page 291.

Lesson 2 (student pages 11–12)
Simple Subjects and Simple Predicates

Objectives
- To learn that the simple subject is the most important word or words in the complete subject, and that in imperative sentences the subject is understood to be *you*
- To learn that the simple predicate is the verb in the complete predicate that tells what the subject did, or

English Language Learners
Read **Practice** aloud. Lead students in a discussion of different words and their characteristics. Record this information in a web or chart on the board.
Reread **Practice**. Have students identify the complete subject and predicate in each sentence and then find the simple subject and predicate. Model testing their answers by simplifying each sentence. (Example: item 1: The kiwi scurries.) Read the sentences that contain understood *you* (5, 9) aloud, with the *you* in place to help students recognize them as commands. Point out that sometimes a simple predicate contains a helping verb, such as *has,* and a main verb. Ask students which sentences have both a helping verb and a main verb. (10, 11, 12) Then have students circle the helping verb and underline the main verb.
For **Apply**, model saying aloud sentences about birds. Encourage students to use the information in the web or chart on the board to write their sentences.
If possible, have students use computers with access to the Internet to carry out **Reinforce**. Tell students to make sure all sentences in their e-mails are complete before identifying simple subjects and predicates.

Speaking and Listening
Have students each find a sentence in a textbook, read it aloud, and identify its simple subject and predicate. Have listeners comment on whether these are correct. You may need to explain that in complex sentences it can be difficult to identify the simple subject and predicate, and that in future lessons students will learn how to analyze these types of sentences more effectively.

(T3)

English Language Learners
Teaching suggestions provide scaffolding for English language learners.

Each lesson plan includes basic information on topics that may be unfamiliar to students.

Speaking and Listening
These activities develop oral communication skills.

Students practice building on others' ideas and expressing their own ideas clearly—skills that are important for meeting the new language standards.

Speaking Alert
The megaphone signals specific skills that relate to both oral and written communication.

When the megaphone appears, encourage students to discuss how the lesson topic applies to their spoken language.

Read and Analyze

Agreement with Compound Subjects
Unit 6: Lesson 68

  a. Vince and Reba live in Florida.
  b. Neither Vince nor Reba visits the Everglades often.

Circle the compound subject in each sentence. Underline the verb in each sentence. Which sentence has a verb that goes with a singular subject? _____

A **compound subject** and its verb must agree. If a compound subject includes the conjunction *and*, the subject is plural and needs a plural verb. If a compound subject includes *or* or *nor*, the verb must agree with the last item in the subject. **Remember to use this information when you speak, too.**

See Handbook | Sections 11, 18f

Practice
Look at the compound subject in each sentence. Draw a box around its conjunction. Then underline the correct verb in parentheses.

1. Each year Mr. White and Ms. Brooks (take/takes) their classes to Everglades National Park.
2. Either January or February (is/are) a good time to visit the park because many tours and programs are offered then.
3. The seventh grade class and the eighth grade class (learn/learns) about this distinctive wetland.
4. A ranger or a park administrator (explain/explains) that during the wet season, the Everglades is a wide, shallow, slow-moving river.
5. Sanje, Petra, and Anya (jot/jots) notes for a class report.
6. The Kissimmee River and smaller tributaries (feed/feeds) into Lake Okeechobee.
7. Rainwater and groundwater from Lake Okeechobee (supply/supplies) the water to the Everglades.
8. Ms. Brooks and the ranger (tell/tells) students how the "river of grass"

Grammar, Usage, and Mechanics
Scope and Sequence

Grade	2	3	4	5	6	7	8
Sentence Structure							
subjects							
subject	•	•	•	•	•	•	•
simple and complete subjects	•	•	•	•	•	•	•
understood *you*					•	•	•
compound subject				•	•	•	•
predicates							
predicate	•	•	•	•	•	•	•
simple and complete predicates	•	•	•	•	•	•	•
compound predicate			•	•	•	•	•
predicate nouns and predicate adjectives			•	•	•	•	•
sentences							
simple sentences	•	•	•	•	•	•	•
compound sentences	•	•	•	•	•	•	•
complex sentences		•	•	•	•	•	•
compound-complex sentences						•	•
complete sentences	•	•	•	•	•	•	•
declarative and interrogative sentences	•	•	•	•	•	•	•
imperative and exclamatory sentences	•	•	•	•	•	•	•
choosing sentence structures						•	•
word order in sentences							•
parallel structure							•
combining sentences	•	•	•	•	•	•	•
producing, expanding, and rearranging sentences	•	•	•	•	•	•	•
phrases and clauses							
prepositional phrases	•	•	•	•	•	•	•
adjectival and adverbial prepositional phrases						•	•
participial phrases						•	•
infinitive phrases						•	•
gerund phrases						•	•
dependent and independent clauses				•	•	•	•
adjective and adverb clauses						•	•
noun clauses							•
restrictive and nonrestrictive clauses					•	•	•
analyzing phrases and clauses						•	•
appositives							
appositives					•	•	•
restrictive vs. nonrestrictive						•	•
correcting sentences							
sentence fragments	•	•	•	•	•	•	•
run-on sentences		•	•	•	•	•	•
comma splice			•	•	•	•	•
ramble-on sentences						•	•
misplaced and dangling modifiers						•	•
misplaced subordinate clauses						•	•
objects							
direct object			•	•	•	•	•

Scope and Sequence (continued) Grade	2	3	4	5	6	7	8
Sentence Structure (continued)							
indirect object				•	•	•	•
object of the preposition				•	•	•	•
object complement							•
Parts of Speech							
nouns							
concrete vs. abstract nouns	•	•	•	•	•	•	•
common nouns, proper nouns	•	•	•	•	•	•	•
singular and plural nouns	•	•	•	•	•	•	•
irregular plural nouns	•	•	•	•	•	•	•
possessive nouns	•	•	•	•	•	•	•
collective nouns	•	•	•	•	•	•	•
verbs							
action verbs and linking verbs	•	•	•	•	•	•	•
simple tense (present, past, future)	•	•	•	•	•	•	•
irregular verbs	•	•	•	•	•	•	•
perfect tenses (present, past, future)					•	•	•
progressive forms (present, past, future)			•	•	•	•	•
main verbs and helping (auxiliary) verbs			•	•	•	•	•
modal auxililaries			•	•	•	•	•
transitive and intransitive verbs						•	•
active and passive voice					•	•	•
shifts in verb tense				•	•	•	•
shifts in verb voice							•
verb moods							•
shifts in verb moods							•
verbals							
gerunds						•	•
participles						•	•
infinitives						•	•
pronouns							
personal pronouns	•	•	•	•	•	•	•
reflexive pronouns	•	•	•	•	•	•	•
intensive pronouns					•	•	•
demonstrative pronouns		•			•	•	•
interrogative pronouns					•	•	•
subject pronouns/subjective case pronouns	•	•	•	•	•	•	•
object pronouns/objective case pronouns	•	•	•	•	•	•	•
possessive pronouns/possessive case pronouns	•	•	•	•	•	•	•
indefinite pronouns	•	•	•	•	•	•	•
relative pronouns		•	•	•	•	•	•
adjectives							
adjectives	•	•	•	•	•	•	•
order of adjectives			•	•	•	•	•
demonstrative adjectives	•	•	•	•	•	•	•
proper adjectives				•	•	•	•
comparative and superlative adjectives		•	•	•	•	•	•
coordinate adjectives						•	•
absolute adjectives						•	•
adverbs							
adverbs	•	•	•	•	•	•	•

Scope and Sequence (continued) **Grade**	2	3	4	5	6	7	8
Parts of Speech (continued)							
comparative and superlative adverbs		•	•	•	•	•	•
relative adverbs			•	•	•	•	•
conjunctions							
coordinating conjunctions	•	•	•	•	•	•	•
subordinating conjunctions		•	•	•	•	•	•
correlative conjunctions					•	•	•
prepositions	•	•	•	•	•	•	•
interjections					•	•	•
Usage							
homophones							
your and *you're*		•	•	•	•	•	•
their, they're, there; its and *it's*	•	•	•	•	•	•	•
whose and *who's*						•	•
to, two, too			•	•	•	•	•
than and *then*						•	•
problem words							
myself and *yourself*	•						
very and *real*				•			
good and *well*			•		•		
who and *whom*					•	•	•
doesn't and *don't*			•		•		
learn and *teach*				•			
set and *sit*				•		•	•
like, you know, go, and *all*					•	•	•
who, which, and *that*					•	•	•
leave, let, rise, and *raise*					•	•	•
lie and *lay*						•	•
less and *fewer; over* and *more than*							•
determiners							
articles: *a* and *an*	•	•	•	•	•	•	•
demonstratives: *this, that, these, those*	•	•	•	•	•	•	•
recognizing variations from standard English					•	•	•
Grammar							
pronouns							
subject and object pronouns	•	•	•	•	•	•	•
pronouns in pairs	•	•	•	•	•	•	•
I and *me*	•	•		•	•	•	•
pronoun-antecedent agreement		•	•	•	•	•	•
correcting vague pronouns					•	•	•
shifts in number and person					•	•	•
avoiding extra pronouns					•	•	•
verbs							
subject-verb agreement	•	•	•	•	•	•	•
subject-verb agreement (special cases)						•	•
using helping (auxiliary) verbs	•	•	•	•	•	•	•
using modal auxiliaries			•	•	•	•	•
agreement with compound subjects					•	•	•
negatives							
avoiding double negatives		•	•	•	•	•	•

Mechanics	2	3	4	5	6	7	8
punctuation							
end marks (question mark, period, exclamation point)	•	•	•	•	•	•	•
with items in a series	•	•	•	•	•	•	•
titles							
books	•	•	•	•	•	•	•
movies, songs, stories, poems, CDs, DVDs			•	•	•	•	•
newspapers and magazines					•	•	•
capitalization							
people's names	•	•	•	•	•	•	•
titles of respect	•	•	•	•	•	•	•
geographic names	•	•	•	•	•	•	•
holidays	•	•	•	•	•	•	•
product names	•	•	•	•	•	•	•
dates: month, day	•	•	•	•	•	•	•
sentences	•	•	•	•	•	•	•
titles of works	•	•	•	•	•	•	•
proper nouns	•	•	•	•	•	•	•
abbreviations of proper nouns	•	•	•	•	•	•	•
proper adjectives					•	•	•
direct quotes	•	•	•	•	•	•	•
abbreviations							
titles of respect, initials	•	•	•	•	•	•	•
streets, cities, states, countries	•	•	•	•	•	•	•
month, day						•	•
kinds of business					•	•	•
acronyms							•
commas							
in a series	•	•	•	•	•	•	•
in addresses		•	•	•	•	•	•
after introductory words (ie., *yes* and *no*) and introductory elements		•	•	•	•	•	•
with tag questions					•	•	•
to indicate direct address			•	•	•	•	•
in compound sentences	•	•	•	•	•	•	•
in dialogue		•	•	•	•	•	•
in direct quotations	•	•	•	•	•	•	•
to mark direct speech			•	•	•	•	•
to mark quotations from a text			•	•	•	•	•
in greetings and closings (letters and e-mails)	•	•	•	•	•	•	•
with nonrestrictive elements					•	•	•
with coordinate adjectives						•	•
semicolons							
in compound sentences			•	•	•	•	•
colons							
to separate independent clauses					•	•	•
before lists					•	•	•
in dialogue						•	
after an introductory phrase						•	•
in business letters					•	•	•
in expressions of time						•	•

Scope and Sequence (continued) Grade	2	3	4	5	6	7	8
Mechanics (continued)							
quotation marks							
direct quotations	•	•	•	•	•	•	•
indirect quotations		•	•	•	•	•	•
in dialogue		•	•	•	•	•	•
to mark direct speech				•	•	•	•
quotations from a text				•	•	•	•
apostrophes							
in possessive nouns	•	•	•	•	•	•	•
in contractions	•	•	•	•	•	•	•
hyphens							
to separate syllables in a word break						•	•
to link some compound words						•	•
to link word pairs or groups of words that precede nouns						•	•
to link the parts of numbers						•	•
dashes							
to set off parenthetical elements					•	•	•
to indicate a pause or break							•
parentheses							
to set off parenthetical elements (i.e., explanations or examples)					•	•	•
ellipses							
to indicate a pause or break							•
to indicate an omission							•
letters and e-mails	•	•	•	•	•	•	•
writing paragraphs						•	•
Spelling							
consonant blends	•						
dipthongs *oi, oy*	•						
dipthongs *ow, ou*	•						
soft *g*	•						
ending rules	•	•					
adding suffixes to base words		•	•	•	•	•	•
word families		•					
position-based spelling (vowel-consonant-*e*)		•					
syllable patterns		•					
meaningful word parts		•	•	•	•	•	•
r-controlled vowels			•				
final -*le*, -*en*			•				
final schwa with *l*				•			
final schwa + *n*				•			
final schwa + *r*				•			
schwa in final syllables					•		
consonant doubling		•			•		
silent consonants						•	•
Greek roots					•	•	
Latin roots					•		
prefixes *uni-, mono-, duo-, bi-*							•
homophones					•	•	•
commonly confused words						•	•
frequently misspelled words							•
consulting references to check and correct spellings	•	•	•	•	•	•	•

Nonfiction Topics by Unit

Each unit of *G.U.M.* features the following nonfiction topics.

Unit 5
Grab Bag:
High-Tech Highlights

Unit 6
Great Getaways:
Rivers of the World

Unit 7
Unforgettable Folks:
Problem Solvers

Correlation to the Conventions of Standard English

Each grade level of *G.U.M.* meets grade-specific language standards as well as the standards for all previous grades, ensuring that students retain and further develop the conventions of standard English taught in previous grades. This cumulative progression of skills prepares students to meet college and career readiness expectations.

Grade 8 Conventions of Standard English	Grade 8 *G.U.M.* Page Numbers
Anchor Standard 1: Demonstrate command of the conventions of standard English grammar and usage when writing or speaking.	
L.8.1a Explain the function of verbals (gerunds, participles, infinitives) in general and their function in particular sentences.	**Student Book:** 23–30, 34, 39, 57, 58, 69, 217, 218, 294–296, 300, 325 **Teacher Edition:** T6–T9, T10, T16, T19, T59
L.8.1b Form and use verbs in the active and passive voice.	**Student Book:** 59, 60, 69, 300 **Teacher Edition:** T16, T19
L.8.1c Form and use verbs in the indicative, imperative, interrogative, conditional, and subjunctive mood.	**Student Book:** 31, 32, 34, 76, 129–132, 142, 256, 296, 312, 313 **Teacher Edition:** T8, T20, T36, T39, T70
L.8.1d Recognize and correct inappropriate shifts in verb voice and mood.	**Student Book:** 133–136, 142, 313 **Teacher Edition:** T37, T39
Anchor Standard 2: Demonstrate command of the conventions of standard English capitalization, punctuation, and spelling when writing.	
L.8.2a Use punctuation (comma, ellipsis, dash) to indicate a pause or break.	**Student Book:** 41, 42, 77, 78, 113, 114, 149, 150, 186, 221, 222, 237–242, 249, 250, 255–258, 330–332 **Teacher Edition:** T10, T20, T29, T30, T40, T41, T50, T60, T66, T67, T69, T71
L.8.2b Use an ellipsis to indicate an omission.	**Student Book:** 239, 240, 249, 250, 330 **Teacher Edition:** T66, T69
L.8.2c Spell correctly.	**Student Book:** 35, 36, 41, 42, 71, 72, 77, 78, 107, 108, 113, 114, 143, 144, 149, 150, 179, 180, 185, 186, 215, 216, 221, 222, 251, 252, 256–258 **Teacher Edition:** T9, T10, T19, T20, T29, T30, T39, T40, T49, T50, T59, T60, T69, T71
Grade 7 Conventions of Standard English	**Grade 8 *G.U.M.* Page Numbers**
Anchor Standard 1: Demonstrate command of the conventions of standard English grammar and usage when writing or speaking.	
L.7.1a Explain the function of phrases and clauses in general and their function in specific sentences.	**Student Book:** 19–28, 33, 34, 45–58, 61, 62, 69, 70, 293–295, 297–300, 301 **Teacher Edition:** T5–T7, T13–T17
L.7.1b Choose among simple, compound, complex, and compound-complex sentences to signal differing relationships among ideas.	**Student Book:** 45, 46, 49, 50, 63, 64, 69, 70, 297, 298, 301 **Teacher Edition:** T13, T14, T17
L.7.1c Place phrases and clauses within a sentence, recognizing and correcting misplaced and dangling modifiers.	**Student Book:** 207, 208, 214, 325 **Teacher Edition:** T57
Anchor Standard 2: Demonstrate command of the conventions of standard English capitalization, punctuation, and spelling when writing.	
L.7.2a Use a comma to separate coordinate adjectives (e.g., *It was a fascinating, enjoyable movie* but not *He wore an old[,] green shirt*).	**Student Book:** 103, 104, 233, 234, 329 **Teacher Edition:** T65
L.7.2b Spell correctly.	**Student Book:** 35, 36, 41, 42, 71, 72, 77, 78, 107, 108, 113, 114, 143, 144, 149, 150, 179, 180, 185, 186, 215, 216, 221, 222, 251, 252, 256–258 **Teacher Edition:** T9, T10, T19, T20, T29, T30, T39, T40, T49, T50, T59, T60, T69, T70
Grade 6 Conventions of Standard English	**Grade 8 *G.U.M.* Page Numbers**
Anchor Standard 1: Demonstrate command of the conventions of standard English grammar and usage when writing or speaking.	
L.6.1a Ensure that pronouns are in the proper case (subjective, objective, possessive).	**Student Book:** 93, 94, 105, 106, 155, 156, 177, 189–192, 213, 306, 315, 321 **Teacher Edition:** T26, T53
L.6.1b Use intensive pronouns (e.g., *myself, ourselves*).	**Student Book:** 91, 92, 105, 305 **Teacher Edition:** T25

Grade 6 Conventions of Standard English *(continued)*	Grade 8 *G.U.M.* Page Numbers
L.6.1c Recognize and correct inappropriate shifts in pronoun number and person.	**Student Book:** 195, 196, 214, 322 **Teacher Edition:** T54
L.6.1d Recognize and correct vague pronouns (i.e., ones with unclear or ambiguous antecedents).	**Student Book:** 193, 194, 197, 198, 213, 214, 322, 323 **Teacher Edition:** T54, T55
L.6.1e Recognize variations from standard English in their own and others' writing and speaking, and identify and use strategies to improve expression in conventional language.	**Student Book:** 161–164, 171–176, 177, 178, 317, 319, 320 **Teacher Edition:** T45, T47, T48
Anchor Standard 2: Demonstrate command of the conventions of standard English capitalization, punctuation, and spelling when writing.	
L.6.2a Use punctuation (commas, parentheses, dashes) to set off nonrestrictive/parenthetical elements.	**Student Book:** 21, 22, 33, 55, 56, 70, 233, 234, 237, 238, 249, 294, 299, 330 **Teacher Edition:** T6, T15, T65, T66
L.6.2b Spell correctly.	**Student Book:** 35, 36, 41, 42, 71, 72, 77, 78, 107, 108, 113, 114, 143, 144, 149, 150, 179, 180, 185, 186, 215, 216, 221, 222, 251, 252, 256–258 **Teacher Edition:** T9, T10, T19, T20, T29, T30, T39, T40, T49, T50, T59, T60, T69, T71

Grade 5 Conventions of Standard English	Grade 8 *G.U.M.* Page Numbers
Anchor Standard 1: Demonstrate command of the conventions of standard English grammar and usage when writing or speaking.	
L.5.1a Explain the function of conjunctions, prepositions, and interjections in general and their function in particular sentences.	**Student Book:** 19, 20, 34, 137–140, 142, 243, 244, 250, 293, 314, 331 **Teacher Edition:** T5, T38, T67
L.5.1b Form and use the perfect (e.g., *I had walked; I have walked; I will have walked*) verb tenses.	**Student Book:** 123, 124, 141, 310 **Teacher Edition:** T34
L.5.1c Use verb tense to convey various times, sequences, states, and conditions.	**Student Book:** 121–124, 131, 132, 141, 142, 310, 312 **Teacher Edition:** T34, T36
L.5.1d Recognize and correct inappropriate shifts in verb tense.	**Student Book:** 127, 128, 142, 311 **Teacher Edition:** T35
L.5.1e Use correlative conjunctions (e.g., *either/or, neither/nor*).	**Student Book:** 139, 140, 142, 314 **Teacher Edition:** T38
Anchor Standard 2: Demonstrate command of the conventions of standard English capitalization, punctuation, and spelling when writing.	
L.5.2a Use punctuation to separate items in a series.	**Student Book:** 191–192, 213, 233–234, 249, 329 **Teacher Edition:** T53, T65
L.5.2b Use a comma to separate an introductory element from the rest of the sentence.	**Student Book:** 47, 48, 233, 234, 249, 329 **Teacher Edition:** T13, T14, T65, T67
L.5.2c Use a comma to set off the words *yes* and *no* (e.g., *Yes, thank you*), to set off a tag question from the rest of the sentence (e.g., *It's true, isn't it?*), and to indicate direct address (e.g., *Is that you, Steve?*).	**Student Book:** 243, 244, 250, 331 **Teacher Edition:** T67
L.5.2d Use underlining, quotation marks, or italics to indicate titles of works.	**Student Book:** 227, 228, 249, 327 **Teacher Edition:** T63
L.5.2e Spell grade-appropriate words correctly, consulting references as needed.	**Student Book:** 36, 41, 42, 72, 77, 78, 108, 113, 114, 143, 144, 149, 150, 180, 185, 186, 216, 221, 222, 252, 257, 258 **Teacher Edition:** T9, T19, T29, T39, T49, T59, T69

Grade 4 Conventions of Standard English	Grade 8 *G.U.M.* Page Numbers
Anchor Standard 1: Demonstrate command of the conventions of standard English grammar and usage when writing or speaking.	
L.4.1a Use relative pronouns (*who, whose, whom, which, that*) and relative adverbs (*where, when, why*).	**Student Book:** 51, 52, 69, 97, 98, 106, 298, 307 **Teacher Edition:** T14, T27
L.4.1b Form and use the progressive (e.g., *I was walking; I am walking; I will be walking*) verb tenses.	**Student Book:** 125, 126, 141, 311 **Teacher Edition:** T35
L.4.1c Use modal auxiliaries (e.g., *can, may, must*) to convey various conditions.	**Student Book:** 211–213, 326 **Teacher Edition:** T58
L.4.1d Order adjectives within sentences according to conventional patterns (e.g., *a small red bag* rather than *a red small bag*).	**Student Book:** 103, 104, 106, 308 **Teacher Edition:** T28
L.4.1e Form and use prepositional phrases.	**Student Book:** 19, 20, 34, 293 **Teacher Edition:** T5
L.4.1f Produce complete sentences, recognizing and correcting inappropriate fragments and run-ons.	**Student Book:** 9, 10, 45–46, 65, 66, 69, 70, 291, 302 **Teacher Edition:** T3, T13, T18

Grade 4 Conventions of Standard English *(continued)*	Grade 8 *G.U.M.* Page Numbers
L.4.1g Correctly use frequently confused words (e.g., *to, too, two; there, their*).	**Student Book:** 153–160, 165, 166, 169, 170, 177, 178, 315, 316, 318, 319 **Teacher Edition:** T43, T44, T46, T47
Anchor Standard 2: Demonstrate command of the conventions of standard English capitalization, punctuation, and spelling when writing.	
L.4.2a Use correct capitalization.	**Student Book:** 41, 77, 113, 149, 185, 221, 225–230, 243, 244, 249, 250, 257, 327, 328 **Teacher Edition:** T10, T20, T30, T40, T50, T60, T63, T64, T67, T71
L.4.2b Use commas and quotation marks to mark direct speech and quotations from a text.	**Student Book:** 243–246, 250, 331, 332 **Teacher Edition:** T67, T68
L.4.2c Use a comma before a coordinating conjunction in a compound sentence.	**Student Book:** 45, 46, 297 **Teacher Edition:** T13
L.4.2d Spell grade-appropriate words correctly, consulting references as needed.	**Student Book:** 36, 41, 42, 72, 77, 78, 108, 113, 114, 143, 144, 149, 150, 180, 185, 186, 216, 221, 222, 252, 257, 258 **Teacher Edition:** T9, T19, T29, T39, T49, T59, T69

Grade 3 Conventions of Standard English	Grade 8 *G.U.M.* Page Numbers
Anchor Standard 1: Demonstrate command of the conventions of standard English grammar and usage when writing or speaking.	
L.3.1a Explain the function of nouns, pronouns, verbs, adjectives, and adverbs in general and their functions in particular sentences.	**Student Book:** 17, 18, 33, 34, 81–104, 105, 106, 117–120, 141, 189, 190, 199, 200, 209–212, 213, 214, 293–295, 303–308, 309, 321, 323, 326 **Teacher Edition:** T5, T23–T28, T33, T53, T55, T58
L.3.1b Form and use regular and irregular plural nouns.	**Student Book:** 81, 82, 105, 303 **Teacher Edition:** T23
L.3.1c Use abstract nouns (e.g., *childhood*).	**Student Book:** 85, 86, 105, 304 **Teacher Edition:** T24
L.3.1d Form and use regular and irregular verbs.	**Student Book:** 121, 122, 141, 165–168, 178, 310, 318 **Teacher Edition:** T34, T46
L.3.1e Form and use the simple (e.g., *I walked; I walk; I will walk*) verb tenses.	**Student Book:** 121, 122, 141, 310 **Teacher Edition:** T34
L.3.1f Ensure subject-verb and pronoun-antecedent agreement.	**Student Book:** 193–196, 201–206, 213, 214, 322–325 **Teacher Edition:** T54, T56, T57
L.3.1g Form and use comparative and superlative adjectives and adverbs, and choose between them depending on what is to be modified.	**Student Book:** 209, 210, 214, 326 **Teacher Edition:** T58
L.3.1h Use coordinating and subordinating conjunctions.	**Student Book:** 137, 138, 142, 314 **Teacher Edition:** T38
L.3.1i Produce simple, compound, and complex sentences.	**Student Book:** 45, 46, 49, 50, 69, 70, 297, 298 **Teacher Edition:** T13, T14
Anchor Standard 2: Demonstrate command of the conventions of standard English capitalization, punctuation, and spelling when writing.	
L.3.2a Capitalize appropriate words in titles.	**Student Book:** 227, 228, 249, 327 **Teacher Edition:** T63
L.3.2b Use commas in addresses.	**Student Book:** 247, 248 **Teacher Edition:** T68
L.3.2c Use commas and quotation marks in dialogue.	**Student Book:** 243, 244, 250, 331 **Teacher Edition:** T67
L.3.2d Form and use possessives.	**Student Book:** 87, 88, 105, 231, 232, 249, 304, 328 **Teacher Edition:** T24, T64
L.3.2e Use conventional spelling for high-frequency and other studied words and for adding suffixes to base words (e.g., *sitting, smiled, cries, happiness*).	**Student Book:** 35, 36, 71, 72 **Teacher Edition:** T9, T19
L.3.2f Use spelling patterns and generalizations (e.g., *word families, position-based spellings, syllable patterns, ending rules, meaningful word parts*) in writing words.	**Student Book:** 35, 36, 71, 72, 107, 108, 143, 144, 179, 180, 215, 216, 251, 252 **Teacher Edition:** T9, T19, T29, T39, T49, T59, T69
L.3.2g Consult reference materials, including beginning dictionaries, as needed to check and correct spellings.	**Student Book:** 36, 41, 42, 72, 77, 78, 108, 113, 114, 144, 149, 150, 180, 185, 186, 216, 221, 222, 252, 257, 258 **Teacher Edition:** T9, T19, T29, T39, T49, T59, T69

Grade 2 Conventions of Standard English	Grade 8 *G.U.M.* Page Numbers
Anchor Standard 1: Demonstrate command of the conventions of standard English grammar and usage when writing or speaking.	
L.2.1a Use collective nouns (e.g., *group*).	**Student Book:** 85, 86, 105, 304 **Teacher Edition:** T24
L.2.1b Form and use frequently occurring irregular plural nouns (e.g., *feet, children, teeth, mice, fish*).	**Student Book:** 81, 82, 105, 303 **Teacher Edition:** T23
L.2.1c Use reflexive pronouns (e.g., *myself, ourselves*).	**Student Book:** 91, 92, 105, 305 **Teacher Edition:** T25
L.2.1d Form and use the past tense of frequently occurring irregular verbs (e.g., *sat, hid, told*).	**Student Book:** 121, 122, 141, 165–168, 177, 178, 310, 318 **Teacher Edition:** T34, T46
L.2.1e Use adjectives and adverbs, and choose between them depending on what is to be modified.	**Student Book:** 99–104, 106, 209, 210, 213, 214, 307, 308, 326 **Teacher Edition:** T27, T28, T58
L.2.1f Produce, expand, and rearrange complete simple and compound sentences (e.g., *The boy watched the movie; The little boy watched the movie; The action movie was watched by the little boy*).	**Student Book:** 9, 10, 12, 14, 22, 24, 26, 29, 30, 31, 32, 33, 34, 45, 46, 50, 52, 54, 58, 68, 69, 291, 296, 297 **Teacher Edition:** T3, T8, T13
Anchor Standard 2: Demonstrate command of the conventions of standard English capitalization, punctuation, and spelling when writing.	
L.2.2a Capitalize holidays, product names, and geographic names.	**Student Book:** 113, 149, 221, 225, 226, 249, 250, 257, 327 **Teacher Edition:** T30, T40, T60, T63, T71
L.2.2b Use commas in greetings and closings of letters.	**Student Book:** 247, 248, 332 **Teacher Edition:** T68
L.2.2c Use an apostrophe to form contractions and frequently occurring possessives.	**Student Book:** 231, 232, 249, 328 **Teacher Edition:** T64
L.2.2d Generalize learned spelling patterns when writing words (e.g., *cage → badge; boy → boil*).	**Student Book:** 36, 72, 108, 144, 180, 216, 252 **Teacher Edition:** T9, T19, T29, T39, T49, T59, T69
L.2.2e Consult reference materials, including beginning dictionaries, as needed to check and correct spellings.	**Student Book:** 36, 41, 42, 72, 77, 78, 108, 113, 114, 144, 149, 150, 180, 185, 186, 216, 221, 222, 252, 257, 258 **Teacher Edition:** T9, T19, T29, T39, T49, T59, T69

Beasts & Critters:
Astounding Animals

Unit 1 Sentence Structure

Building Sentence Awareness

Write these phrases on the board and ask a volunteer to read them aloud:

Zoology, a subcategory of biology.

Zoologists study all kinds of animals.

Ask students to identify the group of words that does not tell a complete thought. (first phrase) Then have students add words to create a sequence of words that makes sense. (Example: Zoology is a subcategory of biology.) Explain to students that in Unit 1 they will learn about the different parts that make up a sentence. They will learn how to combine different parts to create sentences that give clear information. Point out to students that knowing what a sentence is and how to construct sentences will help them become better readers and writers.

Introduce the Unit Theme
Astounding Animals

Explain that Unit 1 gives information about a number of animals whose size, strength, habits, and capabilities are unusual. Invite students to name some animals they think are astounding, and have them tell what makes these animals unusual. List their ideas in a word web with the phrase Astounding Animals at the center.

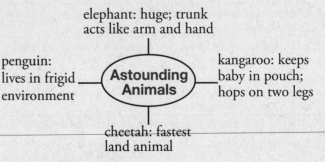

elephant: huge; trunk acts like arm and hand

penguin: lives in frigid environment

Astounding Animals

kangaroo: keeps baby in pouch; hops on two legs

cheetah: fastest land animal

Assessment Options

Unit Pretest

The **Unit Pretest** (pp. 263–266) is intended to be used as a diagnostic assessment to help you determine, prior to instruction, your students' existing knowledge and skill proficiency. Follow this procedure for administering the Unit Pretest:

1. Read aloud the test instructions. (**Note:** For additional scaffolding, you may wish to read the test questions and answer choices aloud.)

2. Tell students that they will have 20 minutes to read and answer the questions independently.

3. When time is up, collect and correct the tests. Use the results to determine which lessons to teach for targeted instruction or which lessons to spend extra time on during whole-class instruction if you are teaching all lessons in the unit.

Unit Posttest

The **Unit Posttest** (pp. 333–336) helps you judge students' achievement while providing students practice for high-stakes tests. When you are ready to administer the test, ask students to carefully tear it out of their books. (**Note:** If the test has already been removed, distribute it to students.) Read aloud the directions for each section and make sure students understand how to answer the questions. Ask students to work independently to complete the test.

Students who miss two questions focusing on the same grammar element may need additional help. Reteach the concept, following this procedure:

1. Review **Read and Analyze**.

2. Review the rule statement for the concept.

3. Guide students through items a second time. Ask the students to explain why each right answer is correct.

4. Refer students to the **G.U.M. Handbook** for further reinforcement.

Complete Subjects and Complete Predicates

Objectives

- To learn that every sentence has a subject and a predicate
- To learn what words make up the complete subject and what words make up the complete predicate
- To identify the complete subject and the complete predicate
- To complete sentences by adding a subject or a predicate
- To write and evaluate original sentences with long or short subjects and predicates

English Language Learners

Invite students to share what they know about penguins and Antarctica. Introduce the words *conditions (climatic conditions), insulation, abdomen,* and *endure.*

Read the sentences in **Practice** aloud and invite volunteers to paraphrase the information. Then reread each sentence, one at a time, and ask students to identify the complete subject and complete predicate in each by asking Whom or what is this sentence about? to identify the subject and What happened? or What did the subject do? to identify the predicate.

Read the phrases in **Apply** aloud, and ask volunteers to suggest a subject or predicate that could complete each phrase. (Example: item 20: The icy waters off the coast *are full of fish and other sea creatures.*) Pair students with English-proficient partners to complete the activity.

For **Reinforce**, read the boxed text and the instructions aloud. Have students work with partners to plan and outline their short paragraphs. Tell them that it may help to compose their sentences orally before they write. Then have students work independently to write their paragraphs and expand them.

Speaking and Listening

Invite volunteers to read aloud the short and long paragraphs they wrote in **Reinforce**. Have students discuss which of each pair they think is more effective and why. Then have volunteers write sentences from their paragraphs on the board. Invite students to identify the complete subject and the complete predicate in each.

Extra Practice

For more practice, see page 291.

Simple Subjects and Simple Predicates

Objectives

- To learn that the simple subject is the most important word or words in the complete subject, and that in imperative sentences the subject is understood to be *you*
- To learn that the simple predicate is the verb in the complete predicate that tells what the subject did, or links the subject to information about it
- To identify simple subjects, the understood subject *you,* and simple predicates in sentence context and to write them in original sentences
- To conduct research and write an e-mail containing simple subjects and simple predicates

English Language Learners

Read **Practice** aloud. Lead students in a discussion of different words and their characteristics. Record this information in a web or chart on the board.

Reread **Practice**. Have students identify the complete subject and predicate in each sentence and then find the simple subject and predicate. Model testing their answers by simplifying each sentence. (Example: item 1: The kiwi scurries.) Read the sentences that contain understood *you* (5, 9) aloud, with the *you* in place to help students recognize them as commands. Point out that sometimes a simple predicate contains a helping verb, such as *has,* and a main verb. Ask students which sentences have both a helping verb and a main verb. (10, 11, 12) Then have students circle the helping verb and underline the main verb.

For **Apply**, model saying aloud sentences about birds. Encourage students to use the information in the web or chart on the board to write their sentences.

If possible, have students use computers with access to the Internet to carry out **Reinforce**. Tell students to make sure all sentences in their e-mails are complete before identifying simple subjects and predicates.

Speaking and Listening

Have students each find a sentence in a textbook, read it aloud, and identify its simple subject and predicate. Have listeners comment on whether these are correct. You may need to explain that in complex sentences it can be difficult to identify the simple subject and predicate, and that in future lessons students will learn how to analyze these types of sentences more effectively.

Extra Practice

For more practice, see page 291.

Lesson 3 (student pages 13–14)
Compound Subjects and Compound Predicates

Objectives

- To learn that a compound subject is two or more subjects joined by a conjunction and that a compound predicate is two or more verbs joined by a conjunction
- To identify the simple subjects in each compound subject and the simple predicates in each compound predicate in sentences
- To combine phrases to form sentences with compound subjects or predicates
- To understand that in a sentence containing both a compound subject and a compound predicate, both parts of the subject must perform both actions in the predicate

English Language Learners

Have students share what they know about Australia. Then tell them that many animals native to Australia are marsupials—animals with pouches in which they keep and feed their babies for a long time. Next, read aloud **Practice**. Help students identify the compound subject or predicate in each sentence. Explain that the conjunctions *and* and *or* are signals to the presence of a compound subject or compound predicate. Have students confirm their responses by restating each sentence as two or more simple sentences. (Example: item 1: Koalas are a kind of marsupial; Kangaroos are a kind of marsupial; Wallabies are a kind of marsupial.)

For **Apply**, help students identify which part of each pair of sentences is the same, the subject or the predicate, before determining how to rewrite each pair as a single sentence.

Rewrite the sentences in **Reinforce** on the board, breaking each down into simple sentences to help students figure out which one is incorrectly written. (Example: The stars sparkled brightly./The wind sparkled brightly./The stars blew softly./The wind blew softly.)

Speaking and Listening

List these words on the board: NOUNS—penguins, kiwis, oropendulas, bowerbirds, kangaroos, koalas, wallabies; VERBS—build, live, have, eat, hop, develop.

Encourage students to use these and other words in oral sentences that contain compound subjects or compound predicates.

Extra Practice

For more practice, see page 292.

Lesson 4 (student pages 15–16)
Direct Objects and Indirect Objects

Objectives

- To learn that a direct object is a noun or a pronoun that receives the action of a verb
- To learn that an indirect object is a noun or a pronoun naming a thing or person to whom something is given, told, or taught, and that it comes before a direct object in a sentence
- To identify direct and indirect objects in sentences
- To complete sentences by adding a direct object or an indirect object
- To learn that an object complement is a noun, pronoun, or adjective that follows a direct object and identifies or describes it
- To identify object complements in sentences

English Language Learners

Invite students to tell what they know about leopards and cheetahs. Record this information in a compare/contrast chart on the board. Then read **Practice** aloud; afterward, call on students to suggest information about each animal that could be added to the compare/contrast chart. Next, help students find the direct object in each sentence and determine whether the sentence has an indirect object; if it does, have students identify it as well.

Read aloud each incomplete sentence in **Apply** and help students decide which word from the word bank fits in the blank. Then have students write the word in the blank and tell whether it is a direct object or an indirect object.

Read aloud the explanation of object complements in **Reinforce**. Help students first find the direct object in each sentence (if it has one) and then find the object complement (if there is one). Have students tell whether each object complement identifies the direct object (the object complement is a noun) or describes it (the object complement is an adjective).

Speaking and Listening

Write these sentence frames on the board:
I gave _____ a _____. I made my friend _____.
Have volunteers complete the first sentence by filling the blanks with nouns, and complete the second by filling the blank with an adjective.

Extra Practice

For more practice, see page 292.

Objectives

- To learn that predicate nouns follow linking verbs and rename the subject, and that predicate adjectives follow linking verbs and describe the subject
- To identify linking verbs, predicate nouns, and predicate adjectives in sentences
- To add predicate nouns or predicate adjectives to complete sentences
- To find words in a word search and use them in sentences that include either a predicate noun or a predicate adjective.

English Language Learners

Pronounce and discuss the meanings of these terms: *invertebrates, terrestrial, cephalopods, mollusks, squid, octopuses.* If possible, show students pictures of mollusks, including octopuses and squids.

Have students read **Practice** silently. Remind them that a noun names a person, place, or thing, while an adjective describes someone or something. Reread each sentence aloud, one at a time. Tell students that the naming words are predicate nouns and the describing words are predicate adjectives. Also explain that a linking verb does not show action; the linking verbs *become, is, are, was,* and *were* link the subject to words that give information about it. Then have students underline the linking verb in each sentence.

For **Apply**, work with students to compose phrases orally to complete the sentences. Then have students write responses.

Read the instructions for **Reinforce** to students. Have a volunteer model finding a word in the puzzle and writing it on the line. Have students work in pairs to complete the activity.

Speaking and Listening

List these linking verbs on the board: is, are, was, were, feel, become, seem. Then display a picture, poster, or painting that shows people on a boat, a pier, or a beach. Encourage students to compose oral sentences about the scene using a linking verb and a predicate noun or a predicate adjective. (Examples: The man *is* a *fisherman.* He *looks peaceful.*)

Extra Practice

For more practice, see page 293.

Objectives

- To learn that a prepositional phrase can tell *how, what kind, when, how much,* or *where*
- To identify prepositions, prepositional phrases, and objects of prepositions in sentence context
- To add prepositional phrases to make sentences give more information
- To differentiate between adjectival and adverbial prepositional phrases

English Language Learners

Encourage students to share what they know about hummingbirds. Have students who have observed these birds describe what they saw and heard.

Read the sentences in **Practice** aloud. Explain that a bird sanctuary is a place where birds and their natural environment are protected. Then reread each sentence and call on volunteers to identify the prepositional phrase, the preposition that begins the phrase, and the object of the preposition.

Read the sentences in **Apply** aloud. Point out that there is more than one way to rewrite each item. Suggest that students work in pairs to select a prepositional phrase for each sentence and then write their responses.

Read aloud the boxed text in **Reinforce**. Then read each sentence in **Reinforce** aloud and have students first identify the prepositional phrase, then tell what word or words it modifies, and finally tell whether the phrase is adjectival or adverbial. As necessary, guide students to identify the part of speech of the word or words modified in order to explain why the phrase is adjectival or adverbial.

Speaking and Listening

Write these prepositional phrases on the board.
near the shore
in the rainforest
at night
through the air
Ask students to incorporate these and other prepositional phrases into original sentences about types of birds. (Example: Eagles soar through the air.)

Extra Practice

For more practice, see page 293.

Objectives

- To discover that an appositive is a phrase that identifies or means the same thing as a noun
- To learn that an appositive follows the noun it identifies and is set off by commas when it is a nonrestrictive element
- To identify appositives in sentences and to rewrite sentences using appositives
- To learn that appositives that are needed to explain who or what a noun is should not be set off by commas

English Language Learners

If possible, use a world globe or a world map on the Internet to show students the location of the Galapagos Islands. Explain that an archipelago is a large group of islands.

Read the sentences in **Practice** aloud and invite students to summarize the information. Have a volunteer reread the first sentence, identify the appositive, and tell which noun it identifies. (a group of islands in the Pacific Ocean; Galapagos Archipelago) Follow a similar procedure for the remaining items. Have students note that each appositive gives additional information about the noun it refers to.

Have volunteers read each of the sentence pairs in **Apply** aloud. Ask other volunteers to tell which words in the underlined sentence give more information that could be added to the other sentence. Have students say the revised sentence aloud with the appositive in place before writing it.

Read aloud the explanation at the beginning of **Reinforce** and help students see that the underlined phrase is necessary in the second sentence but not in the first. Have them determine whether item 21 or 22 should have commas around the appositive and explain why.

Speaking and Listening

Invite each student to briefly describe a friend or favorite relative for the class, using appositives. (Example: My Uncle Rick, *who lives in Iowa,* wrote me a letter.)

Extra Practice

For more practice, see page 294.

Objectives

- To discover that participles are verbals (words formed from verbs) that act as adjectives
- To learn that a participial phrase is made of a participle and other words that complete its meaning
- To identify participial phrases and the participles within them in sentences
- To rewrite confusing sentences by placing the participial phrase in the correct place in a sentence
- To learn that an absolute phrase consists of a noun followed by a descriptive word or phrase, and to rewrite sentences containing absolute phrases

English Language Learners

Read aloud the sentences in **Practice**. Model identifying the participial phrase in item 1; read the sentence without this phrase (Visitors might see elephants.) to show that the subject-verb relationship in the sentence is *visitors/might see*. Call on volunteers to read each remaining sentence and identify the participial phrase and the participle within it.

Next, read aloud the instructions for **Apply** and item 16. Ask students to identify the participial phrase in this sentence and then tell what words it seems to modify. (aunt, uncle, cousins) Point out that these are people, not places, and that the participial phrase should be near the noun *Kenya,* which is a place and is the word the phrase logically modifies. Work through the remaining items in a similar way.

Read aloud the information in the box and the instructions for **Reinforce**. Have students work in pairs to complete the activity.

Speaking and Listening

Have students locate pictures of elephants in magazines or on the Internet. Encourage them to orally compose sentences about these pictures; tell them to include a participial phrase in each sentence they compose.

Extra Practice

For more practice, see page 294.

Objectives

- To learn that an infinitive is a phrase made up of the word *to* followed by the present form of a verb
- To learn that an infinitive phrase includes an infinitive and any other words that complete its meaning
- To identify infinitive phrases in sentences
- To complete sentences by adding infinitives
- To learn about parallel structure as it relates to verbals
- To identify a sentence with nonparallel verbals, and to rewrite it correctly

English Language Learners

Read aloud the sentences in **Practice**. Model looking for the word *to* in item 1, seeing whether it is followed by a verb, identifying the words that complete the phrase, and then stating the whole infinitive phrase. After that, read the same sentence without the infinitive phrase to show that the subject-verb relationship in the sentence is *I/went*. Call on volunteers to read each remaining sentence and identify the infinitive phrase in it.

Read aloud the phrases from the word bank in **Apply** and the items below it. Model choosing a phrase to complete item 16. Then have students work in pairs to complete the remaining items.

For **Reinforce**, read aloud the boxed text. Ask: *Is the sentence* I like singing and to go fishing *a well-written sentence? Why or why not?* (No. The verbals are not parallel.) Then read aloud items 21 and 22. Have volunteers identify the problem sentence and suggest revisions.

Speaking and Listening

Engage students in a conversation about where lizards can be seen in your area. Encourage students to use infinitives, such as *to go, to see, to find,* and *to discover* in their sentences.

Extra Practice

For more practice, see page 295.

Objectives

- To identify simple subjects and simple predicates in sentences with participial phrases or infinitive phrases
- To identify participial phrases and infinitive phrases in sentences
- To complete sentences by adding participles or infinitives
- To identify sentence fragments

English Language Learners

Discuss with students attributes of bears. Encourage students to share what they know about grizzly bears. Then review with students how to identify the simple subject and simple predicate in a sentence, how to recognize a participial phrase, and how to recognize an infinitive phrase.

Read aloud the sentences in **Practice**. Model identifying the subject-verb relationship and then the participial phrase in item 1. Have volunteers identify these elements as well as any infinitive phrases in each remaining sentence.

Read the words in the word bank and the incomplete sentences in **Apply** aloud. Clarify the meaning of each verbal in the word bank before having students work in pairs to complete the activity.

For **Reinforce**, read each item aloud. Ask volunteers to identify the subject-verb relationship (if there is one) in each sentence, and state whether the item is a complete sentence or a sentence fragment. The activity can be extended by having volunteers revise each fragment so it becomes a complete sentence.

Speaking and Listening

Have students orally compose sentences about what it would be like to encounter a grizzly bear. Encourage them to include participial phrases or infinitive phrases in their sentences, and to use proper subject-verb relationships.

Extra Practice

For more practice, see page 295.

Lesson 11 (student pages 29–30)
Expanding and Combining Sentences

Objectives

- To discover that sentences that include descriptive words and words with exact meanings give more information
- To discover that sentences that combine connected ideas make clear important relationships
- To identify paragraphs that effectively present key information
- To rewrite paragraphs so they present more information and make clear important relationships

English Language Learners

Ask students to describe hippopotamuses; list on the board the descriptive words and phrases students give. Tell students that hippos are found in the wild in Uganda, Tanzania, Kenya, Zambia, and several other African nations.

Read aloud the example paragraphs in **Read and Analyze**. Discuss with students what the writer did to change paragraph *a* into a paragraph that presents more information and makes clear important relationships—paragraph *b*. (expanded sentences; combined sentences) Read aloud the rule statement and have students read it with you.

Read aloud the instructions and each pair of paragraphs in **Practice**. Ask volunteers to identify the differences between the two paragraphs, and explain why one is more effective than the other. In item 3 make sure students recognize that although the second paragraph is longer, it is less effective than the first paragraph because the words and phrases added to it do not give important information.

Next, read aloud the instructions and the paragraph in **Apply**. Have students work with English-proficient partners to do the required research and rewrite the paragraph. Note that students will need Internet access to complete this activity.

Have students continue to work with their partners to complete the paragraph revision activity in **Reinforce**. Encourage students to read aloud their paragraph each time they expand a sentence or combine sentences in it.

Speaking and Listening

Encourage students to research the current status of hippopotamus populations in the wild. Then have students discuss ways in which people can support the protection of this vulnerable species.

Extra Practice

For more practice, see page 296.

Lesson 12 (student pages 31–32)
Kinds of Sentences

Objectives

- To learn that every sentence begins with an uppercase letter and ends with an end mark
- To learn that a declarative sentence makes a statement and ends with a period, an interrogative sentence asks a question and ends with a question mark, an imperative sentence gives a command and ends with an exclamation point or a period, and an exclamatory sentence shows excitement and ends with an exclamation point
- To identify kinds of sentences and to add appropriate end marks
- To rewrite each kind of sentence as another kind of sentence
- To analyze the effect of a particular declarative sentence structure

English Language Learners

Ask students to share their knowledge of gorillas. Point out the equator on a map of Africa. Have volunteers name nations adjacent to the equator. Tell students that the world's remaining wild gorillas live in this region.

Have a volunteer read aloud the example paragraph in **Read and Analyze**. Call on students to respond to the prompts. Read aloud the rule statement and have students read it with you.

Read the sentences in **Practice** aloud. Have students work independently to supply end marks and identify the kinds of sentences.

Read aloud each item in **Apply** with vocal expression that helps show what kind of sentence it is. Have students work in pairs to rewrite each sentence as the type indicated. Then call on volunteers to read aloud each sentence with the inflection indicated by the end punctuation—once as it is originally stated and then as they have rewritten it.

Read aloud the statement in **Reinforce**. Have students work in pairs to complete the activity. Encourage students to consider why writers use particular sentence structures when they analyze stories or articles.

Speaking and Listening

Lead students in a discussion of how they might help clear up the misconception that gorillas are violent animals. Encourage interested students to do research to learn more about the realities of gorilla behavior and report to the class on what they learn.

Extra Practice

For more practice, see page 296.

Unit Review (student pages 33–34)

The **Unit Review** allows you to check students' progress and determine when reteaching is necessary. The review pages may be completed in class or as homework. If a student responds incorrectly to two or more items involving the same skill, you may want to work directly with the student to review the relevant lesson. The lesson number to which each review item relates appears in parentheses on the review pages in the Teacher Edition.

Assign the **Extra Practice** activities (pp. 291–296) to reteach targeted skills in a more focused way.

Spelling Practice (student pages 35–36)

Adding Suffixes: *-ary, -ory*

Have students read the example sentences and the directions in **Read and Analyze**. Ask them to identify the suffix in the word in bold type. (-ary) Discuss the meaning of the word. Read the rule statement aloud.

Have students work in pairs to complete the **Word Sort** and share their results with the class. For **Pattern Practice** items 1–8, read aloud the directions and have students work independently. Ask them to present their answers to another student. For **Pattern Practice** items 9–15, read aloud the directions and have students work independently to write the word that completes each sentence. Ask students to identify the suffix in each word they write. (elementary—-ary, mandatory—-ory, migratory—-ory, contrary—-ary, literary—-ary, customary—-ary, complimentary—-ary)

Read aloud the directions in **Use the Dictionary**. Have students work independently to choose the words that best complete the sentences.

English Language Learners

Have students work with a partner who is fluent in English for the spelling activities. The suffixes *-ary* and *-ory* are of Latin origin and have equivalent suffixes in Spanish: *-ario(a)* and *-torio(ia),* respectively. In both cases, the suffix affects the root the same way, and both suffixes are used to create adjectives from verbs. Make sure students identify the exceptions to these rules, such as *expository* and *expositivo, elementary* and *elemental,* and *savory* and *sabroso.*

(you) | Diagram | sentences (student pages 37–38)

Objectives

- To learn that a sentence diagram is a picture of a sentence that shows how its parts fit together
- To place subjects, predicates, adjectives, articles, and direct objects in a sentence diagram

Diagramming Subjects and Verbs

Have students read the information in the box at the top of page 37. Then draw their attention to the first sentence, *Owls hoot.* Have them use the diagram of this sentence to answer questions 1–3. Before students diagram sentences 4–6, help them identify the simple subject and the simple predicate (verb) in each sentence.

① subject
② verb

Diagramming Adjectives and Articles

Ask students to read about where articles and adjectives belong in a sentence diagram and then to explain why the words *the* and *bright* are placed under the word *sun* in the example. (because *the* and *bright* both modify *sun*) Have students work independently to complete the sentence diagrams.

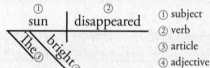

① subject
② verb
③ article
④ adjective

Diagramming Direct Objects

Invite students to read this section and to answer the question. Point out that the line that separates the direct object from the verb does not cross the horizontal line. Student pairs can diagram the remaining sentences. Remind them to look back at earlier sections, if necessary, to recall where adjectives, articles, subjects, and verbs belong in the diagram. Suggest that students use a ruler to draw the diagrams for the sentences at the bottom of page 38.

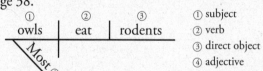

① subject
② verb
③ direct object
④ adjective

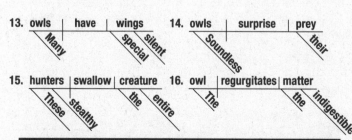

Continued on page T10

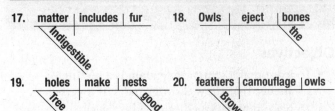

17. matter | includes | fur   18. Owls | eject | bones
    Indigestible   *the*

19. holes | make | nests   20. feathers | camouflage | owls
    Tree   *good*   *Brown*

Writing Sentences (student page 39)

Explain to students that on this page they will practice rewriting sentences that have been poorly written. Ask students to read the directions at the top of the page and then work in pairs to identify the problem in each of the five sentences. Point out that there is more than one way to revise each sentence.

After students have rewritten the sentences, call on several volunteers to read aloud the new sentences. Encourage students to compare and comment on the different solutions.

Direct them to read the description of a paragraph at the bottom of the page. Point out that the kind of paragraph described here is a paragraph of persuasion; explain that paragraphs in narratives (stories) do not need to follow the format described here. Call on volunteers to identify the topic sentence, the supporting sentences, and the concluding sentence in the model paragraph.

Writing a Paragraph (student page 40)

Review with students what a paragraph is. Then work with students to reorder the sentences they wrote on page 39 to form a paragraph with these same elements. Tell students that they may make additional revisions to the sentences if they wish. After students have written their paragraphs, encourage them to compare the finished products.

Students can work independently to write their original paragraphs. Remind them to use the checklist at the bottom of page 40 to evaluate their paragraphs.

Proofreading (student pages 41–42)

English Language Learners

Have students work with a partner who is fluent in English for the proofreading activities.

Proofreading Practice

Ask students to identify the topic of the report on page 41. (whales) Explain that the report contains several mistakes and that as they read, they should look for these mistakes.

Review the **Proofreading Marks** chart and the examples. Remind students that these marks are used by professional writers to check their work before publication. Read the first sentence aloud. Discuss the error (misplaced comma) and how it should be marked. Ask students (in pairs or independently) to mark how the errors should be corrected with proofreading marks. You may wish to have students correct the spelling errors, too.

After they have completed the activity, ask volunteers to read each sentence aloud and to identify errors. Ask students to mark overlooked errors in another color. (**Note:** Some errors can be corrected in more than one way.)

Proofreading Checklist

Ask students to select a recent piece of their own writing and to write the title of that piece at the top of the chart. Have them put a check mark next to each item in the checklist after they have checked it in their work. Students might first work independently and then trade papers with a partner to double-check each other's work. You might model, or ask a student to model, the use of the **G.U.M. Handbook** (beginning on student page 361) to clarify a concept or rule.

Also Remember…

Remind students that capitalization and punctuation are important for clear writing. If necessary, help students use the **G.U.M. Handbook** to clarify when commas should be used and to review the use of uppercase letters.

Your Own List

Suggest that students look at the errors they did not find in the proofreading activity and add them to the checklist. Ask students to think about other kinds of errors they sometimes make and to add these to the checklist.

Ask students to place this page in their writing portfolios. These pages may be used to assess students' progress over the course of the year.

These two pages provide interesting and fun activities that reinforce the skills and concepts students learned in Lessons 1 to 12. These activities give students the opportunity to extend what they have read about in the unit by thinking more about various kinds of animals. You might utilize the **Community Connection** pages in one of the following ways:

- Ask students to take the pages home, select one activity to do, and then share the results of that activity with the class.
- Have pairs of students complete one activity.
- Preview the activities as a class, and then assign the activities to small groups of students to complete cooperatively. Allow time for groups to share the results.

When you are ready to have students select activities, direct them to pages 43–44. Explain that the activities on page 43 will give them an opportunity to think more about astounding animals. Explain that one activity provides an opportunity to find out about jobs in the community that involve working with animals, and a chance to interview a person who does this type of work. Point out that page 44 is a planning guide that will help students take notes as they conduct their interview. Have students carefully tear out the pages, and then explain how you wish students to use them.

The World Outside:
Changes in the Natural World
Unit 2 Sentence Structure

Building Sentence Awareness

Write these words on the board, in a single line with no punctuation marks: events many world our change natural environment and volcanoes earthquakes. Ask students if the words make sense as a complete thought. (no) Then invite students to choose and arrange some of these words to form sentences. (Examples: Many natural events change our environment; Volcanoes and earthquakes change our world.) Point out that word choice and word order are important in forming sentences.

Introduce the Unit Theme
Changes in the Natural World

Ask students to describe changes in the natural world they have learned about. Record their responses in a chart with the words Changes in the Natural World at the top and the words Caused by Natural Processes and Caused by Human Activities in separate columns beneath. Explain that Unit 2 describes some significant changes that have happened or are happening on our planet.

Changes in the Natural World	
Caused by Natural Processes	**Caused by Human Activities**

Have students copy the chart; tell them that as they learn about changes in the natural world from this unit, they should list each one in the proper place in the chart.

Assessment Options
Unit Pretest

The **Unit Pretest** (pp. 267–270) is intended to be used as a diagnostic assessment to help you determine, prior to instruction, your students' existing knowledge and skill proficiency. Follow this procedure for administering the Unit Pretest:

1. Read aloud the test instructions. (**Note:** For additional scaffolding, you may wish to read the test questions and answer choices aloud.)

2. Tell students that they will have 20 minutes to read and answer the questions independently.

3. When time is up, collect and correct the tests. Use the results to determine which lessons to teach for targeted instruction or which lessons to spend extra time on during whole-class instruction if you are teaching all lessons in the unit.

Unit Posttest

The **Unit Posttest** (pp. 337–340) helps you judge students' achievement while providing students practice for high-stakes tests. When you are ready to administer the test, ask students to carefully tear it out of their books. (**Note:** If the test has already been removed, distribute it to students.) Read aloud the directions for each section and make sure students understand how to answer the questions. Ask students to work independently to complete the test.

Students who miss two questions focusing on the same grammar element may need additional help understanding the concept. Reteach the concept, following this procedure:

1. Review **Read and Analyze**.

2. Review the rule statement for the concept.

3. Guide students through items a second time. Ask the students to explain why each right answer is correct.

4. Refer students to the **G.U.M. Handbook** for further reinforcement.

Simple Sentences and Compound Sentences

Objectives

- To learn that a simple sentence (or independent clause) is made up of a subject and a predicate and expresses one thought, and that a compound sentence is made up of two closely related independent clauses joined by a comma and a coordinating conjunction or by a semicolon
- To identify simple and compound sentences and the conjunction or semicolon that joins compound sentences
- To rewrite two simple sentences as a compound sentence
- To conduct research and practice writing compound sentences

English Language Learners

Write the word desertification on the board and have students identify the smaller word in it. (desert) Then invite students to speculate about the meaning of *desertification*.

Read aloud **Practice**. If necessary, clarify the words *diminishing, moisture, nutrients, herbivore,* and *carnivore*. Call on volunteers to tell whether each sentence is simple or compound. To reinforce understanding, have students reread each compound sentence as two simple sentences. Remind students that the conjunction *but* signals a contrast—it links two different things or ideas.

Read aloud the sentences in **Apply** and have students discuss whether to use *and, but,* or a semicolon to join each pair. (Use *but* in 12, 14, and 15; use a semicolon or a comma and *and* in 13; use a comma and *and* in 16.) Explain that a semicolon can be used when two clauses are closely related. (Example: Some deserts form because of human activity; others form naturally.)

Read aloud the instructions for **Reinforce**. Students can work with a partner to conduct the research and write the three compound sentences.

Speaking and Listening

Call on a volunteer to say aloud two simple sentences about deserts. Call on a second volunteer to restate the sentences as a compound sentence. (Example: The desert gets very hot during the day. It can become very cold at night. becomes The desert gets very hot during the day, but it can become very cold at night.)

Extra Practice

For more practice, see page 297.

Dependent Clauses and Independent Clauses

Objectives

- To learn that a dependent clause is a group of words with a subject and a predicate that does not make sense by itself, and that a dependent clause needs to be joined with an independent clause in order to tell a complete thought
- To understand that a dependent clause often begins with a subordinating conjunction such as *although, because, if, as,* or *when*
- To identify dependent clauses, independent clauses, and subordinating conjunctions in sentences
- To match dependent and independent clauses and to work cooperatively to write complex sentences about climate change

English Language Learners

Have students examine the picture of the polar bear on page 47; ask if any students know where these bears live (in the Arctic) and what they eat (seals and fish).

Have students read **Practice** silently. If necessary, clarify the words *abnormal, fluctuations, significant,* and *habitat*. Then reread each sentence aloud, and have students identify the dependent clause in each. To help test their answers, have students read the dependent clause by itself and confirm that it does not make sense.

Then read aloud each dependent clause in **Apply** and help students determine which independent clause matches it. Have students read the complex sentence aloud, emphasizing the pause where the comma belongs, before they write the sentence.

For **Reinforce**, guide students to generate several dependent clauses before having them complete the activity.

Speaking and Listening

Write these dependent clauses on the board: because it rained, although I was tired, when I got home, as I was sleeping. Call on volunteers to brainstorm independent clauses that could be joined with each dependent clause to form complex sentences. (Example: Because it rained, the game was canceled.)

Extra Practice

For more practice, see page 297.

Lesson 15 (student pages 49–50)

Complex and Compound-Complex Sentences

Objectives

- To learn that a complex sentence is made up of an independent clause and a dependent clause
- To learn that a compound-complex sentence is made up of at least two independent clauses and at least one dependent clause
- To distinguish among compound sentences, complex sentences, and compound-complex sentences
- To create complex sentences and compound-complex sentences by joining simple and compound sentences with subordinating conjunctions

English Language Learners

Introduce the concept of Pangaea—an ancient land-mass that included all present-day continents—and ask students to share what they know about it.

Read aloud the example sentences in **Read and Analyze**. Have students follow the marking directions; then have volunteers respond to the questions. Read aloud the rule statement, and have students read it aloud with you.

Read aloud each of the sentences in **Practice**. Clarify unfamiliar terms and then have students summarize the information. Then ask volunteers to tell whether the sentence is compound, complex, or compound-complex. Remind them that subordinating conjunctions (*although, because, if, as, when*) often introduce dependent clauses. Help students confirm their responses by reading each clause separately. If both make sense as separate sentences, the sentence is compound; if one clause cannot stand alone, the sentence is complex or compound-complex.

Model completing **Apply** by rewriting item 11 on the board with the conjunction in place. Have students complete the activity in pairs.

For **Reinforce**, read aloud the passage and then have students each work with an English-proficient partner to complete the writing activity.

Speaking and Listening

Write several coordinating and subordinating conjunctions on separate index cards. Give a card to each student. Then ask students to compose a compound, complex, or compound-complex sentence using the word on their card.

Extra Practice

For more practice, see page 298.

Lesson 16 (student pages 51–52)

Adjective Clauses

Objectives

- To learn that an adjective clause is a dependent clause that describes a noun or pronoun
- To learn that an adjective clause begins with either a relative pronoun or a relative adverb
- To identify adjective clauses in sentences, and indicate whether each begins with a relative pronoun or a relative adverb
- To combine pairs of sentences to create sentences with adjective clauses
- To learn that a noun clause is a dependent clause that acts like a noun
- To identify noun clauses in sentences

English Language Learners

Encourage students to share their knowledge of rain forests.

Read aloud the example paragraph in **Read and Analyze**. Have a volunteer identify the clauses described and the words that begin them. Read aloud the rule statement and have students read it with you.

Read aloud the sentences in **Practice**. Ask students to identify the adjective clause in each sentence. To verify their responses, have students read each sentence aloud without the adjective clause and discuss how the adjective clause adds meaning to the sentence. Then have students work with partners to complete the activity.

Use item 13 to model combining sentences in **Apply**. Point out that the word *people* in the second sentence can be replaced by the relative pronoun *who*. Have students work with partners to rewrite the remaining pairs of sentences.

Read aloud the instructions and sentences in **Reinforce**. Have students continue to work with partners to complete the activity.

Speaking and Listening

List several nouns on the board, such as forest, tree, traveler, monkey, and parrot. Then write these pronouns on separate index cards: who, whom, that, whose, which. Have students take turns drawing a pronoun card and using it in a sentence to begin an adjective clause describing one of the nouns on the board. (Example: The traveler who saw the monkey went home happy.)

Extra Practice

For more practice, see page 298.

Objectives

- To learn that an adverb clause is a dependent clause that tells more about a verb, an adjective, or an adverb
- To learn that an adverb clause can begin with a subordinating conjunction (*than, although, because, if, as, as if, before, while, when, whenever*)
- To identify adverb clauses in sentences and to rewrite pairs of sentences as a single complex sentence containing an adverb clause
- To identify the differences among an adverb, an adverb phrase, and an adverb clause

English Language Learners

Ask students to share what they know about the ozone layer and its importance to life on Earth.

Next, read aloud the rule statement and explain that some of the words listed can also function as other parts of speech, such as prepositions or conjunctions. Have students read **Practice** silently; call on volunteers to summarize the information about the ozone layer. Then read each sentence aloud, one at a time, and have students identify the adverb clause in it. To help them, suggest that they first find the part of the sentence that can stand alone (the independent clause). Explain that the adverb clause is the rest of the sentence.

Model completing items in **Apply** by writing the answer to item 16 on the board. (Because one chlorine atom from CFCs can destroy more than 100,000 ozone molecules, the ozone layer was being destroyed quickly.) Have students complete items 17–20 independently and then read the completed sentences aloud.

Students can complete **Reinforce** in pairs.

Speaking and Listening

Write short, simple sentences on the board, such as: The moon appeared; The stars twinkled; The students slept. Then write these words on separate index cards: because, although, when, before, after, where. Have students select a word card and use it in a complex sentence that incorporates one of the simple sentences on the board. (Example: The stars twinkled *after* the sun had set.)

Extra Practice

For more practice, see page 299.

Objectives

- To learn that a restrictive clause is a dependent clause that is essential to the message its sentence conveys, and that a nonrestrictive clause is a dependent clause that is not essential to the message its sentence conveys
- To learn that a nonrestrictive clause is set off from the rest of its sentence by one or two commas
- To identify restrictive and nonrestrictive clauses in sentences
- To write and correctly punctuate sentences with restrictive clauses and sentences with nonrestrictive clauses

English Language Learners

Ask students how water changes the shape of Earth. Then read aloud the example sentences and questions in **Read and Analyze**. Have volunteers respond to the questions. Read aloud the rule statement and have students read it with you.

Read aloud the instructions and each sentence in **Practice**. Guide a student to identify the dependent clause in the first sentence and the noun it modifies, and tell whether it is a restrictive or nonrestrictive clause. (that falls on hills and mountains; rainwater; restrictive) Then have students work with partners to complete the activity.

Next, read aloud the instructions and sentence pairs in **Apply**. Have volunteers suggest ways each pair of sentences could be combined. Then have students work with English-proficient partners to complete the activity.

Have students work with partners to find the words in the puzzle in **Reinforce**. Encourage students to use a dictionary to learn meanings of unfamiliar words. Then have students work with partners to write the sentences with restrictive and nonrestrictive clauses.

Speaking and Listening

Display a map showing waterways in your region. Have students discuss which small waterways flow together to form larger waterways and which larger waterways flow together to form major rivers. Have students speculate on what landforms these waterways have shaped over the centuries. Encourage interested students to do additional research to learn about the geologic history of your region.

Extra Practice

For more practice, see page 299.

Lesson 19 (student pages 57–58)
Verbals: Gerunds and Gerund Phrases

Objectives

- To discover that gerunds are verbals ending in *-ing* that act as nouns
- To learn that a gerund phrase is made up of a gerund and the other words that complete its meaning
- To identify gerunds and gerund phrases in sentences
- To use gerunds to complete sentences
- To use gerund phrases to rewrite two sentences as one complex sentence

English Language Learners

Direct students' attention to the illustration of the salvinia weevil on page 57, and read the caption aloud. Encourage students to share their knowledge of local plant and animal life.

Read aloud the sentences in **Practice** and clarify these terms: *non-native, species, ecosystem, prey, predator,* and *larvae*. Then reread each sentence aloud, and call on students to identify the gerund and gerund phrase.

For **Apply**, have students work with partners to discuss how to convince a friend not to release goldfish into the wild. Then have students complete the sentences using gerunds.

For **Reinforce**, students can work in pairs to rewrite the two sentences as one complex sentence with at least one gerund phrase.

Speaking and Listening

Invite students to use gerunds and gerund phrases to talk about things that are important to them. (Example: *Taking my dog for a walk* is important. *Going to the park* is our favorite activity.)

Extra Practice

For more practice, see page 300.

Lesson 20 (student pages 59–60)
Active Voice and Passive Voice

Objectives

- To learn that if the subject performs an action, the verb is in the active voice
- To learn that if the subject is acted upon by something else, the verb is in the passive voice
- To discover that in many sentences written in the passive voice, the preposition *by* follows the verb
- To identify the active voice and the passive voice in sentences
- To rewrite sentences from the passive voice to the active voice
- To identify verbs in the active voice in a passage
- To write a sentence with a verb in the passive voice, and then rewrite it so the verb is in the active voice

English Language Learners

Explain to students that earthquakes occur along faults, which are cracks in the plates that form Earth's surface, or boundaries between these plates.

Read the sentences in **Practice** aloud. Help students understand how faults move and form mountains and valleys. Clarify the terms *compress, colliding,* and *rugged*. Call on volunteers to tell whether each sentence is in the active voice or the passive voice. Help them identify sentences in the passive voice; point out the passive voice sentences which contain the preposition *by*.

Students can work in pairs to complete **Apply**. Model revising item 3 in **Practice**, and tell students to write the revised sentence on the lines for item 18. (The land is reshaped drastically at the plates' boundaries. becomes The movement of Earth's plates reshapes the land drastically at the plates' boundaries.)

Read aloud the passage in **Reinforce**. Then have students work with partners to find the verbs in the active voice. As needed, offer help to students as they write their sentences with verbs in the passive voice, and rewrite them as sentences with verbs in the active voice.

Speaking and Listening

Invite students to talk about earthquakes they have experienced, read about, or watched on television. Have them use the active voice to describe these events.

Extra Practice

For more practice, see page 300.

Objectives

- To learn that phrases and clauses function as single parts of speech
- To identify the functions of phrases and clauses
- To identify words modified by phrases and clauses in sentences
- To combine pairs of sentences and identify phrases and clauses and their functions
- To write sentences with specified types of phrases and clauses

English Language Learners

Invite students to share their knowledge of meteors. Ask students why many science-fiction stories have been written about meteors.

Read aloud the example sentences in **Read and Analyze**. Have volunteers respond to the questions. Then read aloud the rule statement and have students read it aloud with you.

Read aloud the instructions and each sentence in **Practice**. Guide a student to identify *of space rock* as a phrase in item 1; explain that this phrase gives more information about the noun *chunk*, and so it is an adjective phrase. Have students work in pairs to complete the activity.

Read aloud the instructions and sentence pairs in **Apply**. Inform students that there are many different ways each pair of sentences could be combined. Model deciding how to combine the two sentences in item 9, and then identify and classify a phrase or clause in the new sentence. Have students work with English-proficient partners to complete the activity.

Have students continue working with their partners on the activity in **Reinforce**. When students finish, have pairs trade papers and check to see that the sentences contain the phrases and clauses specified.

Speaking and Listening

Have students each find in a textbook a sentence with an adjective phrase, an adverb phrase, an adjective clause, or an adverb clause in it. Have students read aloud the sentences, and have listeners identify and classify a phrase or clause in that sentence. (**Note:** The phrase or clause a listener identifies may not be the one the student reading the sentence had identified.)

Extra Practice

For more practice, see page 301.

Objectives

- To learn that simple sentences, compound sentences, complex sentences, and compound-complex sentences can be used to signal different types of relationships among ideas
- To identify sentence structures that effectively communicate ideas and relationships between ideas
- To combine pairs of sentences into sentences with appropriate structures for signaling relationships between ideas
- To recognize that different sentence structures suit different situations and purposes

English Language Learners

Encourage students to share what they know about volcanoes. Guide them to describe how volcanic eruptions build up the land and create new landforms. Have students examine the illustrations and read the captions.

Read aloud the example sentences in **Read and Analyze**. Have volunteers answer the questions. Read aloud the rule statement, and have students read it with you.

Read aloud the instructions and the pairs of sentences in **Practice**. Remind students that longer sentences are not necessarily more informative than short sentences. Next, guide a volunteer to respond to item 1; discuss with students why the first sentence is more effective. (It identifies a set of processes that create landforms, and then gives the scientific term for these processes.) Then have students work with partners to complete the activity.

Read aloud the instructions for **Apply** and the groups of sentences to be combined. Have volunteers suggest ways of combining the sentences in item 7; work with students to analyze the structure of each suggested sentence. Then have students work with English-proficient partners to complete the activity.

Read aloud the instructions and the excerpts in **Reinforce**. Clarify any unfamiliar terms. Students can work with partners to write their paragraphs of comparison.

Speaking and Listening

Have students imagine that they have just spotted a distant volcano beginning to erupt. Invite students to tell you some sentences they might speak at that moment. Write these on the board. Then have students imagine that they have just finished watching a video about a volcanic eruption that took place long ago. Invite students to tell you some sentences they might speak at that moment. Write these on the board and have students discuss differences in length and structure between the two groups of sentences.

Extra Practice

For more practice, see page 301.

Lesson 23 (student pages 65–66)

Avoiding Fragments, Run-ons, Comma Splices, and Ramble-ons

Objectives

- To learn that
  - a sentence fragment does not tell a complete thought
  - a run-on sentence is a compound sentence without a comma and a conjunction
  - a comma splice is a run-on sentence with a comma but no conjunction
  - a ramble-on sentence contains unnecessary words or phrases
- To identify and correctly rewrite sentence fragments, run-ons, comma splices, and ramble-ons
- To rewrite a ramble-on sentence

English Language Learners

Explain to students that this lesson is about how glaciers have shaped landscapes.

Have students read the sentences in **Practice** with partners and decide which kind of error each sentence contains. Then reread each sentence aloud, and call on students to give their answers and to explain why each sentence is incorrectly written.

For **Apply**, model revising the incorrect sentences. Explain that there is more than one way to revise each one. For instance, item 3 could be revised in these ways: Alpine, or mountain, glaciers occur in high, cold mountain valleys; over time these glaciers slowly slide down the mountains. or Alpine, or mountain, glaciers occur in high, cold mountain valleys, and over time these glaciers slowly slide down the mountains.

Guide students to identify the main idea expressed in the monster ramble-on in **Reinforce**. Note that there are several ways students could revise this sentence to make it shorter and clearer. Ask: What can glaciers expose?

Speaking and Listening

Have small groups of students work cooperatively to compose an example of a fragment, a run-on, a comma splice, and a ramble-on sentence. Have groups alternate reading aloud one of their examples. Listeners should identify the error and suggest ways to correct it.

Extra Practice

For more practice, see page 302.

Lesson 24 (student pages 67–68)

Natural, Inverted, and Interrupted Order

Objectives

- To learn that a sentence with natural order follows the subject-verb-object pattern
- To learn that the verb or the object comes before the subject in a sentence with inverted order
- To learn that a sentence with interrupted order contains a dependent clause that interrupts the subject-verb-object pattern
- To identify sentences with natural, inverted, and interrupted order
- To rewrite sentences with natural order as sentences with inverted order
- To rewrite sentences with inverted order as sentences with natural order

English Language Learners

Point out the illustration of the earthworm on page 67, and ask students to share what they know about earthworms.

Read the sentences in **Practice** aloud; guide students to identify the simple subject, simple predicate, and direct object (if there is one) in each sentence. Then have students work with partners to decide which kind of order each sentence has.

For **Apply**, model changing item 16 into an inverted sentence. (Dark is the soil in these hills.) Have students complete items 17–21 in pairs.

Read the two Shakespeare quotes in **Reinforce** aloud, and clarify the words *yonder, thus,* and *hath.* Have students complete the section independently and read their answers aloud. Ask students whether they prefer the inverted or natural sentence; have them explain why.

Speaking and Listening

Have small groups of students work cooperatively to compose one example of a sentence with each type of order (inverted, interrupted, and natural). Have groups alternate reading aloud one of their examples. Listeners should identify the sentence order.

Extra Practice

For more practice, see page 302.

The **Unit Review** allows you to check students' progress and determine when reteaching is necessary. The review pages may be completed in class or as homework. If a student responds incorrectly to two or more items involving the same skill, you may want to work directly with the student to review the relevant lesson. The lesson number to which each review item relates appears in parentheses on the review pages in the Teacher Edition.

Assign the **Extra Practice** activities (pp. 297–302) to reteach targeted skills in a more focused way.

Spelling Practice (student pages 71–72)

Adding Suffixes: -ant, -ance, -ent, -ence

Have students read the example sentence and the directions in **Read and Analyze**. Ask students to identify the word that means "lasting," as well as its suffix. (permanent, -ent) Read the rule statement aloud.

Have students work in pairs to complete the **Word Sort** and share their results with the class. For **Pattern Practice** items 1–7, read aloud the directions and have students work independently. Ask them to present their answers to another student. For **Pattern Practice** items 8–14, read aloud the directions and have students work independently to add the suffix and write each word in the sentence. Ask students to identify the words they formed for each sentence. (observant, attendance, residence, revelance, evidence, observance, resident)

Read aloud the directions in **Use the Dictionary**. Have students work independently to write the words with suffixes.

English Language Learners

Have students work with a partner who is fluent in English for the spelling activities. The suffixes in these activities have similar equivalents in Spanish: -ant is -ante, -ente, or -iente; -ance is -ancia or -encia; -ent is -ante, -ente, or -iente; and -ence is -ancia or -encia. Learning these suffixes will help your Spanish-speaking students understand the meanings of words that contain them.

Objectives

• To learn how to diagram a compound sentence
• To learn how to diagram a complex sentence

Recall with students that a sentence diagram helps to show how different parts of a sentence fit together. Review diagramming a sentence containing a simple subject, a simple predicate, an adjective, an article, and a direct object such as: A hungry rabbit munched a carrot.

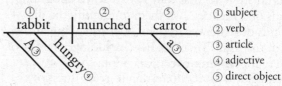

① subject
② verb
③ article
④ adjective
⑤ direct object

Diagramming Compound Sentences

Next, demonstrate how to diagram a compound sentence:

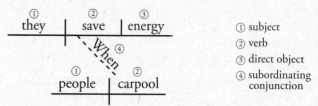

① subject
② verb
③ adjective
④ direct object
⑤ coordinating conjunction

Have students identify the simple subjects and simple predicates in sentences 1–4. Then have students diagram each sentence.

Diagramming Complex Sentences

First, demonstrate how to diagram a sentence with an adverb clause:

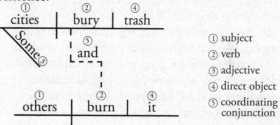

① subject
② verb
③ direct object
④ subordinating conjunction

Then, demonstrate how to diagram a sentence with an adjective clause:

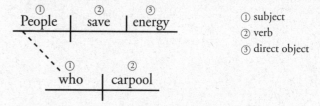

① subject
② verb
③ direct object

Have students identify the dependent clause in sentences 5–7 and decide whether that clause is an adverb clause or an adjective clause. Then have them diagram each sentence.

Language Standard(s): L.8.1, L.8.1a, L.8.1b, L.8.2, L.8.2c

T19

Writing Sentences (student page 75)

Point out to students that on this page they will practice rewriting sentences that have been poorly written. Direct students to read the directions at the top of page 75 and then read the two sentences. Call on volunteers to suggest ways the first sentence might be rewritten. Explain that there is more than one way to revise it.

After students have rewritten the sentences, call on several volunteers to read aloud their revisions. Encourage students to identify the revisions they feel work best and to explain why.

Remind students that they have learned about the four kinds of sentences. Ask them to identify the different kinds of sentences in the model paragraph at the bottom of the page. Then ask how including a variety of sentence types can improve a paragraph. (A variety can make a paragraph more interesting to read; questions and exclamations can grab a reader's attention.)

Writing a Paragraph (student page 76)

Direct students to read the directions at the top of the page. Explain that they will use the sentences they rewrote on page 75 to write a paragraph. Students might work cooperatively to identify statements that could be revised to create questions, commands, or explanations.

Students can work independently or in pairs to write their original paragraphs. Suggest that they look back at the information about changes to the natural world in Unit 2 to help them develop their paragraphs. Also remind them to use the checklist at the bottom of page 76 to evaluate their paragraphs for substance, style, and mechanics.

Proofreading (student pages 77–78)

English Language Learners

Have students work with a partner who is fluent in English for the proofreading activities.

Proofreading Practice

Ask students to identify the topic of the report on page 77. (responsible waste management) Explain that the report contains a number of mistakes and that as they read, they should look for these mistakes.

Review the **Proofreading Marks** chart and the examples. Remind students that these marks are used by professional writers to check their work before publication. Read the first sentence aloud. Discuss the errors (Commas should be placed around the appositive, and *spreading* is spelled incorrectly.) and how they should be marked. Ask students (in pairs or independently) to mark how the errors should be corrected with proofreading marks. You may wish to have students correct the spelling errors as well.

After all students have completed the activity, ask volunteers to read each sentence aloud and to identify errors. Ask students to mark errors they overlooked in another color. (**Note:** Some errors can be corrected in more than one way.)

Proofreading Checklist

Ask students to select a recent piece of their own writing and to write the title of that piece at the top of the chart. Have them put a check mark next to each item in the checklist after they have checked it in their work. Students might first work independently and then trade papers with a partner to double-check each other's work. You might model, or ask a student to model, using the **G.U.M. Handbook** (beginning on student page 361) to clarify a concept or rule.

Also Remember…

Remind students that capitalization and punctuation are important for clear writing. If necessary, help students use the **G.U.M. Handbook** to clarify when commas should be used and to review the use of uppercase letters.

Your Own List

Suggest that students look at the errors they did not find in the proofreading activity and add them to the checklist. Ask students to think about other kinds of errors they make and to add these to the checklist.

Ask students to place this page in their writing portfolios. These pages may be used to assess students' progress over the course of the year.

These two pages provide interesting and fun activities that reinforce the skills and concepts students learned in Lessons 13 to 24. These activities give students the opportunity to extend what they have read about in the unit by finding out more about changes in the natural world. You might utilize the **Community Connection** page in one of the following ways:

- Ask students to take the pages home, select one activity to do, and then share the results of that activity with the class.
- Have pairs of students select one activity to complete together.
- Preview the activities as a class, and then assign the activities to small groups of students to complete cooperatively. Set aside a time for groups to share the results.

When you are ready to have students select activities, direct them to pages 79–80. Explain that the activities on page 79 will give them an opportunity to find out more about the natural world. Explain that one activity gives them a chance to interview a scientist. Point out that page 80 is a planning guide that will help them take notes as they conduct the interview. Have students carefully tear out the pages, and then explain how you wish students to use them.

Timeless Tales:
Myths and Legends

Unit 3 Parts of Speech

Building Grammar Awareness

Write these sentences on the board:

> What is a myth? It is a fanciful tale from an ancient people. It explains something in their world.

Invite volunteers to point to words that name people, places, things, or ideas (myth, tale, people, world); words that take the place of nouns (what, it, it, something, their); and words that describe nouns or pronouns (fanciful, ancient). Inform students that in Unit 3 they will learn about each of these kinds of words. Point out that learning about different kinds of words and using them correctly in sentences helps people better understand what they say and write.

Introduce the Unit Theme

Myths and Legends

Inform students that the title of Unit 3 is "Timeless Tales." Explain that each lesson tells about a story that people in a different culture made up at a different time in history. Some stories are thousands of years old, and others are only decades old. Invite students to share the names of myths or legends they have already heard or read. Record students' responses in a chart using Myth or Legend and Country or Region as headings.

Myth or Legend	Country or Region

Have students copy the chart; tell them that as they learn about different world myths and legends in this unit, they should list each one in the proper place in the chart.

Assessment Options
Unit Pretest

The **Unit Pretest** (pp. 271–274) is intended to be used as a diagnostic assessment to help you determine, prior to instruction, your students' existing knowledge and skill proficiency. Follow this procedure for administering the Unit Pretest:

1. Read aloud the test instructions. (**Note:** For additional scaffolding, you may wish to read the test questions and answer choices aloud.)

2. Tell students that they will have 20 minutes to read and answer the questions independently.

3. When time is up, collect and correct the tests. Use the results to determine which lessons to teach for targeted instruction or which lessons to spend extra time on during whole-class instruction if you are teaching all lessons in the unit.

Unit Posttest

The **Unit Posttest** (pp. 341–344) helps you judge students' achievement while providing them with valuable practice for high-stakes tests. When you are ready to administer the test, ask students to carefully tear it out of their books. (**Note:** If the test has already been removed, distribute it to students.) Read aloud the directions for each section and make sure students understand how to answer the questions. Ask students to work independently to complete the test.

Students who miss two questions focusing on the same grammar element may need additional help understanding the concept. Reteach the concept, following this procedure:

1. Review **Read and Analyze**.

2. Review the rule statement for the concept.

3. Guide students through items a second time. Ask the students to explain why each right answer is correct.

4. Refer students to the **G.U.M. Handbook** for further reinforcement.

Objectives

- To learn that a singular noun names one person, place, thing, or idea, and a plural noun names more than one
- To identify singular and plural nouns in sentences
- To write the plural forms of regular and irregular singular nouns
- To learn that a collective noun names a group of people or things that act as one unit

English Language Learners

Invite volunteers to name any myths or legends they know, either in English or in their native language. If students have no knowledge of myths or legends, provide examples of things ancient people told stories about, such as patterns of stars, mountains that looked like people, or heroes everyone admired.

Read the sentences in **Practice** aloud. Call on volunteers to identify the singular and plural nouns in the sentences. To verify their responses, ask students if each word they have chosen names one or more than one person, place, thing, or idea.

Read aloud the directions for **Apply**. Then have volunteers name the singular common nouns in **Practice**. Discuss which ending should be added to create each plural form.

For **Reinforce**, read aloud the information about collective nouns. Then discuss the meaning of the words in the box. Have volunteers tell which words name a group of people or things. Help students understand that the other words are plural nouns. Have students work with a partner to choose three collective nouns to use in their own sentences.

Speaking and Listening

Have students imagine they are explaining what myths or legends are to a younger student. Ask volunteers to take turns telling what they know. Encourage students to use singular and plural nouns. (Examples: *Cultures* made up *legends*. *Paul Bunyan* is an American *legend*.)

Extra Practice

For more practice, see page 303.

Objectives

- To learn that a common noun names any person, place, thing, or idea
- To discover that a proper noun names a particular person, place, thing, or idea
- To identify common and proper nouns in sentences
- To rewrite sentences, replacing common nouns with proper nouns
- To capitalize proper noun phrases correctly

English Language Learners

Point to Guatemala on a classroom map and explain that for thousands of years the Maya have lived there. Tell students that in this lesson they will read a Mayan legend about a bird called a quetzal. Invite volunteers to share anything they know about the Maya or about the quetzal.

Read aloud **Practice**. If necessary, clarify the words *sacred, shield, wounded, stained,* and *endangered*. Ask volunteers to point out the common and proper noun(s) in each sentence. Remind them that words that name a particular person, place, thing, or idea and begin with a capital letter are proper nouns, and words that name any person, place, thing, or idea are common nouns.

Read aloud the sentences in **Apply**. Have students work with partners to decide which proper noun can replace each common noun. Explain that an indigenous group is a group of people who lived in a place long before other people came there.

For **Reinforce**, read the information in the box. Have students work in pairs to rewrite the sentences.

Speaking and Listening

Distribute index cards that list either a proper noun or a common noun. Call on volunteers to read the word on a card, tell which type of noun it is, and compose an oral sentence using the noun.

Extra Practice

For more practice, see page 303.

Objectives

- To discover that a noun can name a group of people or things
- To discover that a noun can name a thing that can be sensed or an idea
- To identify concrete, abstract, and collective nouns
- To learn that collective nouns that are singular in form are treated as singular nouns in determining subject-verb agreement
- To write verb forms that agree with collective nouns in sentences
- To write a narrative paragraph using abstract, concrete, and collective nouns

English Language Learners

Ask students to tell what they know about William Tell. If necessary, explain that he was a legendary Swiss hero. Point out the location of Switzerland and Austria on a map of Europe.

Read aloud the example sentences and the directions in **Read and Analyze**. Have students reread the example sentences with you and identify the kinds of nouns specified. Read the rule statement aloud, and then have students read it with you.

Next, read the **Practice** instructions and each numbered sentence. Have students read each sentence to themselves, decide which boldfaced noun is the type of noun specified, and circle it.

Read aloud the directions for **Apply**. Explain to students that in sentences in which the things named by a collective noun act together, the collective noun is considered singular and takes the verb form that goes with a singular noun. Read aloud each sentence and have volunteers tell which form of the verb in parentheses should be used to complete the sentence.

Have students work independently to complete the writing task in **Reinforce**. Afterward, have students work with partners to read aloud, expand, and reorder sentences in their paragraphs, and then present them to the class.

Speaking and Listening

Invite any students who have had experiences with the sport of archery to describe to the class what equipment is needed and what skills are involved. If possible, invite an adult involved with the sport of archery to provide more information and answer students' questions.

Extra Practice

For more practice, see page 304.

Objectives

- To learn that a possessive noun shows ownership or close relationship
- To identify singular possessive nouns and plural possessive nouns in sentences
- To rewrite sentences, using possessive nouns
- To find hidden nouns in a word search and to identify the possessive nouns

English Language Learners

Explain that Norse mythology was told in the lands that now include the countries of Norway, Sweden, Iceland, and Denmark. Point to these countries on a class map. Invite volunteers to share anything they know about Norse myths. Explain that Thor was the Norse god of thunder. He lived with other gods and goddesses in a land called Asgard.

Have students read **Practice** aloud. If necessary, clarify the terms *pranks, suspects, hand in marriage, plotters, damsel,* and *smite.* Then ask volunteers to identify the singular possessive and plural possessive nouns in the sentences. Remind students that in most cases the position of the apostrophe, before or after the *s*, can help them figure out whether the word is a singular possessive or a plural possessive noun.

For **Apply** have students work with an English-proficient partner. Explain that they will have to cross out some of the underlined words and rearrange others to create a new sentence that contains a possessive noun.

Have students work in pairs to complete **Reinforce**. Explain that the hidden words go both down and across, and point out an example of each.

Speaking and Listening

Write several short phrases such as these on the board: the hammer of the thunder god, the adventures of the friends, the ending of the story. Have volunteers shorten each phrase to include a possessive noun and use it in an oral sentence. (Examples: *The thunder god's hammer* disappears. *The friends' adventure* takes them to the land of the giants. *The story's ending* is happy.)

Extra Practice

For more practice, see page 304.

Objectives

- To learn that the personal pronouns *I, me, we,* and *us* can be used to refer to oneself and the personal pronouns *she, her, he, him, you, they, them,* and *it* can be used to refer to others
- To identify personal pronouns in sentences
- To write sentences using personal pronouns
- To rewrite sentences replacing the universal pronoun *he*

English Language Learners

Point out China on a world map. Invite volunteers to share anything they know about Chinese myths. Tell students that in this lesson they will read a Chinese myth about the creation of people.

Read aloud the sentences in **Practice.** Call on volunteers to identify the personal pronoun(s) in each sentence. Students can verify their responses by telling to whom the pronoun refers.

For **Apply** have students work with an English-proficient partner. They can begin by reviewing an example of each type of pronoun from the rule statement. Invite students to read their completed sentences aloud.

Read aloud the explanation and solutions for **Reinforce.** Have students work in pairs to rewrite the sentences.

Speaking and Listening

Invite students to create a riddle about one or more mythical characters they have read about, and invite classmates to solve the riddle. (Examples: She formed people out of mud. Who is she? Answer: the Chinese goddess Nuwa; I fought Pedro de Alvarado. Who am I? Answer: The Maya chief, Tecún Umán.)

Extra Practice

For more practice, see page 305.

Objectives

- To learn that compound personal pronouns can be used as reflexive pronouns or intensive pronouns
- To recognize that reflexive pronouns are used to reflect action back to the subject of a sentence
- To recognize that intensive pronouns are used to emphasize the identity of the subject of a sentence
- To recognize reflexive and intensive pronouns and use them correctly in sentences and in a paragraph

English Language Learners

Point to Greece on a world map. Discuss with students the meaning of *loom* ("a device for weaving yarn"). Then ask volunteers to compare weaving to a spider's web-spinning.

Read aloud the example sentences in **Read and Analyze.** Have students then reread the example sentences with you. Ask volunteers to respond to the questions. Read the rule statement aloud, and then have students reread it with you.

Read the **Practice** instructions and each sentence aloud. Guide students to identify *yourself* as a compound personal pronoun in the first sentence and then classify it as a reflexive pronoun. Have students work with partners to identify and classify the compound personal pronouns in the remaining sentences.

Next, read aloud the instructions and sentences in **Apply.** Work as a class to complete item 15. Then have student pairs complete the remaining items.

Finally, read aloud the instructions in **Reinforce.** Have students work independently to write their paragraphs. When they finish, have students work with partners to revise their paragraphs. Encourage them to expand, combine, and move sentences to make their writing more expressive.

Speaking and Listening

Invite students to imagine themselves to be highly skilled at some type of work. Have students take turns boasting about how good they are at this work. Encourage them to exaggerate in humorous ways; tell them to use reflexive and intensive pronouns in their boasts.

Extra Practice

For more practice, see page 305.

Objectives

- To learn that possessive pronouns such as *her, his, its, their, my, our,* and *your* show possession and that possessive pronouns such as *hers, his, theirs, mine, ours,* and *yours* can replace both a possessive noun and the noun that is a possession
- To identify possessive pronouns in sentences
- To rewrite sentences, using possessive pronouns
- To solve a crossword puzzle using possessive pronouns

English Language Learners

Have students imagine what might happen if they made a wish that every vegetable they were served turned to candy. Ask volunteers to speculate on whether this would be a good wish to make and explain why or why not.

Read aloud the sentences in **Practice**. Clarify any unfamiliar words, such as *satyr, (to be) rash,* and *inconsolably.* Have volunteers identify the possessive pronoun(s) in each sentence. Remind them to avoid circling the personal pronouns such as *she* that also appear in the sentences.

Model completing **Apply** using item 17. Clarify the meaning of unfamiliar words, such as *flaw* and *moral.* Have students say their revised sentences aloud before writing them.

Then have each student work with a partner to complete the puzzle in **Reinforce**.

Speaking and Listening

Invite students to suggest other wishes that King Midas could have made. (Examples: I would like my daughter to live a long, happy life. I would like to have the respect of all my friends.) Then have students discuss why each would or would not be a good wish. Encourage them to use as many possessive pronouns as they can.

Extra Practice

For more practice, see page 306.

Objectives

- To learn that indefinite pronouns refer to persons or things that are not identified as individuals
- To identify indefinite pronouns in sentences
- To complete sentences using indefinite pronouns
- To use indefinite pronouns to solve a puzzle

English Language Learners

Tell students that this lesson is about a real person who became an American legend. Explain that this person traveled through Ohio, Indiana, and Pennsylvania planting apple trees. Because he was such an interesting person, people made up many stories about him.

Read aloud the sentences in **Practice**. Clarify any unfamiliar words or terms. Have volunteers reread each sentence aloud and then identify the indefinite pronoun(s).

Students can work in pairs to complete **Apply**. Suggest they complete the sentences orally before writing their responses.

Partners can work cooperatively to complete **Reinforce**. Invite a volunteer to read aloud the answer to the final question.

Speaking and Listening

Have students imagine doing something to help their community. Ask them to describe what they would do and how it would help. Encourage them to use indefinite pronouns in their explanation. (Example: *Nobody* in my neighborhood has a garden. I would help *everyone* plant one.)

Extra Practice

For more practice, see page 306.

Lesson 33 (student pages 97–98)
Relative and Interrogative Pronouns

Objectives

- To learn that when the pronouns *who, whom, whose, which,* and *that* are used to introduce an adjective clause, they are called relative pronouns
- To learn that when the pronouns *who, whom, whose, which,* and *what* are used to begin a question, they are called interrogative pronouns
- To identify relative pronouns and interrogative pronouns in sentences
- To complete sentences, using a relative pronoun or an interrogative pronoun
- To rewrite sentences using correct relative pronouns

English Language Learners

Point to India on a world map. Tell students that this lesson tells about events that take place in a Hindu epic written about 2,000 years ago. Explain that *Hindu* refers to a religion practiced in India and other parts of the world and that an epic is a long poem that tells a story.

Read aloud the sentences from **Practice**. Have volunteers identify each relative pronoun and the noun it modifies. Guide students to see that each adjective clause includes a subject and a verb. Explain that a good way to check the structure of a sentence is to "take out" the adjective clause and read the rest of the sentence aloud. (Example: item 4: Rama sent an army of monkeys to go in search of Sita.) Call on other students to identify the interrogative pronouns. Remind them that an interrogative pronoun begins a question.

Have students work with English-proficient partners to complete **Apply**.

For **Reinforce**, have students work in pairs to rewrite the sentences. Then call on volunteers to tell why the pronoun in the original sentence was wrong and which pronoun they used to correct it. Point out the word *what* in item 25; explain that *what* cannot be used to introduce an adjective clause.

Speaking and Listening

List all the pronouns from the rule statement under two headings on the board: Relative Pronouns and Interrogative Pronouns. Challenge pairs of students to brainstorm questions that include both a relative and an interrogative pronoun. (Example: *What* is the name of the demon *who* kidnapped Sita?)

Extra Practice

For more practice, see page 307.

Lesson 34 (student pages 99–100)
Adjectives and Adverbs

Objectives

- To learn that adjectives modify nouns, pronouns, and other adjectives and that there are different kinds of adjectives
- To learn that adverbs modify verbs or adjectives by explaining how, when, where, or to what extent
- To identify adjectives and adverbs and the words they modify in sentences
- To add adjectives and adverbs to complete sentences
- To identify noun modifiers and use them in sentences

English Language Learners

Ask students if anyone has heard of the mythical hero Hercules. Invite students to share what they know. If necessary, inform students that Hercules was said to be the strongest person on Earth.

Read aloud the sentence in **Read and Analyze**. Have a volunteer identify the words called for. Then read aloud the rule statement and have students read it aloud with you.

Read the sentences in **Practice** aloud and discuss the information in them. Ask students to identify the article and the adverb in item 1, and tell what word each modifies. (the—king; submissively—presented) Have students work in pairs to complete the activity.

Read aloud the instructions, words, and sentences in **Apply**. Have students work as a class to complete item 15. Then have student pairs complete the remaining sentences.

Have students work with partners to complete the word search and write the sentence specified in **Reinforce**. Encourage volunteers to read their completed sentences to the class.

Speaking and Listening

Invite several volunteers to use adjectives to describe an object in the classroom without naming it. Have the other students try to guess what object is being described.

Extra Practice

For more practice, see page 307.

Lesson 35 (student pages 101–102)
Demonstrative Pronouns and Demonstrative Adjectives

Objectives

- To learn that *this, these, that,* and *those* are demonstratives
- To learn that a demonstrative pronoun takes the place of a noun and tells which one
- To identify demonstrative adjectives and demonstrative pronouns in sentences
- To rewrite sentences using demonstrative pronouns or demonstrative adjectives
- To identify demonstrative pronouns in famous quotations and to explain to what they refer

English Language Learners

Point to the city of Puebla, Mexico, on a class map. Tell students that two of the tallest mountains in Mexico are not far from Puebla and that a legend is told to explain how these mountains were created. Ask volunteers to share what they know about the Aztecs or the myth of Popocatépetl.

Read aloud the sentences in **Practice** and have students summarize the events. Clarify unfamiliar terms such as *volcanoes, cunning,* and *tomb.* Ask students to identify the demonstrative adjectives and demonstrative pronouns. Remind them that a demonstrative adjective comes before a noun, while a demonstrative pronoun takes the place of a noun.

Have students work on **Apply** in pairs. Suggest that they say each revised sentence aloud before writing it.

Students can complete **Reinforce** with the help of an English-proficient partner.

Speaking and Listening

Invite students to bring in photographs of a family gathering or magazine pictures of a family doing something together. Have them describe the people and objects in the pictures, using demonstrative pronouns and demonstrative adjectives. (Examples: *This* is a party we had to celebrate Mexican independence. *That* is my Aunt Mari. *These* people are my grandparents.)

Extra Practice

For more practice, see page 308.

Lesson 36 (student pages 103–104)
Ordering Adjectives

Objectives

- To discover that pairs of adjectives should be used in a natural-sounding order
- To learn that coordinate adjectives should be separated with a comma
- To identify pairs of adjectives used in an order that sounds natural and are punctuated properly
- To use pairs of adjectives in a natural-sounding order and punctuate them properly
- To write a paragraph about an inspiring legendary character using adjectives appropriately

English Language Learners

Point out the location of Vietnam on a world map. Inform students that today they will read about a legendary military hero of that country. Have students look at the illustration on page 103. Read the caption aloud. The name *Trieu Thi Trinh* contains sounds that do not exist in English. Here is a rough approximation: *Jeu Tea Gin-Chin.*

Read aloud the example sentences in **Read and Analyze.** Have volunteers respond to the questions. Read aloud the rule statement. Then have students read it with you. You may want to have students examine the chart in Handbook Section 16, which presents guidance on ordering adjectives.

Read aloud each sentence in **Practice** twice, inserting a different answer each time. Ask students to identify which choice produces a more natural-sounding sentence. Have students work independently to complete the activity.

Pair students with English-proficient partners for the activity in **Apply.** Encourage students to read their completed sentences aloud quietly, to make sure they sound natural.

Have students work independently to draft the paragraph specified in **Reinforce.** Afterward, have students join with partners to read aloud, expand, and rearrange sentences to make their paragraphs clearer and more effective.

Speaking and Listening

Play a game in which one student says a noun and other students suggest pairs of adjectives that could be used to modify the noun. The student suggesting the noun must choose one of the pairs of adjectives and write a sentence on the board using those adjectives to modify that noun. Have students check for correct comma usage.

Extra Practice

For more practice, page 308.

Unit Review　　　(student pages 105–106)

The **Unit Review** allows you to check students' progress and determine when reteaching is necessary. The review pages may be completed in class or as homework. If a student responds incorrectly to two or more items involving the same skill, you may want to work directly with the student to review the relevant lesson. The lesson number to which each review item relates appears in parentheses on the review pages in the Teacher Edition.

Assign the **Extra Practice** activities (pp. 303–308) to reteach targeted skills in a more focused way.

Spelling Practice　　　(student pages 107–108)

Prefixes: *uni-, mono-, duo-, bi-*

Have students read the example sentences and the directions in **Read and Analyze**. Ask which word in the sentences contains a prefix meaning "one." (universe) Ask which word in the sentences contains a prefix meaning "two." (dual) Read the rule statement aloud.

Have students work in pairs to complete the **Word Sort** and share their results with the class. For **Pattern Practice** items 1–8, read aloud the directions and have students work independently. Ask them to present their answers to another student. For **Pattern Practice** 9–14, read aloud the directions. Have students work independently to identify the word that completes each sentence. Ask which prefixes appear in the words students selected. (unison—uni-, biannual—bi-, monotone—mono-, bisect—bi-, monorail—mono-, unify—uni-)

Read aloud the directions in **Use the Dictionary**. Have students work independently to choose the correct prefix for each word.

English Language Learners

Have students work with a partner who is fluent in English for the spelling activities. The prefixes *uni-, mono-, duo-,* and *bi-* are commonly used in Spanish. Tell your Spanish-speaking students that the prefixes *uni-* and *duo-* are similar to the number words *uno* and *dos*. Use the words *bilingual/bilingüe* and *monolingual/monolingüe* to explain the meanings of *mono-* and *bi-*. Spanish speakers will recognize words with these prefixes and understand their meanings.

(you) | Diagram | sentences
(student pages 109–110)

Objectives

- To learn how to diagram sentences containing the understood *you*
- To learn how to diagram sentences containing different kinds of pronouns
- To learn how to diagram sentences containing predicate nouns and sentences containing predicate adjectives

Recall with students how to diagram sentences that contain simple subjects and simple predicates as well as those that contain compound subjects and compound predicates. You may wish to use a sentence such as: Danika and Jay enjoy myths.

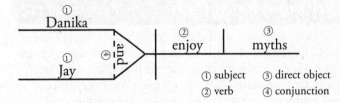

① subject　　③ direct object
② verb　　　④ conjunction

Diagramming Understood *You*

Have students read about where the understood *you* goes in a diagram of an imperative sentence. Ask them where the pronoun *you* would go in each of the three target sentences. Then have them diagram the sentences on the lines provided.

Diagramming Possessive Pronouns

Have students look at the example to find out where possessive pronouns belong in a sentence diagram. Before students complete their sentence diagrams for this section, have them identify the possessive pronoun and the noun to which it refers in each sentence. Point out that item 5 has a compound subject and that they should use what they learned about compound subjects in Unit 1 (pages 13 and 14) to help them diagram the sentence.

Diagramming Predicate Adjectives and Predicate Nouns

Have students look at the examples and identify the predicate adjective and predicate noun in each sentence. Then have students diagram the sentences. Point out that in sentence 10, there is a compound predicate adjective. Tell students to apply what they have learned about how to diagram other compound elements to diagram this sentence correctly.

Writing Sentences (student page 111)

Explain to students that on this page they will rewrite some sentences to provide more information. Ask students to read the directions at the top of page 111 and the five sentences below. Then have students rewrite each sentence so it gives clear, detailed, colorful information.

After students have rewritten the sentences, call on several volunteers to reread items 1 and 2. Encourage the others to identify the elements that were added (adjectives, adverbs, and prepositions) and to tell which revised sentences they like best.

Review the parts of a paragraph with students. (topic sentence, supporting sentences, concluding sentence) Then have students read the model paragraph at the bottom of the page and identify these elements.

Writing a Paragraph (student page 112)

Have students read the directions at the top of the page. Explain that they can adapt one of the sentences as the topic sentence, or they may wish to compose a new topic sentence and a new concluding sentence. Encourage students to share their completed paragraphs.

Students can work independently to compose their original paragraphs. Remind them to use the checklist at the bottom of the page to evaluate their writing. Encourage them to make any necessary revisions.

Proofreading (student pages 113–114)

English Language Learners

Have students work with a partner who is fluent in English for the proofreading activities.

Proofreading Practice

Ask students to identify the topic of the report on page 113. (John Henry) Explain that the report contains a number of mistakes and that as they read, they should look for these mistakes.

Review the **Proofreading Marks** chart and the examples. Remind students that these marks are used by professional writers to check their work before publication. Read the first sentence aloud. Discuss the error (*henry* should be *Henry*) and how each error should be marked for correction.

After they have completed the proofreading activity, ask volunteers to read each sentence aloud and to identify errors. Ask students to mark overlooked errors in another color. (**Note:** Some errors can be corrected in more than one way.)

Proofreading Checklist

Ask students to select a recent piece of their own writing and to write the title of that piece at the top of the chart. Ask students to put a check mark next to each item in the checklist after they have checked it in their work. Students might first work independently and then trade papers with a partner to double-check each other's work. You might model, or ask a student to model, using the **G.U.M. Handbook** (beginning on student page 361) to clarify a concept or rule.

Also Remember…

Remind students that capitalization and punctuation are important for clear writing. If necessary, help students use the **G.U.M. Handbook** to clarify when commas should be used and to review the use of uppercase letters.

Your Own List

Suggest that students look at the errors they did not find in the proofreading activity and add them to the checklist. Ask students to think about other kinds of errors they make and to add these to the checklist.

Ask students to place this page in their writing portfolios. These pages may be used to assess students' progress over the course of the year.

These two pages provide interesting and fun activities that reinforce the skills and concepts students learned in Lessons 25 to 36. These activities give students the opportunity to extend what they have read about in the unit by finding out more about myths and legends. You might utilize the **Community Connection** pages in one of the following ways:

- Ask students to take the pages home, select one activity to do, and then share the results of that activity with the class.
- Have pairs of students select one activity to complete together.
- Preview the activities as a class, and then assign the activities to small groups of students to complete cooperatively. Set aside a time for groups to share the results.

When you are ready to have students select activities, direct them to pages 115–116. Explain that the activities on page 115 will give them an opportunity to connect myths and legends to everyday life. Explain that one activity provides an opportunity to plan an event to celebrate their favorite myths and legends. Point out that page 116 is a planning guide that will help them organize a successful event. Have students carefully tear out the pages, and then explain how you wish students to use them.

Looking Back:
American Journeys

Unit 4 Parts of Speech

Building Grammar Awareness

Write this sentence on the board:

The group hiked determinedly along the Appalachian Trail.

Ask students to find a word that names an action (hiked), a word that tells how (determinedly), and a phrase that tells where (along the Appalachian Trail). Inform students that in Unit 4 they will learn more about verb tenses and parts of speech. Remind students that knowing the parts of speech and how to use them correctly will help others understand what they say and write.

Introduce the Unit Theme

American Journeys

Inform students that the title of Unit 4 is "Looking Back." Explain that the lessons in Unit 4 describe some of the amazing journeys Americans have gone on over the years. Have volunteers describe some American journeys they know about, such as the first trip to the moon. Record their responses in a table on the board and discuss reasons people take journeys.

Type of Journey	Why
space	exploration
ocean	exploration
pioneers	new home/freedom
mountain climbing	personal challenge

Assessment Options

Unit Pretest

The **Unit Pretest** (pp. 275–278) is intended to be used as a diagnostic assessment to help you determine, prior to instruction, your students' existing knowledge and skill proficiency. Follow this procedure for administering the Unit Pretest:

1. Read aloud the test instructions. (**Note:** For additional scaffolding, you may wish to read the test questions and answer choices aloud.)

2. Tell students that they will have 20 minutes to read and answer the questions independently.

3. When time is up, collect and correct the tests. Use the results to determine which lessons to teach for targeted instruction or which lessons to spend extra time on during whole-class instruction if you are teaching all lessons in the unit.

Unit Posttest

The **Unit Posttest** (pp. 345–348) helps you judge students' achievement while providing students practice for high-stakes tests. When you are ready to administer the test, ask students to carefully tear it out of their books. (**Note:** If the test has already been removed, distribute it to students.) Read aloud the directions for each section and make sure students understand how to answer the questions. Ask students to work independently to complete the test.

Students who miss two questions focusing on the same grammar element may need additional help understanding the concept. Reteach the concept, following this procedure:

1. Review **Read and Analyze**.

2. Review the rule statement for the concept.

3. Guide students through items a second time. Ask the students to explain why each right answer is correct.

4. Refer students to the **G.U.M. Handbook** for further reinforcement.

Objectives

- To learn that an action verb shows action
- To learn that a linking verb connects the subject of a sentence to a word or phrase that describes or renames the subject
- To identify action verbs and linking verbs in sentences
- To complete sentences by selecting appropriate action verbs and linking verbs

English Language Learners

Ask students to explain what NASA is. (National Aeronautics and Space Administration—our nation's space exploration agency) Then tell students that the explorer featured in this lesson is not a person—it is a machine with a computer for a brain.

Read the sentences in **Practice** aloud. Call on volunteers to identify the verb in each sentence, tell whether or not it shows action, and then indicate whether it is an action verb or a linking verb.

Have students discuss the information in **Apply** with an English-proficient partner. Then invite students to read their completed sentences to the class.

For **Reinforce**, students should work with partners to figure out whether the verb in each sentence is an action verb or a linking verb. Use item 24 to model the substitution strategy. Tell students that since the sentence makes sense when you replace *looks* with a form of the verb *be,* then *looks* is a linking verb in this sentence.

Speaking and Listening

List some space-related nouns from the lesson on the board: spacecraft, planet, orbit, and mission. Invite students to use these words with action verbs and linking verbs to create original sentences.

Extra Practice

For more practice, see page 309.

Objectives

- To learn that a transitive verb is an action verb that transfers its action to a direct object
- To learn that an intransitive verb does not have a direct object and shows action that the subject does alone
- To identify transitive verbs and their direct objects, and intransitive verbs, in sentences
- To complete sentences using transitive and intransitive verbs correctly
- To write sentences using the same verb in a transitive and an intransitive form

English Language Learners

Ask students to share their knowledge of shipwrecks. Then discuss why people might spend time and money looking for shipwrecks on the bottom of the sea.

Read aloud the sentences in **Practice**. Ask students to identify the transitive verbs and their direct objects, and the intransitive verbs. To help students identify direct objects, suggest that they say the verb and then ask *what?* or *whom?* The answer is the direct object.

For example, in item 1, they can ask *Read what?* The answer is *read stories. Stories* is the direct object of the verb *read*. If there is no answer, there is no direct object and the verb is intransitive.

For **Apply**, have students first determine which of the verbs in the box can take a direct object. Then have partners select the most appropriate verb for each sentence and write it in the blank.

Have students work with an English-proficient partner to complete **Reinforce**. Invite volunteers to read their sentence pairs to the class.

Speaking and Listening

Tell students that searches for shipwrecks are journeys to find relics from the past. Have students discuss other types of journeys for historic artifacts and information. Ask students to identify one transitive and one intransitive verb each speaker uses.

Extra Practice

For more practice, see page 309.

Lesson 39 (student pages 121–122)

The Simple Tenses: Present, Past, and Future

Objectives

- To discover that the present tense indicates that something happens regularly or is true now
- To learn that past tense verbs tell about something that has already happened
- To learn that future tense verbs tell about something that is going to happen
- To identify verbs in past, present, and future tenses in sentences
- To complete sentences using the past, present, and future tense forms of verbs
- To write copy for a brochure using past, present, and future tense verbs

English Language Learners

Ask students if they are familiar with the American explorers Lewis and Clark. Invite students to share what they know. Point out the map on page 122; explain that this shows the route these explorers took on their expedition to find out what the western lands of the Louisiana Purchase were like.

Have students read the sentences in **Practice** aloud. Call on volunteers to identify the verb in each sentence and to tell whether it is in the past, present, or future tense. Remind students that some of the verbs are irregular verbs, so their past tense form will not end in -ed. Point out that *sent* in item 1 and *kept* in item 3 are past tense forms of irregular verbs.

For **Apply**, students can work in pairs to decide which verb belongs in the blank and to use its past, present, or future form to complete the sentence.

For **Reinforce**, students will need to use a computer with Internet access. On the board, model writing an opening sentence for the brochure: How would you like to follow in the footsteps of two of America's greatest explorers? If possible, have peer tutors help students with their writing.

Speaking and Listening

Invite volunteers to discuss what it would be like to venture into a wilderness area with almost no knowledge of what might be there. Direct them to use present, past, and future tense verbs in their discussion.

Extra Practice

For more practice, see page 310.

Lesson 40 (student pages 123–124)

The Perfect Tenses: Present, Past, and Future

Objectives

- To learn that the present perfect tense indicates action that began in the past and was recently completed or is still happening
- To learn that the past perfect tense indicates action that was completed by a certain time in the past
- To learn that the future perfect tense indicates action that will be completed by a certain time in the future
- To learn how to form the perfect tenses by using a form of *have* with the past participle of a verb
- To identify perfect tense verbs in sentences and to complete sentences using them
- To write sentences about events on a timeline using perfect tense verbs

English Language Learners

Explain to students that the North Pole is the northernmost point on our planet and that this point is far beneath the ice-covered surface of the ocean there. Tell students that explorers seeking to reach the North Pole tried to reach the part of the icecap that was directly above the North Pole.

Read **Practice** aloud. Tell students that they can determine the tense of a perfect tense verb by looking at the tense of the helping verb *have*. If the tense is *present* (*have*), then the verb phrase is *present perfect tense*; if it is *past* (*had*), then the verb is *past perfect*; and if it is *future* (*will have*), then the verb is in the *future perfect tense*. Students can work in small groups to identify the perfect tense form of each of the boldfaced words.

For **Apply**, have students work in pairs to determine when the action takes place in each sentence before writing a perfect tense verb. Suggest that they look for clues in the prepositional phrases or in other verb tenses in the sentence.

Invite a volunteer to read aloud **Reinforce**. Have students work with English-proficient partners as they write their sentences.

Speaking and Listening

Ask students to share the most interesting or exciting moment of a journey that they have seen in a movie or read about in a book or magazine. Encourage them to use perfect tense verbs in their accounts.

Extra Practice

For more practice, see page 310.

Lesson 41

(student pages 125–126)

Progressive Verb Forms: Present, Past, and Future

Objectives

- To discover that progressive verb forms show continuing action
- To learn how to form progressive verbs
- To distinguish between present, past, and future progressive verb forms in sentences
- To complete sentences by writing the correct progressive form of the verb
- To identify progressive forms of verbs in crossword puzzle clues and then complete the puzzle

English Language Learners

Ask students whether they would like to learn to fly a plane someday. Then ask students to speculate on why a pilot might want to fly longer or farther than anyone else. (to set a record; to become famous)

Read aloud the sentences in **Practice**. Point out that progressive forms of verbs end in *-ing* and use forms of *be* as helping verbs. Have students reread the first sentence and tell which progressive form is used. (past progressive) Have student pairs complete the remaining items.

For **Apply**, call on volunteers to tell which helping verb is appropriate for each item. Have student pairs complete the sentences.

For **Reinforce**, have volunteers identify the progressive tense verb in each clue. Call on others to answer the clues, and then have students write the answers to the puzzle.

Speaking and Listening

Ask students to describe an airline flight or an auto trip they have taken. Guide them to use progressive verb forms to tell what they were experiencing along the way.

Extra Practice

For more practice, see page 311.

Lesson 42

(student pages 127–128)

Avoiding Inappropriate Tense Shifts

Objectives

- To recognize that verb tenses help establish the time frame of a narrative or a description
- To learn that events happening in the same time frame should be described using verbs in the same tense
- To learn that events happening at different times should be described using verbs in different tenses that make clear the order of these events
- To identify and correct inappropriate tense shifts in sentences and paragraphs
- To write a paragraph using verb tenses correctly to indicate different time frames

English Language Learners

Point out the location of Yosemite National Park on a map of North America. Ask students to share any knowledge they have of the park.

Read aloud the example paragraph in **Read and Analyze**. Have a volunteer respond to the questions and read the corrected sentence aloud. Then read aloud the rule statement, and discuss it with your students.

Read aloud the paragraphs in **Practice**. Guide students to identify and correct the two tense-shift errors in the first paragraph. Then have students work with English-proficient partners to identify and correct the tense-shift errors in paragraph 2.

Next read aloud the instructions and the sentences in **Apply**. Have students continue working with English-proficient partners to complete this activity.

Then read aloud the instructions for **Reinforce**. Have students work with their partners to plan and write drafts. Afterward, have students work with partners to read aloud, expand, and reorder sentences in their paragraphs, paying special attention to correct use of verb tenses.

Speaking and Listening

Write *past* and *future* on several slips of paper and put them in a bag. Have students, in turn, pick a slip from the bag. If the word on the slip says *past,* have them describe an exciting or amusing incident that took place in the recent past. Encourage them to use time-order words to indicate past action. If the slip says *future,* ask them to comment on an upcoming event.

Extra Practice

For more practice, see page 311.

Objectives

- To learn that mood is an aspect of grammar that has to do with a speaker's attitude toward the nature of the information he or she is conveying
- To learn that verbs can change form to reflect these attitudes
- To identify and write verbs in the indicative mood and verbs in the imperative mood
- To write sentences with verbs in the imperative mood

English Language Learners

Point out the state of Utah on a United States map. Explain to students that many members of the Church of Jesus Christ of Latter-Day Saints, often called Mormons, journeyed overland to Utah and settled much of the state in the nineteenth century.

Read aloud the example sentences in **Read and Analyze.** Have a volunteer respond to the questions. Then explain to students that in this lesson and the three that follow, they will learn about how verbs in English indicate mood, which has to do with how close to reality a speaker believes the information in a sentence to be. Read aloud the rule statement, and have students read it aloud with you.

Read aloud the instructions for **Practice.** Then read aloud each sentence. Guide students to decide whether the speaker is expressing information that she or he considers real, or is giving a directive to the reader. Have students work in pairs to complete the activity.

Next read aloud the instructions, the words in the word bank, and the sentences in **Apply.** Complete items 17 and 18 as a class. Have students work with partners to complete the activity.

Have students continue to work with partners to write the sentences specified in **Reinforce.**

Speaking and Listening

Invite students to do research on the Internet to learn more about the pioneer era in the American West. Encourage them to share what they learn with the class.

Extra Practice

For more practice, see page 312.

Objectives

- To learn that mood is an aspect of grammar that has to do with a speaker's attitude toward the nature of the information he or she is conveying
- To learn that verbs can change form to reflect those attitudes
- To identify and write verbs in the subjunctive mood (which is sometimes called the "conditional mood")
- To complete contrary-to-fact statements that include verbs in the subjunctive mood

English Language Learners

Point out the cities of Chicago; St. Louis; Oklahoma City; Amarillo, Texas; Albuquerque, New Mexico; Flagstaff, Arizona; and Los Angeles. Explain to students that in the late 1920s a route connecting these cities was established; it was called Route 66, and many people consider it America's most famous highway.

Read aloud the example sentences in **Read and Analyze.** Have a volunteer respond to the questions. Read aloud the rule statement, and have students read it with you.

Read aloud the instructions for **Practice.** Then read aloud each sentence. Discuss with students whether the sentence states something close to reality, something contrary to fact, or something that a person desires or recommends. Have students work in pairs to complete the activity.

Next read aloud the instructions, the verbs in the word bank, and the sentences in **Apply.** Review the present tense and past tense forms of the verb *be.* Guide volunteers to supply appropriate verb forms for sentences 11 and 12. Have students work with partners to complete the activity.

Have students continue to work with partners to complete the contrary-to-fact statements in **Reinforce.**

Speaking and Listening

Invite students to describe American road trips they would like to take with family members. Instruct listeners to respond with recommendations that include verbs in the subjunctive mood. (Example: I recommend that your family stop at the Corn Palace in Mitchell, South Dakota.)

Extra Practice

For more practice, see page 312.

Lesson 45 (student pages 133–134)
Avoiding Mood Shifts

Objectives

- To recognize that verbs can change form to indicate mood
- To learn that verbs in clauses with similar structure should be consistent in mood
- To identify the mood of verbs in sentences
- To identify and correct inappropriate mood shifts in sentences
- To write sentences with verbs in appropriate moods

English Language Learners

Point out the California coast on a map of the United States. Inform students that California State Highway 1 runs alongside the coast for most of the length of the state, and that many people travel along this road to enjoy the sights and activities the route offers.

Read aloud the example paragraphs in **Read and Analyze.** Have a volunteer respond to the questions. Then read aloud the rule statement and have students read it with you.

Read aloud the instructions and sentences in **Practice.** Guide students to identify the mood of each verb in item 1 (subjunctive; indicative). Have students mark these verbs as indicated. Ask whether there is an inappropriate mood shift in this sentence. (yes) Have students mark the sentence as indicated. Have students work with partners to complete the activity.

Next read aloud the instructions and sentences in **Apply.** Have a volunteer model how to revise item 11 to correct the mood shift. Then have students work with partners to complete the activity.

After that, read aloud the instructions for **Reinforce.** Ask a volunteer to provide a model response. Then have students work with partners to write their sentences.

Speaking and Listening

Encourage students to identify and describe scenic routes in your region. If possible, have students trace the routes they identify on a road map of your region. Guide students to give accurate oral instructions for how to travel from your school to the route they have identified.

Extra Practice

For more practice, see page 313.

Lesson 46 (student pages 135–136)
Avoiding Voice Shifts

Objectives

- To learn that if the subject performs an action, the verb is in the active voice
- To learn that if the subject is acted upon by something else, the verb is in the passive voice
- To identify verbs in the active and passive voices in sentences
- To identify and correct awkward voice shifts in sentences
- To write a sentence using consistent voice

English Language Learners

Have students look at the picture on page 135 and read the caption. Inform students that Marvin Creamer took an amazing sailing trip without using any navigational devices. Invite volunteers to tell what they know about sailing.

Read aloud the example sentences in **Read and Analyze.** Have a volunteer respond to the questions. Read aloud the rule statement and have students read it with you.

Read aloud the instructions and sentences in **Practice.** Have students work with partners to complete the activity.

Next read aloud the instructions and sentences in **Apply.** Have a volunteer model how to revise item 11 to correct the voice shift. Then have students work with partners to complete the activity.

Have students continue to work with partners in **Reinforce** to find the words in the puzzle and write the specified sentence. Encourage interested students to do research to learn about types of boats and ships in the puzzle with which they are not familiar.

Speaking and Listening

Invite students to describe their experiences on boats and ships. Encourage listeners to identify active voice verbs and passive voice verbs in speakers' sentences.

Extra Practice

For more practice, see page 313.

Lesson 47 (student pages 137–138)
Coordinating and Subordinating Conjunctions

Objectives
- To discover that the coordinating conjunctions *and, or,* and *but* connect words or groups of words (including independent clauses) that are similar
- To learn that subordinating conjunctions such as *although, since,* and *before* show how an idea in a dependent clause is related to an idea in an independent clause in a sentence
- To identify coordinating and subordinating conjunctions in sentences
- To complete sentences using the appropriate coordinating or subordinating conjunctions
- To identify subordinating conjunctions in well-known sayings and to write an original saying that includes a subordinating conjunction

English Language Learners
Invite students to share what they know about mountain climbing. Ask students why they think people enjoy this dangerous sport. (Examples: It's challenging. It's great exercise.)

Read aloud the sentences in **Practice**. Call on volunteers to identify the separate independent or dependent clauses in each sentence and to tell whether they are connected by a coordinating or a subordinating conjunction. Have them name the conjunction.

Have student pairs complete **Apply** orally before they write their answers.

Read aloud the statements in the box in **Reinforce**. Clarify the meaning of each saying. Then have partners find the subordinating conjunction and the dependent clause in each sentence. Encourage partners to write original sayings that include a subordinating conjunction.

Speaking and Listening
Write the words and, or, but, although, because, since, and if on the board. Invite students to describe a real or imagined hike on a mountain using these conjunctions. Model, using these examples: Although the path was steep, we were able to climb steadily. We descended quickly because the weather turned bad.

Extra Practice
For more practice, see page 314.

Lesson 48 (student pages 139–140)
Correlative Conjunctions

Objectives
- To learn that correlative conjunctions always appear in pairs and that they connect words or groups of words
- To identify correlative conjunctions in sentences
- To rewrite pairs of sentences as a single sentence with correlative conjunctions
- To identify correlative conjunctions in sentences and then use the sentences to solve riddles

English Language Learners
Inform students that they are going to read about how, before the Civil War, some enslaved people were helped to escape to places where they could enjoy freedom.

Read aloud the sentences in **Practice**. Clarify the meanings of the words *flourished, network, routes, abolitionists, fugitive, enslaved,* and *liberated*. Also discuss the literal and figurative meanings of the word *underground*. Then call on volunteers to name the words that make up each correlative conjunction. Ask others to identify the coordinating conjunctions in the remaining sentences.

Have students work with English-proficient partners to complete **Apply**. Point out that they may have to delete some words and add others when they rewrite each sentence pair as one sentence.

Have partners orally identify the correlative conjunctions in **Reinforce** and then solve the riddles.

Speaking and Listening
Write a pair of correlative conjunctions on index cards. Have student pairs pick a card and use the correlative conjunctions in sentences about events in American history.

Extra Practice
For more practice, see page 314.

The **Unit Review** allows you to check students' progress and determine when reteaching is necessary. The review pages may be completed in class or as homework. If a student responds incorrectly to two or more items involving the same skill, you may want to work directly with the student to review the relevant lesson. The lesson number to which each review item relates appears in parentheses on the review pages in the Teacher Edition.

Assign the **Extra Practice** activities (pp. 309–314) to reteach targeted skills in a more focused way.

Spelling Practice   (student pages 143–144)

Latin Roots: *act, port, dict, ject*

Have students read the example sentence and the directions in **Read and Analyze**. Ask students to identify the Latin root in the word in bold type. (ject) Discuss the meaning of *objective*. Read the rule statement aloud.

Have students work in pairs to complete the **Word Sort** and share their results with the class. For **Pattern Practice** items 1–8, read aloud the directions and have students work independently. Ask them to present their answers to another student. For **Pattern Practice** items 9–17, read aloud the directions and have students work independently to write the words that complete the sentences. Ask students to identify the Latin root in each word. (transaction—act, contradict—dict, unpredictable—dict, objective—ject, reaction—act, activate—act, dejected—ject, rejection—ject, portable—port)

Read aloud the directions in **Use the Dictionary**. Have students work independently to complete the words with Latin roots.

English Language Learners

Have students work with a partner who is fluent in English for the spelling activities. The Latin roots in these activities are part of common words in Spanish, and your Spanish-speaking students will be familiar with most of them. You can use these words to explain the meaning of each root and the meaning of the corresponding English/Spanish cognate. Remind students to pay close attention to minor differences in spelling between both languages, as in *objective* and *objetivo*.

(you) | Diagram | sentences

Objectives
- To learn where to place adverbs and the elements in prepositional phrases in sentence diagrams.

Diagramming Adverbs

Recall with students that in sentence diagrams containing adjectives, the adjective is connected to the noun it modifies by a slanted line below the noun. Have students look at the example; point out that an adverb is connected to the verb, adjective, or adverb it modifies by a slanted line below the modified word. Then have students diagram sentences 1 and 2.

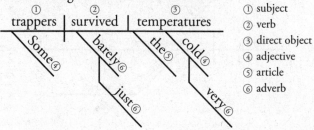

① subject
② verb
③ direct object
④ adjective
⑤ article
⑥ adverb

Diagramming Prepositions and Prepositional Phrases

Remind students that prepositional phrases can act like adjectives and modify nouns, or they can act like adverbs and modify verbs. Have students identify the noun and verb modified in the example. After that, have student pairs identify each adjectival or adverbial prepositional phrase in the numbered sentences. Then have them diagram sentences 3 and 4.

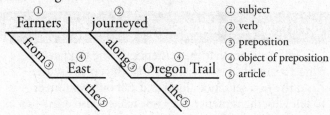

① subject
② verb
③ preposition
④ object of preposition
⑤ article

Have student pairs diagram sentences 5–12 on page 146.

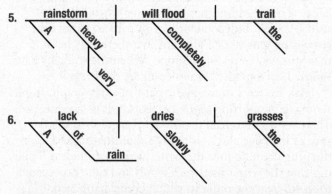

Continued on page T40

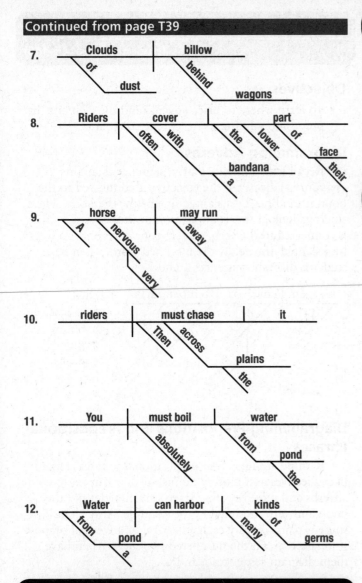

7. Clouds | billow
   of
   dust
   behind
   wagons

8. Riders | cover | part
   often with the lower of
   face
   bandana their
   a

9. horse | may run
   A nervous away
   very

10. riders | must chase | it
    Then across
    plains
    the

11. You | must boil | water
    absolutely from
    pond
    the

12. Water | can harbor | kinds
    from many of
    pond germs
    a

Writing Sentences (student page 147)

Tell students that the sentences at the top part of page 147 need to be revised so that they make sense. Read the first sentence aloud and call on a volunteer to tell why the sentence does not make sense. (The first verb phrase is not in the correct tense.) Point out that *last summer* indicates that the action happened in the past. Then call on another volunteer to correct the sentence. (I went to Guanajuato, Mexico, last summer because my grandmother lives there.) Then have students work independently or in pairs to correct the remaining sentences. Point out that there may be more than one way to revise each one. When the students have finished, encourage them to compare their revisions.

Ask students to name the parts of a paragraph. (topic sentence, supporting sentences, concluding sentence) Then ask them to read the model paragraph at the bottom of the page and to identify subordinating and coordinating conjunctions the writer used to join ideas. Point out that the writer used verb tenses and time expressions to make clear the order in which events happened.

Writing a Paragraph (student page 148)

Ask students to read aloud the instructions at the top of the page and then to write a paragraph using the sentences they revised on page 147. Encourage students to read aloud their complete paragraphs.

Have students work independently to write their personal narratives in the space provided or on another sheet of paper. Remind them to check their work using the checklist at the bottom of the page.

Proofreading (student pages 149–150)

English Language Learners

Have students work with a partner who is fluent in English for the proofreading activities.

Proofreading Practice

Ask students to identify the topic of the report on page 149. (Jedediah Smith) Explain that the report contains several mistakes and that as they read, they should look for these mistakes.

Review the **Proofreading Marks** chart and the examples. Remind students that these marks are used by professional writers to check their work before publication. Read the first two sentences aloud. Discuss the error (*United States* should be capitalized.) and how it should be marked for correction.

After they have completed the proofreading activity, ask volunteers to read each sentence aloud and to identify errors. Ask students to mark overlooked errors in another color. (**Note:** Some errors can be corrected in more than one way.)

Proofreading Checklist

Ask students to select a recent piece of their own writing and to write the title of that piece at the top of the chart. Ask students to put a check mark next to each item in the checklist after they have checked it in their work. Students might first work independently and then trade papers with a partner to double-check each other's work. You might model, or ask a student to model, using the **G.U.M. Handbook** (beginning on student page 361) to clarify a concept or rule.

Also Remember...

Remind students that capitalization and punctuation are important for clear writing. If necessary, help students use the **G.U.M. Handbook** to clarify when commas should be used and to review the use of uppercase letters.

Your Own List

Suggest that students look at the errors they did not find in the proofreading activity and add them to the checklist. Ask students to think about other kinds of errors they make and to add these to the checklist.

Ask students to place this page in their writing portfolios. These pages may be used to assess students' progress over the course of the year.

These two pages provide interesting and fun activities that reinforce the skills and concepts students learned in Lessons 37 to 48. These activities give students the opportunity to extend what they have read about in the unit by thinking more about various kinds of journeys, and why people choose to make them. You might utilize the **Community Connection** pages in one of the following ways:

- Ask students to take the pages home, select one activity to do, and then share the results of that activity with the class.

- Have pairs of students complete one activity.

- Preview the activities as a class, and then assign the activities to small groups of students to complete cooperatively. Allow time for groups to share the results.

When you are ready to have students select activities, direct them to pages 151–152. Explain that the activities on page 151 will give them an opportunity to think more about journeys of various kinds. Explain that one activity provides an opportunity to conduct an interview with a person who helps people make journeys as a part of his or her job. Point out that page 152 is a planning guide that will help students take notes as they conduct their interview. Have students carefully tear out the pages, and then explain how you wish students to use them.

Grab Bag:
High-Tech Highlights

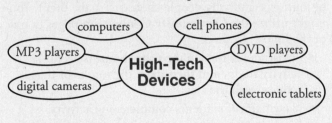

Unit 5 Usage

Building Usage Awareness

Write the following sentences on the board:
Computer programs are not to hard two learn if your a person whose skilled at problem-solving.

Its easy for people to learn new concepts if their curious and eager to discover them on there own.

My computer has over six programs on it, and I've maked stuff with all of them.

Invite a volunteer to read aloud the sentences. Ask students if the words *sound* correct. (Most do.) Then ask them if all the words *look* correct. (Many do not.) Ask volunteers to identify the words that are used incorrectly. (Sentence 1: *to, two, your,* and *whose;* Sentence 2: *Its, their,* and *there*) Ask students what is wrong with the third sentence. (The past participle of *make* is not formed correctly; *stuff* is too vague.) Help students rewrite the sentences correctly. Tell them that in Unit 5 they will learn how to correctly use words that sound alike but have different meanings and spellings. Explain that they will also learn about other words that are often used incorrectly in speaking and writing.

Introduce the Unit Theme
High-Tech Highlights

Inform students that the title of Unit 5 is "Grab Bag" and that each lesson is about a different type of modern technology. Review with students some of the high-tech devices they use or know about: computers, cell phones, MP3 players, DVD players, high-resolution TVs, and so on. Record their responses in a web.

Assessment Options
Unit Pretest

The **Unit Pretest** (pp. 279–282) is intended to be used as a diagnostic assessment to help you determine, prior to instruction, your students' existing knowledge and skill proficiency. Follow this procedure for administering the Unit Pretest:

1. Read aloud the test instructions. (**Note:** For additional scaffolding, you may wish to read the test questions and answer choices aloud.)

2. Tell students that they will have 20 minutes to read and answer the questions independently.

3. When time is up, collect and correct the tests. Use the results to determine which lessons to teach for targeted instruction or which lessons to spend extra time on during whole-class instruction if you are teaching all lessons in the unit.

Unit Posttest

The **Unit Posttest** (pp. 349–352) helps you judge students' achievement while providing them with valuable practice for high-stakes tests. When you are ready to administer the test, ask students to carefully tear it out of their books. (**Note:** If the test has already been removed, distribute it to students.) Read aloud the directions for each section and make sure students understand how to answer the questions. Ask students to work independently to complete the test.

Students who miss two questions focusing on the same grammar element may need additional help understanding the concept. Reteach the concept, following this procedure:

1. Review **Read and Analyze.**

2. Review the rule statement for the concept.

3. Guide students through items a second time. Ask the students to explain why each right answer is correct.

4. Refer students to the **G.U.M. Handbook** for further reinforcement.

Objectives

- To discover that *your* and *you're*, and *their*, *they're*, and *there* sound the same but have different spellings and meanings
- To learn that the words *your* and *their* are possessive pronouns that show ownership; that *you're* and *they're* are contractions of the words *you are* and *they are;* and that *there* refers to a place or introduces a clause
- To select the correct use of *your* or *you're*, and *their*, *they're*, or *there* in sentences
- To use the words *your* and *you're*, and *their*, *they're*, and *there* correctly in sentences
- To learn about homophones

English Language Learners

Tell students that they are going to learn about proper *etiquette*, or polite behavior, when writing an e-mail.

Read aloud **Practice**. Have a volunteer reread the first sentence. Ask students if the possessive pronoun *your* or the words *you are* make sense in the sentence. Tell students that if the words *you are* make sense, then they should use the contraction *you're*. Guide students to complete the rest of **Practice** in a similar manner.

Before students complete **Apply**, read aloud the sentences. Ask pairs to say each answer orally before they write it and then to determine whether *your, you're, their, they're,* or *there* belongs in the sentence.

Emphasize to students the definition of *homophone* in **Reinforce**. Then have partners work together to complete the activity.

Speaking and Listening

Divide the class into two groups: the pronoun *your* group and the contraction *you're* group. Then have a volunteer give oral instructions to the class about an activity or game he or she enjoys doing. Each time the word *your* or *you're* is used in a sentence, the appropriate group should raise their hands. (Example: In the game of tag, if someone touches *your* arm, *you're* "it"!) If time allows, repeat the game with *their* and *they're*.

Extra Practice

For more practice, see page 315.

Objectives

- To discover that *its* and *it's*, and *who's* and *whose* sound the same but have different spellings and meanings
- To learn that *its* and *whose* are possessive pronouns
- To learn that *it's* is a contraction of the words *it is* or *it has,* and *who's* is a contraction of the words *who is* or *who has*
- To select the correct use of *its* or *it's* and *whose* or *who's* in sentences
- To complete sentences using *its* or *it's* and *whose* or *who's*
- To write a cell phone advertisement using the words *its, it's, whose,* and *who's*

English Language Learners

Help students with the first sentence in **Practice** by rereading it aloud and asking whether the possessive pronoun *its* or the words *it is* make sense in the sentence. (*its*) Follow a similar procedure with the remaining sentences before having students underline their answers. Remind students that if the words *it is* or *it has* make sense in a sentence, then they should underline the contraction *it's*; if the phrase *who is* or *who has* makes sense in a sentence, then they should underline the contraction *who's*.

Have students work in pairs to complete **Apply**. Partners should discuss their answers before they write them.

Have students work with English-proficient partners to complete **Reinforce**. Encourage students to discuss the features of a cell phone and then list them before they begin writing their ad. Finally, have students reread their work and check their use of homophones.

Speaking and Listening

Tell students that many people have difficulty remembering when to write *it's* or *its* and when to write *who's* or *whose*. Challenge partners to devise a clever way to help people remember which of these words is spelled with an apostrophe. Have them present their method to the class. After all the ideas have been presented, have students vote for the one they think would be most effective.

Extra Practice

For more practice, see page 315.

Lesson 51 (student pages 157–158)

To, Too, and *Two*

Objectives

- To discover that *to, too,* and *two* sound the same but have different spellings and meanings
- To learn that *to* can be a preposition that means "in the direction of," and can also be used with a verb to form an infinitive
- To learn that *too* is an adverb and means "also" or "excessively"
- To learn that *two* refers to the number 2
- To distinguish among *to, too,* and *two* in sentences
- To complete sentences using *to, too,* or *two*
- To write original riddles based on homophones

English Language Learners

Read aloud the sentences for **Practice**. Clarify unfamiliar terms such as *affordable, access, components, essentials, sturdy, scarce, wind-up crank, gap,* and *prosperous*. Then ask volunteers to read aloud each sentence, identify the word in parentheses that correctly completes that sentence, and explain the reason for their choice.

For **Apply**, have students work in pairs to fill in the blanks. Invite volunteers to read aloud their completed sentences, spelling the word they have written in each blank. Pairs of students might enjoy reading the completed sentences as dialogue.

Have volunteers read aloud the sample riddles in **Reinforce**. Clarify the meanings of the homophones in the example riddles and in the box below. You may wish to work with students to write three group riddles.

Speaking and Listening

Write the words *to, too,* and *two* on index cards and place the cards in a hat or bowl. Have students take turns drawing a card and using that word in a sentence. Listeners should tell how the word should be spelled and why. Cards should be returned to the hat after each turn.

Extra Practice

For more practice, see page 316.

Lesson 52 (student pages 159–160)

Writing About Quantity

Objectives

- To learn that *less* can be used to refer to a smaller amount that is not a sum of items and *fewer* is used to refer to a smaller number of items
- To learn that *over* can be used to refer to a larger amount that is not a sum of items and *more than* is used to describe a larger number of items
- To select the correct form among *less* and *fewer,* and *over* and *more than* in sentences
- To complete sentences using *less, fewer, over,* and *more than*
- To write an e-mail to a friend using *less, fewer, over,* and *more than*

English Language Learners

Explain to students that American writers tend to distinguish between *over* and *more than* when referring to quantity, whereas some other writers do not. Tell students that for the purpose of academic writing, they should know the difference between how these words are used.

Read aloud the sentences for **Practice**. Clarify unfamiliar expressions such as *conduct, results, better-targeted, fluff, database, search engine,* and *wildcard character*. Then ask volunteers to read aloud each sentence, identify the word in parentheses that correctly completes that sentence, and explain the reason for their choice.

For **Apply**, have students work in pairs to fill in the blanks. Ask volunteers to read their completed sentences.

Have students complete **Reinforce** independently or in pairs. Once they have finished writing, have students circle the quantity words they used and check whether they used them correctly.

Speaking and Listening

Distribute a small quantity of countable objects to students, such as marbles, markers, or playing cards. Also distribute something to each student that is not countable but varies in size from that of other students, such as different amounts of water in paper cups. Then guide students to compose sentences using *less, fewer, over,* and *more than*. (For example: Marta has *less* water than Ramon, but Ramon has *fewer* markers. *More than* six students are holding marbles in their hands.)

Extra Practice

For more practice, see page 316.

Objectives

- To learn that a negative word means "no" or "not at all," and that in standard English double negatives should be avoided
- To learn that *doesn't* is used with a singular subject and that *don't* is used with a plural subject
- To discover that *don't* is used with *I* and *you*
- To identify the correct use of negatives in sentences
- To rewrite sentences, replacing double negatives with correct words
- To use negatives to complete a crossword puzzle

English Language Learners

Inform students that they will read about a type of technology that people can use to find various locations; it is called Global Positioning System, or GPS. Explain that this technology depends on satellites—machines that orbit around Earth and send or relay signals that people use for radio, television, and other forms of communication.

Read aloud each sentence in **Practice**, saying both answers in parentheses. Ask students to tell which word or words belong in the sentence and why.

Have students work with English-proficient partners to read and correct the sentences in **Apply**. Ask students to discuss why each sentence is wrong and how to reword the sentence correctly. If your class includes Spanish speakers, explain that unlike in Spanish, double negatives are not used in English.

For **Reinforce**, students can work with a partner to complete the crossword puzzle.

Speaking and Listening

Have groups of students brainstorm rules of behavior for visiting another country. Encourage groups to share their rules with the class. (Examples: *Never* wander away from the adults you are with. *Don't* lose your passport!)

Extra Practice

For more practice, see page 317.

Objectives

- To learn that in academic writing, writers should respect the conventions of standard English and avoid using contractions, shortened forms of words, slang or informal language, and vague words
- To identify in sentences expressions that should be avoided in academic writing
- To rewrite sentences by replacing contractions and informal or vague expressions with more appropriate language
- To learn that writers can strengthen their writing by avoiding the expressions *there is, there are,* and *it is*
- To rewrite sentences to eliminate *there is, there are,* and *it is*

English Language Learners

Ask students if they have read or heard of blogs. Explain that a blog is similar to a diary, but that instead of writing in a book, the writer types words and saves them on a website. Discuss with students what people might write about in their blogs.

Read aloud each sentence in **Practice**. Ask students to tell which word or words do not belong in the sentence and why. Have students make note of which expressions are contractions or shortened forms, which are informal, and which are vague.

Have student pairs work with an English-proficient partner to read and correct the sentences in **Apply**. Ask students to discuss why each sentence is not appropriate for academic writing and how to reword the sentence correctly.

For **Reinforce**, students can work with a partner to rewrite the sentences using more active words.

Speaking and Listening

Have students work in groups to reread the sentences in **Practice**. For each sentence, have students discuss the various ways the writer could have expressed the same idea in proper academic language.

Extra Practice

For more practice, see page 317.

Objectives

- To learn that *lie* and *lay* are different verbs that sound similar; *lay* takes a direct object, but *lie* does not
- To learn that *set* and *sit* are different verbs that sound similar; *set* takes a direct object, but *sit* does not
- To learn that *rise* and *raise* are different verbs that sound similar; *raise* takes a direct object, but *rise* does not
- To distinguish among forms of *sit* and *set, lie* and *lay,* and *rise* and *raise* in sentences
- To rewrite sentences using the correct form of *lie, lay, set, sit, rise* or *raise*
- To learn that the words *raze* and *raise* sound the same but have different spellings and meanings; *raze* means "to destroy"
- To write original sentences using forms of the words *raise* and *raze*

English Language Learners

Read aloud the sentences in **Practice.** Clarify the meaning of unfamiliar terms such as *e-waste, dispose, impact, hazardous, contaminating, groundwater, incinerated, recycled, seep,* and *facilities.* Have a volunteer reread the first sentence, tell which word is correct, and explain why. Have students complete the remaining sentences in pairs. Suggest they refer to the rule statement at the top of the page if they need help remembering the usage of a given word.

Model revising the first sentence in **Apply.** (Change *stayed* to *lain.*) Then have students work with English-proficient partners to rewrite the rest of the sentences.

Students can work with English-proficient partners to complete **Reinforce.**

Speaking and Listening

Ask students to take turns giving commands in a simple game of Simon Says. Have students include the words *lie, lay, sit, set, rise* or *raise* in their commands. (Examples: *Rise* from your chair. *Raise* your hands above your head. *Sit* down.)

Extra Practice

For more practice, see page 318.

Objectives

- To learn that irregular verbs do not add *-ed* in the past tense.
- To identify the correct past tense forms of irregular verbs in sentences
- To complete sentences using the correct form of the irregular verb specified
- To complete a crossword puzzle using the past tense forms of irregular verbs

English Language Learners

Ask students to tell what they know about robots. If necessary, explain that a robot is a machine that people can control through the use of computers; a robot will perform specific jobs that people tell it to do.

Read each sentence in **Practice** aloud twice, saying a different answer choice each time. Have students take turns picking the correct word and rereading the completed sentence aloud. Clarify any unfamiliar words or expressions such as *monitoring robot, weeding robot, mowing robot, computer-controlled device, capacity, turntable,* and *Robot Hall of Fame.*

For **Apply,** have pairs of students complete the sentences orally before writing the correct past tense form of the verb.

Students can work cooperatively to complete the puzzle in **Reinforce.** They may wish to make a chart showing all the tenses of the verb in the word bank before completing the activity. Invite them to substitute verbs orally before writing in their books.

Speaking and Listening

Write two or three irregular verbs on index cards and distribute one card to each student. (The verbs should appear in their present tense form.) Then have students tell a round-robin story about a fictional character's amazing day. Have students take turns using past forms of their verbs to tell about the character's adventures.

Extra Practice

For more practice, see page 318.

Lesson 57 (student pages 169–170)
Easily Confused Words

Objectives

- To learn that people often confuse words that sound alike
- To discover that *then* and *than* are different words that sound similar but have different meanings
- To learn that *than* is a subordinating conjunction used to make comparisons, and *then* can be an adverb that tells about time or can mean "therefore"
- To understand that if one word is easily confused with another, it is wise to look up both words in a dictionary to clarify their meanings
- To complete sentences by identifying the correct word in pairs of easily confused words
- To complete sentences using the correct word in commonly confused word pairs
- To write a paragraph using three easily confused words

English Language Learners

Read aloud the sentences in **Practice**. Clarify the meanings of each pair of words in the exercise, as necessary. Have a volunteer reread the first sentence, tell which word is correct, and explain why. Have students complete the remaining sentences in pairs.

For **Apply**, clarify the meanings of the word pairs in the box. Then have students work with English-proficient partners to choose the correct word to complete each sentence.

Ask volunteers to suggest some things that people could store in a digital archive, such as books, magazines, movies, artwork, and songs. Then have students work in pairs to complete **Reinforce**.

Speaking and Listening

Distribute an index card with one pair of easily confused words to each student. Then have students take turns using each of their words in a sentence. As they say each sentence, students should hold up their card and point to the word they are using. Have the other students raise their hands when a word is used correctly.

Extra Practice

For more practice, see page 319.

Lesson 58 (student pages 171–172)
Frequently Misused Words

Objectives

- To learn that *go* and *went* mean "move(d) from place to place," that *is like* means "resembles something," and that *all* means "the total of something"
- To discover that these words cannot be used to indicate that someone is speaking
- To cross out the incorrect use of these words in sentences
- To correctly rewrite sentences that use *go, went, like,* and *all* incorrectly
- To use a variety of descriptive verbs that can take the place of *said*

English Language Learners

Have volunteers read aloud **Practice**. Clarify any unfamiliar words, such as *physicist, outrageous, manipulate, dwarf, cancerous,* and *tissues.* Have volunteers identify the incorrect uses of *go, went, like,* and *all* in the sentences. Call on others to tell which verbs could be used instead.

Have students work with partners to complete **Apply**. Suggest that pairs first read the sentences as written and then discuss how the sentences should be corrected before rewriting them.

Read aloud **Reinforce**. Have students work with partners to write a different verb for each sentence. Then invite volunteers to read aloud their sentences, using the tone indicated by the verbs. Model the process if necessary. Discuss the different meanings of these verbs.

Speaking and Listening

Write go, went, like, and all on the board. Have students take turns selecting a word and using it in two oral sentences—one using the word correctly and one using it incorrectly. Have listeners identify the correct usage.

Extra Practice

For more practice, see page 319.

Objectives

- To discover that pronouns can take the place of one or more nouns but should follow the rules of standard English: They not be used right after the noun or nouns they could replace
- To identify and delete extra pronouns in sentences and to rewrite sentences to eliminate extra pronouns
- To compose original sentences and reports using subject pronouns correctly

English Language Learners

Direct students' attention to the illustration on page 173. Read aloud the caption. Discuss with students the importance of this relatively simple device.

Read aloud the example sentences in **Read and Analyze.** Have a volunteer respond to the question and then read the identified sentence without the extra subject pronoun. Read aloud the rule statement and then have students read it with you.

Read aloud each sentence in **Practice.** Ask students to raise their hands each time they hear an extra subject pronoun that should be eliminated. Then have students work with partners to complete the activity.

In **Apply,** read the sentences aloud and have students work in pairs to correct and rewrite the sentences.

Have students work independently to do the research and write the reports specified in **Reinforce.** Note that students will need access to computers with Internet availability as well as writing paper to complete this activity.

Speaking and Listening

Offer interested students the opportunity to read about other inventions in the weekly column "Who Made That?" which has appeared in *The New York Times Magazine* for a number of years. Have these students report to the class on the stories they found most interesting.

Extra Practice

For more practice, see page 320.

Objectives

- To discover that facts and ideas should be stated simply and clearly
- To identify and eliminate unnecessary words and redundant information in sentences
- To revise sentences from an essay or a report to eliminate unnecessary words

English Language Learners

Point out the location of Bangalore, India, on a world map. Ask students to share what they know about this city and country.

Read aloud the example sentences in **Read and Analyze.** Have a volunteer respond to the questions. Read aloud the rule statement and then have students read it with you.

Read aloud each sentence in **Practice.** Ask students to raise their hands each time they hear an unnecessary phrase or statement. Then have students work in pairs to complete the activity.

In **Apply,** read the sentences aloud and then have students work in pairs to correct and rewrite the sentences.

Have students work independently to identify and revise sentences as specified in **Reinforce.**

Speaking and Listening

Invite students who have studied mathematics in other countries to compare the way math is taught there with the way math is taught in your school. Alternatively, you might have interested students do research on computational shortcuts and demonstrate one or two of these to the class.

Extra Practice

For more practice, see page 320.

Unit Review (student pages 177–178)

The **Unit Review** allows you to check students' progress and determine when reteaching is necessary. The review pages may be completed in class or as homework. If a student responds incorrectly to two or more items involving the same skill, you may want to work directly with the student to review the relevant lesson. The lesson number to which each review item relates appears in parentheses on the review pages in the Teacher Edition.

Assign the **Extra Practice** activities (pp. 315–320) to reteach targeted skills in a more focused way.

Spelling Practice (student pages 179–180)

Spelling Patterns: Words With Silent Consonants

Have students read the example sentence and the directions in **Read and Analyze**. Ask which words in the sentence have silent consonants. (adolescents, undoubtedly) Have students identify the silent letters. (c, b) Read the rule statement aloud.

Have students work in pairs to complete the **Word Sort** and share their results with the class. For **Pattern Practice** 1–8, read aloud the directions and have students work independently. Ask them to present their answers to another student. For **Pattern Practice** items 9–17, read aloud the directions. Have students work independently to write the word that completes each sentence. Ask students to identify the silent letter in each word they write. (acquaintance—c, discipline—c, subtle—b, adjourn—d, adjust—d, acknowledge—k, miscellaneous—c, raspberry—p, pneumonia—p)

Read aloud the directions in **Use the Dictionary**. Have students work independently to choose the word in each pair that is spelled correctly.

English Language Learners

Have students work with a partner who is fluent in English for the spelling activities. Spelling and pronouncing words with silent letters is difficult for English language learners because there are few silent letters in languages such as Spanish. Practice the words in this unit with your English language learners. Say them aloud and have students repeat them after you. At first, some students may pronounce the silent letter.

(you) | Diagram | sentences (student pages 181–182)

Diagramming Indirect Objects

Recall with students that in a sentence diagram, the direct object is placed on the horizontal line after the verb and is separated by a short vertical line. Ask students where the indirect object is placed in the example. (It is below the verb, connected by a slanted line.) Students can work independently or in pairs to diagram the sentences.

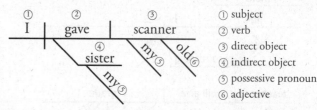

① subject
② verb
③ direct object
④ indirect object
⑤ possessive pronoun
⑥ adjective

Diagramming Sentences With *There*

Have students note where the word *There* appears in a sentence diagram when it begins a sentence. Then have them work in pairs to diagram the sentences in this section.

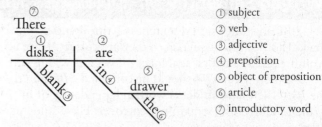

① subject
② verb
③ adjective
④ preposition
⑤ object of preposition
⑥ article
⑦ introductory word

Diagramming Inverted Sentences

Recall with students that they learned to identify sentences with inverted order in Lesson 24 of Unit 2. Read aloud the example sentence. Have a volunteer tell how the sentence could be rewritten with natural order. (My new flat-screen monitor is wonderful.) Tell students that converting an inverted sentence to natural order is the first step in diagramming it. Have students look at the diagram. Explain that *How* is diagrammed as an adverb. Then have students diagram sentences 9–12.

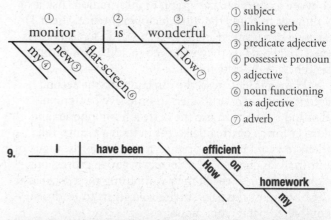

① subject
② linking verb
③ predicate adjective
④ possessive pronoun
⑤ adjective
⑥ noun functioning as adjective
⑦ adverb

Continued on page T50

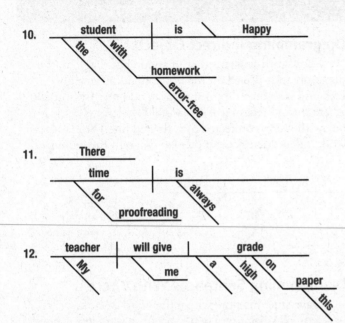

10.

11.

12.

Writing Sentences (student page 183)

Inform students that sentences 1 through 6 on page 183 need to be revised so they are correct. Have a volunteer read the first sentence, tell what is wrong with it, and then tell how it should be corrected. (*Its* should be *It's*.) Then have students work independently or in pairs to correct the remaining sentences. Have students compare their revisions.

Read aloud the informative paragraph at the bottom of the page. Draw students' attention to the introductory sentence, the sentences that give more information, and the concluding sentence. Call on volunteers to name the topic of the paragraph. (how computers help students write reports)

Writing a Paragraph (student page 184)

Have students look back at their revised sentences on page 183. Explain that the sentences can be used to write a complete paragraph of information. Ask a volunteer to name the introductory sentence. (item 1) Then ask students if items 2–6 appear in logical order. (yes) Tell students they will need to add a concluding sentence to the paragraph.

Have students read the directions to the second activity and then write their informative paragraph. Remind students to use the correct homophones and correct forms of irregular verbs in their writing. Tell them to avoid using shortened forms of words, vague or informal language, and incorrect negative expressions. Remind them to check their work using the checklist at the bottom of the page. Invite volunteers to read their completed paragraphs aloud.

Proofreading (student pages 185–186)

English Language Learners

Have students work with a partner who is fluent in English for the proofreading activities.

Proofreading Practice

Ask students to identify the topic of the report on page 185. (how technology helps people solve problems) Explain that the report contains several mistakes and that as students read, they should look for and mark these mistakes.

Review the **Proofreading Marks** chart and the examples. Remind students that these marks are used by professional writers to check their work before publication. Read the first sentence aloud. Discuss the error (*you're* should be *your*) and how it should be marked for correction. You may wish to have students correct the spelling errors as well.

After they have completed the proofreading activity, ask volunteers to read each sentence aloud and to identify errors. Ask students to mark overlooked errors in another color. (**Note:** Some errors can be corrected in more than one way.)

Proofreading Checklist

Ask students to select a recent piece of their own writing and to write the title of that piece at the top of the chart. Ask students to put a check mark next to each item in the checklist after they have checked it in their work. Students might first work independently and then trade papers with a partner to double-check each other's work. You might model, or ask a student to model, using the **G.U.M. Handbook** (beginning on student page 361) to clarify a concept or rule.

Also Remember…

Remind students that capitalization and punctuation are important for clear writing. If necessary, help students use the **G.U.M. Handbook** to clarify when commas should be used and to review the use of uppercase letters.

Your Own List

Suggest that students look at the errors they did not find in the proofreading activity and add them to the checklist. Ask students to think about other kinds of errors they make and to add these to the checklist.

Ask students to place this page in their writing portfolios. These pages may be used to assess students' progress over the course of the year.

These two pages provide interesting and fun activities that reinforce the skills and concepts students learned in Lessons 49 to 60. These activities give students the opportunity to extend what they have read about in the unit by finding out more about high-tech products. You might utilize the **Community Connection** pages in one of the following ways:

- Ask students to take the pages home, select one activity to do, and then share the results of that activity with the class.

- Have pairs of students select one activity to complete together.

- Review the activities as a class, and then assign the activities to small groups of students to complete cooperatively. Set aside a time for groups to share the results.

When you are ready to have students select activities, direct them to pages 187–188. Explain that the activities on page 187 will give them an opportunity to find out more about high-tech products and to use the Internet to learn more about their community. Explain that one activity provides an opportunity to plan a high-tech fair. Point out that page 188 is a planning guide that will help them gather information to plan the fair. Have students carefully tear out the pages, and then explain how you wish students to use them.

Great Getaways:
Rivers of the World
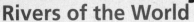

Unit 6 Grammar

River	Area
Mississippi	Eastern United States
Colorado	Southwestern United States
Columbia River	Northwestern United States
Nile	Africa
Amazon	South America
Yangtze	China
Ganges	India

Building Grammar Awareness

Write the following sentence on the board:

Me and Jeff thinks the Amazon is the more impressive river in the world.

Read the sentence aloud and ask students if it sounds correct. (no) Invite volunteers to tell what is wrong with it. (The subject pronoun *I* should be used instead of *me* and it should come after *Jeff;* the verb *thinks* should be *think,* to agree with the plural subject; *most* should be used instead of *more* because the sentence compares more than two things.) Tell students that in Unit 6 they will learn how to use pronouns correctly, how to make verbs agree with their subjects, and how to use helping verbs correctly. Remind them that using words and word forms correctly will help others understand them when they speak and write.

Introduce the Unit Theme
Rivers of the World

Inform students that the title of Unit 6 is "Great Getaways" and that in the unit, they will learn about many great rivers of the world.

Invite students to name great rivers they know of and to name the areas where the rivers are located. You may wish to make a chart on the board noting students' responses. Discuss with students the features of each river and the various reasons why it is important.

Assessment Options
Unit Pretest

The **Unit Pretest** (pp. 283–286) is intended to be used as a diagnostic assessment to help you determine, prior to instruction, your students' existing knowledge and skill proficiency. Follow this procedure for administering the Unit Pretest:

1. Read aloud the test instructions. (**Note:** For additional scaffolding, you may wish to read the test questions and answer choices aloud.)

2. Tell students that they will have 20 minutes to read and answer the questions independently.

3. When time is up, collect and correct the tests. Use the results to determine which lessons to teach for targeted instruction or which lessons to spend extra time on during whole-class instruction if you are teaching all lessons in the unit.

Unit Posttest

The **Unit Posttest** (pp. 353–356) helps you judge students' achievement while providing them with valuable practice for high-stakes tests. When you are ready to administer the test, ask students to carefully tear it out of their books. (**Note:** If the test has already been removed, distribute it to students.) Read aloud the directions for each section and make sure students understand how to answer the questions. Ask students to work independently to complete the test.

Students who miss two questions focusing on the same grammar element may need additional help understanding the concept. Reteach the concept, following this procedure:

1. Review **Read and Analyze**.

2. Review the rule statement for the concept.

3. Guide students through items a second time. Ask the students to explain why each right answer is correct.

4. Refer students to the **G.U.M. Handbook** for further reinforcement.

Lesson 61 (student pages 189–190)
Subject Pronouns and Object Pronouns

Objectives

- To learn that subject pronouns (*I, he, she, we, they*) can take the place of a subject in a sentence
- To learn that object pronouns (*me, him, her, us, them*) can be used after an action verb or a preposition
- To learn that the pronouns *it* and *you* can be either subject or object pronouns
- To identify subject and object pronouns in sentences and to rewrite sentences using subject or object pronouns
- To replace archaic pronouns with modern pronouns in a literary passage

English Language Learners

Read aloud the caption on page 189, and point out the location of London and the Thames River on a world map.

Read aloud **Practice**. Call on a volunteer to reread the first sentence, name the correct pronoun (*I*), tell whether it is a subject or an object pronoun (It is a subject pronoun.), and identify its function in the sentence. (It is the simple subject of the sentence.) Have students work in pairs to complete **Practice**.

Have students work cooperatively to complete **Apply**. Model using item 15 as an example.

Read aloud each quotation in **Reinforce**. Clarify each passage's language and then help students identify the archaic pronouns and suggest replacements.

Speaking and Listening

Have students take turns describing something someone gave them or something they gave someone else. Encourage them to use subject pronouns and object pronouns as they speak. (Example: *I* gave my little brother a catcher's mitt, and *I* taught *him* to catch.)

Extra Practice

For more practice, see page 321.

Lesson 62 (student pages 191–192)
Pronouns in Pairs

Objectives

- To learn that a subject pronoun should be used in a compound subject
- To learn that an object pronoun should be used in a compound direct or indirect object, or in a compound object of a preposition
- To choose appropriate subject or object pronouns to complete sentences
- To rewrite sentences using subject or object pronouns
- To learn that *I* and *me* always come last in a pair with a noun or another pronoun

English Language Learners

Point out the Columbia River on a class map.

Read aloud **Practice**. Clarify the meanings of any unfamiliar words such as *gorge, migrate, spawn, dams,* and *falls*. Ask students to identify which pronoun choice in parentheses is correct in each sentence. To help students determine the correct pronoun, suggest that they say the sentence without the name of the other person. (Example: item 2: Take away *Paul and*; then read the sentence as "*I* love hiking in the woods along the gorge." Then try "*Me* love hiking in the woods along the gorge.")

Have pairs of students complete **Apply**. Suggest that they make a list of subject and object pronouns and then work together to determine which pronoun should replace each boldfaced noun or noun phrase.

Partners can work together to complete **Reinforce**.

Speaking and Listening

Have students compose oral sentences about a time they worked with a friend or sibling to do something, such as completing a class project or making something at home. (Example: Mr. Del Rio asked Hannah and *me* to work together. *She* wrote the first half of the report, and *I* wrote the second half.) Listeners can identify the pronouns being used and tell whether they are subject or object pronouns.

Extra Practice

For more practice, see page 321.

Objectives

- To discover that an antecedent is the word or words that a pronoun refers to and that pronouns and antecedents must agree in number and gender
- To identify pronoun antecedents in sentences
- To complete sentences using appropriate pronouns
- To rewrite a passage using nouns to replace pronouns that have no antecedents

English Language Learners

Point out the Nile River and its two major tributaries—the Blue Nile and the White Nile—on a world map. Explain that the Nile ends in northern Egypt, where it flows into the Mediterranean. Ask volunteers to share their knowledge about Egypt or the Nile.

Read the sentences in **Practice** aloud. Clarify any unfamiliar words, such as *tributaries, originate,* and *expedition.* Call on a volunteer to identify the word or words the boldfaced pronoun in each sentence refers to. Students can verify their responses by replacing the pronoun with its antecedent and rereading the sentence. Model using item 2. (The Nile River system is complex. The *system* has many tributaries.)

For **Apply**, read aloud the first item. Help students decide which pronoun belongs in the blank. (the subject pronoun *They*) Have students complete the remaining sentences in pairs.

For **Reinforce**, explain the meanings of the words *necropolis, temple, obelisks, barges,* and *oarsmen.* Have students circle each subject or object pronoun they find in the passage. Then work with students to choose the correct nouns that take the place of the pronouns without antecedents in the paragraph.

Speaking and Listening

Write several nouns on the board, such as teacher, student, pencil, book, desk, and chalkboard. Have students work in pairs to compose two oral sentences telling about how various objects in the class are used every day. The first sentence should use nouns; the second should replace the nouns with pronouns. (Example: The *teacher* tells the *student* to open his *science book. She* tells *him* to open *it.*)

Extra Practice

For more practice, see page 322.

Objectives

- To learn that an antecedent is the word or words that a pronoun refers to, and that pronouns and antecedents must agree in number and gender
- To select pronoun forms that agree with antecedents in sentences
- To recognize and correct errors involving inappropriate shifts in pronoun number and person
- To write scripts using personal pronouns that agree with their antecedents

English Language Learners

Have students look at the picture on page 195 and read the caption. Encourage students who have visited Washington, D.C., or have spent time near the Potomac River to describe what they saw and experienced.

Next, read aloud the example sentences and the directions in **Read and Analyze.** Have volunteers respond to the directions. Read the rule statement aloud and have students read it with you.

Read aloud each sentence in **Practice** twice, once with the first pronoun choice and once with the second choice. Ask a volunteer to select the correct pronoun choice for item 1 and identify the antecedent. Then have students work in pairs to complete the activity.

Have students each work with an English-proficient partner to complete **Apply.**

Then have students continue working with partners to write the scripts called for in **Reinforce.**

Speaking and Listening

Invite students each to select an important building or monument in Washington D.C., do research to learn about it, and then share the knowledge they gain with the class. Encourage students to explain the significance of each building and monument in United States history and American government.

Extra Practice

For more practice, see page 322.

Lesson 65 (student pages 197–198)
Correcting Vague Pronouns

Objectives

- To learn that personal pronouns and demonstrative pronouns should refer clearly to antecedents
- To recognize pronouns that do not refer clearly to antecedents and to correct these errors by rewriting the sentences in which these appear
- To write a letter in which all personal and demonstrative pronouns have clear antecedents

English Language Learners

Ask a volunteer to point out on a map of Africa the locations and paths of the Congo, Gambia, Niger, and Volta rivers.

Read aloud the example paragraph in **Read and Analyze.** Have volunteers respond to the questions. Then read the rule statement aloud and have students reread it with you.

Read aloud the sentences in **Practice.** Work with students to complete the first item. Point out that the demonstrative pronoun *those* could refer to atlases, guidebooks, or maps. Guide a volunteer to choose one alternative and revise the sentence so this preference is made clear.

Then have students work in pairs to complete the remaining items. When all have finished, call on volunteers to suggest ways of rewriting sentences with vague pronouns to eliminate the confusion those pronouns cause.

Next, read aloud the sentences in **Apply.** Have a volunteer model rewriting sentence 17 to correct the vague pronoun reference in it. Have students work in pairs to complete the activity.

Then have students work independently to write the letter specified in **Reinforce.** Afterward, have students work with partners to read aloud, expand, and reorder sentences in their letters.

Speaking and Listening

Invite pairs of students to compete in your own quizdown on "Great Rivers of the World." Select a committee of quizmasters to prepare questions; encourage them to focus especially on information presented in Lessons 61–65. You may want to stage a second quizdown after students have completed Lessons 66–72.

Extra Practice

For more practice, see page 323.

Lesson 66 (student pages 199–200)
Using *Who* or *Whom*

Objectives

- To use *who* as the subject of a sentence or clause
- To use *whom* as the object of a verb or preposition
- To choose *who* or *whom* in sentences
- To write questions with *who* and *whom*
- To choose *who* or *whom* to write sentences about familiar people

English Language Learners

Point out the St. Lawrence River on a class map. Explain to students that it forms part of the international boundary between Canada and the United States.

Read aloud **Practice.** Then call on volunteers to reread each sentence and to tell whether *who* or *whom* belongs in the sentence. Remind students that *whom* follows a preposition, such as *for* (item 12). *Whom* is also needed when the word is a direct object (item 13: *whom* I spoke with).

Have students work in pairs to complete **Apply.** Model using item 14 as an example.

Read aloud the directions in **Reinforce.** Have students work with an English-proficient partner or an aide to talk about people they know who match the descriptions. Then have them write their sentences.

Speaking and Listening

Invite students to take part in a guessing game. Have volunteers use *Who* and *Whom* to form questions about a famous person or historical figure the class has read about. The rest of the class should then try to guess the answers. (Example: *Who n*amed the St. Lawrence? After *whom* was the river named?)

Extra Practice

For more practice, see page 323.

Lesson 67 (student pages 201–202)
Subject-Verb Agreement

Objectives

- To learn that the subject and the verb in a sentence must agree
- To learn how to make present tense verbs agree with singular and plural subjects
- To choose the verb form that agrees with the subject in sentences
- To complete sentences using the correct present tense form of verbs
- To write present tense sentences that have correct subject-verb agreement

English Language Learners

Point to the picture and read aloud the caption on page 201. Ask students who have gone rafting or boating on a river to share their experiences.

Read aloud **Practice.** Clarify the meaning of *comprise, obstructions, maneuvering, rapids, whirlpools, hazards,* and *scout* (noun and verb). Call on volunteers first to identify the simple subject in each sentence and then to determine whether it is singular or plural. To decide which verb form belongs in the sentences, model reading item 2 without the intervening words between the simple subject and the verb answer choices. (individuals...*want/wants* new challenges) Have student pairs complete the remaining sentences.

Students can work cooperatively with an English-proficient partner to complete **Apply.**

Partners can work together to complete **Reinforce.**

Speaking and Listening

Have each student write the singular and plural forms of a noun from Lesson 67 on an index card. (*trip/ trips, rafter/rafters, river/rivers*) Put the cards in a hat and have students take turns drawing an index card and using the nouns on it as the subjects of two oral sentences, making sure that each subject and verb agree.

Extra Practice

For more practice, see page 324.

Lesson 68 (student pages 203–204)
Agreement With Compound Subjects

Objectives

- To learn that a compound subject and its verb must agree
- To understand that a compound subject is plural when it is joined by *and,* and that the verb must agree with the last item in the subject if the compound subject is joined by *or* or *nor*
- To choose the verb form that agrees with the compound subject in sentences
- To complete sentences using the correct verb forms
- To choose the correct verb in sentences with compound subjects and then to use the clues to solve a puzzle

English Language Learners

Point out the Florida Everglades on a classroom map. Ask students to share anything they know about the Everglades. (**Note:** You may want to point out that "the Everglades" is considered a singular subject because it is one area.)

For **Practice,** ask students to identify the compound subject in each sentence and tell which word joins the different parts of the subject. Call on volunteers to identify the verb that completes each item correctly.

Have students work with partners to complete **Apply.**

Read aloud the clues for **Reinforce.** Have students work with English-proficient partners to select the proper form of the verb and then fill in the missing information to solve the puzzle.

Speaking and Listening

Invite groups of students to describe activities that members of their group enjoy or do not enjoy. (Example: Neither Monica *nor* Wai Lin *plays* sports. Both Erno *and* Raul *play* many sports.) Call on listeners to tell whether the subject and verb agree in each sentence.

Extra Practice

For more practice, see page 324.

Lesson 69 (student pages 205–206)

Subject-Verb Agreement: Special Cases

Objectives

- To discover that there are special cases for the subject-verb agreement rule
- To learn that titles of books, movies, stories, and songs are always considered singular
- To learn that collective nouns are almost always considered singular
- To learn that almost all indefinite pronouns are considered singular
- To complete sentences by selecting the correct verb forms
- To match collective nouns with the groups of animals they name

English Language Learners

Point out the Mississippi River on a map of the United States. Tell students they will read about a famous writer who spent the early part of his life living along the Mississippi. Have students read the caption and notice the illustration on page 206.

Read aloud **Practice**. Help students identify the simple subject in each sentence and tell whether it is a title, a collective noun, or an indefinite pronoun. Then call on volunteers to tell which verb belongs in the sentence.

Have students work with partners to complete **Apply**, following a similar procedure as in **Practice**.

Help students match each collective noun to the group of animals it names in **Reinforce**. Suggest that students consult a dictionary if necessary. Invite volunteers to reread their sentences aloud.

Speaking and Listening

Have students compose oral sentences about one or more groups of animals listed in **Reinforce**. Remind them to be sure that the verb agrees with the collective noun in each sentence they say. (Example: A troop of monkeys lives at the zoo.) Discuss why they think each collective noun was coined for each group of animals.

Extra Practice

For more practice, see page 325.

Lesson 70 (student pages 207–208)

Avoiding Dangling and Misplaced Modifiers

Objectives

- To learn that a verbal phrase always refers to, or modifies, a noun or pronoun in the main part of a sentence
- To learn that a dangling modifier is a phrase that does not refer to any particular word
- To learn that a misplaced modifier is a phrase that seems to refer to the wrong noun or pronoun in a sentence
- To identify dangling and misplaced modifiers in sentences
- To revise sentences containing dangling or misplaced modifiers
- To complete sentences that contain introductory verbal phrases

English Language Learners

Point out the Colorado River and the Grand Canyon on a United States map.

Then read aloud **Practice**. Clarify any unfamiliar phrases. Tell students they should ask themselves *Who?* or *What?* did the action in the verbal phrase. If the question can be answered by the nearest noun or pronoun in the sentence, then the verbal phrase is used correctly. Model item 2 by asking: *What* originates in the Rocky Mountains? (the Colorado River) Explain that the sentence is correct because the verbal phrase modifies the nearby noun *Colorado River*. Help students complete the remaining sentences in the same way.

Pair students with English-proficient partners to read **Apply**. Model correcting item 15. (Winding through rock and sandstone, the Colorado River has cut deep canyons.) Have pairs rewrite the sentences cooperatively. Invite students to read their revised sentences to the class.

Partners can continue to work together on **Reinforce**.

Speaking and Listening

Invite students to talk about something they saw or did while they were doing something else. Ask them to use at least one verbal phrase as they speak. (Example: Seeing my friends in the cafeteria, I sat down to eat with them.)

Extra Practice

For more practice, see page 325.

Objectives

- To learn that comparative forms of adjectives or adverbs compare two people, places, things, or actions, and that the superlative forms compare three or more
- To learn how to create the comparative and superlative forms of adjectives and adverbs
- To discover that the words *better* and *less* compare two things, and that *best* and *least* compare three or more things
- To identify the correct use of comparative adjectives and adverbs in sentences
- To complete sentences using the correct forms of adjectives and adverbs
- To learn that some adjectives are absolute
- To write sentences using absolute adjectives

English Language Learners

Read **Practice** aloud. Ask students to identify how many people or things are being compared in each sentence. Have students complete the section in pairs.

For **Apply**, help students identify what is being compared in each sentence. Help them determine whether they can create the comparative form by adding *-er* or *-est* or the words *more* or *most*. Ask students which word changes spelling when a suffix is added (item 14: *muddy becomes muddiest*). Clarify unfamiliar words such as *diverse* and *impressive*.

Have students work on **Reinforce** with English-proficient partners.

Speaking and Listening

Have students orally compare two rivers they have learned about. Remind them to use comparative adjectives and adverbs correctly as they make their comparisons. (Example: The Amazon is *longer* than the Mississippi. The Amazon is the *most amazing* river in the world.)

Extra Practice

For more practice, see page 326.

Objectives

- To learn that an auxiliary verb, or helping verb, works with a main verb
- To learn that modal auxiliaries such as *could* and *may* refer to a possible action or tell how likely it is that something will happen
- To learn that forms of the auxiliary verbs *do, is,* and *will* indicate the tense of the main verb; they are also used to form negatives and questions
- To identify main verbs and auxiliary verbs in sentences
- To complete sentences using the correct auxiliary verbs
- To find auxiliary verbs in a word search puzzle and then use two to write sentences

English Language Learners

Show students the location of the Ganges River on a world map. Then point out the picture and read the caption on page 211.

Read aloud **Practice**. Have students identify and circle the main verb or verbs in each sentence. For each main verb, have students determine whether an auxiliary verb accompanies it. Have a volunteer identify each auxiliary verb orally before students underline it.

Help students complete **Apply** by writing the auxiliary verbs from the rule box and the word *must* on the board. Have volunteers choose an auxiliary verb from the board to complete the first item. Have pairs complete the remaining items.

To help students complete **Reinforce**, add *is* and *does* to the list of auxiliary verbs you wrote on the board for **Apply**. Help students find the eight auxiliary verbs in the puzzle. Then have students work with a partner to write two original sentences.

Speaking and Listening

Invite students to talk about some of their plans for the next holiday or school vacation. Ask them to use auxiliary verbs as they speak. (Example: I *will* be visiting the Rio Grande during spring break. I *would* like to go rafting on it.)

Extra Practice

For more practice, see page 326.

Unit Review (student pages 213–214)

The **Unit Review** allows you to check students' progress and determine when reteaching is necessary. The review pages may be completed in class or as homework. If a student responds incorrectly to two or more items involving the same skill, you may want to work directly with the student to review the relevant lesson. The lesson number to which each review item relates appears in parentheses on the review pages in the Teacher Edition.

Assign the **Extra Practice** activities (pp. 321–326) to reteach targeted skills in a more focused way.

Spelling Practice (student pages 215–216)

Homophones and Other Commonly Confused Words

Have students read the example sentences and the directions in **Read and Analyze**. Ask which word in bold type means "constantly." (continuously) Ask which word in bold type means "frequently." (continually) Discuss how the two words are alike and different. Read the rule statement aloud.

Have students work in pairs to complete **Words in Context** and share their answers with the class. For **Pattern Practice** 13–18, read aloud the directions and have students work independently. Ask them to present their answers to another student. For **Pattern Practice** 19–24, read aloud the directions. Have students work independently to write the correct words. Have students share their answers. (immigrant, emigrant, persecution, prosecution, devise, device)

Read aloud the directions in **Use the Dictionary**. Have students work independently to choose the word that best completes each sentence.

English Language Learners

Have students work with a partner who is fluent in English for the spelling activities. Have your English language learners practice pronouncing similar-sounding words by using them in sentences. This will facilitate their identification. Tell students they may have to use context clues to figure out the meanings of some of the words in these activities. Practice this by having students write and read sentences that clearly demonstrate and differentiate word meaning and pronunciation.

(you) | Diagram | sentences (student pages 217–218)

Objectives

- To learn how to diagram sentences containing participial phrases
- To learn how to diagram sentences containing infinitive phrases
- To learn how to diagram sentences containing gerund phrases

Diagramming Participial Phrases

Have students read the explanation and sample sentence in the first section. Point out how the participle is placed below the noun it modifies.

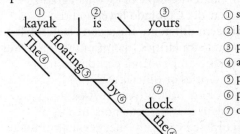

As students diagram items 1–3, have them think about what word the participial phrase modifies. Remind them that a participle can modify a noun in the subject or the predicate.

Diagramming Infinitive Phrases

Draw students' attention to the first sentence diagram and help them notice that the infinitive sits above the line following the verb. Tell students that in this sentence, the infinitive functions as a direct object. Then have pairs of students diagram items 4–6.

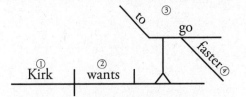

Diagramming Gerund Phrases

Have students look at how a sentence with a gerund phrase is diagramed. Then have pairs of students diagram sentences 7–9. Tell students to ask themselves how each gerund functions before they diagram each item.

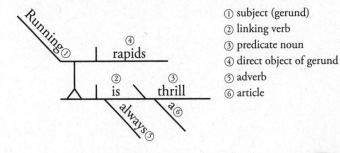

Writing Sentences (student page 219)

Inform students that sentences 1 through 7 on page 219 need to be revised so that the subject and verb agree. Have a volunteer read the first sentence aloud, tell what is wrong with it, and explain how it should be corrected. (*has supported* should be changed to *have supported*) Then have students work independently or in pairs to correct the remaining sentences. Have students compare their revisions.

Writing a Paragraph (student page 220)

Read aloud the paragraphs on page 219. Draw students' attention to each paragraph's topic sentence and to the sentences that give supporting details. Call on volunteers to name the topic of each paragraph. (The first states that the Colorado River and the Columbia River seem different. The second states that they have important similarities.) Point out that a writer may begin a compare-and-contrast composition by stating either similarities or differences.

Have students look back at their revised sentences on page 219. Explain that the sentences are out of order but when ordered correctly, they form a complete paragraph. Ask a volunteer to suggest a topic sentence that could introduce the paragraph. (The Nile and the Ganges are alike in several ways.) Have students write that topic sentence or a similar one. Then have students reorder the supporting sentences in a logical way and write the paragraph. Explain that there is more than one possible order for the supporting sentences.

Have students read the directions to the second activity and then write two paragraphs comparing and contrasting two rivers. Remind them that as they write, they should be sure that all subjects and verbs agree. Remind them to check their work using the checklist at the bottom of the page.

Proofreading (student pages 221–222)

English Language Learners

Have students work with a partner who is fluent in English for the proofreading activities.

Proofreading Practice

Ask students to identify the topic of the report on page 221. (the Mackenzie River) Explain that the report contains several mistakes and that as they read, they should look for these mistakes.

Review the **Proofreading Marks** chart and the examples. Remind students that these marks are used by professional writers to check their work before publication. Read the first sentence aloud. Discuss the error (*Most long* should be *longest*.) and how it should be marked for correction. You may wish to have students correct the spelling errors as well.

After they have completed the proofreading activity, ask volunteers to read each sentence aloud and to identify errors. Ask students to mark overlooked errors in another color. (**Note:** Some errors can be corrected in more than one way.)

Proofreading Checklist

Ask students to select a recent piece of their own writing and to write the title of that piece at the top of the chart. Ask students to put a check mark next to each item in the checklist after they have checked it in their work. Students might first work independently and then trade papers with a partner to double-check each other's work. You might model, or ask a student to model, using the **G.U.M. Handbook** (beginning on student page 361) to clarify a concept or rule.

Also Remember…

Remind students that capitalization and punctuation are important for clear writing. If necessary, help students use the **G.U.M. Handbook** to clarify when commas should be used and to review the use of uppercase letters.

Your Own List

Suggest that students look at the errors they did not find in the proofreading activity and add them to the checklist. Ask students to think about other kinds of errors they make and to add these to the checklist.

Ask students to place this page in their writing portfolios. These pages may be used to assess students' progress over the course of the year.

These two pages provide interesting and fun activities that reinforce the skills and concepts students learned in Lessons 61 to 72. These activities give students the opportunity to extend what they have read about in the unit by learning more about rivers and human activities associated with them. You might utilize the **Community Connection** pages in one of the following ways:

- Ask students to take the pages home, select one activity to do, and then share the results of that activity with the class.

- Have pairs of students select one activity to complete together.

- Review the activities as a class, and then assign the activities to small groups of students to complete cooperatively. Set aside a time for groups to share the results.

When you are ready to have students select activities, direct them to pages 223–224. Explain that the activities on page 223 will give them an opportunity to find out more about rivers of the world. Explain to students that one activity provides an opportunity to learn about a river sport and to present what they have learned to the class. Point out that page 224 is a planning guide that will help them gather information. Have students carefully tear out the pages, and then explain how you wish students to use them.

Unforgettable Folks:
Problem Solvers

Unit 7 Mechanics

Building Mechanics Awareness

Write this sentence on the board and read it aloud:
> i'd like to become a medical researcher in africa asia or south america when im older said carole

Then write the sentence with the correct punctuation and capitalization, and ask a volunteer to read it aloud again. ("I'd like to become a medical researcher in Africa, Asia, or South America when I'm older," said Carole.)

Ask students which sentence is easier to read and why. (the second one, because it has the proper punctuation) Call on volunteers to name the different kinds of punctuation they see. (quotation marks, commas, apostrophes)

Inform students that in Unit 7 they will learn how to use these and other punctuation marks. Explain that they will also learn some rules for capitalizing words, as well as how to write initials, abbreviations, acronyms, titles, quotations, letters, e-mails, and bibliographies correctly. Point out to students that using correct punctuation and capitalization in sentences helps other people understand what they write.

Introduce the Unit Theme
Problem Solvers

Inform students that the title of Unit 7 is "Unforgettable Folks" and that the lessons tell about people who have solved problems so as to make life easier and more rewarding for others. Invite students to name problem solvers they know about; these might include national or international leaders, inventors, medical researchers, nonprofit organizations, local officials, or even family members or friends. In each case ask students to tell what problem the person or people solved, and how that solution helped others.

Assessment Options
Unit Pretest

The **Unit Pretest** (pp. 287–290) is intended to be used as a diagnostic assessment to help you determine, prior to instruction, your students' existing knowledge and skill proficiency. Follow this procedure for administering the Unit Pretest:

1. Read aloud the test instructions. (**Note:** For additional scaffolding, you may wish to read the test questions and answer choices aloud.)

2. Tell students that they will have 20 minutes to read and answer the questions independently.

3. When time is up, collect and correct the tests. Use the results to determine which lessons to teach for targeted instruction or which lessons to spend extra time on during whole-class instruction if you are teaching all lessons in the unit.

Unit Posttest

The **Unit Posttest** (pp. 357–360) helps you judge students' achievement while providing students practice for high-stakes tests. When you are ready to administer the test, ask students to carefully tear it out of their books. (**Note:** If the test has already been removed, distribute it to students.) Read aloud the directions for each section and make sure students understand how to answer the questions. Ask students to work independently to complete the test.

Students who miss two questions focusing on the same grammar element may need additional help understanding the concept. Reteach the concept, following this procedure:

1. Review **Read and Analyze**.

2. Review the rule statement for the concept.

3. Guide students through items a second time. Ask the students to explain why each right answer is correct.

4. Refer students to the **G.U.M. Handbook** for further reinforcement.

Objectives

- To learn that a proper noun names a specific person or product, geographic location, holiday, thing, or idea, and that important words in proper nouns are capitalized
- To learn that proper adjectives are descriptive words formed from proper nouns, and that they are capitalized
- To learn that titles of respect, such as *Mr.* or *Judge,* are used before a person's name and are capitalized
- To correct capitalization errors in sentences
- To add capitalization and punctuation to a passage written in lowercase letters

English Language Learners

Explain to students that when a natural disaster or a war occurs in a region, more medical help may be needed than can be supplied by the countries involved. Tell students that Doctors Without Borders is an organization that was formed to solve this problem.

Read aloud **Practice.** Clarify the meaning of *humanitarian, malnutrition, nutrients, susceptible, war-torn, formula, shelf life,* and *fortified.* Have students work in pairs to identify the words that should be capitalized. Remind them to look for words that begin a sentence and those that name specific people, countries, nationalities, or months.

Have students complete **Apply** in pairs. Explain that *Sahel* is a proper noun because it names a certain region.

Read aloud **Reinforce.** Help students identify and punctuate the five sentences in the passage. Remind them that the subject pronoun *I* should also be capitalized.

Speaking and Listening

Invite students to discuss a current international situation in which large numbers of people have needed help. Discuss the kinds of help they have needed, and the kinds of international organizations that provide such help. Ask students to identify proper nouns when they are mentioned.

Extra Practice

For more practice, see page 327.

Objectives

- To discover that titles of books, movies, magazines, and newspapers should be underlined, and titles of songs, stories, and poems should be in quotation marks
- To learn that titles written with an underline are in italics when they appear in type
- To learn which words in a title should be capitalized
- To identify and add correct capitalization and punctuation to titles in sentences
- To rewrite titles of books and movies using correct capitalization and punctuation
- To write a persuasive paragraph using correct capitalization and punctuation

English Language Learners

Refer students to the illustration on page 227, and if possible, play a recording of a song of social commentary by Woody Guthrie. Ask students to speculate on why a song might be effective in raising people's awareness of a social problem.

Read aloud the first sentence in **Practice.** Demonstrate how to correct the essay title. ("Voices for Social Repairs") Then have students work in pairs to complete the activity.

For **Apply,** have volunteers read aloud the titles on the bookshelf. Then read the first question aloud and ask students which title best answers the question. (<u>Pete Lucky's Happy Accident</u>) Then have students work cooperatively to write the book title with correct capitalization and punctuation. Complete the remaining items the same way.

Have students work on **Reinforce** with an English-proficient partner.

Speaking and Listening

Begin a discussion with students about books, stories, and poems they have read; songs they have heard; or movies they have seen. Then call on volunteers to name their favorite; tell whether it is a book, story, poem, song, or movie; and to write the title on the board. Have the class verify the capitalization and punctuation.

Extra Practice

For more practice, see page 327.

Lesson 75 (student pages 229–230)
Initials, Abbreviations, and Acronyms

Objectives

- To learn that an abbreviation is a shortened form of a word
- To discover that titles of respect, addresses, the names of days and some months, and certain words in the names of businesses can be abbreviated in informal writing
- To learn that an initial can replace a person's name or the name of some places, and that an initial is written as an uppercase letter followed by a period
- To identify and correct abbreviations and initials in sentences
- To rewrite names using abbreviations and initials
- To identify and write acronyms

English Language Learners

Ask students to share what they know about World War II. If necessary, explain that one of the key events in the Allied effort to defeat Germany was the landing of troops in France on D-day, June 6, 1944.

Read aloud **Practice**. Explain the abbreviations *Pres.* (*President*) and *Gen.* (*General*). Have student pairs correct the errors.

Have the same partners complete **Apply**. If necessary, tell them how to abbreviate some less familiar items such as *Mistress* (*Mrs.* or *Miss*), *Company* (*Co.*), *Corporation* (*Corp.*), *Sergeant* (*Sgt.*), and *Incorporated* (*Inc.*). Model completing the activity using item 30 as an example. (Pres. Franklin D. Roosevelt)

Read aloud the information on acronyms and initialisms in **Reinforce**. Guide students to identify the acronym for each term before they write their response.

Speaking and Listening

Have students, in turn, tell the class their address (street, city, state) and the full name of a person they know, using a title of respect. Listeners should tell how each address and name could be abbreviated.

Extra Practice

For more practice, see page 328.

Lesson 76 (student pages 231–232)
Apostrophes in Possessives and Contractions

Objectives

- To learn how to form singular and plural possessive nouns and contractions using apostrophes
- To identify possessive nouns and contractions in sentences
- To rewrite sentences using possessives or contractions
- To analyze how apostrophes are used in informal speech

English Language Learners

Ask students to share what they know about the types and uses of plastic, and the environmental problems that discarded plastic items can cause.

Read aloud the sentences in **Practice**. Clarify unfamiliar words and phrases, such as *resins, properties, shellac, substance, dentures, stable,* and *synthetic.* To help students choose the correct words, rephrase each sentence without the possessive noun or the contraction. (Example: item 1: *Some natural properties of resins* are similar to those of plastics.)

For **Apply** have students work with English-proficient partners to rewrite the sentences using possessive pronouns or contractions. Model using items 16 and 17. Point out that phrases containing *of* should be rewritten as possessives.

Read aloud the background information and the directions in **Reinforce**. Then read aloud the numbered items slowly. Help students identify each word in which the spelling has been altered by substituting an apostrophe for one or more letters.

Speaking and Listening

Invite students to identify and describe items and parts of items in the classroom that are made of plastic; tell students to use possessives and contractions when possible. (Example: *Jacob's* ruler is made of plastic. The ruler *isn't* flexible.) Ask listeners to identify words that contain apostrophes.

Extra Practice

For more practice, see page 328.

Objectives

- To learn that commas are used to separate items in a series, separate coordinate adjectives, set off appositives and nonrestrictive elements, separate clauses in a compound sentence, and set off a long introductory phrase
- To add missing commas to sentences
- To rewrite two or more sentences as one sentence using commas
- To write a description of an item for sale, using commas correctly

English Language Learners

Point to the picture and read aloud the caption on page 233. Ask students to share what they know about eBay and other online auction sites. Have students discuss how buying items on such a site is different from buying items on other types of Internet sites.

Read aloud **Practice.** Clarify unfamiliar words and phrases such as *envisioned, thriving, antiques, microfinance,* and *entrepreneurs.* Then reread each sentence, pausing where a comma should be placed. Ask students whether the sentence lists a series of items or a pair of adjectives; contains an appositive, introductory verbal phrase, or a dependent clause; or is a compound sentence. Have them then tell where commas should be placed.

For each item in **Apply,** have partners decide which words from the second or third sentence repeat information from the previous sentence and which tell more about the subject. Model using item 14. (An auctioneer puts a product up for bid, tracks the bids, and then awards the item to the highest bidder.)

Read aloud the instructions for **Reinforce.** Have a volunteer model a response. Then have students work with partners to complete the writing task. When all have finished, invite volunteers to read their item descriptions to the class.

Speaking and Listening

Place a pile of index cards face down, with one noun written on each card. Invite each student to pick three cards and to compose oral sentences using the words on the cards in a series. Then have each student write his or her sentence on the board as the class verifies the use of the commas.

Extra Practice

For more practice, see page 329.

Objectives

- To learn that a semicolon can be used instead of a comma and a conjunction to join related independent clauses in a compound sentence
- To learn that a colon can be used to join two independent clauses when the second clause explains the first
- To add semicolons or colons to separate clauses in sentences
- To combine sentences using semicolons or colons
- To understand that the colon has many other uses in writing, and to write examples to identify those uses

English Language Learners

Discuss with students the importance of wheelchairs to people whose mobility is otherwise limited. Explain to students that this lesson tells about a person who figured out how to make these devices easier to use.

Read aloud **Practice.** Clarify unfamiliar words and phrases such as *hang-gliding, paraplegic, confronted, tournaments, innovation,* and *sporty-looking.* Be sure students understand that an independent clause is a complete sentence. Then help students identify where the colons or semicolons should be added.

Read aloud **Apply** and help students match the sentences from each column. As you match each pair of sentences, ask volunteers to tell how they know the two sentences go together.

Read aloud each rule in **Reinforce** as students work with partners to identify and call out the sentence that matches the rule. You might compose original sentences as a group activity.

Speaking and Listening

Have students look through textbooks or sets of instructions and find other examples of sentences containing colons or semicolons. Ask students to share their findings and to explain why the semicolons or colons have been used.

Extra Practice

For more practice, see page 329.

Lesson 79 (student pages 237–238)
Hyphens, Parentheses, and Dashes

Objectives
- To learn that hyphens have many uses: to separate syllables at the end of a line, to link some compound words, to link pairs of words that act as adjectives, to link the parts of some numbers
- To learn that parentheses set off an explanation or example
- To identify correct and incorrect use of hyphens and parentheses in sentences
- To add hyphens or parentheses to sentences
- To match rules about dashes with their examples and to write examples for stated rules

English Language Learners
Ask students to share what they know about the first moon landings. If possible, show students still photos or video clips of the landings and moonwalks. Then explain that one of the early missions to the moon nearly ended in tragedy.

Read the sentences in **Practice** aloud. Clarify the meanings of *carbon dioxide, compatible, perish, around-the-clock, top-notch, lithium, hydroxide, canisters, command module,* and *rough-and-ready.* Help students determine which sentences use parentheses or hyphens correctly and which use them incorrectly. Have them explain their reasons. Review the rule box, if necessary.

Read each sentence in **Apply** aloud. Then help students add hyphens or parentheses where they belong.

For **Reinforce,** read aloud the rules for using a dash. Then help students match each rule to its example. Have students work with an English-proficient partner to write a new example for each rule.

Speaking and Listening
Ask each student to find two examples of parentheses, hyphens, or dashes in a book. Then have students present the examples they found and tell why that punctuation was used.

Extra Practice
For more practice, see page 330.

Lesson 80 (student pages 239–240)
Ellipses

Objectives
- To learn that an ellipsis is used to indicate where words have been omitted from a quotation
- To learn that an ellipsis can also be used to signal a pause
- To identify quotations containing ellipses indicating omission of words
- To write quotations using ellipses to indicate where words have been omitted
- To write a paragraph about the inspirational value of a quotation

English Language Learners
Ask students whether scientists are problem solvers. Invite volunteers to give examples of the kinds of problems scientists try to solve.

Read aloud the two versions of a quotation in **Read and Analyze.** Explain to students that the writer uses the word *men* to mean "people." Have a volunteer answer the questions. Ask students whether they agree with what the writer says. Then read aloud the rule statement and have students read it with you.

Read the instructions and the quotations in **Practice** aloud. Have students carry out the tasks for each item; then discuss whether the shortened version of the quotation conveys the same message as the full quotation.

Read aloud the instructions and the quotations in **Apply** aloud. Have students work independently to write the shortened versions of these quotations. Again, discuss with students whether the shortened version of each quotation conveys the same message as the full quotation.

Then read aloud the instructions and the quotation in **Reinforce.** Have students work with English-proficient partners to complete the activity.

Speaking and Listening
Challenge students to paraphrase the quotations presented in the lesson. As an example, you might offer this paraphrase of the Auden quotation: "Scientists are the people whose work has the greatest effect on our lives today."

Extra Practice
For more practice, see page 330.

Objectives

- To learn that long dashes can be used to signal pauses before and after an authorial comment or explanatory phrase
- To learn that commas can be used to signal thoughtful pauses before and after a nonrestrictive phrase or clause
- To learn that an ellipsis can be used to indicate a pause
- To identify punctuation marks signaling pauses
- To insert punctuation marks to signal pauses in sentences
- To write an original sentence using punctuation marks to signal pauses

English Language Learners

Make sure students know that a beetle is a type of insect. Explain that one type of beetle has killed millions of pine trees in the American West.

Read aloud the example sentences in **Read and Analyze**, emphasizing the pauses signaled by the punctuation marks. Have volunteers respond to the questions. Then read aloud the rule statement and have students read it with you.

Read the instructions and sentences in **Practice** aloud, again emphasizing the pauses signaled by the punctuation marks. Have students then identify the punctuation mark that signals each pause.

Read each sentence in **Apply** aloud, pausing where punctuation is needed. Invite volunteers to suggest which punctuation mark would be appropriate to use in each spot. Have students work with partners to complete the activity.

Read the instructions for **Reinforce** aloud. Have partners continue to work together to compose and punctuate paragraphs giving their ideas for new ways to use scrap tires.

Speaking and Listening

Invite students to present to the class their ideas for new ways to use scrap tires. If possible, invite an engineer or a manufacturing professional to discuss and evaluate students' ideas.

Extra Practice

For more practice, see page 331.

Objectives

- To discover that a direct quotation is a speaker's exact words and that quotation marks are used at the beginning and the end of a direct quotation
- To learn that a comma is used to set off an introductory word, a mild interjection, a noun of direct address, or a tag question from the rest of a sentence
- To supply appropriate punctuation for direct quotations
- To rewrite direct quotations using correct punctuation
- To learn that an interjection expresses strong or sudden feeling, and to use interjections correctly as introductory words

English Language Learners

Explain to students that microfinance organizations are helping people in impoverished areas start and expand small businesses.

Then read aloud **Practice**. Have students work with partners to add the missing punctuation. Suggest that they look for key words such as *said, asked, agreed,* and *replied.* Point out that item 17 is an example of an interrupted quotation.

Read aloud the sentences in **Apply**. Clarify the meanings of *finance* and *microloan*. Help students complete items 19 and 20, and have partners complete the remaining items together.

For **Reinforce**, pair students with English-proficient partners to complete the activity.

Speaking and Listening

Invite students to retell a brief conversation they had with a friend. As each student tells what was said, ask the class to decide whether a direct or an indirect quotation was used. (Example: Fran asked, "Have you finished your homework?" I told her that I hadn't.)

Extra Practice

For more practice, see page 331.

Objectives

- To learn that short quotations can be presented in sentences and punctuated as the words of a speaker in dialogue
- To learn that long quotations can be presented as blocks of text set off from the main text
- To learn that information about the source of a quotation must be presented either in a sentence in the main text or in an entry below the quotation
- To decide on how to present quotations of various lengths
- To rewrite quotations in appropriate ways, using correct punctuation

English Language Learners

Briefly discuss these notable individuals whose thoughts are presented in this lesson: Henry Ford, pioneer automobile manufacturer; Henry David Thoreau, author and philosopher; Margaret Mead, anthropologist; Barack Obama, president of the United States of America; and Mark Twain, novelist and humorist.

Read aloud the example quotations in **Read and Analyze**. Point out that each expresses the idea that every person needs to pursue her or his own path to success. Next, have volunteers respond to the questions. Then read aloud the rule statement and have students read it with you.

Read the instructions and quotations in **Practice**. Invite students to paraphrase each and tell whether they agree with its message. Explain to students that although there is no absolute right or wrong way to write particular quotations, writing longer quotations in a block paragraph makes it easier for a reader to concentrate on the ideas presented in the quotation. Then have students work in pairs to complete the activity.

Read aloud the instructions and quotations in **Apply**. Invite students to paraphrase and discuss each quotation. Then have students work independently to complete the activity.

Finally, read the instructions for **Reinforce**. Invite students to share their choices and opinions before they write their short essays. When students finish, have them work with partners to revise and reorder sentences. Have students then produce final drafts, paying special attention to the presentation and punctuation of the quotation.

Speaking and Listening

Invite students each to find and present to the class a quotation that they think is wise and helpful.

Extra Practice

For more practice, see page 332.

Objectives

- To learn that a friendly letter has a heading, a greeting, a body, a closing, and a signature
- To discover that a business letter has the same parts as a friendly letter but also includes an inside address, substitutes a colon for a comma after the greeting, omits paragaph indentations, and aligns all of the letter parts along the left-hand margin
- To learn that an e-mail has these elements: a greeting, a body, a closing, a signature, and an e-mail header containing the e-mail address of the recipient, the date, and a subject line
- To label the five parts of a friendly letter
- To rewrite a business letter correctly
- To write a friendly e-mail

English Language Learners

Ask students if they enjoy writing e-mails and letters, and to whom they like writing the most. Ask them how a letter written to a friend might differ from an e-mail or a letter written to a business.

Read aloud the letter in **Practice**. Have students orally identify each part of the letter before they write their responses.

Read aloud to students the instructions and the text of the letter in **Apply**. Have students discuss what they will do to put this letter into correct business letter form before they complete the activity independently.

Have students work independently on **Reinforce**. If possible, allow students to use computers to create and send their e-mails.

Speaking and Listening

Ask students to bring to class copies of friendly letters, business letters, and e-mails that they have received. Have students display the letters, compare them, and point out the parts.

Extra Practice

For more practice, see page 332.

The **Unit Review** allows you to check students' progress and determine when reteaching is necessary. The review pages may be completed in class or as homework. If a student responds incorrectly to two or more items involving the same skill, you may want to work directly with the student to review the relevant lesson. The lesson number to which each review item relates appears in parentheses on the review pages in the Teacher Edition.

Assign the **Extra Practice** activities (pp. 327–332) to reteach targeted skills in a more focused way.

Spelling Practice (student pages 251–252)

Frequently Misspelled Words

Have students read the example sentence and the directions in **Read and Analyze**. Discuss the meaning of *exhilarating* and why this word is difficult to spell. Explain that a mnemonic device helps someone remember something. Have volunteers share their mnemonic devices with the class. Read the rule statement aloud.

Have students work in pairs to complete **Words in Context** and share their answers with the class. For **Pattern Practice** 11–19, read aloud the directions and have students work independently. Ask them to present their answers to another student. For **Pattern Practice** items 20–25, read aloud the directions. Have students work independently to write an antonym for each word. Ask students to share their answers. (postpone, genuine, familiar, minimum, exhilarating, exhaust)

Read aloud the directions in **Use the Dictionary**. Have students work independently to select the word that is spelled correctly.

English Language Learners

Have students work with a partner who is fluent in English for the spelling activities. Some words may be particularly difficult for Spanish-speaking students to spell and/or pronounce. The word *committee* is difficult to spell because it has three double letters, while the Spanish word, *comité*, has no double letters. The words *jealousy* and *maneuver* may be difficult because they have vowel combinations that are not common in Spanish. Have your Spanish speakers practice the spelling and pronunciation of these and other difficult words.

(you) | Diagram | sentences (student pages 253–254)

Diagramming Adjective Clauses

Review the model diagram in this section. Then have student pairs diagram sentences 2–3.

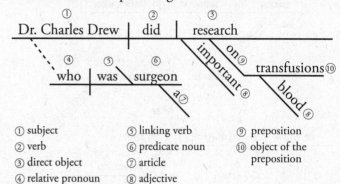

① subject
② verb
③ direct object
④ relative pronoun
⑤ linking verb
⑥ predicate noun
⑦ article
⑧ adjective
⑨ preposition
⑩ object of the preposition

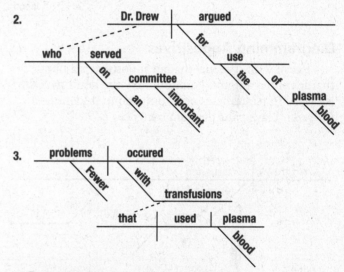

Diagramming Adverb Clauses

Ask a volunteer to describe the diagram in this section. (The subordinating conjunction *When* is written on a dotted line that connects the verb in the clause to the word the clause modifies.) Have students diagram sentences 5–6.

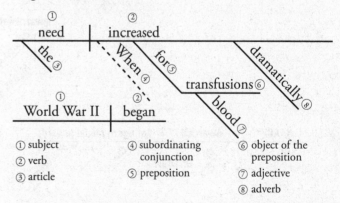

① subject
② verb
③ article
④ subordinating conjunction
⑤ preposition
⑥ object of the preposition
⑦ adjective
⑧ adverb

Continued on page T70

Language Standard(s): L.8.1, L.8.2, L.8.2a, L.8.2b, L.8.2c

T69

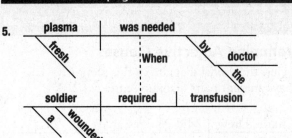

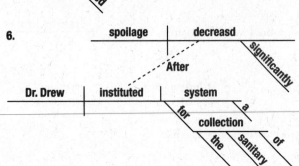

Diagramming Appositives

Recall with students that an appositive is a phrase that identifies a noun. Point out how the noun *specialty* is placed in parentheses next to the noun it identifies (*surgery*). Have pairs diagram sentences 8–9.

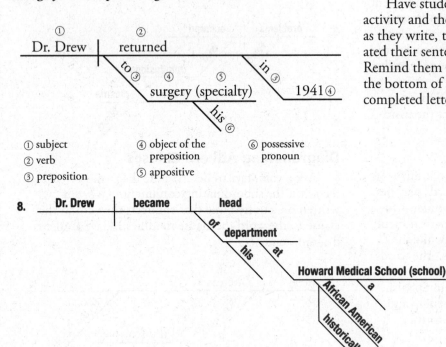

① subject
② verb
③ preposition
④ object of the preposition
⑤ appositive
⑥ possessive pronoun

Writing Sentences (student page 255)

Inform students that sentences 1 through 6 on page 255 need to be revised so that they make sense. Have a volunteer read the first sentence aloud, tell what is wrong with it, and tell how it should be corrected. (*Carved in stone* should be in quotations and *stone* should be capitalized.) Then have students work independently or in pairs to correct the remaining sentences. Have students compare their revisions.

Writing a Paragraph (student page 256)

Read the friendly letter on page 255 aloud. Draw students' attention to the different parts of the letter. Call on volunteers to take turns identifying and then reading aloud the heading, greeting, body, closing, and signature. Ask students to name the topic of the letter. (Sacagawea)

Have students look back at their revised sentences on page 255. Explain that the sentences are out of order, but when ordered correctly they could form the body of a letter. Ask a volunteer to name the introductory sentence. (item 3) Call on others to name, in order, the sentences that give more information. (items 6, 2, 1, 5, and 4) Then ask students to write the revised, corrected letter in the space provided on page 256.

Have students read the directions to the second activity and then write their letters. Remind them that as they write, they should be sure they have punctuated their sentences and used capitalization correctly. Remind them to check their work using the checklist at the bottom of the page. Invite volunteers to read their completed letters aloud.

English Language Learners

Have students work with a partner who is fluent in English for the proofreading activities.

Proofreading Practice

Ask students to identify the topic of the report on page 257. (Florence Nightingale) Explain that the report contains several mistakes and that as they read, they should look for these mistakes.

Review the **Proofreading Marks** chart and the examples. Remind students that these marks are used by professional writers to check their work before publication. Read the first sentence aloud. Discuss the errors (There should be hyphens in *well-to-do*, and *English* should be capitalized.) and how they should be marked for correction. You may wish to have students correct the spelling errors as well.

After they have completed the proofreading activity, ask volunteers to read each sentence aloud and to identify errors. Ask students to mark overlooked errors in another color. (**Note:** Some errors can be corrected in more than one way.)

Proofreading Checklist

Ask students to select a recent piece of their own writing and to write the title of that piece at the top of the chart. Ask students to put a check mark next to each item in the checklist after they have checked it in their work. Students might first work independently and then trade papers with a partner to double-check each other's work. You might model, or ask a student to model, using the **G.U.M. Handbook** (beginning on student page 361) to clarify a concept or rule.

Also Remember...

Remind students that capitalization and punctuation are important for clear writing. If necessary, help students use the **G.U.M. Handbook** to clarify when commas should be used and to review the use of uppercase letters.

Your Own List

Suggest that students look at the errors they did not find in the proofreading activity and add them to the checklist. Ask students to think about other kinds of errors they make and to add these to the checklist.

Ask students to place this page in their writing portfolios. These pages may be used to assess students' progress over the course of the year.

These two pages provide interesting and fun activities that reinforce the skills and concepts students learned in Lessons 73 to 84. These activities give students the opportunity to extend what they have read about in the unit by finding out more about problem solvers in their community. You might utilize the **Community Connection** page in one of the following ways:

- Ask students to take the pages home, select one activity to do, and then share the results of that activity with the class.
- Have pairs of students select one activity to complete together.
- Preview the activities as a class, and then assign the activities to small groups of students to complete cooperatively. Set aside a time for groups to share the results.

When you are ready to have students select activities, direct them to pages 259–260. Explain that the activities on page 259 will give them an opportunity to find out more about various kinds of community problems and the ways in which people try to solve those problems. Explain that one activity provides a chance to learn about job opportunities available to people who want to solve problems. Point out that page 260 is a planning guide that will help students take notes as they conduct their research. Have students carefully tear out the pages, and then explain how you wish students to use them.

Notes

Notes

Notes

Grammar, Usage, and Mechanics

Conventions of Standard English

ZB **Zaner-Bloser**

Grade Level Consultants

S. Elaine Boysworth
Lincolnton, North Carolina

Linda Crawford
Calhoun, Georgia

Martha Swan Novy
Florissant, Missouri

Heather Stanton
Colorado Springs, Colorado

Jaqueline Xavier
Cleveland, Ohio

Illustration: Tom Kennedy, Tracy Greenwalt

ISBN: 978-1-4531-1212-0

ZB Code 16

Zaner-Bloser, Inc.
1-800-421-3018
www.zaner-bloser.com
Printed in the United States of America

1 2 3 4 5 19750 18 17 16 15 14

SFI — Certified Chain of Custody
Promoting Sustainable Forestry
www.sfiprogram.org
SFI-01042

Table of Contents

Unit 1 Sentence Structure

Beasts & Critters: Astounding Animals

Unit 2 Sentence Structure

The World Outside: Changes in the Natural World

Unit 3 Parts of Speech: Nouns, Pronouns, Adjectives, and Adverbs

Timeless Tales: Myths and Legends

Unit 4 Parts of Speech: Verbs and Conjunctions

Looking Back: American Journeys

Unit 5 Usage

Grab Bag: High-Tech Highlights

Unit 6 Grammar

Great Getaways: Rivers of the World

Unit 7 Grammar

Unforgettable Folks: Problem Solvers

Appendix

Unit Pretests

Extra Practice

Unit Posttests

G.U.M. Handbook

Language Index

Read and Analyze

Emperor penguins / live in one of the harshest environments on Earth.
         a.   b.

Which part of this sentence (*a* or *b*) tells whom or what the sentence is about? __a__

Which part of this sentence (*a* or *b*) tells what happens? __b__

Every sentence contains a subject and a predicate. The **complete subject** in a sentence is made up of a noun or pronoun and words that tell about it. The **complete predicate** in a sentence is made up of a verb and words that tell what the subject is, has, or does.

See Handbook | Sections 11, 12

Practice

Underline the complete subject in each sentence once. Underline each complete predicate twice.

1. This species of penguin survives in the extreme conditions of Antarctica.

2. Antarctica is the coldest and windiest continent on Earth.

3. Colonies of Emperor penguins live along the Antarctic coast.

4. Groups of penguins huddle together on the ice.

5. This action protects the penguins against the cold and wind.

6. The body of an Emperor penguin contains a large amount of fat.

7. This body fat provides insulation against the cold.

8. Emperor penguin chicks are born during the long Antarctic winter.

9. The female penguin lays a single egg in mid-May.

10. She goes on a two-month journey to the sea in search of food.

11. The female leaves the egg with her mate.

12. The male penguin balances the egg on his feet.

13. A fold of skin on the male's abdomen covers the egg.

14. This fold protects the egg from the harsh environment.

15. The male penguin eats nothing during this time.

16. The female returns in mid-July from her journey.

17. The male transfers the egg back to his mate.

18. The egg hatches soon after this transfer.

19. The mother penguin feeds her newly hatched Emperor chick.

Emperor penguins endure the severe weather in Antarctica.

Apply   Answers will vary.

Add a subject or a predicate to each phrase to make a sentence. Underline the complete subject in each sentence you write. Circle the complete predicate in each sentence.

20.   the icy waters off the coast _____

_____

21.   eat fish and squid _____

_____

22.   study the penguins' habits _____

_____

23.   strong Antarctic winds _____

_____

Reinforce

Complete subjects and predicates may be very short (*Penguins / swim*) or very long. Short sentences can make a paragraph seem direct and can help focus readers' attention on actions and events. Long sentences in a paragraph can create a smooth flow that carries the reader along from one idea to the next while providing clear descriptions and explanations.

On the lines below write a short paragraph about an unusual animal. Make the subjects and predicates in your sentences short and concise. Then rewrite your paragraph on another sheet of paper, adding words and phrases to make the subjects and predicates longer and more informative. For what purpose might the more concise paragraph be better? For what purpose might the more descriptive paragraph be better?

Answers will vary. _____

_____

_____

_____

_____

_____

_____

_____

_____

_____

_____

_____

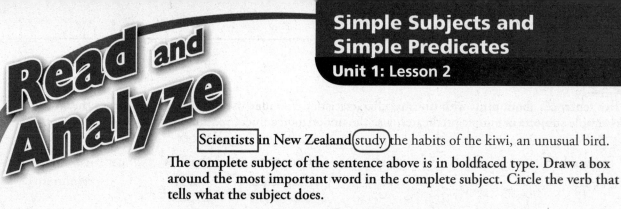

Scientists in New Zealand study the habits of the kiwi, an unusual bird.

The complete subject of the sentence above is in boldfaced type. Draw a box around the most important word in the complete subject. Circle the verb that tells what the subject does.

Do some research on this fascinating creature.

Can you find a subject at the beginning of this sentence? ___no___

Which word below would fit as the subject of the sentence? Circle it.

you   research   kiwi   bird

The **simple subject** is the most important word or words in the complete subject. It is a noun or pronoun that tells whom or what the sentence is about. By identifying the simple subject in a sentence, you can determine whether the subject is singular or plural and choose the correct verb form to use with it. The subject of a request or a command (an imperative sentence) usually is not named. The person being spoken to, *you*, is the **understood subject**. The **simple predicate** is the verb that tells about the subject. It may tell what the subject did or what was done to the subject; or, it may link the subject to words that tell about it.

See Handbook | Sections 11, 12

Practice

Draw a box around the simple subject in each sentence. If the subject is the understood *you*, write *you* on the line. Then underline the simple predicate.

1. The tiny kiwi scurries quickly from place to place. _____

2. The wings of this flightless bird are very small. _____

3. The kiwi has nostrils at the end of its long beak. _____

4. The feathers of the kiwi look much like hair. _____

5. Describe the kiwi's physical appearance. __you__

6. The oropendola is another interesting type of bird. _____

7. This member of the Icterid family lives in Central and

    South American rainforests and grasslands. _____

8. The nest of the oropendola resembles a long hanging sack. _____

9. Notice those long nests hanging from tree branches. __you__

10. That male bowerbird has built a nest with sticks, leaves, and moss. _____

11. He is decorating the nest with pebbles, berries, and shells. _____

12. The elaborate nest will attract a female bowerbird's attention. _____

The kiwi is a flightless bird native to New Zealand.

Apply

Write five sentences about birds with unusual characteristics. You may use nouns and verbs from the word bank as simple subjects or simple predicates. Use the understood subject *you* in one of your sentences.

researchers	fly	beak	hunt	habitat	lives
builds	nest	eats	branches	study	rainforest

13. **Answers will vary.** _____

_____

14. _____

_____

15. _____

_____

16. _____

_____

17. _____

_____

Reinforce Answers will vary.

See Handbook Sections 35, 36, 37

Use the Internet or an encyclopedia to research another unusual bird. Then write an e-mail to a friend or family member describing this bird. Begin with the reason you are e-mailing. Use proper etiquette, such as typing a clear subject line; avoiding special type features and emoticons and using only uppercase letters; and including a detailed salutation (full name and e-mail address). When you have finished your first draft, read your e-mail from beginning to end. Did you achieve your purpose for writing? Proofread for errors in capitalization, punctuation, and spelling. Then print out a hard copy of your final draft. Circle the simple subject in each sentence. Underline each simple predicate.

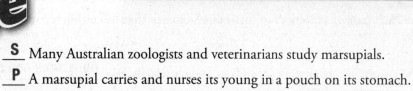
_S_ Many Australian zoologists and veterinarians study marsupials.

_P_ A marsupial carries and nurses its young in a pouch on its stomach.

Write *S* next to the sentence that contains two or more simple subjects.

Write *P* next to the sentence that contains two or more simple predicates.

A **compound subject** is two or more subjects joined by a coordinating conjunction (examples: *and, but, or*). A **compound predicate** is two or more verbs joined by a coordinating conjunction.

See Handbook | Sections 11, 12

Practice

Each sentence below has either a compound subject or a compound predicate. If a sentence has a compound subject, underline the nouns that are the simple subjects. If a sentence has a compound predicate, circle the verbs that are the simple predicates.

1. Koalas, kangaroos, and wallabies are three kinds of marsupials.

2. Koalas live in trees and sleep up to 20 hours a day.

3. They survive on a diet of eucalyptus leaves and drink very little water.

4. Australia and Papua New Guinea are home to kangaroos and wallabies.

5. These marsupials have powerful hind legs and hop from place to place.

6. Baby koalas, kangaroos, and wallabies are called joeys.

7. A joey crawls into its mother's pouch after birth and receives nourishment from her.

8. Wombats and Tasmanian devils are two other kinds of marsupials.

9. Wombats dig and live in burrows.

10. Native grasses and shrub roots are part of the wombat's diet.

11. Tasmanian devils hunt and eat small mammals and birds.

12. The appearance and sound of the Tasmanian devil frightens some people.

13. Tasmanian devils look fierce and screech while eating.

14. Wombats and Tasmanian devils have backward-facing pouches.

15. The newborn wombat makes its way into its mother's pouch

    and stays there for up to ten months.

16. The Tasmanian devil joey enters its mother's pouch

    after birth and remains there for about four months.

**The Tasmanian devil looks ferocious
and has an eerie cry.**

Name _____

Apply Possible answers appear below. Accept all reasonable responses.

Combine each pair of sentences to form one sentence that has either a compound subject or a compound predicate.

17. Opossums are marsupials. Numbats are marsupials, too. **Opossums and numbats are**
    marsupials.

18. The opossum grasps branches with its tail. The animal also carries nesting material with its tail.
    The opossum grasps branches and carries nesting material with its tail.

19. Baby opossums develop inside their mother's pouch. Later they ride on their mother's back.
    Baby opossums grow inside their mother's pouch and later ride on her back.

20. Numbats live in the woodlands of western Australia. They eat termites. **Numbats live in the**
    woodlands of western Australia and eat termites.

21. Dogs prey on the numbat. Foxes prey on this marsupial, too. **Dogs and foxes prey on the numbat.**

Reinforce

It is possible to have both a compound subject and a compound predicate in the same sentence. (*The boys and girls talked and laughed together.*) However, both parts of the compound subject must be performing both actions of the compound predicate. Avoid sentences like this one: *The birds and dogs chirped and barked.* This sentence might make the reader think that the dogs chirped and the birds barked.

On the lines below, rewrite the incorrect sentence as two separate sentences. Write *C* beside the sentence that uses compound subjects and predicates correctly.

22. The campers and counselors swam and splashed in the lake. __**C**__

23. The stars and the wind sparkled brightly and blew softly. _____
    The stars sparkled brightly. The wind blew softly.

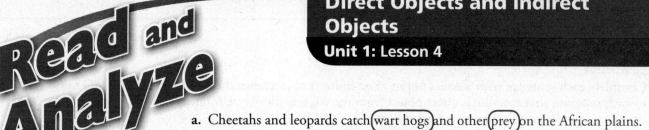

a. Cheetahs and leopards catch (wart hogs) and other (prey) on the African plains.

b. Zookeepers give visitors (information) about these predators.

Circle the nouns in sentence *a* that tell what cheetahs and leopards catch. Circle the noun in sentence *b* that tells what zookeepers give visitors. Draw a line under the noun in sentence *b* that tells *to whom* they give it.

A **direct object** is a noun or pronoun that receives the action of the verb. To find the direct object, say the verb and then ask "What?" or "Whom?" An **indirect object** is a person or thing to whom something is given, told, or taught. The indirect object is a noun or pronoun, and it comes before the direct object. To determine whether a word is an indirect object, move it after the direct object and put the word *to* or *for* in front of it. Example: *Zookeepers give information to visitors*. A sentence may have more than one direct object or indirect object.

See Handbook | Section 21

Practice

Circle each direct object in the sentences below. Underline each indirect object. Be careful. Not all sentences contain indirect objects.

1. The zookeeper gave us a short (lecture) about cheetahs and leopards.

2. The cheetah hunts its (prey) during the daytime.

3. This swift predator catches (creatures) using its strong claws.

4. It holds the doomed (animal) by the neck.

5. The cheetah must eat its (catch) quickly.

6. Other predators may steal its (food.)

7. A cheetah cannot defeat a (lion) or a (pack) of hyenas.

8. The mother cheetah brings her cubs (meat) from her catch.

9. The leopard most often stalks (prey) at night.

10. This carnivore can kill (animals) larger than itself.

11. The leopard keeps its (catch) from other predators in an effective way.

12. It climbs a large, thick-branched (tree) with its catch in its jaws.

13. The leopard then eats its (meal) in the branches, safe from lions and hyenas.

14. The zookeeper gave adults and children more (details) about differences between cheetahs and leopards.

15. Many people asked the zookeeper (questions) after her speech.

The cheetah is the fastest land animal on Earth.

Apply

Complete each sentence with a direct object or an indirect object from the word bank. Write *DO* next to each sentence that contains a direct object from the word bank. Write *IO* next to each sentence that contains an indirect object from the word bank.

teacher	water	class	us	cubs	fur

16. Our teacher gave _____**us**_____ information about the world's wild cats. ___**IO**___

17. Wild cats groom their _____**fur**_____. ___**DO**___

18. Mother cats carry their _____**cubs**_____ with their mouths. ___**DO**___

19. One student asked the _____**teacher**_____ a question about wild cats' dislike of water. ___**IO**___

20. He gave the _____**class**_____ a surprising answer. ___**IO**___

21. Tigers, leopards, and jaguars like _____**water**_____ and are good swimmers. ___**DO**___

Reinforce

See Handbook Section 21

An *object complement* is a noun, pronoun, or adjective that follows a direct object and identifies or describes the direct object. An object complement is often used with verbs that create or nominate, such as *make, name, elect, paint, call,* and so on. In the sentence *He painted the fence white*, for example, the adjective *white* is the object complement, since it describes the direct object *fence*. In the sentence *The team elected her captain*, the noun *captain* is an object complement; it identifies what the direct object *her* has been elected to.

Read the passage below. Find each direct object and underline it. Then put a box around each object complement that identifies or describes the direct object. Be careful. Not all sentences contain object complements. (22–36)

The setting sun turned the African landscape pink. The wildlife photographer spied a cheetah across the plain. This sighting made her happy. She would get a perfect photo of the graceful animal!

Suddenly, storm clouds turned the sky black. This change in the weather made the photographer unhappy: it spoiled her perfect photo opportunity. The cheetah gave a high-pitched call and sprinted away. The photographer expressed disappointment. That photo could have made her an award winner!

Invertebrates are animals without backbones.

Most terrestrial invertebrates are small.

Find the simple subject and the linking verb in each sentence above. Put a box around the boldfaced noun that tells who or what the subject of its sentence is. Circle the boldfaced adjective that gives descriptive information about the subject of its sentence.

A **predicate noun** follows a linking verb and tells more about who or what the subject is. A **predicate adjective** follows a linking verb and describes the subject.

See Handbook | Section 12

Practice

Underline the linking verb in each sentence. Put a box around each predicate noun. Circle each predicate adjective.

1. Cephalopods are an ancient group of marine invertebrates.

2. They are also a class of mollusks.

3. Mollusks are animals with soft bodies and, in most cases, shells.

4. Some marine biologists are experts on cephalopods.

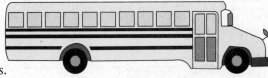

**school bus
length: 40 feet**

5. According to these experts, a cephalopod's brain is relatively large.

6. These creatures are the most intelligent of the invertebrates.

7. Squid and octopuses are one variety of cephalopod.

8. Giant squid and colossal squid are two species of squid.

9. In the past, people were awestruck by tales of giant sea monsters.

**colossal squid
maximum estimated
length: 46 feet**

10. Marine biologists became curious about the existence of gigantic squid.

11. Antarctica's Ross Sea was the site of a major discovery in January 2007.

12. John Bennett is the captain of a New Zealand fishing boat.

13. He was amazed at the sight of a colossal squid tangled in his fishing lines.

14. The adult male squid was enormous—the largest one ever recovered.

15. The creature's weight was about 1,000 pounds.

16. The squid's length was 33 feet.

17. Bennett's capture of the colossal squid was a major contribution to our knowledge of cephalopods.

Apply   Answers will vary.

Write a predicate noun or a predicate adjective to complete each sentence.

18. When I look at the ocean, I feel _____.

19. My favorite sea creature is the _____.

20. Invertebrates are _____.

21. Octopuses are _____.

22. Two species of squid are _____.

23. When the researcher saw the giant squid, he became _____.

24. When marine biologists learned of the discovery of the colossal squid, they felt _____.

Reinforce

Ten nouns from the lesson are hidden in the word search puzzle below. Circle them and list them on the lines. Then use some of these words to write two sentences, one with a predicate noun and the other with a predicate adjective. Do this on another sheet of paper.

C	E	P	H	A	L	O	P	O	D	S	D	B
L	Z	K	R	N	S	C	T	J	M	Q	E	I
A	J	Y	H	I	A	T	L	D	A	U	R	O
S	V	T	D	M	B	O	Q	F	H	I	J	L
S	H	E	L	L	S	P	Z	M	L	D	P	O
D	S	M	O	L	L	U	S	K	S	R	C	G
P	V	C	L	S	C	S	M	Y	H	F	L	I
I	N	V	E	R	T	E	B	R	A	T	E	S
A	N	I	M	A	L	S	L	P	X	Q	V	T
Z	A	Y	I	B	A	C	K	B	O	N	E	S

Nouns

25. _____cephalopods_____

26. _____class_____

27. _____animals_____

28. _____shells_____

29. _____mollusks_____

30. _____invertebrates_____

31. _____backbones_____

32. _____octopuses_____

33. _____squid_____

34. _____biologists_____

The hummingbirds flew around the garden.

Where did the hummingbirds fly? _____ **around the garden** _____

A **prepositional phrase** can tell *how, what kind, when, how much,* or *where.* A prepositional phrase begins with a **preposition,** such as *about, around, at, by, from, in, into, of, on, over, to,* or *with.* It ends with a noun or pronoun that is the **object of the preposition**. The words between the preposition and its object are part of the prepositional phrase. A prepositional phrase can appear at the beginning, middle, or end of a sentence.

See Handbook Section 20

Practice

Underline each prepositional phrase. Circle the preposition that begins each phrase. Put a box around the object of the preposition. There may be more than one prepositional phrase in each sentence.

1. We are learning about different bird species in science class.

2. Last week, a guest speaker from the bird sanctuary visited our class.

3. Our science teacher introduced the guest speaker to us.

4. The speaker gave an interesting talk on his favorite subject—hummingbirds.

5. He is an expert on these tiny, colorful birds.

6. Hummingbirds are the size of a thumb; their wings can beat 80 times per second.

7. The needle-like beak of a hummingbird can reach into long flower blossoms.

8. Hummingbirds can hover in the air and can fly backward.

9. A hummingbird extracts nectar from flowers with its long, thin tongue.

10. This species of bird is found only in North America and South America.

11. The speaker described his recent trip to Ecuador with a research team.

12. Ecuador is located in northwestern South America.

13. This country has 163 species of hummingbird—

    the largest number in any one country.

14. The speaker gave us information about Ecuador's

    hummingbird species.

15. The Esmeraldas Woodstar is a rare hummingbird species

    found in western Ecuador in a fog forest.

16. This tiny bird is dangerously close to extinction.

Hummingbirds fly from flower to flower in search of nectar.

Apply   Possible answers appear below. Accept all reasonable responses.

Rewrite each sentence. Add at least one prepositional phrase to make the sentence give more information. Use prepositional phrases from the work bank, or think of your own.

above the treetops	from the United States	in their natural habitat	in Ecuador
during the day	toward the researchers	near the campground	by plane

17. The researchers traveled to South America. **The researchers traveled to South America from the United States.**

18. They explored the tropical rainforest. **They explored the tropical rainforest during the day.**

19. The colorful hummingbirds flew. **The colorful hummingbirds flew above the treetops.**

20. The researchers observed the hummingbirds. **The researchers observed the hummingbirds in their natural habitat.**

Reinforce

See Handbook Section 20

A prepositional phrase can modify, or tell more about, a noun or pronoun. Prepositional phrases that modify nouns or pronouns are called *adjectival prepositional phrases*. An adjectival prepositional phrase usually comes after the noun or pronoun it modifies. A prepositional phrase can also modify a verb, an adverb, or an adjective. This type of prepositional phrase is called an *adverbial prepositional phrase*. Many adverbial prepositional phrases tell *when, where, how,* or *how long* something was done.

Circle the prepositional phrase in each sentence. Draw an arrow to the word or words it modifies. Then, on the line next to each sentence, write whether the phrase is an adjectival prepositional phrase or an adverbial prepositional phrase.

21. (In 2004,) many scientists visited Germany. **adverbial**

22. A zoologist (from Frankfurt) presented his findings. **adjectival**

23. The discovery (of a possible hummingbird fossil) astounded the scientists. **adjectival**

24. The delicate bones (of hummingbirds) rarely fossilize. **adjectival**

25. The bird fossils were found (in southern Germany.) **adverbial**

26. The tiny skeletons were unearthed (with extreme care.) **adverbial**

a. Lonesome George was a Galapagos giant tortoise.

b. Lonesome George, a Galapagos giant tortoise, lived on an island off the coast of Ecuador.

Draw a box around the phrase in sentence *b* that tells who or what Lonesome George is. What punctuation marks separate this phrase from the rest of the sentence? _____commas_____

An **appositive** is a phrase that identifies a noun. An appositive follows the noun it identifies and is usually separated from the rest of the sentence by commas. (The appositive is set off with commas when it is a nonrestrictive element. A phrase is considered a nonrestrictive element when it gives information that is not essential to the meaning of a sentence.)

See Handbook **Section 24**

Practice

Underline the appositive in each sentence. Draw a box around the noun it identifies.

1. The Galapagos Archipelago, a group of islands in the Pacific Ocean, is located on the equator.

2. Galapagos, a province of Ecuador, is home to a large variety of plants and animals.

3. *Archipelago* comes from the term *galapago,* the Spanish word for *saddle*.

4. The shells of some tortoises on the islands resemble a *galapago,* a type of British riding saddle.

5. Giant tortoises, perhaps the most famous animals in the Galapagos, can weigh over 500 pounds and can live for more than 150 years.

6. One male Galapagos giant tortoise, Lonesome George, was from Pinta Island in the Galapagos.

7. Lonesome George, one of the last known survivors of his species, was thought to be between 60 and 90 years old when he died.

8. Giant tortoises are also found in the Seychelles, a group of islands in the western Indian Ocean.

The Galapagos giant tortoise is one of the largest tortoises on Earth.

9. The Seychelles are located about 1,000 miles east of Kenya, a country in East Africa.

10. The Aldabra Atoll in the outer Seychelles is home to about 152,000 giant tortoises, the world's largest population of the animal.

11. Adwaitya, a giant Aldabra tortoise, died in March 2006 at the age of 255.

12. The tortoise had been living at the Alipore Zoo in Kolkata, an Indian city formerly known as Calcutta.

13. Subir Chowdhury, director of the Alipore Zoo, said records show that the tortoise was born in 1750.

14. The giant tortoise was given as a gift to Robert Clive, one of the founders of British rule in India, in 1875.

15. The tortoise's name, *Adwaitya,* comes from a Sanskrit word meaning "the only one."

Apply   Possible answers appear below. Accept all reasonable responses.

Rewrite each pair of sentences as one sentence. Change the underlined sentence into an appositive.

16. <u>Haller Park is an animal sanctuary in Mombasa, Kenya.</u> Haller Park is home to a giant Aldabra tortoise. **Haller Park, an animal sanctuary in Mombasa, Kenya, is home to a giant Aldabra tortoise.**

17. <u>Dr. Paula Kahumbu is the manager of Haller Park.</u> Dr. Kahumbu described how an orphan baby hippo befriended the tortoise. **Dr. Paula Kahumbu, the manager of Haller Park, described how an orphan baby hippo befriended the tortoise.**

18. <u>Owen is a baby hippopotamus.</u> Owen lost his mother in the devastating tsunami of December 2004. **Owen, a baby hippopotamus, lost his mother in the devastating tsunami of December 2004.**

19. Owen was brought to Haller Park by Dr. Kahumbu and Stephen Tuei. <u>Stephen Tuei is the sanctuary's chief animal caretaker.</u> **Owen was brought to Haller Park by Dr. Kahumbu and Stephen Tuei, the sanctuary's chief animal caretaker.**

20. Owen was released in Haller Park and ran to Mzee. <u>Mzee is the park's 130-year-old giant Aldabra tortoise.</u> **Owen was released in Haller Park and ran to Mzee, the park's 130-year-old giant Aldabra tortoise.**

Reinforce

See Handbook Section 24

The appositives studied so far have been separated from the rest of the sentence by commas. These appositives give more information about the nouns they describe. However, some appositives should *not* be set off by commas. If an appositive is essential to the meaning of a sentence, it should not be set off by commas. Appositives that are essential to the meaning of a sentence are called *restrictive appositives*. Those that simply provide more information about the nouns they describe are called *nonrestrictive appositives*.

| Example | Jeremy Aguilar, <u>my cousin</u>, wrote a report on giant tortoises. |

(The nonrestrictive appositive *my cousin* is not essential to the sentence; it gives more information about Jeremy Aguilar and should be set off by commas.)
My cousin <u>Jeremy Aguilar</u> saw giant tortoises at the San Diego Zoo.
(The restrictive appositive *Jeremy Aguilar* is necessary to explain which cousin is meant.)

If necessary, add commas around the appositives in the following sentences. If no commas are necessary, write *C* on the line next to the sentence.

21. My sister Tamara is the youngest of all my sisters. **C**

22. Tamara my youngest sister plans to visit the Galapagos Islands someday. _____

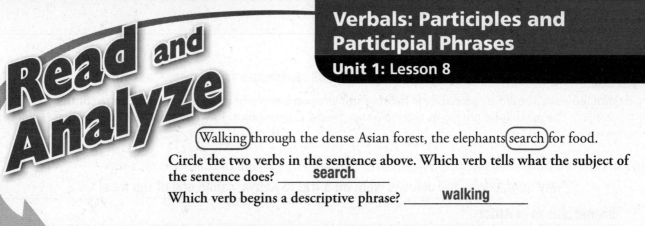

Read and Analyze

(Walking) through the dense Asian forest, the elephants (search) for food.

Circle the two verbs in the sentence above. Which verb tells what the subject of the sentence does? _____search_____

Which verb begins a descriptive phrase? _____walking_____

Sometimes a verb does not act as the simple predicate of a sentence. A **verbal** is a word formed from a verb that plays another role in the sentence. One type of verbal is a **participle**. A participle may be a present participle (*covering*) or a past participle (*consumed*). A **participial phrase** is made of a participle and other words that complete its meaning. A participial phrase can act as an adjective. In the sentence above, *Walking through the dense Asian forest* is a participial phrase that describes *elephants*.

See Handbook Sections 18d, 25a

Practice

Underline each participial phrase. Then circle the participle.

1. Visitors (traveling) to Africa and certain parts of Asia might see elephants.

2. (Identified) as the largest living land mammal, the African elephant is found in the wild only in Africa.

3. (Weighing) about 12,000 pounds, an adult male African elephant stands approximately 11 feet tall at the shoulder.

4. Zoologists (researching) African elephants have determined that there are two different types: bush elephants and forest elephants.

5. The type of African elephant (known) as the bush elephant is found in most countries south of the Sahara.

6. (Inhabiting) the countries of central and western Africa, forest elephants live in forests, grasslands, and mountains.

Elephants are highly intelligent and social animals.

7. The type of elephant (called) the Asian elephant is smaller than the African elephant.

8. (Standing) 9 to 10½ feet tall at the shoulder, an adult male Asian elephant can weigh up to 8,000 pounds.

9. (Found) in parts of India and Southeast Asia, Asian elephants are light gray and may have pink or white spots.

10. Two humps (located) just above the Asian elephant's ears give the animal a distinctive appearance.

11. Scientists (studying) elephants have discovered many amazing things about them.

12. Experts (observing) wild elephants have documented their highly complex societies.

13. (Possessing) special receptors on their feet, elephants can pick up underground vibrations.

14. The animals can sense vibrations (indicating) potential danger.

15. Elephants (living) in seaside areas ran to safety in advance of the deadly Indian Ocean tsunami of December 2004.

Apply   Possible answers appear below. Accept all reasonable responses.

A participial phrase should be placed near the noun or pronoun it modifies so it does not create confusion for the reader. The participial phrase in each sentence below is misplaced. Rewrite each sentence so that it makes sense.

16. Called one of the most scenic places in Africa, my aunt, uncle, and cousins went on a trip to Kenya. **My aunt, uncle, and cousins went on a trip to Kenya, called one of the most scenic places in Africa.**

17. Located near the beaches of Kenya's South Coast, they visited an elephant sanctuary. **They visited an elephant sanctuary located near the beaches of Kenya's South Coast.**

18. Grazing in the tall grass, my cousins Bettina and Kent spied a baby elephant. **My cousins Bettina and Kent spied a baby elephant grazing in the tall grass.**

19. Rolling in the mud, my uncle snapped a picture of a baby elephant. **My uncle snapped a picture of a baby elephant rolling in the mud.**

Reinforce

See Handbook | Section 25b

> An absolute phrase consists of a noun or noun phrase followed by a descriptive word or phrase. Like a participial phrase, an absolute phrase may contain a verbal form ending in –*ing* or –*ed*. It may also contain an adjective, an additional noun phrase, or one or more prepositional phrases.
>
> noun phrase + present participle
> The elephants bathed in the river, <u>their mother watching</u>.
>
> noun phrase + adjective + prepositional phrase
> A hippo swam upstream, <u>its nose visible above the water</u>.
>
> noun phrase + prepositional phrases
> A lioness lay under a tree, <u>her cubs in the grass near her</u>.

Each sentence below is formed incorrectly. Cross out the form of *be* in the second clause to turn the clause into an absolute phrase. Then rewrite each sentence.

20. Sue paddled down the river, her brother ~~was~~ sitting quietly beside her.
    Sue paddled down the river, her brother sitting quietly beside her.

21. Crocodiles slithered along the bank, their bodies ~~were~~ covered in mud.
    Crocodiles slithered along the bank, their bodies covered in mud.

22. Juan photographed the giraffe, its neck ~~was~~ almost too long for the shot.
    Juan photographed the giraffe, its neck almost too long for the shot.

23. The elephants huddled together, the babies ~~were~~ in the center of the group.
    The elephants huddled together, the babies in the center of the group.

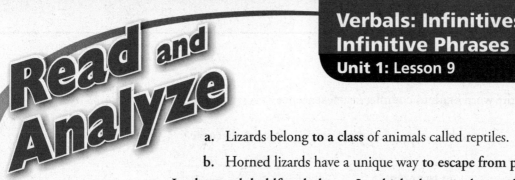

a. Lizards belong **to a class** of animals called reptiles.

b. Horned lizards have a unique way **to escape from predators.**

Look at each boldfaced phrase. In which phrase is the word *to* followed by a verb? ___**b**___

In which phrase is the word *to* followed by an article and a noun? ___**a**___

An **infinitive** is a phrase made up of the word *to* followed by the present form of a verb (*to escape*). Infinitives may act as adjectives, adverbs, or nouns. An **infinitive phrase** is made up of an infinitive and any other words that complete its meaning. In sentence *b* above, *to escape from predators* is an infinitive phrase.

See Handbook Section 25a

Practice

Underline the infinitive phrase in each sentence.

1. I went to the local library <u>to do research on lizards.</u>

2. The librarian helped me <u>to learn the distinguishing characteristics of lizards.</u>

3. I used the library computer <u>to look up information about several lizard species.</u>

4. The largest species of lizard, the Komodo dragon, is able <u>to climb trees.</u>

5. The Komodo dragon's keen sense of smell helps it <u>to find food.</u>

6. When a Komodo dragon bites its prey, deadly bacteria in the lizard's mouth are transmitted to the prey, causing it <u>to die of infection.</u>

7. The flexible skull of the lizard allows it <u>to swallow large chunks of food.</u>

8. Komodo dragons are able <u>to withstand the harsh environment of their habitat.</u>

9. I was amazed <u>to discover that a horned lizard can squirt blood from its eyes.</u>

10. This ability enables the horned lizard <u>to protect itself from predators.</u>

11. The lizard's coloring allows it <u>to blend in with its desert surroundings.</u>

12. The horned lizard's camouflage makes it difficult <u>to spot.</u>

13. During the early part of the day, horned lizards may flatten themselves against rocks <u>to bask in the sun.</u>

14. At night, the lizard uses its spines <u>to dig a hole for itself in the sand.</u>

15. The horned lizard uses its long, sticky tongue <u>to catch ants</u>, its main source of food.

The horned lizard heats itself by basking in the sun.

Apply Answers will vary.

Write an infinitive from the word bank to complete each sentence.

to pursue	to focus	to discover	to become	to study

16. Someone who wants _____**to become**_____ a herpetologist, a scientist who studies reptiles and

    amphibians, must take many science classes.

17. Subjects that herpetologists need _____**to study**_____ in college include biology and chemistry.

18. A person who wishes _____**to pursue**_____ this career needs persistence and determination.

19. Many herpetologists find it exciting _____**to discover**_____ new things about reptiles and

    amphibians.

20. Herpetologists may want _____**to focus**_____ their research on just one species of reptile or

    amphibian.

Reinforce

See Handbook Section 25a

A sentence may contain more than one participial phrase (*Caught off guard and flattered by the attention, she thanked us for the surprise party*) or infinitive phrase (*I like to sing and to go fishing*). Using two verbals of the same type to express similar ideas is using *parallel structure*. Using two verbals of different types to express similar ideas—for example, *I like singing and to go fishing*—is considered poor style. In your writing, use parallel structure when expressing two or more similar ideas.

Read the two sentences below. Rewrite the sentence that is not parallel in structure to make it parallel. Write *C* beside the sentence that is parallel in structure.

21. Observing the lizards and taking notes, Graham began the research for his report. _____**C**_____

    _____

    _____

    _____

22. Iris likes to hike in the woods and riding her bicycle. **Iris likes to hike in the woods and to ride her bicycle.**

    _____

    _____

    _____

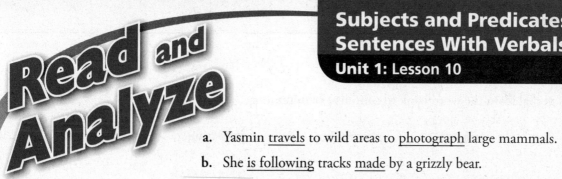

a. Yasmin <u>travels</u> to wild areas to <u>photograph</u> large mammals.

b. She <u>is following</u> tracks <u>made</u> by a grizzly bear.

Which underlined verb in sentence *a* tells what the subject does?
_____ <u>travels</u> **What type of verbal phrase in sentence *a* is the other verb a part of?** __ infinitive phrase __ **Which underlined verb in sentence *b* tells what the subject is doing?** __ is following __ **What type of verbal phrase in sentence *b* is the other verb a part of?** __ participial phrase __

Every sentence has at least one **subject-verb relationship**. The subject tells what the sentence is about. The verb tells what the subject does or what the subject is doing, or links the subject to more information about it. Some sentences also contain verbs that are not part of a subject-verb relationship. These verbs are called **verbals**. **Participles** and **infinitives** are types of verbals. Participles and infinitives usually are parts of phrases that describe.

See Handbook Sections 11, 12, 25a

Practice

Draw one line under the simple subject in each sentence. Draw two lines under the simple predicate. Draw a box around each participial phrase. Circle each infinitive phrase.

1. Living mostly in Alaska and western Canada, <u>grizzlies</u> <u>are</u> a type of brown bear.

2. Weighing around 500 pounds, an adult <u>male</u> <u>can be</u> 6 feet in length.

3. A <u>grizzly</u> standing on its hind paws <u>is surveying</u> the surrounding area.

4. Mother <u>bears</u> carefully <u>supervise</u> their cubs to protect them from other predators.

5. These massive <u>creatures</u> <u>hunt</u> small mammals, hoofed animals, and fish, and gather berries, leaves, and roots to eat.

6. <u>Scientists</u> studying grizzly bears <u>have identified</u> more than 100 plants in western North America as parts of these bears' diet.

7. Feeling hunger, a <u>grizzly</u> <u>will use</u> its sensitive ears and nose to locate food.

8. Concerning locations of past food sources, these <u>bears</u> <u>have</u> excellent memory.

9. <u>Observers</u> studying grizzly bears <u>have described</u> them as intelligent and curious.

10. A <u>grizzly</u> <u>uses</u> its long claws to dig up roots.

11. The <u>hump</u> of muscles extending across the grizzly's shoulders <u>provides</u> extra strength for a dig.

12. To accumulate fat for winter, a <u>grizzly</u> <u>eats</u> up to 90 pounds of food each day.

13. <u>Bears</u> living in very cold climates <u>spend</u> the winter inside their dens or caves.

14. <u>Dens</u> <u>are</u> shelters made of branches or dug out of the ground.

15. <u>Grizzlies</u> typically <u>try</u> to avoid contact with humans.

16. A single <u>attack</u> on a human by a grizzly <u>causes</u> many people to regard these bears as ferocious predators.

A mother grizzly bear is very protective of her cubs.

Name _____

Apply

Write the correct verbal from the word bank to complete each sentence.

to protect	co-existing	according	respecting	to destroy

17. _____**Co-existing**_____ with Native Americans, grizzly bears thrived in North America for

thousands of years.

18. _____**Respecting**_____ grizzly bears, Native Americans admired their intelligence and strength.

19. European settlers killed grizzly bears for their fur and began _____**to destroy**_____ their habitat

in the mid-1800s.

20. _____**According**_____ to biologists, fewer than 1,000 grizzly bears roam the continental United

States today.

21. _____**To protect**_____ those few that remain, conservationists added the grizzly bear to the

endangered species list in 1975.

Reinforce

When a writer uses a verbal phrase instead of a proper subject-verb relationship, the result is a sentence fragment. Identify the sentence fragments below by writing *fragment* on the line. If possible, use a computer's grammar checker to help you do this.

22. Several ways for humans to protect themselves from grizzly bears. _____**fragment**_____

23. Campers should store all food in bear-resistant containers to

keep bears away. _____

24. Attracting grizzly bears, scented items such as chocolate,

candy, or toothpaste. _____**fragment**_____

25. To avoid surprising a grizzly bear, hikers should talk or sing songs. _____

26. Never approach or feed a bear crossing your path. _____

27. Being responsible, keeping both humans and bears safe. _____**fragment**_____

a. Hippopotamuses do look cute. However, they are aggressive and dangerous.

b. Many people see hippopotamuses as cute, humorous, even lovable creatures. In reality, though, hippos are among the most aggressive of all creatures; and, because of their enormous size and considerable speed, they are among the most dangerous.

Which paragraph presents more key information? __**b**__ What are some of the differences between the sentences in paragraph *a* and the sentences in paragraph *b* above? **The sentences in paragraph *b* provide more explanatory and descriptive information and also contain more linking words that indicate relationships between ideas.**

Sentences that include details, descriptive words, and words with precise meanings **give more information.** Sentences that combine connected facts or ideas **make clear important relationships.** Just adding more words to a sentence doesn't make it more effective, however. When you write, **expand or combine sentences** to help readers better understand what you are discussing.

See Handbook Sections 13, 16, 19, 20, 22

Practice

Draw a star by the paragraph in each item that more effectively presents key information.

1. The name *hippopotamus* means "river horse" in Greek. Hippos resemble pigs, but they are most closely related to whales, dolphins, and porpoises.

The ancient Greeks gave this remarkable creature the name *hippopotamus*, meaning "river horse." Many of the hippo's physical features, including its girth, teeth, and toes, resemble those of pigs. Advanced scientific analysis has shown, however, that the hippo's closest relatives are not land animals; they are sea creatures—whales, dolphins, and porpoises! ☆

2. Hippos are the third-largest land creature in size and weight; only elephants and rhinoceroses are larger. Hippos live in warm regions of Africa and spend their days submerged in rivers, lakes, or ponds; the water keeps them cool and helps support their enormous weight. ☆

Hippos are huge. They live in warm parts of Africa. They stay underwater during the day.

3. Hippos emerge from the water at dusk each evening to feed. These herbivores prefer to graze on short grasses, but they eat many other types of plants as well. A feeding session can last as long as six hours. ☆

At the end of the day, hippos leave their watery homes and trot across the land to find grassy areas to graze on. They don't just grab a quick bite; they may spend four, five, or six hours eating before they return to the water. Also, they don't just eat grass. A hungry hippo will eat a wide variety of plants.

Name _____

Apply

Work with a partner to search the Internet to find more information on hippopotamuses in zoos. Then rewrite the paragraph below, expanding and combining sentences so that it gives more information and makes clear important relationships.

> Hippos have been popular animals in zoos for a long time. A hippo in a zoo was kept in a small cemented area with a pool and a patch of grass. Now some zoos have created areas for hippos that are more like their homes in the wild. The Toledo Zoo is one of these.

Answers will vary. Sample response:

Hippos have been popular attractions in zoos for more than 150 years. Obaysch, the first hippo exhibited, drew more than 10,000 visitors a day to its London Zoo home. Until recently, hippos in zoos typically were kept in a small enclosure with a tiny cement pool and a small patch of grass. Recently, though, a number of zoos have built new, larger enclosures that resemble hippos' homes in the wild. One of the first and best of these new exhibits is the Toledo Zoo Hippoquarium; its hippo pond holds 360,000 gallons of water. Underwater and overhead webcams there give people throughout the world the opportunity to see hippos in real time going about their daily activities.

_____

_____

_____

_____

Reinforce

On the lines below, rewrite a paragraph from a report or story you have written recently. Expand and combine sentences so the paragraph helps readers better understand what you are discussing.

Answers will vary.

_____

_____

_____

_____

_____

_____

Read this paragraph. It contains the four kinds of sentences.

Will gorillas be able to survive in the wild? Their numbers have declined sharply in recent years. What a tragedy it would be to have these gentle, intelligent creatures become extinct! Think about what the world's people can do to help ensure gorillas' survival.

Circle the sentence that makes a statement. Draw a box around the sentence that asks a question. Draw two lines under the sentence that gives a command. Draw one line under the sentence that expresses strong emotion.

A **declarative sentence** makes a statement and ends with a period. An **interrogative sentence** asks a question and ends with a question mark. An **imperative sentence** gives a command and ends with a period or an exclamation point. An **exclamatory sentence** shows excitement and ends with an exclamation point. Begin every sentence with an uppercase letter.

See Handbook Section 10

Practice

Add the correct punctuation mark to each sentence. Then label it *declarative, interrogative, imperative,* or *exclamatory.*

1. Where is the region known as Equatorial Africa? __interrogative__

2. It is in the part of Africa nearest the equator. __declarative__

3. Find the nations of Uganda, Rwanda, and Democratic Republic of Congo on a map of Africa. __imperative__

4. Eastern lowland gorillas, one of four subspecies of gorillas, live in these nations. __declarative__

5. Consider the likelihood of survival for the 5,000 Eastern lowland gorillas that remain in the wild. __imperative__

6. How scarce Eastern mountain gorillas have become! __exclamatory__

7. Are there fewer than 1,000 of this subspecies remaining in the world? __interrogative__

8. This tiny population lives in the Virunga mountain area, where the three nations come together. __declarative__

9. Western lowland gorillas face many threats, but their numbers remain in excess of 150,000. __declarative__

10. Will the other subspecies, the Cross River gorilla, be enabled to survive? __interrogative__

11. Picture a population of only 300 gorillas. __imperative__

12. Thank goodness international organizations such as WWF Global are working to protect gorillas and their habitats! __exclamatory__

Name _____

Apply   Answers will vary. Sample responses are shown.

Rewrite each sentence so it is the type of sentence indicated in parentheses.

13. You should read this article about gorilla behavior. (imperative)

    Read this article about gorilla behavior. _____

14. Gorillas' arms are longer than their legs. (interrogative)

    Are gorillas' arms longer than their legs? _____

15. Do gorillas often use both arms and legs in walking? (declarative)

    Gorillas often use both arms and legs in walking. _____

16. Gorillas are shy. (exclamatory)

    How shy gorillas are! _____

17. Do gorillas live in groups of six to twelve, with a large male as the leader? (declarative)

    Gorillas live in groups of six to twelve, with a large male as their leader. _____

18. What great responsibilities the leader has as decision-maker and protector of the group! (interrogative)

    Doesn't the leader have great responsibilities as decision-maker and protector of the group? _____

Reinforce   Answers will vary. Sample responses are shown.

Each kind of sentence can be structured in different ways to achieve different effects. Read the statement below by gorilla researcher Dian Fossey.

> The more you learn about the dignity of the gorilla, the more you want to avoid people.

19. What type of sentence is this? **declarative** _____

20. What does Fossey compare in this sentence? **gorilla behavior and human behavior** _____

21. How does the structure of the sentence emphasize the comparison and increase its impact?

    The two parts of the sentence are parallel in words and structure, and the parallel structure _____

    creates a direct contrast between her positive assessment of gorillas' behavior and her negative _____

    assessment of people's behavior. _____

Review

Subjects and Predicates

Underline the complete subject in each sentence. Circle the simple subject. If the understood subject is *you*, write *you* on the line.

1. Come with us to the marine animal park. ___**you**___ **(2)**

2. The (star) of the show is a bottle-nosed dolphin. _____ **(1, 2)**

Underline the complete predicate in each sentence. Circle the simple predicate.

3. These acrobats of the marine world (leap) in formation. **(1, 2)**

4. Dolphins (swim) in large groups in the wild. **(1, 2)**

Draw one line under each compound subject in these sentences, and circle each simple subject in the compound subject. Draw two lines under each compound predicate, and draw a box around each simple predicate in the compound predicate.

5. A dolphin [breathes] and [expels] water through a blowhole on its head. **(2, 3)**

6. (Herring,) (sardines,) and other (fish) are favorite dolphin foods. **(2, 3)**

7. Agile dolphins [swim] very fast and [leap] high out of the water. **(2, 3)**

8. Happy (passengers) and (members) of the crew spot dolphins in front of their ship. **(2, 3)**

Objects, Predicate Nouns, and Predicate Adjectives

Circle the term in parentheses that correctly describes the boldfaced word in each sentence.

9. Many varieties of tuna are **valuable** to fishermen. (direct object (predicate adjective)) **(5)**

10. Dolphins often accompany the **schools** of tuna. ((direct object) predicate noun) **(4)**

11. One of the tools used to ensnare dolphins is a **net**. (direct object (predicate noun)) **(5)**

12. New kinds of nets give **dolphins** an escape route. ((indirect object) direct object) **(4)**

Appositives

Underline the appositive in each sentence.

13. The sound waves bounce off the object and return to the dolphin, a creature sensitive to such waves. **(7)**

14. From the echoes, the returning sound waves, the dolphin can tell an object's size, shape, and location. **(7)**

15. Bats, flying mammals, use a similar system. **(7)**

Prepositional Phrases

Underline the prepositional phrase or phrases in each sentence. Circle each preposition. Draw a box around its object.

16. Humans have been very fond (of) dolphins (for) a long time. **(6)**

17. Our relationship (with) dolphins is featured (in) many stories. **(6)**

18. (In) one ancient Greek story, a dolphin saves a drowning boy. **(6)**

Circle each adjectival prepositional phrase. Underline each adverbial prepositional phrase. Draw a box around the word each phrase modifies.

19. Dolphins communicate without any vocal cords. **(6)**

20. A dolphin's whistles, squeaks, and clicks apparently transmit information to other dolphins. **(6)**

21. Sounds waves from a dolphin's clicks move outward toward objects. **(6)**

Verbals

Draw one line under the simple subject in each sentence. Draw two lines under the simple predicate. Draw a box around each participial phrase. Circle each infinitive phrase.

22. You can learn (to tell alligators and crocodiles apart.) **(8, 9, 10)**

23. (To see the main difference between a crocodile and an alligator,) you must compare the animals' snouts. **(8, 9, 10)**

24. Looking at the snouts, you will notice a broader snout on the alligator than on the crocodile. **(8, 9, 10)**

25. Dining mostly on fish, alligators also occasionally eat crustaceans, insects, and small animals. **(8, 9, 10)**

Sentences

Expand and combine these sentences so they tell more and make relationships clearer. **Answers will vary.**

26. Sloths move slowly. Predators consider them unappetizing. **(11)**

_____

27. Porcupines move slowly. Their quills discourage most predators. **(11)**

_____

Add the correct punctuation mark to each sentence. Then label it *declarative, interrogative, imperative,* or *exclamatory.*

28. What an awesome sight a moose is!_____exclamatory_____ **(12)**

29. Have you visited Glacier National Park?_____interrogative_____ **(12)**

30. Hikers often see moose there._____declarative_____ **(12)**

31. Bring binoculars and a camera if you go._____imperative_____ **(12)**

Spelling Practice

The speed a running cheetah can achieve is **extraordinary**. This lightning-fast cat can sprint at up to 75 miles per hour.

What is the suffix in the word in bold type? _____**-ary**_____ What does the word mean? ___**very unusual and remarkable**___

Adding Suffixes: *-ary, -ory*

The suffixes *-ary* and *-ory* can be added to the ends of roots and base words to create adjectives, as in *primary* and *satisfactory*. The spelling of the base word sometimes needs to be changed before these suffixes can be added. For example, the silent **e** at the end of *imagine* is dropped before *-ary* is added to form *imaginary*.

Word Sort

Use the words below to complete the word sort.

momentary	honorary	circulatory	preparatory	secondary	advisory
auditory	contrary	sensory	legendary	migratory	customary

Suffix *-ary*	Suffix *-ory*
momentary	circulatory
honorary	preparatory
secondary	advisory
contrary	auditory
legendary	sensory
customary	migratory

Pattern Practice

advisory	legendary	mandatory	customary	literary	migratory
momentary	sensory	involuntary	elementary	contrary	complimentary

Add -ary or -ory to each base word. Change the spelling of the base word as needed.

1. custom _____**customary**_____

2. compliment _____**complimentary**_____

3. advise _____**advisory**_____

4. migrate _____**migratory**_____

5. moment _____**momentary**_____

6. element _____**elementary**_____

7. legend _____**legendary**_____

8. sense _____**sensory**_____

Write the word from the word bank above that best completes each sentence.

9. My sister's _____**elementary**_____ school is two blocks from here.

10. The school has a _____**mandatory**_____ fire drill once a month.

11. These ducks are _____**migratory**_____ birds that summer in the north.

12. Your information is _____**contrary**_____ to everything else I've heard.

13. Anne's _____**literary**_____ club reads and discusses books.

14. It is _____**customary**_____ for Rob's family to eat dinner at 6:00.

15. Quinn's kind remarks were very _____**complimentary**_____.

Use the Dictionary

Circle the word in each pair that best completes the sentence. Use a print or an online dictionary to confirm word meanings.

16. Kyle listens well and is more of an (auditory) sensory learner.

17. Arteries and veins are part of the subsidiary (circulatory) system.

18. I prefer (contemporary) involuntary writing to the classics.

(you) | Diagram | sentences

A **sentence diagram** is a picture of a sentence that shows how the parts of the sentence fit together. Diagramming sentences can help you understand how the words in a sentence are related.

Diagramming Subjects and Verbs

A short sentence consisting of a simple subject and a simple predicate is diagrammed this way:

Owls hoot.   Owls | hoot

Look at the structure of the diagram. Based on its structure, complete these sentences.

1. The simple subject and simple predicate go on a _____**horizontal**_____ line.
   horizontal/vertical

2. A _____**vertical**_____ line separates the subject and predicate.
   horizontal/vertical

3. The subject goes to the _____**left**_____ of the vertical line, and the predicate goes to the
   left/right
   _____**right**_____.
   left/right

Use what you have learned to diagram these sentences. Include only the simple subject and the simple predicate. Ignore all the other words in the sentences.

4. The sun disappeared.   **sun** | **disappeared**

5. The owls awoke.   **owls** | **awoke**

6. Rodents scurried.   **Rodents** | **scurried**

Diagramming Adjectives and Articles

An adjective (describing word) or an article (*a, an, the*) goes on a slanted line below the word it modifies. Look at the way this sentence has been diagrammed.

The bright sun disappeared.   sun | disappeared
                                    The bright

Now diagram these sentences.

7. The sleepy owls awoke.   **owls** | **awoke**
                              The sleepy

8. Hungry rodents scurried.

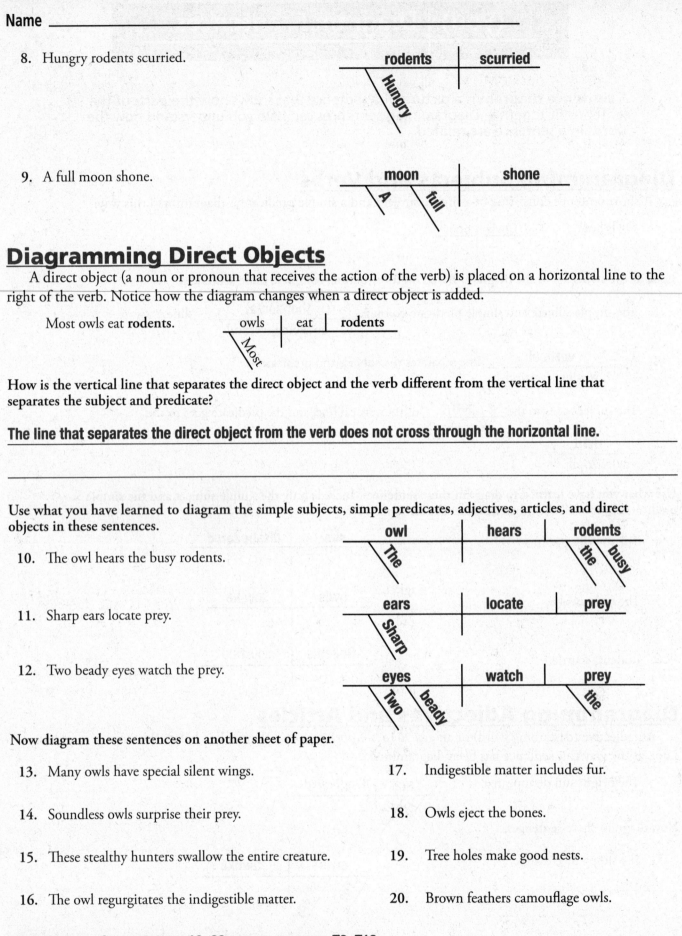

9. A full moon shone.

Diagramming Direct Objects

A direct object (a noun or pronoun that receives the action of the verb) is placed on a horizontal line to the right of the verb. Notice how the diagram changes when a direct object is added.

Most owls eat **rodents**.

How is the vertical line that separates the direct object and the verb different from the vertical line that separates the subject and predicate?

The line that separates the direct object from the verb does not cross through the horizontal line.

Use what you have learned to diagram the simple subjects, simple predicates, adjectives, articles, and direct objects in these sentences.

10. The owl hears the busy rodents.

11. Sharp ears locate prey.

12. Two beady eyes watch the prey.

Now diagram these sentences on another sheet of paper.

13. Many owls have special silent wings.

14. Soundless owls surprise their prey.

15. These stealthy hunters swallow the entire creature.

16. The owl regurgitates the indigestible matter.

17. Indigestible matter includes fur.

18. Owls eject the bones.

19. Tree holes make good nests.

20. Brown feathers camouflage owls.

The diagrams for sentences 13–20 appear on pages T9–T10.

Writing Sentences

Possible answers appear below. Accept all reasonable responses.

These sentences need your help. Rewrite each one so it is clearer and makes better sense.

1. Our city's new aquarium offers amazing sights and sounds, more of them than any other attraction in the area. **Our city's new aquarium offers more amazing sights and sounds than any other attraction in the area.**

2. Visitors find themselves staring down into a pond filled with twenty huge alligators entering the building. **Visitors entering the building find themselves staring down into a pond filled with twenty huge alligators.**

3. In one large gallery visitors can pick up and listen to starfish and the songs of humpback whales. **In one large gallery visitors can pick up starfish and listen to the songs of humpback whales.**

4. A rare opportunity to see nature's marine marvels up close is offered at this wonderful new facility; you should definitely visit it soon. **This wonderful new facility offers a rare opportunity to see nature's marine marvels up close; you should definitely visit it soon.**

5. In another room they can stand in the middle of a great hollow glass cylinder, and big fish swim around and around. **In another room they can stand in the middle of a great hollow glass cylinder and watch big fish swim around and around.**

All the sentences in a paragraph relate to a single topic. A paragraph should have a topic sentence, at least two supporting sentences, and a concluding sentence. Notice these kinds of sentences in this model paragraph. Also notice its purpose: it is trying to persuade readers to do something.

topic sentence
(states the main idea you are making)

supporting sentences
(give details to support your main idea)

concluding sentence
(summarizes the paragraph or restates the topic sentence)

No living room is complete without a fish tank full of guppies. Guppies are energetic, colorful fish that breed easily. Because there are many colors of guppies, you can create an aquarium with a unique look. You can choose blue or red guppies to contrast with your green plants. If you put different colors of guppies together, you will soon have a tank full of multicolored baby guppies. **If you want a truly striking aquarium that catches everyone's eye, you should fill it with guppies.**

Writing a Paragraph

The sentences you repaired on page 39 can be reordered to make a persuasive paragraph. Decide which sentence is the topic sentence, which are the three supporting sentences, and which is the concluding sentence. Reorder the sentences, and write the paragraph on the lines below.

The rewritten sentences should appear in the following order: 1, 2, 3, 5, 4. Students may wish to make

additional revisions in their sentences as they write the paragraph.

_____

_____

_____

_____

_____

_____

Think of a great place for people to go to see astounding animals. Write a paragraph that would convince people to visit that place. Describe some amazing things they might experience there. Be sure to include an enticing topic sentence, at least two vivid supporting sentences, and an enthusiastic concluding sentence.

Answers will vary. _____

_____

_____

_____

_____

_____

_____

_____

Read your paragraph again. Use this checklist to make sure it is complete and correct.

- ❑ My paragraph has a topic sentence.
- ❑ My paragraph has at least two supporting sentences.
- ❑ All my sentences are clear and make sense.

- ❑ I have used prepositional phrases correctly.
- ❑ My paragraph has a concluding sentence.

Proofreading
Practice

Read this passage about whales and find the mistakes. Use the proofreading marks to show how the mistakes should be fixed. Use a dictionary to check and correct spellings. **Suggested answers appear below. Accept all reasonable responses.**

Proofreading Marks

Mark	Means	Example
ℐ	delete	Baleen whales h̶a̶v̶e̶ have no teeth.
∧	add	Baleen whales ∧have no teeth.
≡	make into an uppercase letter	b̲aleen whales have no teeth.
/	make into a lowercase letter	Baleen W̸hales have no teeth.
⊙	add a period	Baleen whales have no teeth⊙
ⓢⓟ	fix spelling	Baleen wails have no teeth.

Whales

The whale may look like a giant fish, but, it is not a fish at all. It is a mamal ⓢⓟ, like a mouse or a human

being. This means that it has to come up to the ocean's surface to breathe, which it does through a blowhole

located at the top of it's ⓢⓟ head. Some whales can hold their breathe ⓢⓟ for up to two hours!

Scientists place whales into two major groups: the baleen whales and the toothed whales. Toothed

whales, as they're ⓢⓟ name suggests, have teeth baleen whales do not have teeth. Instead, they have hundreds of

tall, thin plates/Hanging from the upper jaw. These plates are made of the same material as human fingernails.

The plates, together called the baleen, filter food from water. b̲aleen whales eat mostly plankton, small plant and

anamal ⓢⓟ organisms that float around the ocean. Most toothed whales, on the other hand, eat fish or squid⊙their

diet might even include octopuses or crabs.

Both kinds of whales have a layer of fat, or blubber, under there ⓢⓟ skin. This blubber can be up to

20 inches thick, it helps to keep them warm in cold waters. Because blubber is stored enenrgy ⓢⓟ, whales are able to

go a long time without eating. They do this especially when migrating or breeding.

Proofreading
Checklist

You can use the checklist below to help you find and fix mistakes in your own writing. Write the titles of your own stories or reports in the blanks at the top of the chart. Then use the questions to check your work. Make a check mark (✓) in each box after you have checked that item. **Answers will vary.**

Titles

Proofreading Checklist for Unit 1

Does each sentence have a subject and a predicate?				
Have I used appositives correctly?				
Have I used prepositional, participial, and infinitive phrases to make my writing more precise?				
Have I varied the length and type of sentences to add variety to my writing?				
Do all my sentences state complete thoughts?				

Also Remember…

Does each sentence begin with an uppercase letter?				
Does each sentence end with the right end mark?				
Have I spelled each word correctly?				
Have I used commas correctly?				
Did I use a dictionary to check and correct spellings?				

Your Own List

Use this space to write your own list of things to check in your writing.

Community Connection

In Unit 1 of *Grammar, Usage, and Mechanics,* students learned about **different types of sentences and sentence structures** and used what they learned to improve their own writing. The content of these lessons focuses on the theme **Astounding Animals.** As students completed the exercises, they learned about numerous creatures with remarkable attributes. These pages offer a variety of activities that reinforce skills and concepts presented in the unit. They also provide opportunities for students to make connections between the information presented in the lessons and animal-related activities going on today in the community.

A Pal to a Pet

Find out which pet care facilities in your area allow students to volunteer. You may be able to volunteer at a local Humane Society to play with pets and take them for walks. Dogs and cats need regular human attention and can become stressed and unhappy if left alone for too long. You'll have fun as you perform a valuable service.

Watch the Birds

Go on a bird-watching expedition. Wherever you live, you can easily find somewhere to observe birds. In dense urban areas, birds congregate at places they might find food and water, such as parks, outdoor café tables, and public fountains. In the country, you don't need to look far to find birds. Different types of birds live in fields, scrubby brush, and wetlands. You may even have a bird feeder at your own house. Wherever you go bird watching, take a notebook and a pencil with you and write descriptive information about each bird you see.

Internet Creatures

The Internet contains a vast network of information about nearly every possible topic. Conduct a Web search for "unusual animals" and bookmark your most interesting results. Whenever you find amazing animal pictures, copy the pictures to your desktop. Make an online photo album with these photos to share with friends and family. To make the album instructional, look up each animal in an online encyclopedia and write a short caption to go with each picture.

Habitat Helper—Animal Careers

Learn about job opportunities for people who love animals. Such opportunities may include careers in biology and other life sciences, forestry and park management, veterinary medicine, and pet training, grooming, breeding, and showing. Organizations that can give you more information about animal careers include your local Humane Society, your State Department of Wildlife (which may also be called the Department of Fish and Game), and your nearest zoo. Choose one occupation that interests you and learn more about it.

- What skills are required to do this job?
- What education and training would I need for this job?
- How can I get this education and training?
- How long does it take to become proficient at this work?
- What is a typical working day like in this profession?

If possible, interview an adult you know who has a job working with animals. Take notes during the interview, and share the results of the interview with your class. Use the planning guide on the next page to help you plan the interview and organize your notes.

Name _____

Interview Planner **Answers will vary.**

Person I am interviewing:

Name _____

Age _____

Occupation _____

Number of years employed in that field _____

Date of interview: _____

Questions to ask:

1. _____
   _____

2. _____
   _____

3. _____
   _____

4. _____
   _____

5. _____
   _____

6. _____
   _____

7. _____

8. _____
   _____

Notes:

_____
_____
_____
_____
_____
_____
_____

a. Some deserts were once forests ~~or~~ lakes.

b. Some dry lands are becoming deserts, ~~and~~ some deserts are spreading.

Cross out the boldfaced conjunction in each sentence. Which sentence could be written as two separate sentences? __b__

A **simple sentence** is made up of a subject and a predicate and expresses only one complete thought. It is an *independent clause*. A **compound sentence** is made of two closely related independent clauses. The two clauses can be joined by a comma and a coordinating conjunction (*and, but,* or *or*) or by a semicolon (;).

See Handbook Sections 8, 13, 22

Practice

Write *S* next to each simple sentence. Write *CD* next to each compound sentence. Circle the comma and conjunction or the semicolon in each compound sentence.

1. Not all dry regions are deserts, but all dry regions are fragile ecosystems. __CD__

2. A dry, fragile ecosystem may be threatened by excessive human activities such as cultivation, irrigation, and industry, and it becomes vulnerable to desertification. __CD__

3. *Desertification* refers to the process of dry areas becoming deserts. __S__

4. Water is lost off the land instead of soaking into the soil to provide moisture for plants; this leads to reduced plant and animal life. __CD__

5. Areas with fewer plants cannot sustain existing animal populations; these populations then begin to disappear. __CD__

6. The dry heat also affects the delicate ecosystem. __S__

7. The hot sun heats the exposed rocks, and the rocks eventually crack and crumble. __CD__

8. Wind picks up and smashes the rock pieces, and they become sand. __CD__

9. Desertification exists on every continent except Antarctica, but many people are fighting it. __CD__

10. Desertification can be fought with new plantings of hardy, native trees and shrubs. __S__

11. Water conservation and wise use of resources by humans can stop desertification in some areas. __S__

Camels scavenge for vegetation as a result of desertification in Sudan, Africa.

Apply Possible answers appear below. Accept all reasonable responses.

Rewrite each pair of simple sentences as one compound sentence.

12. Scientists have studied the formation of deserts. They do not completely understand the process yet.

    Scientists have studied the formation of deserts, but they do not completely understand the _____

    process yet. _____

13. Some deserts form because of human activity. Others form naturally. **Some deserts form because of** _____

    human activity; others form naturally. _____

14. Forests once covered much of North Africa. Now, the Sahara desert exists in that same area.

    Forests once covered much of North Africa, but now the Sahara desert exists in that same area. _____

15. The lands in Death Valley National Park in California are bone-dry now. In prehistoric times a huge lake

    existed there. **The lands in Death Valley National Park in California are bone-dry now, but in** _____

    prehistoric times a huge lake existed there. _____

16. The earth's climate grew warmer over time. The lake dried up. **The earth's climate grew warmer over time,** _____

    and the lake dried up. _____

Reinforce

See Handbook Sections 36, 37

Use the Internet or an encyclopedia to research the Dust Bowl period of the 1930s in the United States. Then write three compound sentences about this event.

17. **Answers will vary.** _____

    _____

18. _____

    _____

19. _____

    _____

Although the temperature outside may not feel warm today, <u>average global temperatures are increasing.</u>

Look at the two parts of this sentence, the boldfaced part and the underlined part. Which part makes sense by itself? **the underlined part**

An **independent clause** is a group of words with a subject and a predicate that makes sense by itself. A **dependent clause** has a subject and a predicate, but it does not express a complete thought by itself. It needs—or is dependent on—an independent clause. Often a dependent clause begins with a subordinating conjunction such as *although, because, if, as,* or *when.* When a dependent clause is an introductory element in a sentence, use a comma to separate it from the rest of the sentence.

See Handbook Sections 8, 13, 22

Practice

Draw one line under each independent clause. Draw two lines under each dependent clause. Circle the subordinating conjunction that begins each dependent clause.

1. (Because) average global temperatures are increasing, the earth is experiencing global warming, or climate change.

2. Scientists labeled recent temperature increases abnormal (after) they studied temperature data from the past 1,000 years.

3. (Although) some temperature fluctuations are normal, human activities almost certainly are accelerating the recent increases.

4. (When) the temperature rises, changes to the environment can be significant.

5. Glaciers and sea ice melt (when) temperatures increase.

6. Polar bears could be harmed by this melting (since) sea ice is a critical habitat for them.

7. These hunters spend much of their time on the sea ice (where) they stalk seals.

8. (Because) sea ice now melts sooner in spring and forms later in fall, polar bears have fewer good hunting months.

9. Many polar bears apparently are thinner than normal (because) the sea ice now melts three weeks earlier.

10. (Although) Alaska remains a cold region, average temperatures there have risen.

11. (Even though) an increase of 5.4 degrees sounds small, it can cause big changes.

12. (When) temperatures in the Arctic increase, permanently frozen ground called permafrost thaws.

13. The ground becomes unstable and uneven (as) the permafrost layer softens.

14. (As) the ground shifts, it can twist railroad tracks and damage the foundations of buildings.

15. (While) scientists document these changes, some people are working on solutions.

A polar bear on sea ice watches for seals that come to the surface to breathe.

Name _____

Apply Possible answers appear below. Accept all reasonable responses.

Draw a line to match each dependent clause with an independent clause. Then write the new sentences you have created on the lines. Be sure to add punctuation. (16–20)

Dependent Clauses

when scientists studied climate changes

as the planet warms up

if permafrost thaws

if sea ice melts early

because the environment is so delicate

Independent Clauses

polar bears may go hungry

they found that average global temperatures have increased rapidly recently

a small increase in temperature can have big effects

disruptive events are occurring

structures can be damaged

21. **When scientists studied climate changes, they found that average global temperatures have** _____ **increased rapidly recently.** _____

22. **As the planet warms up, disruptive events are occurring.** _____

_____

23. **If permafrost thaws, structures can be damaged.** _____

_____

24. **If sea ice melts early, polar bears may go hungry.** _____

_____

25. **Because the environment is so delicate, a small increase in temperature can have big effects.** _____

_____

Reinforce Answers will vary.

On the lines below, write three dependent clauses about climate change. (Example: *if the temperatures in Antarctica increase significantly*) Trade papers with a partner. Complete your partner's sentences by writing an independent clause to go with each dependent clause. Trade papers again and read the sentences your partner completed.

26. _____

27. _____

28. _____

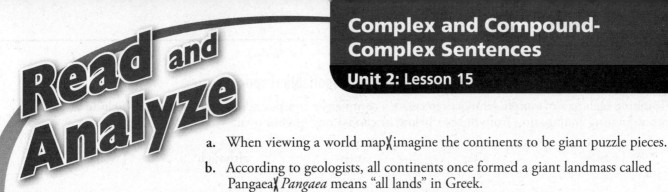

a. When viewing a world map⁄imagine the continents to be giant puzzle pieces.

b. According to geologists, all continents once formed a giant landmass called Pangaea⁄ *Pangaea* means "all lands" in Greek.

Cross out the comma in sentence *a* and the semicolon in sentence *b*. Which sentence begins with words that would *not* be a sentence if a period replaced the crossed-out comma or semicolon? ____a____ Which sentence would become two separate sentences if a period were added at the end of its first clause? ____b____

A dependent clause must be joined with an independent clause to become a sentence. A sentence made up of an independent clause and a dependent clause is a **complex sentence**. A sentence made up of two independent clauses and a dependent clause is a **compound-complex sentence**.

See Handbook Sections 8, 13, 22

Practice

Write *CD* next to each compound sentence. Write *CX* next to each complex sentence. Write *CCX* next to each compound-complex sentence. Then underline each dependent clause and draw a box around each independent clause.

1. Pangaea apparently existed about 200 million years ago; it was surrounded by one ocean, which scientists call Panthalassa. **CCX**

2. After Pangaea had existed for a long time, it split into two separate continents. **CX**

3. The northern continent included present-day North America and Europe, and most of present-day Asia; this ancient continent has been given the name Laurasia. **CD**

4. The southern continent has been given the name Gondwanaland; it included present-day Africa, Antarctica, Australia, South America, and India. **CD**

5. Landmasses move around the globe because they are situated on slabs of rock called plates. **CX**

6. When German scientist Alfred Wegener first proposed the idea of drifting continents in 1912, his peers ridiculed it; however, Wegener had evidence supporting his theory. **CCX**

7. Because fossils in South America match fossils in Africa and Australia, South America probably was connected to those continents long ago. **CX**

8. After two other scientists refined Wegener's theory of continental drift, more researchers found it convincing. **CX**

9. Scientists Harry Hess and Robert Dietz added information about changes in the lands beneath the ocean; according to Hess and Dietz, seafloors spread and continents shift because plates under the ocean floor move against or away from each other. **CCX**

10. When plates move, they can cause earthquakes or create volcanoes. **CX**

Apply Possible answers are shown. Accept all reasonable responses.

Combine each pair of simple sentences to create a complex or compound-complex sentence. Include a subordinating conjunction from the box below, or choose one of your own.

because	after	since	although	if

11. It may not feel like it. Continents continue to shift today. **Although it may not feel like it to us, continents continue to shift today.**

12. You feel an earthquake. You are sensing plate movements. **When you feel an earthquake, you are likely sensing plate movements.**

13. Many scientists believe Africa and South America must have been interlocked. The geological structures of rock in southwest Africa and southeast Brazil are identical. **Many scientists believe that Africa and South America must have been interlocked, since the geological structures of rock in southwest Africa and southeast Brazil are identical.**

14. The theory that Pangaea existed is now widely accepted. Extensive geological evidence supports it. **The theory that Pangaea existed is now widely accepted because extensive geological evidence supports it.**

15. According to some scientists, the continents may drift back together. That day, if it comes, would be very far in the future. **According to some scientists, the continents may drift back together someday, although that day, if it comes, would be very far in the future.**

Reinforce

Write a paragraph about a place in your area where you could go to see evidence of Earth's constant change. Describe what you might see there and what these sights might reveal about change over time. Include at least one complex or compound-complex sentence in your paragraph.

Answers will vary.

_____

_____

_____

_____

_____

_____

_____

_____

Scientists are concerned about the destruction of rain forests, (which) are home to three-quarters of the world's plant and animal varieties. They look forward to a time [when] all nations establish and enforce laws protecting forested regions.

Draw one line under the dependent clause that gives descriptive information about rain forests. Circle the first word in this clause. Draw two lines under the dependent clause that explains what sort of time scientists hope will come. Draw a box around the first word in this clause.

An **adjective clause** is a **dependent clause** that describes a noun or a pronoun. An adjective clause can begin with a **relative pronoun,** such as *that, who, whom,* or *which;* or it can begin with a **relative adverb,** such as *when, where,* or *why.*

See Handbook Sections 8, 13, 17g, 19

Practice

Underline the adjective clause in each sentence. If the first word in the clause is a relative pronoun, circle that word. If the first word in the clause is a relative adverb, draw a box around the word.

1. Rain forests, (which) cover about 2 percent of the earth's surface, are being destroyed.

2. Logging and clearing land for agriculture are two reasons [why] rain forests are being cut down.

3. Destruction of rain forests means loss of habitat for the creatures (that) live there.

4. Tree-dwelling animals cannot remain in areas [where] all vegetation has been removed to create pasture land.

5. When loggers harvest rain forest timber, birds (that) nest in trees must move to other areas.

6. After its big trees have been logged, a forest (that) had been thick and humid becomes thin and dry.

7. Forests [where] large healthy trees have been cut are more vulnerable to fire.

8. *Deforestation,* (which) means "the removal of forests," also affects the soil.

9. Soil in areas [where] rain forest vegetation has been removed loses its nutrients.

10. One reason [why] many scientists oppose rain forest destruction is the loss of potentially valuable plant species.

11. According to botanists (whose) research focuses on tropical plants, many varieties of plants there are undiscovered.

12. Plants (that) grow only in rain forests have yielded several important anti-cancer drugs.

Deforestation causes many changes to the environment and landscape.

Apply   Possible answers appear below. Accept all reasonable responses.

Rewrite each pair of sentences as one complex sentence. Change the underlined sentence into an adjective clause.

13. Deforestation can also devastate people. <u>People live in the rain forests.</u> **Deforestation can also devastate**

    people who live in the rain forest.

14. These people rely on the forest for food and shelter. <u>The forest is the place where they live.</u> **These people**

    rely on the forest where they live for food and shelter.

15. Sometimes loggers damage places. <u>These places are very important to local people for religious reasons.</u>

    Sometimes loggers damage places that are very important to local people for religious reasons.

16. In some cases, though, forest communities want more contact with the modern world. <u>The modern</u>

    <u>world can offer them jobs, roads, schools, and medical care.</u> **In some instances, though, forest**

    people want more contact with the modern world, which can bring them jobs, roads,

    schools, and medical care.

Reinforce

When a dependent clause acts like a noun, it is called a noun clause. The noun clause can be the subject or object of a verb. Words often used to begin noun clauses include *that, whichever, who, what, where, when,* and *why.*

I have learned <u>that rain forests are in danger.</u>

The dependent clause *that rain forests are in danger* functions as a noun: it is the direct object of the verb *have learned.*

Underline each dependent clause in the sentences below. Then write *noun* if the clause is a noun clause, and write *adjective* if the clause is an adjective clause.

17. Scientists have shown <u>that deforestation can cause landslides.</u>   **noun**

18. Without the trees <u>that normally keep a hillside stable</u>, rocks and soil

    can easily slide down.   **adjective**

19. Scientists say <u>that continued deforestation will cause the extinction</u>

    <u>of certain species.</u>   **noun**

20. I will join an organization <u>that opposes harmful deforestation.</u>   **adjective**

The ozone layer is important <u>because it protects us from the sun's ultraviolet rays.</u>

Underline the dependent clause that tells why the ozone layer is important. Does this part of the sentence make sense by itself? <u>no</u>

An **adverb clause** is a dependent clause that tells about a verb, an adjective, or an adverb. Adverb clauses tell *where, when, why,* or *how much*. They often begin with a subordinating conjunction such as *than, although, because, if, as, as if, while, when,* or *whenever.*

See Handbook Sections 8, 13, 22

Practice

Underline the adverb clause in each sentence.

1. <u>Although you cannot see it,</u> the ozone layer exists about 31 miles high in the atmosphere.

2. <u>When the sun is shining,</u> it is sending harmful ultraviolet rays toward Earth.

3. The ozone layer protects us <u>because it absorbs some of these ultraviolet rays.</u>

4. <u>When scientists discovered a thinning of the ozone layer above Antarctica,</u> they called it the ozone hole.

5. The ozone hole occurs every August, <u>when it is spring in the Southern Hemisphere.</u>

6. <u>When there is less ozone in the atmosphere,</u> more ultraviolet rays hit Earth.

7. Ultraviolet rays are a health concern <u>because they can cause skin cancer.</u>

8. Eyes can also be damaged <u>when they are exposed to ultraviolet rays.</u>

9. <u>If ultraviolet rays increase,</u> animals will experience more health problems too.

10. <u>Although it seems that animals in the ocean are safe from the harmful rays,</u> they are not.

11. Crop production can drop <u>when ultraviolet radiation is strong.</u>

12. Humans, plants, and animals are more at risk at high altitudes <u>because less atmosphere exists overhead.</u>

13. <u>When scientists investigated the ozone hole,</u> they concluded that chlorofluorocarbons (CFCs) were destroying the ozone layer.

14. <u>Because these chemicals were widely used in aerosol sprays,</u> large amounts of toxins were swept up by the wind into the atmosphere.

15. <u>When chemicals such as these rise through the atmosphere,</u> they destroy the ozone in the ozone layer.

OZONE LAYER

The ozone layer protects living things from ultraviolet rays.

Apply Possible answers appear below. Accept all reasonable responses.

Rewrite each pair of simple sentences as one complex sentence. Use the word in parentheses to change the underlined sentence into an adverb clause.

16. (because) <u>One chlorine atom from CFCs can destroy more than 100,000 ozone molecules.</u> The ozone layer was being destroyed quickly. **Because one chlorine atom from CFCs can destroy more than 100,000 ozone molecules, the ozone layer was being destroyed quickly.**

17. (as) <u>People realized that chemicals were harming the ozone layer.</u> They sought solutions to the problem. **As people realized that chemicals were harming the ozone layer, they sought solutions to the problem.**

18. (before) They decided to stop making chlorofluorocarbons. <u>It was too late.</u> **They decided to stop making chlorofluorocarbons before it was too late.**

19. (when) <u>Countries around the world signed a treaty called the Montreal Protocol in 1987.</u> They agreed to limit the manufacture of CFCs. **When countries around the world signed a treaty called the Montreal Protocol in 1987, they agreed to limit the manufacture of CFCs.**

20. (because) Scientists expect the ozone layer to heal itself by around 2050. <u>So many countries have limited the production of CFCs.</u> **Scientists expect the ozone layer to heal itself by around 2050 because so many countries have limited the production of CFCs.**

Reinforce

In this activity, you will distinguish among adverbs, adverb phrases, and adverb clauses. Draw a line from each sentence to the correct description of the boldfaced word or words.

21. The ozone layer started disappearing **because chemicals harmed ozone.**   adverb (one word)

22. The ozone layer started disappearing **quickly.**   adverb phrase (no verb)

23. The ozone hole started appearing **in the 1970s.**   adverb clause (has a verb)

24. The sun shines **during the day.**   adverb (one word)

25. The sun shines **although there are some clouds.**   adverb phrase (no verb)

26. The sun shines **brightly.**   adverb clause (has a verb)

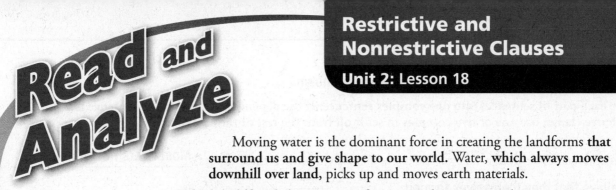
Moving water is the dominant force in creating the landforms **that surround us and give shape to our world.** Water, **which always moves downhill over land,** picks up and moves earth materials.

Which boldfaced clause gives information that is essential in its sentence? <u>**that surround us and give shape to our world**</u> Which boldfaced clause gives information that is not essential in its sentence? <u>**which always moves downhill over land**</u> What punctuation marks are used to set off this clause from the rest of the sentence? <u>**commas**</u>

A **restrictive clause** is a dependent clause that is essential to the meaning its sentence conveys: it gives information about the noun it modifies that is critically important. A **nonrestrictive clause** is a dependent clause that is not essential to the message its sentence conveys: if this clause were left out, the sentence would still convey its message effectively. A nonrestrictive clause is set off from the rest of its sentence by one or two commas, depending on its place in the sentence.

See Handbook Sections 8, 17g

Practice

Read each sentence. Draw a line under the adjective clause and circle the noun it modifies. Write *RC* if it is a restrictive clause and *NC* if it is a nonrestrictive clause.

1. (Rainwater) that falls on hills and mountains moves downslope. **RC**

2. The sheets of water concentrate into (rills,) which then join together to form creeks. **NC**

3. Creeks join together to form small rivers, and these join to form the great (rivers) that eventually flow into the ocean. **RC**

4. Each stream carries solid material with it; some of the (material) that is picked up is deposited elsewhere as the water moves across the land, and some of it is carried all the way to the ocean. **RC**

5. (Water) that is concentrated in linear flows erodes the land beneath it when it flows swiftly. **RC**

6. A slight increase in the speed of a creek's (flow,) which typically happens when rain falls or snow melts, significantly increases the creek's ability to transport material. **NC**

7. A creek swollen by heavy rains can move large rocks as well as massive amounts of sand and gravel; this (process,) which occurs most frequently in winter and spring in many parts of the United States, reshapes the landscape. **NC**

8. Over time, (streams) that flow swiftly carve deep channels for themselves. **RC**

9. Another (factor) that affects the amount of material carried by a stream is the nature of the land beneath it. **RC**

10. A stream flowing over (bedrock,) which is relatively smooth and solid, will not pick up much material. **NC**

11. A (stream) moving at the same pace that flows over land with loose soil will pick up and transport a much greater amount of material. **RC**

12. A (river) that spreads out and slows down will drop much of its load; a swiftly flowing river will carry solids much farther. **RC**

Apply Answers will vary. Sample responses are shown.

Combine each pair of sentences into one complex sentence. If the dependent clause in the sentence is a nonrestrictive clause, use one or two commas to set it off from the rest of the sentence.

13. Most rivers flow through valleys. The rivers themselves formed these valleys. **Most rivers flow through valleys that they themselves formed.**

14. These valleys reflect the size of the rivers in them. The valleys have been formed over long periods of time. **These valleys, which have formed over long periods of time, reflect the size of the rivers in them.**

15. The course of a river changes over time. This river flows through a valley. **The course of a river that flows through a valley changes over time.**

16. This process is quite predictable and happens in stages. The process is called the erosion cycle. **This process, which is called the erosion cycle, is quite predictable and happens in stages.**

17. Over time, a river changes its course from a straight line to a sequence of S curves. These curves become more pronounced as time passes. **Over time, a river changes its course from a straight line to a sequence of S curves, which become more pronounced as time passes.**

Reinforce

Eleven words for natural waterways of various sizes are hidden in the puzzle below. Write these words on the lines provided. Then, on another sheet of paper, write two sentences using some words from the puzzle. Include a restrictive clause in one sentence and a nonrestrictive clause in the other.

W	F	R	E	S	H	E	T	G
S	O	R	C	R	E	E	K	X
T	R	I	B	U	T	A	R	Y
R	K	V	R	N	R	I	L	L
E	B	U	A	N	I	A	Q	B
A	Z	L	N	E	V	H	C	L
M	S	E	C	L	E	D	W	G
M	J	T	H	B	R	O	O	K

Across

18. freshet

19. creek

20. tributary

21. rill

22. brook

Down

23. stream

24. fork

25. rivulet

26. branch

27. runnel

28. river

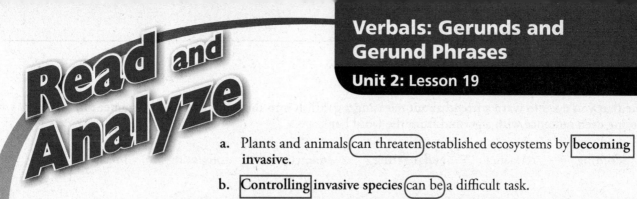

a. Plants and animals (can threaten) established ecosystems by [becoming] invasive.

b. [Controlling] invasive species (can be) a difficult task.

Circle the simple predicate in each sentence. Draw a box around each verb form ending in *-ing*. Is either *-ing* form part of a simple predicate? __no__

Is the boldfaced phrase in sentence *a* the sentence subject, an indirect object, or the object of a preposition? ____the object of a preposition____

Is the boldfaced phrase in sentence *b* the sentence subject, a predicate noun phrase, or the object of a preposition? ____the sentence subject____

A **gerund** is a verbal that acts as a noun. All gerunds are verb forms that end with *-ing*. A **gerund phrase** is made up of a gerund and the other words that complete its meaning. In the sentences above, *becoming invasive* and *Controlling invasive species* are gerund phrases.

See Handbook Section 25a

Practice

Underline each gerund phrase. Draw a box around the gerund itself.

1. Non-native species become invasive by [taking] over resources and by [harming] native species.

2. [Competing] with native species for food is one example of how invasive species can unbalance an ecosystem.

3. Non-native tree frogs called *coqui* are skilled at [hunting] Hawaii's snails, insects, and spiders.

4. These tree frogs may impact native Hawaiian birds by [consuming] the birds' preferred prey.

5. The frogs may also harm native birds by [sustaining] large populations of the birds' predators.

6. Introduced predators can reduce populations of native animals by [preying] on them.

7. The brown tree snake has negatively impacted the ecology of Guam by [eating] large numbers of lizards and birds.

8. [Hanging] on power lines is another way brown tree snakes cause damage.

9. Invasive plant species can harm native plants by [blocking] their sunlight.

10. The salvinia plant presents a threat by [covering] the surfaces of ponds and lakes.

11. The salvinia kills underwater plants by [blocking] off all light.

12. Sometimes scientists can find animals that are ideally suited for [controlling] an invasive species.

13. Scientists have used salvinia weevils to control salvinia by [introducing] the weevil to heavily infested areas.

14. The weevil larvae kill the salvinia plants by [burrowing] into their buds and stems.

The salvinia weevil eats only the salvinia plant, so it is safe to introduce as a biological control agent.

Name _____

Apply

Imagine that you need to warn a friend about releasing a goldfish into the wild. Plan your argument by completing each sentence with a gerund from the word bank.

adopting	releasing	endangering	contacting	competing	breeding

15. I know you want to give your goldfish a larger home, but _____ **releasing** _____ it could cause problems.

16. By _____ **competing** _____ with other fish for survival, your goldfish could harm the ecosystem.

17. Your goldfish may even start a new invasive population by _____ **breeding** _____.

18. There are ways to give your fish a better home without _____ **endangering** _____ the ecosystem.

19. Members of local pet clubs may help you out by _____ **adopting** _____ your fish.

20. _____ **Contacting** _____ them would be a much better solution.

Reinforce   Possible answers appear below. Accept all reasonable responses.

Using gerund phrases is a good way to add variety to the sentence structures in your writing.

Read the sentences below. Rewrite each pair of sentences as a single sentence containing at least one gerund phrase.

21. Zebra mussels can change a lake's ecosystem. They can carpet the bottom of the lake and use up nutrients. **Zebra mussels can change a lake's ecosystem by carpeting the bottom of the lake and using up nutrients.**

_____

22. Zebra mussels suffocate native mussel populations. This is just one of the zebra mussel's destructive effects on lake ecosystems. **Suffocating native mussel populations is just one of the zebra mussel's destructive effects on lake ecosystems.**

_____

Earth's (mountains) were created by plate tectonics. ___**0**___

Plate (tectonics) created the earth's mountains. ___**X**___

Circle the simple subject in each sentence. Write *X* by the sentence in which the subject does something. Write *O* by the sentence in which something is done to the subject.

If the subject performs an action, the verb is said to be in the **active voice**. (*Plate tectonics created.*) If the subject is acted upon by something else, the verb is said to be in the **passive voice**. (*Mountains were created.*) Many sentences in the passive voice have a prepositional phrase that begins with the word *by* and follows the verb.

See Handbook | Sections 18g, 20

Practice

Circle the simple subject in each sentence. Draw a box around the simple predicate. Be sure to include helping verbs. Write *A* if the verb is in the active voice. Write *P* if it is in the passive voice.

1. (Plate tectonics) refers to the movement of chunks of the earth's crust. ___**A**___

2. The earth's (plates) constantly are moving into, away from, or against each other. ___**A**___

3. The (land) is reshaped drastically at the plates' boundaries. ___**P**___

4. (Many) of the earth's mountains were formed by the force of plate movements. ___**P**___

5. These (movements) can push rocks upward. ___**A**___

6. A (plate) also can slide beneath a neighboring plate. ___**A**___

7. The top (plate) can be pushed upward to a great height by the bottom plate. ___**P**___

8. (Plates) also can compress and expand. ___**A**___

9. The (process) of compression and expansion creates breaks, or faults, in the rock layers. ___**A**___

10. Mountain (ranges) can be formed by faults in the middle of plates, far from their colliding edges. ___**P**___

11. (Parts) of the Rocky Mountains were created by compression folds and faults. ___**P**___

12. In the southwest United States, the earth's (crust) has been stretched by the movement of plates. ___**P**___

13. Because of this extension, the Basin and Range (region) is covered by fault-block mountains. ___**P**___

14. The stretching (crust) broke the rocky plates into pieces. ___**A**___

15. Downward-sliding (chunks) formed valleys. ___**A**___

16. The steep (sides) of the remaining rocks stood as mountain ranges. ___**A**___

17. The (process) of extension has been forming these rugged features since the Miocene epoch 25 million years ago. ___**A**___

Name _____

Apply   Suggested answers appear below. Accept all reasonable responses.

Look again at each sentence in the Practice section that has a verb in the passive voice. Rewrite each sentence so the verb is in the active voice.

18. **The movement of Earth's plates reshapes the land drastically at the plates' boundaries.** _____

_____

19. **The force of plate movements formed many of the earth's mountains.** _____

_____

20. **The bottom plate can push the top plate upward to a great height.** _____

_____

21. **Faults in the middle of plates can form mountain ranges far from their colliding edges.** _____

_____

22. **Compression folds and faults created parts of the Rocky Mountains.** _____

_____

23. **In the southwest United States, the movement of plates has stretched the earth's crust.** _____

_____

24. **Because of this extension, fault-block mountains cover the Basin and Range region.** _____

_____

Reinforce

The active voice communicates action briefly and powerfully. Some writers believe that the passive voice should be used only when an action is done by an unknown or unimportant agent—for example, *The ridge had eroded.*

Read the passage below. Notice that all of the sentences are in strong active voice. Then underline each verb in the active voice. (25–26)

At transform plate boundaries, plates <u>grind</u> past each other side by side. This type of boundary <u>separates</u> the North American plate from the Pacific plate along the San Andreas fault, a famous transform plate boundary that is responsible for many of California's earthquakes.

Write a sentence about an earthquake that has its verb in the passive voice. Then rewrite the sentence so the verb is in active voice.

27. **Answers will vary.** _____

_____

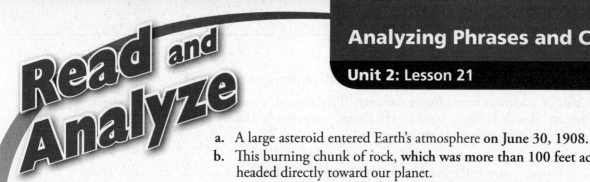

a. A large asteroid entered Earth's atmosphere **on June 30, 1908.**

b. This burning chunk of rock, **which was more than 100 feet across,** was headed directly toward our planet.

c. **Traveling at a speed in excess of 30,000 mph,** the meteor had the potential to do unimaginable damage if it collided with Earth.

d. **Although it exploded before striking Earth,** the Tunguska Fireball (as it came to be called) caused more destruction than any other space object in modern times.

Which sentences above contain boldfaced phrases? __a, c__ Which contain boldfaced clauses? __b, d__ In which sentences do the boldfaced words tell more about a noun? __b, c__ In which do they tell more about a verb? __a, d__

A **phrase** is a group of words that functions as a part of speech. For example, a participial phrase typically functions as an adjective by modifying, or telling more about, a noun. A phrase does not contain a subject-verb combination. A **clause** is a group of words that contains a subject-verb combination. A dependent clause—a clause that cannot stand alone as a sentence—functions as a part of speech also. For example, a dependent clause can function as an adverb by modifying a verb.

See Handbook Sections 13, 17g, 19, 20, 25

Practice

Look at the boldfaced group of words in each sentence. Circle the word or words it modifies. Then identify the structure and function of these words by writing *adjective phrase*, *adverb phrase*, *adjective clause*, or *adverb clause*.

1. The Tunguska Fireball is classified as a meteoroid; a meteoroid is a ⟨chunk⟩ **of space rock** that enters Earth's atmosphere but does not reach its surface. _____**adjective phrase**_____

2. The energy of its explosion was a thousand times more powerful than that of the atomic ⟨bomb⟩ **that was dropped on Hiroshima.** _____**adjective clause**_____

3. The meteoroid ⟨exploded⟩ **near the Podkamennaya Tunguska River** in a thinly inhabited part of Siberia. _____**adverb phrase**_____

4. **If it had occurred in a populous area,** the explosion ⟨would have caused⟩ a tragedy too terrible to imagine. _____**adverb clause**_____

5. The ⟨area⟩ **where the explosion occurred** was so sparsely populated that no deaths are known to have resulted from the blast. _____**adjective clause**_____

6. The blast ⟨did flatten⟩ trees **over an 800-square-mile area.** _____**adverb clause**_____

7. The ⟨heat⟩ **from the blast** was so intense that a worker in a trading post 40 miles away felt that his shirt had caught fire. _____**adjective phrase**_____

8. **Because the site was so far from transportation routes and is so frequently affected by severe weather,** no researcher ⟨reached⟩ it until 1927. _____**adverb clause**_____

The Tunguska fireball damaged many trees when it hit Earth.

Name _____

Apply Suggested answers appear below. Accept all reasonable responses.

Combine each pair of sentences into a single sentence. If the sentence you create contains an adjective phrase, an adverb phrase, an adjective clause, or an adverb clause, underline it and write which it is. (You only need to mark one phrase or clause in each sentence you write.)

9. There is no impact crater at the epicenter of the Tunguska blast. The meteor did not strike Earth.

   There is no impact crater at the epicenter of the Tunguska blast <u>because the meteor did not</u>

   <u>strike Earth.</u> (adverb clause)

10. Asteroids enter Earth's atmosphere. These asteroids are called meteors. Asteroids <u>that enter Earth's</u>

   <u>atmosphere</u> are called meteors. (adjective clause)

11. When a meteor burns up in Earth's atmosphere, it is called a meteoroid. Most meteors do burn

   up in Earth's atmosphere. When a meteor burns up in Earth's atmosphere, <u>as most meteors do,</u>

   it is called a meteoroid. (adverb clause)

12. A few meteors do strike Earth. These are called meteorites. The few meteors <u>that do strike</u>

   <u>Earth</u> are called meteorites. (adjective clause)

13. A meteorite struck a spot in northern Arizona about 49,000 years ago. It created a huge crater there.

   A meteorite <u>that struck a spot in northern Arizona about 49,000 years ago</u> created

   a huge crater there. (adjective clause)

14. This crater is known as the Barringer Meteor Crater. It is almost a mile wide and more than 500 feet deep.

   That crater, <u>called the Barrington Meteor Crater,</u> is almost a mile wide and more than

   500 feet deep. (adjective phrase)

Reinforce

Write four sentences about meteors. Include an adjective phrase in one sentence, an adverb phrase in another sentence, an adjective clause in another, and an adverb clause in the remaining sentence. Be prepared to tell what word or words each phrase or clause modifies.

Answers will vary.

_____

_____

_____

a. Fujiyama is a volcano, and so is Mauna Loa.

b. Fujiyama and Mauna Loa have different shapes.

c. Although Fujiyama and Mauna Loa are both volcanoes, they were formed in different ways.

d. Although Fujiyama and Mauna Loa are both volcanoes, they have different shapes, and they were formed in different ways.

Which sentence is made up of one independent clause? __b__ Which sentence is made up of two independent clauses? __a__ Which sentence is made up of one independent clause and one dependent clause? __c__ Which sentence is made up of two independent clauses and one dependent clause? __d__ Which of these sentences conveys the most information in an effective manner? __d__

Simple sentences, compound sentences, complex sentences, and **compound-complex sentences** offer a writer a variety of ways of stating information and showing relationships. When you write, choose sentence types that enable you to express your ideas clearly and show how they are related to one another.

See Handbook | Section 13

Practice

Read each pair of sentences. Mark a star beside the one that more effectively expresses the idea and shows relationships. If the sentence you choose is a simple sentence, write *S* in the blank. If it is a compound sentence, write *CD*. If it is a complex sentence, write *CX*. If it is a compound-complex sentence, write *CCX*.

1. Many landforms are created when processes occur within Earth; these are called tectonic processes. ☆**CCX**

   Tectonic processes create many of Earth's landforms. _____

2. Diastrophism is the name of a process that changes Earth's surface. _____

   Diastrophism, which is the change of Earth's surface resulting from movements of tectonic plates, is one tectonic process that creates landforms. ☆**CD**

3. Vulcanism produces volcanoes, which are mountains formed by volcanic eruptions; the material that pours forth from a volcano builds up the volcano so it becomes higher than the surrounding land. _____

   Vulcanism is the term for the other tectonic process that creates landforms; volcanoes are the most noticeable products of volcanism. ☆**CD**

4. While some volcanoes are shaped like cones, others are shaped like shields; these different shapes are the result of different processes of formation. ☆**CCX**

   Cone-shaped volcanoes are formed on one way, and shield-shaped volcanoes are formed in another way. _____

5. Cone volcanoes like Fujiyama result from explosive eruptions that typically lay down alternating layers of lava, and of ash and cinders. ☆**CX**

   Explosive eruptions produce cone volcanoes, and Fujiyama is a cone volcano. _____

6. Nonexplosive flows of lava create shield volcanoes like Mauna Loa. _____

   Shield volcanoes like Mauna Loa are created when lava flows but does not explode; shield volcanoes can be many miles wide. ☆**CX**

Apply   Answers will vary. Sample responses are shown.

Rewrite each group of sentences as one sentence. Choose a type of sentence that makes clear the relationships between ideas.

7. The Pacific Ring of Fire is a horseshoe-shaped region. It stretches from the west coast of South America northward to Alaska's Aleutian Islands and then southward off the coast of Asia all the way to Indonesia. **The Pacific Ring of Fire is a horseshoe-shaped region that stretches from the west coast of South America northward to Alaska's Aleutian Islands and then southward off the coast of Asia all the way to Indonesia.**

8. Three-quarters of the world's volcanoes are located along the Pacific Ring of Fire. Some of these volcanoes are active, and others are dormant. **Three-quarters of the world's active and dormant volcanoes are located along the Pacific Ring of Fire.**

9. Japan is home to ten percent of the world's active volcanoes. Japan occupies an area in the Ring of Fire where Earth's crust is particularly unstable. **Japan, which is home to ten percent of the world's active volcanoes, occupies an area in the Ring of Fire where Earth's crust is particularly unstable.**

10. The Hawaiian Islands are not located on the Ring of Fire. They rise in the western Pacific Ocean over a hot spot in Earth's upper layers. **The Hawaiian Islands are not located on the Ring of Fire; they rise in the western Pacific Ocean over a hot spot in Earth's upper layers.**

Reinforce

Different circumstances call for different kinds of sentences. Read these two reports about the eruption of Krakatoa, the most violent eruption in modern times. The first is from the log of a captain whose ship was in the vicinity of the eruption. The second is from the report a British official in the area sent to his superiors in London.

> A fearful explosion. A frightful sound. I am writing this blind in pitch darkness. We are under a continued rain of pumice-stone and dust. So violent are the explosions that the ear drums of over half my crew have been shattered.
>
> —Captain Sampson, from the log of the Norham Castle

> The present [volcanic] outburst commenced on Sunday last, and on that night the inhabitants of nearly the whole of Java and Sumatra were alarmed by loud noises resembling the reports of heavy artillery, which continued through the night and at rarer intervals during Monday. . . .
>
> —Consul Alexander Patrick Cameron, dispatch to Lord Granville

On another sheet of paper, write a paragraph comparing the sentence structure, tone, and purpose of the two reports. Explain whether you think each writer used kinds of sentences appropriate for his purpose.
Answers will vary.

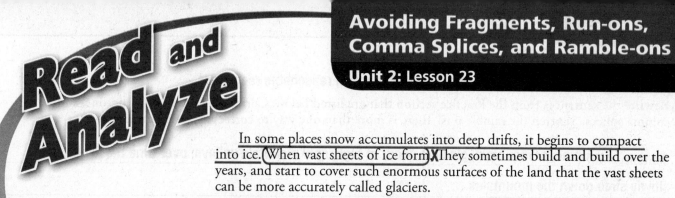
In some places snow accumulates into deep drifts, it begins to compact into ice. (When vast sheets of ice form) X They sometimes build and build over the years, and start to cover such enormous surfaces of the land that the vast sheets can be more accurately called glaciers.

Circle the dependent clause that is missing an independent clause. Underline the sentence that is written incorrectly because it is made up of two independent clauses without a conjunction. Write *X* at the beginning of the sentence that contains unnecessary words and phrases.

A **fragment** does not tell a complete thought. A **run-on sentence** is a compound sentence that is missing a comma and a conjunction. A **comma splice** is a run-on sentence that has a comma but is missing a conjunction. A **ramble-on** sentence is correct grammatically but contains unnecessary words and phrases or includes too many ideas. Avoid fragments, run-ons, comma splices, and ramble-ons in the final versions of your written work.

See Handbook Sections 8, 14, 22

Practice

Write *F* after each fragment. Write *RO* after each run-on. Write *CS* after each comma splice. Write *RA* after each ramble-on sentence.

1. There are two different types of glaciers they are not hard to distinguish. __RO__

2. Alpine and continental glaciers. __F__

3. Alpine, or mountain, glaciers occur in high, cold mountain valleys, over time these glaciers slowly slide down the mountains. __CS__

4. Continental glaciers cover large, flat areas around the earth's poles, it is cold enough for snow to fall throughout the year. __CS__

5. You may be surprised to learn that, like alpine glaciers, continental glaciers, which cover large areas that are often basically just open ocean, are frozen fresh water because they are made by snow falling from above instead of sea water freezing from below. __RA__

6. During colder eras, these glaciers expanded they spread over the Antarctic and Arctic regions like pancake batter. __RO__

7. Alpine glaciers are one of the strongest forces the earth has ever seen; with their might, these powerful glaciers have carved and shaped landforms of all kinds in many parts of our planet. __RA__

8. There are two national parks called Glacier National Park one is in Canada and the other is in the United States. __RO__

9. Glaciers once covered the land in both parks even today there are glaciers for visitors to see. __RO__

10. Carved extraordinary formations out of the land there. __F__

11. These big, heavy rivers of ice, like sandpaper and chisels as they move across the land. __F__

Apply Possible answers appear below. Accept all reasonable responses.

Rewrite the sentences from the Practice section that are listed below. Correct the fragments, run-ons, and comma splices. Shorten the ramble-ons. There is more than one way to correct each sentence. (12–19)

Sentence #3 Alpine, or mountain, glaciers occur in high, cold mountain valleys; over time these glaciers slowly slide down the mountains.

Sentence #4 Continental glaciers cover large, flat areas around the earth's poles, where it is cold enough for snow to fall throughout the year.

Sentence #5 Continental glaciers are frozen fresh water because they are made by snow falling from above.

Sentence #6 During colder eras, these glaciers spread over the Antarctic and Arctic regions like pancake batter.

Sentence #7 Alpine glaciers have carved and shaped landforms in many parts of our planet.

Sentence #9 Glaciers once covered the land in both parks. Even today there are glaciers for visitors to see.

Sentence #10 The glaciers carved extraordinary formations out of the land there.

Sentence #11 These big, heavy rivers of ice act like sandpaper and chisels as they move across the land.

Reinforce

This monster ramble-on sentence contains more than 60 words. Cross out unnecessary words, phrases, and clauses to make the sentence as short as possible. Write your revised sentence below.

~~In some cases, where the rocks contain important clues as to the early geological processes of the earth in past eras,~~ glaciers can ~~come through the area and scrape away rocks, shear rocks in half, and~~ expose ~~whole cliff faces with the result that scientists can access these rocks and find~~ important geological information ~~that they would never have been able to access without the glacier.~~

20. Suggested answer: Glaciers can expose important geological information.

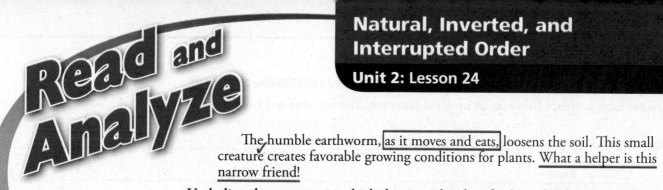

Read and Analyze

The humble earthworm, as it moves and eats, loosens the soil. This small creature creates favorable growing conditions for plants. What a helper is this narrow friend!

Underline the sentence in which the natural order of subject followed by verb is reversed. Draw a box around the clause that interrupts a subject-verb-object pattern. Put a check mark over the sentence that has the subject, verb, and object in that order, with no clause interrupting it.

A sentence with **natural order** follows the subject-verb pattern, with any direct object, predicate noun, or predicate adjective coming after the verb. In a sentence with **inverted order,** a verb, direct object, predicate noun, or predicate adjective comes before the subject. A sentence with **interrupted order** breaks up the subject-verb pattern with a dependent clause.

See Handbook Section 13

Practice

Write *N* after each sentence with natural order. Write *IV* after each sentence with inverted order. Write *IT* after each sentence with interrupted order.

1. Soil, which is necessary for most plant life, is a complex mix of ingredients. **IT**

2. Thousands of kinds of soils cover the surface of the earth. **N**

3. Fortunate are those families with farms on fertile soil! **IV**

4. All soils contain organic matter, rocks, minerals, air, and water. **N**

5. Organic matter, which comes from decaying plants and animals, adds to the soil's fertility. **IT**

6. Earthworms hasten the decomposition of organic matter. **N**

7. How odd it seems that a creature would eat soil! **IV**

8. Soil earthworms do devour. **IV**

9. Their castings they leave on the surface. **IV**

10. Earthworms, as farmers do with plows, turn over soil. **IT**

11. Earthworms make tunnels and burrows. **N**

12. These passageways let air and water into the soil and so improve its ability to sustain plant life. **N**

13. Without burrowing creatures, how desolate the earth would be! **IV**

14. Human activity can also affect soil quality. **N**

15. Cutting down plants, which help to sustain life on Earth, can cause soil to blow or wash away. **IT**

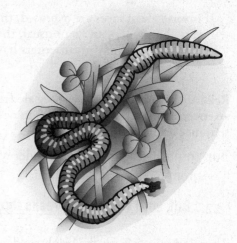

Earthworms enrich the soil by breaking down organic matter, aerating the soil, and acting like tiny plows.

Apply Suggested answers appear below. Accept all reasonable responses.

Rewrite each sentence below as an inverted sentence. The first one has been done for you.

16. The soil in these hills is dark. <u>Dark is the soil in these hills.</u>

     _____

17. The days are long during early summer. <u>**Long are the days during early summer.**</u>

     _____

18. The first shoots of vegetables are green. <u>**Green are the first shoots of vegetables.**</u>

19. The rabbits that raid our garden are clever. <u>**Clever are the rabbits that raid our garden.**</u>

     _____

20. The farmer who buries fencing to keep rabbits out is wise. <u>**Wise is the farmer who buries fencing to**</u>
     <u>**keep rabbits out.**</u>

21. The plants in this fertile soil are so healthy! <u>**How healthy are the plants in this fertile soil!**</u>

     _____

Reinforce

If inverted sentences are overused, they can make a piece of writing sound unnatural. Because inverted sentences are so unusual, though, they can be effective: They draw the reader's attention to the sentences. Many great writers have used inverted sentences to create interesting effects.

Read the two quotes below. They are from works by William Shakespeare. Notice that each of these lines uses an inverted pattern. Rewrite each in natural sentence order. Then decide whether the inverted or the natural sentence order sounds better.

But, soft! what light through yonder window breaks?
   —from *Romeo and Juliet*, II, ii

22. <u>**But, soft! what light breaks through yonder window?**</u>

Thus sometimes hath the brightest day a cloud;
   —from *King Henry VI*, Part II, II, iv

23. <u>**Thus sometimes the brightest day hath a cloud;**</u>

Review

Clauses and Sentence Types

Write *S* next to each simple sentence. Write *CD* next to each compound sentence. Write *CX* next to each complex sentence. Write *CCX* next to each compound-complex sentence.

1. Vikings settled in Iceland and Greenland between A.D. 800 and 1200. __S__ (13)

2. These settlers, who came from northern Europe, were called the Norse; they were looking for farmland, and Iceland and Greenland resembled their home region. __CCX__ (15)

3. Farms could be established in those places because their climates were considerably warmer then. __CX__ (15)

4. The warmer temperatures melted dangerous sea ice, and this made voyages to and from these islands faster and safer. __CD__ (13)

5. After the Vikings arrived in Iceland and Greenland, they raised cattle and crops; they also gathered berries and seaweed and caught fish __CCX__ (15)

Draw one line under the independent clause in each sentence. Draw two lines under the dependent clause.

6. After the Vikings had lived in Iceland and Greenland for several centuries, some unwelcome changes occurred. (14)

7. Crops failed frequently because the climate was becoming colder. (14)

Underline the adjective clause in each sentence. Then circle the noun it modifies.

8. The (crops) that they raised fed their cattle. (16)

9. Their (cattle), which were given less and less food, started dying. (16)

10. The (areas) where survival was becoming most difficult were in Greenland. (16)

Underline the adverb clause in each sentence.

11. Because the climate was colder, dangerous drift ice appeared more frequently in the sea. (17)

12. Although Europe was not far away, the drift ice made voyages there very dangerous. (17)

Gerund Phrases

Underline each gerund phrase.

13. The Little Ice Age lasted from about 1400 to 1850; being cold for 450 years was certainly no fun! (19)

14. Shortening the growing season was one effect of the Little Ice Age. (19)

Active and Passive Voice

Write *A* after each sentence with a verb in active voice. Write *P* after each sentence with a verb in passive voice.

15. Entire villages and nearby farms were covered by expanding glaciers. __P__ (20)

16. The cold temperatures reduced the yields of farms. __A__ (20)

Fragments, Run-ons, Comma Splices, and Ramble-ons

Identify each item as a fragment, run-on, comma splice, or ramble-on by writing *F, RO, CS,* or *RA.*

17. Why the Little Ice Age occurred. __F__ **(23)**

18. Some scientists say that the sun was not shining as brightly during that period of time as it does in normal periods of time, and so it was not providing as much warmth to Earth as it usually provides. __RA__ **(23)**

19. The sun put out less heat energy, weather on Earth became colder. __CS__ **(23)**

20. Some scientists believe ash sent into the atmosphere by erupting volcanoes caused temperatures to drop the ash blocked the sun's rays and kept them from reaching Earth. __RO__ **(23)**

Natural, Inverted, and Interrupted Order

Write *N* next to a sentence if the sentence has natural order. Write *IV* next to a sentence if the sentence has inverted oder. Write *IT* next to a sentence if the sentence has interrupted order.

21. The "year without a summer" 1816 was called. __IV__ **(24)**

22. Frost and snow were on the ground in Europe during the summer months. __N__ **(24)**

Clauses, Phrases, and Sentence Structures

Draw a line under the dependent clause in each sentence. If it is a restrictive clause, write RC after the sentence. If it is a nonrestrictive clause, write NC after the sentence.

23. The cold temperatures of 1816 may have been caused by a volcano <u>whose eruption blasted a huge amount of material into the atmosphere.</u> __RC__ **(18)**

24. That volcanic eruption, <u>which occurred on an island in present-day Indonesia,</u> lowered the world's average temperature by almost one degree Celsius. __NC__ **(18)**

Read each sentence. Circle the word or words modified by the boldfaced phrase or clause. Then identify the boldfaced words as an adjective phrase, an adverb phrase, an adjective clause, or an adverb clause.

25. Krakatoa's eruption (affected) worldwide temperatures **in a similar way.** ___**adverb phrase**___ **(21)**

26. The (material) **that the eruption poured into the atmosphere** blocked some of the sun's rays.
   ___**adjective clause**___ **(21)**

Read each pair of sentences. Mark a star beside the sentence that more effectively expresses ideas. Then label that sentence *S* (simple sentence), *CD* (compound sentence), *CX* (complex sentence), or *CCX* (compound-complex sentence).

27. Because it poses a threat to the communities on its slopes, Mauna Loa has been carefully monitored for more than a century. ☆**CX** **(22)**

   Mauna Loa is a threat. It has been monitored for more than a century. _____ **(22)**

28. Scientists involved in the Decade Volcano project study Mauna Loa and other dangerous volcanoes. _____ **(22)**

   Mauna Loa is now included in the Decade Volcano project, which promotes the study of the world's most dangerous volcanoes; it is one of 16 volcanoes being observed. ☆**CCX** **(22)**

Spelling Practice

With global warming, the polar ice caps we once thought were permanent are melting slowly.

Underline the word in the sentence that means "lasting." Circle the suffix in the word.

Adding Suffixes: *-ant, -ance, -ent, -ence*

The suffixes *-ant* and *-ent* can be added to the ends of roots and base words to create adjectives, as in *abundant* and *evident*. The suffixes *-ance* and *-ence* can be added to the ends of roots and base words to create nouns, as in *abundance* and *evidence*.

Word Sort

Use the words below to complete the word sort. **Answers may be in any order.**

| confidence | competent | relevant | permanent | competence | observant |
| significant | relevance | permanence | observance | significance | confident |

Suffix *-ant*	Suffix *-ance*
significant	significance
observant	observance
relevant	relevance

Suffix *-ent*	Suffix *-ence*
permanent	permanence
competent	competence
confident	confidence

Name _____

Pattern Practice

Write the word in each pair that is spelled correctly. Use a dictionary to check the spellings.

1. intelligance, intelligence _____ **intelligence** _____

2. permanence, permanance _____ **permanence** _____

3. abundent, abundant _____ **abundant** _____

4. inconveniant, inconvenient _____ **inconvenient** _____

5. observance, observence _____ **observance** _____

6. significent, significant _____ **significant** _____

7. competance, competence _____ **competence** _____

Add *-ant, -ent, -ance,* or *-ence* to each base word given. Write the new word in the sentence. Change the spelling of the base word as needed.

8. The _____ **observant** _____ cat notices every tiny noise. (observe)

9. Yoshi has won an award for perfect _____ **attendance** _____. (attend)

10. The Browns still live at this _____ **residence** _____. (reside)

11. It seemed so insignificant that she questioned its _____ **relevance** _____. (relevant)

12. Did the detective find any _____ **evidence** _____ at the crime scene? (evident)

13. That store is closed for the _____ **observance** _____ of the holiday. (observe)

14. That's just our _____ **resident** _____ cricket chirping away. (reside)

15. Living near train tracks can be an _____ **annoyance** _____ to many people. (annoy)

Use the Dictionary

Add *-ant, -ent, -ance,* or *-ence* to each base word and write the new word. Check your spellings in a print or an online dictionary.

16. dominate + ance = _____ **dominance** _____

17. expect + ant = _____ **expectant** _____

18. converge + ent = _____ **convergent** _____

Diagramming Compound Sentences

You have learned that a compound sentence is made of two independent clauses joined by a comma and a coordinating conjunction or by a semicolon.

A compound sentence is diagrammed this way:

Some cities bury trash, and others burn it.

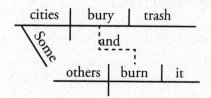

Try diagramming these compound sentences.

1. I visited the dump, but it had closed.

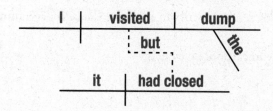

2. Rosa saved newspapers, and Tio recycled them.

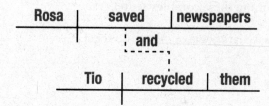

3. Recycling helps, but reducing helps more.

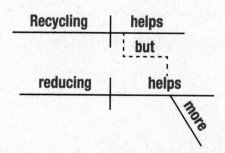

4. Rohit once used many napkins daily, but now he uses just a few.

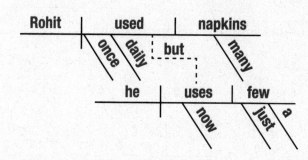

Language Standard(s): L.8.1

73

Diagramming Complex Sentences

You have learned that a complex sentence is made up of an independent clause and a dependent clause. The dependent clause may be an adjective clause that begins with a relative pronoun such as *who, whom, whose, which,* or *that.* Or, it may be an adverb clause that begins with a subordinating conjunction such as *although, if,* or *because,* or a relative adverb such as *when* or *where.*

A complex sentence with an adverb is diagrammed this way:

When people carpool, they save energy.

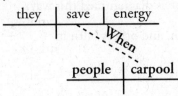

A complex sentence with an adjective clause is diagrammed this way:

People **who carpool** save energy.

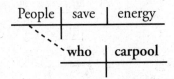

Try diagramming these complex sentences.

5. They save jars because they reuse them.

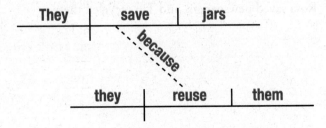

6. I respect people who help the environment.

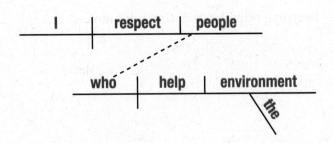

7. As the climate changes, species vanish.

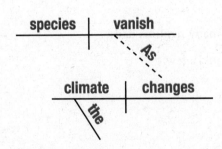

Writing Sentences

Possible answers appear below. Accept all reasonable responses.

The writer of these sentences has tried to include too many ideas. Rewrite each sentence as two or three shorter, clearer sentences. Make sure each sentence you write is complete.

1. The Gulf Stream is a strong current of warm water that flows northward along the eastern coast of North America, and, once it reaches North Carolina, heads to the east to form part of a large clockwise circulation of water in the North Atlantic, although one branch of the Gulf Stream continues north and joins another major current known as the North Atlantic Drift.

   The Gulf Stream is a strong current of warm water that flows northward along the eastern coast of North America. Once it reaches North Carolina, the Gulf Stream heads to the east to form part of a large clockwise circulation of water in the North Atlantic. One branch of the Gulf Stream continues north, however, and joins another major current known as the North Atlantic Drift.

2. Together, the Gulf Stream and the North Atlantic Drift help warm northern Europe by giving off the heat they carry to the surrounding environment, and today, many scientists are concerned that global warming may change the circulation patterns of these currents, and, consequently, cause temperatures in northern Europe to drop; some even predict a mini Ice Age!

   Together, the Gulf Stream and the North Atlantic Drift help warm northern Europe by giving off the heat they carry to the surrounding environment. Today, many scientists are concerned that global warming may change the circulation patterns of these currents, and, consequently, cause temperatures in northern Europe to drop. Some even predict a mini Ice Age!

There are four kinds of sentences—a statement, a question, a command, and an exclamation. Any of these sentences may be simple, compound, or complex. Notice the different types of sentences in this model paragraph.

imperative sentence
(gives a command and ends with a period or an exclamation point)

declarative sentence
(makes a statement and ends with a period)

interrogative sentence
(asks a question and ends with a question mark)

exclamatory sentence
(shows excitement and ends with an exclamation point)

Imagine a great river running through the ocean. This "river" carries warm water from the central Pacific Ocean, passes between Australia and the southern tip of Africa, and then proceeds up to the North Atlantic before looping back and retracing its course south and back to the central Pacific. *What is this "river"?* It is an ocean circulation pattern that is so effective at transporting heat energy that it's sometimes called the Great Ocean Conveyor Belt!

Name _____

Writing a Paragraph

The sentences you repaired on page 75 can be used to make a paragraph. Decide what order the sentences should be in. Then revise at least two of the sentences so your paragraph has a variety of sentence types. Use the model on page 75 as a reference. Write the paragraph on the lines below.

A possible answer appears below. Accept all reasonable responses.

The Gulf Stream is a strong current of warm water that flows northward along the eastern coast of North America. Once it reaches North Carolina, the Gulf Stream heads to the east to form part of a large clockwise circulation of water in the North Atlantic. One branch of the Gulf Stream continues north, however, and joins another major current known as the North Atlantic Drift. Together, the Gulf Stream and the North Atlantic Drift help warm northern Europe. How do they do this? They give off the heat they carry to the surrounding environment. Today, many scientists are concerned that global warming may change the circulation patterns of these currents, and, consequently, cause temperatures in northern Europe to drop. Some even predict a mini Ice Age!

Think of some event or process that has changed the area in which you live. This might be a flood, a fire, an earthquake, or the encroachment of an invasive species. Write a paragraph describing this event or process and its effects. Be sure to include a topic sentence, supporting sentences, and a concluding sentence. Also include at least two different kinds of sentences.

Answers will vary.

_____

_____

_____

_____

_____

Read your paragraph again. Use this checklist to make sure it is complete and correct.

- ❑ My paragraph has a topic sentence.
- ❑ My paragraph has at least two supporting sentences.
- ❑ All my sentences are clear and make sense.

- ❑ I have used at least two types of sentences and punctuated them correctly.
- ❑ My paragraph has a concluding sentence.

Proofreading
Practice

Read this passage about waste management and find the mistakes. Use the proofreading marks to show how the mistakes should be fixed. Use a dictionary to check and correct spellings. **Suggested answers appear below. Accept all reasonable responses.**

Proofreading Marks

Mark	Means	Example
✏	delete	Landfill is a waste management options.
∧	add	Landfill is a waste management option.
≡	make into an uppercase letter	landfill is a waste management option.
/	make into a lowercase letter	Landfill is a Waste management option.
⊙	add a period	Landfill is a waste management option
(sp)	fix spelling	Landfill is a waste managment option.

Responsible Waste Management

Landfill, a method of spreding and compacting solid waste on land and covering it with soil is not a good long-term waste management solution. Landfill generates the greenhouse gases Methane and Carbon dioxide. leakage from landfill can puloot groundwater. population growth requires more and more wild land to be used as dumping grounds. For all these reasons cities across the country are trying to reduce the amount of material that winds up in landfill.

Many cities now offer curbside recycling of used paper, glass, alumanum, steel, and plastic bottles. Recycling offers numerous benafits. Recycling paper products saves trees, Which absorb Carbon Dioxide from the air. Manufacturing with recycled materials uses much less energy than manufacturing with raw materials does, and for example, it takes four to eight times as much energy to extract and process petroleum to make plastic goods as it takes to make plastics from recycled plastic materials.

Many cities also have drop-off centers for the disposal of hazardous waste such as paint and expired medicines. Some comunities even provide drop-off centers for old computers and electronics.

Composting of food scraps and yard trimmings offers another solution composting is the process of decomposing organic matter into a rich soil called compost.

By working together to divert recyclible and compostable materials from landfill, Cities and individuals can play an important role in protecting the environment.

Proofreading
Checklist

You can use the checklist below to help you find and fix mistakes in your own writing. Write the titles of your own stories or reports in the blanks at the top of the chart. Then use the questions to check your work. Make a check mark (✔)in each box after you have checked that item. **Answers will vary.**

Titles

Proofreading Checklist for Unit 2

Have I used phrases and clauses correctly?				
Have I used a comma and coordinating conjunction or semicolon to join independent clauses?				
Have I avoided run-on sentences, comma splices, fragments, and ramble-on sentences?				
Is each simple sentence an independent clause, and does each complex sentence have an independent clause and a dependent clause?				

Also Remember...

Does each sentence begin with an uppercase letter?				
Did I use a dictionary to check and correct spellings?				
Have I used commas correctly?				

Your Own List

Use this space to write your own list of things to check in your writing.

Community Connection

In Unit 2 of *Grammar, Usage, and Mechanics,* students learned about **different types of sentences, phrases, and clauses** and used what they learned to improve their writing. The content of these lessons focuses on the theme **Changes in the Natural World.** As students completed the exercises, they learned about the forces of change that have altered, and may continue to alter, our planet. These pages offer a variety of activities that reinforce skills and concepts presented in the unit. They also provide opportunities for the student to make connections between the information presented in the lessons and their modern surroundings.

Even Small Changes Count

Continents drift, mountains rise and fall, glaciers carve the land, and rivers change course. How have these forces of nature changed your area over the centuries? To find out, take a trip to your local library and ask a librarian for help researching what your area was like in the distant past. Find or draw a picture to show this. Then find or draw a picture of the same area as it looks today. Finally, write a paragraph in which you compare and contrast the two landscapes.

Water Under the Bridge

Water is necessary for all life. It is one of the most powerful agents of change on Earth. Water is constantly shaping the land through erosion. Too little water can also change the land and affect the plants and animals living there. What do you know about the water that is supplied to your community? To find out more, visit your local water department or utilities commission online or in person. Try to find answers to the following questions:

- Does the water in your home come from far away or nearby?
- Does acid rain fall in your area? What contaminants are in your water?
- Does your area experience droughts often? What have been the results of these dry periods?
- What are some things you can do to conserve water?

Preventing, Controlling, Reversing

Some changes, like meteorite hits, seismic activity, and magnetic field reversals, happen to Earth regardless of human existence. Other changes are directly brought about by humans. Learn how humans affect the earth and what people can do to slow down negative changes such as global warming and habitat loss. Search the Internet for websites of organizations that combat global warming, habitat loss, or other negative human impacts on the natural world. Choose one organization that you admire, and prepare a brief speech about how the organization is working toward its goals.

How Do We Know About Changes?

How do scientists find out what the natural world was like long before humans existed on Earth? If possible, interview a science teacher, a science museum curator, or another adult who is knowledgeable in the field of geology, paleontology, or natural history. Before you conduct your interview, collect some questions to ask about how scientists learn about what the earth was like long ago. Use the following list of questions to get started:

- Where can scientists find evidence of how the earth looked long ago?
- Is there anywhere nearby where you can see evidence of geologic changes?
- What kinds of tests can scientists do to learn the age of rocks?
- Does all of our knowledge about extinct species come from fossils?

Use the planning guide below to help you plan the interview. Take notes during the interview, and share the results of the interview with your class.

Interview Planner   Answers will vary.

Topic of interview: _____

Date of interview: _____

Name: _____

Occupation: _____

Experience in field of interest: _____

Questions to ask:

1. _____
   _____

2. _____
   _____

3. _____
   _____

4. _____
   _____

5. _____
   _____

Read and Analyze

Many **cultures** around the (world) have rich story-telling **traditions**.
Circle the boldfaced noun that names a single person, place, or thing.

> A **singular noun** names one person, place, thing, or idea. A **plural noun** names more than one. Most nouns add *-s* or *-es* to form the plural. A small number of nouns have **irregular plurals.** Some nouns change spelling in the plural form (*woman, women*). Some nouns have the same singular and plural form (*deer*).

See Handbook | Section 29

Practice

Circle each singular noun. Underline each plural noun.

1. For centuries, groups across our (planet) have told and retold myths and legends.

2. Myths recount the great feats of supernatural beings, ancestors, and heroes.

3. Ancient groups invented myths to explain the (world) around them, or to explain the (relationship) between gods and humans.

4. The Greeks were fascinated by the stars, so they named each of the constellations and invented stories about them.

5. Many cultures have myths that offer supernatural explanations of how (land,) animals, and humans were created.

The myth of Orion tells how the hunter ended up in the sky.

6. Mythical tales are fantastic and unbelievable.

7. However, they reflect the values of the times in which they were created.

8. Like a (myth,) a (legend) is an unverifiable popular (story) handed down from earlier times.

9. Some legends are based on real individuals or true events.

10. When stories about these folks and events are retold, facts are often embellished and exaggerated.

11. (Johnny Appleseed) was a real (man) who became legendary.

12. (Paul Bunyan) and his (ox,) (Babe,) were imaginary figures.

13. Real boys don't grow so quickly that they wear the clothes of their (father) within five days!

14. Real oxen don't straighten rivers by tugging on them!

15. People are still inventing myths and legends today; only (time) will tell which ones will be retold a (century) from now.

Apply

Write the plural form of each singular common noun you identified in the Practice section. (Names of people or animals are not common nouns.)

16. _____ planets _____   22. _____ stories _____

17. _____ worlds _____   23. _____ men _____

18. _____ relationships _____   24. _____ oxen _____

19. _____ lands _____   25. _____ fathers _____

20. _____ myths _____   26. _____ times _____

21. _____ legends _____   27. _____ centuries _____

Reinforce

See Handbook Section 15

A collective noun names a group of people or things that act as a unit. *Class, flock,* and *team* are collective nouns. Most often, a collective noun is treated as a singular subject:

   The track *team is* the strongest one we've had in years.

Sometimes, if a writer wants to emphasize the different members of a group, he or she may treat the noun as a plural subject:

   The track *team are* congratulating one another on their fine performances.

Circle the words below that are collective nouns. Then use three of them in sentences.

(family)	animals	centuries	(class)	(audience)
gods	myths	(group)	(team)	(company)

28. _Answers will vary._ _____

_____

_____

29. _____

_____

_____

30. _____

_____

_____

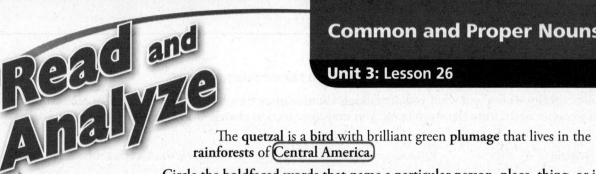

The **quetzal** is a **bird** with brilliant green **plumage** that lives in the **rainforests** of Central America.

Circle the boldfaced words that name a particular person, place, thing, or idea.

A **common noun** names any person, place, thing, or idea. A **proper noun** names a particular person, place, thing, or idea. Proper nouns must be capitalized. A proper noun made of several words (*United Nations* or *Martin Luther King High School*) is considered one proper noun.

See Handbook Section 15

Practice

Circle each common noun in the sentences below. Underline each proper noun.

The quetzal is the national bird of Guatemala.

1. Long ago, the Maya considered the quetzal sacred.

2. They believed that the bird would spread its green wings and use them as a shield to protect their warriors in battle.

3. In the years after the voyage of Christopher Columbus, the Spanish tried to conquer the Maya and seize their gold.

4. Pedro de Alvarado led an attack on Quetzaltenango, a city in the mountains of what is now Guatemala.

5. The Maya fought with spears, clubs, and shields woven out of wicker.

6. The Spaniards fought with swords and guns, and wore thick armor to protect themselves.

7. The chief of the Maya fought against Pedro de Alvarado.

8. As the two men fought, a quetzal darted above them, trying to protect the chief, Tecún Umán.

9. Tecún Umán was ill-equipped to defend himself against the superior arms of his opponent.

10. Pedro de Alvarado wounded Tecún Umán seriously, and the leader of the Maya fell to the ground.

11. It is said that at that moment, the quetzal fell upon Tecún Umán and spread its brilliant green plumes over his chest.

12. The next morning at dawn, the people of Quetzaltenango saw the quetzal rise up from the chief's body.

13. The feathers of the breast of the quetzal were stained with the blood of Tecún Umán.

14. Ever since then, all quetzals have had crimson breasts.

15. Today these exotic birds of Central America are endangered.

Apply   Possible answers appear below. Accept all reasonable responses.

Proper nouns specify whom and what you are talking about. Rewrite each sentence, and replace each common noun with a proper noun from the word bank. You may also need to change other words in your sentences.

Guatemala	Maya	Quetzaltenango	Spanish	*A Guide to Central American Parks*

16. I'm planning a trip to that country. **I'm planning a trip to Guatemala.**

17. The traditions of that indigenous group really interest me. **The traditions of the Maya really interest me.**

18. Outside that city, there's a rainforest that I would like to visit. **Outside Quetzaltenango, there's a rainforest that I would like to visit.**

19. I read all about it in a book. **I read all about it in <u>A Guide to Central American Parks.</u>**

Reinforce

See Handbook Sections 1, 3

To correctly capitalize a proper noun made up of two or more words, capitalize the first word, the last word, and each important word in between. (Don't forget to underline or italicize book and movie titles and to put story titles in quotation marks.)
The National Baseball Hall of Fame
Around the World in Eighty Days

Rewrite these sentences by correctly capitalizing proper nouns.

20. I read a book called aztec and maya myths. **I read a book called <u>Aztec and Maya Myths.</u>**

21. I saw a model of the pyramid of the sun at the national museum of anthropology. **I saw a model of the Pyramid of the Sun at the National Museum of Anthropology.**

22. Students at john f. kennedy middle school put on plays about the history of mexico. **Students at John F. Kennedy Middle School put on plays about the history of Mexico.**

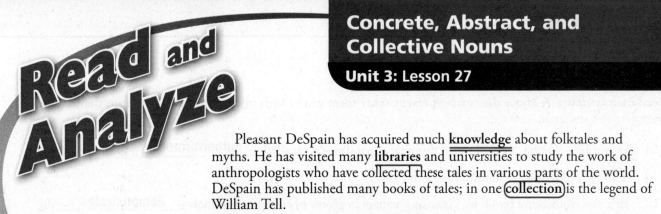

Pleasant DeSpain has acquired much **knowledge** about folktales and myths. He has visited many **libraries** and universities to study the work of anthropologists who have collected these tales in various parts of the world. DeSpain has published many books of tales; in one **collection** is the legend of William Tell.

Circle the boldfaced word that names a group of things. Draw one line under the boldfaced word that names things that can be seen and touched. Draw two lines under the boldfaced word that names an idea.

A **collective noun** names a group of people or things. In most cases, a collective noun that is singular in form should be treated as a singular noun for verb agreement. A **concrete noun** names something you can see, touch, hear, smell, or taste. An **abstract noun** names an idea.

See Handbook | **Section 15**

Practice

Read each sentence. Circle the boldfaced word that is the type of noun listed in parentheses.

1. William Tell had great **skill** with the **crossbow.** (concrete noun)

2. He was a successful hunter, bringing home to his **cottage** food for his **family** regularly. (collective noun)

3. The **people** of the region in which William Tell lived were then ruled by an Austrian governor who was notorious for his **cruelty.** (abstract noun)

4. This governor levied high taxes on the **population** and threw those who could not pay into **jails.** (collective noun)

5. The governor had a red hat placed atop a **pole** in the village near the home of William Tell; the governor said that the hat was a **symbol** of the king of Austria, who then ruled over Switzerland. (concrete noun)

6. The governor then issued an order that everyone had to bow before the **hat** to demonstrate **fidelity.** (abstract noun)

7. One day William Tell walked into the **town** with his son; neither was aware of the **rule,** and both walked past the hat without bowing. (concrete noun)

8. The **pair** were immediately ordered by an Austrian **guard** to bow before the hat. (collective noun)

9. William Tell refused to perform this gesture of **submission,** so the guard blew a **whistle** and several soldiers responded. (abstract noun)

10. William Tell and his son were forced by the **group** to stand before the cruel **governor.** (collective noun)

11. The governor had heard of William Tell's **prowess** as an archer; he asked William Tell whether he could hit an apple with an **arrow** from a distance of 100 yards. (abstract noun)

12. The wicked **governor** then told William that the apple would be placed on his son's head; if William hit the apple, he and his son would regain their **freedom,** but if William missed, the son would be killed. (concrete noun)

13. Showing not just courage but also masterful skill and perfect **concentration,** William sent the arrow right through the **apple.** (abstract noun)

Name _____

Apply

Read each sentence. Choose the correct present-tense form of the verb in parentheses. Write it in the blank to complete the sentence.

14. In real life, a team of people with different capabilities typically _____**outperforms**_____ a group of people who have similar capabilities. (outperform)

15. In a tale from India retold by Pleasant DeSpain, a group of dissimilar animals _____**demonstrates**_____ the ability to solve a variety of problems. (demonstrate)

16. This band of comrades—a crow, a turtle, and a stag—_____**thwarts**_____ a very determined hunter by using individual talents and collective wisdom. (thwart)

Reinforce

William Tell overcame the cruel challenge he faced by performing well under pressure. Think of a time when you performed well under pressure. Write a paragraph describing that situation and telling what enabled you to succeed in that difficult situation. Use at least one abstract noun, one concrete noun, and one collective noun in your paragraph.

Answers will vary. Accept all reasonable responses.

According to Norse mythology, natural phenomena were the results of the **gods'** actions. Thunder was caused by the banging of **Thor's** hammer. The sound of that **god's** hammer usually indicated he was fighting evil-doers.

Circle the part of each boldfaced word that shows ownership.

A **possessive noun** shows ownership or close relationship. **Singular** nouns add an apostrophe and -s to form the possessive (*giant, giant's*). Most **plural** nouns add an apostrophe after the -s to form the possessive (*giants, giants'*). Plurals that don't end in -s (*children, geese*) add an apostrophe and -s (*children's, geese's*) to show possession.

See Handbook Sections 7, 30

Practice

Underline each singular possessive noun. Circle each plural possessive noun. There may be more than one possessive noun in each sentence.

1. One morning everyone in Asgard was awakened by Thor's mighty shout; someone had stolen the thunder god's hammer!

2. Thor's first thought was that the theft might be one of his friend Loki's mischievous pranks.

3. Loki said he knew nothing about the hammer's disappearance, however.

4. Loki suggested that he himself should borrow the goddess Freyja's magic feather coat and use it to fly to the homeland of the giants, the prime suspects.

5. Loki traveled there and discovered the thief to be Thrym, the frost giants' king.

6. Thrym had taken a fancy to the goddess Freyja and refused to return the hammer without a promise of the goddess's hand in marriage.

7. Loki took the giant's message back to Asgard, but Freyja flatly refused to marry Thrym.

8. Thor and Loki hatched a plan: Thor would wear Freyja's dress and cover his face with a veil.

9. Upon the plotters' arrival to the giants' homeland, a great banquet was prepared.

10. Imagine the king's surprise when his bride-to-be ate a whole ox, eight salmon, and many sweets!

11. The fair damsel's maid told Thrym that her lady had not been able to eat for some time because of her excitement about the wedding.

12. Thrym lifted his beloved's veil to peek at her, but dropped it when he saw her eyes' fiery red color.

13. When the ceremony began, Thor's hammer was fetched so the couple could swear vows upon it.

14. Thor immediately grabbed the weapon's handle and used it to smite his enemy; then he and Loki returned victoriously to Asgard.

Apply

Rewrite each sentence, shortening the underlined section by using a possessive noun.

15. The hammer belonging to the thunder god was made by dwarves. __The thunder god's hammer was made by dwarves.__

16. Loki the troublemaker is the favorite Norse god of many people. __Loki the troublemaker is many people's favorite Norse god.__

17. The homeland of the giants was called Jotunheim. __The giants' homeland was called Jotunheim.__

18. Thor wore the necklace belonging to the goddess. __Thor wore the goddess's necklace.__

19. Loki was the friend of Thor, although he often made Thor angry. __Loki was Thor's friend, although he often made Thor angry.__

Reinforce

Circle six nouns hidden in the puzzle. Write each one in the column where it belongs. Then write the possessive form of each noun.

L	E	G	E	N	D	S
R	Q	I	U	E	W	T
H	W	A	C	Q	A	C
O	T	N	Y	J	R	H
U	P	T	V	G	V	O
S	E	W	O	M	E	N
E	O	Z	K	F	S	Y
Z	G	O	D	S	N	T

Note: Students may also find these nouns within the puzzle answers: *leg, end, omen, god, use, ant, war* (singular); *ends, men* (plural).

Singular Nouns		Possessive Forms
20.	house	house's
21.	giant	giant's
Plural Nouns		**Possessive Forms**
22.	legends	legends'
23.	women	women's
24.	gods	gods'
25.	dwarves	dwarves'

Use one of the possessive forms above in a sentence about Thor or Loki.

26. __Answers will vary.__

_____

_____

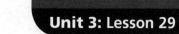

Read and Analyze

(I) enjoy reading Chinese myths.

Circle the word in the sentence above that shows who is speaking.

A **pronoun** can take the place of a noun. **Personal pronouns** can be used to stand for the person speaking, the person spoken to, or the person spoken about. **First person** pronouns refer to the speaker (*I, me*) or include the speaker (*we, us*). **Second person** pronouns refer to the person being spoken to (*you*). **Third person** pronouns refer to the person, place, or thing being spoken about (*he, him, she, her, it, they, them*). ◀◁ **Remember to use this information when you speak, too.**

See Handbook Section 17a

Practice

Circle each personal pronoun. Write *1* if it is a first person pronoun, *2* if it is second person, or *3* if it is third person. Hint: If a sentence has more than one personal pronoun, all are in the same person.

1. Have (you) read any Chinese myths? __2__

2. Dad just gave (me) a book about Chinese gods and goddesses. __1__

3. (I) learned about an important figure in Chinese mythology. __1__

4. (She) was named Nuwa, and (she) was much loved by ancient people. __3__

5. Nuwa was the mother goddess; (she) could change shape and appear in different forms. __3__

6. Myths describe (her) as half-human and half-dragon. __3__

7. Long ago before (we) humans dwelled upon Earth, Nuwa felt very lonely. __1__

8. One day, while walking along the great Yellow River, (she) scooped up some mud and used (it) to form shapes of people. __3__

9. (She) breathed life into (them,) and (they) danced around (her,) giving praise. __3__

10. After (she) had made many figures, (she) took a piece of cane and rolled (it) in the mud and then shook (it) out. __3__

11. Small drops of mud fell off, and (they,) too, turned into men and women. __3__

12. Some myths say that the people (she) formed by hand became aristocrats, or privileged people. __3__

13. (They) say that the people (she) made by shaking the mud off the cane became people who were less fortunate in life. __3__

14. Dad and (I) have asked the librarian to find (us) more books about Chinese myths. __1__

In Chinese mythology, dragons were gods who had special powers.

Apply   Answers will vary.

Write four sentences about a hero of yours, using the types of personal pronouns indicated.

15. first person: _____

_____

16. second person: _____

_____

17. third person singular: _____

_____

18. third person plural: _____

_____

Reinforce

The word *he* once was accepted as a universal pronoun that could refer to anyone, male or female, if a generalization about people was being made.
Example: Myths make a person think about his own cultural beliefs.

Now most writers try to avoid the use of universal *he*. Here are two ways the sentence above might be revised.

Solution #1:

Make the noun and the word
it refers to plural.

Myths make people think about their
own cultural beliefs.

Solution #2:

Replace *his* with *his or her*.

Myths make a person think about his
or her own cultural beliefs.

Try both of these solutions for replacing the universal *he* in these sentences.   **Answers will vary.**

19. Each student chose a myth to write his report about.

The students chose myths to write their reports about.

Each student chose a myth to write his or her report about.

20. The myths a person enjoys depend on his personal taste.

The myths people enjoy depend on their personal taste.

The myths a person enjoys depend on his or her personal taste.

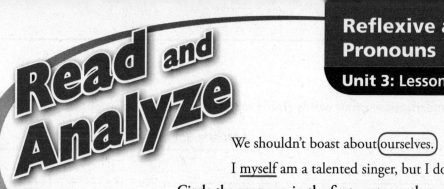

We shouldn't boast about (ourselves.)

I <u>myself</u> am a talented singer, but I don't brag about it.

Circle the pronoun in the first sentence that refers back to the subject. Underline the pronoun in the second sentence that is used for emphasis.

Words such as *myself, herself, itself,* and *themselves* are **compound personal pronouns.** When a compound personal pronoun is used as an object in a sentence and refers back to the subject or another noun, that pronoun is called a **reflexive pronoun.** When a compound personal pronoun is used to emphasize the identity of the sentence subject or another noun, it is called an **intensive pronoun.**

See Handbook Sections 17c, 17e

Practice

Read the sentences below. Underline each compound personal pronoun that is used as a reflexive pronoun. Circle each compound personal pronoun that is used as an intensive pronoun.

1. If you lived in ancient Greece, you would know better than to think <u>yourself</u> superior to a god or goddess.

2. A young weaver named Arachne, however, was as foolish as she was talented; she openly declared that the goddess Athena could not weave as well as she (herself) could.

3. Athena, upon hearing Arachne's words, pulled <u>herself</u> away from important business on Mount Olympus and came to Earth to punish Arachne.

4. Athena offered the girl a chance to prove <u>herself</u> and survive—the two would have a weaving contest.

5. On the fateful day, people came from all over the land to squeeze <u>themselves</u> into the meadow near Arachne's home.

6. Zeus (himself) did not deign to attend the match, but he undoubtedly watched it from above.

7. Arachne was sitting at her loom in front of her cottage when Athena appeared through the clouds and seated <u>herself</u> high on a nearby hilltop.

8. Arachne was the first to weave her tapestry, and so swiftly and deftly did her fingers move that they (themselves) seemed to be part of the loom.

9. The crowd made (itself) heard as it applauded the beauty of Arachne's work.

10. When Athena began weaving, the web in which Arachne had trapped <u>herself</u> became all too clear.

11. Athena's tapestry was breathtaking: The goddess used the sky (itself) to color her threads.

12. That tapestry foretold how we mortals would destroy <u>ourselves</u> through our pride and willfulness.

13. When Athena finished, the people threw <u>themselves</u> to the ground in a demonstration of respect, and Arachne knew she had lost.

14. Rather than end Arachne's life, Athena turned her into a spider that could spin webs for <u>itself.</u>

Apply

Rewrite each sentence, replacing the underlined word or words with a reflexive or intensive pronoun.

15. Arachne got <u>Arachne</u> into trouble by boasting about her weaving. **Arachne got herself into trouble by boasting about her weaving.**

16. Do you sometimes boast about <u>you</u>? **Do you sometimes boast about yourself?**

17. The gods considered <u>the gods</u> to be far superior to mortals. **The gods considered themselves to be far superior to mortals.**

18. Zeus—yes, <u>Zeus</u>—was prideful about his own mighty powers. **Zeus himself was prideful about his own mighty powers.**

Zeus is the king of
the Greek gods.

Reinforce

Imagine that you yourself did something to offend Athena. Write a paragraph telling how you got yourself into and out of trouble. Include at least two reflexive pronouns and one intensive pronoun in your paragraph.

Answers will vary.

_____

_____

_____

_____

_____

_____

_____

_____

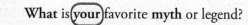

Read and Analyze

What is **your** favorite **myth** or legend?
Circle the boldfaced word that shows ownership or indicates a relationship.

Possessive pronouns show ownership or close relationship. The possessive pronouns *her, his, its, their, my, our,* and *your* can replace possessive nouns. (*The queen's* dress is blue.—*Her* dress is blue.) The possessive pronouns *hers, his, theirs, mine, ours,* and *yours* can replace both a possessive noun and the noun that is a possession. (The blue dress is *the queen's*—The blue dress is *hers*.)

See Handbook Section 17d

Practice

Circle the possessive pronouns. There may be more than one in each sentence.

1. King Midas lived with **his** young daughter in a palace in Greece; **theirs** was a peaceful, happy life.

2. One morning King Midas was walking in **his** garden when he stumbled upon a strange creature—**its** top half was like that of a man, but **its** bottom half looked like that of a goat.

3. King Midas thought the creature might be ill, so he sent it to **his** court physician.

4. Shortly thereafter, the god Dionysus appeared and told King Midas he would grant him one wish for helping **his** friend, a satyr by the name of Silenus.

5. Midas murmured, "Anything I want can be **mine**!"

6. The king thought to himself, "After **my** daughter, the thing I love best is gold," and it was thus that he wished that all he touched would turn to gold.

7. "**Your** wish is a bit rash," Dionysus exclaimed, "but I will honor it all the same."

8. The king ran to touch several fig trees in **his** garden, and each one turned to gold!

9. Laughing with glee, the king ordered a great feast to be prepared in celebration, and soon **his** servants entered the dining hall, **their** arms laden with huge platters of delicious food.

10. King Midas lifted a fig from a tray, but as soon as he touched it, **its** skin turned to gold!

11. The king also discovered that water turned to solid gold as it touched **his** lips.

12. Then **his** daughter ran inside and, before he could stop her, she hugged him and turned to gold.

13. Weeping inconsolably, Midas cried out that he wished **his** terrible curse could be washed away.

14. At that moment, Dionysus reappeared and told Midas he would grant **his** second wish if Midas washed himself in the river Pactolus.

15. Let this story be a lesson to all of us: **our** loved ones are worth far more than gold!

Apply

Rewrite each sentence, replacing each group of underlined words with a possessive pronoun.

16. The legend's moral is "Be careful what you wish for." **Its moral is "Be careful what you wish for."**

_____

17. King Midas's flaw was that he was too greedy. **His flaw was that he was too greedy.**

_____

18. The gods' lessons were sometimes painful ones. **Their lessons were sometimes painful ones.**

_____

19. My book is over here, and the one belonging to you is over there. **My book is over here, and yours is**

over there.

Reinforce

Use what you know about possessive pronouns to complete the puzzle.

Across

1. I wrote _____ own myth!
4. We turned in _____ homework.
5. A peaceful life was _____.
6. The dress is _____.
8. The dog licked _____ paw.

Down

2. Which myth is _____ favorite?
3. They walked in _____ garden.
6. Midas loved _____ young daughter.
7. That gold is _____, not yours!

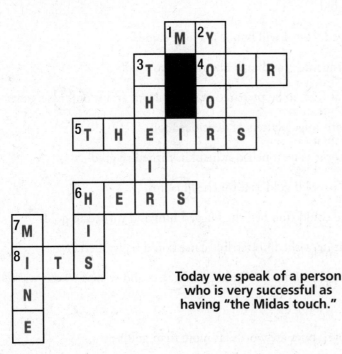

Today we speak of a person who is very successful as having "the Midas touch."

Read and Analyze

Does (anyone) know all the facts behind this American legend?

Circle the pronoun that refers to an unspecified person.

Indefinite pronouns refer to persons or things that are not identified. Indefinite pronouns include *all, anybody, both, either, anything, nothing, everyone, few, most, one, no one, several, nobody, someone,* and *something.*

See Handbook | **Section 17f**

Practice

Circle the indefinite pronouns in these sentences. There may be more than one in each sentence.

1. Have (all) of you heard of Johnny Appleseed?

2. (Most) have heard the name, but (few) if (any) know the real story behind the legend.

3. (Everybody) believes that Johnny Appleseed was a scatterer of seeds, but he was actually a nurseryman.

4. A nurseryman is (someone) who plants seeds, tends plants, and provides young plants to (others.)

5. Does (anybody) know Johnny Appleseed's real name?

6. His name was John Chapman, and almost (nothing) is known about his early life.

7. Practically (everything) written about him is based on guesswork.

8. (Something) we do know, however, is that he was born in Leominster, Massachusetts, on September 26, 1774.

9. We also know that John Chapman had two passions—planting apple trees and being a missionary—and he pursued (both.)

10. (Something) else we know is that for almost 50 years, John Chapman traveled through Ohio, Indiana, and Pennsylvania preaching and establishing apple orchards.

11. Chapman was not the only nurseryman to plant trees and sell them to settlers, but he is the only (one) who achieved legendary stature.

12. (Someone) who always walks barefoot, even in the snow, wears a tin pan as a hat, and makes a sack into a shirt makes a colorful figure for a legend.

13. (Some) claim that he always slept out in his apple nurseries, confident in the belief that (nothing) could harm him as long as he lived in harmony with nature.

14. Because there is such limited information on Chapman's life, (everyone) is free to paint his or her own picture of this colorful American legend.

Johnny Appleseed planted thousands of trees in Ohio, Indiana, and Pennsylvania.

Apply Possible answers appear below. Accept all reasonable responses.

Complete each sentence by writing an indefinite pronoun.

15. Can _____**anyone**_____ tell me anything about Johnny Appleseed?

16. We know some facts about his adult life but _____**few**_____ about his early childhood.

17. Don't believe _____**everything**_____ you hear about him!

18. I'll tell you _____**something**_____ I learned about him, if you promise not to tell anyone else.

19. It's likely that _____**no one**_____ will ever know the entire truth behind the legend.

Reinforce

Circle the indefinite pronoun in each sentence. Then write each letter of the pronoun on the lines provided.

20. There are many stories about Johnny Appleseed, but (few) are true!

    F   E   W
    —   —   —
    1   5

21. According to legend, (everyone) who met Johnny Appleseed liked him.

    E   V   E   R   Y   O   N   E
    —   —   —   —   —   —   —   —
            3   2   9

22. Often Johnny Appleseed would give settlers trees without charging (anything).

    A   N   Y   T   H   I   N   G
    —   —   —   —   —   —   —   —
    6   4

23. (Many) say that Johnny Appleseed never hunted animals or ate meat.

    M   A   N   Y
    —   —   —   —
            8   7

Use the numbered letters to answer this question:

Where is John Chapman buried?

    F   O   R   T   W   A   Y   N   E
    —   —   —   —   —   —   —   —   — , Indiana
    1   2   3   4   5   6   7   8   9

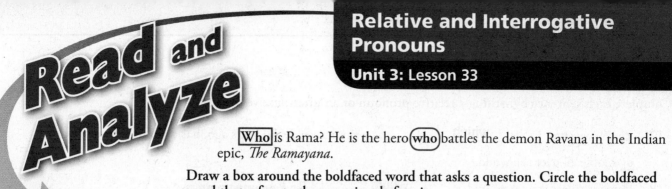

Who is Rama? He is the hero who battles the demon Ravana in the Indian epic, *The Ramayana*.

Draw a box around the boldfaced word that asks a question. Circle the boldfaced word that refers to the noun just before it.

When the pronouns *who, whom, whose, which,* and *that* are used to introduce an adjective clause, they are called **relative pronouns**. A relative pronoun always follows the noun described by the adjective clause it begins. When the pronouns *who, whom, whose, which,* and *what* are used to begin a question, they are called **interrogative pronouns**.

See Handbook Sections 17g, 17h

Practice

Circle each relative pronoun. Underline the noun the adjective clause is describing. Draw a box around each interrogative pronoun.

1. Who knows the story of *The Ramayana*?

2. Rama is the earthly form that the god Vishnu took in order to slay the demon Ravana.

3. Ravana kidnapped Rama's wife Sita and took her away to his home in Lanka, which was across

    a vast ocean.

4. Rama sent an army of monkeys, which was led by Hanuman, to go in search of Sita.

5. The army couldn't cross the ocean, but Hanuman, whose father was the wind god Pavana, could fly.

6. When Hanuman found Sita, she gave him a jewel that would assure Rama she was still alive.

7. Ravana's men captured Hanuman and set his tail on fire, but Hanuman had a blessing that protected him.

8. What did that clever monkey do next?

9. He leapt from roof to roof using his tail, which was still aflame, to set fire to the city of Lanka.

10. When Hanuman returned to Rama, Rama demanded to build a bridge that would reach Lanka.

11. The bridge, which was built in five days, allowed Rama and his army to cross into Lanka.

12. Ravana's army was led by his son, Indrajit, who had the power to make himself invisible.

13. Indrajit was about to perform a ceremony that would give him the power to kill Rama.

14. Rama's brother attacked and killed him, an act that brought Ravana to the battlefield.

15. Ravana and Rama fought intensely until Rama hurled a powerful weapon that he'd been given.

16. Ravana was vanquished, and Rama flew with Sita back to Ayodhya, whose people made Rama king.

Name _____

Apply

Complete each sentence by writing a relative pronoun or an interrogative pronoun.

17. *The Ramayana,* _____ **which** _____ was written over 2,000 years ago, has been read by millions
    of people all over the world.

18. Rama is the character around _____ **whom** _____ *The Ramayana* centers.

19. _____ **What** _____ is the main conflict in the story?

20. The main conflict _____ **that** _____ drives the story is the kidnapping of Rama's wife, Sita.

21. Ravana is the villain _____ **who** _____ kidnaps her.

22. _____ **Who** _____ is Hanuman?

23. He is the son of Pavana, the god
    _____ **who** _____ controls the winds.

24. He's also the one _____ **whose** _____
    ability to fly helps save Sita.

**Temples to honor Hanuman
have been built in India
and Japan.**

Reinforce

Circle the pronoun that is used incorrectly in each sentence. Then rewrite each sentence with the appropriate relative pronoun.

25. My favorite part of *The Ramayana* is the part (what) tells how Hanuman sets fire to Lanka.

    My favorite part of <u>The Ramayana</u> is the part that tells how Hanuman sets fire to Lanka.

    _____

26. Rama's battle with Ravana, (that) happens at the end of the story, is also very exciting.

    Rama's battle with Ravana, which happens at the end of the story, is also very exciting.

    _____

27. People (that) enjoy *The Ramayana* may also enjoy reading Chinese or Aztec myths.

    People who enjoy <u>The Ramayana</u> may also enjoy reading Chinese or Aztec myths.

    _____

Hercules was a noble and mighty warrior.

He labored diligently and fought valiantly.

Circle the two words in the first sentence that tell what kind of warrior Hercules was. Draw a box around the short word that precedes these descriptive words. Underline the two words in the second sentence that tell how Hercules labored and fought.

Adjectives modify nouns, pronouns, and other adjectives. Some adjectives tell what kind. Others tell how many or which one. The articles *a, an,* and *the* are also adjectives. **Adverbs** modify verbs, adjectives, and other adverbs. They tell how, when, where, or to what extent (how much). Many adverbs end in *-ly.* Other common adverbs are *first, very,* and *often.*

See Handbook | Sections 16, 19

Practice

Circle each adjective and draw an arrow to the word it modifies. Draw a box around each adverb and draw an arrow to the word or words it modifies.

1. Hercules submissively presented himself to the king of Mycenae.

2. The wily king assigned Hercules a series of seemingly impossible tasks.

3. One of these labors began when a messenger suddenly entered the royal palace.

4. He breathlessly reported that a huge snake was terrorizing the countryside.

5. The snake was called the Lernaean Hydra; it had nine heads, and one head was immortal.

6. The king sent Hercules to search for this monster, and Hercules departed with his young nephew Iolaus.

7. In a dense forest Hercules found the dark cave where the Hydra lived.

8. He fired three arrows into the cave, and the malevolent Hydra emerged.

9. Its nine heads angrily bobbed and hissed; Hercules obliterated one head, but two heads immediately grew in its place!

10. Hercules desperately turned to Iolaus and gave him instructions.

11. Iolaus ignited a long branch and quickly ran to his uncle's side.

12. Hercules demolished head after head; Iolaus placed the red-hot branch on each open wound, searing it so no new heads could grow.

13. Hercules buried the immortal head under a huge rock to prevent it from causing more harm.

14. Hercules's reappearance surprised and angered the king; he had firmly believed he was sending Hercules on a fatal mission.

One of the Hydra's nine heads was immortal.

Apply

Expand each sentence below by adding one adjective and one adverb. You can use words from the word bank, or use your own words. **Sample responses are shown below. Accept all reasonable responses.**

likely	continually	only	certainly
fierce	dangerous	valiant	hideous

15. The Lernaean Hydra terrorized residents. **The hideous Lernaean Hydra continually terrorized residents.**

    _____

16. This monster seemed invincible. **This fierce monster certainly seemed invincible.**

    _____

17. Without the help of his nephew, Hercules would have lost his battle with the Hydra. **Without the help of his valiant nephew, Hercules would likely have lost his battle with the Hydra.**

18. This task was one of twelve that the king assigned to Hercules. **This dangerous task was only one of twelve that the king assigned to Hercules.**

Reinforce

A noun can also be used to describe another noun.

mountain road	*computer* class	*school* principal

Circle four adjectives and four nouns in the puzzle. Then use the four nouns you circled as noun modifiers in your own sentences. **Sentences will vary. Accept all reasonable responses. Note: Students may also find these words within the puzzle answers:** *victor, lass, danger, mortal, story, amp* **(nouns);** *mortal* **(adjective).**

V	K	B	N	I	G	D	Z	S	A
I	M	M	O	R	T	A	L	H	P
C	S	D	B	U	J	N	V	E	P
T	C	Q	L	R	Z	G	F	C	L
O	L	U	E	V	V	E	B	N	E
R	A	X	J	U	Y	R	L	S	H
I	S	H	I	S	T	O	R	Y	X
O	S	Y	N	W	I	U	G	Y	W
U	Z	K	P	A	B	S	W	X	K
S	W	A	M	P	E	U	K	E	D

19. _____

    _____

20. _____

    _____

21. _____

    _____

22. _____

    _____

(This) picture shows Popocatépetl and Iztaccíhuatl.

<u>Those</u> are two of the tallest mountains in Mexico.

Circle the word that modifies the noun *picture* and tells *which one*. Underline the word that stands for the noun *mountains*.

This, these, that, and *those* are **demonstratives**. **Demonstrative adjectives** describe nouns and tell which one. **Demonstrative pronouns** take the place of nouns. *This* and *these* refer to a thing or things close by. *That* and *those* refer to a thing or things farther away. ◀📢 **Remember to use this information when you speak, too.**

See Handbook Sections 16, 17i

Practice

Underline each demonstrative pronoun. Circle each demonstrative adjective. Draw an arrow from each demonstrative adjective to the noun or pronoun it modifies.

1. (Those) two mountains in the picture are both volcanoes.

2. (This) smaller one nearby is Popocatépetl, and (that) larger one in the distance is Iztaccíhuatl.

3. A legend explains how both of <u>these</u> were formed.

4. (This) legend features a great Aztec warrior by the name of Popocatépetl.

5. (This) young warrior fell in love with an Aztec princess by the name of Iztaccíhuatl, but soon after, he learned he had to leave for battle.

6. <u>That</u> was sad news indeed, but before leaving, our hero received permission to marry the princess upon his return from war.

7. Many men had sought the princess's affections, and one of <u>these</u> was quite jealous of Popocatépetl for winning the right to wed the princess.

8. (That) cunning suitor approached the princess and told her Popocatépetl had been killed in battle.

9. The princess, saddened by (this) report, died from grief!

10. When Popocatépetl returned and learned <u>this</u>, he ordered a great tomb be built for her.

11. Legend has it, in (those) days, it was much easier to move land than it is today, so ten hills were brought together to form one great mountain.

12. No sooner had Popocatépetl laid the dead princess on the top of (that) mountain, than the mountain took on the shape of a sleeping woman.

13. As (this) warrior kneeled before his princess, snow began falling and soon covered both of them.

14. Popocatépetl and Iztaccíhuatl were transformed into (those) two volcanoes that we see today.

Name _____

Apply Possible answers appear below. Accept all reasonable responses.

Rewrite each sentence, replacing the underlined words with a demonstrative pronoun or with a demonstrative adjective and any other words needed. Answers may vary.

15. <u>The drawing I'm pointing to</u> shows Popocatépetl. **This drawing shows Popocatépetl.** _____

_____

16. <u>The mountains shown in the photograph</u> are in Mexico. **Those mountains are in Mexico.** _____

_____

17. <u>The smoke rising from the volcano</u> is called the plume. **This is called the plume.** _____

_____

18. <u>The type of volcano shown in the picture</u> is a cone volcano. **This is a cone volcano.** _____

_____

Reinforce

Circle the demonstrative pronoun in each of the following quotations.

I also grew up, thankfully, with a love of language. (That) may have happened because I was bilingual at an early age.
  —Amy Tan, interview with the Academy of Achievement

I am not one of (those) who in expressing opinions confine themselves to facts.
  —Mark Twain, "Wearing White Clothes" speech

Whose woods (these) are I think I know.
  —Robert Frost, "Stopping by Woods on a Snowy Evening"

Now explain what the demonstrative pronoun refers to in each quotation above.

19. ___*That* refers to growing up with a love of language._____

_____

20. ___*Those* refers to people who confine themselves to facts when expressing opinions._____

_____

21. ___*These* refers to the woods._____

a. Trieu Thi Trinh was a **female brave** warrior said to have lived in the third century.

b. Trieu Thi Trinh was a **brave female** warrior said to have lived in the third century.

c. Her **extraordinary, inspirational** leadership in Vietnam's effort to resist invaders from China has earned her **widespread, long-lasting** admiration.

Read sentences *a* and *b*. Which sentence has the boldfaced adjectives in an order that sounds natural? _____**b**_____ **Read sentence *c*. What punctuation mark is used to separate each pair of boldfaced adjectives?** _____**comma**_____

When you use more than one adjective to describe a noun, put the adjectives in an **order that sounds natural.** When you use **coordinate adjectives**—a pair of adjectives of a similar kind—to describe a noun, place a comma between the adjectives.

See Handbook Sections 8, 16

Practice

Underline the adjectives in parentheses that are written correctly.

1. According to legend, Trieu Thi Trinh stood nine feet tall and had a (<u>loud, clear</u>/loud clear) voice.

2. Some tales say that she rode into battle on an elephant; others claim that she fought atop (<u>an enormous gray</u>/a gray enormous) hippopotamus.

3. Her (older protective/<u>protective older</u>) brother tried to dissuade her from becoming a warrior.

4. She told him she had no intention of being a (submissive typical/<u>typical submissive</u>) female.

5. "I wish to ride the tempest, tame the waves, kill the sharks," she said, and she led her troops to (<u>thirty consecutive</u>/consecutive thirty) victories over the invaders.

6. Legends say that she wore (gold bright/<u>bright gold</u>) armor and carried a sword in each hand.

7. Her opponents feared her (<u>fierce, penetrating</u>/fierce penetrating) gaze; they said, "It would be easier to fight a tiger than to face Lady Trieu in battle."

8. Eventually the invaders sent in such a (well-armored huge/<u>huge well-armored</u>) fighting force that Trieu Thi Trinh could not prevail.

9. Although Lady Trieu perished in that battle, she lives on in (<u>numerous thrilling</u>/thrilling numerous) tales.

10. Most researchers believe that the legends of Trieu Thi Trinh are based on the exploits of a (female real/<u>real female</u>) warrior who led Vietnamese soldiers to victory nineteen centuries ago.

Trieu Thi Trinh is celebrated as a noble hero by the Vietnamese people.

Apply

Expand each sentence below by writing two adjectives on the line. Use an appropriate article in front of the adjectives, if one is needed. Be sure to use the adjectives in a natural-sounding order. If the two adjectives are of a similar kind, use a comma to separate them. **Sample answers are shown. Accept all reasonable responses.**

11. An army led by _____ **a smart brave** _____ individual has the best chance of success.

12. Even _____ **a large, well-equipped** _____ army can be defeated by a clever leader and a disciplined

   group of fighters.

13. Many cultures tell _____ **exciting, inspiring** _____ stories about female warriors.

14. Today _____ **many dedicated** _____ female soldiers help protect their nations as members of

   military units.

15. Perhaps the _____ **remarkable military** _____ accomplishments of some of these women will

   inspire legends that will be told and retold in future centuries.

Reinforce

Which of the legendary characters described in this unit do you think is most inspiring? Write a paragraph in which you describe this individual's traits, talents, and accomplishments, and explain why you admire him or her. Use a pair of adjectives with one of the nouns you include.

Answers will vary. Accept all reasonable responses.

_____

_____

_____

_____

_____

_____

_____

_____

_____

_____

(Numbers in parentheses identify related lessons.)

Nouns

Circle each singular noun. Underline each plural noun.

1. My (aunt) just gave me a (book) of myths and legends. **(25)**

2. It includes many stories of superhuman men and women. **(25)**

Circle the common nouns in the sentences below. Underline the proper nouns.

3. The Vikings told (stories) about a (place) called Valhalla. **(26)**

4. According to (legend), that's where (men) who died bravely in (battle) were taken. **(26)**

Write the correct possessive form for each noun in parentheses.

5. Our class wrote reports on the (world) great myths. _____**world's**_____ **(28)**

6. (Students) reports covered a wide variety of cultures. _____**Students'**_____ **(28)**

7. My (paper) focus was on Japanese myths. _____**paper's**_____ **(28)**

Read each sentence. Circle the boldfaced word that is the type of noun listed in parentheses.

8. Josh Gibson was a real **person** who played for the baseball (team) known as the Homestead Grays. (collective noun) **(27)**

9. His actual **accomplishments** were remarkable, but the legendary feats attributed to him would fill a (book.) (concrete noun) **(27)**

10. One legend says that Gibson hit a **baseball** so high and far one day in Pittsburgh that it did not come down until the next day; its return to earth caused quite a (sensation.) (abstract noun) **(27)**

Pronouns

Circle each personal pronoun. Write *1* if it is a first person pronoun, *2* if it is a second person pronoun, or *3* if it is a third person pronoun.

11. (We) tell myths about how the places in this town came to be. ___**1**___ **(29)**

12. That makes this town seem more interesting than (it) really is. ___**3**___ **(29)**

13. (You) should try making up a myth or legend! ___**2**___ **(29)**

Circle each reflexive pronoun. Draw a box around each intensive pronoun.

14. Adam made (himself) a costume for the play. **(30)**

15. He is playing the role of Theseus; I [myself] am playing Ariadne. **(30)**

16. We must keep (ourselves) calm and focused. **(30)**

17. The play [itself] is not difficult to perform. **(30)**

Pronouns, continued

Circle the phrase that tells what kind of pronoun the boldfaced word is.

18.　Which report is **yours**? (31)

　　　indefinite pronoun　　　　interrogative pronoun　　　(possessive pronoun)

19.　It's the one **that** tells about ancient Greece. (33)

　　　(relative pronoun)　　　　indefinite pronoun　　　　interrogative pronoun

20.　**What** did Alice write her report about? (33)

　　　possessive pronoun　　　(interrogative pronoun)　　　indefinite pronoun

21.　I think she wrote **hers** about Egyptian myths. (31)

　　　indefinite pronoun　　　　interrogative pronoun　　　(possessive pronoun)

22.　Did **anyone** write a report on myths of the Inca? (32)

　　　possessive pronoun　　　(indefinite pronoun)　　　interrogative pronoun

23.　I think Frank is the only student **whose** paper focused on the Inca. (33)

　　　possessive pronoun　　　　interrogative pronoun　　　(relative pronoun)

Adjectives, Adverbs, and Pronouns

Circle each adjective. Draw a box around each adverb.

24.　Johnny Appleseed is a (legendary) character. (34)

25.　People tell ⬜truly (outlandish) stories about him. (34)

26.　Did he ⬜really wear a (battered) pan on his head? (34)

27.　A (real) person, Jonathan Chapman, ⬜apparently was (the) basis for (the) (fabled) wanderer. (34)

Circle each demonstrative pronoun. Underline each demonstrative adjective.

28.　<u>That</u> movie we saw about ancient China was fantastic. (35)

29.　It's got <u>these</u> really amazing special effects. (35)

30.　Do you want to see it again <u>this</u> week? (35)

31.　(That) sounds like a great plan! (35)

Underline the adjectives in parentheses that are written correctly.

32.　One of the (<u>oldest legendary</u>/legendary oldest) characters is the female warrior Queen Semiramis. (36)

33.　She is said to have lived in the ancient city of Babylon almost thirty centuries ago; legends portray her as a

　　　(<u>clever, ruthless</u>/clever ruthless) individual. (36)

Spelling Practice

Read and Analyze

a. Myths offer explanations for things in the **universe**.

b. They have a **dual** purpose of amusing and teaching.

Which sentence contains a word with a prefix meaning "two"? **b**

Which sentence contains a word with a prefix meaning "one"? **a**

> ### Prefixes: *uni-, mono-, duo-, bi-*
> Prefixes are word parts added to the beginnings of words to change their meanings. Some prefixes indicate numbers. The prefixes **uni-** and **mono-** mean "one," as in *unicycle* and *monorail*. The prefix **duo-** means "two," as in *duet,* and the prefix **bi-** means "two" or "twice," as in *bisect*.

Word Sort

Use the words below to complete the word sort. **Answers may be in any order.**

duplication	universe	uniform	biplane	dual	monocle
monopoly	binoculars	monotony	university	biennial	duplex

Prefix *uni-*	**Prefix *mono-***
uniform	monopoly
university	monotony
universe	monocle

Prefix *duo-*	**Prefix *bi-***
dual	binoculars
duplication	biennial
duplex	biplane

Pattern Practice

monotonous	bisect	unique	monotone	bimonthly	unify
monocle	biannual	unison	duplex	duo	monorail

Write the word from the word bank above that solves each riddle.

1. I'm one-of-a-kind. What am I? _____**unique**_____

2. I come around every two months. What am I? _____**bimonthly**_____

3. I'm a group of two. What am I? _____**duo**_____

4. I'm many voices sounding as one. What am I? _____**unison**_____

5. I'll cut something in two. What am I? _____**bisect**_____

6. I'm a single lens for seeing. What am I? _____**monocle**_____

7. I'm two connected apartments. What am I? _____**duplex**_____

8. I'm one thing over and over. What am I? _____**monotonous**_____

Write the word from the word bank above that best completes each sentence.

9. The class recited the pledge in perfect _____**unison**_____.

10. The shelter has a _____**biannual**_____ fundraiser in March and October.

11. The poor presenter spoke in a quiet _____**monotone**_____.

12. _____**Bisect**_____ the blueberry muffin and give me half.

13. We rode a _____**monorail**_____ to the next airport terminal.

14. This agreement is meant to _____**unify**_____ the two countries.

Use the Dictionary

Circle the prefix that best completes each word. Use a print or an online dictionary to check your work.

15. I have the opening (mono)/duologue in the play!

16. Shaun flexed his uni/(bi)ceps as he lifted the weights.

Diagramming Understood *You*

Imperative sentences (commands) usually contain the understood *you* as the subject. When the subject is understood, write (*you*) in the sentence diagram, like this:

Close the door.

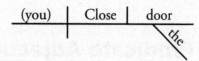

Try diagramming these sentences.

1. Read this book.

2. Do your homework.

3. Come to the party!

Diagramming Possessive Pronouns

Look at the way the possessive pronouns *my* and *their* are diagrammed in these sentences.

My aunt coaches soccer.

We fed **their** dog.

Now diagram these sentences.

4. They joined my class.

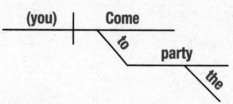

5. His story and her drawings won awards.

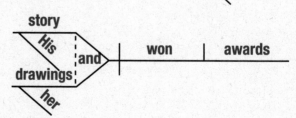

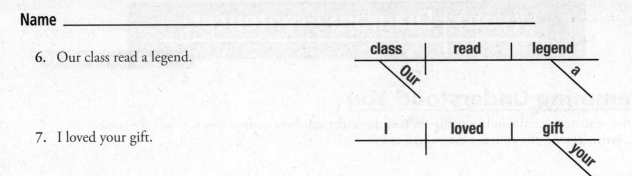

6. Our class read a legend.

7. I loved your gift.

Diagramming Predicate Adjectives and Predicate Nouns

A linking verb, such as *be,* can link the subject of a sentence to an adjective or noun in the predicate. Look at the way *noble* and *a warrior* are diagrammed in these examples:

Predicate adjective:
Hercules was **noble**.

Predicate noun:
Hercules was a **warrior**.

Try diagramming these sentences.

8. Midas was a king.

9. Midas was unwise.

10. Arachne was skillful but boastful.

11. Arachne became a spider.

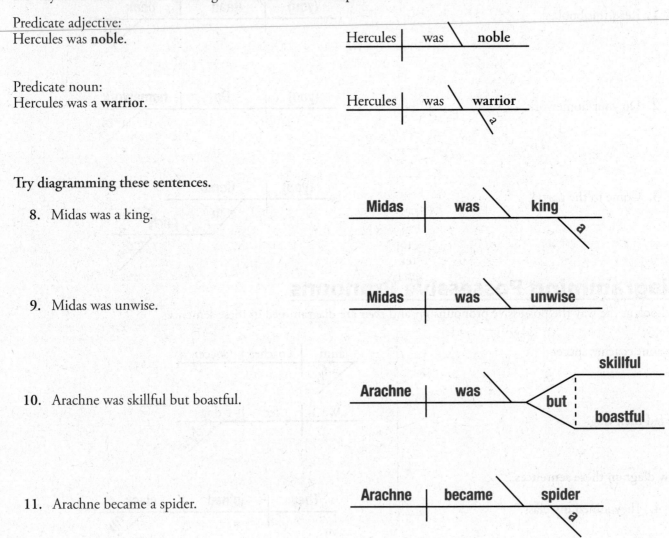

Writing Sentences

Possible answers appear below. Accept all reasonable responses.

These sentences need help! Rewrite them so they give more information about Johnny Appleseed. Refer to Lesson 32 if you need to.

1. Everyone loves the legend. **Everyone loves the legend about Johnny Appleseed, who went around planting apple trees in the early 1800s.**

2. John Chapman was a real-life nurseryman. **John Chapman was the real-life nurseryman who became immortalized in the Johnny Appleseed legend.**

3. He bought up land and planted trees. **He bought up tracts of land, on which he planted thousands of apple trees.**

4. Some stories were quite outlandish. **Some stories that people made up about Johnny Appleseed were quite outlandish.**

5. Most mention his clothes. **Most mention that he wore a tin-pan hat, a shirt made out of a sack, and no shoes.**

When you write a paragraph, always include a topic sentence, two or more supporting sentences that add details about your topic, and a concluding sentence. Your reader will enjoy your paragraph more if you include colorful adjectives and use pronouns and possessives appropriately. Notice how this model paragraph is written.

topic sentence

supporting sentences

colorful adjectives

pronouns and possessives

concluding sentence

My favorite *myth is "Theseus and the Minotaur."* The Minotaur was a **half-bull, half-human** creature *that* lived in a labyrinth. **Fourteen young** men and women were to be given to the Minotaur as a sacrifice. Theseus offered to be *one* of the victims. The princess Ariadne, *who* was in love with Theseus, told *him* to unwind a ball of thread behind *him* as *he* entered the maze. *Everything* worked out as planned. Theseus killed the **savage** Minotaur and found *his* way back out of the maze. *This myth has it all—monsters, drama, and adventure!*

Writing a Paragraph

The sentences you revised on page 111 can be used to write a paragraph. Decide what order the sentences should be in. Write the paragraph on the lines below. Add other words and a concluding sentence, if necessary.

Answers will vary, including the choice of topic sentence.

_____

_____

_____

_____

_____

_____

Write a paragraph about your favorite myth or legend. You might write about one you studied in Unit 3 or about another one you know. Refer to the model paragraph on page 111 if you need help. Be sure to include a variety of interesting adjectives. Use pronouns and possessives when appropriate.

Answers will vary.

_____

_____

_____

_____

_____

_____

_____

Read your paragraph again. Use this checklist to make sure it is complete and correct.

❑ My paragraph has a topic sentence.

❑ My paragraph has at least two
   supporting sentences.

❑ All my sentences are clear and make sense.

❑ I have included colorful adjectives.

❑ I have used pronouns and possessives
   correctly.

❑ My paragraph has a concluding sentence.

Proofreading
Practice

Read this passage about the legendary John Henry and find the mistakes. Use the proofreading marks to show how the mistakes should be fixed. Use a dictionary to check and correct spellings. **Suggested answers appear below. Accept all reasonable responses.**

Proofreading Marks

Mark	Means	Example
❨	delete	John Henry is an ~~old~~ American legend.
∧	add	John Henry is ^an American legend.
≡	make into an uppercase letter	John Henry is an ̲american legend.
/	make into a lowercase letter	John Henry is an American /Legend.
⊙	add a period	John Henry is an American legend⊙
ⓢⓟ	fix spelling	John Henry is an American leg̃und.

The Mighty John Henry

John henry worked on a Chesapeake and Ohio Railroad crew. The crew was divided into teams of four,

and it was each team's job to drive the long iron spikes that connected the rails to the wooden ties. Standing in a

circle, the men would take turns swinging there long-handled hammers until each spike was sunk in place.

Once, the crew was working in the Mountains of west virginia. they had to blast dynamite to carve a

tunel through the mountain. The railroad boss, whose thought the work was going too slowly, brought in a
                                                                              that
speical machine what could drive spikes as it rode along the rails. The men became worried that they would lose
                                         s
their jobs if those machine could do faster work. Than they could.
                    his
John Henry picked up hammer and began racing against the machine. people say he swung his hammer

so hard that sparks shot out as it hit each iron spike. John Henry won the contest; he laid himself fourteen feet of

track and the machine only laid nine. However, John Henry's heart burst from the strain and he died on the spot,
                                                                                      that
hammer in hand. The mens buried him their, and to this day when the trains pass through this tunnel, they blow

their whistles soft and low in solem tribute to the mighty john Henry.

Proofreading
Checklist

You can use the checklist below to help you find and fix mistakes in your own writing. Write the titles of your own stories or reports in the blanks at the top of the chart. Then use the questions to check your work. Make a check mark (✓) in each box after you have checked that item. **Answers will vary.**

Titles

Proofreading Checklist for Unit 3

Have I capitalized proper nouns?				
Have I written plural forms of nouns correctly?				
Have I written possessive forms of nouns correctly?				
Have I used correct forms of personal pronouns?				
Have I used possessive pronouns correctly?				
Have I used appropriate relative pronouns?				

Also Remember…

Does each sentence begin with an uppercase letter?				
Did I use a dictionary to check and correct spellings?				
Have I used commas correctly?				

Your Own List

Use this space to write your own list of things to check in your writing.

Community Connection

In Unit 3 of *Grammar, Usage, and Mechanics,* students learned about different kinds of **nouns, pronouns, and adjectives,** and used what they learned to improve their own writing. The content of these lessons focuses on the theme **Myths and Legends.** As students completed the exercises, they learned about myths and legends from many cultures. These pages offer a variety of activities that reinforce skills and concepts presented in the unit. They also provide opportunities for the student to make connections between the information presented in the lessons and their modern surroundings.

Name That Mythological Character

Greek and Roman myths have been a part of our culture for so long that many words have been derived from mythological characters' names. For example, Arachne's name gave rise to the scientific word for spider: *arachnid.* Collect a list of words and expressions that are derived from Greek and Roman myths; then ask a classmate to guess which mythological character each came from.

Brand New Traditional Tales

Since many myths have no one official version, people are free to reuse plots, themes, and characters, and to retell the myths in new ways. Look for elements of a Greek or Roman myth in modern media. You may consider comic books, movies, television, and recent books and novels. Share your results with the class.

Discovering More Myths and Legends

Choose a region other than Greece or Italy, such as North America, China, India, Peru, West Africa, Mexico, Scandinavia, or the Caribbean. Search for myths and legends from that region. Print out or copy some stories that you particularly like. Arrange to visit a hospital, senior home, or elementary school to read the myths or legends aloud. Alternatively, you can take part in your local library's read-aloud program.

Release Your Inner Mythologist

Try writing a myth or legend in the style of an established mythological tradition. To get yourself started, choose a character from a myth you have read, and imagine a new adventure. To give your myth an interesting plot, you may want to include a problem or moral dilemma that the main character solves at the end. When you have finished your myth, share it with friends and family.

Celebrating Myths and Legends

In this unit, you read summaries and retellings of different myths and legends. Which did you find most interesting? Try to find a published version of that myth or legend. Ask your classmates to find published versions of their favorite myth, as well. Then plan a celebration at which everyone reads aloud his or her favorite myth or legend. Begin by making these decisions:

- When and where will you hold the celebration?
- Which myths and legends, out of those you and your classmates gathered, will be read aloud at the celebration?
- Who will you invite to the celebration, and how will you distribute invitations or announcements?

Use the planning guide on the next page to help you plan your Myth and Legend Celebration.

Name _____

Myth and Legend Celebration Planner Answers will vary.

When the celebration will take place: _____

Where it will take place: _____

List of myths and legends to be
retold at the event:

List of people who will read each aloud:

1. _____   1. _____

   _____   _____

2. _____   2. _____

   _____   _____

3. _____   3. _____

   _____   _____

4. _____   4. _____

   _____   _____

List of celebration invitees:

_____

_____

_____

_____

_____

List of places to announce the event:

1. _____

2. _____

3. _____

4. _____

5. _____

Our class <u>studied</u> Mars.

Mars (is) the fourth planet from the sun.

Underline the verb that shows action. Circle the verb that links the subject of the sentence to words in the predicate that rename and describe it.

An **action verb** shows action. It usually tells what the subject of a sentence or clause is doing, will do, or did. An action verb may include one or more helping verbs in addition to the main verb. A **linking verb** does not show action. It connects the subject of a sentence to a word(s) that describes or renames the subject. Linking verbs are usually forms of *be*. Some common linking verbs are *am, is, are, was, were, been,* and *will be*. The verbs *become, seem, appear,* and *look* can also be used as linking verbs. A linking verb may include one or more helping verbs in addition to the main verb.

See Handbook | Sections 18a, 18c

Practice

Underline each action verb. Circle each linking verb.

1. In 1976, the United States <u>made</u> history when *Viking 1* and *Viking 2* <u>arrived</u> at Mars.

2. NASA <u>launched</u> *Viking 1* on August 20 and *Viking 2* on September 9, 1975.

3. The two parts of each spacecraft (were) an orbiter and a lander.

4. The spacecraft <u>traveled</u> for nearly a year on their way to an orbit around Mars.

5. Once in orbit around that planet, each lander <u>separated</u> from its orbiter.

6. They <u>descended</u> to the surface of the planet.

7. The "brain" of each lander (was) a specially designed computer.

8. The computers <u>commanded</u> the lander's actions.

9. During the mission, the two landers <u>took</u> photographs.

10. They also <u>collected</u> scientific data on the planet's surface.

11. They <u>conducted</u> biology experiments in search of signs of life.

12. The experiments <u>provided</u> important information about the chemical composition of the soil.

13. The soil (was) devoid of living microorganisms.

14. Scientists <u>designed</u> the spacecraft for 90 days of operation.

15. After several years, though, both spacecraft (were) still active!

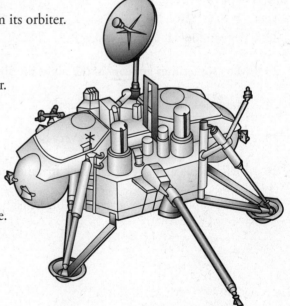

The *Viking* lander was about 10 feet across and 7 feet tall.

Apply

Complete each sentence with a verb or phrase from the box. Underline each action verb you use. Circle each linking verb.

lies	is	may be	explore	want	offers

16. Mars _____（is）_____ a cold desert planet.

17. Even so, the planet _____**offers**_____ exciting possibilities for exploration.

18. Because water is the key to finding out whether there is life on Mars, researchers _____**want**_____ more information about the planet.

19. NASA missions _____**explore**_____ planetary features that might suggest the presence of water.

20. We know that no water _____（lies）_____ on the surface of this planet.

21. However, large amounts of ice _____（may be）_____ underground.

Reinforce

Some verbs, such as *appear, look, smell, feel, grow,* and *taste,* can be either action verbs or linking verbs, depending on how they are used in a sentence. You can test whether a verb is a linking verb by substituting a form of the verb *be* (*am, is, are, was, were, being* or *been*) in its place. If the form of *be* makes sense, the verb probably is a linking verb.

In the sentences below, circle each boldfaced verb that is used as a linking verb. Underline each boldfaced verb that is used as an action verb.

22. Do you **look** at the night sky?

23. Mars sometimes **appears** in the night sky above the United States.

24. Mars（**looks**）red to viewers on Earth.

25. In photos, this planet（**appears**）very dry.

26. I **felt** a replica of a red Mars rock in a museum.

27. Will people someday **grow** food on Mars?

Four days into its maiden voyage, the ocean liner *Titanic* **hit** an iceberg. Two hours and forty minutes later, it **sank** to the bottom of the sea.

Which boldfaced verb says an action the subject did by itself? __sank__

Which boldfaced verb tells about an action the subject did to something else? __hit__

A **transitive verb** is an action verb that transfers its action to a direct object. (*The captain steered the ship.*) An **intransitive verb** does not have a direct object. An intransitive verb shows action that the subject does alone. (*A ship floats.*) Many verbs can be either transitive or intransitive, depending on whether there is a direct object.

See Handbook | Section 18b

Practice

Underline each transitive verb and draw a box around its direct object. Circle each intransitive verb.

1. As a young boy, Robert Ballard <u>read</u> |stories| about the sinking of *Titanic*.

2. Many years later, he (worked) as an oceanographer.

3. In 1985, Ballard and a French scientist <u>took</u> |ships| to the area of *Titanic's* collision.

4. For several weeks, they <u>scanned</u> the ocean |floor| with high-tech tools.

5. They <u>sent</u> an underwater |craft| on a picture-taking expedition along the ocean floor.

6. After several days, metal objects and then a ship's boiler (appeared) on the craft's video screen.

7. The underwater craft <u>had discovered</u> |*Titanic*|!

8. Ballard <u>explored</u> the |site| for several days.

9. Then he (returned) the following year with a different crew.

10. He <u>took</u> |*Alvin,*| a tiny submarine, down to the ocean floor.

11. From the submarine, Ballard <u>sent</u> a small, video-equipped deep-sea |robot| to the site of the wreck.

12. Ballard <u>called</u> the |robot| *Jason Junior,* or *J.J.*

13. The robot's camera (peeked) into many parts of the ship.

14. Ballard <u>left</u> a |plaque| in honor of the victims of *Titanic*.

15. He <u>took</u> |nothing| from that huge underwater museum.

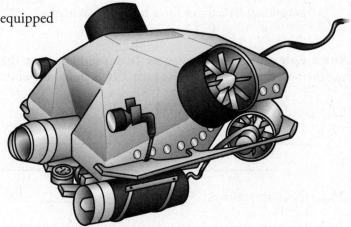

The crew onboard Alvin were able to control the robot J.J. by means of a long cable.

Apply

Write a verb from the word bank to complete each sentence. For each transitive verb you use, write *T*. For each intransitive verb you use, write *I*. Circle the direct object of each transitive verb.

| swam | explored | remove | stole | grew | discovered |

16. Robert Ballard and Jean-Louis Michel _____**discovered**_____ (Titanic) in 1985. __T__

17. They _____**explored**_____ the sunken (ship) with great care. __T__

18. Fish _____**swam**_____ among the ruins of the wreck. __I__

19. A sea plant _____**grew**_____ on a crystal chandelier. __I__

20. The researchers did not _____**remove**_____ (anything) from the ship. __T__

21. Explorers who came in later years _____**stole**_____ many (objects) from the site. __T__

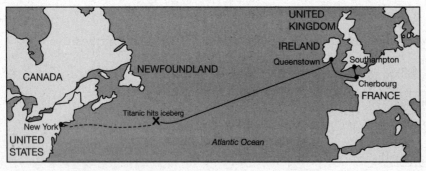

Titanic hit an iceberg about 400 miles off the coast of Newfoundland.

Reinforce

> Many verbs can be transitive or intransitive, depending on whether they are used with a direct object.
>
>   D.O.
> The iceberg *sank* the ship. (transitive)
> *Titanic sank* in about three hours. (intransitive)

Use the verb *sailed* in two sentences. In one sentence, use the verb as a transitive verb with a direct object. In the other, use it as an intransitive verb. Circle the direct object of the transitive verb.

22. sailed (transitive): __**Answers will vary.**_____

_____

_____

23. sailed (intransitive): _____

_____

_____

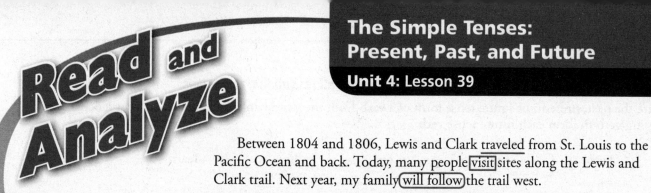

Between 1804 and 1806, Lewis and Clark <u>traveled</u> from St. Louis to the Pacific Ocean and back. Today, many people visit sites along the Lewis and Clark trail. Next year, my family will follow the trail west.

Circle the verb phrase that tells about something that will happen in the future. Underline the verb that tells about something that happened in the past. Draw a box around the verb that tells about something that happens regularly or is true now.

A **present tense verb** indicates that something happens regularly or is true now. A **past tense verb** tells about something that happened in the past. Regular verbs form the past tense by adding *-ed* (*watch, watched*). The spelling of most irregular verbs changes in the past tense (*know, knew*). A **future tense verb** tells what will happen in the future. Add the helping verb *will* to the present tense form of a verb to form the future tense (*visit, will visit*). **Remember to use this information when you speak, too.**

See Handbook Sections 18d, 18e

Practice

Circle the verb in each sentence. (Don't forget to include helping verbs.) Write whether the verb is in the *present, past,* or *future* tense.

1. President Jefferson sent Meriwether Lewis and William Clark on an exploratory journey into the new western territory of the United States. _____**past**_____

2. President Jefferson also asked for meetings with Native American groups from this area. _____**past**_____

3. Lewis and Clark kept detailed journals of their journey. _____**past**_____

4. They made notes about the people, plants, and animals along the way. _____**past**_____

5. The Lewis and Clark National Historic Trail extends through eleven states, from Illinois to the Pacific Ocean. _____**present**_____

6. Lewis and Clark journeyed roughly 3,700 miles from St. Louis to the Pacific Ocean. _____**past**_____

7. Thousands of people travel the Lewis and Clark National Historic Trail each year. _____**present**_____

8. Today, a journey along the entire westward route takes at least two weeks. _____**present**_____

9. Many lovely parks lie along the route of the trail. _____**present**_____

10. Next summer, my family and I will camp at Lewis and Clark Trail State Park. _____**future**_____

11. The park is approximately 25 miles northeast of Walla Walla, Washington, in the southeastern corner of the state. _____**present**_____

12. Meriwether Lewis and William Clark passed through southeastern Washington in the fall of 1805 and the spring of 1806. _____**past**_____

13. My family will spend about a week at this historic park outside Walla Walla. _____**future**_____

Apply Suggested answers appear below. Accept all reasonable responses.

Write the past, present, or future tense form of a verb from the word bank to complete each sentence. Use a helping verb to form each future tense verb.

keep	take	record	be	learn	present

14. Some history websites _____**present**_____ journal entries from the Lewis and Clark expedition.

15. Lewis and Clark _____**took**_____ extensive notes and drew diagrams and sketches of what they saw.

16. Several sergeants on the expedition also _____**recorded**_____ observations in journals.

17. Visitors to these sites _____**learn**_____ about the expedition from primary source materials.

18. It's likely that all expedition journals _____**will be**_____ available online soon.

19. One day I will make a cross-country journey of my own, and I _____**will keep**_____ a journal of my adventures.

Reinforce

See Handbook Section 37

Write the opening paragraph for a brochure about the Lewis and Clark National Historic Trail. Do research on the Internet to learn about this trail. Use past, present, and future tenses in your entry.

Answers will vary.

_____

_____

_____

_____

Astoria

_____

_____

_____

_____

St. Louis

_____

**The Lewis and Clark
National Historic
Trail passes through
eleven states.**

Before the beginning of the twentieth century, no one **had made** an expedition all the way to the North Pole. Since the first successful journey there, nearly 200 people **have explored** the region. Who knows how many people **will have journeyed** the area by the end of this century?

Circle the boldfaced verb phrase that tells about an action that began in the past and continues today. Draw a box around the boldfaced verb phrase that tells about actions that will be complete before a certain time in the future. Underline the boldfaced verb phrase that tells about an action that was completed by a certain time in the past.

The **present perfect** tense (*have explored*) shows an action that started in the past and was recently completed or is still happening. The **past perfect** tense (*had made*) shows action that was completed by a certain time in the past. The **future perfect** tense (*will have journeyed*) shows action that will be complete by a certain time in the future. To form perfect tenses, use a form of *have* with the past participle of a verb. **Remember to use this information when you speak, too.**

See Handbook | Sections 18d, 18e

Practice

Circle each verb in the present perfect tense. Underline each verb in the past perfect tense. Draw a box around each verb in the future perfect tense.

1. My history teacher has asked the class for facts about American explorers.

2. Many people have heard of Commander Robert E. Peary's expedition to the North Pole in 1908–1909.

3. Fewer people have read about Matthew Henson, an assistant to Peary on several historic journeys.

4. Henson had met Peary in Washington, D.C. in 1887, during Peary's preparations for an expedition to Nicaragua.

5. Peary had hired Henson as an expedition member.

6. Henson had acquired seafaring experience as a young ship worker.

7. By the beginning of the North Pole expedition in July 1908, Henson had spent more than twenty years with Peary as an explorer.

8. He, Peary, and four Inuits had reached either the North Pole or a place very near it by the end of the day on April 6, 1909.

9. The National Geographic Society has awarded Matthew Henson the Hubbard Medal posthumously.

Matthew Henson was admired by the Inuit.

10. Winners of this award have earned distinction in exploration, discovery, and research.

11. In 1906 President Theodore Roosevelt had presented Robert E. Peary with the same award.

12. Once I finish my notes on Matthew Henson, I will have created data files on about a dozen explorers.

13. How many explorers will my classmates have researched by the end of the year?

Apply

Write the present perfect form (*has* or *have* + past participle), the past perfect form (*had* + past participle), or the future perfect form (*will have* + past participle) of the verb in parentheses to complete each sentence correctly.

14. Soon it _____**will have been**_____ 110 years since Henson and Peary made their historic North Pole

    expedition. (be)

15. Some scholars _____**have questioned**_____ whether they reached the exact location of the North Pole.

    (question)

16. Others _____**have disputed**_____ whether Henson and Peary were the first to make it so far north.

    (dispute)

17. Perhaps the Inuit _____**had explored**_____ the North Pole long before Peary and Henson. (explore)

18. In 1909 Frederick Cook claimed that he _____**had reached**_____ the North Pole in April of the

    previous year. (reach)

19. Most people _____**have concluded**_____ that Cook's claim was false. (conclude)

Reinforce

Look at the timeline of Matthew Henson's life. Then use the information to write three sentences about him. Use a past perfect tense verb in each sentence to make clear that each event happened before another past time or event.

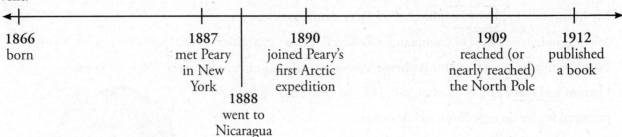

1866
born

1887
met Peary
in New
York

1888
went to
Nicaragua

1890
joined Peary's
first Arctic
expedition

1909
reached (or
nearly reached)
the North Pole

1912
published
a book

20. __**Answers will vary.**_____

    _____

21. _____

    _____

22. _____

    _____

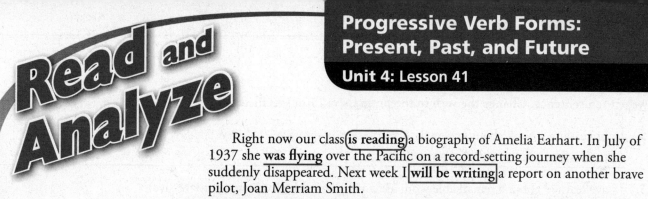

Right now our class is reading a biography of Amelia Earhart. In July of 1937 she **was flying** over the Pacific on a record-setting journey when she suddenly disappeared. Next week I will be writing a report on another brave pilot, Joan Merriam Smith.

Circle the boldfaced verb phrase that tells about an action that is going on now. Underline the boldfaced verb phrase that tells about an action that was happening for a while in the past. Draw a box around the verb phrase that tells about an action that will happen in the future.

Progressive forms of verbs show continuing action. To form a **present progressive** verb, add *am, is,* or *are* to the present participle of a verb (usually the present form + *ing*): *is snoring*. To form a **past progressive** verb, add *was* or *were* to the present participle: *was playing*. To form a **future progressive** verb, add *will be* to the present participle: *will be ringing*. **Remember to use this information when you speak, too.**

See Handbook Sections 18d, 18e

Practice

Underline each progressive verb form. After the sentence, write whether the verb is a *past progressive, present progressive,* or *future progressive* form.

1. The year was 1964, and Joan Smith was planning a solo flight around the world. _____ **past progressive**

2. My computer is listing all successful round-the-world fliers as of January 1, 1964. _____ **present progressive**

3. No woman's name is showing on the list. _____ **present progressive**

4. Joan Smith was retracing Earhart's 1937 round-the-world route. _____ **past progressive**

5. On the day of her disappearance, Earhart was flying over the South Pacific on the final one-third of her journey. _____ **past progressive**

6. On March 17, 1964, friends were waving to Joan Smith on her takeoff from Oakland, California. _____ **past progressive**

7. We are studying a map of Smith's eastward route to Florida. _____ **present progressive**

8. Thunderstorms were raging on her flight from Brazil to Africa. _____ **past progressive**

9. Smith was traveling with nothing but the hum of the plane engine for company! _____ **past progressive**

10. Most likely, people were cheering at the completion of Smith's round-the-world flight on May 12, 1964. _____ **past progressive**

11. I will be studying for my pilot's license at this time next year. _____ **future progressive**

12. I am practicing on flight simulators now. _____ **present progressive**

13. Maybe one day I will be flying over Brazil on a great journey like Smith's. _____ **future progressive**

Name _____

Apply

Rewrite each sentence. Change the verb to the progressive form specified.

14. I was reading a book about great aviators. (present progressive)
I am reading a book about great aviators.

15. I have learned about a remarkable woman named Jerrie Mock. (present progressive)
I am learning about a remarkable woman named Jerrie Mock.

16. Mock flew around the world at the same time as Joan Smith. (past progressive)
Mock was flying around the world at the same time as Joan Smith.

17. She and Smith had taken different routes. (past progressive)
She and Smith were taking different routes.

18. Each woman hoped for success on her potentially historic flight. (past progressive)
Each woman was hoping for success on her potentially historic flight.

19. I will finish the chapter on Jerrie Mock tonight. (future progressive)
I will be finishing the chapter on Jerrie Mock tonight.

Reinforce

Circle the progressive verb form in each clue. Then
write the answers in the puzzle.

Across

2. This is the direction that Smith (was heading.)
4. Many people (are doing) this in the sky right now.
5. She (was trying) to retrace Earhart's flight route.

Down

1. When Smith (was flying) from _____
to Africa, storms were raging.
3. She (was hoping) to fly around the world in 1937.
6. This woman (was circling) the globe at the same
time as Smith.

Joan Merriam Smith
flew 27,000 miles
around the world.

John Muir was born in Dunbar, Scotland, in 1838. At the age of eleven, he moves with his family to the United States. In 1868 Muir traveled to California. After spending several years in Yosemite Valley, Muir married and started a fruit ranch near Martinez, California.

Which verb in this paragraph shifts the time frame in a way that doesn't make sense? _____moves_____ **How should its sentence be rewritten so it stays in the time frame established in the previous sentence?**
At the age of eleven, he moved with his family to the United States.

Choose **verb tenses** carefully so that the verb forms you use work together to indicate time accurately and consistently. When you describe events that happen in the same time frame, do not shift tenses. When you describe events that happen at different times, use verbs in different tenses to indicate the order in which the events happened.

See Handbook | Section 18e

Practice

Read these paragraphs. If the verb in a sentence creates a time shift that doesn't make sense, mark an *X* through the verb. (1–5)

At the age of twenty-nine, John Muir set out on a journey that was to change his life. He had resigned from an industrial engineering job in Indianapolis, Indiana, because that profession did not interest him. He first ~~walks~~ 1,000 miles south to Florida. Then he ~~sails~~ to Cuba. He had planned a journey onward to South America, but he changed his plan because he had read about the natural wonders of a place in California.

On March 28, 1868, Muir arrived in San Francisco. Soon after, he ~~travels~~ east to Yosemite Valley. Four years earlier, conservationists had convinced Congress to set aside Yosemite as public land. Even so, with more settlers coming to California, those wild lands were being cleared and used for grazing. Muir ~~joins~~ the fight to preserve this land as wilderness. He ~~publishes~~ articles, essays, and books about the area. Eventually his efforts led to the creation of Yosemite National Park on October 1, 1890.

Write the correct tense form for each of the crossed out verbs above on the lines that follow.

6. _____walked_____

7. _____sailed_____

8. _____traveled_____

9. _____joined_____

10. _____published_____

John Muir is known for his conservational efforts.

Apply

Rewrite the following sentences so the verbs preserve the time frame established in the first clause of sentence 11. Add the time expressions in parentheses to the sentences to make the time progression clear. **Answers will vary. Sample responses are shown.**

11. Muir devoted his later life to preserving and publicizing wilderness areas; he cofounds the Sierra Club, an environmental protection organization. (in 1892)

    Muir devoted his later life to preserving and publicizing wilderness areas; he cofounded the Sierra

    Club, an environmental protection organization, in 1892.

12. The club leads a fight against a proposed reduction in the size of Yosemite National Park. (that same year)

    That same year the club led a fight against a proposed reduction in the size of Yosemite National Park.

13. Muir serves as president of the Sierra Club. (until his death in 1914)

    Muir served as president of the Sierra Club until his death in 1914.

14. Muir is being honored by having his picture appear on United States stamps. (issued in 1964 and 1998)

    Muir has been honored by having his picture appear on United States stamps issued in 1964 and 1998.

15. The California Legislature establishes April 21 of each year as John Muir Day. (in 1988)

    In 1988 the California Legislature established April 21 of each year as John Muir Day.

Reinforce

Ask someone in your family to tell you about an important or memorable journey that she or he took long ago. Write a paragraph describing this journey. Be sure to use correct verb tenses and include helpful time-order words.

Answers will vary. Accept all reasonable responses.

a. The 1840s was a time when Americans began following trails westward in search of new opportunities.

b. Study this map of pioneer trails.

Which sentence represents something as a fact? _____**a**_____ What is the main verb in this sentence? _____**was**_____ Which sentence gives a directive? _____**b**_____ What is the main verb in this sentence? _____**study**_____

In English, verbs express **mood** as well as tense. Mood as an aspect of grammar has to do with the way different forms of verbs reflect the speaker's attitude toward the information he or she is conveying in a sentence. The most common mood in English is the **indicative mood**. Verbs in the indicative mood represent actions or situations that the speaker believes to be factual or at least close to reality. Verbs in questions that seek real information are usually considered to be in the indicative mood also. (Interrogative sentences are sometimes said to be in the interrogative mood.) Another common mood in English is the **imperative mood**. Commands, requests, warnings, and other directives have verbs in the imperative mood.

See Handbook Section 18h

Practice

Read each sentence. Write whether the boldfaced verb is in the indicative mood or the imperative mood.

1. **Find** Salt Lake City on a map of the United States. _____**imperative**_____

2. Mormon pioneers first **arrived** there in 1846. _____**indicative**_____

3. The church **encouraged** immigration to this new Western community. _____**indicative**_____

4. **Consider** the cost of a covered wagon, oxen, horses, food, and supplies for a journey across half a continent. _____**imperative**_____

5. Many church members **were** recent arrivals from Europe. _____**indicative**_____

6. Their resources **were** insufficient for purchasing a wagon and animals. _____**indicative**_____

7. **Give** thought to possible solutions to this problem. _____**imperative**_____

8. In 1855, church leaders **developed** a plan for emigration from the East without the use of costly wagons and animals. _____**indicative**_____

9. The new pioneers **put** their belongings and supplies into wooden handcarts. _____**indicative**_____

10. **Picture** yourself on a thousand-mile walk, pushing a handcart. _____**imperative**_____

11. An ox **carried** food and provisions for every hundred pioneers. _____**indicative**_____

12. Ten handcart brigades **made** the trip to Salt Lake City between 1856 and 1860. _____**indicative**_____

A crossbar makes it possible to push or pull a handcart.

Apply

Fill each blank with an appropriate verb from the word bank. Circle each verb you write that is in the indicative mood. Draw a box around each verb you write that is in the imperative mood.

put	supplied	meant	faced	gathered	consider

13. Mormon pioneers _____(gathered)_____ in Iowa City.

14. Officials _____(supplied)_____ them with food and supplies for the journey.

15. _____Put_____ yourself in the place of someone at the beginning of a hike across the plains and mountains.

16. A late start _____(meant)_____ traveling through the mountains in severe weather.

17. _____Consider_____ the difficulty of pushing a handcart up a steep trail covered with snow.

18. Few pioneers _____(faced)_____ more severe hardships than did members of the handcart brigades.

Reinforce

Imagine you are a worker in Iowa City in the days when emigrants gathered there to prepare to travel westward. Write six sentences with verbs in the imperative mood in which you direct people to prepare properly for the long and difficult journey.

Answers will vary. Accept all reasonable responses.

a. Rafaela **plans** auto excursions for her family.

b. Her cousin has recommended that Rafaela **plan** a trip along Route 66.

c. "If I **were** you, I would begin your road trip in Chicago," said Alice.

d. "When I **was** in Chicago last year," she continued, "I stood at the corner of Lake Shore Drive and Jackson Boulevard, where Route 66 began."

Look at the boldfaced verb in each sentence. Which sentence has a present tense verb in the indicative mood? ___**a**___ Which has a present tense verb that has an unusual form? ___**b**___ Which sentence has a past tense verb in the indicative mood? ___**d**___ Which has a past tense verb that has an unusual form? ___**c**___

In English, verbs express **mood** as well as tense. Mood has to do with the way different forms of verbs reflect the speaker's attitude toward the information she or he is conveying. Verbs in the **subjunctive mood** (called the conditional mood in certain cases) are used to express conditions contrary to fact (*If I were you* . . . [but I could never be you]). They are also used after verbs of suggesting, representing, or commanding. (*Her cousin Alice has* recommended *that Rafaela* plan *a trip along the path of Route 66.*) Only the present tense has a special subjunctive form (for example, *plan* instead of *plans* as the form that goes with a singular noun). The one exception is the verb *be*: It has both a special present tense form (*be* instead of *is*) and a special past tense form (*were* instead of *was*).

See Handbook | Section 18h

Practice

Read each sentence. Write whether the boldfaced verb is in the indicative mood or the subjunctive mood.

1. "If I **were** a car in 1929, I would have loved Route 66!" said Alice. ___subjunctive___

2. "That **is** a silly thing to say," replied Rafaela. ___indicative___

3. Alice asked that Rafaela **picture** a paved highway with many gas stations and motels. ___subjunctive___

4. "In the 1920s, many roads in America **were** unpaved and did not have facilities for travelers," Alice explained. ___indicative___

5. Rafaela proposed to her family that they **drive** from Chicago to Flagstaff, Arizona, along the roadways that once were part of Route 66. ___subjunctive___

6. "If my vacation **were** longer than a week, I would love for us to take that trip," Rafaela's mother told her. ___subjunctive___

7. "The highway to the Grand Canyon **runs** north from Flagstaff," she continued, "and I have always wanted us to see its grandeur!" ___indicative___

8. "I suggest that your family **travel** as far as Oklahoma City," Alice said to her aunt. ___subjunctive___

9. "Your suggestion **makes** good sense," said Rafaela's mother, "because we can drive there and back in a week and have plenty of time for side trips." ___indicative___

10. "If time **were** not an issue," she continued, "I would take us all the way to Los Angeles—the western terminus of America's Mother Road!" ___subjunctive___

Route 66 was the first great highway from the Midwest to the West Coast.

Apply

Fill each blank with an appropriate form of a verb in the word bank. You can use a verb form more than once. Circle each verb you write that is in the subjunctive mood.

visit	see	stop	be	tour

11. "If I _____ (were) _____ in Oklahoma right now, I would have us visit the Will Rogers Memorial Museum," said Jerome.

12. "I propose that we _____ (stop) _____ there when we take our Route 66 road trip," Rafaela responded.

13. "The George Washington Carver National Monument in Missouri _____ **is** _____ my first choice for a side trip," said Brandon.

14. "If Dr. Carver _____ (were) _____ still alive, I would want to visit him in his laboratory," Alice commented.

15. "This guidebook recommends that every Route 66 traveler _____ (tour) _____ Meramec Caverns, which is also in Missouri," said Jerome.

16. "I _____ **am** _____ not a fan of caves," said Rafaela, "but if everyone else wants to visit that attraction, I will go along."

Reinforce

Complete each contrary-to-fact statement below. Use your imagination.
Answers will vary. Accept all reasonable responses.

17. If I were _____ ,
    I would _____ .

18. If I were a _____ ,
    I would _____ .

19. If I were in _____ ,
    I would _____ .

20. If I were the _____ ,
    I would _____ .

a. Start in San Diego. Head north on the San Diego freeway. Exit that freeway at the turnoff for Doheny Beach.

b. Start in San Diego. Head north on the San Diego freeway. You should exit that freeway at the turnoff for Doheny Beach.

Which paragraph has all verbs in the imperative mood? _____**a**_____ Which paragraph has a verb that is not in the imperative mood? _____**b**_____ What is this verb? _____**should exit**_____

Be careful to **keep the mood of verbs consistent** in clauses that have a similar structure. Do not shift from imperative to subjunctive mood when you are giving instructions. (The modal auxiliaries *should, could, might,* and *may* can be joined with main verbs to create a form of the subjunctive that suggests rather than tells someone what to do.) Do not shift from indicative to subjunctive mood, or from subjunctive to indicative mood, in a compound structure.

See Handbook Section 18h

Practice

Read each sentence. Circle each boldfaced verb that is in the indicative mood. Underline each boldfaced verb that is in the subjunctive mood. Draw a box around each boldfaced verb that is in the imperative mood. If a paragraph contains an inconsistent shift of mood, mark an *X* beside it.

1. "I always recommend that a visitor **rent** a car and (**drives**) north along Highway 1," said Erlinda. ___**X**___

2. "(**Stop**) at Doheny Beach, (**remove**) your shoes, and then you **should stroll** on the wet sand," she continued. ___**X**___

3. "We (**love**) ocean beaches, and we (**find**) marine mammals fascinating," said Ms. Barbaro. _____

4. "I suggest that a family **pause** at Laguna Beach, and (**strolls**) around the old beachside area," Erlinda said. ___**X**___

5. "From there, (**drive**) through Newport Beach, Huntington Beach, and Seal Beach, (**navigate**) through Los Angeles as quickly as possible, and then you **might stop** for a walk at Santa Monica," instructed Erlinda. ___**X**___

6. "The beauty of unspoiled coastal land (**is**) visible to a traveler once she (**passes**) Point Dume," Erlinda continued. _____

7. "If I **were** able to take you with us, you (**will direct**) us to so many amazing spots!" exclaimed Ms. Barbaro. ___**X**___

8. Erlinda smiled and said, "If I **were** on vacation, I **could accompany** you all the way to Eureka!" _____

9. "(**Stay**) overnight somewhere in Big Sur, (**linger**) at beaches between Santa Cruz and Half Moon Bay, and you **should hike** in Mount Tamalpais State Park," Erlinda added. ___**X**___

10. "We (**appreciate**) all your wonderful advice," Ms. Barbaro said to Erlinda, "and we (**will e-mail**) you photographs of our trip! _____

California's Highway 1 offers travelers many dramatic views of the Pacific Ocean.

Apply

Rewrite each sentence below to correct the inconsistent moods of the verbs in it.

Answers will vary. Sample responses are shown.

11. "I insist that a newcomer visit Point Reyes National Seashore and then walks out to the lighthouse there," said Erlinda.

    "I insist that a newcomer visit Point Reyes National Seashore and then walk out to the lighthouse there," said Erlinda.

12. "Wear sensible shoes, carry a bottle of water, and you should bring a jacket, because the wind can be strong and cold," she continued.

    "Wear sensible shoes, carry a bottle of water, and bring a jacket, because the wind can be strong and cold," she continued.

13. "If I were able to build a house anywhere in the world, I will build it atop that cliff," said Ms. Barbaro, pointing to a picture of the coast near the town of Mendocino.

    "If I were able to build a house anywhere in the world, I would build it atop that cliff," said Ms. Barbaro, pointing to a picture of the coast near the town of Mendocino.

14. "I recommend that a traveler drive all the way to the Oregon border and then decides what spot was most inspiring," Erlinda responded.

    "I recommend that a traveler drive all the way to the Oregon border and then decide what spot was most inspiring," Erlinda responded.

15. "Fill your gas tank, wear sunglasses, and you should watch out for road hazards," called Erlinda as she waved goodbye.

    "Fill your gas tank, wear sunglasses, and watch out for road hazards," called Erlinda as she waved goodbye.

Reinforce

Think of a scenic route in your area that you believe a visitor should take. On your own sheet of paper, complete the sentence below with information about that route; use verbs in the subjunctive mood. Then write a second sentence telling three things a traveler on that route should do; use three verbs in the imperative mood in this sentence.

Answers will vary. Accept all reasonable responses.

I recommend that a traveler _____.

a. Sailors must chart their course precisely so that their destination is reached by them.

b. Sailors must chart their course precisely so that they reach their destination.

Which sentence has both verbs in active voice? **b** Which sentence has one verb in active voice and one verb in passive voice? **a** Which sentence sounds awkward? **a**

If the subject of a clause or a sentence performs an action, the verb is said to be in the **active voice**. If the subject of a clause or a sentence is acted on by something else, the verb is said to be in the **passive voice**. In many cases, using one verb in the active voice and one verb in the passive voice in the same sentence can produce an awkward-sounding statement. Be careful to avoid these voice shifts in your writing.

See Handbook Sections 18g, 20

Practice

Read each sentence. Circle each boldfaced verb that is in the active voice. Draw a box around each boldfaced verb that is in the passive voice. If the sentence sounds awkward because of a voice shift, mark an *X* beside it.

1. Ever since Ferdinand Magellan **set** sail in September of 1519, the goal of circumnavigation **has been pursued** by adventurous sailors. ___**X**___

2. Late in the 20th century, Marvin Creamer and a small crew **embarked** on such a journey, but no navigational aids **were carried** by them. ___**X**___

3. Modern sailors **rely** on electronic equipment such as GPS devices to determine location; in previous centuries, compasses, sextants, and clocks **were used** by sailors for this purpose. ___**X**___

4. Creamer **believed** that he **could circumnavigate** the globe without any of these devices. _____

5. In December 1982, a 30-foot cutter named the Globe Star **was launched** by Creamer at National Park, New Jersey; he **stopped** in several ports in the succeeding months to conduct maintenance on it. ___**X**___

6. Creamer **had sailed** for many years, and he **relied** on ambient cues to keep the boat on course. _____

7. He regularly **noted** the position of the stars, the sun, and the planets; the cloud formations, the waves, and the color of the water **were observed** by him as well. ___**X**___

8. He **used** landmarks and the horizon line as navigational aids, and bird sightings also **were noted** by him. ___**X**___

9. Emergency navigational equipment **was carried** on the boat below deck, but Creamer never **used** it. ___**X**___

10. Creamer **returned** to National Park in May of 1984 after seventeen months at sea; he **proved** that sailors can navigate successfully using nothing more than sharp eyes. _____

Marvin Creamer taught at the college where he himself had gone to school.

Apply

Rewrite each sentence below to correct the awkward voice shift in it.
Answers will vary. Sample responses are shown.

11. Marvin Creamer sailed his boat around the world without navigational devices, demonstrating that boats also could have been sailed long distances by ancient mariners using just ambient cues.
Marvin Creamer sailed his boat around the world without navigational devices, demonstrating that ancient mariners also could have sailed their boats long distances using just ambient cues.

12. The ancient Phoenicians sailed their ships around the Mediterranean Sea and beyond, and boats were guided by the Polynesians across vast expanses of the Pacific Ocean long ago.
The ancient Phoenicians sailed their ships around the Mediterranean Sea and beyond, and the Polynesians guided their boats across vast expanses of the Pacific Ocean long ago.

13. Creamer and his crew sailed to South Africa, Australia, and New Zealand without serious mishaps; even treacherous Cape Horn was rounded by them successfully.
Creamer and his crew sailed to South Africa, Australia, and New Zealand without serious mishaps; they even rounded treacherous Cape Horn successfully.

14. Other sailors recognized the significance of Creamer's accomplishment, and he was awarded the Blue Water Medal, sailing's highest honor, by them.
Other sailors recognized the significance of Creamer's accomplishment, and they awarded him the Blue Water Medal, sailing's highest honor.

Reinforce

In the puzzle, circle seventeen words for types of boats and ships. Then, on another sheet of paper, write a compound or complex sentence with two of these words. Make sure your sentence does not have a shift in voice. **Sentences will vary.**

C	H	S	P	E	E	D	B	O	A	T	C	E	F
G	K	K	V	I	D	I	N	G	H	Y	A	R	R
S	A	I	L	B	O	A	T	R	Y	L	R	O	I
L	Y	F	E	R	R	Y	B	A	X	C	A	W	G
O	A	F	T	S	Y	N	S	F	H	A	V	B	A
O	K	B	R	I	G	A	N	T	I	N	E	O	T
P	G	A	L	L	E	O	N	R	J	O	L	A	E
A	R	K	O	U	T	R	I	G	G	E	R	T	Z

In 1953 Edmund Hillary **and** Tenzing Norgay became the first people to reach the summit of Mount Everest. Since then, many others have set out to climb Everest, **but** few have succeeded. Few people can even afford to try **because** an Everest expedition is very costly.

Which boldfaced word links two nouns? _____ **and** _____
Which boldfaced word links two independent clauses? _____ **but** _____
Which boldfaced word begins a dependent clause? _____ **because** _____

Coordinating conjunctions (*and, but, or*) connect words or groups of words (including independent clauses) that are similar. **Subordinating conjunctions** such as *although, because, since, if,* and *before* show how one clause is related to another. Subordinating conjunctions are used at the beginning of adverb clauses.

See Handbook Section 22

Practice

Circle each coordinating conjunction. Draw a box around each subordinating conjunction. Then underline each adverb clause.

1. If you saw Erik Weihenmayer climb a mountain, you would never know he is blind.

2. He has been climbing since he was sixteen years old.

3. In 2001 he climbed Mount Everest, although he could not see the hazards along the route.

4. The summit of Everest stands at 29,035 feet, and it is covered in snow throughout the year.

5. Nearly ninety percent of climbers fail to reach the summit, but Weihenmayer believed he could.

6. He felt confident because he had already climbed four of the world's tallest mountains.

7. Since a climb takes teamwork, he assembled a team of experienced climbers.

8. They would work together, but the climbers ultimately had to look out for themselves.

9. Even a small mistake could cause serious injury, or worse, cost a life.

10. The entire trek took about two months because the climbers had to make back-and-forth trips to move supplies up the mountain.

11. They also had to spend several weeks at the base camp because they needed to acclimate their bodies to the high altitude.

12. Although the team experienced setbacks and weather delays, they successfully reached the summit on May 25, 2001.

13. Because a storm was approaching, Weihenmayer and his team had no time to celebrate.

14. They also knew that the climb wasn't over until they'd made it safely back down the mountain.

Erik Weihenmayer has climbed the Seven Summits, the tallest mountains on each of the seven continents.

Apply

Complete each sentence with a conjunction from the word bank. Write *C* if you used a coordinating conjunction or *S* if you used a subordinating conjunction.

because	but	although	as	and

15. Weihenmayer _____**and**_____ eighteen other team members summited Everest on
    May 25, 2001. __**C**__

16. _____**As**_____ Weihenmayer reached his goal, he got a sudden burst of energy. __**S**__

17. _____**Although**_____ he could not see the view, he says he could hear the flapping of flags planted by
    earlier expeditions. __**S**__

18. The team spent only a short time on the summit _____**because**_____ a storm was approaching. __**S**__

19. It seemed that the trip down would be easier, _____**but**_____ it was just as dangerous. __**C**__

Reinforce

Subordinating conjunctions are commonly used in proverbs, aphorisms, and other wise sayings. In many of these, the subordinating conjunction introduces a clause that tells the conditions under which something is true.

Underline the subordinate clause in each saying below; circle each subordinating conjunction.

Three may keep a Secret, (if) two of them are dead.

(If) you would be wealthy, think of saving, as well as of getting.

—Benjamin Franklin

Now try your hand at writing a proverb, aphorism, or wise saying of your own that includes a subordinating conjunction.

20. __**Answers will vary.**_____

   _____

   _____

   _____

   _____

   _____

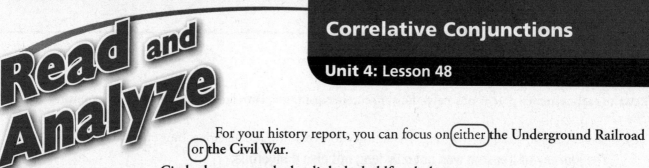

Read and Analyze

For your history report, you can focus on (either) the Underground Railroad (or) the Civil War.

Circle the two words that link the boldfaced phrases.

> **Correlative conjunctions** always appear in pairs. They connect words or groups of words and provide more emphasis than coordinating conjunctions. Some common correlative conjunctions are *both...and, either...or, neither...nor, not only...but (also),* and *whether...or.*

See Handbook | Section 22

Practice

Circle the correlative conjunctions and coordinating conjunctions in these sentences. If a sentence contains correlative conjunctions, write *COR*. If the sentence does not contain correlative conjunctions, write *X*.

1. The Underground Railroad flourished between 1830 (and) 1860. __**X**__

2. It was a network of secret routes (and) safe houses that slaves used to escape to freedom. __**X**__

3. Routes led (not only) north (but also) south. __**COR**__

4. Many escaped slaves fled to (either) Canada (or) Mexico. __**COR**__

5. White abolitionists (and) free African Americans worked together to help the fugitives. __**X**__

6. Abolitionists believed that slavery was wrong, (but) not all wanted to help fugitive slaves. __**X**__

7. Sometimes it was hard for a fugitive to know (whether) to trust a person (or) to avoid him or her. __**COR**__

8. A fugitive seeking shelter might check to see (whether) a lantern outside a safe house was lit (or) unlit. __**COR**__

9. Harriet Tubman (not only) freed herself from slavery (but also) liberated scores of other enslaved people. __**COR**__

10. (Neither) Tubman (nor) any of her underground railroad "passengers" were ever captured. __**COR**__

11. It was (both) Tubman's clever techniques (and) her determination that helped her lead nearly 300 enslaved people to freedom. __**COR**__

12. The Harriet Tubman Home, located in Auburn, New York, preserves Tubman's legacy in the place where she lived (and) died in freedom. __**X**__

During the Civil War, Harriet Tubman served as a nurse, scout, and spy for the Union Army.

Name _____

Apply

Rewrite each sentence pair as one new, shorter sentence using the correlative conjunctions in parentheses.

13. The journey to freedom was long. The journey to freedom was dangerous. (not only/but also)
    The journey to freedom was not only long but also dangerous.

14. The Fugitive Slave Law meant freed slaves were in danger of capture. The Fugitive Slave Law meant free-born African Americans were in danger of capture. (both/and)
    The Fugitive Slave Law meant both freed slaves and free-born African Americans were in danger of capture.

15. Fugitives often fled to Canada. Fugitives fled to Mexico. (either/or)
    Fugitives often fled to either Canada or Mexico.

16. New York was not a slave state. Pennsylvania was not a slave state. (neither/nor)
    Neither New York nor Pennsylvania was a slave state.

Reinforce

Circle the correlative conjunctions in each clue. Then use the clues, along with information from the lesson, to fill in the blanks.

17. This term includes both whites and free African Americans who fought against slavery.
    A B O L I T I O N I S T S

18. Fugitives went either north or south to seek this.
    F R E E D O M

19. Neither New York nor Pennsylvania supported this.
    S L A V E R Y

20. "Conductors" not only hid escaped slaves but also taught them secret codes and phrases to help them find the next safe house along this.
    U N D E R G R O U N D
    R A I L R O A D

Review

(Numbers in parentheses identify related lessons.)

Verbs

Circle each linking verb. Underline each action verb. Then label each action verb as *transitive* (*T*) or *intransitive* (*I*).

1. A journey (is) a long trip, often into the unknown. _____ **(37)**

2. People <u>take</u> journeys for many different reasons. __T__ **(37, 38)**

3. Some individuals <u>travel</u> in the name of science. __I__ **(37, 38)**

4. Many people <u>want</u> adventure. __T__ **(37, 38)**

5. Others <u>seek</u> freedom or a new homeland. __T__ **(37, 38)**

6. Still others <u>love</u> the personal challenges of a journey. __T__ **(37, 38)**

7. Often, journeys (are) quite dangerous. _____ **(37)**

8. Earth (has become) very familiar. _____ **(37)**

9. We <u>have explored</u> almost every corner of our planet. __T__ **(37, 38)**

10. Many future journeys of exploration (will be) to distant worlds. _____ **(37)**

Verb Tenses and Forms

Circle the word or words in parentheses that identify the tense or form of each boldfaced verb.

11. We **are reading** about explorers in social studies. (present/(present progressive)) **(41)**

12. I always **enjoy** books about Lewis and Clark. ((present)/present perfect) **(39)**

13. They **saw** the American West unblemished by cities and freeways. ((past)/present) **(39)**

14. By the end of the expedition, the two leaders **had met** many Native Americans. ((past perfect)/past) **(40)**

15. The tribes **were living** as they had for thousands of years. (past perfect/(past progressive)) **(41)**

16. If I **had lived** in the nineteenth century, I would have journeyed west. ((past perfect)/past progressive) **(40)**

17. The country **has changed** greatly over the past two hundred years. (present/(present perfect)) **(40)**

18. Next summer, my family **will travel** along part of the Oregon Trail. ((future)/future perfect) **(39)**

19. I **will be counting** the days until then. (future/(future progressive)) **(41)**

Verb Forms and Mood

Circle the word in parentheses that identifies the mood of each boldfaced verb.

20. If I **were** living in Alaska, I would learn to drive a dogsled. (indicative (subjunctive)) **(43, 44)**

21. **Watch** this video of a dogsled race. (indicative (imperative)) **(43)**

22. The announcer recommends that each viewer **watch** the lead dog. (imperative (subjunctive)) **(43, 44)**

23. The lead dog pushes forward, and the other dogs **follow**. ((indicative) subjunctive) **(43, 44)**

Avoiding Shifts in Tense, Mood, and Voice

Write an *X* beside each sentence that includes an inappropriate tense shift.

24. Erie Weihenmayer made history on May 25, 2001, when he stands atop Mount Everest. __X__ **(42)**

25. The ascent had been difficult and dangerous for every member of the team, but it had been especially

difficult for Weihenmayer because of his lack of vision. _____ **(42)**

Write an *X* beside each sentence that includes an inappropriate mood shift.

26. "Uncle Steve recommends that my dad get in shape and then hikes the Appalachian Trail," said Marghi to

Evan. __X__ **(45)**

27. "Your dad plays soccer already, so he probably has good stamina," Evan said. _____ **(45)**

Write an *X* beside each sentence that includes an awkward voice shift.

28. My great-great-grandmother rode a train north to Chicago in 1942, and she was followed north by other

family members soon after. __X__ **(46)**

29. My great-great-grandmother quickly found a job in a factory, and she worked there for the next forty

years. _____ **(46)**

Conjunctions

Circle each coordinating conjunction. Underline each subordinating conjunction. Draw boxes around the two
parts of each correlative conjunction.

30. Mysteries remain |not only| in outer space, |but also| in the deepest oceans. **(48)**

31. <u>Because</u> oceans are so deep, many unexplored regions lie beneath their depths. **(47)**

32. Parts of the ocean are as deep as Mount Everest (or) K2 is high. **(47)**

33. Ocean canyons are |not only| extremely deep |but also| totally dark. **(48)**

34. We should support responsible sea exploration (and) use what we learn to protect the oceans. **(47)**

The settlers traveling on the Oregon Trail had one main objective—to start a new, more prosperous life in a new land.

Circle the Latin root in the word in bold type. What does the word mean? **a goal someone works toward**

Latin Roots: *act, port, dict, ject*

Many words in English contain Latin roots. The root **act,** as in *action,* means "to do." The root **port,** as in *export,* means "to carry." The root **dict,** as in *predict,* means "to say." The root **ject,** as in *project,* means "to throw." Knowing the meanings of common Latin roots will help you figure out the meanings of unfamiliar words you may encounter.

Word Sort

Use the words below to complete the word sort. **Answers may be in any order.**

| dictator | objective | activate | reject | transport | dejected |
| enact | reaction | portable | dictate | prediction | transportation |

Latin root *act*	Latin root *port*
activate	transport
reaction	portable
enact	transportation

Latin root *dict*	Latin root *ject*
dictator	objective
dictate	reject
prediction	dejected

Pattern Practice

| objective | portable | contradict | rejection | dejected | reaction |
| react | transaction | activate | unpredictable | dictate | export |

Write the word from the word bank that is an antonym for each word.

1. agree _____**contradict**_____   5. happy _____**dejected**_____

2. import _____**export**_____   6. follow _____**dictate**_____

3. stationary _____**portable**_____   7. ignore _____**react**_____

4. acceptance _____**rejection**_____   8. reliable _____**unpredictable**_____

Write the word from the word bank that best completes each sentence.

9. Using a credit card is a simple, easy _____**transaction**_____.

10. These data _____**contradict**_____ our earlier hypotheses.

11. The weather is so _____**unpredictable**_____ in the spring.

12. My _____**objective**_____ for today is mowing the lawn.

13. Nate had a similar _____**reaction**_____ to the bad news.

14. Lauren logged on to the website to _____**activate**_____ the account.

15. Juan's frown and slumped shoulders showed he felt _____**dejected**_____.

16. Sometimes a writer faces much _____**rejection**_____ before having his or her book published.

17. When camping we use a small _____**portable**_____ stove that is fueled by propane.

Use the Dictionary

Write *act, port, dict,* or *ject* to complete each word so that it matches the definition. Check your work in a print or an online dictionary.

18. _____**port**_____folio: a large, flat case for carrying papers

19. inter_____**ject**_____: say something abruptly that interrupts

20. _____**dict**_____ion: the use of words in speaking and writing

Diagramming Adverbs

You have learned how to diagram sentences containing adjectives (page 37). Like adjectives, adverbs are diagrammed on slanted lines. An adverb is connected to the verb, adjective, or adverb it modifies. This model shows how to diagram adverbs.

Some trappers **just barely** survived the **very** cold temperatures.

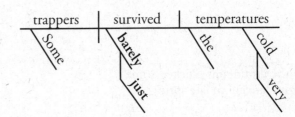

Diagram these sentences to show where the adverbs belong.

1. Beaver pelts brought very high prices then.

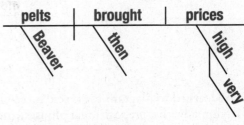

2. Trappers always guarded their pelts carefully.

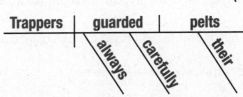

Diagramming Prepositions and Prepositional Phrases

You have learned that many adverbial prepositional phrases tell *how, when, where,* or *to what extent* about verbs. You have also learned that most adjectival prepositional phrases describe nouns. Note how the two types of prepositional phrases are diagrammed in the example.

Farmers **from the East** journeyed **along the Oregon Trail.**

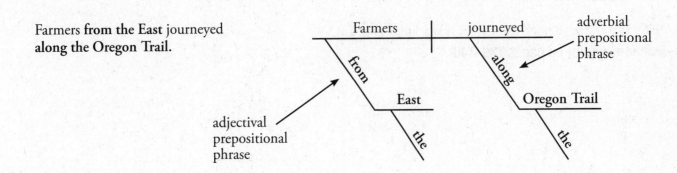

Diagram these sentences. Connect each adverbial prepositional phrase to the verb it tells about. Connect each adjectival prepositional phrase to the noun it tells about.

3. Families with livestock headed for the Willamette Valley.

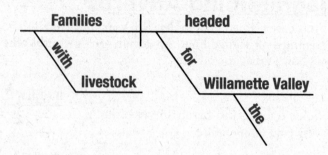

4. Snow in the mountains blocked some passes from late fall to late spring.

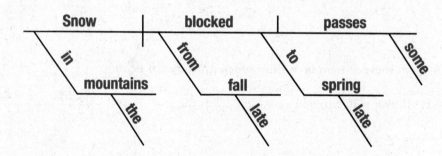

Use what you have learned to diagram these sentences on another piece of paper. Look back at the lesson to recall how to diagram adverbs, prepositional phrases, and correlative conjunctions.

5. A very heavy rainstorm will flood the trail completely.

6. A lack of rain slowly dries the grasses.

7. Clouds of dust billow behind wagons.

8. Riders often cover the lower part of their face with a bandana.

9. A very nervous horse may run away.

10. Then riders must chase it across the plains.

11. You absolutely must boil water from the pond.

12. Water from a pond can harbor many kinds of germs.

Answers appear on pages T39–T40.

Writing Sentences

These sentences need help. Rewrite them so the verbs are in the proper tense.

1. I go to Guanajuato, Mexico, last summer because my grandmother lives there. **I went to Guanajuato, Mexico, last summer because my grandmother lives there.**

2. After Mom and I have flown to Mexico City, we took a bus to Guanajuato. **After Mom and I flew to Mexico City, we took a bus to Guanajuato.**

3. Guanajuato is having a beautiful tree-canopied square in the center of town. **Guanajuato has a beautiful tree-canopied square in the center of town.**

4. In the evenings, we are listening to music in the square. **In the evenings, we listened to music in the square.**

5. I am hoping to visit an old silver mine, but we did not have time. **I was hoping to visit an old silver mine, but we did not have time.**

6. I have gone to Guanajuato again soon. **I will go to Guanajuato again soon.**

When you write a paragraph, always include a topic sentence, two or more supporting sentences that add details about your topic, and a concluding sentence. Your reader will enjoy your paragraph more if you use time expressions, correct verb tenses, colorful adjectives, pronouns, possessives, and conjunctions appropriately. Notice how this model paragraph is written.

topic sentence ─────────────────┐ *Every year my family takes a summer trip.* We *have been* to San Antonio **and** New York. **Last year** we *visited* Washington, D.C. **Neither** my father **nor** my mother *had been* there **before**, **so** we *got lost* a few times. The Smithsonian *is* huge. It *is* **not** one museum **but** a collection of museums. In my opinion the best museum *is* the Smithsonian National Air **and** Space Museum **because** Charles Lindbergh's plane *is* there. He *flew* it across the Atlantic Ocean **in 1927**. The trip to Washington *has been* my favorite vacation, **and** I *hope* I *will visit* it again someday. *It is a wonderful place to learn about history.*

time expressions

verb tense

subordinating and coordinating conjunctions

concluding sentence ─────────────┘

Name _____

Writing a Paragraph

The sentences you revised on page 147 can be used to write a paragraph. Decide whether the order of the sentences makes sense, and if it does not, change it. Write the paragraph on the lines below. Add other words and a concluding sentence, if necessary.

I went to Guanajuato, Mexico, last summer because my grandmother lives there. After Mom and I flew to Mexico City, we took a bus to Guanajuato. Guanajuato has a beautiful tree-canopied square in the center of town. In the evenings, we listened to music in the square. I was hoping to visit an old silver mine, but we did not have time. Hopefully, I will go to Guanajuato again soon.

Write a personal narrative about a trip you have taken. You might write about a family vacation, a visit to a relative's, or another trip. Refer to the model paragraph on page 147 if you need help. Be sure to use the proper verb tenses to make the sequence of events clear. Use subordinating and coordinating conjunctions to make connections between ideas clear.

Answers will vary.

_____
_____
_____
_____
_____
_____
_____
_____
_____
_____

Read your paragraph again. Use this checklist to make sure it is complete and correct.

❑ My paragraph has a topic sentence.

❑ My paragraph has at least two supporting sentences.

❑ All my sentences are clear and make sense.

❑ I have used proper verb tenses.

❑ I have used conjunctions correctly.

❑ My paragraph has a concluding sentence.

Proofreading
Practice

Read this passage about a great explorer. Use the proofreading marks to show how each mistake should be fixed. Use a dictionary to check and correct spellings.

Suggested answers appear below. Accept all reasonable responses.

Proofreading Marks

Mark	Means	Example
ꝰ	delete	Trappers ~~they~~ sought beavers in mountain streams.
∧	add	Trappers sought beavers in ^mountain^ streams.
≡	make into an uppercase letter	t̲rappers sought beavers in mountain streams.
ⓢⓟ	fix spelling	Trappers ⓢⓟ saut beavers in mountain streams.
⊙	add a period	Trappers sought beavers in mountain streams⊙
/	make into a lowercase letter	Trappers sought beavers in M̸ountain streams.

Jedediah Smith, Western Trailblazer

Jedediah Smith ranks as one of America's greatest trailblazers. Not only did he help establish parts of the Oregon Trail and routes across the Great Basin, but he was also the first u̲nited s̲tates citizen to travel overland into California, and the first to cross the lofty Sierra Nevada.

One of Smith's remarkable journeys ~~begins~~ **began** in August 1826. Smith had just attended the annual rendezvous of fur traders in Cache Valley, Utah. Accompanied by seventeen men, he ~~will be heading~~ **headed** south and then west, s̸earching for streams with beavers. Smith's party traveled over dry, sandy plains and rugged hills and then follow^ed^ twisting creeks, but they found no beaver streams. With ⓢⓟ supplys exhausted, Smith decided to move his party westward to a California mission and seek provisions⊙

Smith himself rode ahead of his group to Mission San Gabriel; from there he ~~is sending~~ **sent** a letter to the governor of California (then a part of m̲exico) asking permission to spend time in California. The governor **ordered** ~~orders~~ Smith to San Diego. When Smith arrived, not only did the governor deny Smith's request, but he also accused him of being a spy. After much discussion, T̸he governor agreed not to arrest Smith on condition that he and his party immediate^ly^ leave California by the ⓢⓟ root they entered.

Smith returned to the mission, where his men had been treated well, ~~and~~ **but** he did not obey the agreement. Instead, he led his party north to ~~Californias~~ **California's** San Joaquin River valley to follow its course and trap beavers. A biography about Jedediah Smith ~~had told~~ **will tell** you more about the subsequent̸ly adventures of ~~he~~ **him** and his crew.

Language Standard(s): L.8.2, L.8.2a, L.8.2c

149

Proofreading
Checklist

You can use the checklist below to help you find and fix mistakes in your own writing. Write the titles of your own stories or reports in the blanks at the top of the chart. Then use the questions to check your work. Make a check mark (✓) in each box after you have checked that item. **Answers will vary.**

Proofreading Checklist for Unit 4

	Titles			
Have I used colorful action verbs in sentences?				
Have I used the simple tense, the perfect tense, and the progressive tense correctly?				
Have I avoided inappropriate shifts in verb tense?				
Have I used correlative conjunctions correctly?				

Also Remember...

Have I written complete sentences?				
Does each sentence begin with an uppercase letter?				
Have I included correct end punctuation?				
Did I use a dictionary to check and correct spellings?				

Your Own List
Use this space to write your own list of things to check in your writing.

Community Connection

In Unit 4 of *Grammar, Usage, and Mechanics,* students learned about **forms, moods, and tenses of verbs and about conjunctions,** and they used what they learned to improve their own writing. The content of these lessons focuses on the theme **American Journeys.** As students completed the exercises, they learned about Americans' journeys through and beyond our lands. These pages offer a variety of activities that reinforce skills and concepts presented in the unit. They also provide opportunities for students to make connections between the materials in the lessons and the community at large.

Plan a Sightseeing Trip

Work with a group to identify five interesting places in the United States that you would all like to visit.

- Use a road map of the United States to plan an auto trip from your community to each of these places and then back home. Try to pick the shortest route possible. Make a map of your planned route.

- Next, use an Internet map site to get specific driving instructions for each leg of your journey. These should give mileage and time estimates. Add up the mileage and the estimated number of days needed to make the trip. (Remember to allow time for sleeping, eating, and enjoying each destination!)

- Write a paragraph telling about where you will go on your trip, what you hope to see, how far you will travel on each part, and how much time each segment of the trip will take. Use future tense verbs and future progressive verb forms.

Create a Postcard

Look online or in old magazines for a picture of someone traveling in an unusual way—for instance, by camel, by kayak, in a hot air balloon, on snowshoes, or in a submarine. Print out or cut out this image. Next, do some research on what it is like to travel in this way. Then imagine that you are the person in the picture; write four or five sentences about the journey you were on when the picture was taken. Use past forms of verbs in your sentences.

The Trade of Travel

Learn about job opportunities associated with journeys and travel, such as tour guide, travel agent, rafting guide, travel writer, hotel manager, helicopter pilot, cartographer (map maker), and flight attendant. Choose one occupation that interests you and learn more about it. Try to answer these questions:

- What skills are required to do this job?

- What preparation and training would I need for this job?

- Where is the training available?

- How long does it take to become proficient at this work?

- What is a typical working day like in this profession?

If possible, interview an adult who has a travel-related job you might be interested in. Take notes during the interview, and share the results of the interview with the class. Use the planning guide on the next page to help you plan the interview and organize your notes.

Name _____

Interview Planner Answers will vary.

Person I am interviewing:

Name _____

Age _____

Occupation _____

Number of years employed in that field _____

Date of interview: _____

Questions to ask:

1. _____
   _____

2. _____
   _____

3. _____
   _____

4. _____
   _____

5. _____
   _____

6. _____
   _____

7. _____
   _____

8. _____
   _____

Notes:

_____

_____

_____

_____

_____

_____

_____

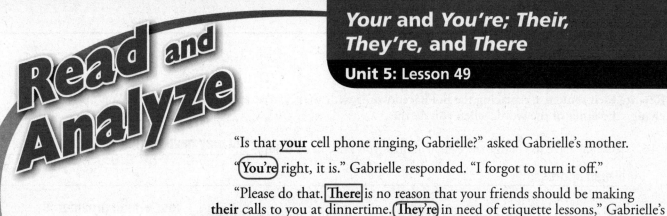

Read and Analyze

"Is that **your** cell phone ringing, Gabrielle?" asked Gabrielle's mother.

"You're right, it is." Gabrielle responded. "I forgot to turn it off."

"Please do that. There is no reason that your friends should be making **their** calls to you at dinnertime. They're in need of etiquette lessons," Gabrielle's mom continued.

Circle the boldfaced words that are contractions. Underline the boldfaced words that show ownership. Draw a box around the boldfaced word that is an introductory word.

Your is a possessive pronoun and shows ownership. **You're** is a contraction made from the words *you* and *are*. **Their** is a possessive pronoun that means "belonging to them." **They're** is a contraction that means "they are." **There** is an adverb and usually means "in that place." *There* may also be used as an introductory word.

See Handbook Section 33

Practice

Read the conversation below. Circle the word in parentheses that completes each sentence correctly. (1–15)

"(Your/You're) going to be happy to hear that we talked about cell phone etiquette today at school," Gabrielle said, switching off her cell phone.

"Well, I am glad. Did you also discuss how important it is to make sure that (your/you're) polite in (your/you're) e-mails?" her mother asked.

"Yes, our teacher said to begin each e-mail with an appropriate greeting and to proofread and spell check e-mails before (their/they're/there) sent," said Gabrielle. "She told us to avoid typing words in all uppercase letters, because (their/they're/there) like shouts. She also said, 'Including a subject line in (your/you're) e-mail is important.'"

"If you follow those rules," her mother said, "I'm sure (your/you're) e-mails will be received more favorably."

"(Their/They're/There) definitely going to be more polite from now on!" said Gabrielle. "My teacher also recommended that we avoid sarcastic remarks. She said that (their/they're/there) often misinterpreted in e-mail."

"(Your/You're) absolutely correct, Gabrielle," her mother said. "(Their/They're/There) have been many misunderstandings because of jokes sent via e-mail."

"Are Jesse and Dad getting home from (their/they're/there) trip tomorrow?" asked Gabrielle. "(Their/They're/There) e-mails should follow the same rules. Jesse is never polite in his e-mails to me!"

"Now that (your/you're) becoming an expert on e-mail etiquette, you can share what you know with your brother," said her mom. "(Their/They're/There) is no need for rudeness."

Name _____

Apply

Rewrite each sentence, replacing the boldfaced words with *your, you're, their, they're,* or *there.* You may need to change the order of the words when you do this.

16. You may have to change **the** e-mail address **you have been using.** <u>**You may have to change your**</u> <u>**e-mail address.**</u>

17. The e-mail provider **you are signed up with** is displaying more and more ads. <u>**Your e-mail provider is**</u> <u>**displaying more and more ads.**</u>

18. **Those ads are** so annoying! <u>**They're so annoying!**</u>

19. Check out these providers; **the** features **that they offer** are better than what you currently have.
<u>**Check out these providers; their features are better than what you currently have.**</u>

20. If you change e-mail providers, **you are** going to have to change your e-mail address. <u>**If you change**</u> <u>**e-mail providers, you're going to have to change your e-mail address.**</u>

21. You'll have to notify people not to write you **at that address** anymore. <u>**You'll have to notify people not**</u> <u>**to write you there anymore.**</u>

Reinforce

Words like *your* and *you're* and *their, they're,* and *there* that sound alike but have different spellings and meanings are called *homophones.* Each sentence below uses one or more homophones incorrectly. Circle the misused word(s) in each one. Then write the correct word(s) on the line.

22. Check out our competitors' rates and features. We'll match what ⟨their⟩ offering. <u>**they're**</u>

23. Stream ⟨you're⟩ favorite videos without interruptions! <u>**your**</u>

24. Quickly download games to ⟨you're⟩ PC. <u>**your**</u>

25. Compare Instanot to other Internet service providers. Find out what ⟨there⟩ doing to protect ⟨you're⟩ privacy.
<u>**they're, your**</u>

26. Look for special offers in ⟨you're⟩ local area. <u>**your**</u>

27. Our support technicans take pride in ⟨they're⟩ work. <u>**their**</u>

28. ⟨Their⟩ aren't many ISP companies that are as reliable as Instanot. <u>**There**</u>

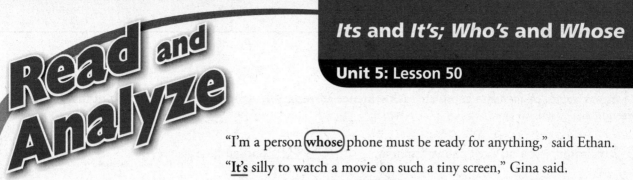

"I'm a person (whose) phone must be ready for anything," said Ethan.

"**It's** silly to watch a movie on such a tiny screen," Gina said.

"I like my phone because (its) battery lasts a long time," Corliss commented.

"**Who's** been using my phone to text message?" wailed Scott.

Underline the boldfaced words that are contractions. Circle the boldfaced words that show ownership.

Its is a possessive pronoun; it means "belonging to it." **It's** is a contraction that means "it is" or "it has." **Whose** shows ownership or possession. **Who's** is a contraction of "who is" or "who has."

See Handbook Section 33

Practice

Underline the correct word in parentheses. (1–15)

The cell phone has become more than just a phone, thanks to (its/it's) tiny but powerful computer hardware and advanced software. (Its/It's) capabilities include taking photos and making short films. If you're a person (who's/whose) interests are technology-related, you'll want a phone with these features.

But if you're someone (who's/whose) a frequent traveler, you may think (its/it's) really convenient to have a phone that can calculate the dollar value of prices in foreign currencies. Before you buy a phone for traveling, though, find out if (its/it's) usable in the countries you'll be visiting.

My sister is someone (who's/whose) easily bored. She says she bought her new phone because (its/it's) like an entertainment center. When she has to wait in line, she takes out her phone and watches video clips on (its/it's) screen.

Nowadays (its/it's) also common to see people listening to music on their cell phones. (Who's/Whose) your favorite group? Would you enjoy listening to (its/it's) greatest hits on your phone? Or would you be too busy using your phone's text messaging feature?

If you're someone (who's/whose) text messaging constantly, your cell phone could hurt you. (Its/It's) common for cell phone texters to have hand and wrist pain. Those (who's/whose) hands are already hurting should try a different use for their cell phone—use it to call people instead of texting them!

The first text message was sent on December 3, 1992.

Apply

Write *its, it's, who's,* or *whose* to complete each sentence correctly. Remember to capitalize a word that begins a sentence.

16. My brother got a new cell phone yesterday. _____**It's**_____ a bright blue phone.

17. With _____**its**_____ camera, he took a picture of a dog.

18. I don't know _____**whose**_____ dog it is.

19. However, his phone displays that picture every time _____**it's**_____ turned on.

20. I wonder _____**who's**_____ the owner of the phone making that horrible sound.

21. _____**It's**_____ my brother's phone; its ringtone is obnoxious.

22. When _____**it's**_____ ringing, the phone sounds like a howler monkey.

23. I've heard howler monkeys _____**whose**_____ cries are much more pleasant than that!

Reinforce Accept all reasonable responses.

Write an ad for a cell phone that has many amazing features. Use *its, it's, who's,* and *whose* in your ad. Then draw a picture of your phone.

_____

_____

_____

_____

_____

_____

_____

_____

_____

_____

_____

_____

_____

Two friends traveled **to** Louisiana for a visit with family. They visited Texas, **too.**

Which boldfaced word means "in the direction of"? ___**to**___ Which names a number? ___**Two**___ Which means "also"? ___**too**___

To can be a preposition that means "in the direction of." *To* can also be used with a verb to form an *infinitive*, as in the sentence *We like to play computer games.* **Too** is an adverb and means "also" or "excessively." **Two** means the number 2.

See Handbook Section 33

Practice

Circle the word in parentheses that correctly completes each sentence.

1. For many people around the world, owning a computer has been (to/**too**/two) expensive.

2. Researchers have developed an affordable laptop so these people can access the Internet, (to/**too**/two).

3. This laptop's (to/too/**two**) components, the hardware and software, feature the bare essentials.

4. Encased in hard plastic, these laptops are designed (**to**/too/two) be sturdy and durable.

5. They can handle high temperatures, (to/**too**/two), unlike most computers marketed today.

6. Because these laptops use far less energy than the average laptop, they are more useful (**to**/too/two) people in areas where power is scarce or expensive.

7. In addition to a plug-in power cord, some of these laptops have (to/too/**two**) other energy sources: batteries and a wind-up crank.

8. The laptops allow students access (**to**/too/two) digital textbooks.

9. The laptops can do (to/too/**two**) other important things for students: they can function as word processors and provide access to the Internet.

10. Some villages in developing countries have purchased one or (to/too/**two**) laptops for sharing.

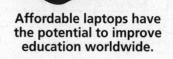

Affordable laptops have the potential to improve education worldwide.

11. The gap between how easily some people are able (**to**/too/two) access technology in developed countries and how hard it is for others to do so in developing countries is called the "digital divide."

12. However, a digital divide exists in developed nations, (to/**too**/two).

13. Perhaps affordable laptops can narrow the digital divide in prosperous nations, (to/**too**/two).

Name _____

Apply

Write *to, too,* or *two* to complete each sentence correctly.

14. "What are you going ___to___ do for the rest of the afternoon, Sumit?" asked Angie.

15. "I have to figure out how ___to___ get rid of my old computer," answered Sumit.

16. "I must finish my homework, ___too___," Sumit continued. "What about you?"

17. "I'm going to visit my ___two___ cousins," Angie said. "What are you thinking of doing with
your computer?"

18. "I don't have any idea! My sister used it for three years, and I've used it for ___two___."

19. "What about donating it? I'm sure someone would be thrilled ___to___ own it," Angie suggested.

20. "That's a great idea. That way I can get rid of it and help someone, ___too___!" Sumit exclaimed.

21. "Exactly," Angie said. "New computers are ___too___ pricey for a lot of people."

22. "This afternoon I'll do research online ___to___ find an organization that accepts old computers,"
Sumit said.

23. "Let me know what you find out. I, ___too___, have an old computer at home," said Angie.

Reinforce

To, too, and *two* are *homophones*: they sound the same but are spelled differently. These riddles are
based on other homophones.
Question: Why was she sore after the race?   Question: What do you call a sweet doe?
Answer: The feat was hard on her feet.   Answer: You call it a dear deer.

Choose three of the following sets of homophones to create your own riddles. Write them on the lines below.
Use a dictionary to check the meaning of any word you don't know.

to/too/two	nose/knows	vain/vein	whale/wail	bored/board
bolder/boulder	peace/piece	pair/pear	heal/heel	see/sea

24. __Answers will vary.__ _____

_____

25. _____

_____

26. _____

_____

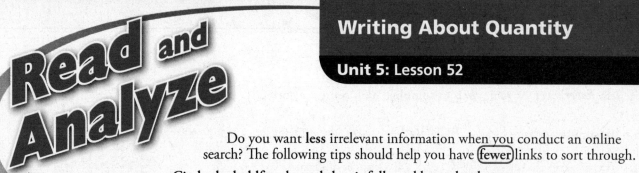

Do you want **less** irrelevant information when you conduct an online search? The following tips should help you have fewer links to sort through.

Circle the boldfaced word that is followed by a plural noun.

The words **less** and **fewer** have similar meanings but are used differently. *Less* can be used to refer to a **smaller amount** that is not a sum of items: *less gasoline; less anger*. *Fewer* is used to refer to a **smaller number** of items: *fewer cars; fewer arguments*.

The word **over** and the phrase **more than** also have similar meanings but are used differently. *Over* can be used to refer to a **larger amount** that is not a sum of items: *over 30 miles; over 200 pounds*. *More than* is used to describe a **larger number** of items: *more than 20 cars; more than 10 packages*.

See Handbook | Section 32

Practice

Circle the word or phrase in parentheses that correctly completes each sentence.

1. Have you ever conducted an online search only to end up with (over/**more than**) the number of results you could handle?

2. Using quotation marks around search terms will help you get (**less**/fewer) fluff in your results.

3. You can also separate your search terms with *and* or *or* for (less/**fewer**) and better-targeted results.

4. It could take you (**over**/more than) an hour or two to research a topic if you do not set a time limit for your search.

5. It may also help to use (over/**more than**) one online database or search engine.

6. However, to obtain (**less**/fewer) useless information, you need to understand how a particular search engine ranks results.

7. Some rank results by how many times each listing has been viewed by users; the first listing is the result that has been viewed (over/**more than**) any other.

8. Other search engines figure out how many of your search terms exist in each result; the results with (less/**fewer**) terms appear toward the bottom of the list.

9. If you want to find (over/**more than**) the number of results your search turned up, try using a wildcard character.

10. The symbols ? and * are wildcard characters, but (over/**more than**) just two of these characters exist.

11. My friend says that using wildcard characters can make your search results (**over**/more than) 20 percent more effective.

12. For example, if you want your search to be (**less**/fewer) rigid and more productive, you can key in "swim*" for results that include *swimming, swimmers, swimsuit,* and even *swim team*.

Apply

Write *less, fewer, over,* or *more than* to complete each sentence correctly.

13. This music website lists _____**more than**_____ 400,000 CDs.

14. The site says that _____**over**_____ 40% of the CDs are

    on sale.

15. It says that items will be shipped in _____**less**_____ than

    a week.

16. I have _____**fewer**_____ than 50 CDs.

17. It costs _____**less**_____ money to download songs from an

    online store than it does to buy CDs.

18. My personal music player weighs _____**less**_____ than

    ten ounces.

19. It has an extra output so that _____**more than**_____ one person

    can listen at a time.

20. I biked _____**over**_____ ten miles to a retail store.

21. The store had _____**fewer**_____ than ten players to choose from.

22. But a trustworthy online store I visited had _____**more than**_____ 50 players available!

Reinforce   Answers will vary.

See Handbook Section 35

Write an e-mail to a friend about an activity that you would like to do more often. In the body of your e-mail, use *less, fewer, over,* and *more than* correctly. Also, be sure to begin with the reason you are e-mailing. Use proper etiquette, such as typing a clear subject line; avoiding special type features, emoticons, or uppercase letters; and including a detailed salutation (full name and e-mail address). When you have finished your first draft, read your e-mail from beginning to end. Did you achieve your purpose for writing? Proofread for errors in capitalization, punctuation, and spelling. Then print a hard copy of your final draft.

a. I haven't never gotten lost before.

b. I don't ever want to get lost, so I won't leave my house without a map.

Which sentence uses too many negative words? _____a_____ Which uses negatives correctly? ___b___

A **negative** is a word that means "no" or "not." The words *no, not, nothing, none, never, nowhere,* and *nobody* are negatives. The negative word *not* is found in contractions such as *don't* and *wasn't*. It is a convention of standard English to **use only one negative word to express a negative idea.** Use the contraction *doesn't* with singular subjects. Use the contraction *don't* with plural subjects and with *I* and *you*. Avoid the use of *ain't*. ◀🔊 **Remember to use this information when you speak, too.**

See Handbook | Section 26

Practice

Circle the correct expression in parentheses to complete each sentence.

1. Throughout the ages, there hasn't been (**anything**/nothing) more dependable for determining location than the position of the moon and stars.

2. However, the technology called Global Positioning System, or GPS, (**isn't**/ain't) dependent on visible objects; it uses satellites and software to give locations.

3. Although the system was developed by the U.S. Department of Defense and is maintained by the U.S. Air Force, users today (doesn't/**don't**) have to be in the military.

4. In fact, it's hard to think of (**an**/no) industry that doesn't benefit from GPS technology.

5. Although GPS devices are easy to use, GPS technology (**isn't**/ain't) easy to understand.

6. Almost nothing (never/**ever**) stops the GPS from working.

7. There are 24 satellites orbiting Earth, none of which (never/**ever**) switch themselves off.

8. A GPS device on Earth measures the time for its signal to travel from four of the satellites and calculates the distance to each satellite; nothing but a computer (**can**/can't) process data that fast.

9. It (don't/**doesn't**) take long for a GPS device to determine a user's location, even if the satellites aren't nearby.

10. While the GPS device (ain't/**isn't**) always perfectly accurate, it's seldom off by more than 33 feet.

11. You can use a GPS device night or day, in any weather, and in almost any place and not worry (none/**at all**) about getting lost.

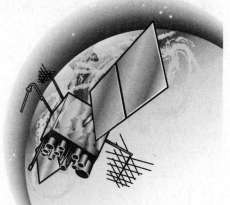

GPS technology relies on satellites to determine a user's location.

Apply Possible answers appear below. Accept all reasonable responses.

Rewrite each sentence so that it uses negatives correctly. Each sentence may be rewritten several ways.

12. Nobody never said that GPS technology was just for travelers. **Nobody ever said that GPS technology was just for travelers.**

13. "Geocaching" is a new game in which players hide prizes in places that ain't easy to locate.
"Geocaching" is a new game in which players hide prizes in places that aren't easy to locate.

14. The coordinates of the prize's location aren't no secret; they are posted on the Internet.
The coordinates of the prize's location aren't secret; they are posted on the Internet.

15. Players don't waste no time trying to locate the prize with their GPS devices. **Players don't waste any time trying to locate the prize with their GPS devices.**

16. The prize is inside a container called a cache; players don't never remove the cache itself.
The prize is inside a container called a cache; players don't ever remove the cache itself.

17. If they did, there wouldn't be nothing for the next player to find. **If they did, there would be nothing for the next player to find.**

18. Players take prizes from caches, but they don't leave no one disappointed. **Players take prizes from caches, but they don't leave anyone disappointed.**

19. They replace the prize inside the cache with one they have brought; ain't that a cool idea?
They replace the prize inside the cache with one they have brought; isn't that a cool idea?

Reinforce

Fill in the crossword puzzle with negatives. Use the clues to help you.

Across

1. I _____ believe our car broke down!
2. We _____ had trouble with it before.
3. _____ expects a car to break down.

Down

4. It _____ an old car.
5. Thankfully the GPS pinpointed our location, even though we were in the middle of _____.
6. And the tow truck was there in _____ time.

Crossword grid:
Across 1: CAN'T
Across 2: HAVE
Across 3: NOBODY
Down 4: ISN'T
Down 5: NOWHERE
Down 6: NO

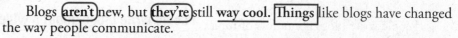

Read and Analyze

Blogs (aren't) new, but (they're) still <u>way cool</u>. [Things] like blogs have changed the way people communicate.

Look at the boldfaced words. Circle each contraction. Underline the expression that is too informal for academic writing. Draw a box around the word that is vague or unspecific.

When you write essays, reports, and other types of compositions for classes, be sure to respect the conventions of standard English. **Avoid the use of shortened forms** of words (*gonna, gotta*); **do not use slang** or informal language (*super, cool, guys, whatever, lots of, okay*); and **replace vague words** (*thing, nice, good, bad*) with more precise terms. In addition, **do not use contractions.**

See Handbook | Section 32

Practice

Underline each expression that should not be used in academic writing. These include contractions, shortened forms, slang, and vague words.

1. Can you imagine what the Internet was like before bloggers started <u>doing their thing</u>?

2. Jorn Barger was among the first <u>dudes</u> to write a blog.

3. He used the word *weblog* to describe the <u>stuff</u> he wrote; later the term was shortened to *blog*.

4. People write blogs about <u>lots of</u> topics.

5. <u>Tons of</u> people use blogs in the way that people have used personal journals in the past.

6. <u>I've</u> kept a handwritten journal, and <u>that's</u> <u>okay</u>, but keeping a blog is <u>way</u> better.

7. Other people use blogs to share opinions on <u>things</u> commonly discussed in letters to the editor of a newspaper.

8. More people seem <u>totally</u> comfortable writing blogs, though, perhaps because they <u>don't</u> feel so much pressure to be grammatically correct.

9. Blogs offer writers a <u>nice</u> way to connect with others interested in the same issues.

10. Blogs have <u>lotsa</u> different looks; some look <u>totally</u> amateurish, and others are quite sophisticated.

11. Bloggers post <u>all kinds of awesome</u> graphics.

12. The <u>thing</u> I like most about blogs is how varied they are.

13. <u>All sorts of</u> people from different backgrounds enjoy blogging.

14. You <u>gotta</u> view blogs with a critical eye, though, or <u>you'll</u> end up with false <u>info</u>.

15. One blogger <u>spilled the beans</u>: "I get my facts from others; if any facts in this blog are wrong, blame them."

16. According to one Internet tracking source, there are more than 100 million blogs. <u>That's</u> <u>a bunch of</u> blogs!

Apply Suggested answers appear below. Accept all reasonable responses.

Rewrite each sentence to eliminate contractions and informal or vague expressions. Each sentence may be rewritten several ways.

17. People write blogs about lots of topics. **People write blogs about a wide variety of topics.**

_____

18. I've kept a handwritten journal, and that's okay, but keeping a blog is way better. **I have kept a handwritten journal, and although I enjoy that, I prefer keeping a blog.**

19. Other people use blogs to share opinions on things commonly discussed in letters to the editor of a newspaper. **Other people use blogs to share opinions on topics commonly discussed in letters to the editor of a newspaper.**

20. Bloggers post all kinds of awesome graphics. **Bloggers post an array of eye-catching graphics.**

_____

Reinforce Suggested answers appear below. Accept all reasonable responses.

See Handbook Section 33

> Writers sometimes think that by using expressions such as *there is, there are,* and *it is* they can make their sentences sound formal and academic. In fact, using such expressions sometimes weakens sentences. Read the following examples and look at how the writer strengthened each sentence by using strong, active words.
>
> | Wordy sentences: | Stronger sentences: |
> |---|---|
> | There are two reasons why I enjoy blogs. | I enjoy blogs for two reasons. |
> | It is unwise for students to reveal personal information in a blog. | Students should not reveal personal information in a blog. |

Rewrite each sentence to eliminate the weak expression *there is, there are,* or *it is.* Each sentence may be rewritten several ways.

21. It is helpful to readers that each blog posting is dated. **Dates help readers track each blog posting.**

_____

22. There are many ways in which people can use blogs. **People can use blogs in many ways.**

_____

23. It is necessary for bloggers to keep up with developments in blogging software. **Bloggers need to keep up with developments in blogging software.**

24. There is a strong possibility that people will continue to invent ways to express themselves on the Internet. **People will probably continue to invent ways to express themselves on the Internet.**

_____

I will **sit** on that chair. You can **set** the computer on the floor. I will **raise** it later. I **laid** the instructions on my desk. You look tired; you should **lie** down. I will tell you when it's time to **rise**.

Which boldfaced word means "to move your body into a chair"? _____ **sit** _____
Which means "to recline"? _____ **lie** _____ Which boldfaced words mean "to place or put something somewhere"? _____ **set** _____ **laid** _____ Which boldfaced word means "to lift something"? _____ **raise** _____ Which boldfaced word means "to move upward"? _____ **rise** _____

Lie and *lay* are different verbs. *Lay* takes a direct object and *lie* does not. *Lie* means "to recline." *Lay* means "to put something down somewhere." *Set* and *sit* are different verbs. *Set* takes a direct object and *sit* does not. If you're about to use *set,* ask yourself, "Set what?" If you can't answer that question, use *sit.* Also, remember that you can't *sit* anything down—you must *set* it down. *Rise* and *raise* are different verbs. *Raise* takes a direct object and *rise* does not. *Rise* means "to move upward." *Raise* means "to lift something." **Remember to use this information when you speak, too.**

See Handbook | Section 32

Practice

Underline the word in parentheses that correctly completes each sentence.

1. (Rise/<u>Raise</u>) your hand if you know what e-waste is.

2. *E-waste,* which stands for "electronic waste," has probably (laid/<u>lain</u>) in your garage for years.

3. Many people have (sat/<u>set</u>) old computers in their home, not knowing how to dispose of them.

4. After you (<u>sit</u>/set) down, I'll tell you about the impact of the improper disposal of e-waste.

5. Because a computer contains hazardous materials, it should not be (sat/<u>set</u>) in unmarked trash cans.

6. Components with heavy metals were (<u>laid</u>/lain) in place when the computer was assembled.

7. Once e-waste has (<u>sat</u>/set) in a landfill, those metals are likely to leak into the ground, contaminating soil and groundwater.

8. If e-waste is improperly incinerated, the fumes that (<u>rise</u>/raise) are likely to be hazardous.

9. The proper way to (<u>lay</u>/lie) your e-waste to rest is to have it recycled safely.

10. Plants have been (sat/<u>set</u>) up in other nations where the e-waste recycling process is less expensive.

11. Some recycling facilities have not (<u>raised</u>/risen) their safety standards high enough.

12. As standards (raise/<u>rise</u>), the health of workers should improve.

13. Recycling facilities need to make sure chemicals do not seep into the soil or (<u>rise</u>/raise) into the air.

14. So don't just (lay/<u>lie</u>) there on the couch.

15. (<u>Rise</u>/Raise) up, gather your e-waste together, and take it to a recycling facility!

Apply

Rewrite each sentence by replacing the underlined word(s) with a form of *lie, lay, set, sit, rise,* or *raise.*

16. Jessica had <u>stayed</u> in bed all morning instead of figuring out what to do with her old computer.

   Jessica had lain in bed all morning instead of figuring out what to do with her old computer.

   _____

17. Finally, she <u>lifted</u> the blinds to let the sun stream in. **Finally, she raised the blinds to let the sun stream in.**

   _____

18. She noticed a brochure her mother had <u>placed</u> on her desk. **She noticed a brochure her mother had**

   set on her desk.

19. She wondered how long it had <u>rested</u> there. **She wondered how long it had lain there.**

   _____

20. Jessica <u>took a seat</u> at her new computer to research disposal options. **Jessica sat at her new computer to**

   research disposal options.

21. After locating a nearby recycling facility, she <u>got up</u> to ask her mother to take her there.

   After locating a nearby recycling facility, she rose to ask her mother to take her there.

   _____

Reinforce

See Handbook Section 33

Raze and *raise* sound the same but have different meanings. *Raze* means "to destroy." The past tense form of *raze* is *razed,* and the past participle form is also *razed.*

Write two sentences about buildings. Use a form of *raise* in one sentence and a form of *raze* in the other.

22. **Answers will vary.**

   _____

23. _____

   _____

Read and Analyze

Who ~~builded~~ that robot? How is it **held** together?

Cross out the boldfaced word that is an incorrect verb form.

Many verbs are **irregular;** they do not add *-ed* in the past tense. Here are some of those verbs:

Present	Past	With *has, have,* or *had*
go	went	gone
hold	held	held
build	built	built
make	made	made
find	found	found

📢 **Remember to use this information when you speak, too.**

See Handbook | Sections 18d, 18e

Practice

Circle the correct verb form in parentheses in each sentence.

1. You have (heard/heared) of robots vacuuming, but what about robots parking cars or weeding gardens?

2. Robots have been (builded/built) for many different tasks.

3. A weeding robot pulled out weeds that had (taken/took) over our garden.

4. Our mowing robot (cut/cutted) our grass before we rose this morning.

5. A monitoring robot had (brought/bringed) polluted air to people's attention, but it was unable to smell the difference between mint and a banana.

6. Has anyone in your family (left/leaved) a car in a parking garage operated by a robot?

7. Robotic garages have (became/become) more common because they can fit in more cars.

8. One parking area that had (holded/held) only 24 cars was made into a robotic garage.

9. Thanks to a computer-controlled device that slides cars into vacant parking spots, the area's capacity has (rised/risen) to 67.

10. To park our car, the robot (gone/went) sideways.

11. Before our car was returned to us, it had been (spun/spinned) around on a turntable so that it faced the exit.

12. I wonder if the Robot Hall of Fame in Pittsburgh has (showed/shown) a parking robot in a display.

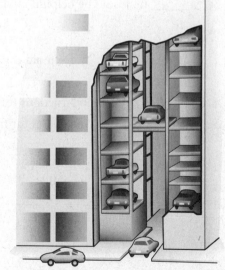

A robotic parking garage can hold more cars than an ordinary parking garage.

Apply

Fill in the blank with a past tense form of the verb in parentheses.

13. My family and I _____**went**_____ to see an exhibit about robots. (go)

14. Not only have scientists built robots, but artists and others have _____**built**_____ them, too. (build)

15. Some robots have been _____**made**_____ of discarded electronic pieces. (make)

16. We _____**heard**_____ loud noises coming from a nearby room. (hear)

17. When we looked in, we _____**saw**_____ two robots in the middle of a battle. (see)

18. Competitors had _____**brought**_____ dozens of robots to this exhibit. (bring)

19. The sound of metal robots crashing into one another _____**hurt**_____ our ears. (hurt)

20. At the show, I learned that Leonardo da Vinci had _____**drawn**_____ plans for an armored humanoid machine in 1495. (draw)

21. The first humanoid robot, called Elektro, was _____**shown**_____ in 1939. (show)

22. The robot exhibit _____**gave**_____ me the idea to build my own robot. (give)

23. I have already _____**begun**_____ my research. (begin)

Reinforce

Use forms of the verbs in the word bank to complete the clues and solve the crossword puzzle.

know	bring	do	write	build	ring

Across

1. My dream robot had _____ the doorbell to be let inside.
2. He _____ me my slippers.
3. I _____ he would be helpful!

Down

2. My robot was _____ from old car and computer parts.
4. I had _____ down instructions for him.
5. He has just _____ my chores for me!

In the book I'm reading, the main character becomes lost in a barren **desert**. She immediately begins dreaming of having ice cream for **dessert**.

Which boldfaced word means "a sweet treat"? _____ **dessert** _____

Which boldfaced word means "an extremely dry place"? _____ **desert** _____

People often confuse similar-sounding words. For example, they confuse **than** and **then,** which sound similar but are different words with different spellings and meanings. *Than* is a subordinating conjunction used to make comparisons, as in the sentence *Kendra is taller than Roger. Then* can be an adverb that tells about time. It can also mean "therefore." If you think you might be confusing one word with another, look up both words in a dictionary.

See Handbook | Sections 32, 33

Practice

Circle the correct word in parentheses to complete each sentence.

1. A great library once existed in Alexandria, Egypt; it had many (aisles/isles) containing hundreds of thousands of documents.

2. That library was (razed/raised) one day, probably by fire, and the world lost all its documents.

3. Now a book's words can be (preserved/persevered) even if the book itself is destroyed.

4. With (currant/current) scanning technology, we can convert the text of books to digital files.

5. These files can then be (dispersed/disbursed) to secure computers.

6. Scanning every book in the world would be quite a (feat/feet)!

7. Preservation is only one reason to create digital books from (physical/fiscal) books.

8. Some people prefer to have (excess/access) to books in a digital format.

9. Reading books on a digital (device/devise) helps save paper.

10. Those who follow technology trends say we are not just going through a (phase/faze).

11. They believe that reading books online is the (weigh/way) of the future.

12. Still, many people (prefer/proffer) printed books.

13. Internet (sites/cites) are also being preserved digitally.

14. The CyberCemetery at the University of North Texas archives (officious/official) government websites and makes them permanently available to the public.

15. Another digital archive (perpetuates/perpetrates) patriotic images.

16. This (faculty/facility) stores and displays U.S. posters from the First and Second World Wars.

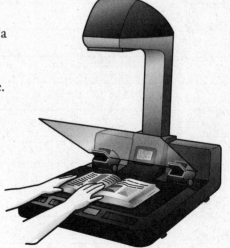

Book scanners help preserve text and save paper.

Apply

Fill each blank with an appropriate word from the word bank. (17–26)

compliments	stationary	bazaar	fare	capitol	then
complements	stationery	bizarre	fair	capital	than

While she was away with her family, Amber used her favorite _____**stationery**_____ to write a letter to her best friend:

Today we explored the _____**capital**_____ city. We took a boat ride along the river; the _____**fare**_____ was reasonable. We also visited an Internet cafe. Later we went into a _____**bazaar**_____ to do some shopping. A beautiful bedspread caught my eye. I purchased it because it _____**complements**_____ the rug my sister and I have in our bedroom. The shopkeeper gave me a _____**fair**_____ price. _____**Then**_____ our family went to dinner, and the meal was so tasty that we gave _____**compliments**_____ to the chef. As we walked back to our hotel we noticed something _____**bizarre**_____. A person painted silver was completely _____**stationary**_____. Then we saw a hat filled with coins and realized he was a street performer.

Reinforce

Write a paragraph about something you think should be preserved in a digital archive. Correctly use at least three easily confused words from this lesson.

Answers will vary.

_____
_____
_____
_____
_____
_____
_____
_____
_____
_____
_____
_____

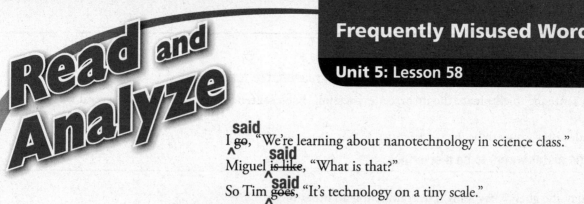
said
I ~~go~~, "We're learning about nanotechnology in science class."
  ^
      said
Miguel ~~is like~~, "What is that?"
       ^
        said
So Tim ~~goes~~, "It's technology on a tiny scale."
        ^

Has this conversation been written in formal language or informal language?
_____ **informal** _____ **Cross out the words that indicate that someone is speaking. Write** *said* **above the words you crossed out.**

Go and *went* mean "move(d)." *Is like* means "resembles something." *All* means "the total of something." In your written work and in polite conversation, avoid using *goes, is all,* or *is like* to mean "said." Also be careful not to insert the word *like* where it doesn't belong, as in the sentence *This is, like, the fastest computer I have ever seen.* **Remember to use this information when you speak, too.**

See Handbook Section 32

Practice

Circle *go, went, all,* **and** *like* **if these words are used incorrectly. (If the word** *was* **is part of the incorrect expression, circle it also.) (1–12)**

Miguel (went), "Sounds interesting. I like doing experiments. What have you learned?"

Tim (was all) "Listen to this: An American physicist named Richard Feynman came up with the outrageous idea in 1959 that scientists would eventually be able to manipulate atoms and molecules. That's, (like), happening today!"

"Wow! How tiny are these particles?" asked Miguel.

(I go), "*Nano* means 'dwarf' in Greek. A nanometer is one billionth of one meter, which is like comparing the size of one marble to the size of Earth."

"And one strand of hair would be like a huge river," Tim added.

So then I (went), "We're learning about how nanotechnology will soon be, (like), everywhere."

And then Tim (goes), "Scientists have used nanotechnology to help your clothes resist stains and spills."

I (was like), "Nanotechnology may help us, (like), cure cancer by sending tiny nano-missiles into the body to kill the cancerous cells while leaving the healthy ones untouched."

Tim (was all), "Nanotechnology may help scientists create artificial human tissues."

Miguel (went), "This is, (like), making me want to be a scientist!"

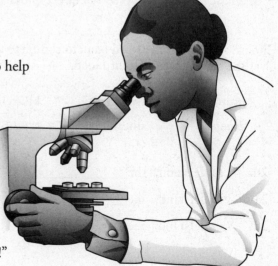

Language Standard(s): L.8.1

Name _____

Apply Possible answers appear below. Accept all reasonable responses.

Rewrite each sentence to eliminate the incorrect expression. Each sentence may be rewritten several ways.

13. My little sister wants to be, like, a scientist.

    My little sister wants to be a scientist.

14. Yesterday she goes, "Stay away! I'm conducting an experiment!"

    Yesterday she said, "Stay away! I'm conducting an experiment!"

15. I was all, "What are you doing?"

    I asked, "What are you doing?"

16. She was like, "I can't tell you, because it's top secret."

    She answered, "I can't tell you, because it's top secret."

17. I went, "Now I know what to get you for your birthday!"

    I retorted, "Now I know what to get you for your birthday!"

18. Intrigued, she went, "What are you going to get me?"

    Intrigued, she asked, "What are you going to get me?"

19. "I can't tell you. It's, like, top secret," I replied.

    "I can't tell you. It's top secret," I replied.

Reinforce Answers will vary.

Many verbs, including *asked, answered, replied, added, exclaimed, remarked, suggested, began, continued, cried, whispered, grumbled,* and *yelled,* may be used to tell how a character is speaking. Using a variety of verbs for this purpose not only makes writing more interesting but also has a dramatic effect on the mood of direct quotations.

Choose verbs from the word bank to complete the sentence frame in six different ways. Notice how each verb gives the sentence a different mood.

| muttered | chuckled | blurted | hissed | sighed | mumbled |
| sneered | thundered | grumbled | whispered | giggled | shrieked |

20. "I understand," she _____.

21. "I understand," she _____.

22. "I understand," she _____.

23. "I understand," she _____.

24. "I understand," she _____.

25. "I understand," she _____.

a. The mouse it is one of the most widely used devices invented in the second half of the 20th century.

b. It enables people to give a computer a command just by rolling and clicking.

Which sentence makes sense if you take out the word *it*? _____a_____

A **subject pronoun** takes the place of one or more nouns in the subject of a sentence or a subordinate clause. Follow the conventions of standard English in your writing: Do not use a subject pronoun right after the noun it stands for.

📢 **Remember this information when you speak, too.**

See Handbook | Section 17b

Practice

Read each sentence. Draw a line through a subject pronoun if it is not needed.

1. In the 1950s, computers ~~they~~ were huge and slow.

2. Doug Engelbart ~~he~~ was an electrical engineer who worked with computers then.

3. In addition to understanding the properties of electricity, Engelbart was a great solver of mechanical problems.

4. He believed that computers ~~they~~ would become faster and more useful.

5. Computer users ~~they~~ would soon need a way of giving commands to the machine quickly and easily.

6. Engelbart ~~he~~ set up an experiment in his lab on the San Francisco Peninsula.

7. For several months he put volunteers in front of a computer screen.

8. The volunteers ~~they~~ were given different types of devices to use to control the cursor on the screen.

9. One device ~~it~~ was a knee pointer; another was a helmet with a pointer attached to it.

10. Volunteers moved the knee pointer with a knee and the helmet pointer with the head; the movements made the cursor move on the screen.

11. The best controlling device turned out to be a box on wheels that Engelbart himself built.

12. A volunteer ~~she~~ would roll it around the top of a desk, and the cursor would move around the screen in the same way.

13. This device ~~it~~ was connected to the computer by a wire.

14. Other researchers in Engelbart's lab began calling the device a mouse, because it was small and had a tail.

15. Engelbart ~~he~~ thought the name *mouse* sounded unprofessional; he called his device the "*x-y* position indicator for a display system."

The computer mouse was invented by Doug Engelbart about 50 years ago.

16. The public has shown their strong preference for the engineers' name over the past fifty years.

Apply

Cross out the extra pronoun in each sentence. Then write the sentence correctly.

17. The trackball ~~it~~ was invented a decade before Doug Engelbart invented the mouse.

   The trackball was invented a decade before Doug Engelbart invented the mouse.

   _____

18. Two Canadian engineers ~~they~~ invented the trackball while working on improving a radar system.

   Two Canadian engineers invented the trackball while working on improving a radar system.

   _____

19. This invention ~~it~~ is used as the controller in many laptops.

   This invention is used as the controller in many laptops.

   _____

20. Touchscreen technology for mobile devices ~~it~~ was developed by Dr. Andrew Hsu.

   Touchscreen technology for mobile devices was developed by Dr. Andrew Hsu.

   _____

Reinforce

New technology is continually being developed and brought to market by innovative companies. Do an Internet search to learn about a technology or a device that is of particular interest to you. Then on the lines below, write a paragraph that includes at least three facts you discovered about this technology or device. Use subject pronouns correctly in your paragraph.

Accept reasonable responses._____

_____

_____

_____

_____

_____

_____

_____

_____

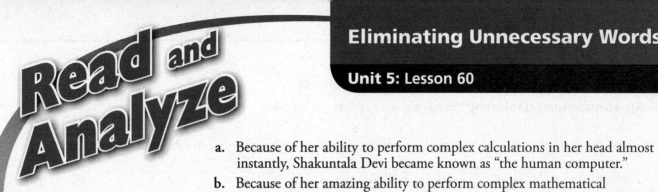

a. Because of her ability to perform complex calculations in her head almost instantly, Shakuntala Devi became known as "the human computer."

b. Because of her amazing ability to perform complex mathematical calculations in her head without the use of a calculator or even pencil and paper almost instantly, Shakuntala Devi became known, not surprisingly, as "the human computer."

Which sentence above communicates information more effectively? ____a____
Why? <u>Unlike sentence *b*, sentence *a* does not include unnecessary words and phrases.</u>

Effective writers **use the fewest words possible** to convey facts and ideas clearly. When you write, first decide what information you need to communicate, and then **state the information as simply and directly as you can**. When you edit, identify and **eliminate unnecessary words and repetitive ideas**.

See Handbook Section 14

Practice

Draw a line through unnecessary words in the sentences below.

1. Shakuntala Devi demonstrated an amazing ~~and surprising~~ ability to memorize numbers, an ability that young children almost never possess, when she was three.

2. By age five, Shakuntala Devi had learned to solve complex math problems ~~that were very difficult~~.

3. A year later, her father, a lion tamer and trapeze artist, arranged for Shakuntala Devi to give public demonstrations of her skills ~~in front of audiences~~ throughout India.

4. When she was eleven, Shakuntala Devi toured ~~the continent of~~ Europe and demonstrated her computational skills.

5. At least twice she was told by math experts that an answer she had given was incorrect, only to have the math experts reverse themselves when they rechecked their calculations and discovered errors ~~in their work~~.

6. In 1977, at Southern Methodist University in Texas, Ms. Devi competed against a computer ~~in a contest~~ to see whether she could solve a math problem faster than it could.

7. Ms. Devi extracted the 23rd root of a 201-digit number in 50 seconds; the computer needed 62 seconds to solve the problem, ~~which meant that Ms. Devi had beaten it by 12 seconds~~.

8. Ms. Devi was so talented that she could ~~use her math talents to~~ multiply a 13-digit number by another 13-digit number almost instantly; this feat earned her a listing in the Guinness World Records.

9. If a person gave Ms. Devi any date ~~in any week, month, or year~~ in the twentieth century, she could tell that person what day of the week it fell on.

10. Ms. Devi wanted to simplify math for students, and she published several books on math skills for young audiences ~~to help them solve math problems more easily~~.

Apply Answers will vary. Sample responses are shown.

Rewrite each sentence, eliminating the unnecessary words.

11. Shakuntala Devi was born in Bangalore, India; it is a city that has become an international center for

    information technology companies from all over the world.

    Shakuntala Devi was born in Bangalore, India, a city that has become an international center for

    information technology companies.

12. Shakuntala Devi developed her math skills and learned to do complex calculations without ever

    attending school.

    Shakuntala Devi developed her math skills without ever attending school.

13. She discovered quick, effective shortcuts that enabled her to solve certain types of problems more quickly

    than she could have if she had used standard computational methods.

    She discovered shortcuts that enabled her to solve certain types of problems very quickly.

14. Ms. Devi helped many students conquer their fear of mathematics and gain confidence as they learned to

    solve challenging math problems successfully.

    Ms. Devi helped many students conquer their fear of mathematics as they learned to solve

    challenging math problems.

Reinforce Answers will vary.

Look over an essay or a report you have written this year. Identify two sentences that have unnecessary words
in them. Copy each sentence on the lines below, and rewrite each to be shorter and more effective.

15. Original sentence: _____

    New Sentence: _____

16. Original sentence: _____

    New sentence: _____

Review

(Numbers in parentheses identify related lessons.)

Usage

Circle the word in parentheses that correctly completes each sentence.

1. How many electronic devices are in (**your**/you're) home? **(49)**

2. Many homes have one or (to/too/**two**) computers. **(51)**

3. Do you know anyone (**who's**/whose) still without a cell phone? **(50)**

4. Many people today depend greatly on (there/**their**/they're) high-tech gadgets. **(49)**

5. If (there/their/**they're**) in an area without cell phone reception, they become uneasy. **(49)**

6. If (there/**their**/they're) Internet connection is down, they feel out-of-touch. **(49)**

7. They cannot jog or ride the bus without listening (**to**/too/two) an MP3 player. **(51)**

8. Are people (to/**too**/two) dependent on these high-tech devices? **(51)**

9. It's true that technology has (**its**/it's) negative effects. **(50)**

10. A person (**who's**/whose) at a computer all day may develop wrist pain. **(50)**

11. A company (who's/**whose**) computer files are not properly backed up may lose data. **(50)**

12. People using (there/**their**/they're) cell phones in public places may annoy others. **(49)**

13. For all the disadvantages of technology, (its/**it's**) also brought many benefits. **(50)**

14. Think of all the ways that technology has made (**your**/you're) life more convenient. **(49)**

15. Can you imagine having (**to**/too/two) type a report on a typewriter? **(51)**

16. If you're someone (**who's**/whose) often late, a cell phone is invaluable. **(50)**

Circle the correct word or words to complete each sentence.

17. Not (**everybody**/nobody) in our class has an MP3 player. **(53)**

18. However, (over/**more than**) fifteen students have them. **(52)**

19. There are (less/**fewer**) students with CD players than with MP3 players. **(52)**

20. I have purchased (**less**/fewer) music than my friend has. **(52)**

Expressions to Avoid in Academic Writing

Circle the correct expression to complete each sentence.

21. Technology has provided students with (stuff/**tools**) they didn't have in earlier years. **(54)**

22. Technology is (cool/**motivating**) for students because it allows them to learn independently. **(54)**

23. They can (**perform tasks**/do things) and acquire information at their own pace. **(54)**

24. The technical skills they learn are (**going to**/gonna) prepare them for joining the workforce. **(54)**

Lie and *Lay*; *Set* and *Sit*; *Rise* and *Raise*; More Irregular Verbs; Easily Confused Words

Circle the correct word to complete each sentence.

25. There's a glare on my screen because someone (rised/**raised**) the blinds. **(55)**

26. (**Then**/Than) why don't you lower them? **(57)**

27. If you need more room, you can (sit/**set**) your laptop here. **(55)**

28. (Wear/**Where**) did I put the power cord? **(57)**

29. Has someone (**taken**/took) it? **(56)**

30. Oh, I think you're (**sitting**/setting) on it! **(55)**

31. I need (**current**/currant) information on several topics. **(57)**

32. Completing my research by Friday will be quite a (feet/**feat**). **(57)**

33. How can I gain (**access**/excess) to this website? **(57)**

34. Isn't the computer a marvelous (devise/**device**)? **(57)**

Frequently Misused Words   Answers will vary. Accept all reasonable responses.

Cross out each incorrect use of *go, went, like,* and *all.* (If the word *was* is part of the incorrect expression, cross that out also.) Write a correct word to replace the incorrect expression, if a replacement is needed. Try not to use the same word as a replacement more than once.

35. John ~~was all~~, "Let's check out the new computer store." _____**said**_____ **(58)**

36. I ~~went~~, "We don't even know if it's open on Sunday." _____**replied**_____ **(58)**

37. John said, "It is~~, like,~~ sure to be open on Sunday." _____ **(58)**

38. Then I ~~was like~~, "Why don't you check store hours online?" _____**asked**_____ **(58)**

Eliminating Words

Read each sentence. Draw a line through any words that are not needed.

39. Deanna ~~she~~ is fascinated by online shopping. **(59)**

40. Some shopping services ~~they~~ offer free delivery. **(59)**

41. Because Deanna is on a tight budget ~~and must carefully control her spending~~, she never makes a purchase the first time she visits a website ~~she has not visited before~~. **(60)**

42. She also waits at least one day before purchasing a product ~~that is for sale~~. **(60)**

Spelling Practice

Many adoles©ents today will undou☐tedly choose to do their reading on a tablet instead of in a book.

Underline the two words in the sentence that have a silent consonant. Circle each silent consonant.

Spelling Patterns: Words With Silent Consonants

Some words have **silent consonants** that are not pronounced. For example, the *g* is silent in *gnarled* and *resign,* the *c* is silent in *fascinate* and *discipline,* and the *p* is silent in *raspberry* and *pneumonia.*

Word Sort

Use the words below to complete the word sort. **Answers may be in any order.**

| adjust | campaign | psychology | miscellaneous | subtle | acknowledgement |
| ascend | mortgage | undoubtedly | adjoin | raspberry | adjourn |

Silent *c* or *k*	Silent *p* or *t*
miscellaneous	psychology
acknowledgement	mortgage
ascend	raspberry
Silent *d* in the first syllable	**Silent *b* or *g***
adjust	campaign
adjoin	subtle
adjourn	undoubtedly

Pattern Practice

acquisition	undoubtedly	acknowledge	adjourn	psychology
adolescent	discipline	acquaintance	subtle	miscellaneous
raspberry	fascinate	pneumonia	adjust	

Write the word above that belongs in each group. Circle the silent consonant.

1. cranberry, blueberry, strawberry _____ ras**p**berry
2. positively, certainly, definitely _____ undou**b**tedly
3. biology, geology, zoology _____ **p**sychology
4. assorted, diverse, various _____ mis**c**ellaneous
5. addition, purchase, possession _____ a**c**quisition
6. hypnotize, captivate, interest _____ fas**c**inate
7. juvenile, youth, minor _____ adoles**c**ent
8. influenza, measles, mumps _____ **p**neumonia

Write the word above that best completes each sentence.

9. Sanjay is a new _____ acquaintance _____ I met at summer camp.
10. It takes a lot of time and _____ discipline _____ to learn a new language.
11. The lemon flavor is so _____ subtle _____ I can hardly taste it.
12. The class will _____ adjourn _____ for the day at noon.
13. You can _____ adjust _____ the volume with this remote control.
14. Mr. Ito didn't _____ acknowledge _____ the whispering in the back of the room.
15. Two quarters, a gum wrapper, and a receipt are among the _____ miscellaneous _____ items in my pocket.
16. A _____ raspberry _____ is a type of fruit that grows on a bush.
17. It is important to go to the doctor right away if you think you have _____ pneumonia _____.

Use the Dictionary

Circle the word in each boldfaced pair that is spelled correctly. Check your work in a print or an online dictionary.

18. Trevor's **asma**/**asthma** keeps him from playing soccer.
19. We'll have to **hussle**/**hustle** to get to the movie on time.
20. Your blouse will go perfectly with my **khaki**/**kahki** pants.

Diagramming Indirect Objects

You have learned where to place a direct object in a sentence diagram. Here's how to diagram an indirect object. (The indirect object is in boldfaced type in this example.)

I gave my **sister** my old scanner.

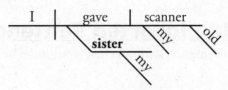

Try diagramming these sentences.

1. Uncle Leo bought me a new graphics program.

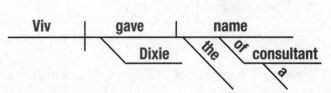

2. I lent Mom my new laptop.

3. She bought us a faster modem.

4. Viv gave Dixie the name of a consultant.

Diagramming Sentences with *There*

When the word *there* is used to begin a sentence, place it on a separate line above the subject.

There are blank disks in the drawer.

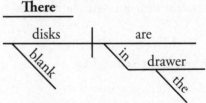

Diagram these sentences.

5. There is enough paper in the printer.

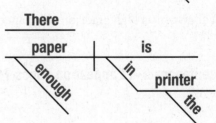

6. There is an ant on your mouse!

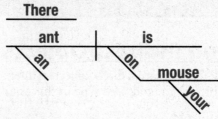

Diagramming Inverted Sentences

You learned about sentences with inverted word order in Unit 2. This model shows how to diagram an inverted sentence.

How wonderful my new flat-screen monitor is!

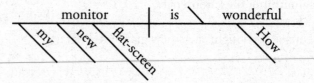

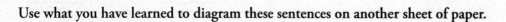

Try diagramming these sentences.

7. Fortunate are those with high-speed connections!

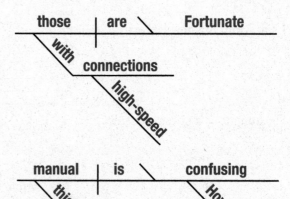

8. How confusing this manual is!

Use what you have learned to diagram these sentences on another sheet of paper.

9. How efficient I have been on my homework!

10. Happy is the student with error-free homework!

11. There is always time for proofreading.

12. My teacher will give me a high grade on this paper.

The diagrams for sentences 9–12 appear on pages T49–T50.

Writing Sentences

These sentences need your help. Rewrite each one so that homophones, problem words, and irregular verbs are used correctly.

1. Its important to evaluate the reliability of the information you find on the Internet. **It's important to evaluate the reliability of the information you find on the Internet.**

2. First, you should think about whose written the website and what they're motives and qualifications are. **First, you should think about who has written the website and what their motives and qualifications are.**

3. Try to find out if the sight has been updated in the passed year. **Try to find out if the site has been updated in the past year.**

4. Notice the domain name of the website your exploring; .gov or .edu cites are usually more reliable then .com cites. **Notice the domain name of the website you are exploring; .gov or .edu sites are usually more reliable than .com sites.**

5. Look for footnotes and, like, links to other cites. **Look for footnotes and links to other sites.**

6. If possible, find out whether an author has wrote other articles on the same topic. **If possible, find out whether an author has written other articles on the same topic.**

An informative paragraph's purpose is to inform readers. It should contain several important facts about a particular topic. The paragraph begins with an introductory sentence and ends with a concluding sentence. In between are sentences providing more information about the topic. Read this informative paragraph.

introductory sentence ⎯⎯⎯⎯⎯

sentences that give more information about the topic ⎯⎯⎯⎯⎯

concluding sentence ⎯⎯⎯⎯⎯

Computers have revolutionized the way students write reports. Students now do much of their research online. They read articles, locate primary sources, view videos, and access library databases all on the Internet. Drafting and publishing a report is much easier using a word processing program. Students have many options for formatting their reports. Most programs include automatic footnote and endnote features. **Computers aid students in many ways; still, a successful report requires original thinking and clear writing on the part of the student.**

Writing a Paragraph

A suggested answer appears below. Accept all reasonable responses.

The sentences you repaired on page 183 can be used to make an informative paragraph. Write the paragraph below. You will need to add your own concluding sentence.

It's important to evaluate the reliability of the information you find on the Internet. First, you should think about who has written the website and what their motives and qualifications are. Try to find out if the site has been updated in the past year. Notice the domain name of the website you are exploring; .gov or .edu sites are usually more reliable than .com sites. Look for footnotes and links to other sites. If possible, find out whether an author has written other articles on the same topic. By taking certain precautions, you can be more confident about the reliability of the information you locate.

Write an informative paragraph about how using a computer has helped you or someone you know accomplish a specific task. Use the paragraph at the bottom of page 183 as a model.

Answers will vary.

_____

_____

_____

_____

_____

_____

Reread your paragraph. Use this checklist to make sure it is complete and correct.

- ❑ My paragraph contains an introductory sentence and a concluding sentence.
- ❑ My paragraph provides several interesting facts about a topic.
- ❑ I have used homophones and problem words correctly.
- ❑ I have used irregular verbs correctly.
- ❑ I have used negatives correctly.

Proofreading
Practice

Read this passage about how technology is helping to tackle environmental challenges, and find the mistakes. Use the proofreading marks below to show how each mistake should be fixed. Use a dictionary to check and correct spellings.

Proofreading Marks

Suggested answers appear below. Accept all reasonable responses.

Mark	Means	Example
⌐	delete	Saving the planet is everyone's responsibility.
∧	add	Saving the planet *is* everyone's responsibility.
≡	make into an uppercase letter	saving the planet is everyone's responsibility.
/	make into a lowercase letter	Saving the Planet is everyone's responsibility.
⊙	add a period	Saving the planet is everyone's responsibility⊙
˅	add an apostrophe	Saving the planet is everyones responsibility.
sp	fix spelling	Saving the planet is everyone's responsability.

Technology as Environmental Problem-Solver

Have you ever thought about how you're [your] computer could help tackle environmental challenges the world is

now facing? Although computers and other technological equipment can pollute soil and water when their [they're] not

disposed of properly, these machines give us the means to solve difficult enviromental [sp] problems⊙

For example, thanks too [to] technology, sum [some] people are able to skip there [their] commute to the office and work

from home. Its called telecommuting, or teleworking, and it saves gassaline [sp] and cuts emissions. Many people

who work from home are, like, more productive because of lesser [fewer] distractions. Telephones, fax machines, and

computers all help make working from a remote location simpel [sp]. Some who work at home use less paper then [than]

they would if they were working in an office. So, telecommuting can save trees, to [too].

Improvements on old tecnologies [sp] have also enabled americans [≡] to use fewer [less] energy. Engineers have made

standard car engines more efficient and have also developed the Hybrid [/] engine, which gets better mileage. Over [More than]

100 people in our community now drive Hybrids [/], which means we're saving tons [a large amount] of gasoline. Its just a matter of

time before researchers find even more ways to protect the environment.

Proofreading
Checklist

You can use the list below to help you find and fix mistakes in your own writing. Write the titles of your own stories or reports in the blanks at the top of the chart. Then use the questions to check your work. Make a check mark (✓) in each box after you have checked that item. **Answers will vary.**

Proofreading Checklist for Unit 5

	Titles			
Have I used *your* and *you're* correctly?				
Have I used *their, they're,* and *there* correctly?				
Have I used *its* and *it's* correctly?				
Have I used *who's* and *whose* correctly?				
Have I used *to, too,* and *two* correctly?				
Have I used other easily confused words correctly?				
Have I used correct forms of irregular verbs?				
Have I used appropriate academic language?				
Have I used negatives correctly?				

Also Remember...

Does each sentence begin with an uppercase letter?				
Did I use a dictionary to check and correct spellings?				
Have I used commas correctly?				

Your Own List
Use this space to write your own list of things to check in your writing.

Community Connection

In Unit 5 of *Grammar, Usage, and Mechanics,* students learned how to use **easily confused words, quantity words, negatives,** and **irregular verbs** correctly. They also learned to avoid using **inappropriate expressions in academic writing.** The content of these lessons focuses on the theme **High-Tech Highlights.** As students completed the exercises, they learned about different types of technology, such as GPS devices and robots, and how new technologies have affected daily life. These pages offer a variety of activities that reinforce skills and concepts presented in the unit. They also provide opportunities for students to make connections between the material in the lessons and their community at large.

Your Town Online

Most communities have a presence in the virtual world of the Internet. Find out what your community's online profile is like by looking it up on the Internet. Type the name of your city and state into a browser's search engine and see what comes up. You may find that your town has its own website and that several other websites link to it.

Bird's Eye View

Have you ever wondered what your community looks like from the air? Type your city and state name into a search engine that links to satellite maps or street maps. Use the arrow buttons to zoom in on ten important places in the community, such as schools, shopping districts, parks, and hospitals. If possible, print out the map and label the places you located.

Tech Fair

Think about what you might include in a school technology fair, and make a plan for holding one. Answer these questions to help you plan the event.

- Where and when will you hold the tech fair?
- What kinds of devices and technologies do you want to include?
- Which tech companies would you invite to participate? What specific devices would you ask each company to bring?
- Will your tech fair include demonstrations? If so, what kinds of equipment and seating arrangements will you need?
- What kinds of furnishing will you need, such as tables, shelves, and movable walls for displays?
- How would you advertise the fair? Be specific.
- How much would you charge fair-goers in order to cover the cost of putting on the fair?

When you have finished working out your plan, develop a flier to advertise the event.

The Planning Stage

The planners of a school fair must make sure they follow school rules about holding events on school property. Talk with your teacher or principal about the rules you would need to comply with in order to hold a tech fair at your school. Use the Tech Fair Planner on the next page to help you organize what you learn.

Name _____

Tech Fair Planner Answers will vary.

When the fair will be held: _____

Where it will be held: _____

School rules the fair must comply with:

_____

_____

_____

Other considerations (such as how many exhibits or people the space can hold):

_____

_____

_____

Companies to Contact:	Contact Information:	Equipment/Furniture Needed:

Advertising Strategies:

_____

_____

_____

a. Mr. Young taught our class about rivers.

b. He taught **us** about **them**.

Which boldfaced word replaces the word *rivers*? __them__

Which boldfaced word replaces the phrase *Mr. Young*? __He__

Which boldfaced word replaces the phrase *our class*? __us__

Subject pronouns include *I, he, she, we,* and *they*. Subject pronouns can be the subject of a clause or sentence. **Object pronouns** can be used after an action verb or a preposition. Object pronouns include *me, him, her, us,* and *them*. The pronouns *it* and *you* can be either subjects or objects. ◀ **Remember to use this information when you speak, too.**

See Handbook Section 17b

Practice

Circle the correct pronoun in parentheses. Write *S* if you circled a subject pronoun. Write *O* if you circled an object pronoun.

1. (I/me) am reading about great rivers of the world in social studies. __S__

2. Our teacher explained to (we/us) that many civilizations developed along rivers. __O__

3. The cities of London, Paris, Moscow, and Tokyo all have rivers running through (they/them). __O__

4. Our teacher wants (we/us) to create a guide for a major city on a river. __O__

5. In the guide (we/us) must explain how the river has affected the city's development. __S__

6. I'm writing about the Thames River because (us/we) visited London last year. __S__

7. My friend Araceli is working with (I/me); she has been there, too. __O__

8. (Her/She) and her family took a boat ride down the Thames. __S__

9. Araceli has brought (I/me) maps and brochures about London. __O__

10. London has a multitude of famous structures, and many of (they/them) are along the Thames. __O__

11. On both sides of the Thames (we/us) saw historic buildings. __S__

12. Our parents wanted us to see Shakespeare's Globe Theatre, so (they/them) took us across the river to visit it. __S__

13. Then they treated (we/us) to a ride on the London Eye. __O__

14. From atop the Eye, (we/us) could see the Thames snaking its way to the sea. __S__

The London Eye is a giant slow-moving Ferris wheel on the bank of the Thames River.

Name _____

Apply

Rewrite each sentence. Replace each boldfaced phrase with a pronoun. Circle each subject pronoun you write. Draw a box around each object pronoun.

15. **The Thames River** flows through London on its way to the English Channel. (It) flows through London on its way to the English Channel.

16. **My friend Araceli** took a boat ride on the Thames. (She) took a boat ride on the Thames.

17. I wish I could have gone with **Araceli and her family.** I wish I could have gone with [them.]

18. **My classmates and I** have read about London's struggle to keep its river clean. (We) have read about London's struggle to keep its river clean.

19. Heavy rainfall causes sewers to overflow into **the river.** Heavy rainfall causes sewers to overflow into [it.]

20. **London officials** monitor levels of contamination and keep the public informed. (They) monitor levels of contamination and keep the public informed.

Reinforce

Forms of personal pronouns in English have changed over the years. Until the sixteenth century the word *thou* was used as a subject pronoun to indicate the person being spoken to, and the word *thee* was used as the object form. Either *thy* or *thine* was used to show possession. Since that time, people have used the word *you* as both a subject and an object pronoun to indicate the person being spoken to; *your* has been used to show possession. Yet many writers continued to use *thou* and *thee* well into the nineteenth century.

Read the following quotations. Circle each pronoun that is no longer commonly used. Then write the modern English pronoun that would be used instead of each of these archaic pronouns.

This above all: to (thine) own self be true,

And it must follow, as the night the day,

(Thou) canst not then be false to any man.

— William Shakespeare

How do I love (thee)? Let me count the ways.

— Elizabeth Barrett Browning

21. ____ **your**

22. ____ **you**

23. ____ **you**

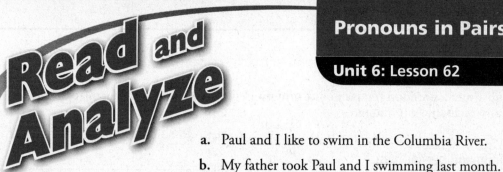

a. Paul and I like to swim in the Columbia River.

b. My father took Paul and I swimming last month.

If you delete "Paul and" from each sentence, which sentence sounds correct? __a__

Use a **subject pronoun** in a compound subject. Use an **object pronoun** in a compound direct object, a compound indirect object, or a compound object of a preposition. If you are unsure which pronoun form to use, say the sentence with only the pronoun part of the compound: For example, *He told Carmen and I about his vacation* becomes *He told I about his vacation*. You can hear that *I* should be replaced with *me*. 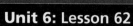 **Remember to use this information when you speak, too.**

See Handbook | Section 17b

Practice

Circle the correct pronoun in each pair. Write *S* if you chose a subject pronoun and *O* if you chose an object pronoun.

1. My parents took Paul, Rosa, and (I/**me**) on a ride along the Columbia River Gorge. __**O**__

2. Paul and (**I**/me) love hiking in the woods along the Gorge. __**S**__

3. Rosa came along because (her/**she**), Paul, and I are writing reports on the Columbia River salmon run. __**S**__

4. Mr. Tanaka had told Paul and (she/**her**) that salmon born in the Columbia River Basin migrate all the way to the Pacific Ocean. __**O**__

5. (**He**/Him) and his aide showed a DVD of salmon swimming upstream to their birthplace. __**S**__

6. When Paul asked why the salmon migrate, Mr. Tanaka told Rosa and (he/**him**) that the adult fish swim upstream to spawn, or lay eggs. __**O**__

7. Mr. Tanaka told (she/**her**) and Paul that dams on the Columbia disturb this migration. __**O**__

8. Dad said that (**he**/him) and Mom had seen the river churning with salmon. __**S**__

9. My parents, my friends, and (**I**/me) visited Bonneville Dam, on the Columbia River. __**S**__

10. Engineers there told Paul, Rosa, and (I/**me**) what they are doing to protect salmon. __**O**__

11. Then (**we**/us) and my parents traveled to Multnomah Falls. __**S**__

12. Paul, Dad, and (**I**/me) climbed to the top of the falls. __**S**__

13. Rosa is afraid of heights, so (her/**she**) and Mom stayed below. __**S**__

14. Dad took a photograph of Paul and (I/**me**) at the top of the falls. __**O**__

15. I told (he/**him**) and Paul that the falls are 620 feet high. __**O**__

16. Paul and (**he**/him) asked how I knew that, and I pointed to a sign. __**S**__

Apply

Rewrite these sentences. Substitute a pronoun for each boldfaced noun or phrase. Circle each subject pronoun you write. Draw a box around each object pronoun.

17. Rosa is working on her report, and she has asked **Paul** and **Mom** for help. Rosa is working on her report, and she has asked him and her for help.

18. Years ago, **Mom** and **Dad** saw waters churning with salmon. Years ago, she and he saw waters churning with salmon.

19. Mr. Tanaka had told **Paul** and **other students** that many dams had been built along the Columbia for hydroelectric power. Mr. Tanaka told him and them that many dams had been built along the Columbia for hydroelectric power.

20. **Ms. Vu and Mr. Tanaka** have studied how dams disrupt the migratory patterns of salmon. She and he have studied how dams disrupt the migratory patterns of salmon.

21. According to **Ms. Vu** and **Mr. Tanaka**, salmon are better adapted to cold, fast-moving water than to lakes and reservoirs. According to her and him, salmon are better adapted to cold, fast-moving water than to lakes and reservoirs.

22. **Mr. Johnson** and **other engineers** are seeking ways to save endangered salmon. He and they are seeking ways to save endangered salmon.

23. **A fish slide** and **other devices** help juvenile fish slide over the dam spillway. It and they help juvenile fish slide over the dam spillway.

24. **Mr. Johnson** and **the other engineers** explained that underwater screens guide fish away from the dam's dangerous turbines. He and they explained that underwater screens guide fish away from the dam's dangerous turbines.

Reinforce

When *I* or *me* is used in a pair with a noun or another pronoun, the pronoun *I* or *me* should come last (*Paul and me*, NOT *me and Paul*).

Circle the choice that completes each sentence correctly.

25. (I and Rosa/Rosa and I) presented what we knew about salmon migration to the class.

26. The class had many questions for (Rosa and me/me and Rosa).

27. The questions gave (Rosa and me/me and Rosa) a great idea.

28. (Paul, I, and Rosa/Paul, Rosa, and I) will plan a field trip to a salmon hatchery.

The Nile is a river in Africa. **It** flows north through much of the continent.

Circle the proper noun that the boldfaced pronoun replaces. Draw an arrow from the pronoun to that name.

An **antecedent** is the word or words a pronoun refers to. When you write a pronoun, be sure its antecedent is clear. A pronoun must also **agree** with its antecedent. An antecedent and pronoun agree when they have the same number (singular or plural) and gender (male or female). **Remember to use this information when you speak, too.**

See Handbook Section 17c

Practice

Circle the antecedent of each boldfaced pronoun.

1. The Nile River flows over 4,100 miles through Africa. Near Alexandria, Egypt, **it** empties into the Mediterranean Sea.

2. The Nile River system is complex. **It** has many tributaries.

3. To find the source of a river mapmakers search for the source of the longest tributary that feeds into **it**.

4. There are two major tributaries of the Nile. **They** are the White Nile and the Blue Nile.

5. The waters of the Blue Nile originate high in the mountains of Ethiopia. **They** are replenished each year by seasonal rains.

6. The White Nile flows from Lake Victoria and beyond. **It** supplies most of the Nile's water.

7. The two rivers flow together in Sudan. **They** meet near the capital city of Khartoum.

8. Later they are joined by a third major tributary. **It** is the Atbara River, which also flows out of Ethiopia.

9. For centuries, explorers searched for the source of the Nile. Many of **them** met with frustration.

10. A priest named Pedro Páez may have been the first European to reach the source of the Blue Nile. **He** traveled there in the early seventeenth century.

11. In 1858, John Hanning Speke saw a great lake. **It** fed the White Nile at Jinja, Uganda.

12. Speke named the lake after Queen Victoria. **She** ruled England at that time.

13. In 2004, members of the White Nile Expedition navigated the length of the Nile. The journey took **them** through remote parts of Africa.

14. Natalie McComb was part of that team. **She** was a tour guide based in Kampala, Uganda.

15. In recent years, other teams have navigated the Nile. **They** have braved many dangers to trace the course of this river.

The Nile River runs through the city of Cairo, Egypt.

Apply

Write a pronoun that relates to each boldfaced antecedent. Capitalize each word that begins a sentence.

16. Many **people** have explored the Nile. Mostly likely, ___**they**___ have been motivated by adventure as much as a search for knowledge.

17. In 2004, two **men** traveled the Blue Nile. No one before ___**them**___ had paddled its entire length.

18. Their **trip** was long and grueling. ___**It**___ took them 148 days.

19. Today, explorers still disagree over the true **source** of the White Nile. Some claim ___**it**___ lies in Burundi, and others claim ___**it**___ is in Rwanda.

20. In 2006, **Neil McGrigor** took a team with ___**him**___ to what he claimed was its true source.

21. McGrigor wanted to prove to **geographers** that the Nile was longer than ___**they**___ had believed.

22. Burundi is farther from Egypt than Rwanda is. However, the **tributary** in Rwanda twists back and forth, which makes ___**it**___ longer than the tributary in Burundi.

23. To measure the length precisely, the **explorers** took a GPS and a laptop computer with ___**them**___.

24. The "true **source** of the Nile" lay deep in the Nyungwe Forest. ___**It**___ was little more than a muddy hole.

Reinforce A possible answer appears below. Accept all reasonable responses.

The word part *ante* in *antecedent* means "before." A pronoun's antecedent should come before the pronoun so that the reader knows which word the pronoun replaces. Rewrite the paragraph below so that every pronoun has a clear antecedent. You will need to replace some pronouns with nouns, and some nouns with pronouns.

It lies on the west bank of the Nile. A necropolis is where pharaohs were buried. Around 1470 B.C. she erected a huge temple there. Queen Hatshepsut also erected four obelisks. On the wall of her temple there is a painting of how they were transported down the Nile on barges. Two obelisks were placed end to end on a barge. Each barge was towed by many boats rowed by them. It may have taken as many as 1,000 oarsmen to do the job.

A necropolis lies on the west bank of the Nile. It is where pharaohs were buried. Around 1470 B.C.

Queen Hatshepsut erected a huge temple there. She also erected four obelisks. On the wall of Queen

Hatshepsut's temple there is a painting of how the obelisks were transported down the Nile on barges.

Two obelisks were placed end to end on a barge. Each barge was towed by many boats rowed by oarsmen.

It may have taken as many as 1,000 to do the job.

_____

_____

_____

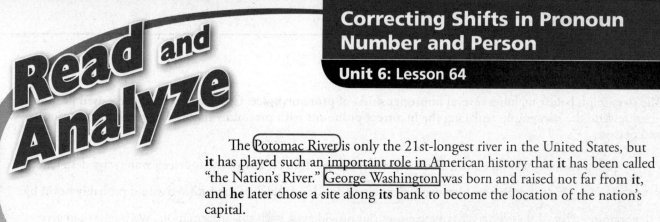

The (Potomac River) is only the 21st-longest river in the United States, but **it** has played such an important role in American history that **it** has been called "the Nation's River." [George Washington] was born and raised not far from **it**, and **he** later chose a site along **its** bank to become the location of the nation's capital.

Circle the words that the pronouns *it* and *its* stand for in this paragraph. Draw a box around the words that the pronoun *he* stands for.

Pronouns must agree with their **antecedents** in number (singular or plural) and gender (male or female). When you use a pronoun to establish a point of view, be careful not to shift to a pronoun of a different number and person.

See Handbook | Section 17c

Practice

In each item below, circle the pronoun form that agrees with its antecedent. Then underline the antecedent.

1. The Potomac River got its name from an Algonquian tribe that lived in its basin in colonial times. (He/**It**) had the name Patawomeck.

2. John Smith was the leader of the first successful colony in Virginia. (**He**/They) spelled the name "Patawomeke" on a map he drew.

3. On a map you can see that the Potomac has two sources, the North Branch and the South Branch. (You/**They**) converge near Green Spring in West Virginia.

4. George Washington's parents were plantation owners in the Potomac Basin. (His/**Their**) son George was born and grew up on that plantation in the 1730s.

People can take a boat ride on the Potomac in Washington, D.C.

5. Members of the United States Congress developed a plan for a new capital in 1790. (It/**They**) then decided to build this new city somewhere along the Potomac River on land that belonged to the federal government.

6. George Washington, who had just become America's first president, was asked to choose the precise location because (they/**he**) knew the Potomac region so well.

7. One of the most important events leading up to the Civil War took place where the Shenandoah River joins the Potomac. (**It**/They) involved the abolitionist John Brown, who led a raid on the United States arsenal there in the village of Harper's Ferry.

8. The Potomac River was a dividing line between the Union and the Confederacy in the Civil War; the Confederate General Robert E. Lee crossed (**it**/them) twice to invade Northern territory.

9. The Potomac has provided drinking water for residents of Washington, D.C., since the time of the Civil War. People in the region have used (**it**/them) for recreation activities for an even longer time.

10. President Bill Clinton named the Potomac an American Heritage River in 1998. (**He**/It) highlighted its great importance to our country by doing so.

Apply

The paragraph below includes several improper shifts of pronoun voice. Circle each improperly used pronoun. Then rewrite the paragraph, replacing the incorrect pronouns with pronouns that indicate the correct number and person.

What if someone offered you an all-expense-paid vacation on any of the fourteen waterways designated as American Heritage Rivers? How would (someone) decide which river to visit? (We) would probably begin by obtaining a list of these rivers. Many websites can provide you with this information. (We) might then give the list a quick look to see if any of the rivers are among your favorites. If not, the next step (someone) should take would be to decide which part of the United States you would most like to visit and see which rivers on the list are in that region. If (they) are an outdoor enthusiast, (they) might select the Far West for its verdant wild areas and mild weather. (We) would quickly notice that only one of the rivers on the list, the Willamette River, is in the Far West. Having identified this river as a possible destination, (we) would want to do research to learn about popular vacation areas and activities there. A few visits to Oregon websites would tell (us) that if (we) like fishing, swimming, boating, hiking, cycling, camping, or sightseeing, you are likely to have a great time on a Willamette River vacation!

Answers will vary. Sample response:

What if someone offered you an all-expense-paid vacation on any of the fourteen waterways designated as American Heritage Rivers? How would you decide which river to visit? You would probably begin by obtaining a list of these rivers. Many websites can provide you with this information. You might then give the list a quick look to see if any of the rivers are among your favorites. If not, the next step you should take would be to decide which part of the United States you would most like to visit and see which rivers on the list are in that region. If you are an outdoor enthusiast, you might select the Far West for its verdant wild areas and mild weather. You would quickly notice that only one of the rivers on the list, the Willamette River, is in the Far West. Having identified this river as a possible destination, you would want to do research to learn about popular vacation areas and activities there. A few visits to Oregon websites would tell you that if you like fishing, swimming, boating, hiking, cycling, camping, or sightseeing, you are likely to have a great time on a Willamette River vacation!

Reinforce

On another sheet of paper, write a script for a 30-second TV commercial for a vacation area on a river located in or near your community. Use at least two personal pronouns in your commercial. Be careful not to shift pronoun voice in your script. **Answers will vary.**

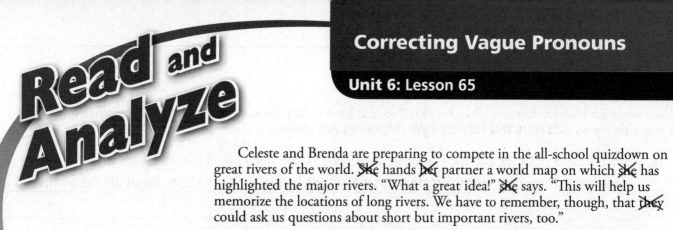

Celeste and Brenda are preparing to compete in the all-school quizdown on great rivers of the world. ~~She~~ hands ~~her~~ partner a world map on which ~~she~~ has highlighted the major rivers. "What a great idea!" ~~She~~ says. "This will help us memorize the locations of long rivers. We have to remember, though, that ~~they~~ could ask us questions about short but important rivers, too."

Can you tell from these sentences who highlighted the rivers on the world map? ___no___ Can you tell who talked about the need to study small but important rivers? ___no___ Does this speaker make clear who will ask the questions in the quizdown? ___no___ Mark an X through each pronoun that does not have a clear antecedent.

Each **personal pronoun** and each **demonstrative pronoun** you use should have a **clear antecedent**. If you see that you have written a sentence with a pronoun that does not refer clearly to an antecedent, you should rewrite the sentence.

See Handbook Sections 17a–c, 17i

Practice

Circle the antecedent for each boldfaced pronoun. If a boldfaced pronoun does not have a clear antecedent in the sentence, mark an X through it.

1. The library has many (reference materials); Celeste wants to study **those** first.

2. Celeste and Brenda will also use the library's computers to find out more about ~~**them**~~.

3. (Arnold and Zack) arrive at the library; **they** will be competing in ~~**it**~~, too.

4. At first, ~~**they**~~ pretend ~~**they**~~ don't see ~~**their**~~ competitors.

5. Since all the (students) need to use the same books and maps, though, **they** eventually have to acknowledge **their** competitors' presence.

6. "Are you using ~~**those**~~?" ~~**he**~~ asks.

7. (Celeste and Brenda) look at each other, and then ~~**she**~~ says, "We need ~~**these**~~, but you can have ~~**those**~~."

8. Arnold and Zack carry ~~**them**~~ to another table, but then ~~**he**~~ walks over to a computer and logs on.

9. "What have **you** learned about the Congo River?" ~~**he**~~ asks (Brenda and Celeste).

10. "I know it's the most important river in West Africa." ~~**he**~~ responds.

11. "What about the Niger, the Gambia, and the Volta?" ~~**she**~~ adds.

12. "We are studying (the Niger, the Gambia, and the Volta), too, but the Congo is far more important than **those**," ~~**he**~~ responds.

13. "Okay, I will test ~~**you**~~ with a question," (Brenda) says.

14. "What huge carnivorous fish lives in the Congo River?" ~~**she**~~ asks ~~**him**~~.

15. At first neither Arnold nor Zack responds, but then (Arnold) smiles, raises **his** index finger, and says, "The answer to ~~**your**~~ question is the giant tigerfish!"

Apply

Each sentence below contains a pronoun that does not have a clear antecedent. Rewrite each sentence to correct the error. **Answers will vary. Sample responses are shown.**

16. When Arnold and Zack quiz each other, he always begins with questions about the Congo River.
    When Arnold and Zack quiz each other, Arnold always begins with questions about the Congo River.

17. "How did you find out that they would focus on that river at the quizdown?" his partner finally asks.
    "How did you find out that the judges would focus on that river at the quizdown?" Arnold's partner finally asks.

18. "Oh, I just made that up," he responds with a smile.
    "Oh, I just made that up," Arnold responds with a smile.

19. "I think the Congo is the most interesting river in the world," he continues.
    "I think the Congo is the most interesting river in the world," Arnold continues.

20. "So you don't really care about winning the quizdown?" he asks him.
    "So you don't really care about winning the quizdown?" Zack asks Arnold.

21. "Oh, I would like to win, but I also want to satisfy my curiosity about that great and mysterious river," he concludes.
    "Oh, I would like to win, but I also want to satisfy my curiosity about that great and mysterious river," Arnold concludes.

Reinforce

Choose a river outside North America that you would like to visit and explore. Do some research to find five interesting facts about that river. Write the facts on the lines below. Then, on another sheet of paper, write a letter to a friend in which you try to convince her or him to join you on a trip to that river. Include the five facts you found, and make sure the personal pronouns and demonstrative pronouns you use have clear antecedents. **Answers will vary.**

Fact 1: _____

Fact 2: _____

Fact 3: _____

Fact 4: _____

Fact 5: _____

Are you the one **who** wrote this report? _____subject_____

The people **whom** you described are quite colorful. _____object_____

Underline the clause in each sentence that includes *who* or *whom*. Which boldfaced word is the *subject* in its clause? _____who_____ Which boldfaced word is an *object* in its clause? _____whom_____ After each sentence, write whether the boldfaced word is a subject or an object.

Use *who* as the **subject** of a sentence or a clause. Use *whom* as the **object** of a verb or of a preposition. ◀📢 **Remember to use this information when you speak, too.**

See Handbook | Sections 17b, 17h

Practice

Underline the clause in each sentence that includes the words in parentheses. Decide whether the word in parentheses should be a subject or an object. Circle *who* or *whom* to complete each sentence correctly.

1. (Who/Whom) can point out the St. Lawrence River on the class map?

2. The first known European to travel up the St. Lawrence was Jacques Cartier, (who/whom) claimed the river's shores for the French crown in the early 1500s.

3. (Who/Whom) can point out Lake Ontario, where the St. Lawrence River originates?

4. The area from Lake Ontario to the sea was inhabited by Native Americans (who/whom) were members of the Iroquois nation.

5. The Mohawk, Seneca, and Oneida were Iroquois groups (who/whom) lived in North America then.

6. In 1608 Samuel de Champlain, (who/whom) wanted to establish French rights to the fur trade, founded Quebec City on the St. Lawrence.

7. Eventually control of the St. Lawrence passed to the British, (who/whom) defeated the French in 1763 in the French and Indian War.

8. The Canadians, (who/whom) wanted to open the Great Lakes to sea traffic, began building canals.

9. The U.S. Congress, (who/whom) formed a partnership with the Canadians, agreed to help construct the St. Lawrence Seaway.

10. In 1959 Queen Elizabeth II of Great Britain dedicated the seaway, along with Dwight Eisenhower, (who/whom) was president of the United States then.

11. The U.S. and Canada, (who/whom) oversee the waterway jointly, regulate traffic through it.

12. The two nations, for (who/whom) construction was costly, set tolls to help pay for the project.

13. A Canadian (who/whom) I spoke with said that sea traffic along the St. Lawrence amounts to about 50 million tons a year.

Name _____

Apply Possible answers appear below. Accept all reasonable responses.

Write a question to go with each statement. Include *who* or *whom* in your question. Be sure to end each sentence with a question mark. The first one is done for you.

14. I read a book about Jacques Cartier. **About whom did you read a book?** _____

15. I wrote a report about fur traders on the St. Lawrence. **About whom did you write a report?** _____

16. Samuel de Champlain wanted to establish France's claims to the St. Lawrence.
Who wanted to establish France's claims to the St. Lawrence? _____

17. The English took control of New France in 1763. **Who took control of New France in 1763?**

18. Canada worked with the United States to construct the St. Lawrence Seaway.
With whom did Canada work to construct the St. Lawrence Seaway? _____

19. President Eisenhower dedicated the seaway with Queen Elizabeth II.
With whom did President Eisenhower dedicate the seaway? _____

20. The U.S. government formed a partnership with the Canadians to run the seaway.
With whom did the U.S. form a partnership to run the seaway? _____

Reinforce Answers will vary. Accept all reasonable responses.

Read the descriptions below. Think of someone you know for whom each description is true. Write the person's name on the line.

Think of someone...

whom you admire _____

who is a great athlete _____

who lives near you _____

with whom you spend Saturdays _____

who has musical talent _____

Now, use your list to write five complete sentences using *who* or *whom*. (*Example: My grandmother is a person whom I admire.*)

21. _____

22. _____

23. _____

24. _____

25. _____

a. Many **people** <u>enjoy</u> white-water rafting.

b. The **sport** <u>becomes</u> more popular every year.

Underline the verb in each sentence. Then look at each boldfaced subject.

Which verb goes with a singular subject? __becomes__

Which verb goes with a plural subject? __enjoy__

The **subject** and its **verb must agree**. Add *-s* or *-es* to a verb in the present tense when the subject is a singular noun or *he, she,* or *it.* Do not add *-s* or *-es* to a verb in the present tense when the subject is a plural noun or *I, you, we,* or *they.* Singular forms of the verb *be* are *is, am,* and *was.* Plural forms are *are* and *were.* Be sure the verb agrees with its subject and not with an object of a preposition that comes before the verb. **Remember to use this information when you speak, too.**

See Handbook | Section 18f

Practice

Circle the correct expression in parentheses to complete each sentence.

1. White-water rafting trips (**offer**/offers) people an opportunity to enjoy wild areas in an exciting way.

2. With interest in extreme sports on the rise, individuals in the U.S. (**want**/wants) new challenges.

3. The International Scale of River Difficulty (rank/**ranks**) rivers by how difficult they are to paddle.

4. Six levels of difficulty (**compose**/composes) this scale.

5. Rivers with a Class I rating (is/**are**) the easiest to navigate.

6. Such a river (**has**/have) few obstructions, though it may have a swift current.

7. Rapids on a Class III river (**require**/requires) careful maneuvering.

8. Steep rapids, powerful and irregular waves, dangerous rocks, and whirlpools (is/**are**) features of Class IV and V rivers.

9. For Class IV through VI rivers, inspections of hazards from the riverbank (is/**are**) mandatory the first time the river is run.

The Gauley River in West Virginia is one of the most advanced white-water runs in the U.S.

10. Class VI rivers, the most difficult kind, (is/**are**) unrunnable, or runnable only by experts.

11. A run on any of these rivers (require/**requires**) taking extreme precautions.

12. A team of rafters never (run/**runs**) a Class VI river if water level or weather is unfavorable.

13. Rafting companies often (**send**/sends) experienced rafters to scout new rivers for rafting trips.

14. Scouts on a new river (**note**/notes) the types of hazards and the number of portages required.

15. Rafters on a portage (**carry**/carries) their raft or boat over land to a safer spot downriver.

16. If the number of hazards (**is**/are) too high, a company will not send rafters there.

Apply

Circle the simple subject in each sentence. Then write the correct form of the verb in parentheses to complete the sentence.

17. Our (team) of expert rafters _____**scouts**_____ new rivers for commercial rafting. (scout)

18. The (rafters) in our company _____**paddle**_____ a river before recommending it to others. (paddle)

19. A (group) of experts _____**decides**_____ on a classification for a river. (decide)

20. Many (aspects) of a river _____**affect**_____ its relative safety. (affect)

21. The (number) of rapids, whirlpools, eddies, and boulders _____**increases**_____ a river's rating. (increase)

22. (Members) of a classification team also _____**consider**_____ the location of the river. (consider)

23. Any classification (system) that makes use of opinions _____**is**_____ imperfect. (be)

24. Sometimes (people) with similar qualifications _____**have**_____ different opinions about a river's difficulty. (have)

25. Risk (factors) such as the amount of water flow _____**are**_____ not constant. (be)

Reinforce Answers will vary. Accept all reasonable responses.

Imagine that you are watching a group of river rafters trying to run some difficult rapids. Write five sentences about what you see. Use present tense verbs in your sentences, and check subject-verb agreement.

26. _____

_____

27. _____

_____

28. _____

_____

29. _____

_____

30. _____

_____

a. (Vince and Reba) live in Florida.

b. (Neither Vince nor Reba) visits the Everglades often.

Circle the compound subject in each sentence. Underline the verb in each sentence. Which sentence has a verb that goes with a singular subject? **b**

A **compound subject** and its verb must agree. If a compound subject includes the conjunction *and,* the subject is plural and needs a plural verb. If a compound subject includes *or* or *nor*, the verb must agree with the last item in the subject.
📢 **Remember to use this information when you speak, too.**

See Handbook Sections 11, 18f

Practice

Look at the compound subject in each sentence. Draw a box around its conjunction. Then underline the correct verb in parentheses.

1. Each year Mr. White ⬚and⬚ Ms. Brooks (take/takes) their classes to Everglades National Park.

2. Either January ⬚or⬚ February (is/are) a good time to visit the park because many tours and programs are offered then.

3. The seventh grade class ⬚and⬚ the eighth grade class (learn/learns) about this distinctive wetland.

4. A ranger ⬚or⬚ a park administrator (explain/explains) that during the wet season, the Everglades is a wide, shallow, slow-moving river.

5. Sanje, Petra, ⬚and⬚ Anya (jot/jots) notes for a class report.

6. The Kissimmee River ⬚and⬚ smaller tributaries (feed/feeds) into Lake Okeechobee.

7. Rainwater ⬚and⬚ groundwater from Lake Okeechobee (supply/supplies) the water to the Everglades.

8. Ms. Brooks ⬚and⬚ the ranger (tell/tells) students how the "river of grass" drains into Florida Bay and the Gulf of Mexico.

9. Shallow water ⬚and⬚ sawgrass (cover/covers) much of the northern part of the Everglades.

10. Saltwater marshes ⬚and⬚ mangrove swamps (form/forms) the southern border of the Everglades.

11. A red mangrove ⬚or⬚ a white mangrove (thrive/thrives) in tidal water.

12. Live oak, mastic, ⬚and⬚ royal palm (grows/grow) on mounds of earth called tree islands.

13. Shark Valley, the Anhinga Trail, ⬚or⬚ Eco Pond (is/are) a good place for viewing alligators.

14. Look over there! A heron ⬚or⬚ an egret (is wading/are wading) in the water!

The blue heron is commonly found wading in the Everglades.

Apply

Write the correct present tense form of the verb in parentheses to complete each sentence.

15. Sanje, Petra, and Anya carefully _____**research**_____ their report on the Everglades. (research)

16. Plants and animals in this region _____**are**_____ interconnected in a fragile ecosystem. (be)

17. A young shrimp or bonefish _____**needs**_____ the shelter offered by a mangrove swamp. (need)

18. Wading birds and alligators _____**snack**_____ on fish and smaller animals. (snack)

19. Small animals and deer _____**are**_____ prey to Florida panthers. (be)

20. Agricultural runoff and other pollutants _____**contaminate**_____ the water and threaten wildlife. (contaminate)

21. Neither the alligator nor the Florida panther _____**thrives**_____ in the Everglades as in the past. (thrive)

22. Disruption of water flow and invasion of non-native plant species _____**damage**_____ the ecosystem in the Everglades. (damage)

23. Canals and levels _____**divert**_____ water from the Everglades for agricultural and urban use. (divert)

24. Neither the Brazilian pepper tree nor the paperbark tree _____**is**_____ native to the Everglades; both have displaced native species there. (be)

Reinforce

Use the information in this lesson to fill in the puzzle. Some answers will be part of a compound subject. Then circle the correct verb in parentheses to complete each clue.

Across

2. Residents and visitors alike (enjoy/enjoys) the _____ Everglades.

4. Neither extreme cold nor sudden temperature change (characterize/characterizes) the climate of the _____.

6. Salt marshes and _____ forests (lie/lies) on the southern border of the Everglades.

7. The _____ River and other tributaries (feed/feeds) into Lake Okeechobee.

Down

1. Either a deer or a smaller animal (make/makes) a meal for a Florida _____.

3. Birds, fish, and _____ (thrive/thrives) in the wetlands.

5. Herons and _____ (is/are) wading birds.

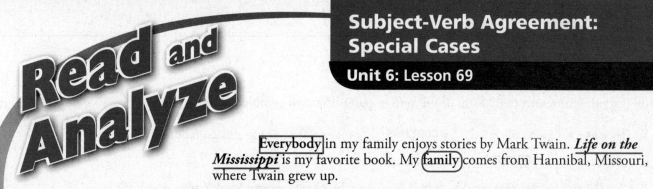

Everybody in my family enjoys stories by Mark Twain. *Life on the Mississippi* is my favorite book. My family comes from Hannibal, Missouri, where Twain grew up.

Look at the boldfaced subjects of these sentences. Circle the noun that refers to more than one person but is considered singular. Underline the book title. Draw a box around the indefinite pronoun. Are the verbs that follow these subjects used with singular subjects or with plural subjects?

<u>**with singular subjects**</u>

The **subject** and its **verb must agree**. There are special rules for certain kinds of subjects. Titles of books, movies, stories, or songs are considered singular even if they end in -*s*. (The Borrowers *is my little brother's favorite book.*) A **collective noun,** such as *collection, group, team, country, kingdom, family, flock,* or *herd,* names more than one person or object acting together as one group. These nouns are almost always considered singular. (*Katie's* <u>team</u> *wins every game.*) Most **indefinite pronouns,** including *everyone, nobody, nothing, something,* and *anything,* are considered singular. (<u>Everybody</u> *likes pizza.*) A few indefinite pronouns, such as *many* and *several,* are considered plural. (<u>Many</u> *like spaghetti.*)

📢 **Remember to use this information when you speak, too.**

See Handbook | Sections 15, 17f, 18f

Practice

Underline the simple subject in each sentence. Circle the correct form of the verb in parentheses.

1. <u>Everyone</u> in my class (is/are) reading *The Adventures of Tom Sawyer*.

2. <u>Many</u> (is/are) aware that Samuel Clemens used the name *Mark Twain* as a pseudonym, or pen name.

3. <u>Nobody</u> in my class (know/knows) what that name means.

4. The <u>phrase</u> *mark twain* (refer/refers) to the second mark on a stick used by riverboat crews to measure the depth of the Mississippi River.

5. A <u>shout</u> of "mark twain" (mean/means) the river is deep enough for a steamboat to pass.

6. My favorite <u>collection</u> of Mark Twain's writings (is/are) the book *Life on the Mississippi*.

7. *Life on the Mississippi* (describe/describes) Twain's experiences learning to pilot a steamboat.

8. My <u>family</u> (has/have) copies of several of Twain's works.

9. Not <u>everybody</u> in my family (enjoy/enjoys) Twain's memoirs as much as I do.

10. <u>Many</u> of us (love/loves) his humorous stories, though.

11. "<u>The Celebrated Jumping Frog of Calaveras County</u>" (is/are) one of our favorites.

12. Right now my mother's book <u>group</u> (is/are) reading Twain's book about King Arthur.

13. *<u>A Connecticut Yankee in King Arthur's Court</u>* (tell/tells) the story of a young American who finds himself transported back to medieval England.

14. *<u>The Prince and the Pauper</u>* (is/are) a fun movie to watch.

Apply

Write the correct present tense form of the verb in parentheses to complete each sentence.

15. That Mark Twain collection _____**contains**_____ many entertaining stories. (contain)

16. My family _____**enjoys**_____ it very much. (enjoy)

17. *The Prince and the Pauper* _____**is**_____ my brother's favorite Mark Twain novel. (be)

18. My class at school _____**likes**_____ *The Adventures of Tom Sawyer*. (like)

19. *The Adventures of Tom Sawyer* _____**tells**_____ about a boy growing up on the Mississippi. (tell)

20. Joe Harper and Huckleberry Finn _____**are**_____ Tom's friends. (be)

21. Tom, Joe, and Huck _____**enjoy**_____ pretending to be pirates. (enjoy)

22. Tom and his friends often _____**get**_____ into mischief. (get)

23. Nobody in my class _____**knows**_____ how the story will end. (know)

24. Everyone _____**wonders**_____ if Tom will get out of trouble. (wonder)

Mark Twain published more than thirty books throughout his career.

Reinforce

Flock and *herd* are not the only collective names that can refer to a group of animals. Groups of certain kinds of animals can be named by special collective nouns. Some of these nouns may be familiar to you, but others are used very rarely.

Match the collective nouns below with the animal groups they refer to. Write the correct letter in the blank.

a. oxen   d. owls   g. bats   i. crows

b. crocodiles e. gorillas   h. whales   j. lions

c. monkeys   f. wolves

25. colony _**g**_   28. team _**a**_   31. parliament _**d**_   33. troop _**c**_

26. band _**e**_   29. pod _**h**_   32. bask _**b**_   34. pack _**f**_

27. pride _**j**_   30. murder _**i**_

Now use one of these collective nouns in a sentence. Remember that a collective noun is almost always singular even when it is followed by a prepositional phrase *(Example: A pride of lions is sleeping near that tree.)*

35. **Answers will vary.** _____

_____

a. Rafting down the Colorado River, Amanda saw many gorgeous sights.

b. Forgetting to use sunscreen, her nose got sunburned.

c. Filled with equipment, Amanda learned to pilot the raft.

Who went rafting down the Colorado River in sentence *a*? _____**Amanda**_____

Does sentence *b* tell who was forgetting to use sunscreen? _____**no**_____

Who or what does sentence *c* seem to say was filled with equipment?
_____**Amanda**_____

Verbal phrases must always refer to, or modify, a nearby noun or a pronoun in the main part of a sentence. **Dangling modifiers** are phrases that do not clearly refer to any particular word in a sentence. **Misplaced modifiers** are phrases that seem to refer to the wrong noun or pronoun in a sentence. When you begin a sentence with a verbal phrase such as "Traveling down the Colorado River," make sure that the question "Who is traveling?" is answered clearly in the first part of the rest of the sentence.

See Handbook Sections 25a, 25b, 31

Practice

Underline the verbal phrase that begins each sentence. Circle the simple subject or subjects of the clause it introduces. If the underlined phrase modifies the subject(s) you circled, write *C* on the line. If the phrase is a dangling modifier or a misplaced modifier, write *X* on the line.

1. Visiting Arizona last year, I rafted down part of the Colorado River. __C__

2. Originating in the Rockies, the Colorado River flows 1,450 miles to the Gulf of California. __C__

3. Winding through rock and sandstone, deep canyons have been cut by the Colorado River. __X__

4. Stretching 277 miles, the Grand Canyon is the largest and most impressive of these. __C__

5. Encompassing more than 1,200,000 acres, Grand Canyon National Park lies on the Colorado Plateau in northwestern Arizona. __C__

6. Considered an example of arid-land erosion, the guide told us about the geology of the area. __X__

7. Averaging 4,000 feet deep, the widest point is fifteen miles across. __X__

8. Known for its geologic importance, we read why the Grand Canyon has been designated a World Heritage Site. __X__

9. Blocked by dams, the guide said that the water flow of the Colorado has been reduced. __X__

10. Needing water from the river, ranchers, farmers, and city-dwellers compete for water allocations. __C__

11. Stopping the raft to point out petroglyphs, we learned about ancient cultures from our guide. __X__

12. Wanting to capture their beauty, I took several photographs. __C__

13. Leaning down to feel the cool water, my camera fell into the river. __X__

14. Trying to grab the camera, my sister almost fell overboard! __C__

Name _____

Apply Possible answers appear below. Accept all reasonable responses.

Each of these sentences from the Practice section has a dangling or misplaced modifier. Rewrite each so that the error is corrected. There is more than one way to rewrite each sentence.

15. Winding through rock and sandstone, deep canyons have been cut by the Colorado River. **Winding through rock and sandstone, the Colorado River has cut deep canyons.**

16. Considered an example of arid-land erosion, the guide told us about the geology of the area.

    The guide told us about the geology of the Grand Canyon, which is considered an example of arid-land erosion.

17. Averaging 4,000 feet deep, the widest point is fifteen miles across. **Averaging 4,000 feet deep, the Grand Canyon is fifteen miles across at its widest point.**

18. Known for its geologic importance, we read why the Grand Canyon has been designated a World Heritage Site. **Known for its geologic importance, the Grand Canyon has been designated a World Heritage Site.**

19. Blocked by dams, the guide said that the water flow of the Colorado has been reduced.
    Blocked by dams, the Colorado has had its water flow reduced.

    _____

20. Stopping the raft to point out petroglyphs, we learned about ancient cultures from our guide.
    Stopping the raft to point out petroglyphs, our guide told us about ancient cultures.

21. Leaning down to feel the cool water, my camera fell into the river. **Leaning down to feel the cool water, I dropped my camera into the river.**

Reinforce Answers will vary.

Use your imagination to think of an independent clause to complete each sentence below. Write the clause on the line. Make sure the noun or pronoun that the verbal phrase modifies is near the introductory phrase.

22. Planning a trip to the river, _____.

23. Swimming in the river, _____.

24. Rafting down the river, _____.

25. Leaving the river, _____.

The Amazon River is (more powerful) than the Missouri River. The Amazon is the **most powerful** river in the world.

Circle the boldfaced words that compare the Amazon River with the Missouri River. Underline the boldfaced words that compare the Amazon River with more than one other river.

The **comparative form** of an **adjective** or **adverb** compares two people, places, things, or actions. Add *-er* to short adjectives and adverbs to create the comparative form. Use the word *more* before long adjectives and adverbs to create the comparative form (*more powerful*). The **superlative form** compares three or more people, places, things, or actions. Add *-est* to create the superlative form of short adjectives and adverbs. Use the word *most* before long adjectives and adverbs to create the superlative form (*most powerful*). Use *better* and *less* to compare two things. Use *best* and *least* to compare three or more things.

📣 **Remember to use this information when you speak, too.**

See Handbook | Section 27

Practice

Think about how many things are being compared in each sentence. Then underline the correct form of the adjective or adverb in parentheses.

1. For many years, geographers agreed that the Nile River was the (longer/longest) river in the world.

2. In 2007, some Brazilian scientists claimed that the Amazon River stretched slightly (farther/farthest).

3. Geographers have yet to agree on the Amazon's precise length, but they have proven that it carries (more water/most water) than any other river.

4. In fact, the volume of water flowing through the Amazon is (greater/greatest) than the volume of water in the Nile, the Mississippi, and the Yangtze rivers combined.

5. The Amazon begins in the Andes Mountains of Peru, at a site (higher/highest) than 17,000 feet in elevation.

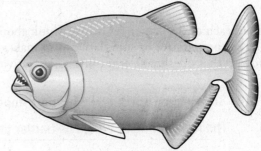

About 20 species of piranha live in the Amazon.

6. As the Amazon wends its way toward the Atlantic Ocean, more than 200 (smaller/smallest) rivers flow into it.

7. Many unusual fish live in the Amazon; piranha are among the (fiercer/fiercest) fish on the planet.

8. One of the (larger/largest) freshwater fish of South America, the pirarucú, lives in the Amazon.

9. The rainforest that covers the Amazon River Basin is the world's (larger/largest) tropical rainforest.

10. Some of its birds are the (more colorful/most colorful) species ever seen.

11. Today, many scientists have called for the Amazon basin's resources to be guarded (more carefully/most carefully) than they have been in the past.

Name _____

Apply

Write the correct form of the adjective or adverb in parentheses.

12. The Amazon may not be the _____**longest**_____ river in the world, but it is longer than the Mississippi. (long)

13. The volume of water flowing through the mouth of the Amazon is _____**greater**_____ than the volume that flows through the mouth of the Nile. (great)

14. The Amazon looks brown at times, but it's not the world's _____**muddiest**_____ river; that is probably the Yellow River in China. (muddy)

15. Plant and animal life in the Amazon basin is _____**more diverse**_____ than in any other area. (diverse)

16. What do you think is the _____**most impressive**_____ feature of the Amazon? (impressive)

17. Would you boat down the Amazon _____**more eagerly**_____ than you would down the Nile? (eagerly)

Reinforce   Possible answers appear below. Accept all reasonable responses.

Some adjectives are *absolute*: either they describe a thing or they do not. They cannot properly be put into the comparative form. For example, a plant is either dead or alive; it does not make sense to say "That plant is the *deadest* of all."

Read each of the sentences below. Think about each boldfaced adjective. Decide whether putting that adjective in the comparative or superlative form makes sense. If it does not, rewrite the sentence with an adjective or an adverb that does make sense in a comparative expression.

18. The Amazon River would be **more impossible** to swim than the Nile.

   The Amazon River would be harder to swim than the Nile.

19. Rain gear is **more sensible** to take on an Amazon journey than on a Nile expedition.

   (Original sentence makes sense.)

20. The story you wrote about the Amazon was the **most unique** I have ever read.

   The story you wrote about the Amazon was the most unusual I have ever read.

21. I think the **most perfect** vacation would be to canoe down the Amazon.

   I think the perfect vacation would be to canoe down the Amazon.

Read and Analyze

I **have** read quite a bit about the Ganges River in India.

It **might** be the river I most want to visit.

Circle the main boldfaced verb in each sentence. Underline the boldfaced auxiliary verb that works with each main verb.

An **auxiliary verb**, or **helping verb**, works with a main verb. Auxiliary verbs have different purposes. Some auxiliary verbs, such as *do, are, have,* and *will,* help indicate the tense of the main verb. They can also be used to form negatives and questions. Other auxiliary verbs carry special meanings; these are called *modal auxiliaries. Could, should, would, might,* and *may* are used to refer to a possible action, or to tell how likely it is that something will happen. *May* is also used to express permission. *Can* expresses ability.

See Handbook Sections 18c, 18e

Practice

Circle the main verb or verbs in each sentence. Then underline each auxiliary verb. Not every main verb will have an auxiliary.

1. We are writing reports about India in my social studies class.

2. I will write a report about the Ganges River.

3. Do you know that the Ganges is considered the greatest river in India?

4. I can tell you why.

5. The Ganges has created a fertile river valley where many crops are grown.

6. Some of India's largest cities have been built along the banks of the Ganges.

7. The Ganges has been sacred to Hindus for thousands of years.

8. Every year pilgrims travel great distances so they can bathe in it.

9. Many believe that the river can cure ailments.

10. I will visit the Ganges as a tourist one day.

11. I may visit ancient sites along its banks.

12. I might even see a rare Ganges river dolphin.

13. My classmates did not know that some types of dolphins live in freshwater.

14. Today the Ganges river dolphin population may number only 2,000.

Many people travel to the city of Varanasi to bathe in the Ganges.

15. If conservation measures are taken soon, the species might be saved.

Apply Possible answers appear below. Accept all reasonable responses.

Complete each sentence with an auxiliary verb. Some sentences have more than one correct answer.

16. I wish that I _____**could**_____ visit the Ganges River.

17. I _____**can**_____ imagine how exciting that would be!

18. I _____**would**_____ trace its course from high in the Himalayas all the way to the Bay of Bengal.

19. My family _____**may**_____ go to India next year to visit our relatives.

20. We _____**have**_____ not seen them in nearly five years.

21. We _____**might**_____ stay with my aunt and uncle in Kolkata, one of the biggest cities in the world.

22. You _____**may**_____ not know that Kolkata used to be known as Calcutta.

23. In that city, my sister and I _____**could**_____ visit the Indian Botanic Garden.

24. My family _____**could**_____ also visit Varanasi, the holiest Hindu city along the Ganges.

25. I _____**do**_____ not know how many people bathe in the Ganges at Varanasi.

26. It _____**must**_____ be more than 50,000 every day.

27. I _____**will**_____ research more sights along the Ganges.

28. Then I _____**can**_____ persuade my parents to take us there.

Reinforce

Find eight helping verbs in the puzzle and circle them.

O	M	R	I	C	A	N	Q
Z	I	B	S	R	D	L	X
W	G	U	K	F	H	C	M
I	H	A	V	E	P	U	G
K	T	I	H	M	O	X	I
J	N	M	V	U	Q	S	L
D	C	A	Q	W	V	E	D
O	V	Y	A	I	X	Z	V
E	P	X	S	L	G	Y	Y
S	H	O	U	L	D	K	K

Now imagine taking a trip along a famous river. Write two sentences about your trip, using helping verbs you found in the puzzle.

29. **Answers will vary.** _____

_____

30. _____

Review

(Numbers in parentheses identify related lessons.)

Subject and Object Pronouns

Circle each boldfaced word that is a subject pronoun. Underline each boldfaced word that is an object pronoun.

1. **I** am doing a report on the Amazon River Basin. **(61)**

2. Peter is working with **me** to research and write **it**. **(61)**

3. **We** are going to describe the plants and animals in the basin. **(61)**

Pronouns in Pairs

Circle the correct pronoun or pronouns in parentheses.

4. Peter and (**I**/me) are going to split the research. **(62)**

5. Our teacher told (me and him/**him and me**) to include a map of the river. **(62)**

6. I really hope that Peter and (**I**/me) are happy with our finished report. **(62)**

Pronoun-Antecedent Agreement

Circle the antecedent of each boldfaced pronoun.

7. The **source** of the Amazon is high in the Andes, which makes **it** hard to reach. **(63)**

8. The Amazon has many **tributaries**; **they** join the river at different points. **(63)**

9. Last year my **uncle** visited Brazil, and **he** took a boat ride on the Amazon. **(63)**

Who and *Whom*

Write *who* or *whom* to complete each sentence correctly.

10. Many European explorers _____who_____ sighted natural features gave them new names. **(66)**

11. John Hanning Speke was the man _____who_____ named Lake Victoria. **(66)**

12. The person after _____whom_____ the lake was named was Queen Victoria. **(66)**

Verbs

Circle the correct form of each verb in parentheses.

13. Neither the Amazon nor the Nile (**is**/are) easy to navigate. **(68)**

14. The film *Mystery of the Nile* (tell/**tells**) of two men's trip down the Blue Nile. **(69)**

15. The story about their adventures (**is**/are) very exciting. **(67)**

16. Challenges of the worst kind (**face**/faces) the explorers on their journey down the river. **(67)**

17. They (have withstand/**must withstand**) extreme temperatures and violent sandstorms. **(72)**

18. A crocodile attack and exposure to malaria (is/**are**) two other challenges. **(68)**

19. I (have travel/**would travel**) down the Nile or the Amazon if I had the chance. **(72)**

20. Nobody (love/**loves**) adventure more than I do. **(69)**

Dangling and Misplaced Modifiers

Underline the verbal phrase that begins each sentence. If the phrase is a dangling or misplaced modifier, write *X* on the line. If the phrase is used correctly, circle the word it modifies and write *C* on the line.

21. Researching the Amazon, (I) learned many facts I did not know before. __C__ **(70)**

22. Flowing more than 4,000 miles, many explorers have traveled that great river. __X__ **(70)**

23. Winding through dense rainforest, countless species inhabit the Amazon. __X__ **(70)**

Comparative and Superlative Adjectives and Adverbs

Circle the correct form of the adjective or adverb in parentheses.

24. Some scientists are trying to prove that the Amazon is the (longer/(longest)) river on Earth. **(71)**

25. They claim that the Nile is ((shorter)/shortest) than the Amazon. **(71)**

26. Without a doubt, the Amazon carries the (more/(most)) water of any river. **(71)**

Revising Sentences Possible answers appear below. Accept all reasonable responses.

Rewrite each sentence so that it is correct. Be sure to replace vague pronouns.

27. My story about Amazon adventures are called "A Week With Crocodiles." **My story about Amazon adventures is called "A Week With Crocodiles." (69)**

28. In the story, a doctor, an extreme athlete, and a spy travels down the river. **In the story, a doctor, an extreme athlete, and a spy travel down the river. (68)**

29. The group are being chased by villains. **The group is being chased by villains. (69)**

30. Neither the doctor nor the extreme athlete know about the pursuers. **Neither the doctor nor the extreme athlete knows about the pursuers. (68)**

31. The spy is carrying a priceless mineral that the leader of the villains want. **The spy is carrying a priceless mineral that the leader of the villains wants. (67)**

32. Chasing the heroes in a boat, crocodiles eat the villains. **Chasing the heroes in a boat, the villains are eaten by crocodiles. (70)**

33. My neighbors Luis and Hector Flores own a digital movie camera, and they like my story; he wants to film some scenes from "A Week With Crocodiles." **My neighbors Luis and Hector Flores own a digital movie camera, and they like my story; they want to film some scenes from "A Week With Crocodiles." (64)**

34. They have found spots along a nearby creek that they think we can use as locations for Amazon River scenes. **Luis and Hector have found spots along a nearby creek that they think we can use as locations for Amazon River scenes. (65)**

35. It is exciting, and I am looking forward to working on it with them. **The idea of filming scenes from my story is exciting, and I am looking forward to working on that project with Luis and Hector. (65)**

Spelling Practice

The river flows (continuously).

The animals **continually** visit the river.

Circle the word in bold type that means "constantly." Underline the word in bold type that means "frequently."

Frequently Misspelled Words

Homophones, such as *assent* and *ascent,* and words that sound alike, such as *continually* and *continuously,* can cause confusion. One way to know which word to use is to consider the context of the sentence.

Words in Context

Write the word that best completes each sentence. Use a dictionary if you need help.

disburse	confidently	morale	canvas	moral	compliment
discrete	canvass	disperse	confidentially	complement	discreet

1. Politicians _____**canvass**_____ our neighborhood during campaign season.

2. Do you have anything made of _____**canvas**_____?

3. Is it ever _____**moral**_____ to borrow money and not return it?

4. Our team's _____**morale**_____ was low after we lost the game.

5. The police came to _____**disperse**_____ the crowd.

6. The club treasurer will _____**disburse**_____ the necessary funds.

7. My art teacher paid me a nice _____**compliment**_____ on my painting today!

8. A speaker strode _____**confidently**_____ on stage.

9. Speak to Dr. Kangas _____**confidentially**_____.

10. Are you _____**discreet**_____ enough to keep a secret?

11. The new mechanism has six _____**discrete**_____ parts.

12. *Sweet* and *salty* are flavors that _____**complement**_____ each other well.

Pattern Practice

ascent	affect	persecution	descent
immigrant	device	dissent	emigrant
assent	effect	prosecution	devise

Each of the boldfaced words in Sentences 13–18 has some letters missing. Finish the correct spelling of each word, using the word bank and a dictionary for help, as needed. Then correctly answer each question by circling *Yes* or *No*.

13. Would a climber make an **as____cen____t** up a mountain? (**Yes**/No)

14. Would you camp at the top of a mountain before starting your **d____esc____ent**? (**Yes**/No)

15. Do people ever **d____iss____ent** from others' opinions? (**Yes**/No)

16. Do disobedient children **as____sen____t** to their parents' requests? (Yes/**No**)

17. Does sunlight ____**af**____fect plant growth? (**Yes**/No)

18. Does studying usually have a negative ____**ef**____fect on a student's grade? (Yes/**No**)

For Items 19–24, fill in each blank as directed, using a word from the word bank. Consult a dictionary if you need help.

19. Write a word that means "a person who migrates to." _____**immigrant**_____

20. Write a word that means "a person who migrates from." _____**emigrant**_____

21. Write a word that means "abuse." _____**persecution**_____

22. Write a word that has to do with court proceedings. _____**prosecution**_____

23. Write a word that means "to imagine or plan." _____**devise**_____

24. Write a word that means "an instrument or a tool." _____**device**_____

Use the Dictionary

Circle the word in each pair that best completes each sentence. Use a print dictionary or an online dictionary if you need help.

25. The color red has a (denotation/**connotation**) of danger.

26. Their arrival home is (**imminent**/eminent).

27. The gracious leader bowed (**respectfully**/respectively)

Diagramming Participial Phrases

You have learned that participial phrases function as adjectives. They are diagrammed as shown below.

The kayak **floating by the dock** is yours.

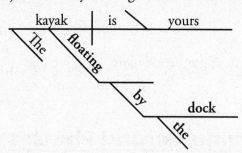

Diagram these sentences. Refer to the model if you need help.

1. The woman carrying paddles is our instructor.

2. We must avoid people behaving foolishly.

3. Rafters paddling together control their boat effectively.

Diagramming Infinitive Phrases

An infinitive phrase can function as a noun. The infinitive phrase in the sentence below functions as the direct object of the verb *wants*. Study how this type of phrase is diagrammed.

Kirk wants **to go faster**.

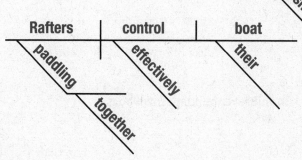

Diagram these sentences. Refer to the model if you need help.

4. The other rafters prefer to go slower.

5. I have to help my brother into the boat.

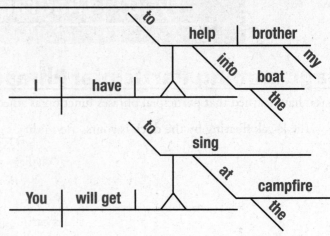

6. You will get to sing at the campfire.

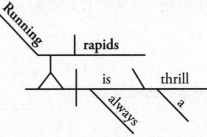

Diagramming Gerund Phrases

You have learned that gerund phrases function as nouns. The gerund phrase in the sentence below functions as the subject. Notice how it is diagrammed.

Running rapids is always a thrill.

Diagram these sentences. Note that in one sentence the gerund phrase is the subject, in another it is a direct object, and in another it is the object of a preposition.

7. Bonnie loves building small boats.

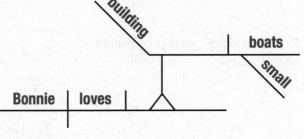

8. Packing the car will take hours.

9. The task of washing the oars is easy.

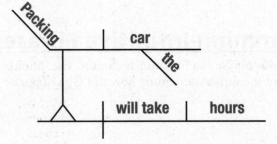

Writing Sentences

These sentences need your help. Rewrite each one so that the subject and verb agree.

1. The Nile and the Ganges has supported great civilizations for thousands of years. **The Nile and the Ganges have supported great civilizations for thousands of years.**

2. Likewise, the Ganges and its many tributaries carries nutrient-laden soil from high in the Himalayas to the delta far below. **Likewise, the Ganges and its many tributaries carry nutrient-laden soil from high in the Himalayas to the delta far below.**

3. Each of the two rivers supply fertile soil in which to grow crops. **Each of the two rivers supplies fertile soil in which to grow crops.**

4. Floods along the Nile replenishes the soil with rich silt carried from high in the mountains. **Floods along the Nile replenish the soil with rich silt carried from high in the mountains.**

5. Both the Ganges and the Nile is central to the cultural heritage of the surrounding regions. **Both the Ganges and the Nile are central to the cultural heritage of the surrounding regions.**

6. The two rivers has long been important means of transportation through their respective continents. **The two rivers have long been important means of transportation through their respective continents.**

7. The tombs of many Egyptian pharaohs is located near the Nile, and thousands of Hindus take their dead to the Ganges because they view the river as sacred. **The tombs of many Egyptian pharaohs are located near the Nile, and thousands of Hindus take their dead to the Ganges because they view the river as sacred.**

A piece of writing that compares the characteristics of two people, places, or things may be divided into two paragraphs. The first paragraph may describe how the two things being compared are alike or how they are different. The second paragraph should describe the opposite. Each paragraph should have a topic sentence stating its main idea. Notice the structure of this model.

At first glance, the Colorado River and the Columbia River seem to be very different. The lower Columbia River flows through the lush green hills, fern-lined gorges, and evergreen forests of the Pacific Northwest on its way to the sea. The Colorado River winds through the desert valleys and immense rock and sandstone canyons of the Southwest. Each river supports distinct ecosystems.

A closer look reveals several important similarities between the two rivers. Each river has supported Native American populations for thousands of years. Both rivers serve as partial natural borders between states. The Columbia provides much of the border between Washington and Oregon. The Colorado River divides Arizona from the southeast corner of California. A number of dams have been constructed along both rivers to provide water and hydroelectric power to surrounding communities. Today, many people use these rivers for recreational activities, including rafting, fishing, and swimming.

Writing a Paragraph

A suggested answer appears below. Accept all reasonable responses.

The sentences you repaired on page 219 can be reordered to make one paragraph describing similarities between the Nile and the Ganges rivers. Write a topic sentence to introduce the paragraph. Then reorder the supporting sentences, and write the paragraph on the lines below.

The Nile and the Ganges are alike in several ways. Each of the two rivers supplies fertile soil in which to grow crops. Floods along the Nile replenish the soil with rich silt carried from high in the mountains. Likewise, the Ganges and its many tributaries carry nutrient-laden soil from high in the Himalayas to the delta far below. The two rivers have long been important means of transportation through their respective continents. The Nile and the Ganges have supported great civilizations for thousands of years. Both the Ganges and the Nile are central to the cultural heritage of the surrounding regions. The tombs of many Egyptian pharaohs are located near the Nile, and thousands of Hindus take their dead to the Ganges because they view the river as sacred.

Write two paragraphs of your own in which you compare and contrast two rivers you have learned about or have visited. Be sure to use a topic sentence and supporting examples in each paragraph. Use the model paragraphs on page 219 as a guide. Continue writing on a separate sheet of paper if you need more room.

Answers will vary.

_____

_____

_____

_____

_____

_____

Reread your composition. Use this checklist to make sure it is complete and correct.

❑ My composition has a clear main idea.

❑ Each paragraph contains a topic sentence and supporting details.

❑ I have described both similarities and differences.

❑ The subject and verb in each sentence agree.

❑ I have included comparative adjectives and other words used to compare, such as *alike, different, both,* and *neither.*

Proofreading
Practice

Read this passage about the Mackenzie River in Canada and find the mistakes. Use the proofreading marks below to show how each mistake should be fixed. Use a dictionary to check and correct spellings.

Proofreading Marks

Suggested answers appear below.
Accept all reasonable responses.

Mark	Means	Example
୶	delete	The Mackenzie River flow~~es~~ through Alberta.
∧	add	The Mackenzie ∧River flows through Alberta.
≡	make into an uppercase letter	The Mackenzie river flows through Alberta.
/	make into a lowercase letter	The MacKenzie River flows through Alberta.
⊙	add a period	The Mackenzie River flows through Alberta⊙
sp	fix spelling	The Mackenzie River flows thru Alberta.

The Mackenzie River

Can you identify the ~~most long~~ **longest** river in Canada? ~~Its~~ **It's** the Mackenzie River, and it's 1,025 miles long. The river originates at Great Slave Lake, which ~~are~~ **is** located in the Northwestern Territories of Canada, and ~~flow~~ **flows** north to the Arctic Ocean⊙

Because it runs through some of the most remote parts of the country⊙ The Mackenzie is known as canada's last truly wild river. Even so, the Mackenzie ~~was~~ **has** been important to indigenous peoples, European explorers, fur traders, and miners. Alexander Mackenzie, the man after ~~who~~ **whom** the river was named, traveled to the river in 1789 as he ~~is~~ **was** attempting to reach the Pacific Ocaen (sp). Before Mackenzie arrived, native people refered (sp) to the river as *Deh Cho,* ~~that~~ **which** means "big river."

In the summer, the river delta of the Mackenzie pruvides (sp) habitat for migrating snow geese and tundra swans. The estuary, or place ~~weat~~ **where** the Mackenzie meets the ocean, ~~are~~ **is** a calving area for Beluga whales. The river is only navigable for about five months of the year. The waters of the Mackenzie ~~freeze~~ **freeze** over in October most years and ~~remains~~ **remain** frozen until May. During the winter, sections of the river ~~is~~ **are** used as ice roads. Ice bridges are also constructed ~~too~~ **to** carry truck traffic. In both summer and winter, the river serves as an important means of transportasion (sp).

Proofreading
Checklist

You can use the list below to help you find and fix mistakes in your own writing. Write the titles of your own stories or reports in the blanks at the top of the chart. Then use the questions to check your work. Make a check mark (✔) in each box after you have checked that item. **Answers will vary.**

	Titles			
Proofreading Checklist for Unit 6				
Have I used the correct subject and object pronouns?				
Have I made sure that all pronouns agree with their antecedents in number and gender?				
Does every verb agree with its subject?				
Have I avoided dangling and misplaced modifiers?				

Also Remember…

Does each sentence begin with an uppercase letter?				
Did I use a dictionary to check and correct spellings?				
Have I used commas correctly?				

Your Own List

Use this space to write your own list of things to check in your writing.

Community Connection

In Unit 6 of *Grammar, Usage, and Mechanics,* students learned more about **grammar,** and they used what they learned to improve their own writing. The content of these lessons focuses on the theme **Rivers of the World.** As students completed the exercises, they learned about several of the world's major rivers. They also read about the importance of rivers for transportation, economic development, and recreation. These pages offer a variety of activities that reinforce skills and concepts presented in the unit. They also provide opportunities for students to make connections between the content of the lessons and the community at large.

Water Works

Invite an official from a local water agency to come to class. Have him or her speak about how that agency goes about providing water for residents, businesses, and farms in the area. Prior to the official's visit, prepare a list of questions to ask him or her. After the visit, write a summary of what you learned.

A River Profile

Choose a river that is important to people in your region. Do research in a library or on the Internet to find out as much as you can about the river. Try to answer these questions: Where is the river's source? How long is the river? How did it get its name? What cities and towns have been built along its course? How do people use its water? What dams have been built on it? How clean is its water? What types of wildlife depend on it? Create and present a display about this river. Use an electronic presentation program if possible. Be sure to include a map; also include photos and other graphics.

River Trivia

Work with a group to prepare 50 questions about rivers. Use facts from the lessons as well as facts from original research. Write each question and its answer on an index card or slip of paper. Rate each question as *easy, average,* or *difficult.* Then decide on rules for a trivia game. You can play just among the group; or you can play against other groups, mixing your questions with theirs.

River Sport Speech

Choose one of these river sports to learn more about:

- rowing
- windsurfing
- water skiing
- wakeboarding
- fishing
- kayaking
- canoeing
- rafting

Find out about this sport by conducting an Internet search, looking at books and magazines about this activity, or interviewing at least one local person involved with this activity. Then write a speech describing the activity and explaining what type of person would be likely to enjoy it. Use the speech planner on the following page to help you organize your ideas.

Name _____

River Sport Speech Planner Answers will vary.

Sport to be profiled: _____

What the sport involves: _____

_____

_____

What equipment is required: _____

_____

_____

What skills must be learned: _____

_____

_____

What safety rules must be followed: _____

_____

_____

Where this activity can be done: _____

_____

_____

Why this activity is fun: _____

_____

_____

Why this activity can be healthful and educational: _____

_____

_____

What kind of person should choose this activity (for example, nature lover, adventurer, athlete, thrill seeker): _____

_____

_____

_____

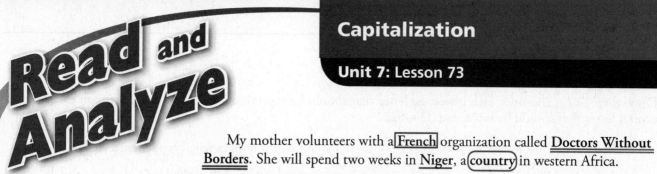

My mother volunteers with a **French** organization called **Doctors Without Borders**. She will spend two weeks in **Niger**, a **country** in western Africa.

Circle the boldfaced word that does not refer to a specific nation. Draw one line under the boldfaced word that names a specific nation. Draw two lines under the boldfaced phrase that names a specific organization. Draw a box around the boldfaced word that is an adjective.

Proper nouns are the names of particular people, places, or things. Capitalize each important word in the names of people, geographic locations, important events, holidays, periods of time, organizations, companies, and products. **Proper adjectives** are descriptive words formed from proper nouns. They must be capitalized. A **title of respect,** such as *Mr.* or *Judge,* is capitalized when it is used directly in front of a person's name.

See Handbook Sections 1, 2, 3, 15

Practice

Draw three lines (≡) under each lowercase letter that should be capitalized. (1–34) Then circle each proper noun and draw a box around each proper adjective.

Doctors without borders is an international humanitarian organization. Started in France in december of 1971, the organization now has offices in the united states, japan, canada, sweden, and many other countries. this organization's doctors are working to fight malnutrition in children under five years of age in Africa and Southeast asia. As dr. christophe fournier points out, young children who do not receive the right vitamins and nutrients are more susceptible to disease.

Fortunately a new food product called Plumpy'nut is helping in the fight against malnutrition. It was invented by french scientist dr. andré Briend he got the idea from a european nut spread named Nutella. plumpy'nut which is a combination of the words *plump* and *peanut,* is a mixture of peanut butter, powdered milk, and powdered sugar that is fortified with vitamins and minerals.

Foods such as plumpy'nut, which do not require refrigeration, are very useful in war-torn places such as Somalia and Sudan Plumpy'nut costs less than milk formula, does not need to be mixed with anything, and has a shelf life of two years.

In october 2007 doctors without borders urged the united nations and the United States to contribute more money for the purchase of ready-to-use food. Currently one company, nutriset is manufacturing Plumpy'nut. companies in malawi and in niamey, the capital of Niger, are making versions of the product as well. Chief nutritionist dr. Milton Tectonidis says that if the United states and the european union would spend more food aid on fortified foods, more companies would want to produce them.

Apply

Draw three lines (≡) under each lowercase letter that should be capitalized. Draw a line (/) through each capital letter that should be lowercase. (35–52)

On wednesday ms. lopez's social studies class learned about world hunger relief. Students created a map showing the three Regions where acute malnutrition is most prevalent: the Sahel, the Horn of africa, and southeast asia. The sahel is a vast dry region in Africa. It borders the atlantic ocean and extends east to the other side of the continent. Among the nations in this Region are senegal, mauritania, mali, Niger, Chad, and Sudan. The Horn of Africa refers to the large Peninsula of east africa that juts into the Arabian Sea. Countries in the Horn of Africa include ethiopia, eritrea, and Somalia.

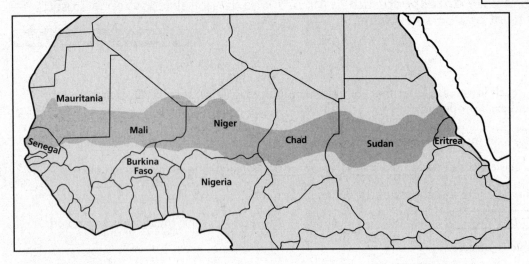

AFRICA

Mauritania

Mali

Niger

Senegal

Burkina Faso

Chad

Sudan

Eritrea

Nigeria

Reinforce

See Handbook Section 35

Today it is common for friends to exchange e-mails that do not include proper capitalization. Read this passage from a friendly e-mail. Then rewrite it with correct capitalization and punctuation. Afterward, discuss with a partner which version you prefer and why.

do you want to see the movie this saturday?? sam saw it and really liked it maybe we could catch the two o'clock show...i have to finish my report about africa first, but i should finish by noon let me know what you think...

Do you want to see the movie this Saturday? Sam saw it and really liked it. Maybe we could catch

the two o'clock show. I have to finish my report about Africa first, but I should finish by noon. Let me know

what you think.

Read and Analyze

"The Sinking of the Reuben James" is a song by Woody Guthrie. I saw a documentary film about Guthrie called American Masters: Woody Guthrie. Circle the film title. Draw a box around the title of the song. How are they written differently? **The song is in quotation marks, and the film is underlined.**

Underline the **titles** of **books, magazines, newspapers, movies, CDs,** and **DVDs**. These are written in italics in printed text. Use quotation marks around the titles of **songs, stories,** and **poems**. **Capitalize** the first word and the last word in titles. Capitalize all other words except articles, short prepositions, and coordinating conjunctions. Remember to capitalize short verbs, such as *is* and *are*.

See Handbook Section 3

Practice

Draw three lines (≡) under each lowercase letter that should be an uppercase letter. Underline or add quotation marks to titles.

1. I'm writing an essay called "voices for social repairs," which focuses

   on writers and musicians who have used their compositions

   to highlight social injustice.

2. For example, Upton Sinclair's book the jungle exposed sanitation problems in

   the American meatpacking industry.

3. Woody Guthrie's song "this land is your land" was a reminder that America's

   wonders belong to all its people.

Woody Guthrie wrote and sang songs that covered political topics and traditional themes.

4. I read a biograpy about him called This land was made for you and me.

5. There is also a CD called bound for glory: songs and stories of woody guthrie.

6. Have you seen the movie the grapes of wrath? It was based on John Steinbeck's

   novel about refugees who came west from Oklahoma during the Great Depression.

7. to kill a mockingbird is a book that tells about injustice toward African Americans in the South

   during the 1930s.

8. Langston Hughes's poem "mother to son" encourages readers not to let life's burdens wear them down.

9. Many songs written in the 1960s protested the poor treatment of individuals and groups. A time magazine

   article from 1963 describes this phenomenon.

10. A TV show called bob dylan: live in newport 1963–1965 highlights several of his protest songs, which call

    for an end to prejudice, injustice, and aggression.

11. In 1972, Helen Reddy's song "i am woman" became an anthem of the women's movement to achieve equality.

Apply

Read the titles of the works on the library shelf. Look back at the titles of works mentioned in the Practice section. Then answer each question. Use correct capitalization and punctuation in each title.

12. Which book is probably a fiction book? **Pete Lucky's Happy Accident**

13. Which DVD probably shows live music performances? **The Folk Concert of the Century**

14. Which DVD might contain information about Albert Einstein? **Great Thinkers of the Twentieth Century**
_____

15. Which book might you use to research a report on creative people? **Seven Creative Geniuses**
_____

16. Write the title of one song you might hear on *Strong Voices of the 1970s*. **"I Am Woman"**
_____

17. Which CD presents a recorded version of a book? **Pete Lucky's Happy Accident**

18. Which book might outline sources of air pollution? **What You Can Do for the Environment Today**
_____

19. Which book would likely be a good source for help with algebra problems? **Math Problems Can Be Easy to Solve**

20. Which book might have information about the American civil rights movement? **A Social History of the 1960s**

Reinforce Answers will vary.

A Hollywood film studio is interested in turning your book about a famous artist, musician, dancer, or athlete into a major motion picture. On another sheet of paper, write a paragraph to convince the company to do so. Include the title of the book, and create an exciting movie title. Use correct capitalization and punctuation.

(Thurs.), (Oct.) 10 ☆

9:00 — Report on Franklin D. Roosevelt due.

3:30 — Checkup at <u>Dr.</u> Turner's office, 220 Houston Blvd.

Underline a short way to write *Doctor*. Draw a square around a short way to write *Boulevard*. Circle short ways to write *Thursday* and *October*. Draw a star above a letter that stands for a name.

An **abbreviation** is a shortened form of a word. **Titles of respect** are usually abbreviated. So are words in **addresses,** such as *Street (St.), Avenue (Ave.),* and *Boulevard (Blvd.).* The names of **days,** the names of some **months,** and certain words in the names of **businesses** are often abbreviated in informal notes. These abbreviations begin with a capital letter and end with a period. An **initial** can replace a person's or a place's name. It is written as an uppercase letter followed by a period.

See Handbook Section 2

Practice

Draw three lines (≡) under each lowercase letter that should be a capital letter. Draw a line (/) through each capital letter that should be a lowercase letter. Add periods where they are needed. (1–29)

World War II began in Sept. 1939, but it wasn't until the Japanese attack on Pearl Harbor on Dec. 7, 1941, that the U.S. finally joined the Allies in battle.

Two years later, on Dec. 24, 1943, Pres. Franklin D. Roosevelt named Gen. Dwight D. Eisenhower as Supreme Commander of the Allied Expeditionary Force in Europe. The Allies' plan was to cross the English Channel and take control of France from the Germans. Gen. Eisenhower's job was to see to it that the armies and navies of the U.S., Great Britain, and the other Allies worked together as one force. Toward this end, he worked closely with leaders such as British Prime Minister mr. Winston Churchill, Admiral Bertram H. Ramsay in charge of Allied naval forces, and Sir Trafford Leigh-Mallory in charge of air forces.

On the eve of the invasion, gen. Eisenhower faced a tough decision. Bad weather had already postponed the operation one day. To pursue the Assault in bad weather would put thousands of Troops in jeopardy, but delaying the landing could mean losing the element of surprise. Fortunately the weather cleared somewhat, and gen. Eisenhower gave the go-ahead. Early the morning of Tues. June 6, 1944, the D-day invasion began. Some 130,000 troops stormed five beaches from about 3,500 landing craft, including ships designed for carrying tanks (LCTs) and those designed for carrying infantry (lcis). They were supported by some 11,000 planes.

The Germans fought fiercely, but by the time night fell, the Allies had a strong hold along sixty miles of Normandy coastline. D-day provided the foothold in France that the Allies needed. On Aug. 25, Gen. George S. Patton Jr. led the U.S. Third Army into Paris to reclaim the city. In less than a year, Germany was forced to surrender to the Allies.

Apply

Rewrite each item below, using abbreviations and initials for the underlined words.

30. <u>President</u> Franklin <u>Delano</u> Roosevelt   **Pres. Franklin D. Roosevelt**

31. 1600 Pennsylvania <u>Avenue</u>   **1600 Pennsylvania Ave.**

32. <u>Mistress</u> Mamie <u>Geneva</u> Eisenhower   **Mrs. Mamie G. Eisenhower**

33. Kaiser Shipbuilding <u>Company</u>   **Kaiser Shipbuilding Co.**

34. <u>Tuesday</u>, June 6, 1944   **Tues., June 6, 1944**

35. <u>Sergeant</u> Edward <u>Allen</u> Carter <u>Junior</u>   **Sgt. Edward A. Carter, Jr.**

36. <u>General</u> George <u>Catlett</u> Marshall   **Gen. George C. Marshall**

37. 10 Downing <u>Street</u>   **10 Downing St.**

38. <u>August</u> 25, 1945   **Aug. 25, 1945**

39. Army Navy <u>Drive</u> and Fern <u>Street</u>   **Army Navy Dr. and Fern St.**

40. <u>September</u> 2, 1945   **Sept. 2, 1945**

41. GenCorp <u>Incorporated</u>   **GenCorp Inc.**

42. Winston <u>Leonard</u> Churchill   **Winston L. Churchill**

43. <u>Doctor</u> Hattie Alexander   **Dr. Hattie Alexander**

44. <u>December</u> 7, 1941   **Dec. 7, 1941**

45. General Motors <u>Corporation</u>   **General Motors Corp.**

Reinforce

See Handbook Section 2

An acronym is formed from the first letters of a pair or group of words. Some acronyms, such as *NASA* (National Aeronautics and Space Administration), are written in all uppercase letters. Others, such as *scuba* (self-contained underwater breathing apparatus), are written as regular, lowercase words. Like an acronym, an initialism is also formed from the first letters of a pair or group of words. An initialism differs from an acronym in that it does not form a word; instead, each letter in the initalism is pronounced, as in *USA* (which stands for "United States of America") or *PDF* (which stands for "portable document format").

Read each phrase below and use its first letters to write a shortened form. Check a dictionary to make sure each acronym or initialism you write is correct.

46. light amplification by stimulated emission of radiation   **laser**

47. frequently asked questions   **FAQ**

48. radio detecting and ranging   **radar**

49. North Atlantic Treaty Organization   **NATO**

50. digital video disk   **DVD**

Are these bracelets from the 1920s made of ivory? No, **they're** made from Bakelite. Today Bakelite bracelets are **collectors'** items.

Which boldfaced word shows possession or ownership? _____**collectors'**_____

Which boldfaced word is a combination of two words? _____**they're**_____

To form the **possessive** of a singular noun, add an **apostrophe** and *-s* (*girl's shoe*). For plural nouns that end in *-s*, add an **apostrophe** (*birds' nests*) to form the possessive. For plural nouns that do not end in *-s*, add an **apostrophe** and *-s* (*children's boots*). **Apostrophes** are also used in **contractions,** two words that have been shortened and combined.

See Handbook | Sections 7, 26, 28, 30

Practice

Circle the correct word in parentheses. If the answer is a possessive, write *possessive*. If the answer is a contraction, write the two words from which the contraction was made.

1. Some natural (resin's/resins') properties are similar to those of plastics. ___**possessive**___

2. One (material's/materials') properties made it ideal for items such as brush handles. ___**possessive**___

3. That material was called lac; (lac's/lacs') purified form was called shellac. ___**possessive**___

4. Unfortunately, natural materials that could be molded (werent'/weren't) easy to find. ___**were not**___

5. Some (product's/products') compositions made them turn brittle over time. ___**possessive**___

6. Many (researcher's/researchers') efforts focused on altering natural materials. ___**possessive**___

7. One (man's/mans') efforts to create a more useful material produced a substance later called celluloid.
___**possessive**___

8. The (substance's/substances) uses included products such as dentures and photographic films. ___**possessive**___

9. (Celluloid's/Celluloids') advantages were that it was hard and it could be easily molded when hot.
___**possessive**___

10. Unfortunately, it (wasn't/wasnt') stable around heat. ___**was not**___

11. One (chemist's/chemists') goal was to make a useful synthetic shellac. ___**possessive**___

12. Leo Baekeland mixed two chemical compounds, but he (didn't/did'nt) come up with what he was after.
___**did not**___

13. Instead, he created the first pure plastic; this (product's/products') name became *Bakelite*. ___**possessive**___

14. Soon many household items—from telephones to cooking (utensil's/utensils') handles—were made of Bakelite. ___**possessive**___

15. (Baekeland's/Baekelands') discovery gave rise to the plastics industry. ___**possessive**___

off **Name** _____

Apply

Rewrite these sentences. Replace boldfaced words with possessives or contractions.

16. Leo Baekeland **could not** have realized just how widespread plastics would become. <u>Leo Baekeland</u> <u>couldn't have realized just how widespread plastics would become.</u>

17. **The homes of most people** are filled with plastic goods. <u>Most people's homes are filled with</u> <u>plastic goods.</u>

18. **The adaptability of plastic** allows it to be shaped into almost any form. <u>Plastic's adaptability allows it to</u> <u>be shaped into almost any form.</u>

19. **The toughness or softness of a plastic product** can vary, depending on its chemical composition. <u>A plastic product's toughness or softness can vary, depending on its chemical composition.</u>

20. Unfortunately, plastics **do not** decompose quickly. <u>Unfortunately, plastics don't decompose quickly.</u>

21. **One of the biggest environmental problems of today** is how to dispose of used plastic. <u>One of today's</u> <u>biggest environmental problems is how to dispose of used plastic.</u>

Reinforce

Writers sometimes use contractions to reflect the way that words are pronounced in informal speech. These contractions sometimes look like possessives. Read the following examples. The first sentence contains a possessive noun. The second sentence contains a contraction.

1. My friend's bicycle has a flat.　　　　The bicycle of my friend has a flat.
2. My friend's coming over.　　　　My friend is coming over.

Read each sentence below. Then rewrite the sentence by replacing the possessive noun or contraction with an expression having the same meaning.

22. "This book's plot is quite gripping," said Ralph. <u>"The plot of this book is quite gripping," said Ralph.</u>

23. "The heroine's trying to find a secret formula," he continued. <u>"The heroine is trying to find a secret</u> <u>formula," he continued.</u>

24. "The mad scientist's a dangerous character," he added. <u>"The mad scientist is a dangerous character,"</u> <u>he added.</u>

25. Ralph concluded by saying, "The heroine's quick thinking saves her from the mad scientist's evil plan." <u>Ralph concluded by saying, "The quick thinking of the heroine saves her from the evil</u> <u>plan of the scientist."</u>

a. My dad says that eBay, the Internet auction site, represents a historic advance in commerce.

b. My uncle has sold items on eBay, and my cousin bought a lamp there.

c. I would like to buy and sell comic books, posters, and baseball cards.

In which sentence do commas separate three items in a series? ____**c**____

In which sentence do commas set off words that rename a noun? ____**a**____

In which sentence does a comma help separate the clauses in a compound sentence? ____**b**____

> Commas are used to **separate items in a series** of three or more words, phrases, or clauses. A comma is used to separate **coordinate adjectives**—pairs of similar adjectives. Commas are used to set off most **appositives,** as well as **nonrestrictive adjective clauses** and other nonrestrictive elements. A comma is used before a conjunction that joins the clauses in a **compound sentence.** A comma is also used after an **introductory element** in a sentence, such as a long prepositional or verbal phrase.

See Handbook | Sections 8, 16, 24, 25a

Practice

Add the missing comma to each sentence.

1. Pierre Omidyar loves solving problems, and he enjoys solving them in new ways.

2. In 1995 the young, energetic computer scientist had a plan.

3. He wanted to use the Internet to help common, ordinary individuals do business.

4. He didn't want business on the Internet to be dominated by wealthy, powerful companies.

5. He envisioned a website for buying and selling items, and he believed users would treat each other fairly.

6. He held another job, but he spent weekends creating his auction website.

7. The new site, which was an immediate success, grew very rapidly.

8. Omidyar knew he had created a thriving business, so he quit his other job.

9. People use eBay to buy and sell antiques, clothes, electronics, and much more.

10. After completing a transaction, the buyer and the seller can post information about each other, which helps ensure honesty.

11. Omidyar, who has made billions from his idea, is looking for worthwhile ways to spend his money.

12. Knowing that he has considerably more than he needs, he wants to help others.

13. He has donated $100 million for microfinance, the making of small loans to poor entrepreneurs.

Pierre Omidyar created the website that became the world's largest electronic marketplace.

Apply Suggested answers appear below. Accept all reasonable responses.

Combine each group of sentences to form one sentence. Add, delete, or change words as necessary. Add commas where needed.

14. An auctioneer puts a product up for bid. He or she tracks the bids. He or she awards the item to the highest bidder. **An auctioneer puts a product up for bid, tracks the bids, and then awards the item to the highest bidder.**

15. I watched an alert auctioneer at work last Saturday. The auctioneer was also quick-witted. **I watched an alert, quick-witted auctioneer at work last Saturday.**

16. In some ways eBay is like a live auction. In other ways it is different. **In some ways eBay is like a live auction, but in other ways it is different.**

17. You can buy antiques on eBay. You can buy collectibles on eBay, too. You can also buy other secondhand items there. **You can buy antiques, collectibles, and other secondhand items on eBay.**

18. Users can browse merchandise by categories. They can search by keyword. They can look up items of a particular seller. **Users can browse merchandise by categories, search by keyword, or look up items of a particular seller.**

Reinforce Answers will vary.

Think of an imaginary item you would like to sell. Write a description of this item that includes the following:

- an appositive that renames the item
- a pair of similar adjectives that describe the object
- three or more phrases in a series that tell what the item does

Be sure to use commas correctly.

_____

_____

_____

_____

_____

_____

_____

a. Marilyn Hamilton is an amazing woman, she turned a tragedy into an opportunity.

b. Some people have that gift: they find a way to make the most of a bad situation.

c. They learn from their own misfortune; they use what they learn to benefit others.

In which sentence are two independent clauses separated incorrectly with only a comma and no conjunction? ___a___

What punctuation marks are used to separate the independent clauses in the other two sentences? ___:___ ___;___

A **semicolon** (;) can be used instead of a comma and conjunction to separate the independent clauses in a **compound sentence**. A **colon** (:) can be used to separate two independent clauses when the second explains the first. It can also be used to introduce a list at the end of a sentence, to separate parts of references in a bibliography, and to separate hours and minutes in an expression of time.

See Handbook Sections 8, 13

Practice Answers will vary.

Write a colon or a semicolon to separate the clauses in each sentence.

1. Marilyn Hamilton was a very active young woman;she enjoyed tennis and hang-gliding.

2. In 1978 an accident changed her life:she crashed her glider into a mountain.

3. Hamilton became paraplegic:she lost the use of her legs.

4. She confronted another problem:her wheelchair was too bulky.

5. A standard wheelchair weighed about fifty pounds;she wanted a lighter one.

6. She sought the aid of two friends;both were weekend inventors.

7. The two men designed gliders;Hamilton asked them to build a wheelchair out of hang-gliding material.

8. The new wheelchair was a vast improvement;it weighed only twenty-six pounds.

9. It looked sleek and sporty;it had a compact frame and an angled back.

10. Hamilton could return to sports;she began competing in tournaments.

11. She became a national tennis champion;she also joined the U.S. Disabled Ski Team.

12. Hamilton and her two friends went into business:they began making wheelchairs.

13. Her partners focused on design and manufacturing;Hamilton focused on marketing.

14. In response to customers' requests, she made another innovation:she offered wheelchairs in bright colors.

15. Soon the sporty-looking chairs were not just for sports:they were for everyday use.

Hamilton used a sports wheelchair to win the 1983 U.S. Women's Open Wheelchair Tennis Championships.

Apply

Draw a line from each item on the left to an item on the right to make a simple or compound sentence. Then rewrite each pair as one sentence. Use a semicolon or a colon to separate independent clauses. Use a colon to introduce a list.

The Paralympic Games are held every two years

Marilyn Hamilton competed in the 1984 Winter Paralympic Games

The Summer Paralympic Games include the following sports

she won a silver medal in skiing

cycling, judo, swimming, and wheelchair basketball

they take place in the same city as the Olympic Games

16. **The Paralympic Games are held every two years; they take place in the same city as the Olympic Games.**

17. **The Summer Paralympic Games include the following sports: cycling, judo, swimming, and wheelchair basketball.**

18. **Marilyn Hamilton competed in the 1984 Winter Paralympic Games; she won a silver medal in skiing.**

Reinforce

The colon has many uses in writing. Think about how the colon is used in these examples. Then draw a line from each example to the rule it matches. (19–23)

BEN: What sports do you play?
GISELLE: Baseball and soccer.

Use a colon to separate hours and minutes in an expression of time.

The judo competition will begin at 3:30 P.M.

Use a colon after the speaker's name in a play.

Many cultures follow this basic rule:
"Treat others the way you want them to treat you."

Use a colon to separate the place of publication and the name of publisher in a book reference in a bibliography.

Bailey, Steve. *Athlete First: A History of the Paralympic Movement.* West Sussex, Eng.: John Wiley & Sons, 2008.

Use a colon to introduce a list or series at the end of a sentence.

I enjoy four sports: football, soccer, basketball, and baseball.

Use a colon to introduce a quotation.

On another sheet of paper, write an example of your own to match each rule.

Answers will vary.

a. The first successful moon landing (the culmination of the *Apollo 11* mission) took place in 1969.

b. *Apollo 12*, the follow-up mission, was also a success.

In which sentence are parentheses ( ) used to enclose information that explains an idea? __a__

In which sentence is a hyphen used to join a word pair that precedes a noun? __b__

Hyphens and **parentheses** are used to make writing clearer. Use a **hyphen** to
- separate the syllables in a word when you must break a word at the end of a line of text.
- link the parts of some compound words, such as *behind-the-scenes.*
- link some word pairs or groups of words that precede a noun and act as an adjective, such as *best-selling novel.*
- link the parts of numbers (written as words) between twenty-one and ninety-nine.

Use **parentheses** to set off an explanation or example.

See Handbook | Section 9

Practice

Write *C* beside each sentence or sentence pair in which hyphens and parentheses are used correctly. Cross out hyphens and parentheses that are used incorrectly. If you are not sure whether a hyphen should be used to link parts of a compound word or adjective phrase, check a dictionary.

1. ~~(~~On April 15, 1970~~)~~ Ed Smylie was at home watching television when he learned of an explosion on board *Apollo 13.* _____

2. Smylie knew he was needed ~~(~~at the Houston Space Center~~)~~ as soon as possible. _____

3. He oversaw a top-notch team of engineers in NASA's crew systems division. __C__

4. He soon discovered that ~~(~~the spacecraft~~)~~ was losing oxygen, electricity, light, and water. _____

5. There was also a problem with the square lithium hydroxide canisters. (The canisters, which were used to cleanse carbon dioxide from the air, had square openings.) __C__

6. Smylie and his staff had to find a way to make the square canisters compatible with the openings in the command module (which were round). __C__

7. Also, they had to use only materials available on board the spacecraft to repair the problems. (If they did not succeed, the crew would perish within a day or two.) __C__

8. The engineers devised a rough-and-ready contraption out of plastic bags, cardboard, and duct tape. __C__

9. After testing their invention, they guided ~~(~~the astronauts~~)~~ to find the same materials on board~~-~~the~~-~~spacecraft. _____

10. Their around-the-clock efforts paid off: the astronauts made it home safely. __C__

Apply

Add hyphens or parentheses where they belong.

11. Duct tape is not what comes to mind when you think of space-age repair tools.

12. Still, duct tape has helped other astronauts besides those on board *Apollo 13.* (In one instance, astronauts used it to do quick-and-dirty repairs to their air-filtering system.)

13. In 2006 the shuttle *Discovery* was on a 13-day mission to the International Space Station.

14. The latches on the jet-propelled backpack belonging to an astronaut (Piers Sellers) somehow came loose.

15. The backpack (used only in emergency situations) allows an astronaut to move backward or forward.

16. Mission Control guided the astronauts to make a quick-fix repair that allowed Sellers to take the planned spacewalk.

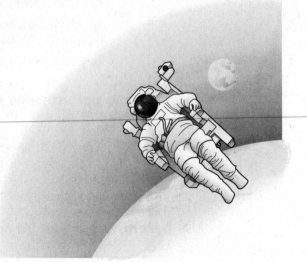

Reinforce

See Handbook Section 9

A dash is a punctuation mark used to signal a pause. A dash is longer than a hyphen. Think about how dashes are used in the sentences in the left-hand column. Then draw a line from each sentence to the rule it matches.

This was the moment I had been waiting for—the spacewalk.

Use dashes to set off a phrase or an independent clause that interrupts an otherwise complete sentence.

I looked at the distant blue orb—Earth was 220 miles away—and wished my friends could see me.

Use a dash to mark an interrupted or unfinished sentence.

Then I recalled the incident at Mission Control. If only—

Use a dash to stress one or more words at the end of a sentence.

On the lines below, write your own example for each rule about the use of dashes.

17. **Answers will vary.** _____

_____

18. _____

_____

19. _____

_____

a. The true men of action in our time, those who transform the world, are not the politicians and statesmen, but the scientists.

—W. H. Auden, *The Dyer's Hand*

b. The true men of action . . . are not the politicians and statesmen, but the scientists.

—W. H. Auden, *The Dyer's Hand*

How is sentence *b* different from sentence *a*? <u>**Sentence b does not contain some of the words that are in sentence a.**</u> What punctuation mark is used to signal this? <u>**Three spaced periods take the place of the missing words.**</u>

An **ellipsis**, a group of three spaced periods, is used to mark the omission of words from a quotation. An ellipsis can also be used to signal a pause. When you use an ellipsis after words that are not a complete sentence, leave a space before the first spaced period. When you use an ellipsis after a sentence, use the sentence's end mark, and leave a space between it and the first spaced period.

See Handbook Section 9

Practice

Read both versions of each quotation. Place an *X* by the one that has words left out. Circle the marks that indicate this. Then, in the full version of the quotation, underline the words that were replaced by the marks.

1. **a.** <u>The reasons we know that we will discover things we can't describe now is that</u> this has been the history of science. We do things to learn something we can define, and we wind up knowing things we never imagined asking about.

    b. (. . .) This has been the history of science. We do things to learn something we can define, and we wind up knowing things we never imagined asking about. **X**

    —Maxine Singer, in *A World of Ideas*, by Bill Moyers

2. **a.** Not many appreciate the ultimate power and potential usefulness of basic knowledge accumulated by obscure, unseen investigators (. . .) who go on seeking answers to the unknown without thought of financial or practical gain. **X**

    b. Not many appreciate the ultimate power and potential usefulness of basic knowledge accumulated by obscure, unseen investigators <u>who, in a lifetime of intense study, may never see any practical use for their findings but</u> who go on seeking answers to the unknown without thought of financial or practical gain.

    —Eugenie Clark, *The Lady and the Sharks*

Apply

Rewrite each quotation, replacing the boldfaced words with an ellipsis.

3. We live in a scientific age, yet we assume that knowledge of science is the prerogative of only a small number of human beings isolated and priestlike in their laboratories. **That is not true. The materials of science are the materials of life itself.** Science is part of the reality of living; it is the what, the how, and the why for everything in our experience.

    —Rachel Carson, in *The House of Life,* by Paul Brooks

    We live in a scientific age, yet we assume that knowledge of science is the prerogative of only a small number of human beings isolated and priestlike in their laboratories. . . . Science is part of the reality of living; it is the what, the how, and the why for everything in our experience.

    —Rachel Carson, in The House of Life, by Paul Brooks

4. . . . Science is one of the grand human activities. **It uses the same kind of talent and creativity as painting pictures and making sculptures. It's not really very different except that you do it from a base of technical knowledge. Science is not an inhuman or superhuman activity.** It's something that humans invented, and it speaks to one of our great needs—to understand the world around us.

    —Maxine Singer, in *A World of Ideas,* by Bill Moyers

    . . . Science is one of the grand human activities. . . . It's something that humans invented, and it speaks to one of our great needs—to understand the world around us.

    —Maxine Singer, in A World of Ideas, by Bill Moyers

Reinforce

Read the quotation below by American geneticist and Nobel Prize winner Barbara McClintock. Circle the ellipsis that signals a pause.

   If you know you are on the right track, if you have this inner knowledge, then nobody can turn you off (. . .) no matter what they say.

On the lines below, write a paragraph telling how these words could inspire someone trying to solve a problem or make a discovery. Use the quotation in your paragraph. **Answers will vary.**

_____

_____

_____

_____

The mountain pine beetle—a terribly destructive pest—has killed many millions of trees in the West in recent years. The Lipson family, Montana landowners and operators of a resort, had more than 10,000 beetle-killed pine trees on their land. The Lipsons needed to remove the dead trees to fight the infestation and reduce fire danger, but felling and hauling away so many trees would have been an unmanageable expense . . . unless there was some way to make money selling the lumber.

What punctuation mark is used to signal pauses in the first sentence? _____ **long dashes** _____ What punctuation mark indicates pauses in the second sentence? _____ **commas** _____ What punctuation mark signals a long pause in the third sentence? _____ **an ellipsis** _____

> Three types of punctuation marks can be used to signal pauses: **Long dashes** can signal pauses before and after an authorial comment or an explanatory phrase in a sentence. A long dash can also be used to signal a sudden interruption in a statement. **Commas** can be used to signal thoughtful pauses between groups of words. An **ellipsis** can be used in a sentence to indicate a long pause.

See Handbook | Sections 8, 9

Practice

Read each sentence quietly to yourself. Circle each punctuation mark that indicates where you should pause.

1. The Lipsons first had to identify infested pines—an easy task, since their needles turned burnt red—and then cut and haul away both the damaged trees and the healthy ones growing near them.

2. This process stopped the infestation in their forest . . . but it left them with a huge amount of beetle-damaged timber.

3. Larry Lipson was determined to find a use—a use that would generate income—for these felled trees.

4. He learned that lumber from beetle-killed pine trees was as strong as any other pine lumber, as long as it had not begun to rot.

5. Larry Lipson sent a small amount of his timber to a sawmill to be cut into boards . . . and what came back certainly surprised him.

6. The wood had an almost-iridescent blue tinge to it which, he later learned, was produced by a fungus carried by the beetles.

7. The Lipson family decided to use this lovely lumber to make accessories for tablets and smartphones—primarily stands and backs.

8. They started a company called Bad Beetle—a name chosen to raise people's awareness of the beetle problem—and set up a website to sell their products.

9. Several other companies now produce a range of products, from kitchen cabinets to tree houses, using the blue-tinged wood.

10. You may have heard the saying, "If you're given lemons, make lemonade," and that is what Larry Lipson and other entrepreneurs are doing with timber formerly regarded as worthless.

This smartphone stand is made out of lumber from trees killed by the mountain pine beetle.

Name _____

Apply

Add long dashes, commas, and ellipses where they are needed in these sentences.
Answers will vary. Sample responses are shown.

11. Scrap tires, too worn for road use, were formerly thrown into landfills.

12. The large number of tires discarded in America—almost 300 million a year at present—makes it imperative that good uses for these items be discovered.

13. Scientists and engineers, as well as officials in the Environmental Protection Agency's Office of Research and Development, have developed a wide array of new uses.

14. Almost half of America's scrap tires are now burned as fuel—a beneficial use, since tires produce more energy and fewer emissions than coal produces.

15. Tires are also used in civil engineering projects, from erosion barriers for bridge piers to noise-absorbing walls alongside highways.

16. In addition, scrap tires are used to manufacture rubberized asphalt for paving roads . . . roads that become remarkably smooth and quiet with their new surface.

17. One project now underway, sponsored by the Department of Energy's Office of Energy Efficiency and Renewable Energy, involves developing treatments for the rubber in scrap tires.

18. This rubber, after being treated, can be used to make gaskets, sealants, and adhesives.

Reinforce

Research some other ways that artists and communities have reused old tires. Write a paragraph about your findings. Use punctuation marks to signal pauses in your paragraph.

Answers will vary.

_____

_____

_____

_____

_____

_____

_____

_____

_____

_____

a. "Would you like to start your own Web-based organization?" asked Sid.

b. "Sure, but I don't know what type of organization I would start," answered Lyn.

Circle the marks that begin and end each quotation. Draw a box around the introductory word in the quotation in sentence *b*. Write the punctuation mark that follows that introductory word. ___,___ Write the punctuation mark that comes before the last quotation mark in sentence *b*. ___,___

A **direct quotation** is a speaker's exact words. Use **quotation marks** at the beginning and end of a direct quotation. Use a comma to separate direct speech, or a speaker's exact words, from the rest of the sentence. Begin a direct quotation with an uppercase letter. Add end punctuation (period, question mark, exclamation point, or comma in place of a period) before the last quotation mark. Use a comma to set off an introductory word such as *Yes*, a mild interjection such as *Oh*, a noun of direct address, or a tag question from the rest of a sentence.

See Handbook Sections 4, 8

Practice

Add quotation marks and commas to these sentences to make them correct.

1. Terry, I heard about this great microfinance organization said Senko.

2. Microfinance is the process of giving small loans to people to start businesses isn't it? asked Terry.

3. Yes, that's more or less what it means Senko agreed.

4. Well, what is this organization you heard about? asked Terry.

5. It's called *Kiva,* which means "agreement" or "unity" in Swahili Senko explained.

6. Then Terry asked What impresses you about this organization?

7. It takes a slightly different approach to solving the problem of poverty answered Senko.

8. Aren't there other microfinance organizations? Terry asked skeptically.

9. Sure but Kiva arranges and manages its loans through a website said Senko.

10. Tell me more said Terry, who was now curious.

11. Kiva operates a person-to-person model Senko pointed out.

12. Local microfinance institutions post received loan applications on the Internet he continued.

13. Okay, then what happens? asked Terry.

14. On the Kiva website, people read descriptions of the loan requests said Senko.

15. He added Then they decide which loan or loans to fund.

16. Lenders can ask questions of the borrowers, can't they? Terry wondered aloud.

17. Yes, they can replied Senko, and borrowers send updates on how their businesses are progressing.

18. Hey, that sounds like a great system! exclaimed Terry.

Name _____

Apply

Rewrite the sentences, adding correct punctuation to the dialogue. Be sure to use commas correctly.

19. Fiona do you want to help finance a small business loan? asked Bobby. **"Fiona, do you want to help finance a small business loan?" asked Bobby.**

20. Yes that sounds like a great idea Fiona replied. **"Yes, that sounds like a great idea," Fiona replied.**

21. We could ask friends in the neighborhood if they want to join us Bobby added. **"We could ask friends in the neighborhood if they want to join us," Bobby added.**

22. Hey we could give a presentation to our parents and grandparents suggested Fiona. **"Hey, we could give a presentation to our parents and grandparents," suggested Fiona.**

23. Let's browse the microloan website and find a business to support said Bobby. **"Let's browse the microloan website and find a business to support," said Bobby.**

24. Why don't you come over after school so we can do online research together? Fiona suggested. **"Why don't you come over after school so we can do online research together?" Fiona suggested.**

Reinforce Suggested answers appear below. Accept all reasonable responses.

See Handbook | Sections 23

An *interjection* is a word used to express strong or sudden feeling. Interjections are sometimes used as introductory words. If an interjection is said with force or strong feeling, it is followed by an exclamation mark; if a sentence follows this type of interjection, the first word of the sentence begins with a capital letter. If an interjection is not said with force or strong feeling, it is followed by a comma, and the word after the comma is not capitalized.

Choose an interjection from the word bank to complete each item. Add appropriate punctuation. Draw three lines (≡) under the first letter of any word that should be capitalized.

ugh	shh	bravo	alas	yikes	eureka

25. ____**Bravo!**____ that was an amazing performance!

26. ____**Eureka!**____ I've found just what I was looking for.

27. ____**Shh,**____ my new puppy is sleeping.

28. ____**Alas,**____ we didn't make the championships.

29. ____**Yikes!**____ that's a snake!

30. ____**Ugh!**____ we've got tons of chores to do.

a. In an article published in the October 1928 issue of *Forum,* automobile manufacturing pioneer Henry Ford said, "The whole secret of a successful life is to find out what is one's destiny to do, and then do it."

b. Here is another great American's thought on individuality and success:

> Why should we be in such desperate haste to succeed, and in such desperate enterprises? If a man does not keep pace with his companions, perhaps it is because he hears a different drummer. Let him step to the music which he hears, however measured or far away.
>
> —Henry David Thoreau, in *Walden*

Which quotation is longer? **b** How is it presented? **as a block of text separate from the main text, with the name of its author and its source given below** How is the other quotation presented? **as part of a sentence that gives information about it**

Write a **short quotation** as you would the words of a speaker: Use **quotation marks** at the beginning and end of the quotation. Use a comma to separate the words of the quotation from the rest of the sentence. Write a **long quotation** as a block of text, indented and set off from the body of what you are writing by a line of space. Do not use quotation marks at the beginning or end of the quotation. Provide source information below the quotation.

See Handbook Section 4

Practice Answers will vary. Sample responses are shown.

Read each quotation below. Decide whether you would present it within a sentence or as a block of text if you were including it in a report or a composition. Circle your choice.

1. I must admit that I personally measure success in terms of the contributions an individual makes to her or his fellow beings.

   —Margaret Mead, in *Redbook,* November 1978

   (in a sentence)   as a block of text

2. I come to embrace the notion that I haven't done enough in my life; I heartily concur; I come to affirm that one's title, even a title like President of the United States, says very little about how well one's life has been led—that no matter how much you've done, or how successful you've been, there's always more to do, always more to learn, and always more to achieve.

   —Barack Obama, in "Arizona State University Commencement Address," May 2009

   in a sentence   (as a block of text)

3. Success is more a function of consistent common sense than it is of genius.

   —An Wang, in *Boston Magazine,* December 1986

   (in a sentence)   as a block of text

Apply

Rewrite each short quotation as part of a sentence. Rewrite each long quotation as a block of text. You may add words to introduce the quotation to the reader.

4. There is nothing mysterious about originality. Originality is merely the step beyond.

       —Louis Danz, *Dynamic Dissonances in Nature and the Arts*

Sentences will vary. The quotation should be part of the sentence.

_____

_____

_____

_____

5. Creativeness often consists merely of turning up what is already there. Did you know that right and left

shoes were thought up only a little more than a century ago?

      —Bernice Fitz-gibbon, in *Peter's Quotations*, by Dr. Laurence J. Peter

Sentences will vary. The quotation should be a block of text.

_____

_____

_____

_____

_____

6. We should be careful to get out of an experience only the wisdom that is in it—and stop there; lest we be

like the cat that sits on a hot stove-lid. She will never sit on a hot stove-lid again—and that is well; but also

she will never sit on a cold one anymore.

      —Mark Twain, *Following the Equator*

Sentences will vary. The quotation should be a block of text.

_____

_____

_____

_____

_____

Reinforce   Answers will vary.

Select one of the quotations from this lesson, or find a quotation about success, creativity, or problem-solving in another source. On another sheet of paper, write a brief essay in which you present the quotation, explain what you think it means, and tell why you agree or disagree with it.

700 Franklin Drive
St. Louis, MO 63101
February 25, 20__

Dear Brenda,

Since we talked on the phone, I've been thinking about the trouble you're having making free throws. Here's my advice: Take a deep breath, bend your knees, and then straighten up and release the ball in one smooth motion.

As for your wanting to improve your defense, I think a coach will be able to give you the advice you need. Good luck!

Your friend,
Heather

There are five different parts of this letter. Two have already been circled. Circle the other three.

A **friendly letter** has five parts: the **heading**, the **greeting**, the **body**, the **closing**, and the **signature**. A friendly letter may include informal language. A **business letter** is a formal letter written to an employer or a business. It has the same parts as a friendly letter, but it also includes the address of the person to whom the letter will be sent. Use a colon after the greeting in a business letter. Omit paragraph indentations and align all letter parts along the left-hand margin. A formal **e-mail** is similar to a letter, but it usually has only four parts: a greeting, a body, a closing, and your name. An e-mail header contains your **e-mail address**, the e-mail address of the person you are writing to, the date, and a **subject line**.

See Handbook Sections 2, 8, 34, 35

Practice

Use the appropriate boldfaced words in the rule box above to label the five parts of this friendly letter.

1. _____**heading**_____   253 Third Street
   Kansas City, KS 66101
   March 3, 20__

Dear Heather, _____**greeting**_____ 2.

I really appreciated your advice on how to perfect my free-throw style. It's helping! Also, I've asked the basketball coach at the community center to give me defensive pointers. He says that he can help me after practice on Tuesday.

How is your gymnastic routine coming along?

3. _____**body**_____

4. _____**closing**_____ Your friend,

5. _____**signature**_____ Brenda

Name _____

Apply

Rewrite this business letter correctly on the lines below. (Hint: The sender's address and the date go first. The inside address goes second.)

    Mr. Dan Kinney Fairview Community Center 2300 Baxter Avenue Kansas City, KS 66101 March 10, 20__ Dear Mr. Kinney I play on the Cougars basketball team in the C league. We have had a really great season. Would you consider moving our team to the B league next year? I think that playing better teams will push us to improve our skills. Thank you for considering this request. Sincerely Brenda Tyler 253 Third Street Kansas City, KS 66101

253 Third Street

Kansas City, KS 66101

March 10, 20__

Mr. Dan Kinney

Fairview Community Center

2300 Baxter Avenue

Kansas City, KS 66101

Dear Mr. Kinney:

I play on the Cougars basketball team in the C league. We have had a really great season. Would you

consider moving our team to the B league next year? I think that playing better teams will push us to

improve our skills. Thank you for considering this request.

Sincerely,

Brenda Tyler

Reinforce Answers will vary.

See Handbook | Section 35

Think of an activity that you enjoy, such as playing a sport, practicing a hobby, or playing an instrument. Then think of someone you know who is more skilled than you are at that activity. Write that person an e-mail requesting advice about how to improve your skills. Be sure to begin with the reason you are e-mailing; type a clear subject line; avoid special type features, emoticons, or using all uppercase letters; and include a detailed salutation (full name and e-mail address). When you have finished your first draft, read your e-mail from beginning to end. Proofread for errors in capitalization, punctuation, and spelling. Then print out a copy of your final draft.

(Numbers in parentheses identify related lessons.)

Capitalization

Draw three lines (☰) under each letter that should be capitalized.

1. people at the united nations are working to end world hunger. **(73)**

2. The sahel and the Horn of africa are two regions of malnutrition. **(73)**

Titles, Initials, Abbreviations, and Acronyms

Draw three lines (☰) under each letter that should be capitalized. Add underlines, quotation marks, and periods where they are needed.

3. A book called <u>Children of the Depression</u> has photos from the 1930s. **(74)**

4. It includes photos by ms dorothea lange and mr walker evans. **(75)**

5. The wpa (Works progress Administration) offered a solution. **(75)**

Punctuation

Underline the correct word in each pair. Write *C* if the word is a contraction or *P* if the word is a possessive.

6. I (had'nt/<u>hadn't</u>) heard of the WPA before. __C__ **(76)**

7. The (<u>agency's</u>/agencies') projects included bridges, parks, and airports. __P__ **(76)**

Add commas, semicolons, and colons where they are needed. (Only one item requires a colon.)

8. WPA-sponsored artists created murals, sculptures, and paintings. **(77)**

9. Writers compiled oral histories; they also wrote books. **(78)**

10. These are two famous WPA writers: John Steinbeck and Studs Terkel. **(78)**

Add hyphens, parentheses, and dashes where they are needed.

11. The National Youth Administration (NYA) sought to employ young people. **(79)**

12. The NYA combined economic relief with on-the-job training. **(79)**

13. Congress—by then focusing solely on winning World War II—abolished the program in 1943. **(79)**

Add dashes, commas, and ellipses where they are needed in these sentences.

14. Finding ways to recycle plastic containers—millions of which now end up in landfills every year—should be at the top of every environmental problem-solver's to-do list. **(81)**

15. Tons of plastic and other trash now circulate in the middle of the Pacific Ocean . . . a terrible, overwhelming problem requiring a brilliant solution. **(80)**

Punctuating Dialogue

Add quotation marks and other marks where they are needed. Draw three lines (≡) under each letter that should be capitalized.

16. Peggy asked Philip, "do you have a summer job lined up?" **(82)**

17. "yes, I'm going to mow lawns," he answered. **(82)**

Ellipses

Rewrite the quotation, replacing the boldfaced words with an ellipsis.

18. We know what a person thinks, **not when he tells us what he thinks, but** by his actions. **(80)**

—Isaac Bashevis Singer, in *The New York Times Magazine,* November 26, 1978

We know what a person thinks . . . by his actions.

Quotations From a Text Answers will vary. Sample responses are shown.

Rewrite each short quotation as part of a sentence. Rewrite each long quotation as a block of text. You may add words to introduce a quotation to the reader.

19. You cannot shake hands with a clenched fist.

—Indira Gandhi, in a press conference in New Delhi **(83)**

Indira Gandhi said, "You cannot shake hands with a clenched fist."

20. Rhetoric is a poor substitute for action, and we have trusted only to rhetoric. If we are really to be a great nation, we must not merely talk, we must act big.

—Theodore Roosevelt, in the September 1917 issue of *The Metropolitan* **(83)**

Theodore Roosevelt believed that leaders should be decisive:

Rhetoric is a poor substitute for action, and we have trusted only to rhetoric. If we are really to be a great nation, we must not merely talk, we must act big.

—Theodore Roosevelt, in The Metropolitan, September 1917

Letters and E-mails

Rewrite this business letter correctly on a separate sheet of paper. **Students should use the correct format for a business letter.**

21. 637 Lennox Street Fargo, ND 58102 April 17, 20__ Hank's Historical Poster Company 333 Douglas Avenue Little Rock, AR 72201 Dear Sir or Madam: I am enclosing a poster I received from you. It had a tiny tear when I received it. Would you please replace it? Sincerely yours, Paul Wingate **(84)**

Spelling Practice

It must have been an **exhilarating** experience to be a part of the team that put the first person on the moon.

The word in bold type means "exciting and uplifting." Create a rule or mnemonic device to help you remember how to spell it.
Answers will vary.

Frequently Misspelled Words

Some words are more difficult to spell than others. For example, words that are commonly mispronounced, such as **irrelevant,** are often misspelled. Words with silent letters, such as **exhaust,** are also a challenge. And sometimes the sounds of words such as **jealousy** give no real clue to the spelling.

Words in Context

Write the word that best completes each sentence. Use a dictionary if you need help.

familiar	committee	minimum	forehead	luxury
prejudice	procedure	genuine	frivolous	postpone

1. Getting to know many different kinds of people prevents __prejudice__.

2. I will need a __minimum__ of four correct answers to pass the test.

3. It is __frivolous__ to buy two new dresses for the party.

4. Baking the scones is a fairly simple __procedure__.

5. Are you __familiar__ with this new young adult series?

6. Ordering dessert was a rare __luxury__ for us.

7. If this rain continues, they will __postpone__ the parade.

8. Dad has joined a __committee__ that plans the annual block party.

9. Is this __genuine__ leather, or is it imitation?

10. The nurse felt my __forehead__ and determined I had a fever.

Name _____

Pattern Practice

numerous	minimum	familiar	irrelevant	pursue	exhilarating
reliable	exhaust	genuine	maneuver	postpone	spontaneous

Replace the underlined word or phrase with a word from above that means the same thing. Use a dictionary if you need help.

11. Unfortunately, my feelings were <u>unimportant</u>. _____**irrelevant**_____

12. We took a <u>sudden</u> detour and got lost. _____**spontaneous**_____

13. There are <u>many</u> reasons why I've chosen to leave. _____**numerous**_____

14. This computer is a very <u>trustworthy</u> product. _____**reliable**_____

15. Cody practiced that skateboard <u>move</u> for hours. _____**maneuver**_____

16. Molly will <u>work toward</u> a career in journalism. _____**pursue**_____

17. I will <u>delay</u> my doctor appointment until next week. _____**postpone**_____

18. Skydiving must be an <u>exciting</u> experience! _____**exhilarating**_____

19. This coin is a <u>real</u> artifact from the Civil War Era. _____**genuine**_____

Write the word from above that is an antonym of each word. Use a dictionary if you need help.

20. speed up _____**postpone**_____

21. fake _____**genuine**_____

22. foreign _____**familiar**_____

23. maximum _____**minimum**_____

24. depressing _____**exhilarating**_____

25. enliven _____**exhaust**_____

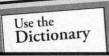

Use the
Dictionary

Circle the word in each pair that is correctly spelled. Check your work in a print or an online dictionary.

26. (courtesy)   curtesy

27. liaeson   (liaison)

28. picnicing   (picnicking)

29. (cancellation)   canselation

Diagramming Adjective Clauses

You have learned that an adjective clause is a dependent clause that describes a noun or pronoun and begins with a relative pronoun such as *who, that,* or *which.* Notice the way an adjective clause is diagrammed. In this sentence, the relative pronoun *who* is the subject of the adjective clause.

Dr. Charles Drew, **who was a surgeon,** did important research on blood transfusions.

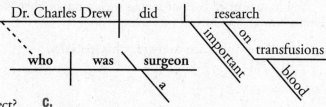

1. Which sentence elements does the dashed line connect? _____**c.**_____

   a. two nouns in the sentence

   b. the direct object and the relative pronoun *who*

   c. the relative pronoun *who* and the noun to which it refers

In the example to the right, the relative pronoun *which* refers to *blood,* the object of the preposition in the independent clause.

At the time, blood transfusions were done with whole blood, **which caused severe problems in some cases.**

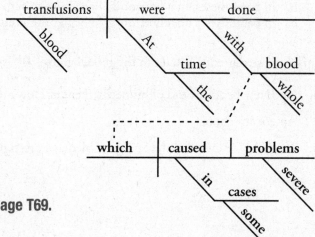

Try diagramming these sentences. **Answers appear on page T69.**

2. Dr. Drew, who served on an important committee, argued for the use of blood plasma.

3. Fewer problems occurred with transfusions that used blood plasma.

Diagramming Adverb Clauses

You have learned that an adverb clause is a dependent clause that tells about a verb, an adjective, or an adverb, and that an adverb clause often begins with a subordinating conjunction such as *although* or *because,* or with a relative adverb such as *when* or *where.*

When World War II began, the need for blood transfusions increased dramatically.

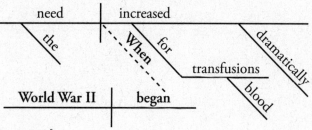

4. Where is the relative adverb *When* placed in this diagram? _____**b.**_____
   a. on a slanted line below the simple subject
   b. on a slanted dotted line connecting the verb in the clause to the word the clause modifies
   c. on a dotted line connecting two subjects

Diagram these sentences. Refer to the model on the previous page. Answers appear on page T70.

5. When a wounded soldier required a transfusion, fresh plasma was needed by the doctor.

6. After Dr. Drew instituted a system for the sanitary collection of blood, spoilage decreased significantly.

Diagramming Appositives

You have learned that an appositive is a phrase that identifies a noun.
Here is how an appositive is diagrammed:

Dr. Drew returned to surgery, **his specialty,** in 1941.

7. Where is the noun in the appositive placed in the diagram? _____ c. _____
   a. on its own diagonal line below the noun it identifies
   b. in parentheses on a horizontal line after the verb
   c. in parentheses on a horizontal line after the noun it identifies

Diagram these sentences. Refer to the model above. Answers appear on page T70.

8. Dr. Drew became head of his department at Howard Medical School, a historically African

   American school.

9. The NAACP awarded the Spingarn Medal, a prestigious award, to Dr. Drew.

Writing Sentences

Possible answers appear below. Accept all reasonable responses.

Rewrite each sentence so that it makes sense. Make each one easier to understand by using correct punctuation and capitalization.

1. I've decided to title my paper Carved in stone. **I've decided to title my paper "Carved in Stone."**

2. I'm focusing on the reasons civic group's choose to erect statues. **I'm focusing on the reasons civic groups choose to erect statues.**

3. I'm sorry to take so long to write, but I've been working on a report for mr wongs class. **I'm sorry to take so long to write, but I've been working on a report for Mr. Wong's class.**

4. I'll leave you with two words before I sign off write soon! **I'll leave you with two words before I sign off: write soon!**

5. When I told my dad the title, he said you're a regular chip off the old block! **When I told my dad the title, he said, "You're a regular chip off the old block!"**

6. The report is about civic art. Works of art installed in public spaces in cities and towns. **The report is about civic art, works of art installed in public spaces in cities and towns.**

A friendly letter has a heading, greeting, body, closing, and signature. A well-written letter has a friendly tone, includes specific information, uses description to create pictures in the mind of its reader, and asks the reader questions to give him or her ideas for writing a letter in return. As you read the model letter below, notice the use of details and questions to the reader.

120 Fern Creek Avenue
Vancouver, WA 98660
March 7, 20__

Dear Wendy,

Your report sounds like it's going to be very interesting. I just saw the Sacagawea statue at Washington Park in Portland, Oregon, last weekend. As you know, Sacagawea was the Shoshone woman who accompanied her husband, Toussaint Charbonneau, on the Lewis and Clark Expedition. Along the way she acted as an interpreter, found plants to eat, and served as a symbol of peace—other tribes saw her and did not view the expedition as hostile.

Here's a fun fact for you: supposedly there are more statues of Sacagawea in the United States than of any other woman. Perhaps you can include information about her in your report.

Your friend,

Mimi

Name _____

Writing a Paragraph

The sentences you revised on page 255 can be used as the body of a friendly letter. Decide in what order the sentences should be. Write them on the lines below. Then add a heading, greeting, closing, and signature.

Answers will vary. Accept all reasonable responses.

_____
_____
_____

_____   _____

_____
_____
_____
_____
_____

Think of an individual who has been commemorated in your community. Write a letter to a friend, telling him or her about this individual. Include facts and descriptions to make your letter interesting. Use the model on page 255 as your guide.

Answers will vary.

_____
_____

_____   _____
_____
_____
_____
_____

Reread your letter. Use this checklist to make sure it is complete and follows the friendly letter form.

❑ Does my letter have all five parts?

❑ Have I punctuated the greeting and closing correctly?

❑ Have I included specific information?

❑ Have I used abbreviations correctly?

❑ Have I capitalized proper nouns?

❑ Have I asked questions my reader will want to answer in a return letter?

❑ Have I used commas, semicolons, hyphens, parentheses, and dashes correctly?

Proofreading
Practice

Read this passage about Florence Nightingale and find the mistakes. Use the proofreading marks to show how the mistakes should be fixed.

Suggested answers appear below. Accept all reasonable responses.

Proofreading Marks

Mark	Means	Example
ℒ	delete	Florence Nightingalee was an English nurse.
∧	add	Florence Nightingale was ᵃⁿ English nurse.
≡	make into an uppercase letter	Florence Nightingale was an english nurse.
/	make into a lowercase letter	Florence Nightingale was an English Nurse.
⊙	add a period	Florence Nightingale was an English nurse⊙
ⓢⓟ	fix spelling	Florence Nightingale was an ˢᵖ Inglish nurse.

Florence Nightingale, Originator of Modern Nursing

Florence Nightingale was born into a well-to-do english family in 1820. She was educated mostly by her

father, William e. Nightingale. He taught her history philosophy and mathematics. He also taught her several

world langauges Greek, Latin, french, German, and italian.

Young florence Nightingale developed an interest in nursing but there were no nursing programs in England

at that time. In 1850, she entered a nursing program in germany. When she returned to London in 1853, she was

employed by the Institution For The Care Of Sick Gentlewomen. As superintendent at the institution, she made

many posative changes. Still, she wanted to do more.

In 1854, war broke out on the Crimean peninsula—an area on the northern coast of the Black sea—between

russia and Great Britain and its allies. Nightingale was asked to take charge of the military hospitals in turkey.

When she and a large party of nurses arrived there on nov 5, 1854, she was appalled by the poor conditions at

the hospital great numbers of sick and wounded soldiers lay on filthy straw mattresses there was insufficient clean

water and the place was infested with rats and fleas. Nightingale imediatly set people to work cleaning the place.

She created a nursing schedule, and she wrote nummerous letters demanding supplies. She worked long hours

and made nightly rounds in the wards thus earning the nickname "The Lady with the Lamp"

At the wars end two years later, Nightingale she returned to england, where she continued to work on behalf

of the helth and welfare of british soldiers. In 1860, she established the Nightingale school for nurses at

St thomas's Hospital, the first quality nursing program in the world.

Proofreading
Checklist

You can use the list below to help you find and fix mistakes in your own writing. Write the titles of your own stories or reports in the blanks at the top of the chart. Then use the questions to check your work. Make a check mark (✓) in each box after you have checked that item. **Answers will vary.**

Titles

Proofreading Checklist for Unit 7

Have I capitalized proper nouns and proper adjectives?				
Have I capitalized and punctuated titles of works correctly?				
Have I used commas correctly?				
Have I used apostrophes correctly in possessives and contractions?				
Have I used colons and semicolons correctly?				
Have I used hyphens, dashes, and parentheses correctly?				
Have I punctuated direct and indirect quotations correctly?				

Also Remember…

Does each sentence begin with an uppercase letter?				
Did I use a dictionary to check and correct spellings?				
Have I used the right end marks at the end of sentences?				

Your Own List
Use this space to write your own list of things to check in your writing.

Community Connection

In Unit 7 of *Grammar, Usage, and Mechanics,* students learned about **capitalization, punctuation, and other aspects of writing mechanics,** and used what they learned to improve their writing. The content of these lessons focuses on the theme **Problem Solvers.** As students completed the exercises, they learned about individuals and groups of people who have solved problems to make life easier and more rewarding for others. These pages offer a variety of activities that reinforce skills and concepts presented in the unit. They also provide opportunities for the student to make connections between the materials in the lessons and the community at large.

Problems in the News

Read a print or online newspaper that serves your area. Find one article about a community problem that needs to be solved and one article about a problem that has already been solved. Discuss these articles with family members or classmates. Identify the people involved with the problem that has been solved, and decide whether they qualify as unforgettable folks. Then come up with a list of possible solutions for the unsolved problem.

Help the Problem Solvers

Choose one organization in your community that helps people with problems of a particular kind. This might be a group that helps people with disabilities, a group that provides free tutoring help to students, or a group that identifies and tries to solve environmental problems. Visit, call, or read about the group to find out more about the work it does. If possible, spend time volunteering for the organization. Then write an advertisement to convince others to become donors or volunteers for the organization.

Seekers of Solutions

It usually takes careful scientific research to find solutions to serious medical problems. Find out where in your area doctors and scientists do research to find vaccines, treatments, and cures for diseases. Browse that facility's website and read about one of the types of research it is doing. Write a letter or an e-mail to a friend, summarizing what you learn.

Family Report

Brainstorm with a relative about a problem affecting your family. Then work together to devise a solution to the problem. Answer each of these questions to help you formulate a plan of action.

- What is the problem?
- Which family member(s) are affected by it? Are there other relatives who could help solve the problem?
- What are some possible solutions? Could the problem be solved by developing a new process, such as planting a garden to save money; by creating an invention, such as a time-saving device; or by working to increase family communication?
- What are the advantages and disadvantages of each possible solution?

Choose the solution that you feel will work best, and write the details of your plan in a "family report." Then distribute the report to each family member.

Name _____

Jobs for Problem Solvers   Answers will vary.

List some of the job opportunities available for people who want to solve problems in your community. Find out about employment in at least two fields such as product development, scientific research, medicine, environmental science, or social services. Then do research to learn more about careers in the field that interests you most. Find out what education and skills are needed in this field and what types of jobs you might someday quality for. Use the planner that follows to help organize the information you find.

I. First Field Researched: _____

    A. Types of Jobs Available:

        1. _____

        2. _____

        3. _____

    B. Most Interesting Type: _____

    C. Kinds of Problems to Be Solved: _____

_____

_____

    D. Education and Skills Required: _____

_____

_____

II. Second Field Researched: _____

    A. Types of Jobs Available:

        1. _____

        2. _____

        3. _____

    B. Most Interesting Type: _____

    C. Kinds of Problems to Be Solved: _____

_____

_____

    D. Education and Skills Required: _____

_____

_____

Appendix Table of Contents

TEST TIP: Be sure to read all four answer choices carefully before choosing and marking the answer you think is correct.

(Numbers in parentheses identify related lessons.)

Read each item carefully. Fill in the circle next to the best answer.

1. Read this sentence.

   > A casual observer might mistake a red fox for a small furry dog.

   Which of the following is the complete predicate of the sentence? **(1)**

   (A) casual observer might mistake
   (B) mistake a red fox
   (C) might mistake a red fox for a small furry dog
   (D) mistake a red fox for a small furry dog

2. Read this sentence.

   > These members of the dog family can live in a variety of environments.

   What are the simple subject and the simple predicate of the sentence? **(2)**

   (A) family; can
   (B) family; can live
   (C) members; can live
   (D) family can; live

3. Read this sentence.

   > The Arctic fox and the fennec of the desert live and thrive in extreme environments.

   Which of the following is a correct statement about the sentence? **(3)**

   (A) It has a compound subject and a simple predicate.
   (B) It has a simple subject and a compound predicate.
   (C) It has a simple subject and a simple predicate.
   (D) It has a compound subject and a compound predicate.

4. Read this sentence.

   > A red fox can hear the peep of a chick from a distance of 90 feet.

   Which word in the sentence is a direct object? **(4)**

   (A) hear
   (B) peep
   (C) chick
   (D) distance

5. Read this sentence.

   > Unlike other canines, gray foxes are climbers of trees.

   Which of the following is a predicate noun in the sentence? **(5)**

   (A) canines
   (B) foxes
   (C) climbers
   (D) trees

6. Read this sentence.

   > A mated pair of foxes often hunt together and always protect each other.

   Which of the following is a prepositional phrase in the sentence? **(6)**

   (A) of foxes
   (B) often
   (C) always
   (D) each

Read each item carefully. Fill in the circle next to the best answer.

7. Read this sentence.

> Wolves, coyotes, and foxes are all canines, members of the dog family, and have many similar characteristics.

Which group of words from the sentence is an appositive? **(7)**

- Ⓐ coyotes, and foxes
- Ⓑ all canines
- Ⓒ members of the dog family
- Ⓓ many similar characteristics

8. Read this sentence.

> Foxes raising pups live in family groups and stay in large dens.

Which group of words from the sentence is a participial phrase? **(8)**

- Ⓐ foxes raising pups
- Ⓑ raising pups
- Ⓒ live in family groups
- Ⓓ stay in large dens

9. Read this sentence.

> Quick reactions and incredibly sharp senses enable foxes to hunt effectively.

Which of the following is an infinitive phrase in the sentence? **(9)**

- Ⓐ quick reactions
- Ⓑ incredibly sharp senses
- Ⓒ enable foxes
- Ⓓ to hunt effectively

10. Read this sentence.

> A bat-eared fox running at top speed can change course suddenly.

What is the simple predicate of the sentence? **(10)**

- Ⓐ running
- Ⓑ top speed
- Ⓒ can change
- Ⓓ change

11. Read each sentence. Which sentence provides the most useful information? **(11)**

- Ⓐ Llamas and alpacas are related to camels.
- Ⓑ Llamas and alpacas live in South America.
- Ⓒ The Incas, whose empire once stretched throughout the mountains and lowlands of western South America, domesticated the llama and the alpaca.
- Ⓓ One was a pack animal, and the other provided wool.

12. Read this sentence.

> What a soft coat the alpaca has!

What type of sentence is this? **(12)**

- Ⓐ declarative
- Ⓑ interrogative
- Ⓒ imperative
- Ⓓ exclamatory

13. Read this sentence.

> Neither the llama nor the alpaca is found in the wild, but their relatives the vicuña and the guanaco roam the slopes of the Andes.

What type of sentence is this? **(12)**

- Ⓐ declarative
- Ⓑ interrogative
- Ⓒ imperative
- Ⓓ exclamatory

Read each item carefully. Fill in the circle next to the best answer.

14. Read this sentence.

> Serious birdwatchers study the only creatures on Earth with feathers.

Which of the following is the complete predicate of the sentence? **(1)**

(A) serious birdwatchers
(B) study the only creatures
(C) study the only creatures on Earth with feathers
(D) the only creatures on Earth

15. Read this sentence.

> Nearly all birds outside Antarctica construct nests of twigs or mud.

What are the simple subject and the simple predicate of the sentence? **(2)**

(A) birds; nests
(B) birds; construct
(C) Antarctica; construct
(D) construct; nests

16. Read this sentence.

> The ostrich and the cassowary have wings but cannot fly.

Which of the following is a correct statement about the sentence? **(3)**

(A) It has a compound subject and a simple predicate.
(B) It has a simple subject and a compound predicate.
(C) It has a simple subject and a simple predicate.
(D) It has a compound subject and a compound predicate.

17. Read this sentence.

> Some birds waterproof their feathers with oil from a special gland.

Which word in the sentence is a direct object? **(4)**

(A) waterproof
(B) feathers
(C) oil
(D) gland

18. Read this sentence.

> An ancestor of modern chickens became an important domestic animal about 5,500 years ago.

Which of the following is a predicate noun in the sentence? **(5)**

(A) chickens
(B) domestic
(C) animal
(D) years

19. Read this sentence.

> All birds' offspring grow and develop inside hard-shelled eggs.

Which group of words from the sentence is a prepositional phrase? **(6)**

(A) all birds' offspring
(B) grow and develop
(C) and develop
(D) inside hard-shelled eggs

Name _____

Read each item carefully. Fill in the circle next to the best answer.

20. Read this sentence.

> Ornithologists, scientists who study birds, are interested in understanding more about how birds navigate.

Which group of words from the sentence is an appositive? **(7)**

(A) scientists who study birds
(B) are interested
(C) understanding more
(D) birds navigate

21. Read this sentence.

> Guided by the sun, stars, wind, and an internal compass, migratory birds can travel long distances to the same destination year after year.

Which group of words from the sentence is a participial phrase? **(8)**

(A) guided by the sun, stars, wind, and an internal compass
(B) an internal compass
(C) travel long distances
(D) to the same destination year after year

22. Read this sentence.

> A variety of birds, from colorful parrots to gray and white mockingbirds, have learned to imitate other birdcalls and noises.

Which of the following is an infinitive phrase in the sentence? **(9)**

(A) a variety of birds
(B) to gray and white mockingbirds
(C) have learned to imitate
(D) to imitate other birdcalls and noises

23. Read this sentence.

> Wearing a down coat, you are warmed by duck or goose feathers.

What is the simple predicate of the sentence? **(10)**

(A) wearing
(B) warmed
(C) are warmed
(D) warmed by

24. Read each sentence. Which sentence provides the most useful information? **(11)**

(A) Grebes are aquatic birds.
(B) Grebes are very capable swimmers but cannot move well on land; consequently, they seldom come ashore.
(C) Grebes build floating nests.
(D) They anchor their nests to plants.

25. Read this sentence.

> Notice that the grebe by that small island has a baby on its back.

What type of sentence is this? **(12)**

(A) declarative
(B) interrogative
(C) imperative
(D) exclamatory

 **TEST TIP:** Don't spend too much time on one item.

(Numbers in parentheses identify related lessons.)

Read each item carefully. Fill in the circle next to the best answer.

1. **Which of the following sentences is a compound sentence? (13)**

   Ⓐ Some processes build up Earth's surface, and others break it down.
   Ⓑ Volcanism, or volcanic eruptions, builds up the surface of our planet.
   Ⓒ Earth's surface is also built up when crustal movements cause warping or buckling.
   Ⓓ If you place your hands flat on the edges of a sheet of paper and gently move them toward the middle, you will see a simple form of buckling.

2. **Read this sentence.**

   > After a volcano erupts, lava, ash, and cinders add to Earth's surface.

   What types of clauses are in the sentence? (14)

   Ⓐ The first is an independent clause; the second is dependent.
   Ⓑ The first is a dependent clause; the second is independent.
   Ⓒ Both are dependent clauses.
   Ⓓ Both are independent clauses.

3. **Which of the following is a complex sentence? (15)**

   Ⓐ Some volcanic eruptions are explosive, but others are not.
   Ⓑ Cone-shaped volcanoes typically have explosive eruptions.
   Ⓒ Mount Vesuvius, which is in Italy, erupted explosively in A.D. 79.
   Ⓓ The eruption covered the surrounding lands with many feet of lava, ash, and cinders.

4. **Which sentence has an adjective clause underlined? (16)**

   Ⓐ Gravity is one process <u>that breaks down surface features</u>.
   Ⓑ Gravity constantly <u>pulls on a rock overhang</u>.
   Ⓒ At some point, the force of gravity will cause <u>the rock overhang to fall</u>.
   Ⓓ Loose materials on mountainsides also move downward, <u>particularly after they are disturbed by wind or rain or animal movements</u>.

5. **Which sentence has an adverb clause underlined? (17)**

   Ⓐ Water is <u>a very important cause of change on Earth's surface</u>.
   Ⓑ A hard rain can break <u>bits of rock off cliff sides</u>.
   Ⓒ <u>After rainfall hits Earth</u>, it carries grains of rock with it.
   Ⓓ These tiny bits of rock eventually are carried <u>all the way to the sea</u>.

6. **Which of the following sentences has a restrictive clause underlined? (18)**

   Ⓐ Wildfires, <u>which are becoming more frequent in the western United States</u>, cause changes to the landscape.
   Ⓑ Many wild creatures flee; <u>some are unable to escape from the flames</u>.
   Ⓒ Vegetation is obliterated, <u>which leaves hillsides barren</u>.
   Ⓓ Hills <u>that are bare</u> usually suffer significant erosion during rainstorms.

Read each item carefully. Fill in the circle next to the best answer.

7. **Which sentence has a gerund phrase underlined? (19)**

   (A) Plant roots grow <u>downward into cracks in rocks</u>.

   (B) <u>As plants grow</u>, roots expand and push against rocks.

   (C) People are also <u>contributing to the breakdown</u> of surface materials.

   (D) <u>Hiking up a mountain</u> breaks down rock on the trail.

8. **Which of these sentences is in the passive voice? (20)**

   (A) Boulders can be broken apart by frost action.

   (B) First, water enters and fills a crack in a boulder.

   (C) The water in the crack freezes and expands.

   (D) The powerful force of that expansion can crack a huge boulder in two.

9. **Read this sentence.**

   > Ocean waves erode seaside cliffs <u>over time</u>.

   What type of phrase or clause is underlined in this sentence? (21)

   (A) adjective phrase

   (B) adverb phrase

   (C) adjective clause

   (D) adverb clause

10. **Read this sentence.**

    > <u>If sea level rises throughout the world</u>, coastal areas will flood more frequently.

    What type of phrase or clause is underlined in this sentence? (21)

    (A) adjective phrase

    (B) adverb phrase

    (C) adjective clause

    (D) adverb clause

11. **Which of the following sentences shows the relationship between ideas most effectively? (22)**

    (A) Wind is another force that causes changes in the landscape; strong winds can pick up loose soil particles and deposit them hundreds of miles away.

    (B) Wind can change the landscape.

    (C) Wind can move loose soil particles long distances.

    (D) Wind can change the landscape by moving loose soil particles.

12. **Which of the following sentences is written correctly? (23)**

    (A) The study of processes that change Earth's surface.

    (B) I want to learn more about forces that change our Earth's surface, I'm really interested in Earth processes.

    (C) I would study physical geography I might also study geology.

    (D) Physical geography is the study of the lands and waters of Earth; geology involves the study of Earth's structure and surface.

13. **Read this sentence.**

    > Powerful are the physical forces of change.

    In what order are the words in the sentence? (24)

    (A) natural order

    (B) inverted order

    (C) interrupted order

    (D) None of the above

14. **Which of the following sentences is a compound sentence? (13)**

    (A) Decomposers are living things that break down dead plants or animals for food.

    (B) These organisms also break down waste produced by plants and animals.

    (C) An earthworm is a decomposer, and so is a banana slug.

    (D) Which are decomposers, algae or fungi?

268

Read each item carefully. Fill in the circle next to the best answer.

15. Read this sentence.

> Mushrooms are a type of fungi; many kinds of mushrooms grow on dead trees.

What types of clauses are in the sentence? **(14)**

(A) The first is an independent clause; the second is dependent.

(B) The first is a dependent clause; the second is independent.

(C) Both are dependent clauses.

(D) Both are independent clauses.

16. Which of the following is a complex sentence? **(15)**

(A) Mushrooms get nourishment from dead trees, and they break it down into bits of organic material.

(B) If fungi did not break down dead plant material, forest soil would likely be less fertile.

(C) Worms also make soil fertile, but most do their work underground.

(D) Most people do not appreciate the important work done by decomposers.

17. Which sentence has an adjective clause underlined? **(16)**

(A) The planet that we live on spins like a top.

(B) Because Earth spins around once every 24 hours, that is the length of a day.

(C) This spinning motion is called rotation; Earth rotates on its axis.

(D) Earth's axis is an imaginary line running from the North Pole to the South Pole.

18. Which sentence has an adverb clause underlined? **(17)**

(A) Our planet moves in another way, too: it moves in a circle around the sun.

(B) Planet Earth makes one complete circle every 365¼ days.

(C) People define a year as 365 days, although this is not quite accurate.

(D) To make up for this inaccuracy, we add one day to each fourth year.

19. Which of the following sentences has a nonrestrictive clause underlined? **(18)**

(A) We use a calendar that is based on the movement of Earth around the sun.

(B) Other peoples have developed calendars that are based on the movement of the moon around Earth.

(C) These calendars, which are known as lunar calendars, have months of 29 or 30 days.

(D) The time from one new moon to the next is the time that a month lasts in the traditional Chinese calendar.

20. Which sentence has a gerund phrase underlined? **(19)**

(A) The sun appears to move across the sky each day.

(B) The apparent movement of the sun across the sky is the result of Earth's rotation.

(C) Seeing long shadows tells you that the sun is low in the sky.

(D) The sun is low in the sky after dawn and before sunset.

Read each item carefully. Fill in the circle next to the best answer.

21. **Which of these sentences is in the passive voice? (20)**

    (A) Most units of time relate to Earth's movements.
    (B) Seconds, minutes, and hours represent divisions of the length of one rotation.
    (C) Some cultures use the moon's movements to measure units of time.
    (D) A lunar calendar is used by several Asian cultures.

22. **Read this sentence.**

    > A number of calendars <u>that make use of lunar months</u> are actually lunisolar calendars: extra months are added to some years to keep the calendar year aligned with the solar year and the seasons.

    What type of phrase or clause is underlined in this sentence? (21)

    (A) adjective phrase
    (B) adverb phrase
    (C) adjective clause
    (D) adverb clause

23. **Which of the following sentences shows the relationship between ideas most effectively? (22)**

    (A) The Gregorian calendar, a solar calendar, is in use throughout the world today.
    (B) Although the Gregorian calendar, a solar calendar, is in use throughout the world today, the dates on which important holidays in many cultures are celebrated are dictated by those cultures' traditional lunar calendars.
    (C) The dates on which important holidays in many cultures are celebrated are not the same year after year, because even though those people use the Gregorian calendar, which is a solar calendar, they still use their traditional lunar calendar sometimes.
    (D) Important holidays in many cultures are celebrated according to their traditional lunar calendar.

24. **Which of the following sentences is written correctly? (23)**

    (A) The change of seasons, probably the most easily recognizable cycle in nature.
    (B) Spring always follows winter, and spring always brings longer, warmer days.
    (C) When spring arrives seeds sprout, leaves begin to grow, many plants produce blossoms.
    (D) These changes happen every year at about the same time, how difficult life would be if we could not depend on the seasons!

25. **Read this sentence.**

    > In the early days of spring, the hills turn green.

    In what order are the words in the sentence? (24)

    (A) natural order
    (B) inverted order
    (C) interrupted order
    (D) None of the above

 **TEST TIP:** Eliminate answer choices that you know are incorrect.

(Numbers in parentheses identify related lessons.)

Read each item carefully. Fill in the circle next to the best answer.

1. Read this sentence.

   > Many storytellers specialize in telling tales from a particular culture.

   Which of these words is a singular noun in the sentence? (25)

   (A) many
   (B) storytellers
   (C) tales
   (D) culture

2. **Read this sentence.**

   > Irina moved from Kiev to Oklahoma City; she tells tales from Ukraine.

   Which of these words is a common noun in the sentence? (26)

   (A) Irina
   (B) Kiev
   (C) tales
   (D) Ukraine

3. **Read this sentence:**

   > Our class has several skillful storytellers and comedians, but Irina is the most popular entertainer of all.

   Which of these words from this sentence is a collective noun? (27)

   (A) class
   (B) storytellers
   (C) comedians
   (D) entertainer

4. Read this sentence.

   > People of all ages love to listen to _____ tales.

   Which of these words would correctly complete the sentence? (28)

   (A) Irinas   (C) Irinas'
   (B) Irina's   (D) Irinases'

5. Read this sentence.

   > She is teaching <u>us</u> how to be better storytellers.

   What kind of personal pronoun is underlined? (29)

   (A) first person
   (B) second person
   (C) third person singular
   (D) third person plural

6. Read this sentence.

   > I myself practice telling tales in front of a mirror, to make my expressions and gestures more effective.

   Which word from the sentence is an intensive pronoun? (30)

   (A) I
   (B) myself
   (C) to
   (D) my

7. Read this sentence.

   > After I tell you my tale, you should tell me _____.

   Which of these is the correct pronoun form to use to complete the sentence? (31)

   (A) your   (C) yours
   (B) you're   (D) your's

271

Read each item carefully. Fill in the circle next to the best answer.

8. Read this sentence.

> In my opinion, anyone who practices reading tales expressively can become an effective storyteller.

Which word from the sentence is an indefinite pronoun? **(32)**

Ⓐ my
Ⓑ anyone
Ⓒ who
Ⓓ become

9. Read this sentence.

> What is the other skill necessary for a person who wants to become a storyteller?

What types of pronouns are *what* and *who* in the sentence? **(33)**

Ⓐ **what**—interrogative pronoun; **who**—relative pronoun.
Ⓑ **what**—relative pronoun; **who**—interrogative pronoun.
Ⓒ Both **what** and **who** are interrogative pronouns.
Ⓓ Both **what** and **who** are relative pronouns.

10. Read this sentence. Look at the underlined words in it.

> A good storyteller can memorize details quickly and accurately.

Which underlined word in this sentence is an adjective? **(34)**

Ⓐ good
Ⓑ can
Ⓒ quickly
Ⓓ accurately

11. Read this sentence. Look at the underlined words in it.

> A person who speaks clearly and has a resonant voice can gain the attention of an audience.

Which underlined word in this sentence is an adverb? **(34)**

Ⓐ who
Ⓑ clearly
Ⓒ resonant
Ⓓ attention

12. Read this sentence.

> I have memorized the two tales in this book, but I haven't memorized any of _____ in that book.

Which of these words would correctly complete the sentence? **(35)**

Ⓐ this
Ⓑ that
Ⓒ these
Ⓓ those

13. Read this sentence.

> If you were asked to name three, legendary heroes as your favorites, which brave clever characters would you choose?

How should this sentence be rewritten? **(36)**

Ⓐ If you were asked to name legendary three heroes as your favorites, which clever brave characters would you choose?
Ⓑ If you were asked to name legendary, three heroes as your favorites, which brave clever characters would you choose?
Ⓒ If you were asked to name three legendary heroes as your favorites, which brave, clever characters would you choose?
Ⓓ The sentence should not be rewritten. It is correct as written.

Read each item carefully. Fill in the circle next to the best answer.

14. Read this sentence.

> Theater troupes in many parts of the world present plays based on timeless tales.

Which of these words is a singular noun in the sentence? **(25)**

(A) troupes
(B) parts
(C) world
(D) plays

15. Read this sentence.

> Mario Lamo, who came from Colombia to California, writes delightful stories.

Which of these choices is a common noun in the sentence? **(26)**

(A) Mario Lamo
(B) who
(C) Colombia
(D) stories

16. Read this sentence:

> Mario uses a book of folktales, a laptop, a keyboard, and his imagination to create puppet plays.

Which of these words from this sentence is an abstract noun? **(27)**

(A) book
(B) laptop
(C) keyboard
(D) imagination

17. Read this sentence.

> Some theater troupes read many _____ published tales to find new material.

Which of these words would correctly complete the sentence? **(28)**

(A) storytellers
(B) storyteller's
(C) storytellers'
(D) storytellerses'

18. Read this sentence.

> A member of a theater troupe read one of Mario's stories, loved it, and contacted <u>him</u>.

What kind of personal pronoun is underlined? **(29)**

(A) first person
(B) second person
(C) third person singular
(D) third person plural

19. Read this sentence.

> Mario himself gave permission to have his story made into a play, and he gave the troupe suggestions on what changes to make.

Which word from the sentence is an intensive pronoun? **(30)**

(A) Mario
(B) his
(C) he
(D) himself

Read each item carefully. Fill in the circle next to the best answer.

20. Read this sentence.

> Mario was excited about the troupe's plan to present _____ story as a puppet play.

Which of these is the correct pronoun form to use to complete the sentence? (31)

- (A) him
- (B) his
- (C) his's
- (D) he's

21. Read this sentence.

> Not everyone who writes a story wants it performed by puppets.

Which word from the sentence is an indefinite pronoun? (32)

- (A) everyone
- (B) who
- (C) story
- (D) it

22. Read this sentence.

> Who among you has seen puppets that are ten feet tall?

What types of pronouns are *who* and *that* in the sentence? (33)

- (A) **who**—interrogative pronoun; **that**—relative pronoun.
- (B) **who**—relative pronoun; **that**—interrogative pronoun.
- (C) Both **who** and **that** are interrogative pronouns.
- (D) Both **who** and **that** are relative pronouns.

23. Read this sentence. Look at the underlined words in it.

> The puppet <u>performance</u> of <u>Mario's</u> story was a <u>huge</u> success: audiences and reviewers praised it <u>enthusiastically</u>.

Which underlined word in the sentence is an adjective? (34)

- (A) performance
- (B) Mario's
- (C) huge
- (D) enthusiastically

24. Read this sentence.

> _____ puppets here are easy to move; those over there are more difficult.

Which of these words would correctly complete the sentence? (35)

- (A) This
- (B) That
- (C) These
- (D) Those

25. Read this sentence.

> The puppet wearing the bright green cloak is a wise, patient woman who saves her village from a monster.

How should this sentence be rewritten? (36)

- (A) The puppet wearing the bright, green cloak is a wise, patient woman who saves her village from a monster.
- (B) The puppet wearing the bright green cloak is a wise patient woman who saves her village from a monster.
- (C) The puppet wearing the green, bright cloak is a patient wise woman who saves her village from a monster.
- (D) The sentence should not be rewritten. It is correct as written.

 **TEST TIP:** Read every choice before deciding on an answer.

(Numbers in parentheses identify related lessons.)

Read each item carefully. Fill in the circle next to the best answer.

1. Read these sentences.

> In 1916 the federal government passed the Federal Aid Road Act. Thanks to this law, money for new highways became available to states.

What kinds of verbs are in the sentences? **(37)**

- Ⓐ first sentence—action verb; second sentence—linking verb
- Ⓑ first sentence—linking verb; second sentence—action verb
- Ⓒ both sentences—action verbs
- Ⓓ both sentences—linking verbs

2. Read each sentence. Which sentence has an intransitive verb? **(38)**

- Ⓐ In that era the use of automobiles grew rapidly.
- Ⓑ Drivers throughout America wanted better roads.
- Ⓒ Local and state officials chose routes for new roads.
- Ⓓ Then, with federal money, the states built the new roads.

3. Read this sentence.

> A new form of transportation changes patterns of life.

In what tense is the underlined verb? **(39)**

- Ⓐ past
- Ⓑ present
- Ⓒ future
- Ⓓ None of the above

4. Read this sentence.

> Before the advent of the automobile, most farmers had lived isolated lives.

In what tense is the underlined verb? **(40)**

- Ⓐ past perfect
- Ⓑ present perfect
- Ⓒ future perfect
- Ⓓ None of the above

5. Read this sentence.

> By the 1920s some Americans were commuting from outlying communities to cities each day for work.

In what form is the underlined verb? **(41)**

- Ⓐ past progressive
- Ⓑ present progressive
- Ⓒ future progressive
- Ⓓ None of the above

6. Which sentence has an inappropriate tense shift? **(42)**

- Ⓐ In 1920 less than 2% of America's highways had well-paved surfaces, so driving long distances was difficult.
- Ⓑ As autos traveled on dirt roads, they created clouds of dust.
- Ⓒ Sharp rocks punctured tires, and flying pebbles smash windshields.
- Ⓓ Roads became impassable in rainstorms, when dirt turned to mud.

7. Read this sentence.

> Congress significantly **modified** the federal road law in 1921.

In what mood is the boldfaced verb? **(43)**

- Ⓐ indicative
- Ⓑ imperative
- Ⓒ subjunctive
- Ⓓ It is not in any mood.

Read each item carefully. Fill in the circle next to the best answer.

8. Read this sentence.

> I recommend that a modern driver
> <u>consider</u> how difficult automobile
> travel was a century ago.

In what mood is the underlined verb? **(44)**

(A) indicative

(B) imperative

(C) subjunctive

(D) It is not in any mood.

9. Which sentence has an inappropriate mood shift? **(45)**

(A) Our mechanic insists that my mom use one particular brand of gasoline and brings the car in for an oil change every 5,000 miles.

(B) Our car runs well, and that is important to us.

(C) My mom drives herself and several coworkers to their office every day; car trouble creates serious problems.

(D) Put on an old shirt, grab a sponge, and help me wash this beautiful automobile!

10. Which sentence has an awkward voice shift? **(46)**

(A) Today America has an extensive network of highways, and that network facilitates the movement of goods.

(B) Prior to the 1920s almost all freight in America was shipped by rail; freight could not be transported by truck efficiently because of the poor condition of most roads.

(C) America needed better roads in 1921, and the new law required states to build them.

(D) All across the country, workers widened, leveled, and smoothed roadbeds, and then the roadbeds were paved by them using huge machines.

11. Read this sentence.

> Although the law required
> construction of highways connecting
> states, it did not specify routes.

Which of these words is a subordinating conjunction in the sentence? **(47)**

(A) although

(B) required

(C) connecting

(D) not

12. Read each sentence. Which sentence has a pair of correlative conjunctions? **(48)**

(A) Cy Avery of Tulsa, Oklahoma, emerged as a highway specialist.

(B) Avery was not only a successful business owner but also a strong supporter of highway improvement.

(C) Avery was given the task of mapping out what would become the United States Highway System.

(D) He planned a highway route that would connect Chicago with Los Angeles.

13. Read these sentences.

> The first part of Avery's new route ran
> south from Chicago to St. Louis. That
> stretch of the route utilized part of an
> existing highway.

What kinds of verbs are in the sentences? **(37)**

(A) first sentence—action verb; second sentence—linking verb

(B) first sentence—linking verb; second sentence—action verb

(C) both sentences—action verbs

(D) both sentences—linking verbs

Read each item carefully. Fill in the circle next to the best answer.

14. **Read each sentence. Which sentence has an intransitive verb? (38)**

    Ⓐ The route then ran in a southwestward direction to Oklahoma City.

    Ⓑ Avery ran this stretch of the road right past his own service station near Tulsa, Oklahoma.

    Ⓒ The next stretch crossed the Texas Panhandle.

    Ⓓ It then ascended the mountains of New Mexico and Arizona.

15. **Read this sentence.**

    > The final stretch of the route <u>traversed</u> desert lands in southern California.

    In what tense is the underlined verb? (39)

    Ⓐ past

    Ⓑ present

    Ⓒ future

    Ⓓ None of the above

16. **Read this sentence.**

    > Some readers <u>will have guessed</u> the identity of this great American road by now.

    In what tense is the underlined verb? (40)

    Ⓐ past perfect

    Ⓑ present perfect

    Ⓒ future perfect

    Ⓓ None of the above

17. **Read this sentence.**

    > This narrative <u>is telling</u> about Route 66.

    In what form is the underlined verb? (41)

    Ⓐ past progressive

    Ⓑ present progressive

    Ⓒ future progressive

    Ⓓ None of the above

18. **Which sentence has an inappropriate tense shift? (42)**

    Ⓐ On November 11, 1926, a committee of local and national highway officials met and approved Avery's plan for Route 66.

    Ⓑ About 800 miles of the 2,500-mile route were already paved, and more are being prepared for paving at that time.

    Ⓒ Cy Avery recommended "The Main Street of America" for the new road's nickname, and the representatives approved it.

    Ⓓ Author John Steinbeck later called it "the Mother Road," and that nickname became popular, too.

19. **Read this sentence.**

    > If I <u>were</u> a college student, I would study civil engineering.

    In what mood is the underlined verb? (44)

    Ⓐ indicative

    Ⓑ imperative

    Ⓒ subjunctive

    Ⓓ It is not in any mood.

20. **Read this sentence.**

    > <u>Imagine</u> being part of a team that designs and constructs highways!

    In what mood is the underlined verb? (43)

    Ⓐ indicative

    Ⓑ imperative

    Ⓒ subjunctive

    Ⓓ It is not in any mood.

Read each item carefully. Fill in the circle next to the best answer.

21. Which sentence has an inappropriate mood shift? (45)

Ⓐ To prepare yourself for this career, develop your math skills, study hard in science classes, and you should talk with engineers.

Ⓑ My next-door neighbor is an engineer; he recommends that an engineering student work on construction crews during summer breaks.

Ⓒ Today's road-building machines are much more powerful than the machines of the 1920s were.

Ⓓ Although they did not have sophisticated equipment, yesterday's engineers built roads through incredibly challenging terrain.

22. Which sentence has an awkward voice shift? (46)

Ⓐ Workers built and paved more roads, and drivers experienced fewer mishaps.

Ⓑ Trucks could travel farther and faster, and so they began to haul more freight.

Ⓒ More people purchased automobiles, and these autos were used by people for vacation travel as well as everyday transportation.

Ⓓ Motels and drive-in restaurants sprang up along highways; travelers found them affordable and convenient.

23. Read this sentence.

> Many of America's highways passed through scenic areas, but drivers were not always able to enjoy the natural beauty because newly constructed billboards blocked the view.

Which of these words is a coordinating conjunction in the sentence? (47)

Ⓐ through
Ⓑ but
Ⓒ to
Ⓓ because

24. Read this sentence.

> As workers paved more stretches, representatives from the Route 66 states told the rest of America about the wonderful new highway.

Which of these words is a subordinating conjunction in the sentence? (47)

Ⓐ as
Ⓑ more
Ⓒ from
Ⓓ about

25. Read each sentence. Which sentence has a pair of correlative conjunctions? (48)

Ⓐ Traffic on the new national highway increased rapidly.

Ⓑ Both business travelers and sightseers used Route 66.

Ⓒ Singer Nat "King" Cole had a number one hit with a song about Route 66.

Ⓓ For about 50 years "The Main Street of America" moved motorists back and forth across the West.

 **TEST TIP:** Mark your answers neatly. If you erase, erase completely and clearly without smudging.

(Numbers in parentheses identify related lessons.)

Read each item carefully. Fill in the circle next to the best answer.

1. Which of the following sentences has *your* or *you're* used *incorrectly*? **(49)**

   Ⓐ Your new mobile phone is an amazing device!
   Ⓑ I'm surprised at the quality of you're photos.
   Ⓒ You're really good at typing messages on its little keyboard.
   Ⓓ When you're browsing the Internet with your phone, how hard is it to read the pages?

2. Which of the following sentences has *its* or *it's* used *incorrectly*? **(50)**

   Ⓐ It's likely that future cell phones will have additional capabilities.
   Ⓑ I want a phone with GPS as one of its capabilities.
   Ⓒ It's possible that a future phone will have temperature sensors.
   Ⓓ Then it's screen could display the temperature as well as the time.

3. Read each sentence. Look at the underlined word in it. Which sentence is written *incorrectly*? **(51)**

   Ⓐ Jelani thinks that fancy cell phones are <u>to</u> expensive.
   Ⓑ He places calls <u>to</u> family members and friends with his plain old cell phone.
   Ⓒ He says that phone screens are <u>too</u> small to display Web pages.
   Ⓓ He says he doesn't need his cell phone to be an MP3 player because his family already has <u>two</u> of those.

4. Read this sentence.

   > When I was young, our family would usually take _____ 25 pictures during a vacation.

   Which of these choices would correctly complete the sentence? **(52)**

   Ⓐ less
   Ⓑ fewer
   Ⓒ less than
   Ⓓ fewer than

5. Read each sentence. Which sentence is written *incorrectly*? **(53)**

   Ⓐ Nowadays it's not unusual for our family to take 1000 photos during a vacation.
   Ⓑ It's not difficult to delete the ones that aren't good.
   Ⓒ We don't never upload photos to an Internet photo storage site until we have deleted the bad ones.
   Ⓓ We haven't ever ordered more than 25 prints of any vacation.

6. Read this sentence.

   > In my report on technological gadgets, which I wrote for science class, I discussed several things.

   Which word or words in the sentence do not belong in academic writing? **(54)**

   Ⓐ technological gadgets
   Ⓑ science class
   Ⓒ several
   Ⓓ things

Read each item carefully. Fill in the circle next to the best answer.

7. Read each sentence. Look at the underlined word in it. Which sentence is written *incorrectly*? **(55)**

    (A) Our new big-screen TV <u>sets</u> on a strong table.
    (B) It took two of us to <u>raise</u> it from the floor.
    (C) We <u>set</u> it carefully on the table.
    (D) When I <u>sit</u> in the big blue chair, I can see the picture clearly.

8. Read each sentence. Look at the underlined word in it. Which sentence is written *incorrectly*? **(56)**

    (A) My grandfather <u>built</u> the table we are using for the big-screen TV.
    (B) The table has always <u>held</u> heavy things well, because it's so sturdy.
    (C) Grandfather <u>maked</u> a cabinet for the cable box, too.
    (D) We have <u>found</u> that low-tech skills like his make living with high-tech equipment more pleasant.

9. Read each sentence. Look at the underlined word in it. Which sentence is written *incorrectly*? **(57)**

    (A) If you want to get a good job in a high-tech company, you should <u>persevere</u> in your math studies.
    (B) Most people who <u>devise</u> high-tech methods use math in the process.
    (C) Many high-tech jobs involve <u>fiscal</u> management; companies have to be careful with their money!
    (D) Accounts payable departments <u>disperse</u> money only for invoices with purchase order numbers.

10. Read each sentence. Look at the underlined word(s) in it. Which sentence is written *incorrectly*? **(58)**

    (A) Meg and Heather <u>went</u> to a high-tech job fair.
    (B) Meg <u>was all</u>, "I'm not leaving until I get a job offer!"
    (C) Heather replied, "If I don't find a job that I think I will <u>like</u>, I'm not signing anything."
    (D) "How do <u>you know</u> what a job will be like until you start it?" asked Meg.

11. Read each sentence. Look at the underlined word in it. Which sentence is written *incorrectly*? **(59)**

    (A) Jacob has discovered that <u>he</u> really enjoys physics.
    (B) <u>He</u> has already taken the only physics course his high school offers.
    (C) Jacob's counselor has suggested to Jacob that <u>he</u> take a free physics MOOC.
    (D) Jacob <u>he</u> is very excited to take a course taught by a famous physicist.

12. Read each sentence. Which sentence contains words that are unnecessary and should be eliminated? **(60)**

    (A) For those of you who don't already know, MOOC stands for massive open online course.
    (B) Many universities now offer MOOCs for free.
    (C) Students typically do not receive academic credit.
    (D) For students willing to work hard, MOOCs offer a chance to learn from top-level instructors.

13. Which of the following sentences has *there, they're,* or *their* used *incorrectly*? **(49)**

    (A) A list of upcoming physics MOOCs is posted over there.
    (B) The courses are challenging, but their likely to be fascinating.
    (C) Prospective astronomers may want to expand their knowledge by taking "Dark Matter in Galaxies."
    (D) More and more professors are planning MOOCs; they're excited to be able to offer large numbers of people the opportunity to learn about important topics.

Read each item carefully. Fill in the circle next to the best answer.

14. **Which of the following sentences has** *your* **or** *you're* **used** *incorrectly?* **(49)**

    Ⓐ Your a big music fan, aren't you?
    Ⓑ Would you like to play the solos your favorite guitarist plays?
    Ⓒ If so, you're someone who might enjoy learning to play a real guitar.
    Ⓓ You're also a prospective customer for a certain type of video game.

15. **Which of the following sentences has** *its* **or** *it's* **used** *incorrectly?* **(50)**

    Ⓐ It's amazingly easy to play great guitar solos using that video game.
    Ⓑ That certainly explains its popularity.
    Ⓒ Its not easy to train your brain and fingers to play a real guitar well.
    Ⓓ If guitar games continue to improve, it's possible that fewer people will take time to learn to play the real instrument.

16. **Read each sentence. Look at the underlined word in it. Which sentence is written** *incorrectly?* **(51)**

    Ⓐ I am talking <u>to</u> my friend Miriam in Kenya.
    Ⓑ She lives in a village that is <u>two</u> hundred miles from Nairobi.
    Ⓒ You might think such a village would be <u>too</u> remote for the use of cell phones.
    Ⓓ Many remote villages are linked <u>too</u> the rest of the world by cell phones.

17. **Read this sentence.**

    According to the electronic scale, the weight of my suitcases is _____ the limit.

    Which of these choices would correctly complete the sentence? (52)

    Ⓐ over
    Ⓑ more
    Ⓒ more than
    Ⓓ None of the above

18. **Read each sentence. Which sentence is written** *incorrectly?* **(53)**

    Ⓐ Cell phone use is not allowed during an airline flight.
    Ⓑ My friend wasn't paying attention when the announcement about cell phones was made.
    Ⓒ Although he didn't hear the announcement, I did.
    Ⓓ I told him to turn off his phone, because I didn't want it to cause no problems.

19. **Read this sentence.**

    Modern automobiles have stuff that makes them safer and more efficient to drive.

    Which word or words in the sentence do not belong in academic writing? (54)

    Ⓐ modern
    Ⓑ stuff
    Ⓒ safer
    Ⓓ more efficient

Read each item carefully. Fill in the circle next to the best answer.

20. **Read each sentence. Look at the underlined word in it. Which sentence is written *incorrectly*? (55)**

    (A) Computers <u>rise</u> the efficiency of automobile engines.

    (B) You can <u>set</u> a desired speed, and cruise control will maintain the speed automatically.

    (C) When you <u>sit</u> in a front seat, a computer senses your presence and warns you to buckle up via an alarm.

    (D) If you fasten your seat belt or <u>rise</u> from the seat, the alarm stops.

21. **Read each sentence. Look at the underlined word in it. Which sentence is written *incorrectly*? (56)**

    (A) My parents <u>took</u> me with them to a new car dealership.

    (B) We <u>seen</u> a car with a rear-view camera.

    (C) It <u>showed</u> on a small screen what was behind the car.

    (D) Will this device <u>cut</u> the number of accidents that occur when drivers go in reverse?

22. **Read each sentence. Look at the underlined word in it. Which sentence is written *incorrectly*? (57)**

    (A) Shopping on the Internet is like visiting a great <u>bazaar</u>.

    (B) You can find pillows that <u>compliment</u> the color of your couch.

    (C) You can design your own <u>stationery</u> and have it printed and sent to you very quickly.

    (D) You can find items cheaper on the Internet <u>than</u> at local stores.

23. **Read each sentence. Look at the underlined word in it. Which sentence is written *incorrectly*? (58)**

    (A) Lily <u>went</u>, "The Internet is a great homework helper."

    (B) "My assignments <u>are all</u> posted on our school's website," she continued.

    (C) Estrella said that she goes to the library as often as she <u>goes</u> online for information.

    (D) "I <u>like</u> doing research in the library more than on the Internet," she added.

24. **Read each sentence. Look at the underlined word in it. Which sentence is written *incorrectly*? (59)**

    (A) Rita and Jackie <u>they</u> love to visit travel websites.

    (B) Although they cannot afford to travel to far-off places now, <u>they</u> dream of doing so someday.

    (C) The travel sites let <u>them</u> see fascinating buildings and breathtaking landscapes.

    (D) Both of <u>them</u> have long lists of countries they hope to visit.

25. **Read this sentence.**

    Rita and Jackie have discovered websites that enable travelers to find the most economical airline flights at the lowest cost, discover reasonably priced hotels in good locations, and buy specially priced train and bus passes in advance.

    Which words in this sentence are unnecessary and should be eliminated? (60)

    (A) that enable travelers

    (B) at the lowest cost

    (C) in good locations

    (D) in advance

 **TEST TIP:** Change an answer only if you are sure that your first choice is wrong.

(Numbers in parentheses identify related lessons.)

Read each item carefully. Fill in the circle next to the best answer.

1. Read this sentence.

> Those of us who love fishing have learned to analyze rivers.

Which word in the sentence is an object pronoun? (61)

Ⓐ those   Ⓒ who
Ⓑ us   Ⓓ None of the above

2. Read each sentence. **Which sentence is written** *incorrectly*? **(62)**

Ⓐ My sister and me have learned to read rivers.
Ⓑ The ripples on a river's surface tell her and me about the location of the main channel.
Ⓒ When she and I are in a canoe on a river, we know where to steer.
Ⓓ We and our parents go fishing every year.

3. Read this sentence.

> My dad caught a salmon and had to work hard to reel <u>it</u> into the boat.

Which is the antecedent for the underlined pronoun? (63)

Ⓐ year   Ⓒ salmon
Ⓑ dad   Ⓓ boat

4. **Each of these sentences is from the same paragraph. Read each sentence, and look at the underlined word. Which sentence is written incorrectly? (64)**

Ⓐ How does a stream biologist prepare <u>herself</u> to conduct a research project?
Ⓑ First, <u>she</u> selects a stream and uses what she knows about it to establish a hypothesis.
Ⓒ For example, <u>she</u> might hypothesize that a stream is polluted.
Ⓓ <u>You</u> would then spend time researching what is already known about the stream.

5. **Read each sentence. Look at the underlined word. Which sentence has a pronoun that does not have a clear antecedent? (65)**

Ⓐ Robert's cousin, Dr. Robin Lynn, is a stream biologist; he invited <u>her</u> to speak at his school.
Ⓑ Robert and other interested students listened to Dr. Lynn talk about her stream studies, and <u>they</u> asked her some good questions.
Ⓒ After the talk, <u>they</u> walked to a nearby creek.
Ⓓ The students stood by the creek as Robert demonstrated techniques for collecting water samples from <u>it</u>.

6. **Read each sentence. Look at the underlined word. Which sentence is** *not* **correct? (66)**

Ⓐ <u>Who</u> has observed a waterfall?
Ⓑ I met a photographer <u>who</u> has photographed more than 100 waterfalls.
Ⓒ To <u>who</u> is she sending that photo?
Ⓓ My aunt is the person with <u>whom</u> I traveled to Niagara Falls.

7. **Read each sentence. Look at the underlined verb. Which sentence is** *not* **correct? (67)**

Ⓐ A river in the mountains <u>runs</u> swiftly.
Ⓑ The slope of its bed <u>is</u> generally fairly steep.
Ⓒ When a river flowing through mountains <u>reach</u> a cliff, a waterfall results.
Ⓓ A waterfall on the plains <u>is</u> a relatively rare sight.

Read each item carefully. Fill in the circle next to the best answer.

8. Read each sentence. Look at the underlined verb. Which sentence is *not* correct? **(68)**

    (A) Neither Kansas nor Nebraska <u>have</u> many waterfalls.
    (B) Washington and the other Pacific states <u>have</u> many dramatic waterfalls.
    (C) At the bottom of a waterfall, binoculars or a camera lens <u>becomes</u> wet from the mist.
    (D) Spray or bubbles <u>are</u> fascinating to watch.

9. Read each sentence. Look at the underlined verb. Which sentence is *not* correct? **(69)**

    (A) Everyone in these canyons <u>fear</u> floods.
    (B) All of us <u>know</u> how high the river can get.
    (C) Anyone whose cabin has been flooded <u>prepares</u> for flood season.
    (D) "Tips for Avoiding Flood Damage" <u>is</u> a helpful pamphlet.

10. Read each sentence. Which sentence is *not* correct because of a dangling or misplaced modifier? **(70)**

    (A) Fearing damage from spring floods, we remove items from our cabin in the fall.
    (B) Checking weather reports regularly, we know when floods are likely to occur.
    (C) Hearing a prediction of heavy rains last week, we drove to our cabin.
    (D) Loading up the car with furniture, the flood did little damage to our cabin.

11. Read this sentence.

    | What is the _____ river you have ever swum in? |

    Which choice would complete the sentence correctly? **(71)**

    (A) colder
    (B) more cold
    (C) coldest
    (D) most cold

12. Read this sentence.

    | I actually have never swum in a really cold river. |

    Which word in the sentence is an auxiliary verb? **(72)**

    (A) actually
    (B) have
    (C) never
    (D) swum

13. Read this sentence.

    | Ricardo has measured the temperature of this river, and now he must decide whether to swim in it. |

    Which word in this sentence is a modal auxiliary? **(72)**

    (A) has
    (B) must
    (C) to
    (D) swim

Read each item carefully. Fill in the circle next to the best answer.

14. **Read this sentence.**

> My friend Lesley quizzed me about rivers, and I answered most questions correctly.

Which word in the sentence is an object pronoun? **(61)**

Ⓐ my
Ⓑ me
Ⓒ I
Ⓓ most

15. **Read each sentence. Which sentence is written *incorrectly*? (62)**

Ⓐ Then she and I switched roles, and I asked her questions.
Ⓑ She also did well, so her and me felt well prepared for the geography test.
Ⓒ Billy and she answered all the test questions correctly.
Ⓓ They were trailed closely by Njoki and me; we each missed only one question.

16. **Read these sentences.**

> What is the largest river in Africa that empties into the Atlantic Ocean? It is the Congo River, which drains the Congo Basin.

Which is the antecedent for the underlined pronoun? **(63)**

Ⓐ river
Ⓑ Africa
Ⓒ Atlantic Ocean
Ⓓ Congo Basin

17. **Each of these sentences is from the same paragraph. Read each sentence. Look at the underlined word in it. Which sentence is written incorrectly? (64)**

Ⓐ You can access satellite images to learn about rivers far from where you live.
Ⓑ Imagine that you want to learn about South America's Orinoco River.
Ⓒ We can find satellite images of it on websites such as zonu.com.
Ⓓ You will notice that NASA is the source of many satellite images of rivers.

18. **Read each sentence. Look at the underlined word. Which sentence has a pronoun that does not have a clear antecedent? (65)**

Ⓐ Christopher Columbus made Europeans aware of the mouth of the Orinoco after he viewed it at the end of the 15th century.
Ⓑ The source of this long river was not identified until 1951, more than 450 years after Columbus visited it.
Ⓒ They found its origin at a spot along the border between Venezuela and Brazil.
Ⓓ From its origin, the Orinoco flows northward into the center of Venezuela, and then curves toward the east, eventually reaching the Atlantic near the Guyana border.

19. **Read each sentence. Look at the underlined word. Which sentence is *not* correct? (66)**

Ⓐ Who can name a song about the Mississippi River?
Ⓑ To whom are you listening on your MP3 player?
Ⓒ I am listening to Johnny Cash; he's the singer from who I learned "Big River."
Ⓓ Was Jimmie Rodgers the musician who wrote "Miss the Mississippi and You"?

Read each item carefully. Fill in the circle next to the best answer.

20. **Read each sentence. Look at the underlined verb. Which sentence is *not* correct? (67)**

    (A) Rivers in the Midwest <u>are</u> the subjects of many songs.

    (B) This song from pioneer days <u>has</u> the Ohio River as its setting.

    (C) Several songs by songwriters from Texas <u>mentions</u> rivers in the Lone Star State.

    (D) A song by Stephen Foster, one of America's best-loved songwriters, <u>celebrates</u> the Suwannee River, which flows through Georgia and Florida.

21. **Read each sentence. Look at the underlined verb. Which sentence is *not* correct? (68)**

    (A) Neither the Colorado River nor the Rio Grande <u>is</u> as long as the Yukon River.

    (B) Canada's Yukon Territory and the state of Alaska <u>are</u> crossed by the mighty Yukon.

    (C) The Missouri River and the Mississippi River <u>are</u> each longer than the Yukon.

    (D) The Hudson River or the Delaware River <u>are</u> where my aunt will go to kayak this year.

22. **Read each sentence. Look at the underlined verb. Which sentence is *not* correct? (69)**

    (A) Almost everyone in the United Kingdom <u>knows</u> the location of the Thames River.

    (B) Anyone who has visited the west coast of Ireland <u>has</u> an idea of where the river Shannon is.

    (C) *Great Rivers of the British Isles* <u>have</u> information about these and other major rivers.

    (D) Several of us <u>are</u> planning a summer trip to the U.K.

23. **Read each sentence. Which sentence is *not* correct because of a dangling or misplaced modifier? (70)**

    (A) Seeking shade from the desert sun, we were hiking in a dry desert canyon.

    (B) Hearing thunder in the distance, we quickly climbed up to high ground.

    (C) Sitting in a safe place, a torrent of water flooded the canyon.

    (D) Watching the flash flood, we were very thankful that we had heeded the thunder's warning.

24. **Read this sentence.**

    > The great rivers in Siberia are _____ than those in almost any other region.

    Which choice would complete the sentence correctly? (71)

    (A) longer
    (B) more long
    (C) longest
    (D) most long

25. **Read this sentence.**

    > Have you ever heard of the Ob, the Yenisey, or the Lena?

    Which word in the sentence is an auxiliary verb? (72)

    (A) have
    (B) you
    (C) ever
    (D) heard

TEST TIP: Review your work. If you finish the test before time is up, go back and check your work.

(Numbers in parentheses identify related lessons.)

Read each item carefully. Fill in the circle next to the best answer.

1. Read this sentence.

> Tom Cuthbertson, a writer who lived in Santa Cruz, California, helped people become Problem Solvers.

Which term should *not* be capitalized? **(73)**

Ⓐ Tom Cuthbertson   Ⓒ California
Ⓑ Santa Cruz   Ⓓ Problem Solvers

2. Read each sentence. Which sentence has the title in it written correctly? **(74)**

Ⓐ Tom wrote "Anybody's Bike Book," a book on how to repair bicycles.
Ⓑ His book My Lawnmower Hates Me explains how to fix lawnmowers.
Ⓒ Tom wrote a biography of a famous gardener; its appendix, entitled Gardening Procedures, has excellent tips for gardeners.
Ⓓ Tom's short article entitled "Bicycles have come a long way" describes problems that early bicycle designers had to solve.

3. Read each sentence. Which sentence is written *incorrectly*? **(75)**

Ⓐ We went for a bike ride on Dec. 31, 2007.
Ⓑ My bike chain came off when we were riding on Seabright Ave.
Ⓒ I borrowed some tools from Mr Paul Sanchez.
Ⓓ I repaired my bike, and then we rode to Dwight D. Eisenhower Memorial Park.

4. Read each sentence. Look at the underlined word. Which sentence is written *incorrectly*? **(76)**

Ⓐ I save money by solving my bike's problems myself.
Ⓑ I use Tom Cuthbertson's book as a guide.
Ⓒ The book's section on adjusting brakes is easy to understand.
Ⓓ I have repaired several friend's bikes, too.

5. Read each sentence. Look at the commas. Which sentence is written *incorrectly*? **(77)**

Ⓐ Most oceanographers, scientists who study the ocean, believe that global warming is affecting Earth's oceans.
Ⓑ These scientists need more data to draw conclusions, and they are working hard to gather and share information.
Ⓒ They began sending streaming video of the ocean floor in 2005, and the videos were very interesting!
Ⓓ In addition to pictures, oceanographers can receive current physical, geological, and, biological data from an area via the Internet.

6. Read this sentence.

> The transmission of data from the ocean floor is part of a large ocean research effort the name of the project is the Ocean Observatories Initiative.

Where should a semicolon be placed in this sentence? **(78)**

Ⓐ after **data**   Ⓒ after **effort**
Ⓑ after **floor**   Ⓓ after **project**

7. Read each sentence. Which sentence is *not* punctuated correctly? **(79)**

Ⓐ The home of the Ocean Observatories Initiative (OOI) project is the University of California, San Diego.
Ⓑ The data generated will be available (to anyone with an Internet connection).
Ⓒ This amazing real-time data will be provided at no cost!
Ⓓ Science classes all across America—perhaps including yours—will soon be able to study the same data that top oceanographers study.

Read each item carefully. Fill in the circle next to the best answer.

8. Read this quotation:

> In an age when man has forgotten his origins and is blind even to his most essential needs for survival, water **along with other resources** has become the victim of his indifference.
>
> —Rachel Carson,
> *The Silent Spring*

If you were to write a shortened version of this quotation, leaving out the boldfaced phrase, which punctuation mark should you insert in place of that phrase? **(80)**

- Ⓐ comma
- Ⓑ long dash
- Ⓒ colon
- Ⓓ ellipsis

9. Read each sentence. Which sentence has a punctuation mark in it that signals a pause? **(81)**

- Ⓐ I do not live near the ocean, but I would like to be able to study it.
- Ⓑ The tides, the wind, the waves . . . to me, these are beautiful mysteries.
- Ⓒ Scientific study—hypothesizing, observing, measuring, documenting—is what I would like to do as my work.
- Ⓓ All three sentences above have punctuation marks that signal pauses.

10. Read each sentence. Which sentence is *not* punctuated correctly? **(82)**

- Ⓐ "I'm excited about being able to study the sea floor," said Sharon.
- Ⓑ Beth said that "Amazing creatures live deep in the ocean."
- Ⓒ "I would rather study Mars," said Pete.
- Ⓓ "You can do that on the Internet for free, too," said Sharon.

11. Read this business letter.

> 2550 Clark Avenue
> Nampa, ID 83653
> August 22, 20__
> Dear Professor Sowers:
> I saw an odd creature swim into the ocean sector shown on your streaming video yesterday at 3:56 P.M. Could you tell me what that creature was?
> Sincerely,
> Laura Herbst

Which part of the letter is missing? **(84)**

- Ⓐ inside address
- Ⓒ greeting
- Ⓑ heading
- Ⓓ closing

12. Read this sentence.

> In the April 1976 issue of *Fortune Magazine*, Frederick Seitz said, "A good scientist is a person in whom the childhood quality of perennial curiosity lingers on. Once he gets an answer, he has other questions".

What should be done to make this sentence correct? **(83)**

- Ⓐ Remove the quotation marks.
- Ⓑ Replace the quotation marks with long dashes.
- Ⓒ Move the second quotation mark so it follows the period.
- Ⓓ Nothing should be done. The sentence is correct as written.

13. Read this sentence.

> Dr. Helen Taussig and Dr. Alfred Blalock saved the lives of many Children at Johns Hopkins Hospital in Baltimore, Maryland.

Which term should *not* be capitalized? **(73)**

- Ⓐ Dr. Helen Taussig
- Ⓑ Children
- Ⓒ Johns Hopkins Hospital
- Ⓓ Baltimore, Maryland

Read each item carefully. Fill in the circle next to the best answer.

14. **Read each sentence. Which sentence has the title in it written correctly? (74)**

(A) You can read about the heart procedure these doctors invented in the book "The Miracle Finders."

(B) Another excellent book about great problem solvers is <u>Black Pioneers of Science and Invention</u>.

(C) Have you read the poem <u>On the Completion of the Pacific Telegraph</u>, by Jones Very?

(D) It appears in the book The Treasury of American Poetry.

15. **Read this sentence. Which sentence is written** *incorrectly*? **(75)**

(A) Can a U.S. president be a problem solver?

(B) The residents of 1600 Pennsylvania Ave have always had to face serious problems.

(C) Lyndon B. Johnson tried to solve the problem of civil rights abuses in America.

(D) Richard M. Nixon worked to improve relations with China.

16. **Read each sentence. Look at the underlined word. Which sentence is written** *incorrectly*? **(76)**

(A) One of the <u>world's</u> most serious ongoing problems is conflict in the Middle East.

(B) <u>America's</u> thirty-ninth President, Jimmy Carter, worked hard to bring peace to that region.

(C) He brought together two Middle East <u>nation's</u> leaders, Anwar Sadat of Egypt and Menachem Begin of Israel.

(D) The two signed an agreement that brought peace to the <u>region's</u> peoples for a while.

17. **Read each sentence. Look at the commas. Which sentence is written** *incorrectly*? **(77)**

(A) Granville T. Woods, a noted inventor, was born in 1856.

(B) He worked on ships and trains in his youth and, he became trained in engineering.

(C) Woods opened a factory that made telegraph, telephone, and other electrical equipment.

(D) Soon he began creating innovative, effective communications equipment.

18. **Read this sentence.**

> Woods received a patent for a device that "sent speech" over telegraph lines the American Bell Telephone Company purchased the rights to this invention.

Where should a semicolon be placed in this sentence? (78)

(A) after **patent**   (C) after **lines**

(B) after **speech**   (D) after **Company**

19. **Read each sentence. Which sentence is** *not* **punctuated correctly? (79)**

(A) A wireless method of communication—railway telegraphy—was invented by Woods in 1887.

(B) With this invention—moving trains could send messages to railway stations and other trains, and receive messages from them as well.

(C) Woods's device sent telegraph messages (via static electricity) from the train to the telegraph lines that paralleled most tracks.

(D) Workers at railway stations could use this invention to warn the engineers of life-threatening situations, such as tornadoes and washed-out bridges.

Read each item carefully. Fill in the circle next to the best answer.

20. Read this quotation:

> For the story—from *Rumpelstiltskin* to *War and Peace*—is one of the basic tools invented by the mind of man, for the purpose of gaining understanding. There have been great societies that did not use the wheel, but there have been no societies that did not tell stories.
>
> —Ursula K. LeGuin,
>
> "On Fantasy and Science Fiction"

Which is a correctly written shortened version of the first sentence in this quotation? (80)

(A) For the story . . . is one of the basic tools invented by the mind of man, for the purpose of gaining understanding.

(B) For the story—is one of the basic tools invented by the mind of man, for the purpose of gaining understanding.

(C) For the story, is one of the basic tools invented by the mind of man, for the purpose of gaining understanding.

(D) For the story; is one of the basic tools invented by the mind of man, for the purpose of gaining understanding.

21. Read this sentence.

> Imagine living in a world without electronic communication a world in which no news could travel faster than a horse could gallop.

Where should an ellipsis be inserted in this sentence to signal a pause? (81)

(A) between **world** and **without**

(B) between **communication** and **a**

(C) between **world** and **in**

(D) between **faster** and **than**

22. **Read each sentence. Which sentence is *not* punctuated correctly? (82)**

(A) Alvin said that "he wanted to learn Morse code."

(B) "What is that?" asked Kijana.

(C) "It is a system for transmitting words with electronic pulses," Alvin answered.

(D) He then explained that in Morse code, each letter of the alphabet is represented by one to four dots, dashes, or dots and dashes.

23. **Read each sentence. Which sentence is *not* punctuated correctly? (82)**

(A) "I thought wireless communication was a recent development," said Tonya.

(B) Martin said that he was surprised that static electricity could be useful.

(C) Mr. Bell said, You should both read more about the history of technological progress.

(D) "You'll be surprised by almost every article," he continued.

24. Read this quotation.

> "I admire machinery as much as any man, and am as thankful to it as any man can be for what it does for us. But it will never be a substitute for the face of a man, with his soul in it, encouraging another man to be brave and true."
>
> —Charles Dickens,
>
> *Wreck of the Golden Mary*

What should be done to make this a correctly written quotation? (83)

(A) Replace the periods with ellipses.

(B) Place quotation marks around *Wreck of the Golden Mary*.

(C) Remove the quotation marks.

(D) Place a comma after *admire*.

Lesson 1 Circle the complete subject in each sentence. Underline the complete predicate.

1. (I) am taking swimming classes.
2. (Classes) are held every Friday after school.
3. (This class) will make me a stronger swimmer.
4. (My blue swimsuit) has big white polka dots on it.
5. (The temperature of the pool) is usually very warm.
6. (My goggles) provide protection from the chemicals in the pool water.
7. (My swimming teacher) demonstrated the backstroke for the first time last Friday.
8. (Most of that class time) was spent on the mechanics of the stroke.
9. (A new stroke) can be challenging.
10. (I) noticed my improvement after each lap.
11. (The other students in the class) are developing their swimming skills, too.
12. (A group of us) calls ourselves "the sharks."
13. (My teacher) often uses a stopwatch to time us.
14. (My muscles) feel sore sometimes after a long class.
15. (Hard work) is making me a better swimmer.

Lesson 2 Circle the simple subject in each sentence. If the subject is understood *you*, write *you* on the line. Underline the simple predicate.

1. A (visit) to the library is always an adventure. _____
2. The (library) is a great destination for after school. _____
3. Be quiet! **you**
4. Tall (shelves) full of so many books can intimidate a visitor. _____
5. A (patron) can find mystery, science fiction, and nonfiction books. _____
6. Some (libraries) have DVDs and comic books, too. _____
7. A special (section) for teens exists at some libraries. _____
8. Ask a librarian for a book recommendation. **you**
9. Tell the librarian about your favorite book. **you**
10. (Some) of the most popular books might be temporarily unavailable. _____
11. Other (patrons) may have borrowed them. _____
12. Search the shelves for other interesting books. **you**
13. Reference (librarians) can help with any research project. _____
14. A library (card) is a passport to the world of knowledge. _____
15. Enjoy your books! **you**

Lesson 3 Each sentence has a compound subject or a compound predicate. Circle the two or three simple subjects that make up each compound subject. Underline the two verbs that make up each compound predicate.

1. (Brittany,) (Kevin,) and (I) went ice-skating on Saturday.

2. The (Polar Bears) and the (Walruses) were finishing their hockey game.

3. We <u>watched</u> the end of the game and <u>huddled</u> together for warmth.

4. Then we <u>laced</u> our skates and <u>stepped</u> onto the ice.

5. I <u>slipped</u> on the ice and <u>fell</u>.

6. The ice <u>was</u> cold and <u>soaked</u> my clothes.

7. (Kevin) and (Brittany) helped me back onto my feet.

8. I <u>gripped</u> the ice rink wall and <u>steadied</u> myself.

9. My (friends) and (I) skated in large circles around the ice rink.

10. Kevin <u>skated</u> backward and <u>impressed</u> us with other fancy moves.

11. (Brittany) and (Kevin) suggested some hot chocolate as a treat.

12. I carefully <u>hopped</u> off the ice and <u>followed</u> my friends to the cafeteria.

13. The ice sweeper <u>drove</u> onto the ice and <u>smoothed</u> its surface.

14. Loud music <u>blared</u> from speakers and <u>beckoned</u> us back onto the ice.

15. We <u>were</u> tired but <u>skated</u> until closing time.

Lesson 4 Circle each direct object in each sentence. If the sentence contains an indirect object, underline it.

1. Hank wags his (tail) impatiently.

2. Roger walks (him) every day after school.

3. Today Roger is taking (Hank) to a park several blocks away.

4. Well-behaved Hank puts his (leash) in his mouth.

5. Scents along the way distract (Hank.)

6. He sniffs every (shrub,) (tree,) and (rock) enthusiastically.

7. A mother with a stroller approaches (Hank) and (Roger) cautiously.

8. Hank's large size intimidates most (people) and even other (dogs.)

9. Nobody has any (reason) for fear, in Roger's opinion.

10. Roger tells the <u>mother</u> (stories) about sweet Hank.

11. She finally allows her (child) out of his stroller.

12. The happy child pets (Hank) lovingly.

13. Hank thoroughly enjoys this (attention) from the child.

14. Roger has taught <u>Hank</u> some (tricks.)

15. Roger gives <u>Hank</u> a (treat) and a (pat) on the head after each trick.

Extra Practice

Lesson 5 Underline each predicate noun and predicate adjective in the sentences below. Write *PN* after each sentence with a predicate noun. Write *PA* after each sentence with a predicate adjective. Circle the linking verb in each sentence.

1. Paul (is) late for a movie date on his birthday. _____**PA**_____
2. Paul's friends (are) worried about his late arrival. _____**PA**_____
3. Movie previews (are) a well-known interest of Paul's. _____**PN**_____
4. His friends (are) generous with praise for the previews. _____**PA**_____
5. He (feels) sad about his tardiness. _____**PA**_____
6. The audience for the evening's feature film (is) mostly teenagers. _____**PN**_____
7. A comic book superhero (is) the subject of the movie. _____**PN**_____
8. Suddenly the theater speakers (become) fountains of noise. _____**PN**_____
9. An enormous beetle (becomes) the center of attention on the screen. _____**PN**_____
10. The beetle (becomes) a black-caped superhero in the blink of an eye. _____**PN**_____
11. The superhero (is) beloved throughout the city. _____**PA**_____
12. The ending of the movie (is) a shock. _____**PN**_____
13. Paul and his friends (are) hungry for birthday cake after the movie. _____**PA**_____
14. The beetle-shaped chocolate cake (is) the best after-movie treat ever. _____**PN**_____
15. The birthday present from his friends (is) a superhero poster! _____**PN**_____

Lesson 6 Underline each prepositional phrase. Circle the preposition that begins each phrase. Draw a box around the object of the preposition. There may be more than one prepositional phrase in a sentence.

1. I ride my bike (through) a forest (to) my grandmother's house.
2. My grandmother lives (in) a small cottage (with) her dog.
3. The trees (in) the forest are very thick (above) my head.
4. The sun does not show (through) their branches.
5. Moss grows (on) the trees and hangs (from) the branches.
6. (At) the river, I must bike (across) a narrow bridge.
7. The fish (in) the river glide (through) the water.
8. The road runs (along) the river bank (for) almost a mile.
9. (At) the forest edge, I turn left (on) another road.
10. This new road takes me (through) an apple orchard and (up) a small hill.
11. (After) my bike ride, I will run (with) my grandmother's dog.
12. Finally my grandmother's house comes (into) view.
13. I pedal faster (toward) the gate and don't skid (to) a stop (until) the last second.
14. I lean (against) the heavy gate and then step (into) the garden.
15. My grandmother opens the front door and greets me (with) a big hug.

Extra Practice

Lesson 7 Underline the appositive phrase in each sentence.

1. Mike, a student who had a report due the next day, was panicking.

2. His computer, a usually dependable machine, had suddenly locked up.

3. Scary buzzing sounds, ones that made him fear a crash, were coming from the computer.

4. After Mike restarted it, the computer made reassuring noises, normal warm-up sounds.

5. However, Mike's report, a nearly finished assignment, had disappeared.

6. The research report, a ten-page paper on the pyramids of Egypt, had taken him all week to write.

7. What was Mike, a worrywart by nature, going to do now?

8. Ms. Spiker, his teacher, never accepted late homework.

9. Then the doorbell rang, and Mike saw Melissa, his neighbor, on the front stoop.

10. She had already finished her homework, a report on the Colosseum in Rome.

11. Mike told Melissa, a computer whiz, about his lost pyramid report.

12. She went to the computer table, a place messy beyond belief, and looked at the computer.

13. She spotted an earlier draft of the paper, a copy decorated with scribbled edits.

14. Mike, a hopelessly slow typist, was still frantic.

15. Melissa, a quick thinker, decided that the task would go faster if she read aloud while Mike typed.

Lesson 8 Underline the participial phrase in each sentence. Circle the participle.

1. (Running) through the house, Lucy grabbed her lunch and her backpack.

2. The front door slammed behind her, (making) a noise like a small explosion.

3. She glanced at her watch, (knowing) she would only see bad news.

4. (Discovering) she was disastrously late, Lucy picked up the pace.

5. (Rounding) the corner, she saw the taillights of her bus.

6. She ran with all her might, (powered) by fear of tardiness.

7. (Called) "Dasher" by her track coach, Lucy was a champion sprinter.

8. (Seeing) a green light change to yellow, Lucy slowed her pace.

9. (Watching) the same light, the bus driver accelerated.

10. The bus sailed through the intersection, (leaving) Lucy behind.

11. (Frustrated) by the experience, she nervously checked her watch again.

12. She waited impatiently for the next bus, (breathing) fast from her run.

13. (Standing) on her tiptoes, Lucy saw another bus on its way toward her.

14. (Stepping) off the bus in front of school, Lucy heard the clang of the warning bell.

15. (Thrilled) with her on-time arrival, Lucy gave herself a pat on the backpack.

Lesson 9 Underline the infinitive phrase in each sentence.

1. A gardener has just gone to the nursery to select new plants for her garden.

2. She puts on gardening gloves to protect her hands from thorns.

3. She has many thorny bushes to rip out.

4. The bushes were just thick enough to be home to small critters.

5. Some insects poke their heads out to see what is going on.

6. Certain insects are necessary to keep a garden healthy.

7. The gardener clears the garden of weeds to make room for her new plants.

8. She mixes fertilizer into the soil to add nutrients.

9. The gardener prepares to plant a small apple tree.

10. She uses a shovel to dig a hole.

11. To stabilize the tree in the hole, she puts earth back around the base.

12. The gardener brings the hose closer to water the newly planted tree.

13. Sunshine and water are needed to make the tree grow.

14. Someday the tree will provide shade to protect garden visitors from the sun.

15. In future years, the gardener will pick the tree's apples to make jams and pies.

Lesson 10 Draw one line under the simple subject in each sentence. Draw two lines under the simple predicate. Circle each participial phrase. Draw a box around each infinitive phrase.

1. My sisters traveled to the desert to see the stars.

2. Gazing at the night sky, they became silent.

3. Countless points of light twinkled, creating an unforgettable sight.

4. To get the best view, the girls had hiked to the highest point around.

5. In the city, we see far fewer stars twinkling above.

6. To stargaze properly, you must go to a place far from city lights.

7. The bright desert stars seemed to be out just for my sisters.

8. The temperature dropped dramatically, chilling the girls thoroughly.

9. Setting up camp earlier, they had been assaulted by the hot sun.

10. Desert nights tend to be quite cold.

11. The girls were happy to wrap themselves in more blankets.

12. The girls began to invent new constellations.

13. Soon they became too sleepy to continue the game.

14. Packed together for warmth inside the tent, all three girls soon were asleep.

15. Yipping mournfully, a coyote bid them good night.

Extra Practice

Lesson 11 Combine the information in each group of sentences to write one sentence.
   Possible answers appear below. Accept all reasonable responses.

1. The platypus is a mammal. It can be found in Australia. It also lives in Tasmania. It is a very strange-looking animal. **The platypus is a strange-looking mammal found in Australia and Tasmania.**

2. The male platypus has a spur on its hind foot. This spur contains poison. This poison can hurt people and animals. Most people don't know this about the platypus. **Most people don't know that the male platypus has a poisonous spur on its hind foot that can hurt people and animals.**

3. The platypus is covered in fur. The fur is dense and dark brown. The thick fur traps heat. This phenomenon keeps the platypus warm. **The platypus is covered in a thick, dark brown fur that traps heat to keep the animal warm.**

4. The platypus is a good swimmer. It lives near streams. It is in the water most of the day swimming and looking for food. It eats worms, shrimp, and crayfish. **A good swimmer, the platypus lives near streams and spends most of the day in the water looking for worms, shrimp, and crayfish to eat.**

5. People used to hunt the platypus. They wanted it for its fur. The platypus is now protected. There are laws that prohibit hunting the platypus. **People used to hunt the platypus for its fur, but it is now protected by laws that prohibit hunting.**

Lesson 12 Add the correct punctuation mark to each sentence. Then label each sentence *declarative, interrogative, imperative,* or *exclamatory.*

1. Would you like to see a movie with me**?** **interrogative**
2. Yes, that would be fun**!** **exclamatory**
3. Find out what is playing**.** **imperative**
4. What kinds of movies do you like**?** **interrogative**
5. I like animated movies the best**. or !** **declarative or exclamatory**
6. Animated movies are so childish**! or .** **exclamatory or declarative**
7. Could we see a comedy instead**?** **interrogative**
8. Sure, I like comedies, too**. or !** **declarative or exclamatory**
9. Let me use your computer to look up movie times**.** **imperative**
10. Here's a good comedy that starts in 30 minutes**.** **declarative**
11. Do you think we can make it**?** **interrogative**
12. We can if we leave right now**. or !** **declarative or exclamatory**
13. Slow down or we'll be in an accident**. or !** **imperative or exclamatory**
14. Wow, what a long line**!** **exclamatory**
15. It has to be a good movie if so many people are waiting to see it**! or .** **exclamatory or declarative**

Lesson 13 Write *S* next to each simple sentence and *CD* next to each compound sentence. Circle the comma and conjunction or the semicolon in each compound sentence.

1. Emily is enjoying a summer day at the beach. __S__
2. Hearing waves crash onto the shore is soothing, (and) watching them is mesmerizing. __CD__
3. The sand is warm from the sun, (and) Emily feels warm, too. __CD__
4. She takes out her sandwich; she has also packed a book. __CD__
5. What a perfect lazy day it is! __S__
6. A toddler waddles toward Emily, (and) she smiles at him. __CD__
7. He wobbles, (but) he catches himself. __CD__
8. He seems keenly interested in Emily. __S__
9. She smiles and says hello. __S__
10. The wobbly toddler is startled, (and) he runs toward his parents. __CD__
11. Emily waves good-bye, (and) then she turns back to watch the waves. __CD__
12. The beach is not always this sunny and pleasant. __S__
13. Clouds block the sun, (and) a cold wind blows on many days. __CD__
14. The wind can kick up the sand, (and) a visitor can be freezing cold even with a parka on. __CD__
15. Emily finishes her sandwich and opens her book. __S__

Lesson 14 Draw one line under each independent clause and two lines under each dependent clause. Circle the subordinating conjunction that begins each dependent clause.

1. (After) I pulled on my rain boots, I stepped outside.
2. I take long walks (when) it rains.
3. (Although) most people avoid the rain, it's wonderful to me.
4. (Though) I like the rain, I do not like water inside my shoes.
5. (When) that happens, my socks get wet and chill my feet.
6. I wear my rain boots (because) they prevent that.
7. The sky becomes dark (before) a rainstorm begins.
8. My town looks very different (when) rain pours down.
9. It looks different (because) not many people come out.
10. They stay indoors (until) the rain stops.
11. (While) I walk, my imagination takes me to a new town.
12. I explore it (as) I listen to the rain.
13. (When) I return home, I notice a slug on the front step.
14. (Although) some animals avoid the rain, others move about in it.
15. (When) I remove my boots, I find two warm and dry feet.

Lesson 15 Write *CD* next to each compound sentence and *CX* next to each complex sentence. Write *CCX* next to each compound-complex sentence.

1. When her parents announced a plan for a family camping trip, Gloria groaned. ____**CX**____

2. Her parents and her younger brother were excited, but Gloria did not feel that way at all. ____**CD**____

3. This year the family would camp for a whole week; they usually went for just a few days. ____**CD**____

4. When they had camped in the hills last year, a bee had stung Gloria. ____**CX**____

5. The sting had hurt, and the site had swelled up because she is allergic to bee stings. ____**CCX**____

6. It had been on her cheek, and it had itched and throbbed even though she put lotion on it. ____**CCX**____

7. When she thought about camping, Gloria could only think of that sting. ____**CX**____

8. Her parents were sympathetic, but they wanted her with the family. ____**CD**____

9. When they expressed their feelings to Gloria, she began to think of all the fun she had last year. ____**CX**____

10. They had lounged in the sun, and they had told stories by candlelight while stars twinkled above. ____**CCX**____

11. She had ridden bikes with her brother, and they had explored all around the lake. ____**CD**____

12. She had made s'mores with her favorite kind of chocolate, and she had swum in the creek. ____**CD**____

13. Cooking outside had been fun, and she had enjoyed bird songs in the mornings. ____**CD**____

14. As she thought about these events, Gloria had a change of heart; maybe camping wasn't so bad. ____**CCX**____

15. If there were morning birdsongs and s'mores ahead, Gloria was ready to go. ____**CX**____

Lesson 16 Underline the adjective clause in each sentence. Circle the noun it describes. Draw a box around the relative pronoun or the relative adverb that begins the clause.

1. (Larry) [who] is a strong, quick player, passed the ball to Mike.

2. Mike caught the pass right at the (moment) [when] it seemed it would zip past him.

3. The two were practicing for the championship (tournament,) [which] their school had never reached before.

4. The team had a great record during a (season) [when] other local teams had faltered.

5. Mike fired a (shot) [that] touched nothing but net.

6. The few (students) [who] were still sitting in the bleachers cheered loudly.

7. Larry and Mike had stayed after (practice,) [which] had ended at 5 p.m.

8. Their coach had given them permission; there was no (reason) [why] they shouldn't practice a bit more.

9. They had until (6 p.m.,) [which] was minutes away.

10. Mike lofted a (jump shot) [which] swished through the net.

11. Suddenly the (gym) [which] had been brightly lit, was plunged into darkness.

12. (Larry) [whose] sense of humor was well known, complimented Mike on his "lights-out" shooting.

13. The (students) [who] were still in the stands groaned.

14. Suddenly a flashlight beam appeared in the (corner) [where] the coach had his office.

15. The coach walked the students out to a (bus stop) [where] they could catch a ride home.

Lesson 17 Underline the adverb clause in each sentence. Draw a box around the subordinating conjunction that begins the clause.

1. ☐Because☐ Clarissa hopes to become an elite gymnast, she works hard in her gymnastic classes.

2. She goes to class three times a week ☐after☐ she finishes school.

3. ☐When☐ the final bell rings, she always feels a surge of energy.

4. Clarissa stretches ☐before☐ she practices any of her moves.

5. Her favorite event is the balance beam, ☐while☐ her least favorite is the horse.

6. ☐Before☐ the gymnasts begin the rings, the coach describes the workout for the day.

7. The rings are hard for many gymnasts ☐because☐ they require much strength.

8. ☐Although☐ the rings are still difficult for her, Clarissa feels stronger as a result of so much practice.

9. ☐After☐ everyone has had a turn on the rings, the gymnasts move to the uneven bars.

10. ☐As☐ Clarissa twirls around the high bar, she mentally prepares for the dismount.

11. Now Clarissa is excited ☐because☐ it is time for the balance beam.

12. ☐When☐ it is her turn, she executes two perfect somersaults on the balance beam.

13. Something terrible happens ☐when☐ Clarissa begins her work on the horse.

14. ☐When☐ she runs and leaps, she overshoots the horse and falls onto the mat.

15. ☐Although☐ she is a bit sore and embarrassed, she quickly lines up for another try.

Lesson 18 Read each sentence. Draw a line under the dependent clause and circle the noun it modifies. Write *RC* if it is a restrictive clause and *NC* if it is a nonrestrictive clause.

1. The (woman) who runs this tennis camp is my mother's oldest friend. __RC__

2. She coaches tennis at the local (college,) which is known for its excellent team. __NC__

3. There was a (time) when she played professionally all over the world. __RC__

4. But playing competitive (tennis,) which can be grueling, was not for her. __NC__

5. She hopes this camp will instill in students the (love) for tennis that she has always had. __RC__

6. My (mother,) who also plays tennis, signed me up immediately. __NC__

7. I'll likely enjoy playing this (sport,) which I have watched on television for years. __NC__

8. Do you have any (relatives) who have played tennis in the past? __RC__

9. My mother will probably give me some (tips) that will help me improve as well. __RC__

10. The camp used to be held on the (courts) where the college students play. __RC__

11. Now we will meet at the city (courts,) which are not kept up as well. __NC__

12. I will be using an older (racquet) that my mother loaned to me. __RC__

13. I will purchase my own racquet at a (time) when I have more money. __RC__

14. The (coach,) who can seem rather strict at times, is a very caring teacher. __NC__

15. This camp will be a great (experience) that we won't soon forget. __RC__

Lesson 19 Underline each gerund phrase. Draw a box around the gerund.

1. [Building] a gingerbread house is a lot of work.

2. [Mixing] all the ingredients of the gingerbread batter is the first step.

3. Next comes [pouring] the batter into large, flat pans.

4. [Baking] the gingerbread is the easiest part of the process.

5. [Smelling] the delicious scent of the spices is a treat.

6. While the gingerbread cools, [sneaking] a piece is not allowed!

7. The walls and roof of the house are made by [cutting] the hard, flat bread into rectangles.

8. A special icing is used for [gluing] the walls and candy pieces together.

9. [Spreading] icing along the edges of the walls and roof is the next step.

10. The job of [putting] the house together requires skill and patience.

11. [Collecting] all the candy pieces is the best part.

12. [Attaching] the candy pieces onto the gingerbread house is also a lot of fun.

13. The hardest part is [making] all the candy pieces stick.

14. [Standing] back for a better view of the finished house is a satisfying experience.

15. [Creating] something from scratch can be very rewarding.

Lesson 20 Write *A* if the verb in the sentence is in the active voice. Write *P* if the verb in the sentence is in the passive voice.

1. Alex was being followed. ___P___

2. He sensed it. ___A___

3. He swiftly turned around. ___A___

4. A dog stopped in its tracks. ___A___

5. The dog was surprised by Alex's sudden movement. ___P___

6. Alex and the dog stared at each other. ___A___

7. Neither of them moved. ___A___

8. Then the dog cocked its head in a quizzical gesture. ___A___

9. Why was Alex being followed by this dog? ___P___

10. A friendly little whine was produced by the dog. ___P___

11. Alex interpreted the sound as a plea for food. ___A___

12. The next day a dog treat was packed in Alex's backpack by his mother. ___P___

13. The treat would be given to the dog by Alex. ___P___

14. On his walk home from school, Alex saw the dog up ahead. ___A___

15. This time the dog was being followed by Alex. ___P___

Extra Practice

Lesson 21 Look at the boldfaced group of words in each sentence. Underline the word or words it modifies. Then write *PH* if it is a phrase or *CL* if it is a clause.

1. Mr. Irwin has volunteered to help me build a <u>bookcase</u> **for my books**. ___PH___

2. My old <u>bookcase</u>, **which I have had for years**, has become too small. ___CL___

3. The <u>shelves</u>, **sagging under the weight of many books**, are no longer sound. ___PH___

4. I <u>asked</u> Mr. Irwin to help me **because he has all the tools we'll need**. ___CL___

5. He is also a skilled <u>woodworker</u> **who has made all kinds of furniture**. ___CL___

6. Mr. Irwin thinks it would be best to <u>build</u> the bookcase **with oak**. ___PH___

7. <u>Furniture</u> **made of a solid wood** will last for many years. ___PH___

8. **Because I lack experience**, I <u>warned</u> Mr. Irwin that I couldn't offer much help. ___CL___

9. He said there were probably many <u>things</u> **that I could do to assist him**. ___CL___

10. For example, I <u>can hold</u> the ends of the boards **while he saws them**. ___CL___

11. I <u>can</u> also <u>keep</u> the shelves in place **until Mr. Irwin has tightened the screws**. ___CL___

12. We <u>will paint</u> the bookcase **with a dark stain** before we are finished. ___PH___

13. I <u>selected</u> the color myself **when we went to the hardware store**. ___CL___

14. **Hoping to start as soon as possible**, <u>Mr. Irwin</u> has suggested that we meet tomorrow. ___PH___

15. His <u>workshop</u> is **next to my school**, so I will just walk there. ___PH___

Lesson 22 Read each pair of sentences. Mark a star beside the one that more effectively expresses the idea and shows relationships. Then label the sentences *S* for simple, *CD* for compound, *CX* for complex, or *CCX* for compound-complex.

1. We consider Europeans such as Columbus and Captain Cook to be great navigators; the ancient Polynesians were perhaps even more impressive. ___CD___

   Though Europeans such as Columbus and Captain Cook are considered great navigators, the ancient Polynesians of the South Pacific were even more impressive. ___☆ CX___

2. Because they lived on islands surrounded by water, the Polynesians had much experience with water travel. ___CX___

   The island-dwelling Polynesians had much experience with water travel. ___☆ S___

3. The Polynesians' islands became overpopulated; when there was no more room on their islands, they sailed far away in search of new island homes. ___CCX___

   When their islands became overpopulated, the Polynesians sailed far away in search of new island homes. ___☆ CX___

4. The Polynesians had a knack for navigation, but they were also smart inventors who developed a special double canoe. ___☆ CCX___

   The Polynesians were good navigators and smart inventors. ___S___

Lesson 23 Label each item *F* (fragment), *RO* (run-on), *CS* (comma splice), or *RA* (ramble-on).

1. It was a beautiful day, Damian was going to take advantage of it. **CS**

2. Damian decided it was perfect for a bike rally he invited some friends to the park. **RO**

3. His friends, Marcus, Jennifer, and Martin, thought a bike rally was a great idea when Damian told them about it over the phone, and they talked about what they would wear and eat. **RA**

4. The neighborhood park not far from Damian's house. **F**

5. Martin wore his new baseball cap he bought some raisins on his way to the park. **RO**

6. Jennifer baked brownies, she wrapped them carefully in foil. **CS**

7. Marcus wearing his lime green biking shirt. **F**

8. Damian planned the route, it was going to be challenging! **CS**

9. The four friends met up at one o'clock in a sunny area by the large rock near the playground in between the maple grove and the tennis courts. **RA**

10. A quick snack before hitting the road. **F**

11. Some curious squirrels and pigeons approached they were looking for leftovers. **RO**

12. Jennifer threw some sunflower seeds to a pigeon soon there were pigeons everywhere. **RO**

13. Marcus led the way on the first part of the rally, it was an easy ride along shady streets. **CS**

14. Jennifer the leader on the steep ride up to the lookout point. **F**

15. The group then followed Marcus, they rode back to the park. **CS**

Lesson 24 Write *N* after each sentence with natural order. Write *IV* after each sentence with inverted order. Write *IT* after each sentence with interrupted order.

1. Dorothy, Vikash, and Patrick had a decision to make. **N**

2. The friends, who had planned a pizza party, could not agree on toppings. **IT**

3. Empty were their stomachs! **IV**

4. Sharp were their arguments! **IV**

5. Patrick, who hated olives, wanted pepperoni and mushrooms. **IT**

6. Vikash liked pepperoni but despised mushrooms. **N**

7. How ill Dorothy became at the suggestion of anchovies! **IV**

8. On and on went the debate, with rejection after rejection. **IV**

9. Suddenly Dorothy snapped her fingers and suggested pineapple and ham. **N**

10. This combination, which was called "Hawaiian pizza" on the menu, won unanimous approval. **IT**

11. That pizza the friends ordered. **IV**

12. Patrick felt relieved that everyone seemed happy. **N**

13. The pizza, which looked absolutely delicious, was cut into six pieces. **IT**

14. Tangy was the sauce! **IV**

15. Tasty was the topping! **IV**

Lesson 25 Write each noun in parentheses in its correct plural form.

1. Two (week) ago my (parent), my sister, and I went camping. _____ weeks, parents _____

2. Our little car was stuffed with our tent, sleeping (bag), and (box) of food. _____ bags, boxes

3. We took our two (dog) along, which turned out to be a bit of a mistake. _____ dogs _____

4. They kept jumping around and wagging their (tail) in our (face). _____ tails, faces _____

5. Dusty chased the (bird) away, and Red scared the (deer) with his barking. _____ birds, deer _____

6. We had a lot of fun, though, especially with some (child) at the next campsite. _____ children _____

7. At night, we all played (game) and sang (song) by the fire. _____ games, songs _____

8. We found (stick) and used them to roast (marshmallow) over the coals. _____ sticks, marshmallows _____

9. We were not bothered by (fly) or (mouse) on the trip. _____ flies, mice _____

10. Mom taught us the (name) of many of the (tree) and (plant) in the area. _____ names, trees, plants

11. We walked through (valley) and (canyon) and listened for (echo). _____ valleys, canyons, echoes _____

12. Dad taught us to use (compass), but we still got lost a couple of (time). _____ compasses, times _____

13. I've got lots of (photograph) that we took during the trip. _____ photographs _____

14. My family will be telling (story) about this trip and enjoying (memory) of it for years.
    _____ stories, memories _____

Lesson 26 Underline each proper noun. Circle each common noun.

1. William H. Johnson was born in Florence, South Carolina.

2. Johnson received a lot of encouragement from teachers in high school.

3. When he was still a teenager, he moved to New York City to study art.

4. He studied at the National Academy of Design, and his works received many awards.

5. Johnson then went to France, where he studied the works of great artists such as Cezanne and Gauguin.

6. He visited museums all over Europe.

7. Johnson was considered an expressionist.

8. Over the years, Johnson deliberately chose to paint in a style known as "primitive."

9. He painted objects and people in a colorful, two-dimensional way.

10. His subjects were often African Americans.

11. One of his most famous paintings is titled *Going to Church*.

12. During the Great Depression and World War II, Johnson worked for the Works Progress Administration.

13. That was a program that gave many artists and writers employment.

14. Johnson sold few of his paintings but he exhibited his works often and received much critical acclaim.

15. Johnson donated his works to the National Museum of Art, which is a part of the Smithsonian Museum in Washington, D.C.

Lesson 27 Read each sentence. Circle the boldfaced word that is the type of noun listed in parentheses.

1. My merry (band) of friends and I went to the Renaissance festival in the **fairgrounds**. (collective)

2. To our **amazement**, the (fairgrounds) had been transformed into an English village from the 1500s. (concrete)

3. (Troupes) of actors roamed the **grounds** dressed as lords and ladies. (collective)

4. The (hilarity) of the **skits** was rewarded with laughter. (abstract)

5. We really admired the **knights** for their wit—and their (bravery). (abstract)

6. In the main field, (knights) were jousting with long wooden poles for the **victory**. (concrete)

7. The **knights** were dressed from head to toe in an (array) of armored gear. (collective)

8. We smiled with (amusement) as we watched them try to mount their **horses**. (abstract)

9. The field was decorated with a **variety** of colorful (flags) featuring various coats of arms. (concrete)

10. These elaborate **pictures** were (symbols) of the famous families of England. (abstract)

11. The **festival** also featured (carts) selling authentic foods. (concrete)

12. My stomach rumbled with (hunger) as I smelled the roasting **turkey**. (abstract)

13. A small (crowd) had gathered around the artisans selling **crafts**. (collective)

14. I was attracted by **thoughts** of purchasing the lovely (necklaces) for sale. (concrete)

15. The (artistry) displayed by these beautiful **pieces** was impressive. (abstract)

Lesson 28 Write the possessive form of each noun in parentheses. Circle each plural possessive noun you write.

1. Airplanes are one of (humankind) greatest inventions. _____**humankind's**_____

2. I enjoy sailing through the clouds thousands of miles above (Earth) surface. _____**Earth's**_____

3. I really like looking out through the (cabin) windows. _____**cabin's**_____

4. Houses and cars look like little toys, and fields resemble a patchwork (quilt) squares. _____**quilt's**_____

5. I love to see a (city) outline from the air. _____**city's**_____

6. Most (travelers) minds wander as they look out the window. ___(**travelers'**)___

7. The hum of the (aircraft) engines is oddly soothing. _____**aircraft's**_____

8. Sometimes (people) conversations can make it hard to sleep, though. ___(**people's**)___

9. (Airlines) food offerings are limited, so it's wise to carry snacks onboard. ___(**Airlines'**)___

10. I've noticed that (passengers) responses to rough weather are very different. ___(**passengers'**)___

11. Once we flew through a storm, and the (wings) vibrations made me a little nervous. ___(**wings'**)___

12. Another time, the (brakes) squeals made me slightly uneasy. ___(**brakes'**)___

13. Fortunately, the (attendants) calm words helped reassure me. ___(**attendants'**)___

14. At the (journey) end, I'm usually a little tired, but excited to be in a new place. _____**journey's**_____

15. Hopefully, next (year) vacation will involve flying someplace. _____**year's**_____

Lesson 29 Circle each personal pronoun. Write *1* if it is a first person pronoun, *2* if it is a second person pronoun, and *3* if it is a third person pronoun.

1. Marty and (I) played chess on Saturday. __1__

2. (He) is a pretty good player. __3__

3. Do (you) agree? __2__

4. (You) are better, though. __2__

5. Mai beat (him) last month. __3__

6. (She) is an incredible player. __3__

7. Did Marty challenge (her)? __3__

8. Yes, (they) played after school. __3__

9. (She) won in fewer than 30 minutes. __3__

10. Am (I) as good as Mai? __1__

11. (You) are good, but Mai seems unbeatable. __2__

12. (We) should watch more of Mai's matches. __1__

13. Maybe (I) could learn something. __1__

14. Marty told (me) that Mai is playing Tony soon. __1__

15. Do (you) want to watch that match? __2__

Lesson 30 Read each sentence. Underline each compound personal pronoun that is a reflexive pronoun. Circle each compound personal pronoun that is an intensive pronoun.

1. Seth tried to teach <u>himself</u> to make raviolis, but the venture was a disaster.

2. He admitted to <u>himself</u> that he needed help from a master—his grandma.

3. "I (myself) was a novice once," Nana said with a chuckle.

4. "First we need to clear <u>ourselves</u> a large space on the counter," she said.

5. Seth (himself) organized the kitchen clutter and wiped the marble surface.

6. Nana wrapped <u>herself</u> in a giant apron and got down to work.

7. "When making raviolis, the dough (itself) often presents a challenge," she said.

8. "Remind <u>yourself</u> to always keep the dough as cold as possible," she suggested.

9. Seth (himself) had found rolling the dough difficult, so this advice was perfect.

10. Soon Nana was expertly wielding the rolling pin and covering <u>herself</u> in flour.

11. Seth (himself) was coated in the white stuff after rolling his dough.

12. "Clean <u>yourself</u> off and start cooking mushrooms in the skillet," Nana said.

13. "Add some cheese, and we will have (ourselves) a tasty filling," she added.

14. Seth and Nana both cut and filled their own raviolis by <u>themselves</u>.

15. When they were finished, Nana (herself) couldn't tell which ones were hers!

Lesson 31 Circle each possessive pronoun.

1. Ray's bike is newer than (mine.)
2. (His) is red and black.
3. I don't like it as well as (yours.)
4. Tammy's bike is blue, and (its) handlebars are flecked with gold.
5. I wish (my) bike had thicker tires.
6. Ray's bike has twenty speeds, but (mine) has only ten.
7. (Your) bike is just fine!
8. (Its) brakes are squeaking a bit.
9. Have you checked (their) pads?
10. If you fix (your) brakes, do you want to join us on Saturday?
11. What's (your) plan?
12. Sam and Ngoc want to train for (their) race, so we're all biking a 20K.
13. Should I meet you at (your) house or at (theirs?)
14. Why don't you come over to (my) place?
15. Then we'll head over to (their) house together.

Lesson 32 Circle each indefinite pronoun.

1. (Everyone) in my family loves chili.
2. (Nobody) uses the same recipe as (anyone) else uses.
3. My uncle thinks his chili is the best that (anyone) has ever tasted.
4. (Most) of us prefer my aunt Ruth's chili.
5. I am glad to be served (either.)
6. (Both) are very delicious.
7. (Everyone) in my family enjoys spicy food.
8. (Few) can eat chili as hot as my dad makes it, though.
9. (All) of us are afraid to ask him to make it milder.
10. (None) of us wants to hurt Dad's feelings.
11. I wish (someone) had the courage to tell him, though.
12. Now, (everybody) just takes a gulp of water after every spoonful.
13. There's (nothing) else we can do.
14. Maybe (somebody) should hide the peppers next time Dad cooks.
15. That way (everyone) can enjoy Dad's chili.

Lesson 33 Circle each relative pronoun and underline the noun it refers to. Draw a box around each interrogative pronoun.

1. [What] is a hybrid?
2. It is a type of <u>car</u> (that) runs on two kinds of power.
3. The hybrid has an <u>engine</u> (that) uses fuel such as gasoline.
4. It also has a <u>motor</u> (that) uses electricity.
5. Each hybrid has a <u>generator</u> (that) powers the motor.
6. [Who] has ridden in a hybrid?
7. One <u>thing</u> (that) you will notice is the silence.
8. [What] is the reason for this?
9. The <u>energy</u> (that) is produced in the generator is stored in a battery.
10. The gasoline <u>engine</u>, (which) is the noisiest part of the car, shuts off at lower speeds.
11. The only thing propelling the car at these speeds is the quiet electric <u>motor</u>, (which) draws power stored in the battery.
12. <u>People</u> (who) drive hybrids should watch carefully for pedestrians.
13. Visually impaired <u>people</u>, (who) rely on noise to know when a car is near, may not hear a hybrid coming.
14. [Which] of the hybrids gets good gas mileage?
15. Hybrids emit less pollution than do most other <u>cars</u>, (which) makes hybrids easier on the environment.

Lesson 34 Underline each adjective, including each article. Circle each adverb.

1. Fiji is <u>an</u> <u>island</u> nation in <u>the</u> <u>southern</u> Pacific Ocean.
2. It is <u>a</u> <u>popular</u> destination for tourists who (dearly) love <u>the</u> tropics.
3. People flock to Fiji to enjoy <u>the</u> <u>white</u>, <u>sandy</u> beaches and <u>sparkling</u> waters.
4. They (enthusiastically) soak up <u>the</u> <u>warm</u> sunshine, which persists (year-round).
5. Tourists (often) rent scuba gear and go for dives in <u>the</u> <u>clear</u> water.
6. Divers can (easily) see <u>colorful</u> <u>coral</u> reefs and schools of <u>exotic</u> fish.
7. Fiji (also) features <u>dense</u> <u>tropical</u> forests and <u>volcanic</u> mountains.
8. It consists of hundreds of islands, but <u>the</u> <u>main</u> ones are Viti Levu and Vanua Levu.
9. Fiji has <u>860,000</u> residents who live (permanently) on <u>the</u> <u>major</u> islands.
10. <u>The</u> <u>many</u> tourists add to <u>this</u> population throughout <u>the</u> year.
11. Fiji (mostly) depends on tourism to support its economy.
12. <u>Fijian</u> farmers (also) grow sugar to export to <u>other</u> countries.
13. <u>Popular</u> <u>Fijian</u> foods include seafood and cassava, <u>an</u> <u>edible</u>, <u>starchy</u> root.
14. Because residents are (constantly) surrounded by water, fishing is <u>common</u>.
15. Fiji's mix of <u>native</u>, <u>European</u>, <u>Indian</u>, and <u>Chinese</u> cultures makes <u>the</u> country <u>an</u> <u>interesting</u> place to live.

Extra Practice

Name _____

Lesson 35 Circle each demonstrative adjective. Underline each demonstrative pronoun.

1. <u>This</u> is a photo album I made in my art class.
2. I decorated it with (these) shells I found on the beach.
3. I wish I had some shells like <u>those</u>!
4. Where did you find (this) one?
5. I found (that) one at Stinson Beach.
6. (These) others my sister gave to me.
7. How did you get (those) shells to stick to your album cover?
8. They sell (this) special glue at the craft store.
9. I'm really impressed with all the work you've put into (this) album.
10. Will you show me (those) pictures?
11. Who is <u>that</u>?
12. <u>This</u> is my Aunt Lupe.
13. <u>These</u> are my cousins.
14. <u>That</u> looks like a fun game they're playing.
15. I'll teach you how to play after I show you (these) pictures.

Lesson 36 Underline the adjectives in parentheses that are written correctly.

1. It was (an autumn gorgeous/<u>a gorgeous autumn</u>) day in mid-October.
2. We decided to explore the (Vermont scenic/<u>scenic Vermont</u>) countryside.
3. Everyone hopped in the (<u>reliable blue</u>/reliable, blue) minivan, and we were off.
4. The (<u>bright afternoon</u>/afternoon bright) sun shone in our faces.
5. The (<u>cool, crisp</u>/cool crisp) air made us shiver, so we rolled up the windows.
6. There are many (narrow winding/<u>narrow, winding</u>) roads outside of town.
7. We took one that leads to (<u>several small</u>/small several) lakes.
8. The birch trees lining the road had (yellow large/<u>large yellow</u>) leaves.
9. Their (<u>delicate white</u>/white, delicate) branches quivered in the breeze.
10. A flock of (honking twenty/<u>twenty honking</u>) geese flew overhead.
11. They were heading south to escape the (<u>harsh Canadian</u>/Canadian harsh) winter.
12. The trees surrounding the lakes were an (intense fiery/<u>intense, fiery</u>) red.
13. We could see their reflections in the (<u>clear, calm</u>/clear calm) water.
14. A (steep, tree-covered/<u>steep tree-covered</u>) hill rose behind the lake.
15. With its many colors, it looked like my (patchwork old/<u>old patchwork</u>) quilt.

Lesson 37 Underline each action verb. Circle each linking verb.

1. *Pathfinder* (was) a Mars mission.

2. It <u>launched</u> in 1996.

3. The craft <u>had</u> a lander and a rover.

4. The lander <u>communicated</u> information to NASA.

5. The name of the rover (was) *Sojourner*.

6. The six-wheeled rover (looked) like a toy.

7. It (was) about the size of a microwave oven.

8. The machine (was) able to move over small boulders.

9. After landing, *Pathfinder* <u>had</u> modem trouble.

10. Scientists at NASA <u>corrected</u> the problem.

11. *Pathfinder* <u>sent</u> many images back to NASA.

12. Possibly, Mars (was) once a wet planet.

13. At some point, it (became) a cold, dry desert.

14. The *Pathfinder* mission (was) very successful.

15. Like *Viking 1* and *Viking 2*, *Pathfinder* <u>outlasted</u> its design life.

Lesson 38 Underline each transitive verb and draw a box around its direct object. Draw a circle around each intransitive verb.

1. I <u>love</u> the ocean.

2. In the summer, my family often (goes) to the beach.

3. Mom (naps) under an umbrella.

4. My little sister and I (wade) in the water.

5. Then we <u>gather</u> seashells.

6. Last summer, I <u>found</u> a sea star.

7. It (lay) near a piece of driftwood.

8. I <u>keep</u> the sea star on my dresser at home.

9. Sometimes we (stay) at the beach until dark.

10. Once we <u>built</u> a bonfire.

11. On rare occasions, a pod of whales (swims) by.

12. One day, I <u>will take</u> a long voyage.

13. I (will go diving) far beneath the waves.

14. I <u>may see</u> strange fish and amazing plants.

15. Perhaps I <u>will discover</u> a wrecked ship!

Extra Practice

Lesson 39 Circle each present tense verb. Underline each past tense verb. Draw a box around each future tense verb.

1. Last month my community center group <u>took</u> a trip to Maine.

2. I almost <u>stayed</u> home.

3. Many bears (wander) around the woods there.

4. My best friend <u>laughed</u> at my fears.

5. That journey <u>was</u> my first camping trip.

6. The Maine wilderness (is) very beautiful.

7. We <u>hiked</u> through meadows and forests.

8. Fortunately, I <u>had</u> no encounters with bears.

9. We <u>saw</u> many of them, but from a safe distance.

10. The community center group [will go] again next year.

11. Next time, I [will take] a camera.

12. I <u>forgot</u> it this time.

13. The gift shops (sell) a lot of postcards.

14. I <u>bought</u> some as souvenirs.

15. I (want) my own pictures for my blog, though.

Lesson 40 Circle the boldfaced verbs in present perfect tense. Underline the boldfaced verbs in past perfect tense. Draw a box around the boldfaced verbs in future perfect tense.

1. Recently, I (**have started**) a scrapbook of great journeys.

2. I never <u>**had enjoyed**</u> scrapbooks before.

3. Back in sixth grade I <u>**had made**</u> a scrapbook of a trip I took.

4. The project <u>**had bored**</u> me thoroughly.

5. Something about the journey's topic (**has made**) me think differently.

6. The scrapbook (**has grown**) quite thick since I started it.

7. After I add details about Lewis and Clark, I [**will have included**] more than twenty journeys.

8. I (**have found**) a really great map of their expedition.

9. I (**have added**) many pages to my scrapbook, but I need to add more.

10. Soon I [**will have used**] all the available space.

11. By the time I finish this project, I [**will have learned**] a great deal about different journeys.

12. I (**have enjoyed**) all the research I've done about explorers' lives.

13. I <u>**had heard**</u> of only a few of the explorers before I began my report.

14. My teacher (**has asked**) to see the scrapbook.

15. None of her students (**has created**) a scrapbook like mine before.

Lesson 41 Circle each boldfaced verb that is a progressive form. Cross out each boldfaced verb that is not a progressive form.

1. I (am writing) a science-fiction story.

2. This ~~is~~ a summary of the story so far.

3. Vin (was flying) over the equator when suddenly he had engine trouble.

4. He ~~saw~~ a stretch of deserted beach.

5. Vin (was attempting) an emergency landing there when his radio died.

6. Just before that, Vin ~~had heard~~ shouts and strange crackling sounds.

7. What Vin did not know was that Martians (were attacking) Earth.

8. The second chapter of the story (is giving) me some problems.

9. I am not sure what ~~will happen~~ next.

10. My writing group (will be discussing) the story tomorrow.

11. The story (is taking) me a long time to write.

12. I ~~have made~~ many revisions to it already.

13. I (am looking) forward to the group's feedback.

14. They ~~have given~~ me sound advice in the past.

15. They gave me a good deal of support while I (was writing) my last story.

Lesson 42 Read each sentence. If a verb in the sentence creates a time shift that doesn't make sense, mark an X through the verb. Write the correct tense of the verb on the line.

1. Brandon was trying to study when he ~~hears~~ a tap on his window. _____heard_____

2. He saw his friend Max peering in from the bushes outside his room. _____

3. He sighed as he abandoned the books on his desk and ~~goes~~ to open the window. _____went_____

4. "What's up, Max?" he ~~says~~. "Why aren't you home studying for the science exam?" _____said_____

5. Though he got very good grades, Max never seemed to study much at all. _____

6. He ~~has~~ an annoying habit of distracting Brandon right before a test. _____had_____

7. Brandon did well in school too, but his success ~~requires~~ more time and effort. _____required_____

8. "Martin and I are going to a movie," Max said. "Are you in?" _____

9. Brandon rolled his eyes in frustration and ~~will point~~ to the books on his desk. _____pointed_____

10. "You know I have to study, Max," he ~~says~~. "Why do you always do this?" _____said_____

11. "Oh, that test will be easy. You can study later," Max replied with a grin. _____

12. "It's almost six, and we'd be out until at least eight or nine," Brandon said. _____

13. "Go and ask your mom," Max ~~will plead~~. "You know you want to go." _____pleaded_____

14. Brandon protested again and promptly ~~shuts~~ the window on his friend. _____shut_____

15. Max shrugged his shoulders and went to join Martin. _____

Name _____

Lesson 43 Read each sentence. Write whether the mood of the boldfaced verb is *indicative* or *imperative*.

1. The Mount Rushmore National Memorial **is** near the town of Keystone, South Dakota. ____indicative____

2. Its sixty-foot carvings of four presidents **compose** an iconic national image. ____indicative____

3. The memorial **was built** to bring tourists to the American West. ____indicative____

4. **Consider** its popularity and you will agree the project was a success. ____imperative____

5. The sculptor, Gutzon Borglum, **chose** the men to be represented: Washington, Jefferson, Roosevelt, and Lincoln. ____indicative____

6. In 1927, he and 400 workers **began** carving the faces into the granite cliffs. ____indicative____

7. **Imagine** how much work it took to create such gigantic sculptures. ____imperative____

8. Originally, the face of Jefferson **was supposed** to be to the right of Washington's. ____indicative____

9. But the rock **was** not stable enough to support the carving. ____indicative____

10. **Look** carefully at the memorial and **picture** what Jefferson would have looked like in a different position. ____imperative____

11. The first face, that of Washington, **was completed** in 1934. ____indicative____

12. The three other faces **were finished** by 1939. ____indicative____

13. Original plans to also carve the presidents' bodies **were abandoned** because of a lack of funds. ____indicative____

14. **Visit** this spectacular sight as soon as you have an opportunity. ____imperative____

15. **Leave** plenty of time to tour the museum and visitors' center as well. ____imperative____

Lesson 44 Read each sentence. Write whether the mood of the boldfaced verb is *indicative* or *subjunctive*.

1. "If I **were** you, I would definitely go," Ella said to her friend Cara. ____subjunctive____

2. The girls **were discussing** Cara's invitation to visit her aunt in Spain. ____indicative____

3. Cara **was** not sure whether she wanted to spend the summer in a strange country. ____indicative____

4. "But I **am** totally unfamiliar with the language and the customs," Cara protested. ____indicative____

5. "If I **were** fluent in Spanish, things would be different," she added. ____subjective____

6. "I suggest that you **stop** thinking about reasons you can't go," Ella said. ____subjunctive____

7. "This **is** a wonderful opportunity that you can't pass up," Ella asserted. ____indicative____

8. Ella **was** shocked that Cara could consider staying home. ____indicative____

9. "A little preparation **will help** you feel more comfortable," she said. ____indicative____

10. Then Ella proposed that they **meet** every weekend to learn some Spanish together. ____subjunctive____

11. She suggested that they also **find** some books about Spanish culture and cuisine. ____subjunctive____

12. "If there **were** a Spanish restaurant in town, we could go there too," Ella concluded. ____subjunctive____

13. Cara **was changing** her mind about this possible adventure. ____indicative____

14. "If I **were** more knowledgeable, I think I could overcome my fear," she said. ____subjunctive____

15. "Bueno," Ella replied. "See? I **am teaching** you already." ____indicative____

Lesson 45 Underline each boldfaced verb that is in the indicative mood. Circle each boldfaced verb that is in the imperative mood. Draw a box around each boldfaced verb that is in the subjunctive mood. If a sentence contains an inappropriate mood shift, mark an *X* beside it.

1. I suggest that you [drive] to the orchard and [pick] apples. _____

2. It <u>is</u> a beautiful day, and the place <u>is bursting</u> with fruit. _____

3. If I [were] available, I <u>will love</u> to go with you. **X**

4. (Take) the freeway south, (exit) onto Wyatt Road, and then I suggest that you [turn] right. **X**

5. The orchard <u>sits</u> at the top of the hill; its driveway <u>is</u> on the left. _____

6. I recommend that you [arrive] early and [park] in the grass near the farmhouse. _____

7. (Find) the owner, Mr. Kay, and then I recommend that you [ask] him for a bushel basket. **X**

8. The basket <u>looks</u> really big, but you <u>will have</u> no trouble filling it. _____

9. If I [were] you, I <u>will start</u> by picking a few Granny Smith apples. **X**

10. This tart green fruit <u>is</u> perfect for making pies and <u>tastes</u> good, too. _____

11. (Gather) some Honeycrisp apples, and then you <u>will grab</u> some Red Delicious as well. **X**

12. (Take) your basket back to the farmhouse and (pay) Mr. Kay promptly. _____

13. I also suggest that you [talk] with Mr. Kay and [ask] him to show you around the farm. _____

14. He <u>raises</u> goats and <u>grow</u> acres of pumpkins as well. _____

15. (Enjoy) your day and (tell) me all about it when you get back! _____

Lesson 46 Underline each boldfaced verb that is in the active voice. Circle each boldfaced verb that is in the passive voice. If a sentence contains a voice shift, mark an *X* beside it.

1. Like many young Victorian women, Mary Kingsley <u>stayed</u> home, and her parents (were nursed) by her. **X**

2. But Mary <u>loved</u> to read about nature, and she <u>yearned</u> to travel around the world. _____

3. By 1892, fate <u>granted</u> her wish, and a boat to Africa (was boarded) by this brave woman. **X**

4. Mary <u>explored</u> Africa's rivers in canoes, and she often <u>traveled</u> by herself. _____

5. Her trip (was funded) by trading; she <u>exchanged</u> cloth for rubber and ivory. **X**

6. English merchants <u>clamored</u> for these rare goods, and she <u>sold</u> them at a good price. _____

7. Mary <u>befriended</u> many Africans, and their unfamiliar ways (were understood) by her. **X**

8. She <u>wrote</u> a respectful book about their culture, but people back in England <u>reacted</u> with disapproval. _____

9. In 1894, Mary (was hired) by the British Museum; she <u>collected</u> African plants and animals for them. **X**

10. Mary <u>found</u> a new species of fish, and the fish (was named) after Mary by scientists. **X**

11. Mary also <u>encountered</u> some dangerous situations, for she <u>refused</u> to let anything hold her back. _____

12. She once <u>met</u> a dangerous hippo, but the creature (was) somehow (tamed) by her. **X**

13. She (was) also (surprised) by an angry gorilla, but she <u>survived</u> to tell the tale. **X**

14. Mary <u>climbed</u> Mt. Cameroon before any European woman, and she <u>lived</u> with the Fang people. _____

15. She <u>spoke</u> to the British about Africa, and much (was learned) about this place because of her. **X**

Lesson 47 Underline each coordinating conjunction. Circle each subordinating conjunction.

1. I auditioned for the school play, <u>and</u> I was shocked to get a part.

2. (Although) I was trying for a small role, I got the lead.

3. Everyone told me I would be great, <u>but</u> I was absolutely terrified.

4. The director gave us scripts on Friday, <u>and</u> I read the entire play.

5. That put me into a panic (because) my character had more than fifty lines!

6. (When) my father saw my nervousness, he read through the play with me.

7. He coached me all weekend, (although) I said he didn't have to.

8. He cued me (when) I had trouble remembering a line.

9. That helped me, <u>and</u> I began to feel more confident.

10. (After) we had our first practice, I discovered the value of my hard work.

11. (Because) I had read the play so many times, I knew other actors' lines, too.

12. I could whisper a line to them (if) they forgot it in rehearsal.

13. We will perform the play on Saturday, (after) we have a dress rehearsal.

14. I'm still nervous, <u>but</u> I'm nervous in a good way.

15. (If) I don't trip on stage, I'll do just fine!

Lesson 48 Circle each conjunction. If a sentence contains correlative conjunctions, write *CC* on the line.

1. I don't know (whether) to write my essay about my summer trip (or) about my winter trip. __**CC**__

2. My summer trip was to the Maryland shore, (and) my winter trip was to Atlanta. _____

3. (Either) the Maryland shore (or) Atlanta would be interesting to write about. __**CC**__

4. We stayed with Grandma in Maryland, (and) we stayed in a motel in Atlanta. _____

5. (Both) staying with Grandma (and) visiting a big city were fun. __**CC**__

6. (Because) the motel in Atlanta had a heated pool, we swam a lot. _____

7. We drove through North Carolina (and) South Carolina on our way to Atlanta. _____

8. At the Maryland shore, we hiked on the beach (or) went shopping each day. _____

9. We (not only) hiked (but also) played miniature golf. __**CC**__

10. (Neither) I (nor) my sister made a hole-in-one. __**CC**__

11. I took only a few pictures at the beach, (but) they turned out great! _____

12. (Both) Nina (and) Wing have asked me about my trips. __**CC**__

13. (Neither) Nina (nor) Wing has been to Maryland (or) Georgia. __**CC**__

14. I like to learn (and) have fun on a vacation. _____

15. (After) I write my essay, I will print a copy with digital photographs. _____

Lesson 49 Circle the correct word in parentheses.

1. Where are you and (**your**/you're) family going this weekend?

2. Will you visit (**your**/you're) grandparents?

3. I'm sure (there/their/**they're**) going to be delighted to see you.

4. (There/**Their**/They're) eyes will surely light up.

5. (Your/**You're**) going to take the train, aren't you?

6. I hope you enjoy the trip (**there**/their/they're).

7. Be sure to take (**your**/you're) camera.

8. I'm sure (your/**you're**) going to get some great shots.

9. (**There**/Their/They're) may be snow along the way.

10. The trees will have lost (there/**their**/they're) leaves in that area.

11. Do (**your**/you're) grandparents have many animals on their farm?

12. (There/Their/**They're**) really lucky to live in such a great place.

13. Could we visit (there/**their**/they're) place someday?

14. I will ask them for (there/**their**/they're) permission.

15. Maybe I can go with you and (**your**/you're) parents next time you visit.

Lesson 50 Circle the correct word in parentheses.

1. (Who's/**Whose**) bike is parked outside?

2. It looks like (**its**/it's) front tire is flat.

3. Oh, you're the one (**who's**/whose) got the flat?

4. If you want to borrow my pump, (its/**it's**) in the garage.

5. (Its/**It's**) a good idea to carry extra tire patches around with you.

6. A tire can lose (**its**/it's) tread quickly on these rough roads.

7. I think (its/**it's**) helpful to learn basic bike repair.

8. (**Who's**/Whose) going to fix your bike for you out in the middle of nowhere?

9. (Its/**It's**) not that hard to fix a flat tire.

10. If the chain falls off (**its**/it's) track, that's an easy repair, too.

11. If you're someone (who's/**whose**) bike often has flats, you should learn to fix them.

12. A person (**who's**/whose) prepared to make minor repairs can feel more secure.

13. (Its/**It's**) a shame that basic bike repair isn't taught at our school.

14. Your tire looks like (its/**it's**) fixed for the time being.

15. (**Its**/It's) inner tube doesn't appear to be leaking.

Extra Practice

Lesson 51 Circle the word in parentheses that correctly completes each sentence.

1. Do you like (**to**/too/two) do research on the Internet?

2. I think articles are (to/**too**/two) difficult to read online.

3. I know several tricks (**to**/too/two) use to make Internet research more efficient.

4. Can you tell me how (**to**/too/two) use a search engine?

5. Use at least (to/too/**two**) keywords together to narrow your search.

6. Do you use quotation marks (**to**/too/two) narrow your search even further?

7. That helps, (to/**too**/two).

8. I never know how (**to**/too/two) recognize the most reliable information.

9. There are (to/too/**two**) kinds of sites that are particularly reliable.

10. What are the (to/too/**two**) you recommend?

11. Government sites are very useful, and educational sites can be, (to/**too**/two).

12. Are sites ending in **.com** good ones (**to**/too/two) use for research?

13. They may be unreliable, or they may be (to/**too**/two) biased.

14. Wow, there's a lot (**to**/too/two) know about using the Internet!

15. Yes, sometimes I think there's (to/**too**/two) much to learn.

Lesson 52 Circle the word or phrase in parentheses that correctly completes each sentence.

1. (Over/**More than**) a dozen kids in our class are collecting state coins.

2. That's (**over**/more than) 40% of the entire class.

3. (Less/**Fewer**) students are collecting stamps.

4. You have (over/**more than**) 30 United States quarters in your collection.

5. That's well (**over**/more than) the number that Ted Brown has.

6. I have (less/**fewer**) quarters than either of you.

7. It will probably take me (**over**/more than) a year to complete my collection.

8. I am still hunting for (over/**more than**) 20 state quarters.

9. I have spent (**less**/fewer) time collecting coins than you have.

10. You have been gathering coins for (**over**/more than) a year now.

11. Did you know that there were (over/**more than**) six billion quarters minted in 2000?

12. That's two billion (over/**more than**) the number of quarters our nation minted in 1999.

13. (Less/**Fewer**) state quarters were minted in subsequent years.

14. The U.S. Mint produces (**less**/fewer) coinage for some states than for others.

15. For example, Delaware has (less/**fewer**) state quarters in circulation than Connecticut has.

Lesson 53 Circle the correct expression in parentheses to complete each sentence.

1. Our basketball team has not lost (**any**/no) games this year.

2. We haven't (**ever**/never) had such a good year before.

3. Last year, our team did not play well (**anywhere**/nowhere) except at home.

4. This year, the team has not lost (**any**/no) confidence while on the road.

5. Our team (ain't/**isn't**) afraid of any other team.

6. I've never seen (**anyone**/nobody) better than our center, Jerome Lee.

7. He never shoots (no/**any**) air balls.

8. No opposing player has been able to block (**any**/none) of his shots.

9. There isn't (**anyone**/no one) else on our team who shoots as well as Jerome.

10. He isn't a bad rebounder, (**either**/neither).

11. None of our players lets (no one/**anyone**) on the other team have an easy shot.

12. Last Saturday, the other team didn't score (**any**/no) points in the second quarter.

13. I didn't see (**anybody**/nobody) on the other team who was thrilled about it.

14. No one wants to miss (none/**any**) of the action in Saturday's play-off game.

15. There's not going to be (**anywhere**/nowhere) to sit if we don't get there early.

Lesson 54 Circle the expression in parentheses that is appropriate to use in academic writing.

1. This report explains why computers are such (awesome/**valuable**) inventions.

2. Before we had computers, we (**could not**/couldn't) do many of the activities we do today.

3. Today (we're/**we are**) able to communicate with friends through the use of computers.

4. Most (folks/**people**) I know use e-mail to stay in touch with friends and family.

5. People can buy various (stuff/**items**) for their computers over the Internet.

6. The Internet makes it (**quite**/way) easy to find information.

7. Some sites provide (**abundant**/tons of) information.

8. You can (check out/**look up**) when the next bus is coming.

9. You can (gripe about/**critique**) movies and restaurants.

10. I like to (**read**/check out) the statistics about my favorite sports teams.

11. More and more books are (gonna/**going to**) be available online in the next ten years.

12. My friends and I listen to some very (cool/**innovative**) music on the Internet.

13. The Internet has (a whole lot of/**800 million**) users.

14. Can you imagine how your life (**would have**/would've) been without the Internet?

15. I wonder what new (things/**features**) the Internet will offer in the next ten years.

Lesson 55 Circle the word in parentheses that correctly completes each sentence.

1. Where did I (sit/**set**) my yoga mat?
2. Oh, I (lied/**laid**) it over there near the door.
3. Are you going to (**lie**/lay) there, or are you going to do yoga with me?
4. All right, (sit/**set**) your mat next to mine.
5. You can (rise/**raise**) the blinds if it seems too dark in here.
6. Stand up and (rise/**raise**) your arms above your head.
7. When you (**rise**/raise) from this forward lunge, your leg muscles might be tired.
8. Now let's (**sit**/set) quietly and take deep breaths.
9. Slowly (rise/**raise**) your left leg and then your right.
10. You may want to (lie/**lay**) a pillow under your neck for this next pose.
11. My favorite pose is the one where we (**lie**/lay) still and close our eyes.
12. Once I (lie/**lay**) down and fell asleep!
13. The person (**sitting**/setting) next to me woke me when I started snoring.
14. Even if I'm tired before stretching, I always (**rise**/raise) afterward feeling refreshed.
15. Some enthusiasts do stretches as soon as they (**rise**/raise) in the morning.

Lesson 56 Write the correct past tense form of the verb in parentheses to complete each sentence.

1. Everyone _____**said**_____ the school musical was a huge success. (say)
2. The Art Club had _____**built**_____ amazing sets. (build)
3. The music director had _____**held**_____ plenty of rehearsals. (hold)
4. This year, all of the performers _____**came**_____ to practice on time. (come)
5. Everyone _____**brought**_____ their scripts along with them. (bring)
6. As a result, no one _____**forgot**_____ his or her lines. (forget)
7. The rehearsals all _____**went**_____ very smoothly. (go)
8. That _____**gave**_____ everyone confidence. (give)
9. We all _____**overcame**_____ our stage fright. (overcome)
10. My mother had never _____**heard**_____ such a strong lead singer. (hear)
11. The band had _____**taken**_____ pains to learn each song. (take)
12. No one _____**left**_____ during the intermission. (left)
13. Everyone _____**thought**_____ that the musical was the best in years. (think)
14. At the closing curtain, the audience _____**gave**_____ us a standing ovation. (give)
15. The local music critic _____**wrote**_____ a glowing review of the musical. (write)

Lesson 57 Circle the word in parentheses that correctly completes each sentence.

1. This (**past**/passed) summer I began helping out at my parents' grocery store.

2. It's at the end of the colorful downtown (bizarre/**bazaar**).

3. Like my parents, I (**wear**/ware) a smock when I'm at work.

4. I help my parents keep the (isles/**aisles**) stocked with groceries.

5. It's quite a (feet/**feat**) to maintain the proper inventory.

6. My parents don't want the store shelves to be (bear/**bare**).

7. They arrange merchandise so that customers can (**access**/assess) it easily.

8. My parents pride themselves on the freshness of their (wears/**wares**).

9. Sometimes my parents let me (wring/**ring**) up groceries.

10. Working the cash register is harder (then/**than**) it seems.

11. You have to quickly count the change people (**pour**/poor) into your hand.

12. You need to (way/**weigh**) all of the produce and punch in the right prices.

13. I bagged a senior's groceries and (**then**/than) helped her to her car.

14. She gave me (**compliments**/complements) on my good work.

15. The next day she wrote a thank-you note on her personal (stationary/**stationery**).

Lesson 58 Cross out each incorrect usage of *go, went, all,* and *like.* (If the word *was* is part of the incorrect expression, cross that out also.) Write correct words to replace the crossed out words if a replacement is needed. **Answers will vary. Accept all reasonable responses.**

1. Lily ~~was all~~, "How can we raise money for new softball uniforms?" _____**asked**_____

2. Ty ~~went~~, "I don't have a single good idea." _____**replied**_____

3. "We could have a raffle," Miriam ~~went~~. _____**suggested**_____

4. I ~~was all~~, "Then we've got to offer really good prizes." _____**said**_____

5. Ty ~~went~~, "Selling raffle tickets is no fun!" _____**exclaimed**_____

6. Then Miriam ~~was like~~, "Why don't we have a car wash?" _____**added**_____

7. I ~~went~~, "That's an excellent idea!" _____**replied**_____

8. Lily was, ~~like,~~ skeptical at first, but she finally agreed. _____

9. Then Ty ~~went~~, "Where will we have it?" _____**inquired**_____

10. Miriam ~~was all~~, "At the school, of course!" _____**answered**_____

11. Then I said I was, ~~like,~~ willing to make the signs. _____

12. At first Ty thought supplies would be, ~~like,~~ too expensive. _____

13. Then Miriam said she could, ~~like,~~ borrow buckets from her parents' nursery. _____

14. I ~~was like~~, "We can all bring a few rags and sponges from home." _____**said**_____

15. Finally, Lily ~~was like~~, "This is going to be fun!" _____**shouted**_____

Name _____

Lesson 59 Draw a line through each unneeded pronoun. Note: Some sentences are correctly written.

1. The painting *Washington Crossing the Delaware* ~~it~~ is a famous work of art.

2. It depicts General Washington and his troops crossing the Delaware River during the Revolutionary War.

3. Washington ~~he~~ hoped to surprise the enemy with an attack in the winter of 1776.

4. Surprisingly, this painting ~~it~~ was not completed until 1851.

5. It was painted by a German American artist named Emanuel Gottlieb Leutze.

6. Leutze ~~he~~ was actually in Germany when he began work on the first version.

7. Europeans fighting in the revolutions of 1848 ~~they~~ inspired him.

8. The first version was destroyed in a World War II air raid on a German museum.

9. Luckily, Leutze ~~he~~ had painted a second copy.

10. Visitors ~~they~~ can still see the painting today.

11. Critics have noted a number of inaccuracies in *Washington Crossing the Delaware*.

12. The American flag shown ~~it~~ had not yet been designed in 1776.

13. And all the men depicted in the boat ~~they~~ would have easily sunk such a small vessel.

14. The real crossing actually took place at night and in the rain.

15. However, Leutze ~~he~~ painted Washington's face lit up by the rising sun of dawn.

Lesson 60 Draw a line through unnecessary words in each sentence.

1. One of the most impressive World's Fairs in history was held in Chicago in 1893, ~~well over 100 years ago~~.

2. The fair's official name, ~~or the name it is called in important records~~, was the World's Columbian Exposition.

3. It marked the 400th anniversary of Columbus's arrival in the Americas ~~after his ocean journey~~.

4. People came from almost 50 countries to share aspects of ~~and things about~~ their culture with visitors.

5. Organizers ~~and people in charge~~ oversaw the building of an entire city on the fairgrounds.

6. Most of the structures were designed ~~and conceived~~ in a neoclassical style that recalled ancient Greek buildings.

7. The display was called the White City because the buildings were white, ~~not dark and dreary~~.

8. They were also lit up by many electric lights, ~~so they were really bright~~.

9. The structures, ~~which were not meant to last forever~~, were intended to be only temporary.

10. They were composed ~~and made~~ of plaster instead of brick and stone, harder substances.

11. There were many other celebrated attractions at the fair ~~that drew people to it~~.

12. The first Ferris wheel took riders 264 feet into the air ~~above the fair below~~.

13. Early electric companies ~~that were the first ones in America~~ demonstrated their technologies.

14. And many artists and inventors showed off their creations, ~~the things they made~~.

15. The fair ran from ~~the month of~~ May through October and had 26 million visitors.

Lesson 61 Circle each boldfaced word that is a subject pronoun. Underline each boldfaced word that is an object pronoun.

1. What did **you** do last weekend?
2. **I** took my little brother to see a movie.
3. **I** told **him** to keep quiet.
4. **He** often talks to **me** during the most suspenseful part of the movie.
5. People shush **us** if **we** make too much noise.
6. That embarrasses **me**, so **I** try to be as quiet as possible.
7. Do **you** eat popcorn when **you** see a movie?
8. If **I** see people with popcorn, **I** try not to sit by **them**.
9. The crunching drives **me** crazy.
10. To **me**, crunching is worse than my little brother's whispers.
11. **I** will give **you** a piece of advice.
12. If **you** eat candy in a movie, take **it** out of the wrapper before the movie starts.
13. My mom says **she** finds the rustling of candy wrappers distracting.
14. A family sat behind **me** once, and all of **them** were eating.
15. **They** crunched, rustled, and slurped their way through the whole film.

Lesson 62 Circle the correct pronoun in each pair. Write *S* if you chose a subject pronoun and *O* if you chose an object pronoun.

1. Rob and (**I**/me) wanted to go hiking last Saturday. ___S___
2. (**He**/Him) and I asked Mom if we could go. ___S___
3. (**She**/Her) and my dad were cleaning the garage. ___S___
4. Dad said that (**he**/him) and Mom were almost finished. ___S___
5. Mom asked Rob and (I/**me**) if she could hike with us. ___O___
6. (**Rob and I**/Me and Rob) told her she could. ___S___
7. Dad told (**Mom and me**/Mom and I) that we should phone Uncle Tim and my cousin. ___O___
8. Cousin Mara said that (her/**she**) and her dad would love to come. ___S___
9. So they joined Mom, Rob, and (I/**me**) at Pine Ridge Park. ___O___
10. Uncle Tim and Mara hadn't eaten, so we gave (**him**/he) and her lunch. ___O___
11. Then Mom and (**I**/me) led everyone on our favorite trail. ___S___
12. Uncle Tim said that (**he and Mara**/Mara and him) had never gone that way. ___S___
13. Rob, Mara, and (me/**I**) raced to the top of a hill. ___S___
14. Rob said that (him and Mara/**Mara and he**) had tied for first. ___S___
15. Mara said that (her/**she**) had beaten him by a nose. ___S___

Extra Practice

Lesson 63 Circle the antecedent or antecedents of each boldfaced pronoun.

1. (Kay) and her friend (Liam) got lost as **they** were going to the mall.
2. They missed their (bus stop) although the driver called **it** out.
3. (Liam) was talking on his cell phone, so **he** didn't hear the driver.
4. (Kay) was daydreaming, so **she** didn't hear the driver either.
5. Once the two (friends) realized their error, **they** asked the driver what to do.
6. He gave them (directions,) but they forgot **them** as soon as they got off the bus.
7. They boarded another (bus,) but **it** had a different number.
8. The bus took a different (route;) **it** was longer than the way they had come.
9. Finally Kay spotted (River Park Mall;) the bus dropped them off in front of **it.**
10. As soon as (Kay) and (Liam) got off the bus, **they** hurried inside the mall.
11. Kay wanted to buy her (father) a present because **he** had a birthday coming.
12. (Kay) was drawing a blank, so **she** asked Liam to help her.
13. Liam led her into a department (store;) **it** was having a sale.
14. (Liam) fell behind a crowd of shoppers, and Kay worried that she had lost **him.**
15. Kay found a fishing (hat) on sale; she decided **it** was just what her dad needed.

Lesson 64 Circle the pronoun that agrees with the antecedent in each pair of sentences.

1. Liz and Eric went to a hockey game downtown. (They/(It)) was the last game of the season.
2. Thousands of fans streamed into the arena. ((They)/It) wore jerseys and sweatshirts with the team colors.
3. Eric insisted on buying a program. (It/(He)) wanted to read about all the players.
4. Liz's and Eric's seats were in the top level of the arena. (It/(They)) had to climb many steps to get to them.
5. Liz got a little dizzy looking down at the ice. (She/(It)) was so far below them!
6. "The Star-Spangled Banner" was sung by two local music students. ((They)/We) sounded like professional singers.
7. Everyone applauded when the students finished. The team will likely ask (him/(them)) to sing again next year.
8. The crowd cheered when the players took the ice. ((They)/It) spent a few minutes warming up.
9. Both teams took their positions when the buzzer sounded. (She/(It)) was so loud it startled Eric.
10. Liz was impressed with the players' skills. (They/(She)) knew how difficult skating was.
11. Liz had taken skating lessons before. After falling repeatedly, she had learned that the sport was not for ((her)/it).
12. Eric admired the players, too. While watching (him/(them)), he dreamed of playing himself.
13. After ten minutes, the home team scored. Eric and Liz jumped out of (its/(their)) seats.
14. The noise from the crowd was louder than ever. In fact, ((it)/they) was deafening.
15. The whole arena seemed to shake. Eric had to cover ((his)/their) ears.

Lesson 65 Read each boldfaced pronoun. If the pronoun does not have a clear antecedent, mark an *X* through it.

1. There is a farmers' market in our town every Saturday. ~~They~~ hold it in the town square.

2. At least two dozen farmers sell their fruits and vegetables. ~~They~~ are always nice to see.

3. Dad and I try to arrive early at the market each week. **We** want to have the best selection possible.

4. Dad chats with Mr. Ruiz and buys some of his eggs. ~~It~~ is his first priority.

5. Dad knows Mr. Ruiz from high school when ~~he~~ was on the wrestling team.

6. Though he is a farmer and Dad can't even grow a houseplant, **they** are still friends.

7. Mr. Ruiz's children help him sell beans and tomatoes as well. ~~They~~ are always fun to see.

8. If the tomatoes seem ripe enough, Dad and I will buy **them** for making salsa.

9. The woman in the stall next door sells berries. **She** always smiles and waves us over.

10. She tells Dad how pretty I am and gives me a raspberry. ~~It~~ is the highlight of my day.

11. "~~She~~ is the loveliest person," Dad always says with a grin.

12. Next we usually fill our bags with melons and potatoes. ~~They~~ are always so heavy!

13. Our last stop is the Mexican food truck where ~~they~~ make the best tamales.

14. There is always a long line of people waiting for this treat. ~~It~~ is pretty impressive!

15. Dad and I appreciate the market because **we** love buying from local farmers.

Lesson 66 Circle the pronoun in parentheses that completes each sentence correctly.

1. (**Who**/Whom) is that sitting over there on the grass?

2. To (who/**whom**) are you pointing?

3. I am pointing to the man (**who**/whom) is talking to Mr. Chen.

4. Do you mean the one (**who**/whom) is wearing the blue baseball cap?

5. Yes, that is the person to (who/**whom**) I'm referring.

6. Isn't he the guy (**who**/whom) plays his saxophone here on weekends?

7. No, I think the man (**who**/whom) plays sax is taller and has darker hair.

8. That person looks familiar, though; to (who/**whom**) is he talking now?

9. He is talking to a woman (**who**/whom) comes to the park often.

10. Yes, she's someone (who/**whom**) I've seen here many times before.

11. She's the one (**who**/whom) sits at the other end of the park.

12. Is she the one (**who**/whom) paints portraits for twenty dollars?

13. Yes! Maybe the man to (who/**whom**) I was pointing wants his portrait painted.

14. We are the ones (**who**/whom) should have our portrait painted.

15. Then we could give it to Mom, (**who**/whom) has always wanted to have a portrait of us.

Name _____

Lesson 67 Circle the simple subject in each sentence. Then underline the correct form of each verb in parentheses.

1. This (can) of clams (smell/**smells**) fishy!
2. (Clams) (is/**are**) supposed to smell fishy.
3. Fresh (clams) from New England (**taste**/tastes) great in chowder.
4. When fresh clams aren't available, (chowder) made with canned clams (**is**/are) just fine.
5. The (students) in my cooking class (**make**/makes) chowder with fresh fish.
6. Clam (juice) from bottles (enhance/**enhances**) the chowder's flavor.
7. Too much (liquid) in chowder (make/**makes**) the broth watery.
8. (Chunks) of potato (**help**/helps) to thicken the broth.
9. The (broth) in these bowls (seem/**seems**) too thin.
10. But thick and lumpy (soup) (do/**does**) not appeal to me, either.
11. The (pot) full of vegetables (**is**/are) bubbling vigorously.
12. (Cooks) with experience (**stir**/stirs) chowder to keep solid ingredients from sticking.
13. (Chowder) without salt and pepper (taste/**tastes**) bland.
14. A (package) of oyster crackers (**is**/are) served with each bowl of chowder.
15. The (ingredients) in this soup (was/**were**) the freshest the cook could find.

Lesson 68 Look at the compound subject in each sentence. Circle the conjunction(s). Then underline the correct verb.

1. Ben (and) his sister Veronica (is/**are**) very active on weekends.
2. A bike ride, a swim, (or) a hike (**is**/are) likely to be their choice this weekend.
3. Sometimes Rene (and) Jaime (**go**/goes) biking or swimming with them.
4. (Neither) Rene (nor) Jaime (enjoy/**enjoys**) hiking, though.
5. Veronica, Ben, Jaime, (and) Rene often (bike/**bikes**) to the neighborhood park.
6. Bike lanes (and) paths (**make**/makes) their rides at the park safe and pleasant.
7. On occasion, (either) Ben (or) Jaime (bring/**brings**) along a soccer ball.
8. Veronica (and) her brother also (**like**/likes) rainy days.
9. On those days, (either) Veronica (or) Ben (bake/**bakes**) cookies.
10. Peanut butter (or) oatmeal (**is**/are) the kind Veronica usually makes.
11. Shortbread (or) ginger snaps (**is**/are) more to Ben's liking.
12. Sometimes Veronica, Ben, (and) their little brother Freddy (watch/**watches**) TV.
13. Ben (or) Freddy usually (pick/**picks**) the show.
14. Veronica (and) her two brothers (**prefer**/prefers) classic cartoons to new ones.
15. Now and then, Freddy (or) Ben (choose/**chooses**) a nature show.

Lesson 69 Circle the simple subject in each clause. Then underline the correct form of each verb in parentheses.

1. (The Lincoln Pool Rays) (<u>is</u>/are) the name of our water polo team.

2. Our (team) (<u>is</u>/are) the best one that Lincoln High School has had in years.

3. Almost (no one) ever (defeat/<u>defeats</u>) us.

4. (Nothing) (stop/<u>stops</u>) us once we start scoring.

5. (All) of the players (<u>follow</u>/follows) the rules in a book our coach recommended.

6. (*Water Polo for Winners*) (describe/<u>describes</u>) how to raise the level of your game.

7. (Everything) about offensive and defensive plays (<u>is</u>/are) clearly explained.

8. (Many) of our competitors (<u>use</u>/uses) this book, too.

9. (Few) of them (<u>succeed</u>/succeeds) the way we do, though.

10. At the dinner table, our (family) (talk/<u>talks</u>) about our matches.

11. The whole (group) (travel/<u>travels</u>) to tournaments to cheer for our team.

12. Sometimes the school's (band) (play/<u>plays</u>) at our matches.

13. Not (all) of the members (<u>come</u>/comes), though.

14. The (group) (perform/<u>performs</u>) between periods.

15. The (horn section) (play/<u>plays</u>) loudly to encourage us.

Lesson 70 Underline the verbal phrase that begins each sentence. If the phrase is a dangling or misplaced modifier, write *X* on the line. If the phrase is used correctly, circle the word it modifies and write *C* on the line.

1. <u>Having forgotten to set his alarm</u>, (Ed) overslept. __**C**__

2. <u>Worried about being late for school</u>, (Ed) sprang out of bed. __**C**__

3. <u>Getting dressed quickly</u>, his socks were mismatched. __**X**__

4. <u>Tying his shoes</u>, Ed's shoelaces broke. __**X**__

5. <u>Forgetting the bread in the toaster</u>, the toast was burned. __**X**__

6. <u>Dropping his cereal bowl</u>, (Ed) splashed milk and cereal everywhere. __**C**__

7. <u>Darting under his feet</u>, Ed tripped over the new puppy. __**X**__

8. <u>Hurrying out the door</u>, the sack lunch was left on the counter by Ed. __**X**__

9. <u>Running for the bus</u>, Ed's hat fell off his head. __**X**__

10. <u>Bending to pick it up</u>, (Ed) dropped all of his books. __**C**__

11. <u>Stopping to retrieve everything</u>, the bus left without Ed. __**X**__

12. <u>Determined to get Ed to school on time</u>, a shortcut was taken by Ed's mother. __**X**__

13. <u>Sitting in heavy traffic</u>, (Ed) and his (mother) felt anxious. __**C**__

14. <u>Pulling into the parking lot</u>, Ed thanked his mother and leaped from the car. __**X**__

15. <u>Beating the final bell</u>, class started with Ed in his seat. __**X**__

Lesson 71 Think about how many things are being compared in each sentence. Then underline the correct form of the adjective or adverb in parentheses.

1. Thuy is a (<u>better</u>/best) pitcher than Leah is.

2. Leah's pitches are a bit (<u>slower</u>/slowest) than Thuy's.

3. I am a (<u>worse</u>/worst) pitcher than either of them.

4. Both of them pitch (<u>more accurately</u>/most accurately) than I do.

5. I'm not a great pitcher, but I am the (better/<u>best</u>) catcher on the team.

6. I can keep the (faster/<u>fastest</u>) runners from stealing bases.

7. Marina has a (<u>stronger</u>/strongest) arm than Fia has.

8. Paula steals bases (<u>more often</u>/most often) than Thuy does.

9. Anne is the (more powerful/<u>most powerful</u>) hitter in our league.

10. She is a (<u>better</u>/best) bunter than anyone else, too.

11. There is no player who is (<u>more committed</u>/most committed) to winning than Rhea.

12. She is also the (more conscientious/<u>most conscientious</u>) about showing up for practice.

13. Tanya is the (more relaxed/<u>most relaxed</u>) player on the team.

14. Even in the (trickier/<u>trickiest</u>) situations, she never loses her cool.

15. We are definitely (<u>better</u>/best) prepared than we were last year!

Lesson 72 Underline the correct auxiliary verb in each sentence.

1. (<u>Have</u>/Could) you tried the new Thai restaurant on Grove Street?

2. If you enjoy Thai food, you (have/<u>might</u>) be interested in trying it.

3. I don't think I (<u>have</u>/might) ever tasted better Thai food.

4. You (<u>would</u>/have) enjoy it, too, I'm sure.

5. Your family (had/<u>should</u>) take you there some time.

6. The reviews of the restaurant (might/<u>have</u>) all been exceptionally good.

7. We (can/<u>must</u>) have ordered six dishes!

8. All of the dishes (have/<u>were</u>) made with the freshest ingredients.

9. The Thai noodles (<u>may</u>/should) be the best I have ever eaten.

10. My mother (could/<u>had</u>) never tasted such delicious coconut soup.

11. If you go there on a Saturday, you (have/<u>might</u>) need a reservation.

12. I (can/<u>do</u>) not know whether it is open on Sundays.

13. There (should/<u>might</u>) have been people eating there last Sunday.

14. My mom has said that I (do/<u>may</u>) invite a friend next time we go.

15. (<u>Would</u>/Can) you enjoy joining us for dinner there on Saturday?

Lesson 73 Draw three lines (≡) under each lowercase letter that should be capitalized. Draw a line (/) through each uppercase letter that should be lowercase.

1. I would like to visit several Countries in africa one day.

2. One country I would visit is the Republic of senegal.

3. Senegal lies on the coast of the atlantic ocean.

4. Some of its neighboring countries are Guinea-Bissau, guinea, mauritania, and mali.

5. The senegal river runs along the northern Border of senegal.

6. Like many other countries in africa, Senegal is a former french colony.

7. Its people celebrate Independence Day on april 4.

8. President abdoulaye wade took office on April 1, 2000, and was reelected in march 2007.

9. the capital city of dakar lies on the Cape Verde Peninsula.

10. Senegal is slightly smaller than the State of south dakota.

11. This tropical land experiences a rainy season from may through november.

12. The dry season lasts from december through april.

13. The official language of Senegal is french, but several other languages are spoken, including wolof.

14. About 350 miles off the Coast of the country lie the Cape verde Islands.

15. People in this island Nation speak cape Verde Creole and portuguese.

Lesson 74 Draw three lines (≡) under the letters that should be capitalized. Underline or add quotation marks where they are needed in titles.

1. My little brother just read the book The Great Broccoli Mystery by Edna Gernert.

2. Another great book by Edna Gernert is Streets Paved With Chocolate.

3. The movie version was called Fantastic Chocolate March.

4. Better Brush Your Teeth was a popular song from the movie.

5. I wrote a funny short story titled Orville and the Organic Farm.

6. If it's ever made into a movie, the theme song will be the veggie Guy.

7. The song at the end will be Lettuce all be friends.

8. Someday I will publish all my writing in a book titled Selected works of Matt Thompson.

9. My mother, who's a chef, wrote the cookbook artichoke artistry.

10. She was inspired to write it by the Pablo Neruda poem Ode to an Artichoke.

11. My mother says I eat wholesome foods because she read the methods of healthful cooking to me as a baby.

12. Dad says it's because he read me the poem It Mighta Been a Vitamin.

13. Maybe it's because I watched reruns of Julia Child and Company with my grandma.

14. My grandpa was fond of the movie Sylvester Graham and His Amazing Crackers.

15. I think that the next movie I watch will be attack of the brutal zucchini.

Lesson 75 Rewrite each item below. Use initials and abbreviations where you can.

1. Doctor Judith Anne Green — **Dr. J. A. Green**
2. Mister Tristan Scott Reese — **Mr. T. S. Reese**
3. Lindbergh Drive — **Lindbergh Dr.**
4. Mount Whitney — **Mt. Whitney**
5. Courtland Street — **Courtland St.**
6. Mistress Melissa Eve Choy — **Miss/Mrs. M. E. Choy**
7. Rotund Rock Corporation — **Rotund Rock Corp.**
8. General Lloyd Henry MacIntyre — **Gen. L. H. MacIntyre**
9. Oak Glen Boulevard — **Oak Glen Blvd.**
10. Mister Alberto Jose Lopez — **Mr. A. J. Lopez**
11. Green Meadow Road — **Green Meadow Rd.**
12. Doctor Elija Bergman — **Dr. E. Bergman**
13. Spiffy Sports Shoes Incorporated — **Spiffy Sports Shoes Inc.**
14. Sixteenth Avenue — **Sixteenth Ave.**
15. Parent Teacher Association — **PTA**

Lesson 76 Underline the correct word in parentheses. If the word is a possessive, write *P*. If the word is a contraction, write the two words it was made from.

1. My (brother's/brothers') teacher wants him to enter the science fair. **P**
2. The (fair's/fairs') application deadline is next Tuesday. **P**
3. Wade (didn't/did'nt) know what to create. **did not**
4. We had looked in books but (hadn't/had'nt) come up with a project idea. **had not**
5. My (dad's/dads') suggestion was to make a robot. **P**
6. I told him that (wasn't/was'nt) a very realistic suggestion. **was not**
7. My mother said that Wade could simulate a (volcano's/volcanos') eruption. **P**
8. That idea, while achievable, certainly (isn't/is'nt) an original one. **is not**
9. (There's/Theres') always at least one erupting volcano at every science fair. **There is**
10. Then I had the idea of using the (Internet's/Internets') resources. **P**
11. Wade and I went online, and within one (hours'/hour's) time, we had a great idea. **P**
12. Wade will determine which is cleaner, (dog's/dogs') mouths or the mouths of people. **P**
13. First, he will get cotton swab samples of several (people's/peoples') mouths. **P**
14. Then, he'll swab our dog (Red's/Reds') mouth. **P**
15. Finally, he will examine each (sample's/samples') bacteria under a microscope. **P**

Lesson 77 Add commas where they belong. Remember that a comma is needed to separate pairs of similar adjectives.

1. I went to the flea market with my mom, and we found some great stuff.

2. She bought a used blender, a stew pot, and a set of cups.

3. I found some tools, a pair of in-line skates, and an old camera.

4. It was fun to walk around and look at all the affordable, low-priced goods.

5. There was such a bright, colorful array of kitchen items.

6. Despite the gray weather, there were many buyers and sellers.

7. We saw antiques, used clothing, cookware, and a lot more.

8. I looked at vintage posters, old photographs, postcards, and sheet music.

9. The colorful, treasure-laden stalls were packed with goods.

10. Food vendors were there as well, so we sampled their wares.

11. We ate hot pretzels, corn on the cob, and hot dogs.

12. A few raindrops fell in the afternoon, but it was not enough to slow things down.

13. My sweet, soft-spoken mother is quite a shrewd bargainer.

14. Thanks to her skills, we got everything for less than the asking price.

15. There was a lively, energetic feel to the place.

Lesson 78 Add a colon or a semicolon to punctuate each sentence correctly.

1. Joe helped his parents paint the living room; it really needed it.

2. First, they moved out the furniture; they stored it in the garage.

3. Next, they removed the light fixtures; they also took the covers off the light switches.

4. They bought supplies: paint, drop cloths, brushes, rollers, and so on.

5. Joe's parents had trouble deciding on the paint color; his father wanted white, and his mother wanted color.

6. Joe considered the options; he chose a soft blue.

7. The prep-work was tedious; the family members had to mask all the windows with tape.

8. They washed the walls; then they sanded them.

9. They did what's called "cutting in"; that is the process of carefully painting the places where walls meet.

10. Joe liked the roller work; it went more quickly than the brush work.

11. At the end of the day, they surveyed their work; the room needed a second coat.

12. On day two, Joe had to paint the window frames and trim; he didn't enjoy that.

13. His spirits lifted when his parents ordered the best pizza ever: mushroom and pepperoni.

14. The family members were finished painting by 6:30, just in time to watch the football game.

15. Joe looked at the windows he'd painted; he was proud of his handiwork.

Lesson 79 Cross out hyphens, parentheses, and dashes that are used incorrectly. Add hyphens, parentheses, and dashes where they belong.

1. The word *astronaut* is derived from the Greek words *astron* ("star") and *nautes* ("sailor").

2. Becoming an astronaut—a dream for many young people—is not easy to do.

3. Astronauts need to be physically fit. (Much stamina is required for space travel.)

4. Astronauts also need to be highly qualified, self-motivated individuals.

5. A background in the sciences (either biological or physical) is highly desirable.

6. Math and engineering are two other valuable fields of study.

7. Candidates must exhibit a "can-do" attitude.

8. Space exploration is a multinational endeavor—astronauts from several nations often fly together—so it's desirable for astronauts to be bilingual.

9. Finalists undergo a week-long interview and orientation process.

10. Those selected for the program report to the Lyndon B. Johnson Space Center (NASA headquarters).

11. They embark on a two-year training and evaluation program.

12. Astronauts accumulate a number of flight hours in high-performance jet aircraft.

13. To experience the zero gravity sensation of outer space, astronauts ride in a special four-engine jet.

14. A series of steep climbs and dives forces passengers to float in mid-air for up to 30 seconds at a time!

15. Do you think you have what it takes to be an astronaut?

Lesson 80 Read each pair of quotations below. The first one is complete. The second one features an ellipsis that replaces a part of the first one. Mark an *X* if the ellipsis is used incorrectly.

1. "A visit to Niagara Falls during any season of the year is a pure pleasure," says travel writer Ned Minor in *Best American Vacations*.

   "A visit to Niagara Falls . . . is a pure pleasure," says travel writer Ned Minor in *Best American Vacations*.

   _____

2. "Make time to ride the *Maid of the Mist*, a boat that takes tourists along the bottom of the falls, if you want to feel their power up close," he suggests.

   "Make time to ride the *Maid of the Mist* . . . a boat that takes tourists along the bottom of the falls . . . if you want to feel their power up close," he suggests. **X**

3. "There are also parks and observation towers on both sides of the border that offer stunning views of the falls from all angles," Minor adds.

   "There are also parks and observation towers . . . that offer stunning views of the falls from all angles," Minor adds. _____

4. Minor warns, "This is a very popular destination, especially in the summer. Make sure you book your hotel early."

   Minor warns, "This is a very popular destination, especially in the summer. Make sure you. . . ." **X**

Lesson 81   Each sentence below is missing one or two punctuation marks. Rewrite the sentence. Insert the punctuation mark in parentheses to correctly indicate a pause. You may use the mark more than once.

1. Last weekend, we saw an excellent new film *Beyond the Night* at the local theater. (,)
    Last weekend, we saw an excellent new film, <u>Beyond the Night,</u> at the local theater.

2. I found the movie very entertaining and it made me want to be an astronaut. (. . .)
    I found the movie very entertaining . . . and it made me want to be an astronaut.

3. The first scene surely one of the best in history shows two NASA crew members in space. (—)
    The first scene—surely one of the best in history—shows two NASA crew members in space.

4. The two women young astronauts on their first mission are repairing a satellite. (,)
    The two women, young astronauts on their first mission, are repairing a satellite.

5. It could be just a routine day or it could be a day that will change their lives forever. (. . .)
    It could be just a routine day . . . or it could be a day that will change their lives forever.

6. Ominous music I think it was also composed by the director rises in the background. (—)
    Ominous music—I think it was also composed by the director—rises in the background.

7. Sensing some horrible accident would befall them I felt my heart racing and my palms sweating. (,)
    Sensing some horrible accident would befall them, I felt my heart racing and my palms sweating.

8. I won't reveal anything more about the film that would be cruel of me until you've seen it. (—)
    I won't reveal anything more about the film—that would be cruel of me—until you've seen it.

Lesson 82   Add the missing quotation marks and/or commas to each sentence.

1. "Have you seen that new kung fu movie, Juan?" Lee asked.

2. "You mean the one that takes place at the space station, don't you?" asked Juan.

3. "Yes, I've heard that the special effects are amazing," Lee replied.

4. "I haven't seen it, but I read good reviews of it," Juan answered.

5. "Slow motion takes on new meaning in outer space, doesn't it?" Lee said.

6. Juan answered with a laugh, "I guess there's faster action inside the station."

7. "Let's see the movie this weekend," Lee suggested.

8. "Hey, our social studies reports are due Monday," Juan reminded him.

9. "Ugh, you're right!" groaned Lee as he slumped in his chair.

10. "You haven't started writing yours yet, have you?" Juan inquired.

11. "I've only done the outline," answered Lee, a worried frown on his face.

12. "Let's work together on Saturday," Juan suggested.

13. "If we finish," he continued, "maybe we can see the movie Sunday."

14. "Wow, that's a great idea!" exclaimed Lee.

15. "The thought of seeing the movie will motivate us to work efficiently," said Juan.

Lesson 83 Read each direct and indirect quotation from a text and add the correct punctuation. (Hint: Not all sentences need punctuation added.)

1. The author of *Spotlight* makes his theme clear when he writes "Lacey would find that friendship was the most important thing."

2. When he introduces his heroine, she has just told her best friend Meg that she is on the verge of realizing her dream of becoming a movie star.

3. "Soon everyone in the world will know me, and I'll have a million friends," she announces to Meg.

4. Meg is skeptical and a little jealous when she replies, "Yes, but only your true friends will be there when you need them."

5. The author hints that Lacey will learn this lesson the hard way when he later says, "As her name grew bigger, Lacey's old friends played a smaller part in her life. She couldn't believe it, but she was lonely."

6. He wants the reader to understand that there is a difference between people in our lives and real friends we can count on.

7. Luckily, Lacey shows she realizes this too when she says, "I took friendship for granted. I need it more than fame."

8. Lacey later apologizes to Meg and tries to explain that she let fame get the better of her.

9. Meg has trouble forgiving Lacey, and says, "I warned you not to leave your old friends behind."

10. In the end, however, the author writes, "Lacey finally learned how to live in the spotlight and keep the people she loved in her life."

Lesson 84 Rewrite this business letter in correct letter form. Add in missing punctuation marks.
Made Swift Sports Uniforms 9800 Settler Boulevard Denver, CO 80002 Dear Sir or Madam My soccer team is interested in purchasing new uniforms. Will you please send me a copy of your latest catalog? Sincerely yours Diana Hughes 253 Sunrise Avenue Greenville, SC 29602 May 12, 20__

253 Sunrise Avenue _____

Greenville, SC 29602 _____

May 12, 20__ _____

Made Swift Sports Uniforms _____

9800 Settler Boulevard _____

Denver, CO 80002 _____

Dear Sir or Madam: _____

My soccer team is interested in purchasing new uniforms. Will you please send me a copy of your latest

catalog? _____

Sincerely yours, _____

Diana Hughes _____

Read this text and answer the questions on the next page.

China's Mighty Ships

1   <u>The *Niña*, the *Pinta*, and the *Santa María* Columbus's legendary ships</u>

2   <u>may be world-famous, but they were neither the first nor the largest vessels to</u>

3   <u>explore the unknown.</u> <u>For thousands of years, Chinese sailors had been</u>

4   <u>commanding ships called junks, which were massive enough to carry hundreds</u>

5   <u>of people and many tons of cargo.</u> <u>In particular, the junks using in the 1405</u>

6   <u>expedition of Zheng He overshadowed any Western boat of that time.</u> Some

7   are thought to have been over 400 feet long and almost 200 feet wide. <u>Putting</u>

8   <u>this size in perspective, Columbus's *Pinta* was only about 56 feet long.</u>

9   Nearly 100 years before the Italian's voyage, Zheng He and his fleet began

10   a series of journeys that would take them to Africa, India, and other parts of

11   Asia. The fleet included over 300 ships and nearly 30,000 men. <u>It must have</u>

12   <u>been quite an extraordinary sight, even at the vast ocean.</u> There were boats for

13   carrying supplies, boats for horses, boats for soldiers, warships, and boats that

14   transported only fresh water for drinking.

15   <u>Zheng He traded China's silk and fine pottery for African and Middle</u>

16   <u>Eastern spices, ivory, wood, and gems?</u> He brought novel items back to his

17   native land to the delight and wonder of the emperor and his court. During a

18   trip to Africa, he collected lions, zebras, and a giraffe. <u>Zheng He not only oversaw</u>

19   <u>the exchange of goods and ideas between China and the world and he also</u>

20   <u>spread the influence of his empire far and wide.</u>

21   <u>After Zheng He died in 1433, China began a period of isolation that would</u>

22   <u>last for centuries!</u> The mighty expeditions of Chinese explorers were forgotten.

(Numbers in parentheses identify related lessons.)
Read each item carefully. Fill in the circle next to the best answer.

1. What change, if any, should be made to the underlined words in lines 1–3? **(7)**

   Ⓐ NO CHANGE
   Ⓑ Columbus's legendary ships,
   Ⓒ , Columbus's legendary ships
   Ⓓ , Columbus's legendary ships,

2. What change, if any, should be made to the underlined words in lines 3–5? **(11)**

   Ⓐ NO CHANGE
   Ⓑ junks, which, were
   Ⓒ junks which, were
   Ⓓ junks which were

3. What change, if any, should be made to the underlined words in lines 5–6? **(8, 10)**

   Ⓐ NO CHANGE
   Ⓑ used in the
   Ⓒ were used in the
   Ⓓ to use in the

4. What change, if any, should be made to the underlined words in lines 7–8? **(9, 10)**

   Ⓐ NO CHANGE
   Ⓑ Put this size
   Ⓒ After putting this size
   Ⓓ To put this size

5. What change, if any, should be made to the underlined words in lines 11–12? **(6)**

   Ⓐ NO CHANGE
   Ⓑ under the vast ocean
   Ⓒ on the vast ocean
   Ⓓ through the vast ocean

6. What change, if any, should be made to the underlined words in lines 15–16? **(12)**

   Ⓐ NO CHANGE
   Ⓑ and gems;
   Ⓒ and gems.
   Ⓓ and gems!

7. What change, if any, should be made to the underlined words in lines 18–20? **(11)**

   Ⓐ NO CHANGE
   Ⓑ world, or he
   Ⓒ world but he
   Ⓓ world, but he

8. What change, if any, should be made to the underlined words in lines 21–22? **(12)**

   Ⓐ NO CHANGE
   Ⓑ for centuries.
   Ⓒ for centuries?
   Ⓓ for centuries:

Read each item carefully. Fill in the circle next to the best answer.

9. Read the following sentences.

> <u>Observed under a microscope, snowflakes</u> look like works of art. Each crystal is a unique six-sided marvel.

What part of the first sentence is underlined? **(1, 2)**

- Ⓐ complete subject
- Ⓑ complete predicate
- Ⓒ simple subject
- Ⓓ simple predicate

10. Read the following sentences.

> Loons are aquatic <u>birds</u> found in North America. These black-and-white swimmers dive underwater to catch fish.

What part of the first sentence is underlined? **(4, 5)**

- Ⓐ direct object
- Ⓑ indirect object
- Ⓒ predicate noun
- Ⓓ predicate adjective

11. Read the following sentences.

> I'm going to loan <u>you</u> my umbrella for the afternoon. Those dark clouds look threatening.

What part of the first sentence is underlined? **(4, 5)**

- Ⓐ direct object
- **Ⓑ** indirect object
- Ⓒ predicate noun
- Ⓓ predicate adjective

12. Read the following sentences.

> The magnolia, <u>a flowering tree</u>, is common throughout the South. With its large waxy leaves and even larger blossoms, it is hard to miss.

What part of the first sentence is underlined? **(2, 3, 6, 7)**

- Ⓐ appositive
- Ⓑ prepositional phrase
- Ⓒ compound subject
- Ⓓ simple subject

13. Read the following sentences.

> Sparky grabbed the bone and ran to the back of the yard. She immediately started burying her treat <u>in the soft earth</u>.

What part of the second sentence is underlined? **(2, 3, 6, 7)**

- Ⓐ appositive
- **Ⓑ** prepositional phrase
- Ⓒ compound predicate
- Ⓓ simple predicate

14. Read the following paragraph.

> [1] Joe and Mario want to earn money this summer. [2] They racked their brains to think of jobs they could do. [3] Mario's dad suggested that they do yard work for neighbors. [4] Now Mario and Joe are mowing grass and watering flowers for Mrs. Tran.

Which sentence has a compound predicate? **(3)**

- Ⓐ sentence 1
- Ⓑ sentence 2
- Ⓒ sentence 3
- **Ⓓ** sentence 4

Read each item carefully. Fill in the circle next to the best answer.

15. Read the following sentences.

> The students <u>playing in the orchestra</u> are all excellent musicians. They were chosen after several rigorous auditions.

What part of the first sentence is underlined? **(8–10)**

- Ⓐ participial phrase
- Ⓑ prepositional phrase
- Ⓒ appositive
- Ⓓ infinitive phrase

16. Read the following sentences.

> Many birds migrate, or relocate to a different area, for a certain season. Some fly thousands of miles <u>to reach their destinations.</u>

What part of the second sentence is underlined? **(8–10)**

- Ⓐ participial phrase
- Ⓑ prepositional phrase
- Ⓒ appositive
- Ⓓ infinitive phrase

17. Read the following sentences.

> Althea has sent a care package <u>to her sister</u> in college. It is her first year away from home, and Althea misses her terribly.

What part of the first sentence is underlined? **(8–10)**

- Ⓐ participial phrase
- Ⓑ prepositional phrase
- Ⓒ appositive
- Ⓓ infinitive phrase

18. Read the following paragraph.

> [1] Congratulations, you have been voted student of the month! [2] Come to the principal's office this afternoon to receive your prize. [3] There will be a photographer from the local paper there as well.

Where is the best place to add the following sentence? **(12)**

> Do you mind if she takes your picture?

- Ⓐ Before sentence 1
- Ⓑ After sentence 1
- Ⓒ After sentence 2
- Ⓓ After sentence 3

19. Read the following sentences.

> [1] Wilson must choose an activity for next fall. [2] He might play lacrosse. [3] He might play the drums in the marching band. [4] No matter which activity he chooses, he will be busy.

What is the best way to combine sentences 2 and 3? **(11)**

- Ⓐ He might play lacrosse and play drums in the marching band.
- Ⓑ He might play lacrosse or he might play the drums in the marching band.
- Ⓒ He might play lacrosse, or he might play the drums in the marching band.
- Ⓓ He might play lacrosse or, he might play the drums in the marching band.

20. Read the following sentences.

> I smell something cooking in the kitchen. <u>Did you start making dinner already?</u>

Which kind of sentence is underlined? **(12)**

- Ⓐ exclamatory
- Ⓑ interrogative
- Ⓒ declarative
- Ⓓ imperative

336

Read this text and answer the questions on the next page.

Not Just a Falling Apple

1   Sir Isaac Newton, famed victim of that falling apple, gave much more to

2 science than a funny story about observing gravity. <u>Though his many ideas and</u>

3 <u>theories greatly advanced our understanding of how the world works, he is</u>

4 <u>mostly remembered for, watching a piece of fruit drop from a nearby tree.</u> Some

5 versions of the tale even describe the apple hitting him on the head!

6   <u>Newton did tell others about this experience, but it is not likely, that he</u>

7 <u>developed his theory of gravitation in an instant.</u> <u>The apple anecdote has lived</u>

8 <u>on; because it is amusing.</u> It also helps us hold on to a myth we enjoy about

9 scientists: they come upon their ideas in a sudden moment of inspiration. In

10 reality, scientific discovery takes a lot of thought and work. <u>It involves trial and</u>

11 <u>error, which takes time.</u> Newton carefully formed his theory over many hours.

12 <u>He stated that all bodies with mass have a certain force that attracts them to</u>

13 <u>each other, it is this force that causes an apple to always fall to the earth.</u>

14   Newton thought of other laws that describe how and why objects move.

15 <u>Although they aren't linked to a legend about fruit, they are very important.</u>

16 These basic ideas are still considered in scientific study and still taught to every

17 student in science class. <u>Are the three universal laws of motion.</u> The first

18 law states that an object will continue moving or resting unless it is acted upon

19 by an outside force. The second law describes how a moving object accelerates,

20 or changes its speed. The third law says that when an object exerts a force on

21 another object, the second object pushes back with an equal force. <u>Remember</u>

22 <u>these laws when you think of Newton next to them, that apple means nothing.</u>

(Numbers in parentheses identify related lessons.)

Read each item carefully. Fill in the circle next to the best answer.

1. What change, if any, should be made to the underlined words in lines 2–4? **(19, 21)**

   - (A) NO CHANGE
   - (B) remembered, for watching
   - (C) remembered for watching
   - (D) remembered; for watching

5. What change, if any, should be made to the underlined words in lines 12–13? **(23)**

   - (A) NO CHANGE
   - (B) other. It is
   - (C) other it is
   - (D) other; is

2. What change, if any, should be made to the underlined words in lines 6–7? **(15, 18)**

   - (A) NO CHANGE
   - (B) likely; that he
   - (C) likely. That he
   - (D) likely that he

6. What change, if any, should be made to the underlined words in line 15? **(14, 22)**

   - (A) NO CHANGE
   - (B) fruit they are
   - (C) fruit; they are
   - (D) fruit. They are

3. What change, if any, should be made to the underlined words in lines 7–8? **(14, 17)**

   - (A) NO CHANGE
   - (B) lived on, because
   - (C) lived on: because
   - (D) lived on because

7. What change, if any, should be made to the underlined words in line 17? **(23)**

   - (A) NO CHANGE
   - (B) Are three
   - (C) The three
   - (D) They are the three

4. What change, if any, should be made to the underlined words in lines 10–11? **(16, 18)**

   - (A) NO CHANGE
   - (B) error. Which takes
   - (C) error; which takes
   - (D) error which takes

8. What change, if any, should be made to the underlined words in lines 21–22? **(23)**

   - (A) NO CHANGE
   - (B) Newton, next to
   - (C) Newton, Next to
   - (D) Newton. Next to

Read each item carefully. Fill in the circle next to the best answer.

9. Read the following sentences.

> Jane Austen wrote several novels, but she is most remembered for _Pride and Prejudice._ It is the story of five sisters living in England at the turn of the nineteenth century.

What kind of sentence is underlined? **(13, 15)**

Ⓐ simple
Ⓑ compound
Ⓒ complex
Ⓓ compound-complex

10. Read the following sentences.

> Although darkness will come sooner tomorrow, I am glad that daylight saving time is ending. We will gain an extra hour of sleep tonight.

Which part of the first sentence is underlined? **(14, 21)**

Ⓐ prepositional phrase
Ⓑ participial phrase
Ⓒ dependent clause
Ⓓ independent clause

11. Read the following sentences.

> [1] The flowers are perennials. [2] They grow in front of Sasha's house. [3] They bloom every year at the beginning of June.

What is the best way to combine sentences 1 and 2? **(11, 14, 16)**

Ⓐ The flowers, they grow in front of Sasha's house.
Ⓑ The flowers that grow in front of Sasha's house are perennials.
Ⓒ The flowers that grow, in front of Sasha's house are perennials.
Ⓓ The flowers are growing perennials in front of Sasha's house.

12. Read the following sentences.

> Set up your tents and gather some kindling. We'll build the campfire after the sun has gone down.

Which part of the second sentence is underlined? **(16–18)**

Ⓐ independent clause
Ⓑ adjective clause
Ⓒ adverb clause
Ⓓ nonrestrictive clause

13. Read the following sentences.

> The counselor who works at our school is my aunt, Fiona. She has an advanced degree in psychology.

Which part of the first sentence is underlined? **(16–18)**

Ⓐ nonrestrictive clause
Ⓑ restrictive clause
Ⓒ adverb clause
Ⓓ independent clause

14. Read the following paragraph.

> [1] It is true that Orville and Wilbur were in the Kitty Hawk area on that day in 1903. [2] The famous flight, however, took place closer to Kill Devil Hills. [3] This lesser-known town is several miles south of Kitty Hawk.

Where is the best place to add the following sentence? **(13, 15)**

> Kitty Hawk, North Carolina, is often cited as the place where the Wright brothers first flew their plane.

Ⓐ Before sentence 1
Ⓑ After sentence 1
Ⓒ After sentence 2
Ⓓ After sentence 3

Read each item carefully. Fill in the circle next to the best answer.

15. Read the following sentences.

> Writing words with suffixes can be quite challenging. The spelling of the base word is often changed.

What kind of phrase is underlined? **(19)**

Ⓐ appositive
Ⓑ infinitive
Ⓒ gerund
Ⓓ participial

16. Read the following sentences.

> Springtime, when tree branches are still bare, is the perfect time for birding. Birds are more easily spotted, and great numbers of them are on the move.

Which part of the first sentence is underlined? **(18, 21)**

Ⓐ independent clause
Ⓑ nonrestrictive clause
Ⓒ prepositional phrase
Ⓓ appositive

17. Read the following sentences.

> I agree with the moral of this folktale. Wise is the person who chooses happiness over material wealth.

Which kind of order is represented by the underlined sentence? **(24)**

Ⓐ natural
Ⓑ inverted
Ⓒ chronological
Ⓓ interrupted

18. Read the following sentences.

> Mosquitoes, which can carry a disease called malaria, are a danger in tropical areas. Make sure you use repellent and sleep inside protective netting.

Which kind of order is represented by the underlined sentence? **(24)**

Ⓐ natural
Ⓑ inverted
Ⓒ chronological
Ⓓ interrupted

19. Read the following sentences.

> The first federal United States postage stamp was issued on July 1, 1847. Before the national government _____ could be bought only from private printers.

Which words and punctuation best complete the second sentence? **(22, 23)**

Ⓐ sold stamps, they
Ⓑ sold stamps they
Ⓒ sold stamps; they
Ⓓ sold stamps: they

20. Read the following paragraph.

> [1] The art show features many of the artists in our class. [2] Devon sculpted that figure out of clay. [3] The giant mural was painted by Tonya and Wang Li. [4] Tim took those photographs of the old factory downtown.

Which sentence is written in the passive voice? **(20)**

Ⓐ sentence 1
Ⓑ sentence 2
Ⓒ sentence 3
Ⓓ sentence 4

Read this text and answer the questions on the next page.

Local Landmark Stirs Debate

1   Is a piece of civic history worth saving? <u>This was the question submitted

2   for debate at last nights well-attended Ridgeville city council meeting.</u> Over 75

3   citizens packed into the small council chamber to offer opinions concerning the

4   fate of the 100-year-old city hall building. <u>Though it is a downtown noted

5   landmark, the "Old Hall," as it is popularly called, has been abandoned for nearly

6   five years.</u> The brick facade is crumbling, and there is likely toxic mold growing in

7   the basement. Should the city allocate funds for the restoration of this grand old

8   structure, or should the Old Hall be torn down? There are good arguments for

9   both courses of action, as council members found out yesterday.

10   The loudest and most enthusiastic proponent of saving the building was

11   <u>Dr. James Jackson, President of the Ridgeville Historic Preservation Society.</u> He

12   gave an impassioned speech about the importance of restoring and reusing our

13   historic structures. <u>He also argued that destroying the Old Hall would deprive

14   Ridgeville citizens of a source of beauty and pride it has counted on for

15   decades.</u> "The Old Hall is the most elegant example of neoclassical architecture

16   for miles around. It gives our city character and a claim to fame," he asserted.

17   <u>"I would save it myself, if I could, but we need the city to do the right thing."</u>

18   Jackson's words inspired cheers from the crowd, but some are still

19   skeptical. Leading the opposition is business owner Darlene Hill. "The building

20   is quickly becoming an eyesore. <u>Why pour money into something so obsolete?</u>

21   <u>Those voting to save it will not be heros in my eyes," she said.</u> <u>Whom made the

22   strongest case?</u> Ridgeville will find out when the council votes next Tuesday.

Name _____

Read each item carefully. Fill in the circle next to the best answer.

1. What change, if any, should be made to the underlined words in lines 1–2? **(28)**

   Ⓐ NO CHANGE
   Ⓑ at last nights'
   Ⓒ at last nights's
   Ⓓ at last night's

2. What change, if any, should be made to the underlined words in lines 4–6? **(34, 36)**

   Ⓐ NO CHANGE
   Ⓑ noted, downtown landmark
   Ⓒ downtown, noted landmark
   Ⓓ noted downtown landmark

3. What change, if any, should be made to the underlined words in lines 10–11? **(26)**

   Ⓐ NO CHANGE
   Ⓑ Dr. James Jackson, president
   Ⓒ dr. James Jackson, President
   Ⓓ Dr. james jackson, president

4. What change, if any, should be made to the underlined words in lines 13–15? **(29)**

   Ⓐ NO CHANGE
   Ⓑ she has counted on
   Ⓒ they have counted on
   Ⓓ them have counted on

5. What change, if any, should be made to the underlined words in line 17? **(30)**

   Ⓐ NO CHANGE
   Ⓑ save me it
   Ⓒ save itself
   Ⓓ myself save it

6. What change, if any, should be made to the underlined words in line 20? **(32)**

   Ⓐ NO CHANGE
   Ⓑ into someone
   Ⓒ into everything
   Ⓓ into nothing

7. What change, if any, should be made to the underlined words in line 21? **(25)**

   Ⓐ NO CHANGE
   Ⓑ hero in my eyes
   Ⓒ hero's in my eyes
   Ⓓ heroes in my eyes

8. What change, if any, should be made to the underlined words in lines 21–22? **(33)**

   Ⓐ NO CHANGE
   Ⓑ Whose made the
   Ⓒ Who made the
   Ⓓ Which made the

Read each item carefully. Fill in the circle next to the best answer.

9. Read the following sentences.

> "Yes, I am very fortunate," said Rashida, winner of the city spelling bee. "But it was skill, not <u>luck</u>, that helped me today."

What kind of noun is underlined? **(26, 27)**

Ⓐ proper
Ⓑ concrete
Ⓒ collective
Ⓓ abstract

10. Read the following sentences.

> Carla's dad is a soldier who is stationed overseas. He joins his <u>division</u> in Japan again in a couple of weeks.

What kind of noun is underlined? **(26, 27)**

Ⓐ proper
Ⓑ plural
Ⓒ collective
Ⓓ abstract

11. Read the following sentences.

> Dwight D. Eisenhower was a general who commanded _____ in the United States Army during World War II. He became president of the United States in 1953.

Which word best completes the first sentence? **(25, 28)**

Ⓐ troop
Ⓑ troops
Ⓒ troop's
Ⓓ troops'

12. Read the following sentences.

> "Oh, the honor is all _____," said Ariel. She was excited to be meeting her best friend's parents at last.

Which pronoun best completes the first sentence? **(31)**

Ⓐ my
Ⓑ me
Ⓒ mine
Ⓓ myself

13. Read the following paragraph.

> [1] Finn's favorite extracurricular activity is playing hockey. [2] Since his first glide on the ice, he has been in love with the sport. [3] Leah spends a lot of her time writing prose and verse.

Where is the best place to add the following sentence? **(28, 31)**

> Her poems' themes often involve strength and bravery.

Ⓐ Before sentence 1
Ⓑ After sentence 1
Ⓒ After sentence 2
Ⓓ After sentence 3

14. Read the following sentences.

> Acadia National Park, <u>which</u> is in Maine, is the oldest national park east of the Mississippi River. It features forests, mountains, and coastal areas.

What kind of pronoun is underlined? **(30, 32, 33)**

Ⓐ relative
Ⓑ reflexive
Ⓒ indefinite
Ⓓ intensive

Read each item carefully. Fill in the circle next to the best answer.

15. Read the following sentences.

> Olive made an amazing copy of her friend's original drawing. The artist <u>herself</u> couldn't tell the difference between the two pictures.

What kind of pronoun is underlined? **(30, 32, 33)**

- (A) relative
- (B) reflexive
- (C) indefinite
- (D) intensive

16. Read the following sentences.

> Mr. Soto loaned David a jacket for his campaign speech. "Wear <u>this</u>," he said, "and you will be the most impressive candidate for class president."

What kind of pronoun is underlined? **(32, 33, 35)**

- (A) demonstrative
- (B) interrogative
- (C) indefinite
- (D) relative

17. Read the following sentences.

> [1] The United States headed toward a divisive civil war. [2] It needed someone wise to take over as president. [3] Luckily, Abraham Lincoln was elected in 1860.

What is the best way to combine sentences 1 and 2? **(11, 15, 17)**

- (A) When the United States headed toward a divisive civil war it needed someone wise to take over as president.
- (B) The United States headed toward a divisive civil war but it needed someone wise to take over as president.
- (C) As the United States headed toward a divisive civil war, it needed someone wise to take over as president.
- (D) The United States needed someone wise to take over as president.

18. Read the following sentences.

> "I can't eat all of _____ carrot sticks," Ada said as she handed me a bag of the orange vegetables. "Would you like some?"

Which demonstrative adjective best completes the first sentence? **(35)**

- (A) this
- (B) that
- (C) these
- (D) those

19. Read the following sentences.

> The quarterback made _____ attempts to pass for a touchdown during the final seconds of the game. Unfortunately, his team still lost by six points.

Which pair of adjectives completes the first sentence and is written correctly? **(36)**

- (A) several, desperate
- (B) several desperate
- (C) desperate several
- (D) desperate, several

20. Read the following paragraph.

> [1] Jaya played her trombone noisily in her room. [2] Max pounded at his drum set in the basement. [3] "I can't stand another minute of this clamor!" said Tara. [4] With her hands over her ears, she swiftly ran from the house.

Which sentence does NOT contain an adverb? **(34)**

- (A) sentence 1
- (B) sentence 2
- (C) sentence 3
- (D) sentence 4

Read this text and answer the questions on the next page.

Lost!

1   The sun was sinking lower in the sky, and Charlotte was worried. "How

2 could I have let myself get separated from the group?" she said out loud. The

3 dense thicket of conifers in front of her will not respond. Charlotte had

4 wandered in what seemed like circles for three hours, and now she had to admit

5 that she was lost, darkness was coming, and her only companions were these

6 trees. As these realizations washes over her, worry quickly turned to panic.

7   "Get a grip, Lottie." She again speaks to herself, this time in a whisper. She

8 sat down on a nearby log, took a few deep breaths, and looked carefully at the

9 surrounding forest. She tried to remember the moment when she will have first

10 found herself alone and cut off from her friends. She had stopped, for only

11 a moment, to investigate an unusual wildflower a few yards off the trail.

12 She had taken several pictures of the blossom so she could identify it later.

13 And then, suddenly, she had noticed the silence around her.

14   "I should have just retraced my steps back to camp," Charlotte thought,

15 "but instead I ran blindly through the woods after my friends. I wish I could see

16 just one familiar landmark that would help me get on the right track. These

17 trees all look exactly alike!" More shadows gathered. The light was fading.

18   Frantically, Charlotte thought of her older brother, an Eagle Scout. "If I

19 was Drew, what would I do?" she asked. Then it hit her. The sun was setting in

20 the west, and the camp was on the western edge of the park. "I'll walk toward

21 the sun!" she said, her feet already blazing a trail through the underbrush. A

22 half hour later, she is relieved to see the camp lights twinkling in the dusk.

(Numbers in parentheses identify related lessons.)
Read each item carefully. Fill in the circle next to the best answer.

1. What change, if any, should be made to the underlined words in line 1? **(41)**

   (A) NO CHANGE
   (B) The sun is sinking
   (C) The sun were sinking
   (D) The sun will have sunk

2. What change, if any, should be made to the underlined words in lines 2–3? **(39)**

   (A) NO CHANGE
   (B) is not responding
   (C) does not respond
   (D) did not respond

3. What change, if any, should be made to the underlined words in line 6? **(39)**

   (A) NO CHANGE
   (B) washed over her
   (C) wash over her
   (D) will wash over her

4. What change, if any, should be made to the underlined words in line 7? **(42)**

   (A) NO CHANGE
   (B) She again has spoken
   (C) She again spoke
   (D) She again is speaking

5. What change, if any, should be made to the underlined words in lines 9–10? **(40)**

   (A) NO CHANGE
   (B) when she had first
   (C) when she has first
   (D) when she was first

6. What change, if any, should be made to the underlined words in line 12? **(40)**

   (A) NO CHANGE
   (B) She has taken
   (C) She is taken
   (D) She will have taken

7. What change, if any, should be made to the underlined words in lines 18–19? **(44)**

   (A) NO CHANGE
   (B) If I will be Drew
   (C) If I were Drew
   (D) If I am Drew

8. What change, if any, should be made to the underlined words in lines 21–22? **(42)**

   (A) NO CHANGE
   (B) she has been relieved
   (C) she will be relieved
   (D) she was relieved

Read each item carefully. Fill in the circle next to the best answer.

9. Read the following sentences.

> Ellen <u>could</u> not <u>sleep</u> because she <u>was</u> anxious about her track meet. She <u>tossed</u> and turned all night.

Which underlined word is a linking verb? (37)

Ⓐ could
Ⓑ sleep
Ⓒ was
Ⓓ tossed

10. Read the following sentences.

> Kudzu is an invasive vine that <u>grows</u> mainly in the southeastern United States. It <u>has</u> <u>become</u> an undesirable plant because it <u>strangles</u> the surrounding flora.

Which underlined word is a transitive verb? (38)

Ⓐ is
Ⓑ grows
Ⓒ has become
Ⓓ strangles

11. Read the following sentences.

> The Farmville Humane Society _____ popcorn and hot dogs at tomorrow's carnival. All money raised will go toward building a new animal shelter.

Which verb best completes the first sentence? (40, 41)

Ⓐ was selling
Ⓑ will be selling
Ⓒ has sold
Ⓓ had sold

12. Read the following sentences.

> Marco's teacher suggested that he <u>interview</u> a geologist before writing his research paper. Professional scientists can be great resources with up-to-date information.

Which mood is expressed by the underlined verb? (43, 44)

Ⓐ indicative   Ⓒ imperative
Ⓑ interrogative   Ⓓ subjunctive

13. Read the following sentences.

> "<u>Read</u> this book if you like mysteries," Xavier said. "I couldn't put it down."

Which mood is expressed by the underlined verb? (43, 44)

Ⓐ indicative   Ⓒ imperative
Ⓑ interrogative   Ⓓ subjunctive

14. Read the following paragraph.

> [1] In 1588, Philip II of Spain attempted to invade England and overthrow Queen Elizabeth. [2] He hoped the Spanish Armada would be the invincible weapon that achieved this goal. [3] The Spanish Armada was so large. [4] This caused it to take two days to leave the port in Lisbon.

What is the best way to combine sentences 3 and 4? (11, 15, 18, 43)

Ⓐ The Spanish Armada took two days to leave the port in Lisbon and it was so large.
Ⓑ The Spanish Armada was so large because it took two days to leave the port in Lisbon.
Ⓒ The Spanish Armada took two days to leave the port in Lisbon because it was so large.
Ⓓ Because it was so large the Spanish Armada took two days to leave the port in Lisbon.

347

Read each item carefully. Fill in the circle next to the best answer.

15. Read the following sentences.

> <u>Brainstorm</u> a topic for your report, and then <u>look</u> for appropriate resources at the library. <u>Write</u> important facts on note cards, and you <u>should remember</u> to include bibliographical information as well.

Which underlined verb represents a shift in mood? **(45)**

- Ⓐ Brainstorm
- Ⓑ look
- Ⓒ Write
- Ⓓ should remember

16. Read the following sentences.

> "If I were you, I'd _____ French," Aunt Susan said. "It's such a beautiful language."

Which verb best completes the first sentence? **(44)**

- Ⓐ take
- Ⓑ takes
- Ⓒ took
- Ⓓ taken

17. Read the following sentences.

> "Chocolate is my favorite flavor, _____ I think I'll try strawberry today," Jill said as she peered into the ice cream case. She was in the mood for something different.

Which word is a coordinating conjunction that correctly completes the first sentence? **(47)**

- Ⓐ though
- Ⓑ but
- Ⓒ and
- Ⓓ since

18. Read the following sentences.

> <u>When</u> a storm forms in the warm waters <u>near</u> the equator, it <u>can</u> become a hurricane. The heat fuels the storm, <u>and</u> wind patterns cause the air to swirl.

Which underlined word is a subordinating conjunction? **(47)**

- Ⓐ When
- Ⓑ near
- Ⓒ can
- Ⓓ and

19. Read the following sentences.

> _____ you ride the subway or take the bus, you will still arrive in plenty of time. The concert doesn't start for several hours.

Which correlative conjunction best completes the first sentence? **(48)**

- Ⓐ Either
- Ⓑ Neither
- Ⓒ Not only
- Ⓓ Whether

20. Read the following paragraph.

> [1] Several local bands marched in the Independence Day parade. [2] Carriages and floats were pulled by beautiful draft horses. [3] The grand marshal, the town's mayor, rode in a shiny convertible. [4] She waved and threw candy to the spectators.

Which sentence contains a shift to passive voice? **(46)**

- Ⓐ sentence 1
- Ⓑ sentence 2
- Ⓒ sentence 3
- Ⓓ sentence 4

Read this text and answer the questions on the next page.

Facing a Fear

1   <u>Mrs. Jones paused outside her daughter's room and listened to the high,</u>

2 <u>sweet voice raising and falling on the other side of the door.</u> "That girl can really

3 sing," she thought to herself with a sad smile. "I wish she had the courage to let

4 the world hear it."

5   <u>Keisha Jones she was known as the quietest girl in her class.</u> She might

6 have even been the biggest wallflower in all of James Madison Middle School.

7 Speaking in class made her tremble, and talking to strangers made her blush.

8 <u>Shy Keisha thought and felt many things she could not bring herself to say out</u>

9 <u>loud.</u> She was an avid reader and a history buff. She loved jazz music, and, when

10 she was alone, she could belt out a tune like a professional singer. <u>Few people</u>

11 <u>known, of course, about her amazing vocal talent.</u>

12   <u>Mrs. Jones wrapped softly on Keisha's door and entered the room.</u> "Are

13 you practicing something special, honey?" she asked. "It sounds wonderful."

14   "Oh, I'm just imagining what it would be like to try out for the school

15 musical," Keisha replied. "I'd never get the part, but it's fun to dream, right?"

16   <u>Mrs. Jones was all, "What makes you think you wouldn't get the part?"</u>

17   <u>"Well, there are over a dozen girls trying out for one thing," Keisha</u>

18 <u>replied.</u> "And then there's the fact that singing in public is terrifying."

19   "I know expressing yourself is scary, Keisha, but maybe it's time you

20 faced that fear. <u>It's a shame that nobody can't ever hear that lovely voice."</u>

21   "You think my voice is lovely?" Keisha reddened a little, but then she

22 looked determined. "I'll think about trying out." It was definitely a start.

(Numbers in parentheses identify related lessons.)
Read each item carefully. Fill in the circle next to the best answer.

1. What change, if any, should be made to the underlined words in lines 1–2? **(55)**

   (A) NO CHANGE
   (B) sweet voice razing
   (C) sweet voice rising
   (D) sweet voice risen

2. What change, if any, should be made to the underlined words in line 5? **(59)**

   (A) NO CHANGE
   (B) Keisha she was
   (C) Keisha Jones was
   (D) Keisha Jones her was

3. What change, if any, should be made to the underlined words in lines 8–9? **(51)**

   (A) NO CHANGE
   (B) bring herself too say
   (C) bring herself two say
   (D) bring her to say

4. What change, if any, should be made to the underlined words in lines 10–11? **(56)**

   (A) NO CHANGE
   (B) Few people knowed
   (C) Few people knewed
   (D) Few people knew

5. What change, if any, should be made to the underlined words in line 12? **(57)**

   (A) NO CHANGE
   (B) rapt softly
   (C) rapped softly
   (D) wraps softly

6. What change, if any, should be made to the underlined words in line 16? **(58)**

   (A) NO CHANGE
   (B) Mrs. Jones asked
   (C) Mrs. Jones went
   (D) Mrs. Jones was like

7. What change, if any, should be made to the underlined words in lines 17–18? **(52)**

   (A) NO CHANGE
   (B) more then a dozen girls
   (C) higher than a dozen girls
   (D) more than a dozen girls

8. What change, if any, should be made to the underlined words in line 20? **(53)**

   (A) NO CHANGE
   (B) nobody can never hear
   (C) nobody can ever hear
   (D) anybody can't never hear

Read each item carefully. Fill in the circle next to the best answer.

9. Read the following sentences.

> "This essay has _____ mistakes than your last one did," said Mr. Travers. "Your writing is really improving."

Which word best completes the first sentence? **(52)**

(A) less
(B) littler
(C) fewer
(D) smaller than

10. Read the following sentences.

> I have no idea _____ going to win the top prize at the science fair. There are so many excellent projects this year.

Which word best completes the first sentence? **(50)**

(A) whose
(B) whom
(C) who's
(D) whom's

11. Read the following sentences.

> The little tabby's kittens just opened _____ eyes yesterday. They sleep together in a fuzzy ball.

Which word best completes the first sentence? **(49, 50)**

(A) it's
(B) its
(C) their
(D) they're

12. Read the following sentences.

> Dad and I spent the afternoon sketching the natural scenes around us. "It's nice to see _____ artistic side," he said.

Which word best completes the second sentence? **(49)**

(A) you
(B) you's
(C) you're
(D) your

13. Read the following sentences.

> Kevin was nervous about his job interview scheduled for the following day. He _____ out his clothes, résumé, and bus fare so he would be ready in the morning.

Which word best completes the second sentence? **(55)**

(A) lay
(B) laid
(C) lain
(D) lied

14. Read the following paragraph.

> [1] Mahatma Gandhi was a leader of the early twentieth-century movement to end British rule of India. [2] He organized large demonstrations to protest taxes and other injustices imposed on his people. [3] This guy believed that much could be accomplished through nonviolent actions. [4] He was often imprisoned, however, for challenging the government.

Which sentence contains a word or words that should be avoided in academic writing? **(54)**

(A) sentence 1
(B) sentence 2
(C) sentence 3
(D) sentence 4

Read each item carefully. Fill in the circle next to the best answer.

15. Read the following sentences.

> Lamar had so much nervous energy that he could not _____ still. He stood up and began pacing back and forth.

Which word best completes the first sentence? **(55)**

- (A) sit
- (B) sat
- (C) set
- (D) sets

16. Read the following sentences.

> Elizabeth Blackwell _____ to study medicine at a time when only men were accepted as physicians. In 1849, she became the first woman in the United States to earn a medical degree.

Which word best completes the first sentence? **(56)**

- (A) choose
- (B) chose
- (C) chosen
- (D) choosed

17. Read the following sentences.

> [1] Jeff pulled his laundry out of the dryer. [2] He had a look of horror on his face. [3] His favorite sweater had shrunk to half its original size!

What is the best way to combine sentences 1 and 2? **(11, 15, 17)**

- (A) Jeff pulled his laundry out of the dryer, he had a look of horror on his face.
- (B) When Jeff pulled his laundry out of the dryer he, had a look of horror on his face.
- (C) Jeff pulled his laundry out of the dryer, because he had a look of horror on his face.
- (D) When Jeff pulled his laundry out of the dryer, he had a look of horror on his face.

18. Read the following sentences.

> Langston Hughes saw his first book of poetry, *The Weary Blues*, published in 1926. He went on to _____ plays, novels, short stories, and more poems.

Which word best completes the second sentence? **(57)**

- (A) right
- (B) rite
- (C) wright
- (D) write

19. Read the following paragraph.

> [1] She loves tromping through the snow and feeling the icy breeze on her face. [2] Rhett, on the other hand, prefers the summer months. [3] He spends as much time as he can out in the sun.

Where is the best place to add the following sentence? **(59)**

> Karen is always happiest during the winter.

- (A) Before sentence 1
- (B) After sentence 1
- (C) After sentence 2
- (D) After sentence 3

20. Read the following sentences.

> Mount Kilimanjaro, in Tanzania, is the tallest mountain in the continent of Africa. With a peak 19,341 feet above sea level, it is also the tallest free-standing mountain in the world.

Which underlined words are unnecessary? **(60)**

- (A) in Tanzania
- (B) the continent of
- (C) above sea level
- (D) in the world

Read this text and answer the questions on the next page.

Little Italy, 1905

1   It has been two years since we arrived here in New York City, but it is still

2   difficult to call it home. Papa assures me that we had to leave our friends and

3   family in Italy. He says that life here is not perfect, but there are many more

4   opportunities. This optimism has never wavered, despite the fact that Papa lost

5   his job at the shoe factory several months ago. Mama has tried to support us by

6   sewing shirts and petticoats at home, but I can tell by the anxious look he always

7   wears that our situation is becoming desperate.

8   The air in our small flat are very oppressive, both literally and figuratively.

9   We share one floor of a ten-story building with three other families. Our two

10   rooms consist of a kitchen and a bedroom where Papa, Mama, Luciana, Natalia,

11   Ernesto, and I sleep. The single window provides little breeze, and the flat is

12   often hot and smoky. Just outside, the smells of garbage and manure from the

13   streetcar horses assaults me as soon as I leave the building.

14   My one refuge is school, where I am learning English, mathematics, and

15   science. It is my favorite subject, and my teacher thinks I have a natural talent

16   for it. The school is also kind enough to provide a free hot lunch. Ernesto and me

17   are so grateful for the meal because it ensures that we will not take food from

18   the mouths of our sisters and parents.

19   I am afraid, however, that the time has come to put aside my education.

20   I am almost fifteen and perfectly capable of finding work. I love my studies, but

21   my family need me. Maybe things will begin looking up for us, as Papa says, and

22   he will be able to open his store. Until then, hope is all we have.

(Numbers in parentheses identify related lessons.)
Read each item carefully. Fill in the circle next to the best answer.

1. What change, if any, should be made to the underlined words in lines 3–4? **(61, 63)**

   (A) NO CHANGE
   (B) You say that
   (C) It says that
   (D) She says that

2. What change, if any, should be made to the underlined words in lines 4–5? **(67, 72)**

   (A) NO CHANGE
   (B) had never wavered
   (C) have never wavered
   (D) was never wavered

3. What change, if any, should be made to the underlined words in lines 5–7? **(63, 64)**

   (A) NO CHANGE
   (B) she always wears
   (C) they always wear
   (D) it always wears

4. What change, if any, should be made to the underlined words in line 8? **(67)**

   (A) NO CHANGE
   (B) were very oppressive
   (C) is very oppressive
   (D) was very oppressive

5. What change, if any, should be made to the underlined words in lines 12–13? **(67)**

   (A) NO CHANGE
   (B) was assaulting me
   (C) has assaulted me
   (D) assault me

6. What change, if any, should be made to the underlined words in lines 15–16? **(65)**

   (A) NO CHANGE
   (B) Mathematics is my
   (C) They are my
   (D) School is my

7. What change, if any, should be made to the underlined words in lines 16–18? **(62)**

   (A) NO CHANGE
   (B) Me and Ernesto
   (C) Ernesto and I
   (D) I and Ernesto

8. What change, if any, should be made to the underlined words in lines 20–21? **(69)**

   (A) NO CHANGE
   (B) family have needed me
   (C) family needs me
   (D) family are needing me

Read each item carefully. Fill in the circle next to the best answer.

9. Read the following sentences.

> Louisa May Alcott, _____ wrote the classic *Little Women*, was born in 1832. The novel is based on her life with her three sisters.

Which word best completes the first sentence? **(66)**

A that
B whose
C who
D whom

10. Read the following sentences.

> Avery told her friend Warren that she was moving to another state. He looked devastated after she broke the news to him.

Which underlined word is an object pronoun? **(61)**

A her
B she
C He
D him

11. Read the following sentences.

> Neither Talia nor Akira _____ action movies. Maybe we should think of something else to see.

Which verb best completes the first sentence? **(68)**

A like
B likes
C are going to like
D have liked

12. Read the following sentences.

> [1] Nobody admires a sore loser. [2] Smile at your opponent. [3] Give him or her a handshake.

What is the best way to combine sentences 2 and 3? **(11, 13)**

A Smile at your opponent, give him or her a handshake.
B Smile at your opponent and, give him or her a handshake.
C Smile at your opponent, and give him or her a handshake.
D Smile at your opponent but give him or her a handshake.

13. Read the following paragraph.

> [1] They look like icicles, but they are actually made of minerals. [2] Stalactites are often found in caves made of limestone. [3] Water drips from the ceiling and leaves long tubular deposits of calcite.

Where is the best place to add the following sentence? **(63, 64)**

> Stalactites are formations that hang from the ceilings of caves.

A Before sentence 1   C After sentence 2
B After sentence 1   D After sentence 3

14. Read the following sentences.

> I promised my brother that I would take _____ to the park later. I couldn't tell who was more excited—little boy or dog.

Which words best complete the first sentence? **(62)**

A he and Scruffy
B him and Scruffy
C his and Scruffy
D himself and Scruffy

Read each item carefully. Fill in the circle next to the best answer.

15. Read the following sentences.

> *Romeo and Juliet* _____ one of today's most popular Shakespearean plays. The tragic story of star-crossed lovers is read and performed in high schools everywhere.

Which verb best completes the first sentence? **(67, 69)**

(A) were
(B) was
(C) are
(D) is

16. Read the following sentences.

> Thanks, Julie, for the wool socks you knitted for me. _____ will keep my feet toasty all winter.

Which pronoun best completes the second sentence? **(63)**

(A) You
(B) She
(C) They
(D) We

17. Read the following sentences.

> Violet clasped her hands together and gave Dad her most pleading look. "_____ I go to the concert?" she asked.

Which auxiliary verb best completes the second sentence? **(72)**

(A) Can
(B) May
(C) Must
(D) Could

18. Read the following paragraph.

> [1] The sights and sounds of the rain forest were almost overwhelming. [2] The loud squawking of exotic birds filled the air. [3] Swinging from tree to tree, we saw the cutest monkeys. [4] And when we listened closely, we could hear the roar of a distant waterfall.

Which sentence contains a misplaced modifier? **(70)**

(A) sentence 1
(B) sentence 2
(C) sentence 3
(D) sentence 4

19. Read the following sentences.

> The Charleston was the _____ dance of the 1920s. It involved twisting the feet and kicking them forward and backward.

Which word or words best complete the first sentence? **(71)**

(A) popularest
(B) most popular
(C) more popular
(D) popularer

20. Read the following sentences.

> Marisol is clearly the more conscientious twin. She checked her homework <u>more carefully</u> than Miranda did.

What part of the second sentence is underlined?

(A) comparative adverb   **(71)**
(B) comparative adjective
(C) superlative adverb
(D) superlative adjective

Read this text and answer the questions on the next page.

Folk Art's Great Grandma

1   Most artists know at an early age that they want to spend their lives

2 drawing, painting, sculpting, designing, or composing. As soon as they can hold

3 a brush or a pencil, they begin to create art. The iconic American painter known

4 as Grandma Moses took a very different path. Her career as an artist began in

5 the late 1930s . . . when she was 76 years old!

6   Anna Mary Robertson Moses was born in greenwich, New York, in 1860.

7 She attended a one room country schoolhouse, worked on a farm, married, and

8 then farmed with her husband in Virginia and New York. She had no formal

9 artistic training: but she enjoyed embroidery, the art of decorating fabric with

10 yarn and thread. When Moses was in her seventies, her hands were afflicted

11 with arthritis—this hardship turned into a stroke of luck—and she took up

12 painting because she could still hold a brush. She mostly painted country and

13 farm scenes that she remembered from her already long life. Her subjects were

14 depicted going about their daily activities, such as collecting maple sugar and

15 bringing in hay, all against the backdrop of scenic hills and forests.

16   In 1938, Louis J Calder an art collector, was driving through a nearby town

17 and saw some of Moses's paintings displayed in a drugstore. He was charmed

18 by their joyfulness and beautiful simplicity and bought several on the spot.

19 Soon Grandma Moses saw her paintings exhibited at New Yorks Museum Of

20 Modern Art. They were featured on greeting cards fabrics, and, decorative tiles.

21 One of her works, *Fourth of July*, even hangs in the White House. Moses painted

22 until her death at age 101. This late bloomer completed more than 1,600 works!

(Numbers in parentheses identify related lessons.)
Read each item carefully. Fill in the circle next to the best answer.

1. What change, if any, should be made to the underlined words in lines 4–5? **(80, 81)**

   Ⓐ NO CHANGE
   Ⓑ 1930s-when she
   Ⓒ 1930s (when she
   Ⓓ 1930s; when she

2. What change, if any, should be made to the underlined words in line 6? **(73)**

   Ⓐ NO CHANGE
   Ⓑ Greenwich, new york
   Ⓒ greenwich, new york
   Ⓓ Greenwich, New York

3. What change, if any, should be made to the underlined words in lines 7–8? **(79)**

   Ⓐ NO CHANGE
   Ⓑ one-room country schoolhouse
   Ⓒ one—room country schoolhouse
   Ⓓ (one room) country schoolhouse

4. What change, if any, should be made to the underlined words in lines 8–10? **(77)**

   Ⓐ NO CHANGE
   Ⓑ training but, she
   Ⓒ training but she
   Ⓓ training, but she

5. What change, if any, should be made to the underlined words in lines 10–12? **(79, 81)**

   Ⓐ NO CHANGE
   Ⓑ stroke of luck and
   Ⓒ stroke of luck, and
   Ⓓ stroke of luck . . . and

6. What change, if any, should be made to the underlined words in lines 16–17? **(75, 77)**

   Ⓐ NO CHANGE
   Ⓑ Louis J. Calder an art collector
   Ⓒ Louis J. Calder, an art collector,
   Ⓓ Louis j. Calder, an art collector

7. What change, if any, should be made to the underlined words in lines 19–20? **(73, 76)**

   Ⓐ NO CHANGE
   Ⓑ New York's Museum of Modern Art
   Ⓒ New Yorks' museum of Modern Art
   Ⓓ New York's Museum of modern art

8. What change, if any, should be made to the underlined words in line 20? **(77)**

   Ⓐ NO CHANGE
   Ⓑ cards fabrics and decorative tiles
   Ⓒ cards, fabrics and decorative, tiles
   Ⓓ cards, fabrics, and decorative tiles

Read each item carefully. Fill in the circle next to the best answer.

9. Read the following sentences.

> The famous lines that appear on the Statue of Liberty's pedestal were written by Emma Lazarus. They are from an 1883 poem called _____

Which title completes the second sentence and is correct? (74)

(A) *The New Colossus.*
(B) "*The New Colossus.*"
(C) "The New Colossus."
(D) The New Colossus.

10. Read the following sentences.

> The North Atlantic Treaty Organization is a group of countries, mainly in Europe and North America, that are allies. _____ was formed in 1949.

Which acronym completes the second sentence and is correct? (75)

(A) nato
(B) NATO
(C) N.A.T.O
(D) Nato

11. Read the following sentences.

> Many of the _____ toys were left scattered all over the floor. I almost tripped over a set of blocks!

Which word best completes the first sentence? (76)

(A) childrens
(B) childrens'
(C) children's
(D) childrens's

12. Read the following sentences.

> "This weather _____ prevent us from getting to the cabin," Mr. Kim said confidently. "I have very good snow tires!"

Which contraction best completes the first sentence? (76)

(A) won't
(B) willn't
(C) wasn't
(D) would've

13. Read the following sentences.

> [1] I thought New Mexico would be a hot, dusty wasteland. [2] I was wrong. [3] The mountains and piñon trees are gorgeous.

What is the best way to combine sentences 1 and 2? (11, 15, 77)

(A) I thought New Mexico would be a hot, dusty wasteland so I was wrong.
(B) I thought New Mexico would be a hot, dusty wasteland, but I was wrong.
(C) I thought New Mexico would be a hot, dusty wasteland and I was wrong.
(D) I thought New Mexico would be a hot, dusty wasteland because I was wrong.

14. Read the following paragraph.

> [1] Travis an obsessive planner, was bothering us again. [2] "I think we need to make a list of things to take on the camping trip, don't you?" he said. [3] Too tired to argue, we nodded our heads. [4] Travis immediately found a pen, paper, and his travel guide.

Which sentence is missing a comma? (77, 82)

(A) sentence 1
(B) sentence 2
(C) sentence 3
(D) sentence 4

Read each item carefully. Fill in the circle next to the best answer.

15. Read the following sentences.

> Stephanie is allergic to peanuts_____
> therefore, we should plan to make a
> different kind of dessert. This recipe
> for chocolate cream pie looks good.

Which punctuation mark best completes the first sentence? **(78)**

- Ⓐ colon
- Ⓑ semicolon
- Ⓒ comma
- Ⓓ no punctuation

16. Read the following sentences.

> John Quincy Adams _____ the son
> of John Adams _____ was the sixth
> president of the United States. He
> was later elected to the House of
> Representatives.

Which punctuation marks best complete the first sentence? **(79–81)**

- Ⓐ hyphens
- Ⓑ ellipses
- Ⓒ parentheses
- Ⓓ apostrophes

17. Read the following sentences from a business letter.

> I am writing to inform you that the
> swings in Creekside Park are in need
> of repair. As you are the director of
> the Hale Recreation Department, I
> hope you will remedy this dangerous
> situation.

Which greeting should be used in this letter? **(84)**

- Ⓐ Dear Lois,
- Ⓑ Dear Ms Santorini:
- Ⓒ Dear Ms. Santorini,
- Ⓓ Dear Ms. Santorini:

18. Read the following sentences.

> "Yes, I would love to go to the
> beach with _____ said. "Just let me
> grab my towel and sunscreen."

Which words and punctuation best complete the first sentence? **(82)**

- Ⓐ you Rosa," Molly
- Ⓑ you, Rosa." Molly
- Ⓒ you, Rosa," Molly
- Ⓓ you, Rosa, Molly

19. Read the following sentences.

> This book I'm reading about Native
> American myths and legends is
> so interesting. The author _____
> told stories of two giant birds who
> created thunder and lightning."

Which words and punctuation best complete the second sentence? **(83)**

- Ⓐ writes "The Choctaw
- Ⓑ writes, "The Choctaw
- Ⓒ writes, The Choctaw
- Ⓓ writes: The Choctaw

20. Read the following paragraph.

> [1] Thea pulled a book out of her
> bag and showed it to Danny. [2]
> "This novel about a girl searching
> for her brother is really inspiring,"
> she said. [3] Then she pointed to a
> page that said, "While finding my
> brother, I also found myself."

Where is the best place to add the following sentence? **(82, 83)**

> Danny replied to Thea's
> announcement with a quizzical look.

- Ⓐ Before sentence 1
- Ⓑ After sentence 1
- Ⓒ After sentence 2
- Ⓓ After sentence 3

Grammar, Usage, and Mechanics Handbook
Table of Contents

Mechanics

Sentence Structure and Parts of Speech

(Continued on page 362)

(Continued from page 361)

Usage

Letters and E-mails

Research

Guidelines for Listening and Speaking

<u>(you)</u> | Diagram | sentences

Mechanics

- **Capitalize the first word in a sentence.**   <u>T</u>he kangaroo rat is an amazing animal.
- **Capitalize all *proper nouns*, including people's names and the names of particular places.**
  <u>G</u>regory <u>G</u>ordon   <u>W</u>ashington <u>M</u>onument
- **Capitalize titles of respect.**   <u>M</u>r. Alvarez   <u>D</u>r. Chin   <u>M</u>s. Murphy
- **Capitalize family titles used just before people's names and titles of respect that are part of names.**
  <u>U</u>ncle <u>F</u>rank   <u>A</u>unt <u>M</u>ary   <u>G</u>overnor <u>A</u>damson
- **Capitalize initials of names.**
  <u>T</u>homas <u>P</u>aul <u>G</u>erard (<u>T</u>. <u>P</u>. <u>G</u>erard)
- **Capitalize place names.**   <u>F</u>rance   <u>U</u>tah   <u>C</u>hina   <u>B</u>altimore
- **Capitalize *proper adjectives*, adjectives that are made from proper nouns.**
  <u>C</u>hinese   <u>I</u>celandic   <u>F</u>rench   <u>L</u>atin <u>A</u>merican
- **Capitalize the months of the year and the days of the week.**
  <u>F</u>ebruary   <u>A</u>pril   <u>M</u>onday   <u>T</u>uesday
- **Capitalize important words in the names of products and companies.**
  <u>B</u>lue <u>B</u>rook <u>C</u>heese <u>S</u>pread   <u>H</u>eart of <u>G</u>old <u>A</u>pplesauce
  <u>L</u>ittle <u>H</u>ills <u>B</u>akery   <u>A</u>nderson and <u>M</u>umford, <u>I</u>nc.
- **Capitalize important words in the names of organizations.**
  <u>A</u>merican <u>L</u>ung <u>A</u>ssociation   <u>V</u>eterans of <u>F</u>oreign <u>W</u>ars
- **Capitalize important words in the names of holidays.**
  <u>V</u>eterans <u>D</u>ay   <u>F</u>ourth of <u>J</u>uly
- **Capitalize the first word in the greeting or closing of a letter.**
  <u>D</u>ear Edmundo,   <u>Y</u>ours truly,
- **Capitalize the word *I*.**   Frances and <u>I</u> watched the movie together.
- **Capitalize the first, last, and most important words in a title. Be sure to capitalize all verbs, including *is* and *was*.**
  <u>I</u>sland of the <u>B</u>lue <u>D</u>olphins   *<u>A</u>way <u>I</u>s a <u>S</u>trange <u>P</u>lace to <u>B</u>e*
- **Capitalize the first word in a direct quotation.**
  Aunt Rose said, "<u>P</u>lease pass the clam dip."

Abbreviations are shortened forms of words. Many abbreviations begin with an uppercase letter and end with a period.
- **You can abbreviate words used in addresses when you write.**
  Street (**St.**)   Avenue (**Ave.**)   Route (**Rte.**)   Boulevard (**Blvd.**)   Road (**Rd.**)   Drive (**Dr.**)
- **Use postal abbreviations for names of states in addresses.**

Note: State names are abbreviated as two uppercase letters, with no periods.

Alabama (AL)	Idaho (ID)	Missouri (MO)	Pennsylvania (PA)
Alaska (AK)	Illinois (IL)	Montana (MT)	Rhode Island (RI)
Arizona (AZ)	Indiana (IN)	Nebraska (NE)	South Carolina (SC)
Arkansas (AR)	Iowa (IA)	Nevada (NV)	South Dakota (SD)
California (CA)	Kansas (KS)	New Hampshire (NH)	Tennessee (TN)
Colorado (CO)	Kentucky (KY)	New Jersey (NJ)	Texas (TX)
Connecticut (CT)	Louisiana (LA)	New Mexico (NM)	Utah (UT)
Delaware (DE)	Maine (ME)	New York (NY)	Vermont (VT)
District of	Maryland (MD)	North Carolina (NC)	Virginia (VA)
Columbia (DC)	Massachusetts (MA)	North Dakota (ND)	Washington (WA)
Florida (FL)	Michigan (MI)	Ohio (OH)	West Virginia (WV)
Georgia (GA)	Minnesota (MN)	Oklahoma (OK)	Wisconsin (WI)
Hawaii (HI)	Mississippi (MS)	Oregon (OR)	Wyoming (WY)

- **You can abbreviate titles of address and titles of respect when you write.**
  Mister (**Mr.** Brian Davis)　　Mistress (**Miss** or **Mrs.** Maria Rosario)　　General (**Gen.** Robert E. Lee)
  Doctor (**Dr.** Emily Chu)　　Junior (Everett Castle **Jr.**)　　Saint (**St.** Andrew)

Note: *Ms.* is a title of address used for women. It is not an abbreviation, but it requires a period (**Ms.** Anita Brown).

- **You can abbreviate certain words in the names of businesses when you write.**
  Pet Helpers, Incorporated (Pet Helpers, **Inc.**)　　Zykar Corporation (Zykar **Corp.**)

- **You can abbreviate days of the week when you take notes.**

Sunday (**Sun.**)	Wednesday (**Wed.**)	Friday (**Fri.**)
Monday (**Mon.**)	Thursday (**Thurs.**)	Saturday (**Sat.**)
Tuesday (**Tues.**)		

- **You can abbreviate months of the year when you take notes.**

January (**Jan.**)	April (**Apr.**)	October (**Oct.**)
February (**Feb.**)	August (**Aug.**)	November (**Nov.**)
March (**Mar.**)	September (**Sept.**)	December (**Dec.**)

  (May, June, and July do not have abbreviated forms.)

- **You can abbreviate directions when you take notes.**
  North (**N**)　　East (**E**)　　South (**S**)　　West (**W**)

An *initial* is the first letter of a name. An initial is written as an uppercase letter and a period. Sometimes initials are used in the names of countries or other places.
　　Michael Paul Sanders (**M. P.** Sanders)　　United States of America (**U. S. A.**)
　　Washington, District of Columbia (Washington, **D. C.**)

An *acronym* is a special type of abbreviation that is formed from the first letters of a group of words. Some acronyms, such as *NASA* (National Aeronautics and Space Administration), are written in all capitals. Others, such as *scuba* (self-contained underwater breathing apparatus), are written as regular words, in all-lowercase letters.

Section 3 Titles

- **Underline titles of books, newspapers, TV series, movies, and magazines.**
  <u>Island of the Blue Dolphins</u>　　<u>Miami Herald</u>　　<u>I Love Lucy</u>

Note: These titles are written in italics in printed text.

- **Use quotation marks around articles in magazines, short stories, chapters in books, songs, and poems.**
  "This Land Is Your Land"　　"The Gift"　　"Eletelephony"

- **Capitalize the first, last, and most important words in titles. Articles, short prepositions, and conjunctions are usually not capitalized. Be sure to capitalize all verbs, including forms of the verb** *be* (*am, is, are, was, were, been*).
  A Knight in the Attic　　　　*My Brother Sam Is Dead*

Section 4 Quotations and Quotation Marks

- **Put quotation marks ("　") around the titles of articles, short stories, book chapters, songs, and poems.**
  My favorite short story is "Revenge of the Reptiles."

- **Put quotation marks around a** *direct quotation,* **a speaker's exact words or direct speech.**
  "Did you see that alligator?" Max asked.

- **Do not put quotation marks around an** *indirect quotation,* **a person's words retold by another speaker. An indirect quotation is often signaled by** *whether* **or** *that.*
  Max asked Rory whether he had seen an alligator.

Writing a Conversation

- Put quotation marks around the speaker's words. Begin a direct quotation with an uppercase letter. Use a comma to separate the quotation from the rest of the sentence.
  Rory said, "There are no alligators in this area."

- When a direct quotation comes at the end of a sentence, put the end mark inside the last quotation mark.
  Max cried, "Look out!"

- When writing a conversation, begin a new paragraph with each change of speaker.
  Max panted, "I swear I saw a huge scaly tail and a flat snout in the water!"

  "Relax," Rory said. "I told you there are no alligators around here."

- Put quotation marks around a quotation from a text. Include information on the source of the quotation.
  In his letter from the Birmingham jail, which was reprinted in the *Atlantic Monthly* (August 1963), the great civil rights leader Martin Luther King Jr. wrote, "Injustice anywhere is a threat to justice everywhere."

Writing a Long Quotation From a Text

- Set off a lengthy quotation from the rest of an essay or a report, either by indenting the whole block of text or by printing it in smaller type. Do not use quotation marks at the beginning and end of the quotation.
- Give source information either in the sentence that precedes the quotation or in indented lines below the quotation.

  And then as the little plane climbed higher and Olive saw spread out below them fields of bright and tender green in this morning sun, farther out the coastline, the ocean shiny and almost flat, tiny white wakes behind a few lobster boats—then Olive felt something she had not expected to feel again: a sudden surging greediness for life. She leaned forward, peering out the window: sweet pale clouds, the sky as blue as your hat, the new green of the fields, the broad expanse of water—seen from up here it all appeared wondrous, amazing. She remembered what hope was, and this was it. That inner churning that moves you forward, plows you through life the way the boats plowed the shiny water, the way the plane was plowing forward to a place new, and where she was needed.

  —Elizabeth Strout,
  Olive Kitteridge

Section 5 Spelling

Use these tips if you are not sure how to spell a word you want to write:
- Say the word aloud and break it into syllables. Try spelling each syllable. Put the syllables together to spell the whole word.
- Write the word. Make sure there is a vowel in every syllable. If the word looks wrong to you, try spelling it other ways.
- Think of a related word. Parts of related words are often spelled the same.
  Decide is related to *decision*.

Correct spelling helps readers understand what you write. Use a dictionary when you need help. When you use the word-processing function of a computer to write something, you can use the spell-check feature. It will identify possible spelling errors in your writing. A spell checker will not catch errors with homophones, though. For example, if you type *break* instead of *brake*, the spell checker will not catch the mistake, because the word is spelled correctly.

Every sentence must end with a period, an exclamation point, or a question mark.

- Use a *period* at the end of a statement (declarative sentence) or a command (imperative sentence).

  Dad and I look alike. (*declarative*)   Step back very slowly. (*imperative*)

- Use an *exclamation point* at the end of a firm command (imperative sentence) or at the end of a sentence that shows great feeling or excitement (exclamatory sentence).

  Get away from the cliff! (*imperative*)   That is an incredible sight! (*exclamatory*)

- Use a *question mark* at the end of an asking sentence (interrogative sentence).

  How many miles is it to Tucson? (*interrogative*)

Section 7 Apostrophes

An apostrophe (') is used to form the possessive of a noun or to join words in a contraction.

- Possessives show ownership. To make a singular noun possessive, add *'s*.

  The bike belongs to Carmen. It is Carmen's bike.

- To form a possessive from a plural noun that ends in *-s*, add only an apostrophe.

  Those books belong to my sisters. They are my sisters' books.

- Some plural nouns do not end in *-s*. To form possessives with these nouns, add *'s*.

  The children left their boots here. The children's boots are wet.

- Use an apostrophe to replace the dropped letter(s) in a contraction.

  it's (it is)   hasn't (has not)

Section 8 Commas, Semicolons, and Colons

Commas in Sentences

- Use a comma after an introductory word in a sentence.

  Yes, I'd love to go to the movies.   Actually, we had a great time.

- Use a comma after a mild interjection at the beginning of a sentence.

  Oh, it has started raining.   Hey, just grab an umbrella!

- Use a comma to separate items in a series. A series is a list of three or more items. Put the last comma before *and* or *or*. A comma is not needed to separate two items.

  Shall we eat cheese, bread, or fruit?   Let's eat cheese and fruit.

- Use a comma to separate a noun of direct address from the rest of a sentence.

  Akila, will you please stand up?   We would like you to sing, Akila.

- Use a comma to separate a tag question from the rest of a sentence.

  "It's a hot day, isn't it?" remarked Jill.

- Use a comma to separate a direct quotation, or direct speech, from the rest of a sentence.

  Joe asked, "How long must I sit here?"   "You must sit there for one hour," Vic said.

- Use a comma with the conjunction *and, or,* or *but* when combining independent clauses in a compound sentence.

  Lisa liked the reptiles best, but Lyle preferred the amphibians.

- Use a comma to separate a dependent clause at the beginning of a sentence from the rest of the sentence.

  Because Lisa likes reptiles, she is considering a career as a herpetologist.

- Use a comma to separate coordinate adjectives—a pair of adjectives of a similar kind. To decide whether to put a comma between adjectives, try reading the sentence with the word *and* inserted between the adjectives. If the word *and* sounds natural there, you should use a comma.

  Reptiles have dry, scaly skin. (*needs a comma*)

  Look at that big green lizard! (*does not need a comma*)

- Use commas to set off a clause or phrase that presents information that is not necessary for understanding the main idea of a sentence.

  Alaska, the largest state in the Union, offers summer visitors the opportunity to see the midnight sun.

- Use commas to set off a nonrestrictive adjective clause. A nonrestrictive clause is one that adds information about the word it modifies but is not essential to the meaning of the sentence. Walt Jackson, <u>who sold me a turtle last year,</u> has a new pet gecko. (*The adjective clause just tells more about the noun it modifies. Because the information in the clause is not essential, the clause is nonrestrictive. Commas are needed.*)

  The woman <u>who runs the pet store</u> offered me a job. (*The adjective clause tells which woman is being talked about. Because the information in the clause is essential, no commas are used.*)

Semicolons and Colons in Sentences

- You may use a semicolon in place of a comma and a conjunction when combining independent clauses.
  Lisa likes reptiles; Lyle prefers amphibians.
- A colon can be used when the second clause states a direct result of the first or explains the first.
  Lisa owns reptiles: she has two pet snakes.
- Use a colon to introduce a list or series.
  I like three kinds of cheese: cheddar, Swiss, and colby.
- Use a colon to introduce a quotation.
  Cory always follows this motto: "A penny saved is a penny earned."
- Use a colon after the speaker's name in a play.
  LOGAN: Where were you on the night of October 5th, when the gold bullion was stolen?
  BLAKE: I was attending the opening night of *Carmen* at the opera house.
- Use a colon to separate hours and minutes in an expression of time.
  8:15 P.M.   11:45 A.M.
- Use a colon between the city of publication and the publisher in a bibliographic entry.
  O'Dell, Scott. *The Cruise of the Arctic Star.* Boston: Houghton Mifflin, 1973.

Commas With Dates and Place Names

- Use a comma to separate the day from the date and the date from the year.
  We clinched the division championship on Saturday, September 20, 20___.
- Use a comma to separate the name of a city or town from the name of a state.
  I visited Memphis, Tennessee.

Commas and Colons in Letters

- Use a comma after the greeting and the closing of a friendly letter.
  Dear Reginald,   Your friend, Deke
- Use a colon after the greeting of a business letter. Use a comma after the closing.
  Dear Ms. Brocklehurst: Sincerely,

Section 9 | Hyphens, Parentheses, Dashes, and Ellipses

Hyphens in Sentences

- When you break a word at the end of a line, use a hyphen to separate the syllables.
  There is no single "perfect food." Milk, for example, contains most of the nutrients needed by the human body, but it lacks enough iron.
- Use hyphens to link the parts of some compound words.
  <u>son-in-law</u>   <u>city-state</u>
- Use hyphens to link some pairs or groups of words that precede a noun and act as an adjective.
  a <u>family-style</u> meal   a <u>horse-drawn</u> carriage   an <u>up-to-date</u> schedule
- Use hyphens to link the parts of numbers between twenty-one and ninety-nine.
  eighty-two   fifty-seven   seventy-six   thirty-five

Parentheses in Sentences

- Use parentheses to set off an explanation.
  I interviewed my uncle <u>(he raises goats for a living)</u> for my report on animal husbandry.
  Rolf and Dana's farm is 100 miles <u>(160 km)</u> outside of Chicago.
- Use parentheses to set off an example.
  Many types of cheese <u>(chèvre, for example)</u> are made with goats' milk.

Dashes in Sentences

- Use a long dash to signal a pause.
- Use long dashes to set off some types of nonessential information from the other parts of a sentence. An authorial comment may be set off with long dashes.
  Tall sunflowers—my personal favorite among American wildflowers—grow on prairies across much of the United States.
- Use a long dash to mark an unfinished sentence.
  The door slowly opened, and—
- Use a long dash to stress a word or phrase at the end of a sentence.
  Only one thing can make me happy—a victory.

Ellipses in Sentences

- An ellipsis is a series of three spaced periods.
- Use an ellipsis to mark the omission of words from a quotation.
  No man can always be right. So the struggle is to do one's best; to keep the brain and conscience clear; never to be swayed by unworthy motives or inconsequential reasons, but to strive to unearth the basic factors involved and then do one's duty.
  —Dwight D. Eisenhower,
in a letter to Mamie Eisenhower
  No man can always be right. So the struggle is to do one's best; to keep the brain and conscience clear . . . to strive to unearth the basic factors involved and then do one's duty.
  —Dwight D. Eisenhower,
in a letter to Mamie Eisenhower
- Use an ellipsis to signal a pause.
  We were told that the speaker would step onto the stage momentarily. We waited . . . and waited . . . and waited.
- When you use an ellipsis after words that are not a complete sentence, leave a space before the first spaced period.
  Our conservation must be . . . a creative conservation of restoration and innovation.
  —Lyndon B. Johnson,
in a message to Congress,
February 8, 1965
- When you use an ellipsis after a sentence, use the sentence's end mark, and leave a space between it and the first spaced period.
  Vigorous writing is concise. . . . This requires not that the writer make all his sentences short, or that he avoid all detail and treat his subjects only in outline, but that every word tell.
  —William Strunk Jr.
The Elements of Style

Sentence Structure and Parts of Speech

Section 10 The Sentence

A *sentence* is a group of words that tells a complete thought. A sentence has two parts: a *subject* and a *predicate*.

- The subject tells *whom* or *what* the sentence is about. The swimmers race.
- The predicate tells what the subject *is* or *does*. The judges watch carefully.

There are four kinds of sentences: *declarative, interrogative, imperative,* and *exclamatory.*

- A *declarative sentence* makes a statement and ends with a period.
  Jake swam faster than anyone.

- An *interrogative sentence* asks a question and ends with a question mark.
  Did Sammy qualify for the finals?

- An *imperative sentence* gives a command and usually ends with a period; a firm command can end with an exclamation point.
  Keep your eyes on the finish line.   Watch out for that bee!

- An *exclamatory sentence* ends with an exclamation point.   Jake has won the race!

Section 11 Subjects

The *subject* of a sentence tells whom or what the sentence is about.

- A sentence can have one subject.   Mary wrote a book.
- A sentence can have a *compound subject,* two or more subjects that are joined by a conjunction (*and, or*) and that share the same predicate.
  Alex and Mark have already read the book.

- Imperative sentences have an unnamed *understood subject,* the person being spoken to. This subject is referred to as "understood *you.*"   Give me the book, please.
- The *complete subject* includes all the words that name and tell about the subject.
  Many students have borrowed the book.
- The *simple subject* is the most important noun or pronoun in the complete subject.
  Many students have borrowed the book.   They discussed the book yesterday.

  Note: Sometimes the simple subject and the complete subject are the same.

  Ricardo is writing a book.

Section 12 Predicates

The *predicate* of a sentence tells what happened. The *complete predicate* includes a verb and all the words that tell what happened or tell more about the subject.

- A complete predicate can include an action verb to tell what the subject of the sentence did.
  Mary *won* an award.
- A complete predicate can include a linking verb to tell more about the subject.
  Mary *is* a talented writer.

The *simple predicate* is the verb that goes with the subject. It generally tells what the subject did, does, or will do.

  Celia won an award for her performance.

  She will receive a trophy next week.

A *compound predicate* is two or more predicates that share the same subject. Compound predicates are often joined by the conjunction *and* or *or.*

  Ramon sang and danced in the play.

  Mary wrote the play and directed it.

A *predicate noun* follows a linking verb and renames the subject.

  Mary is a writer.   Ramon is a singer.

A *predicate adjective* follows a linking verb and describes the subject.

  Mary is talented.   Ramon is clever.

Section 13 Clauses and Sentence Types

A *simple sentence* tells one complete thought.

> Arthur has a rock collection.

A *compound sentence* is made up of two simple sentences (or *independent clauses*) whose ideas are related. The clauses can be joined by a comma and a conjunction (*and, or, but*).

> Arthur has a rock collection**, and** Mary collects shells.

The two independent clauses in a compound sentence can also be joined by a semicolon.

> Arthur collects rocks**;** Mary collects shells.

Two clauses in a compound sentence can be separated by a colon when the second clause is a direct result of the first clause.

> Arthur enjoys visiting new places**:** he can hunt for rocks to add to his collection.

A *complex sentence* is made up of one independent clause and at least one dependent clause.
A *dependent clause* is a group of words that has a subject and a predicate, but it cannot stand on its own.

> Dependent Clause: when Arthur visited Arizona
> Independent Clause: He learned a lot about desert plants.
> Complex Sentence: When Arthur visited Arizona, he learned a lot about desert plants.

A *compound-complex sentence* includes two or more independent clauses and at least one dependent clause.

> Independent Clauses: Arizona is proud of its saguaro cactus.
>   The saguaro cactus can grow up to sixty feet tall.
> Dependent Clause: which is also called the giant cactus
> Compound-complex Sentence: Arizona is proud of its saguaro cactus; the saguaro, which is also called the giant cactus, can grow up to sixty feet tall.

An *adjective clause* is a dependent clause that describes a noun or pronoun. An adjective clause always follows the word it describes and begins with a relative pronoun such as *who, whom, whose, which,* or *that*.

> My cousin Arthur, **who has a rock collection**, visited the Arizona desert. (*describes* Arthur)
> He studied the interesting rock formations **that rise above the desert floor**. (*describes* formations)

An *adverb clause* is a dependent clause that tells more about a verb, an adjective, or an adverb. Adverb clauses tell *where, when, why,* or *how much*. They often begin with a subordinating conjunction such as *after, since, where, than, although, because, if, as, as if, while, when,* or *whenever*.

> **Whenever Arthur came across an unfamiliar rock**, he took a photograph of it.
>
> (*tells* when *Arthur* took *a photograph*)
>
> Arthur didn't take any rocks away **because the desert environment is fragile**.
>
> (*tells* why *Arthur* didn't take *rocks away*)

A *noun clause* is a dependent clause that functions as the subject of a sentence or the object of a verb. A noun clause begins with a relative pronoun.

> She said **that the floor was slippery**. (*The noun clause* that the floor was slippery *is the direct object of the verb* said.)

Most simple sentences and independent clauses follow what is called the *natural order* of sentence elements: first the subject; then the verb; then the direct object, predicate noun, or predicate adjective.

> S   V   DO   S V   DO
> I will take the turkey with me; I will leave the yams behind.
>
>   S LV PA
> The leaves are green.

In some simple sentences and independent clauses, a verb, direct object, predicate noun, or predicate adjective comes before the subject. A sentence with this order of elements is said to have *inverted order*.

>   DO S V   DO S V
> The turkey I will take with me; the yams I will leave behind.
>
>   PA LV   S
> Green are the leaves.

A sentence in which a dependent clause appears between the subject and the verb is said to have *interrupted order.*

| S | DC | LV | PN |

Thanksgiving, which came early this year, is my favorite holiday.

Section 14 Fragments, Run-ons, Comma Splices, and Ramble-ons

A *fragment* is an incomplete sentence that does not tell a complete thought.
> Sumi and Ali. (*missing a predicate that tells what happened*)
> Went hiking in the woods. (*missing a subject that tells who went hiking*)

A *run-on sentence* is two complete sentences that are run together. To fix a run-on sentence, use a comma and a conjunction (*and, or, but*) to join the two sentences. (You may also join the sentences with a semicolon.)

| Incorrect: | Sumi went hiking Ali went swimming. |
| Correct: | Sumi went hiking, **but** Ali went swimming. |

A *comma splice* is two complete sentences that have a comma between them but are missing a conjunction (*and, or, but*). To fix a comma splice, add *and, or,* or *but* after the comma.

| Incorrect: | Sumi went hiking yesterday, Ali went swimming. |
| Correct: | Sumi went hiking yesterday, **and** Ali went swimming. |

A *ramble-on sentence* is grammatically correct but contains extra words that don't add to its meaning.

| Incorrect: | Hiking through the wilderness to enjoy nature is my favorite outdoor sports activity, probably because it is so enjoyable and such good exercise, and because I enjoy observing wild animals in the wilderness in their natural environment. |
| Correct: | Hiking through the wilderness to enjoy nature is my favorite outdoor sports activity. I enjoy observing wild animals in their natural environment. |

Try not to string too many short sentences together when you write. Instead, combine sentences and take out unnecessary information.

| Incorrect: | I stared at him and he stared at me and I told him to go away and he wouldn't so then I called my big sister. |
| Correct: | We stared at each other. I told him to go away, but he wouldn't. Then I called my big sister. |

Section 15 Nouns

A *common noun* names any person, place, thing, or idea.
> Ira visited an auto <u>museum</u> with his <u>friends</u>. Ira has always had an <u>interest</u> in <u>cars</u>. He likes that blue <u>convertible</u>.

A *proper noun* names a certain person, place, thing, or idea. Proper nouns begin with an uppercase letter. A proper noun that is made up of two or more words is considered one noun.
> <u>Ira</u> wants to visit the <u>Sonoran Desert</u> in <u>Mexico</u> in <u>April</u>.
> He is reading a guidebook about the region entitled ***The Undiscovered Desert***.

A *collective noun* names a group of people or things that act as one unit.
> jury   family   committee   audience   crowd

- Most often, a collective noun is treated as a singular subject.
  The **track** <u>**team is**</u> the strongest one we've had in years.

- Sometimes, if a writer wants to emphasize the different members of a group, he or she may treat the noun as a plural subject.
  The **track** <u>**team are**</u> congratulating one another on their fine performances.

- A noun can also be used to describe another noun:
  <u>freeway</u> exit
  <u>eye</u> chart
  <u>ocean</u> current

A *concrete noun* names something you can see, touch, hear, smell, or taste.
> dog   meadow   pebble   stove

An *abstract noun* names an idea, a quality, or a characteristic.
> freedom   bravery   freshness   excellence

An *adjective* is a word that tells more about a noun or a pronoun.

- Some adjectives tell what kind.
  Jim observed the <u>huge</u> elephant. The <u>enormous</u> beast towered above him.

- Some adjectives tell how many.
  The elephant was <u>twelve</u> feet tall. It weighed <u>several</u> tons.

- A *predicate adjective* follows a linking verb and describes the subject.
  Jim was <u>careful</u> not to anger the elephant. He was <u>happy</u> when the trainer led it away.

- *A, an,* and *the* are special kinds of adjectives called *articles*. Use *a* and *an* to refer to any person, place, thing, or idea. Use *the* to refer to a specific person, place, thing, or idea. Use *a* before a singular noun that begins with a consonant sound. Use *an* before a singular noun that begins with a vowel sound.
  <u>An</u> elephant is heavier than <u>a</u> rhino. <u>The</u> elephant in this picture is six weeks old.

- A *demonstrative adjective* tells which one. *This, that, these,* and *those* can be used as demonstrative adjectives. Use *this* and *these* to talk about things that are nearby. Use *that* and *those* to talk about things that are farther away.
  <u>This</u> book is about rhinos.   <u>These</u> rhinos just came to the zoo.
  <u>That</u> rhino is enormous!   <u>Those</u> funny-looking creatures are wildebeests.

  Note: Never use *here* or *there* after the adjectives *this, that, these,* and *those.*

- A *proper adjective* is made from a proper noun. Capitalize proper adjectives.
  <u>Italian</u> cooking   <u>Democratic</u> convention   <u>Apache</u> legend

- Two or more adjectives can be used to describe a noun. When you use two or more adjectives to describe a noun, put the adjectives in an order that sounds natural. This chart can help you.

how many	what quality	how big	how old	what shape	what color	what material	→ noun
three	*beautiful*	*small*	*new*	*round*	*pink*	*silken*	→ *petals*

Section 17 Pronouns

A *pronoun* can replace a noun.

17a Personal Pronouns

Personal pronouns include *I, me, you, we, us, he, him, she, her, it, they,* and *them.* Personal pronouns can be used to stand for the person speaking, the person spoken to, or the person spoken about.

- *First-person pronouns* refer to the speaker (*I, me*) or include the speaker (*we, us*).
  Let <u>me</u> know when <u>I</u> am next at bat.   It took <u>us</u> hours, but <u>we</u> managed to get to the stadium.

- *Second-person pronouns* refer to the person or people being spoken to (*you*).
  Are <u>you</u> going to the game?   I asked Marisa to give the bases to <u>you</u>.

- *Third-person pronouns* refer to the person, people, or thing(s) being spoken about (*he, him, she, her, it, they, them*).
  <u>They</u> played well.   Pass the ball to <u>him</u>.   Kick <u>it</u> to <u>her</u>.

- The third-person pronoun *he* (with *him* and *his*) was once accepted as a universal pronoun that could refer to anyone, male or female, if a generalization about people was being made. Now most writers try to avoid the use of universal *he.*
  One solution to this pronoun problem is to make the pronoun and the word it refers to plural.
  When a chef cooks, <u>he</u> displays creativity. **becomes:** When chefs cook, <u>they</u> display creativity.
  Each player should bring <u>his</u> own racket. **becomes:** Players should bring <u>their</u> own rackets.
  Another solution is to replace *he* with *he or she,* or replace *his* with *his or her.*
  Each player should bring <u>his</u> own racket. **becomes:** Each player should bring <u>his or her</u> own racket.

17b Subject and Object Pronouns

A *subject pronoun* takes the place of the subject of a sentence. Subject pronouns are said to be in the *nominative case*. Subject pronouns include *I, you, he, she, it, we,* and *they*.

<u>Rita</u> is an excellent soccer player. <u>She</u> never lets the other team score.

Note: Do not use both the pronoun and the noun it replaces together.

Incorrect: <u>Rita she</u> made the team.

Correct: <u>Rita</u> made the team. OR She made the team.

An *object pronoun* replaces a noun that is the object of a verb or a preposition. Object pronouns are said to be in the *objective case*. Object pronouns include *me, him, her, us,* and *them*.

Rita's team played the Bobcats. Rita's team beat <u>them</u>.

The pronouns *it* and *you* can be either subjects or objects.

<u>It</u> was a close game. (*subject pronoun*)   The Bobcats almost won <u>it</u>. (*object pronoun*)

- Use a subject pronoun as part of a compound subject. Use an object pronoun as part of a compound object. To test whether a pronoun is correct, say the sentence <u>without</u> the other part of a compound subject or object.
  Incorrect: Rita told Ellen and <u>I</u> it was a close game. (Rita told <u>I</u> it was a close game.)
  Correct: Rita told Ellen and <u>me</u> it was a close game. (Rita told <u>me</u> it was a close game.)

- When the pronouns *I* and *me* are used in a compound with a noun or another pronoun, *I* or *me* always comes second in a pair or last in a series of three or more.
  Incorrect: The coach gave the Most Improved Players awards to <u>me and Carlos</u>.
  Correct: The coach gave the Most Improved Players awards to <u>Carlos and me</u>.

17c Pronoun Antecedents

An *antecedent* is the word or words a pronoun refers to. The antecedent is almost always a noun.

The <u>Bobcats</u> are excellent players. They won every game last season.

- A pronoun must agree with its antecedent. An antecedent and a pronoun agree when they have the same *number* (singular or plural) and *gender* (male or female).
  Nick's <u>mother</u> cheered. <u>She</u> was very excited.

17d Possessive Pronouns

Possessive pronouns show ownership.

- The possessive pronouns *my, your, his, her, its, their,* and *our* replace possessive nouns.
  Those skates belong to <u>my</u> brother Jorge.
  Those are <u>his</u> kneepads, too. (*The pronoun* his *replaces the possessive noun* Jorge's.)

- The possessive pronouns *mine, ours, yours, hers, his, its,* and *theirs* replace both a possessive noun and the noun that is possessed.
  Alisha's kneepads are blue. <u>Mine</u> are red and <u>hers</u> are blue.
  (*The possessive pronoun* hers *replaces both the possessive noun* Alisha's *and the noun* kneepads.)

- *Whose* is the possessive form of the relative pronoun *who*. It is also used as the possessive form of the relative pronoun *which*.
  The skaters <u>whose</u> parents cannot pick them up at 6 P.M. must wait inside the office.
  (Whose *indicates that the parents belong to the skaters.*)

17e Compound Personal Pronouns

Compound personal pronouns can be used as *reflexive pronouns* or *intensive pronouns*.

- A *reflexive pronoun* refers back to the subject of a sentence.
  My brother bought <u>himself</u> a new puck. We cheered for <u>ourselves</u>.

- An *intensive pronoun* emphasizes the identity of the sentence subject.
  I <u>myself</u> am not a hockey fan.

17f Indefinite Pronouns

Indefinite pronouns refer to persons or things that are not identified as individuals. These pronouns include *all, anybody, both, anything, few, most, no one, either, nothing, everyone, one, several, none, everybody, nobody, someone, everything, something, anyone,* and *somebody.*

> <u>Somebody</u> lost the ball. We can't play <u>anything</u> until we find it.

17g Relative Pronouns

When the pronouns *who, whom, whose, which,* and *that* are used to introduce an adjective clause, they are called *relative pronouns.* A relative pronoun always follows the noun it refers to.

> The player <u>who brought the volleyball</u> can serve first.

> I joined the team <u>that chose me.</u>

> This net, <u>which I found in my closet,</u> will be perfect for our volleyball game.

> **Note:** For more information on using *who, whom, which,* and *that,* see Section 32, Problem Words.

17h Interrogative Pronouns

When the pronouns *who, whom, which,* and *what* are used to begin a question, they are called *interrogative pronouns.*

> <u>Who</u> has brought the volleyball?   <u>What</u> is a wicket used for?
> <u>Which</u> is the net for volleyball?   To <u>whom</u> did you hit the ball?

17i Demonstrative Pronouns

This, that, these, and *those* can be used as *demonstrative pronouns.*

- Use *this* and *these* to talk about one or more things that are nearby.
  > <u>This</u> is a soft rug.   <u>These</u> are sweeter than those over there.
- Use *that* and *those* to talk about one or more things that are far away.
  > <u>That</u> is where I sat yesterday.   <u>Those</u> are new chairs.

Section 18 Verbs

18a Action and Linking Verbs

An *action verb* shows action.

> Scientists <u>study</u> the natural world.   They <u>learn</u> how the laws of nature work.

A *linking verb* does not show action. It connects the subject of a sentence to a word or words in the predicate that tell about the subject. Linking verbs include *am, is, are, was, been,* and *were. Seem, appear,* and *become* can be used as linking verbs, too.

> Explorers <u>are</u> brave.   That route <u>seems</u> long and dangerous.

Some verbs, such as *appear, look, smell, feel, grow, sound,* and *taste,* can be either action verbs or linking verbs, depending on how they are used. You can test whether a verb is a linking verb by substituting a form of the verb *be* (*am, is, are, was,* or *were*) in its place. If the form of *be* makes sense, the verb probably is a linking verb.

> I <u>looked</u> at the bear. (*"I was at the bear" does not make sense:* looked *is an action verb.*)

> The bear <u>looked</u> hungry. (*"The bear was hungry" makes sense:* looked *is a linking verb.*)

18b Transitive and Intransitive Verbs

A *transitive verb* is an action verb that transfers its action to a direct object.

> The polar bear <u>watched</u> a seal's air hole in the ice.   The polar bear <u>caught</u> the seal.

An *intransitive verb* does not have a direct object. An intransitive verb shows action that the subject does alone.

> The bear <u>waited</u> patiently.   Suddenly the bear <u>struck.</u>

Many verbs can be either transitive or intransitive, depending on whether or not there is a direct object.

> The bear <u>ate</u> the seal. (*Seal is the direct object:* ate *is a transitive verb.*)

> The bear <u>ate</u> hungrily. (*Hungrily is an adverb, and there is no direct object:* ate *is an intransitive verb.*)

18c Main Verbs and Auxiliary Verbs

A *main verb* is the most important verb in a sentence. An *auxiliary verb,* or helping verb, comes before the main verb to help it show action. Auxiliary verbs such as *had, are,* and *will* indicate the tense of the main verb. Others, such as *could, might,* and *may,* show how likely it is that something will happen.

Certain auxiliary verbs have special functions. The auxiliary verbs *may* and *might* can be used to ask or give permission. The auxiliary verbs *can* and *could* can be used to indicate ability. The auxiliary verbs *should* and *must* can be used to communicate a duty or an obligation. The auxiliary verbs *may, might, could, should,* and *will* can be used to indicate possibility—how likely something is to happen. Auxiliary verbs that have these special functions are called *modal auxiliaries.*

> Scientists **are** <u>studying</u> glaciers.   The studies **may** <u>help</u> us learn more about Earth.

18d The Principal Parts of a Verb

Each verb has three *principal parts:* its *present form,* its *past form,* and its *past participle form.*
- Most verbs add *-ed* to the present form to create both the past form and the past participle form. These verbs are called *regular verbs.*
- *Irregular verbs* form their past and past participle forms in other ways. The chart below shows the principal parts of several common irregular verbs.

Present	Past	Past Participle
arise	arose	arisen
(be) is	was	been
blow	blew	blown
bring	brought	brought
build	built	built
cut	cut	cut
drive	drove	driven
eat	ate	eaten
fall	fell	fallen
fly	flew	flown
give	gave	given
go	went	gone
grow	grew	grown
have	had	had
hear	heard	heard
hide	hid	hidden
hold	held	held
know	knew	known
lay	laid	laid
leave	left	left
lie	lay	lain
light	lit	lit
make	made	made
ring	rang	rung
run	ran	run
say	said	said
see	saw	seen
shake	shook	shaken
sing	sang	sung
swim	swam	swum
take	took	taken
tell	told	told

(Continued on page 376)

(Continued from page 375)

Present	Past	Past Participle
think	thought	thought
throw	threw	thrown
wear	wore	worn
write	wrote	written

- Almost all verbs add -*ing* to the present form to create the *present participle* form: *sing/singing; talk/talking.*

18e Verb Tense

Verb tense places an action in time.

- The *present tense* is used to show that something happens regularly or is true now.
  Squirrels <u>bury</u> nuts each fall.

- Add -*s* to most verbs to show present tense when the subject is *he, she, it,* or a singular noun. Add -*es* to verbs ending in -*s*, -*ch*, -*sh*, -*x*, or -*z*. Do not add -*s* or -*es* if the subject is a plural noun or *I, you, we,* or *they.*

add -*s*	add -*es*	change *y* to *i*
speak/speak<u>s</u>	reach/reach<u>es</u>	carry/carr<u>ies</u>

- The *past tense* shows past action. Add -*ed* to most verbs to form the past tense. Verbs that do not add -*ed* are called *irregular verbs.*
  reach/reach<u>ed</u> (regular)   speak/<u>spoke</u> (irregular)
  Note: You can find the past and past participle forms of an irregular verb in a dictionary.

- The *future tense* shows future action. Use the verb *will* to form the future tense.
  Mom <u>will visit</u> Antarctica next year.   She <u>will photograph</u> penguins.

- The *present perfect tense* shows action that began in the past and may still be happening. To form the present perfect tense, add the helping verb *has* or *have* to the past participle of a verb.
  Mom <u>has studied</u> Antarctica for years.   Her articles <u>have appeared</u> in science journals.

- The *past perfect tense* shows action that was completed by a certain time in the past. To form the past perfect tense, add the helping verb *had* to the past participle of a verb.
  Before she visited Antarctica, Mom <u>had imagined</u> it as a wasteland.

- The *future perfect tense* shows action that will be complete by a certain time in the future. To form the future perfect tense, add the helping verbs *will have* to the past participle form of a verb.
  By the end of next year, Mom <u>will have published</u> a book on Antarctic wildlife.

- *Progressive forms* of verbs show continuing action. To form a *present progressive* verb, add *am, is,* or *are* to the *present participle* of a verb (usually the present form + -*ing*). To form the *past progressive* verb, add *was* or *were* to the present participle. To form a *future progressive* verb, add *will be* to the present participle.
  Scientists <u>are learning</u> new facts about Antarctica every day. (*present progressive*)
  When Mom <u>was traveling</u> in Antarctica, she saw its beauty. (*past progressive*)
  Someday soon I <u>will be visiting</u> Antarctica with Mom. (*future progressive*)

- Choose verb tenses carefully so that the verb forms you use work together to indicate time accurately and consistently. When you describe events that happen in the same time frame, do not shift tenses. When you describe events that happen at different times, use verbs in different tenses to indicate the order in which the events happened.
  Malcolm wanted to stay dry on the hike, so he <u>packed</u> a poncho. (not <u>packs</u>)
  The doves begin their calls early in the morning, and they <u>continue</u> them past noon. (not <u>continued</u>)

18f Subject and Verb Agreement

The subject and its verb must agree in number. Be sure that the verb agrees with its subject and not with the object of a preposition that comes before the verb.

> An Antarctic explorer needs special equipment.

> (*singular subject:* **An Antarctic explorer;** *singular verb* [*verb* + *-s or -es*]: **needs**)

> Explorers in Antarctica carry climbing tools and survival gear.

> (*plural subject:* **Explorers;** *plural verb* [*verb without -s or -es*]: **carry**)

A *compound subject* and its verb must agree.

- Compound subjects joined by *and* are usually plural.
  Snow and ice <u>make</u> exploration difficult.

- If a compound subject is joined by *or* or *nor,* the verb must agree with the last item in the subject.
  Either the helpers or the leader <u>checks</u> the weather report.

There are special rules for agreement with certain kinds of subjects.

- Titles of books, movies, magazines, newspapers, stories, and songs are always considered singular, even if they end in *-s.*
  The Secret Life of Penguins is the title of Mom's book.

  "Ice and Darkness" is the name of a poem I wrote.

- Collective nouns, such as *collection, group, team, country, kingdom, family, flock,* and *herd,* name more than one person or object acting as a group. These nouns are usually considered singular.
  My <u>family</u> lives in southern Australia.   A <u>flock</u> of seagulls is flying overhead.

- Most indefinite pronouns, including *everyone, nobody, nothing, everything, something,* and *anything,* are considered singular.
  <u>Somebody</u> has left the tent flap open.   Is <u>anything</u> missing?   <u>Everything</u> is fine.

- Some indefinite pronouns that clearly refer to more than one, such as *many, most, few,* and *both,* are considered plural.
  <u>Many</u> are interested in Antarctica, but <u>few</u> are able to make the journey there.

18g Active and Passive Voice

A verb is in *active voice* if its subject performs an action. A verb is in *passive voice* if its subject is acted upon by something else. Many sentences in the passive voice have a prepositional phrase that begins with the word *by* and follows the verb.

> Explorers <u>plan</u> trips months in advance. (*active voice*)

> Trips <u>are planned</u> by explorers months in advance. (*passive voice*)

The active voice can communicate action briefly and powerfully. In most cases, the active voice is stronger and clearer than the passive voice. Try to write most of your sentences in the active voice.

> Strong active voice: The penguin <u>snapped</u> up the fish.

> Weak passive voice: The fish was <u>snapped up</u> by the penguin.

Some writers believe that the passive voice should be used only when an action is done by an unknown or unimportant agent.

> The tent flap <u>was left</u> open. (*The agent who left the tent flap open is unknown.*)

18h Mood of Verbs

Mood as an aspect of grammar has to do with the way different forms of verbs reflect a speaker's attitude toward the information he or she is conveying in a sentence.

- The *indicative mood* is the most common mood in English. Verbs in the indicative mood represent actions or situations the speaker believes to be factual or at least close to reality.
  Kathryn Sullivan **was** the first American woman to walk in space.

  As a scientist, she **has studied** the lands and the ocean here on Earth.

- Verbs in questions that seek real information are usually considered to be in the **indicative mood.**
  Which President **appointed** Dr. Sullivan Chief Scientist of the National Oceanic and Atmospheric Administration (NOAA)?
  Note: Some grammarians consider verbs in questions to be in another mood, the interrogative mood.
- The *imperative mood* is another common mood in English. Commands, requests, warnings, and other directives have verbs in the imperative mood.
  Go to the NOAA website.
- The *subjunctive mood* is the other mood in English. Verbs in the subjunctive mood (sometimes called the *conditional mood*) are used to express conditions contrary to fact.
  If I **were** you, I would join the Science Club. (*Were* expresses a condition contrary to fact: I can never be you.)
- Verbs in the subjunctive mood are also used after verbs of suggesting, representing, or commanding.
  I recommend that Rob **join** the Science Club, too.
- Only the third-person present tense has special subjunctive forms. (The verb *be* is an exception.)
  Sue **joins** many clubs. (indicative)
  I recommend that Sue **join** the Science Club. (subjunctive)
- Verbs in other tenses that are in the subjunctive mood have the same form as verbs in the indicative mood.
  The twins **join** many clubs. (indicative)
  I recommend that the twins **join** the Science Club. (subjunctive)
- The verb *be* has special present tense and past tense forms for the subjunctive mood. The form *be* is used with first, second, and third person pronouns in the present tense.
  The coach insisted that I **be** ready to play. (first person)
  She insisted that they **be** ready, too. (third person)
- The form *were* is used with first, second, and third person pronouns in the past tense.
  If I **were** the coach, I would tell everyone to be ready. (first person)
  If she **were** the coach, she would tell everyone to be ready. (third person)
- The modal auxiliaries *should, could, might,* and *may* can be joined with main verbs to create a form of the subjunctive that suggests rather than tells someone what to do.
  You **might check** with the custodian to see if he found your backpack in the gym.
- Be careful to keep the mood of verbs consistent in clauses that have a similar structure. Do not shift from imperative to subjunctive when you are giving instructions.

  Incorrect: Unlock the door, turn on the light, and you should open a window.

  Correct: Unlock the door, turn on the light, and open a window.

  Do not shift from subjunctive to indicative mood in a compound structure.

  Incorrect: I suggest that a passenger read a book or listens to music.

  Correct: I suggest that a passenger read a book or listen to music.

Section 19 Adverbs

An *adverb* describes a verb, an adjective, or another adverb. Adverbs tell how, when, where, or to what extent.

- Many adverbs end in *-ly*. Some adverbs do not end in *-ly*. These include *now, then, very, too, often, always, again, sometimes, soon, later, first, far, now,* and *fast*.
  Andrew approached the snake cage <u>slowly</u>. He knew that snakes can move <u>fast</u>.
- Some adverbs tell *how*.
  She spoke <u>confidently</u>.   He <u>eagerly</u> bit into the sandwich.
- Some adverbs tell *when*.
  <u>Then</u> the bell rang.   School ended <u>yesterday</u>.   I eat pizza <u>only</u> on Friday.

- Some adverbs tell *where*.

  We went **inside**.   They built a house **there**.   Come **here**.

- Some adverbs tell *to what extent*.

  It is **very** quiet.   I am **almost** finished.

- When the word *when, where,* or *why* begins a dependent clause that tells about a place, a time, or a reason, it is called a *relative adverb*.

  Tucker Avenue is a street **where** many accidents happen. (place)

  Friday is the day **when** my report is due. (time)

  This article gives five reasons **why** you should drink water instead of soda. (reason)

  Note: A word that is a relative adverb can also be classified as a subordinating conjunction.

Section 20 Prepositions

A *preposition* shows a relationship between a word in a sentence and a noun or pronoun that follows the preposition. Prepositions tell when, where, what kind, how, or how much.

- Prepositions include the words *after, in front of, without, above, down, among, with, of, from, for, about, such as, throughout, into, onto, inside, in, at, under, over, on, through, to, across, around, by, beside, during, off,* and *before*.

  Jeff left the milk **on** the table.   He knew it belonged **in** the refrigerator.

- A *prepositional phrase* is a group of words that begins with a preposition and ends with its object. The object of a preposition is a noun or a pronoun. A prepositional phrase can be at the beginning, middle, or end of a sentence.

  Jeff's mom would be home **in five minutes**. **Within three minutes** he had put it away.

- Prepositional phrases that modify (or tell more about) nouns or pronouns are called *adjectival prepositional phrases*. An adjectival prepositional phrase usually comes after the noun or pronoun it modifies. Adjectival prepositional phrases often tell *which*.

  The milk **in the refrigerator** is spoiled. (*modifies the noun* milk *and tells* which milk)

  I can't stand the odor **of spoiled milk**! (*modifies the noun* odor *and tells* which odor)

- *Adverbial prepositional phrases* modify a verb, an adverb, or an adjective. Many adverbial prepositional phrases tell *when, where, how,* or *how long* something was done.

  Jeff usually drinks orange juice **before breakfast**. (*modifies the verb* drinks *and tells* when)

  He says his mom's fresh-squeezed orange juice is the best **in the world**. (*modifies the adjective* best *and tells* where)

  Late **in the evening** I heard a knock at my door. (*modifies the adverb* late *and tells* when)

Section 21 Direct Objects and Indirect Objects

A *direct object* is the noun or pronoun that receives the action of the verb. Direct objects follow action verbs. To find the direct object, say the verb and then "Whom?" or "What?"

  Jacques painted a **picture**. (Painted whom or what? Picture. *Picture* is the direct object.)

- A *compound direct object* occurs when more than one noun or pronoun receives the action of the verb.

  He used a **brush** and oil **paints**. (*Brush* and *paints* compose the compound direct object.)

- A sentence with a direct object may also have an *indirect object*. An indirect object is a noun or pronoun and usually tells to whom something is given, told, or taught.

  Jacques gave his **mom** the painting.

- A direct object may be modified by an *object complement*. An object complement is a noun, pronoun, or adjective that follows a direct object and identifies or describes it. Object complements are often used with verbs such as *make, name, elect, paint,* and *call*.

  The new grass turned the hills **green**. (*Green* describes what color the hills turned.)

  The officer called Javier a **hero**. (*Hero* identifies what Javier was called.)

Section 22 | Conjunctions

The words *and, or,* and *but* are *coordinating conjunctions.*

- Coordinating conjunctions may be used to join words within a sentence.
  My favorite reptiles are snakes **and** lizards.   Najim doesn't like snakes **or** lizards.

- A comma and a coordinating conjunction can be used to join two or more simple sentences.
  (The conjunction *and* does not need a comma if both sentences are short.)
  I like snakes, **but** he says they're creepy.   We can get a snake, **or** we can get a lizard.

A *subordinating conjunction* relates one clause to another. Dependent clauses begin with a subordinating conjunction. Subordinating conjunctions include *because, if, although, when, where, as, while, though, than, as if, whenever, since, wherever, after, often, over,* and *before.*

   Before his mom left, Bo cleaned his room. **Because** he had a favor to ask, he vacuumed, too.

Correlative conjunctions always appear in pairs. They connect words or groups of words and provide more emphasis than coordinating conjunctions. Some common correlative conjunctions are *both . . . and, either . . . or, neither . . . nor, not only . . . but (also),* and *whether. . . or.*

   She is **not only** a good singer **but also** an excellent athlete.

   Neither Raj **nor** Chris came to the concert.

Section 23 | Interjections

An *interjection* expresses emotion and is not part of any independent or dependent clause.
   Wow! This bread is delicious.   **Mmmm**, this bread tastes good!

Section 24 | Appositives

An *appositive* is a phrase that identifies a noun or pronoun.
   My favorite snack, **cornbread with honey**, is easy to make.

- Most appositives are separated from the rest of a sentence by commas. These appositives, called *nonrestrictive appositives,* just give more information about the nouns or pronouns they describe.
  Tara, **my friend who figure skates**, is traveling to Dallas for a competition.

- Some appositives should not be set off by commas. A *restrictive appositive* is an appositive that is vital to the meaning of a sentence; therefore, it should not be set off by commas.
  His book ***The Basics of Automobile Maintenance*** tells how to take care of a car.

  My sister **Katie** likes to read on the porch.

Section 25 | Verbals and Absolutes

25a Verbals

Sometimes a verb does not act as a predicate. *Verbals* are forms of verbs that play other roles in sentences.

- One type of verbal, a *participle,* acts as an adjective. A participle may be the present participle or the past participle form of a verb. (See Handbook Section 18d.)
  George heard the bell **ringing**. (*acts as an adjective describing the noun* bell)

  A **shivering** child stood at the door. (*acts as an adjective describing the noun* child)

  A *participial phrase* is made up of a participle and other words that complete its meaning.
  Filled with pride, Angela accepted her medal. (*acts as an adjective modifying the noun* Angela)

  Matt noticed a skunk **waddling** through the bushes. (*acts as an adjective modifying the noun* skunk)

- An *infinitive* is a phrase made up of the word *to* followed by the present form of a verb (*to defend*). Infinitives may act as adjectives, adverbs, or nouns. An *infinitive phrase* is made up of an infinitive and other words that complete its meaning.
  I like **to walk** in the woods. (*acts as a noun; the direct object of the verb* like)

  This is a good way **to appreciate** nature. (*acts as an adjective modifying the noun* way)

  I listen carefully **to hear** the sounds of woodland creatures. (*acts as an adverb modifying the verb* listen)

- A *gerund* is a verbal that acts as a noun. All gerunds are present participles. (See Handbook Section 18d.)

  My brother enjoys **swimming**. (*acts as a noun; the direct object of the verb* enjoys)

  A *gerund phrase* is made up of a gerund and the other words that complete its meaning.
  Riding the waves on a surfboard is his great ambition. (*acts as the subject of the sentence*)

- A sentence may contain more than one participial or infinitive phrase. Using two verbals of the same type to express similar ideas is using *parallel structure*.
  Warmed by the sun and **cooled by sea breezes,** Smith Beach is the perfect place for a vacation. (two participial phrases)

  Mac wants **to paddle a kayak,** but Ruthann wants **to swim**. (two infinitive phrases)

25b Absolutes

An *absolute phrase* consists of a noun or noun phrase followed by a descriptive word or phrase.

- An absolute phrase may contain a present or past participle.
  Her face **glowing**, Sue looked as happy as she felt. (*noun phrase plus a present participle*)

  The general, his army **defeated**, prepared to surrender. (*noun phrase plus a past participle*)

- An absolute phrase may also contain an adjective, a noun, or a prepositional phrase.
  Teri woke from a deep sleep, her mind and body **alert**. (*noun phrase plus an adjective*)

  Melissa, good grades **her prime objective,** never went out on a school night. (*noun phrase plus a noun phrase*)

  Teri rode home, her guitar **across her back**. (*noun phrase plus a prepositional phrase*)

Usage

Section 26 Negatives

A *negative word* means "no" or "not."

- The words *no, not, nothing, none, never, nowhere,* and *nobody* are negatives.

  The notebook was <u>nowhere</u> to be found.   <u>Nobody</u> wanted to miss the party.

- Often negatives are in the form of contractions.

  Do <u>not</u> enter that room.   <u>Don't</u> even go near the door.

- In most sentences it is not correct to use two negatives.

Incorrect	Correct
We <u>can't</u> see <u>nothing</u>.	We <u>can't</u> see anything.
We <u>haven't</u> got <u>no</u> solution.	We <u>haven't</u> got a solution.

- Some sentences express ideas that require the use of two negative words.

  <u>No one</u> will work for you for <u>nothing</u>. (*In other words, anyone who works will expect to be paid.*)

  I <u>couldn't</u> *not* say hello to her. (*In other words, the speaker had to say hello, even if the speaker might not have wanted to.*)

- Do not use the word *ain't.*

Section 27 Comparisons

- The *comparative form* of an adjective or an adverb compares two people, places, or things. The comparative form is often followed by "than." To compare two people, places, or things, add *-er* to short adjectives and adverbs.

  An elephant is <u>tall</u>. A giraffe is <u>taller</u> than an **elephant**. (*Giraffe is compared with* elephant.)

  A lion runs <u>fast</u>. A cheetah runs <u>faster</u> than **any other animal**. (*Cheetah is compared with* any other animal.)

- The *superlative form* of an adjective or an adverb compares three or more people, places, or things. The article *the* usually comes before the superlative form. To compare three or more items, add *-est* to short adjectives and adverbs.

  The giraffe is the <u>tallest</u> land animal.   The cheetah runs the <u>fastest</u> of any animal on land.

- When comparing two or more persons, places, or things using the ending *-er* or *-est*, never use the word *more.*

Incorrect	Correct
She is <u>more faster</u> than he is.	She is <u>faster</u> than he is.

- The word *more* is used with longer adjectives to compare two persons, places, or things. Use the word *most* to compare three or more persons, places, or things.

  Mario is <u>excited</u> about the field trip.

  Duane is <u>more excited</u> than Mario.

  Kiki is the <u>most excited</u> student of all.

- Sometimes the words *good* and *bad* are used to compare. These words change forms in comparisons.

Mario is a <u>good</u> athlete.	The basketball court is in <u>bad</u> shape.
Kiki is a <u>better</u> athlete.	The tennis court is in <u>worse</u> shape than the basketball court.
Bill is the <u>best</u> athlete of all.	The ice rink is in <u>worst</u> shape of all.

  Note: Use *better* or *worse* to compare two things. Use *best* or *worst* to compare three or more things.

Section 28 Contractions

When two or more words are combined to form one word, one or more letters are dropped and replaced by an apostrophe. These words are called *contractions*. For example, when *he will* becomes the contraction *he'll,* the apostrophe replaces *wi.*

- Here are some other common contractions.

can't (cannot)	**haven't** (have not)	**she'd** (she would)
couldn't (could not)	**I'll** (I will)	**they've** (they have)
doesn't (does not)	**it's** (it is, it has)	**we're** (we are)

Section 29 Plural Nouns

- A *singular noun* names one person, place, thing, or idea.
  girl   pond   arrow   freedom
- A *plural noun* names more than one person, place, thing, or idea. To make most singular nouns plural, add -*s.*
  girl<u>s</u>   pond<u>s</u>   arrow<u>s</u>   freedom<u>s</u>
- For nouns ending in -*sh,* -*ch,* -*x,* or -*z,* add -*es* to make the word plural.
  bush/bush<u>es</u>   lunch/lunch<u>es</u>   quiz/quizz<u>es</u>   box/box<u>es</u>

  For nouns ending in a consonant and -*y,* change the *y* to *i* and add -*es.*
  penny/penn<u>ies</u>   army/arm<u>ies</u>
- For some nouns that end in -*f* or -*fe,* replace -*f* or -*fe* with -*ves* to make the noun plural.
  shelf/shel<u>ves</u>   wife/wi<u>ves</u>   (Exceptions: cliff/cliff<u>s</u>; reef/reef<u>s</u>; cafe/cafe<u>s</u>)
- Some words change spelling when the plural is formed. These plurals are called *irregular plurals.*
  man/m<u>e</u>n   woman/wom<u>e</u>n   mouse/m<u>i</u>ce   goose/g<u>ee</u>se
- Some words have the same singular and plural form. These plurals are also called *irregular plurals.*
  deer   sheep   offspring   scissors

Section 30 Possessive Nouns

A *possessive* shows ownership.

- To make a singular noun possessive, add an apostrophe and *s.*
  John<u>'s</u> bat   the girl<u>'s</u> bike
- When a singular noun ends in -*s,* add an apostrophe and *s.*
  Ross<u>'s</u> project   James<u>'s</u> glasses
- To make a plural noun that ends in -*s* possessive, add an apostrophe.
  the soldiers<u>'</u> songs   the girls<u>'</u> bikes
- When a plural noun does not end in -*s,* add an apostrophe and *s* to show possession.
  the men<u>'s</u> ideas   the children<u>'s</u> shoes

Section 31 Dangling Modifiers and Misplaced Modifiers

A verbal phrase acting as an adjective must modify, or refer to, a specific word in the main part of a sentence. A *dangling modifier* is a phrase that does not refer to any particular word in the sentence. A *misplaced modifier* is a phrase that seems to refer to the wrong word in a sentence.

Incorrect: <u>Walking down the street</u>, deep thoughts come to mind.

(Are deep thoughts walking down the street? No. This verbal phrase does not refer to any particular word in the main part of the sentence: it is a dangling modifier.)

Dangling and misplaced modifiers make your writing unclear, so avoid them. When you begin a sentence with a verbal phrase such as "Walking down the street," make sure that the question "Who is walking down the street?" is answered clearly in the first part of the rest of the sentence.

Correct: <u>Walking down the street</u>, I often think deep thoughts.

(<u>Who</u> is walking down the street? I am. This verbal phrase clearly relates to the pronoun I.)

When you proofread your work, check to make sure you have not written any sentences with dangling or misplaced modifiers. If you have, rewrite those sentences so modifiers appear near the words they describe.

These words are often misused. Be sure to use them correctly when you speak and when you write.

sit	*Sit* means "rest or stay in one place." <u>Sit</u> down and relax for a while.
sat	*Sat* is the past tense of *sit*. I <u>sat</u> in that chair yesterday.
set	*Set* is a verb meaning "put." <u>Set</u> the chair here.
lay	*Lay* means "to put something down somewhere." It takes a direct object. The past tense form of *lay* is *laid,* and the past participle form of *lay* is also *laid.* Each day I <u>lay</u> a tablecloth on the table. Yesterday I <u>laid</u> the yellow tablecloth. I had never <u>laid</u> that one on the table before.
lie	*Lie* means "to recline." It does not take a direct object. The past tense form of *lie* is *lay,* and the past participle form of *lie* is *lain.* Most mornings I <u>lie</u> half awake just before the alarm rings. Early this morning I <u>lay</u> with my eyes open, waiting for the alarm. I had <u>lain</u> there for a few minutes before I realized that it was Saturday.
may	*May* is used to ask permission or to express a possibility. <u>May</u> I have another hot dog? I <u>may</u> borrow that book someday.
can	*Can* shows that someone is able to do something. I <u>can</u> easily eat three hot dogs.
learn	*Learn* means "to get knowledge." Who will help you <u>learn</u> Spanish?
teach	*Teach* means "to give knowledge." Never use *learn* in place of *teach*. **Incorrect:** My sister will <u>learn</u> me to speak Spanish. **Correct:** My sister will <u>teach</u> me to speak Spanish.
is	Use *is* to tell about one person, place, or thing. Alabama <u>is</u> warm during the summer.
are	Use *are* to tell about more than one person, place, or thing. Also use *are* with the word *you*. Seattle and San Francisco <u>are</u> cool during the summer. You <u>are</u> welcome to visit me anytime.
doesn't	The contraction *doesn't* is used with the singular pronouns *he, she,* and *it*. He <u>doesn't</u> like sauerkraut. It <u>doesn't</u> agree with him.
don't	The contraction *don't* is used with the plural pronouns *we* and *they*. *Don't* is also used with *I* and *you*. They <u>don't</u> like Swiss cheese. I <u>don't</u> care for it, either.
I	Use the pronoun *I* as the subject of a sentence. When using *I* or *me* with another noun or pronoun, always name yourself last. <u>I</u> am going to basketball camp. Renée and <u>I</u> will ride together.
me	Use the pronoun *me* after action verbs. Renée will call <u>me</u> this evening. Also use *me* after a preposition, such as *to, at,* and *with*. Pass the ball to <u>me</u>. Come to the game with Renée and <u>me</u>.
good well	*Good* is an adjective. *Well* is an adverb. These words are often used incorrectly. **Incorrect:** Renée plays <u>good</u>. **Correct:** Renée is a <u>good</u> basketball player. She plays <u>well</u>.

raise	*Raise* must be followed by a direct object. I <u>raise</u> the flag every morning.
rise	*Rise* is not used with a direct object. I <u>rise</u> at dawn every morning.
like	*Like* means "similar to" or "have a fondness for." Do not use *like* to indicate a pause or to mean "says." Incorrect: I enjoy, <u>like</u>, all kinds of water sports. He was <u>like</u>, "Swimming is fun." Correct: I <u>like</u> swimming and water polo. He said, "I <u>like</u> the water."
go	*Go* means "move from place to place." Don't use *go* or *went* to mean "says" or "said." Incorrect: She <u>went</u>, "The swim meet was yesterday." Correct: She said, "I <u>went</u> to the swim meet."
all	*All* means "the total of something." Avoid using *was all* to mean "said." Incorrect: He <u>was all</u>, "Everyone likes swimming." Correct: He said, "Everyone likes swimming."
you know	Use the phrase *you know* only when it helps a sentence make sense. Try not to use it in places where it does not belong. Incorrect: We can, <u>you know</u>, go canoeing. Correct: Did <u>you know</u> that my family has a canoe?
let	*Let* is a verb that means "allow." Please <u>let</u> me go to the mall with you.
leave	*Leave* is a verb that means "go away from" or "let stay." We will <u>leave</u> at noon. <u>Leave</u> your sweater here.
was	*Was* is a past tense form of *be*. Use *was* to tell about one person or thing. Hana <u>was</u> sad yesterday.
were	*Were* is also a past tense form of *be*. Use *were* to tell about more than one person or thing. Also use the word *were* with *you*. Hana and her friend <u>were</u> both unhappy. <u>Were</u> you home yesterday?
has	Use *has* to tell about one person or thing. Rory <u>has</u> a stamp collection.
have	Use *have* to tell about more than one. Also use *have* with the pronoun *I*. David and Lin <u>have</u> a rock collection. I <u>have</u> a bottle cap collection.
who	*Who* is in the nominative case and should be used as the subject of a clause. Use *who* to refer to people. The man <u>who</u> picked me up is my father.
whom	*Whom* is in the objective case and should be used as a direct or indirect object or as the object of a preposition. Use *whom* to refer to people. To <u>whom</u> am I speaking?
which	Use *which* to refer to things. His rear tire, <u>which</u> was flat, had to be repaired.
that	*That* can refer to people or things. Use *that* instead of *which* to begin a clause that is necessary to the meaning of the sentence. The picture <u>that</u> Stephen drew won first prize.
very	*Very* is an adverb. It means "extremely." I was <u>very</u> tired after the hike.
real	*Real* is an adjective. It means "actual." Never use *real* in place of *very*. Incorrect: The hike was <u>real</u> long. Correct: I used a <u>real</u> compass to find my way.

less	*Less* can be used to refer to a *smaller amount* that is not a sum of items.	
	If you want to use <u>less</u> gasoline, buy a hybrid.	
fewer	*Fewer* is used to refer to a *smaller number* of items.	
	Be aware that there will be <u>fewer</u> cars from which to choose.	
over	*Over* can be used to refer to a *larger amount* that is not a sum of items.	
	We drove <u>over</u> 30 miles, then biked the rest of the way.	
more than	*More than* is used to describe a *larger number* of items.	
	<u>More than</u> 20 cars remained on the lot.	

In academic writing, avoid *contractions; shortened forms* of words (*gonna, gotta, wanna*); *slang* or *informal language* (*stuff, cool, guy, way* or *totally* for *very, lots of, okay*); and *vague words* (*thing, nice, good, bad*).

Section 33 Homophones

Homophones sound alike but have different spellings and meanings.

are	*Are* is a form of the verb *be.*	We <u>are</u> best friends.
our	*Our* is a possessive pronoun.	<u>Our</u> favorite color is green.
hour	An *hour* is sixty minutes.	Meet me in an <u>hour</u>.

its	*Its* is a possessive pronoun.	The horse shook <u>its</u> shaggy head.
it's	*It's* is a contraction of the words *it is* or *it has*.	<u>It's</u> a beautiful day for a ride.

there	*There* is an adverb that usually means "in that place." It can also be used in the expressions "there is" and "there are."	
	Please put the books <u>there</u>.	<u>There</u> are three books on the table.
	<u>There</u> is an aquarium nearby.	
	Note: Using the expressions *there is, there are,* and *it is* sometimes weakens sentences; try to avoid these expressions in academic writing.	
their	*Their* is a possessive pronoun. It shows something belongs to more than one person or thing.	
	<u>Their</u> tickets are in my pocket.	
they're	*They're* is a contraction made from the words *they are*.	
	<u>They're</u> waiting for me inside.	

two	*Two* is a number.	Apples and pears are <u>two</u> fruits I like.
to	*To* can be a preposition meaning "toward." *To* can also be used with a verb to form an infinitive.	
	I brought the pot <u>to</u> the stove. (*preposition*) I like <u>to</u> cook. (*infinitive*)	
too	*Too* means "also."	I'd like some lunch, <u>too</u>.
	Too can mean "more than enough."	That's <u>too</u> much pepper!

your	*Your* is a possessive pronoun.	
	Where are <u>your</u> socks?	
you're	*You're* is a contraction made from the words *you are*.	
	<u>You're</u> coming with us, aren't you?	

whose	*Whose* is a possessive pronoun. It can refer to people or things.	
	<u>Whose</u> raincoat is this?	The raincoat <u>whose</u> buttons are blue is mine.
who's	*Who's* is a contraction made from the words *who* and *is* or *who* and *has*.	
	<u>Who's</u> at the front door?	<u>Who's</u> taken my book?

than	*Than* is used to make comparisons.	
	We waited for more **than** an hour.	She is taller **than** you.
then	*Then* can be an adverb that tells about time. It can also mean "therefore."	
	Then I went home.	
	If you like mangoes, **then** you should try this mango ice cream.	
principal	A *principal* is a person with authority.	
	The **principal** made the rule.	
principle	A *principle* is a general rule or code of behavior.	
	He lived with a strong **principle** of honesty.	
waist	The *waist* is the middle part of the body.	
	She wore a belt around her **waist**.	
waste	To *waste* something is to use it in a careless way.	
	She would never **waste** something she could recycle.	
aloud	*Aloud* means "out loud" or "able to be heard."	He read the poem **aloud**.
allowed	*Allowed* is a form of the verb *allow*.	We were not **allowed** to swim after dark.
raise	*Raise* is a verb that means "lift up."	We **raise** the American flag each morning.
raze	*Raze* is a verb that means "destroy."	Bulldozers **raze** old buildings so that new ones can be built.

Letters and E-mails

Section 34 Letters

A *friendly letter* is an informal letter written to a friend or a family member.
In a friendly letter, you might send a message, invite someone to a party, or thank someone for a gift.
A friendly letter has five parts.

- The *heading* gives your address and the date.
- The *greeting* includes the name of the person you are writing to. It begins with an uppercase letter and ends with a comma.
- The *body* of the letter gives your message.
- The *closing* is a friendly or polite way to say good-bye. It ends with a comma.
- The *signature* is your name.

35 Rand Street
Chicago, IL 60606
July 15, 20___

Dear Kim,

    Hi from the big city. I'm spending the summer learning to skateboard. My brother Raj is teaching me. He's a pro.
    I have one skateboard and hope to buy another one soon. If I can do that, we can practice together when you come to visit.

      Your friend,

      Art

A *business letter* is a formal letter.
You would write a business letter to a company, an employer, a newspaper, or any person you do not know well. A business letter looks a lot like a friendly letter, but a business letter substitutes a colon for a comma after the greeting, omits paragraph indentations, and aligns all of the letter parts along the left-hand margin.

35 Rand Street
Chicago, IL 60606
July 15, 20___

Swenson Skateboard Company
10026 Portage Road
Lansing, MI 48091

Dear Sir or Madam:

Please send me your latest skateboard catalog. I am particularly interested in your newest models, the K-7 series.

Thank you.

Sincerely yours,
Arthur Quinn
Arthur Quinn

The envelope below shows how to address a letter. A friendly letter and a business letter are addressed the same way.

ARTHUR QUINN
35 RAND ST
CHICAGO IL 60606

          KIM LEE
          1555 MONTAGUE BLVD
          MEMPHIS TN 38106

Section 35 | E-mails

An *e-mail* is a note sent from one person to another person, a group, or a company through a computer network. Today, many people use e-mail to stay in touch with friends and family. An e-mail should contain five parts, like a letter does.

- An e-mail contains a *greeting*, a *body*, a *closing*, and your *name*.
- An e-mail *header* contains your e-mail address, the e-mail address of the person you are writing to, the date, and a subject line.

| Send | Save as a Draft | Cancel |

From:	arthur_quinn@communicago.net
To:	info@swenskate.com
Date:	July 15, 20__
Subject:	Skateboard catalog

Attach Files

Dear Sir or Madam:

Please send me your latest skateboard catalog. I am particularly interested in your newest models, the K-7 series.

My address is 35 Rand Street, Chicago, IL 60606. Thank you.

Sincerely,
Arthur Quinn

Research

Section 36 | Library Research

You can find information for a report or a project in a library.

- Many libraries have an information desk. The person at the desk can help you look for information.
- Libraries have many reference books, including dictionaries, thesauruses, and encyclopedias. You can use these to find information about words and basic information about topics.
- Libraries have nonfiction books about all kinds of subjects. You can find books on a particular subject by entering that subject into a computer connected to the library's database. This database lists all the publications in the library. The computer will usually list several books on the subject you entered. Each listing will have a code that tells where in the library that book can be found.

Section 37 Internet Research

You can use online dictionaries, thesauruses, and encyclopedias to find basic information about words and topics. You can also find information for a report or a project by using an Internet *search engine*.

- Think of **key words** that describe what you are looking for. For example, if you need information on animals that live in the rainforest, you might use the key words **rainforest animals**. Type these words into the search engine's text box.
- The search engine will provide you with links to **websites**. You can click on a link to visit a website.
- When you get to the website, you need to judge whether it will be a good source of information.
  - —Notice the last three letters of the website's Internet address. Sites with **.gov** and **.edu** are usually more reliable than sites with **.com**.
  - —Think about who has written the information. Is the writer an expert on the topic? Is the writer giving facts, or just expressing opinions?
  - —Check to see if the information is up-to-date. The site should tell you when it was last updated.

Internet Safety

Be sure to follow safety rules whenever you use the Internet. These rules will help you keep personal information private.

- When you log on to a school computer, you may type your own name as a username. However, when you go on the Internet, you use a screen name. That should never be your real name or nickname. You will also use a password, a secret word or symbol that identifies who you are. Keep your password safe. Do not share it with anyone. Never use your address, birthday, phone number, or pet's name as a password. Those are too easy for someone else to figure out.
- Have you ever received e-mail with an attachment? Usually you must click the attachment to load it into your computer. Never download attachments from strangers. These may harm your computer.

Section 38 Bibliographies

A *bibliography* is an alphabetical list of all sources used when gathering information for a report or an essay. The models below demonstrate how to create bibliographic entries.

- **Encyclopedia Article or Dictionary Entry**
  "Asteroid." The Columbia Encyclopedia. 6th ed. 2007.
- **Magazine or Newspaper Article**
  Bridges, Andrew. "Deadly Space Threats Get More Attention." The Columbus Dispatch. 13 May 2010: C4.
- **Website**
  Britt, Robert Roy. "Asteroid Discoveries May Outpace Ability to Assess Threat to Earth." Space.com. 19 Oct. 2001. Imaginova Corp. 1 Apr. 2008 <http://space.com/scienceastronomy/solarsystem/asteroid.html>.
- **Book**
  Miller, Ron. Asteroids, Comets, and Meteors. Twenty-First Century: Minneapolis, 2006.

Guidelines for Listening and Speaking

Section 39 | Listening

These steps will help you be a good listener:

- **Listen carefully** when others are speaking.
- **Keep in mind your reason for listening.** Are you listening to learn about a topic? To be entertained? To get directions? Decide what you should get out of the listening experience.
- **Look directly at the speaker.** Doing this will help you concentrate on what he or she is saying.
- **Do not interrupt** the speaker or talk to others while the speaker is talking.
- **Ask questions** when the speaker is finished talking if there is anything you do not understand.

Section 40 | Speaking

Being a good speaker takes practice. These guidelines can help you become an effective speaker:

Giving Oral Reports

- **Be prepared.** Know exactly what it is that you are going to talk about and how long you will speak. Have your notes in front of you.
- **Speak slowly** and **clearly.** Speak **loudly** enough so everyone can hear you.
- **Look** at your audience.

Taking Part in Discussions

- **Listen** to what others have to say.
- **Disagree politely.** Let others in the group know you respect their point of view.
- **Try not to interrupt** others. Everyone should have a chance to speak.

(you) | Diagram | sentences

A sentence diagram is a map of a sentence. It shows how the parts of a sentence fit together and how the individual words in a sentence are related. Sentence diagrams can represent every part of speech and every type of sentence. The models below demonstrate how to create sentence diagrams, beginning with the simplest kinds of sentences.

- In a sentence consisting of a subject and an action verb, the subject and the verb are separated by a vertical line that bisects the horizontal line.
  Rain fell. Rain | fell

- An adjective (or article) that modifies a noun or pronoun belongs on a slanted line below the word it modifies.
  A **cold** rain fell.

  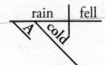

- An adverb that modifies a verb belongs on a slanted line below the verb it modifies.
  A very cold rain fell **steadily**.

- A direct object is placed on a horizontal line to the right of the verb. It is separated from the verb by a short vertical line that does not bisect the horizontal line.
  The downpour drenched the **land**.

  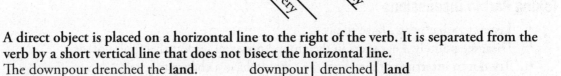

- An indirect object goes below the verb to show *who* or *what* receives something.
  It gave the **crops** a welcome soaking.

- Two separate horizontal lines show a compound predicate. The conjunction joins the verbs.
  Seedlings **uncurled** and **grew**.

- A compound subject is placed on two horizontal lines with a conjunction joining the subjects.
  Leaves and **flowers** glistened.

- A compound sentence is diagrammed as two sentences with a conjunction joining them.
  The rain stopped and the sun appeared.

- A demonstrative pronoun takes the place of a noun. It belongs wherever the noun it replaces would go in the diagram.

  This prompted a collective cheer.

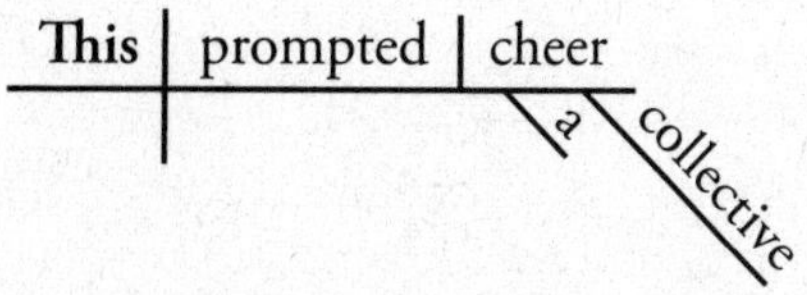

  This | prompted | cheer
  a \ collective

- A possessive pronoun belongs on a slanted line under the noun that is the possession.

  The children left **their** homes gleefully.

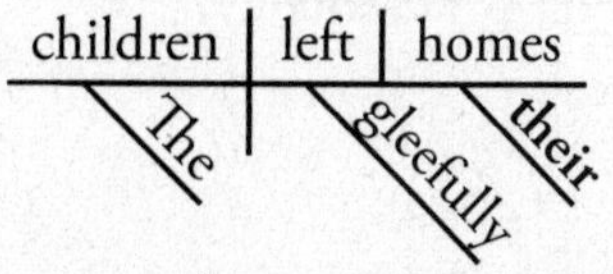

  children | left | homes
  The \ gleefully \ their

- An indefinite pronoun, a subject pronoun, or an object pronoun also belongs wherever the noun it replaces would go.

  Someone started a soccer game.

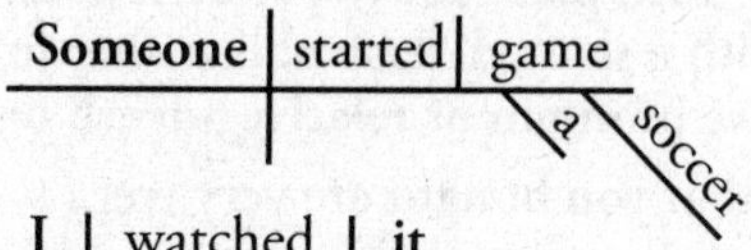

  Someone | started | game
  a \ soccer

  I watched **it**.

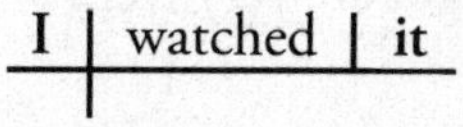

  I | watched | it

- The understood *you* belongs where the subject of the sentence would go. It is written in parentheses.

  Remove your muddy shoes.

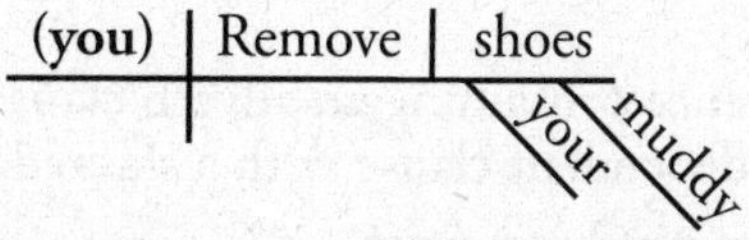

  (you) | Remove | shoes
  your \ muddy

- A linking verb has the same position in a diagram that an action verb has, but the linking verb is separated from the predicate adjective or predicate noun by a diagonal line instead of by a vertical line.

  Your clothes **are** incredibly muddy.

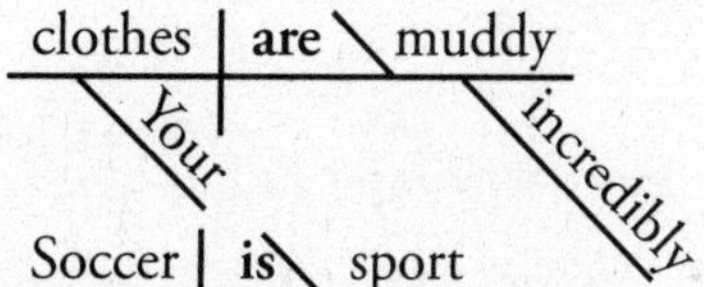

  clothes | are \ muddy
  Your \ incredibly

  Soccer **is** a rough sport.

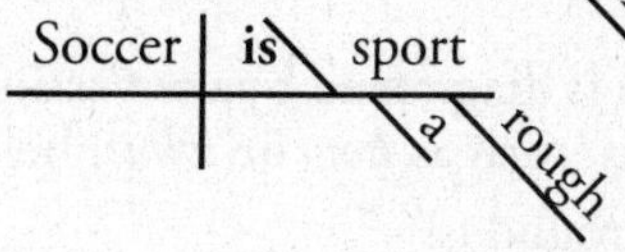

  Soccer | is \ sport
  a \ rough

- An adverbial prepositional phrase that modifies a verb is connected to that verb.

  Leave your shoes **on the porch**.

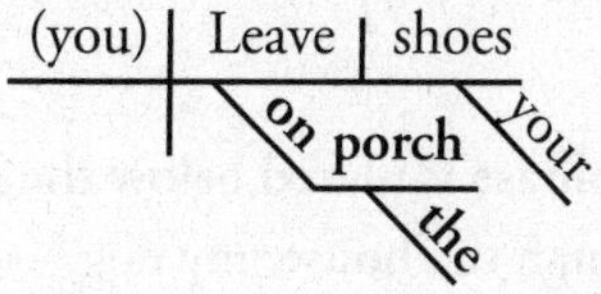

  (you) | Leave | shoes
  on porch \ your
  the

- An adjectival prepositional phrase that modifies a noun is connected to that noun.

  The mud **in the field** is quite deep.

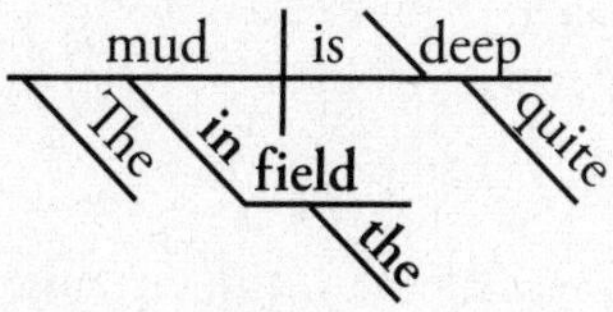

  mud | is \ deep
  The \ in field \ quite
  the

- When *there* begins a sentence, it is placed on a separate line above the rest of the diagram.

  There are fresh towels inside the house.

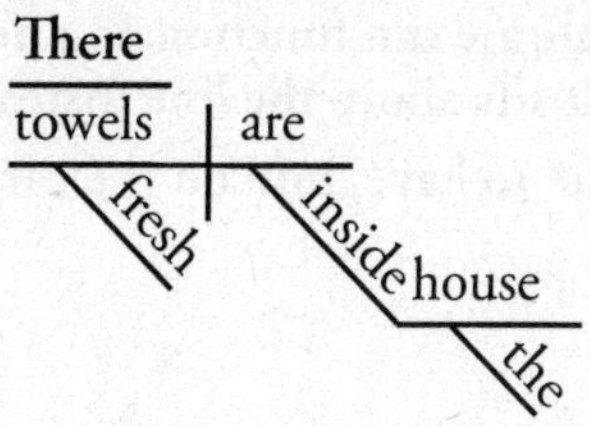

  There
  towels | are
  fresh \ inside house
  the

393

- **An adjective or an adverb is written on a slanted line and is connected to the word it modifies.**

  The **bright** green towel is mine.

- **To diagram a sentence containing an adjective clause, first identify the independent clause and diagram it. Then place the dependent clause below the first diagram. Connect it to the first diagram with a slanted, dashed line that joins the clause to the noun it modifies. Write the relative pronoun or relative adverb on the dashed line.**

  The new shoes **that you bought** are very wet.

- **Diagram a sentence containing an adverb clause in a similar way, but connect the dependent clause to the independent clause with a slanted, dashed line connecting to the verb.**

  They looked nice **until you wore them in the mud.**

- **An inverted sentence is diagramed by converting the sentence to natural word order and then by placing the adverb (such as *how* or *what*) below the word it modifies.**

  How soggy the wet ground is!

- **A participial phrase is placed below the noun it modifies.**

  Running through the house, my dog muddied the floors.

- **An infinitive phrase can function as a noun. It belongs wherever a noun would go in the diagram, but it sits above the line instead of on it.**

  My parents hate **to have mud on the carpet.**

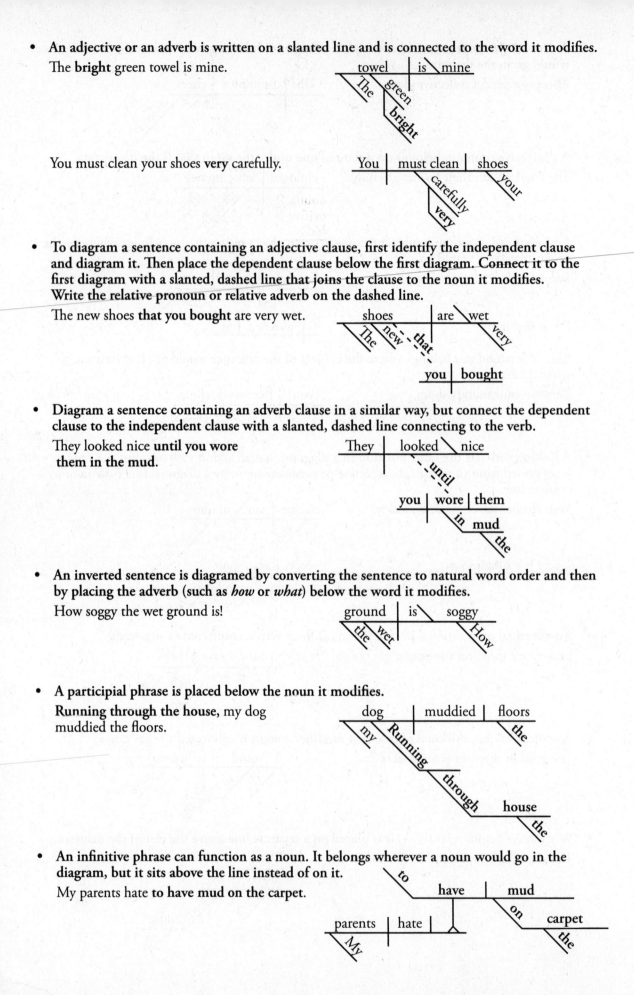

- A gerund phrase functions as a noun. It belongs wherever a noun would go in the diagram, but it sits above the line instead of on it.

Cleaning the carpet is never a fun chore.

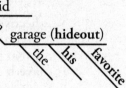

- An appositive is a phrase that identifies a noun. The noun in an appositive is placed in parentheses next to the noun that the appositive identifies.

My dog hid in the garage, his favorite hideout.

Language Index

Conventions of Standard English